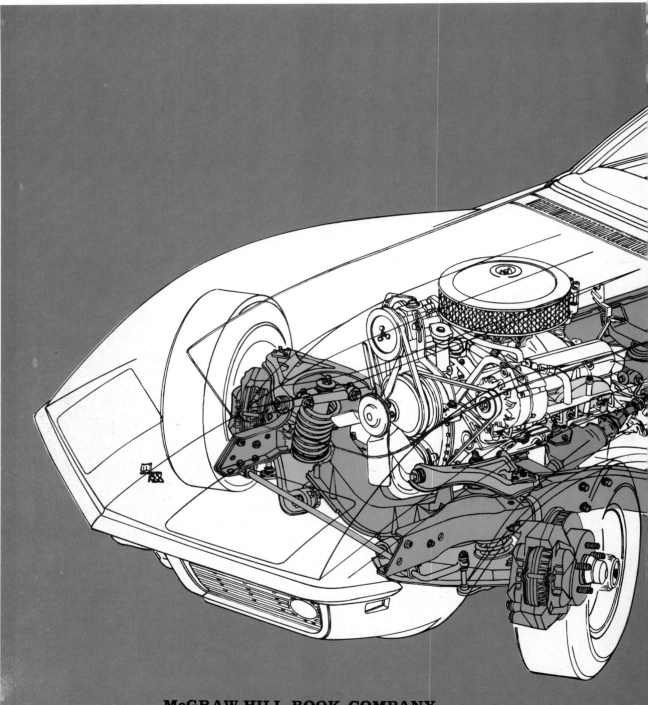

McGRAW-HILL BOOK COMPANY

New York, St. Louis, San Francisco, Dallas
Dusseldorf, London, Mexico, Panama, Sydney, Toronto

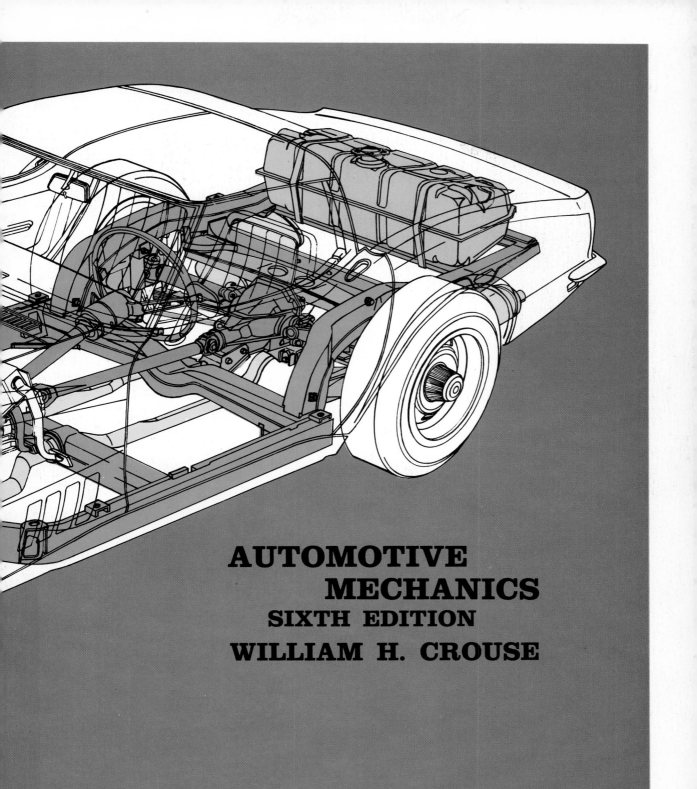

AUTOMOTIVE
MECHANICS
SIXTH EDITION
WILLIAM H. CROUSE

ABOUT THE AUTHOR

Behind William H. Crouse's clear technical writing is a background of sound mechanical engineering training as well as a variety of practical industrial experiences. He spent a year after finishing high school working in a tinplate mill. Summers, while still in school, he worked in General Motors plants, and for three years he worked in the Delco-Remy Division shops. Later he became Director of Field Education in the Delco-Remy Division of General Motors Corporation, which gave him an opportunity to develop and use his natural writing talent in the preparation of service bulletins and educational literature.

During the war years, he wrote a number of technical manuals for the Armed Forces. After the war, he became Editor of Technical Education Books for the McGraw-Hill Book Company. He has contributed numerous articles to automotive and engineering magazines and has written several outstanding books which are listed below. He was formerly Editor-in-Chief of the *McGraw-Hill Encyclopedia of Science and Technology.*

William H. Crouse's outstanding work in the automotive field has earned for him membership in the Society of Automotive Engineers and in the American Society for Engineering Education.

BOOKS BY WILLIAM H. CROUSE

McGraw-Hill Automotive Mechanics Series
  Automotive Chassis and Body
  Automotive Electrical Equipment
  Automotive Engines
  Automotive Fuel, Lubricating, and Cooling
    Systems
  Automotive Transmissions and Power Trains
Automotive Engine Design
Electrical Appliance Servicing
Everyday Automobile Repairs
Everyday Household Appliance Repairs
General Power Mechanics
Science Marvels of Tomorrow
Tests for use with Automotive Mechanics
Understanding Science
Shop Workbook for Automotive Chassis
Shop Workbook for Automotive Electricity
Shop Workbook for Automotive Engines
Shop Workbook for Automotive Service
  and Trouble-shooting
Shop Workbook for Automotive Tools

Automotive Mechanics

ISBN 07-014668-3

5 6 7 8 9 10   VHVH   79 78 77 76 75 74 73 72

PREFACE

This is the sixth edition of *Automotive Mechanics*. It has been largely rewritten and completely reset in a modern, more readable type. Hundreds of new illustrations have been added. All illustrations have been reworked to utilize the second color. A portion of the book has been printed in full color. Many other innovations will be found.

The "CAUTIONS" and other important notices are indicated in a second color for quick student recognition. Related publications are available to assist the student and teacher. A student study guide is being prepared which will provide the student with much self-help material. It outlines each chapter in *Automotive Mechanics,* lists the new terms introduced which the student should learn, provides added explanations of difficult points, and has a variety of tests the students can take (with answers in the back of the guide) so he can check himself on his progress.

In addition, a revised edition of the widely used *Tests for use with Automotive Mechanics* has been prepared, correlated to the sixth edition of the textbook. This provides the instructor with ready-made and convenient tests so he can check the progress of his students.

Also, an *Instructor's Guide for Automotive Mechanics* has been prepared for the sixth edition. This guide will provide the instructor with additional insight into the structure of the textbook and how it was designed to be used for both the classroom and the shop. The answers to the tests in the test book are included in the instructor's guide.

New editions of the five *Automotive Mechanics Shop Workbooks* have also been prepared. These are correlated to the *Automotive Mechanics* textbook, and also to the five textbooks in the *Automotive Mechanics Series.*

Current technical and service literature issued by automotive manufacturers both here and abroad was analyzed during the revision to assure proper coverage of all new developments. In addition, the author visited automotive manufacturers' service research facilities to study the latest in servicing techniques. As a result, the most modern testing equipment and procedures are covered in the book. At the request of many teachers, the fundamentals behind automotive operation—the physical principles—have been strengthened. Also, much new material on new automotive developments has been included. Anti-skid devices, new piston rings, high-performance pistons, smog control, overhead-camshaft engines, thermostatically controlled air cleaners, new automatic transmissions and disk brakes, new tires, and much more are to be found in the new edition.

During the revision, the author and publisher consulted with scores of classroom teachers who used the previous edition. Their day-to-day experience in teaching from the book enabled them to offer many excellent suggestions. Thus, many of the improvements found in the present edition are directly attributable to these interested and helpful teachers. To these many friends, the author wishes to express his deep appreciation. Special thanks are due to William L. MacNeal, Joseph G. McCabe, and Richard Ranft for taking time out from busy schedules to participate in a lengthy round-table discussion of the plans for the new edition. Their many years of experience in teaching and supervising automotive mechanics gave the author and publisher new insights into the needs in this field. The results of their cooperative efforts are evident in the improved appearance, coverage, reading level, and teachability of the new edition of *Automotive Mechanics.*

Automotive Mechanics provides a complete introductory course on the subject. It covers the theory of operation and the construction, maintenance, repair, and adjustment of automotive components. With minor exceptions, it covers the full content of the automotive courses listed in the *Automotive Industry–Vocational Education Conference's Standards for Automotive Service Instructions in Schools.* The student who completes the *Automotive Mechanics* textbook, therefore, covers the full basic curriculum established by the top authorities in vocational education and in the automotive industry. No additional textbooks are required for the student to meet the standards set by the automotive industry and the American Vocational Association.

WILLIAM H. CROUSE

CONTENTS

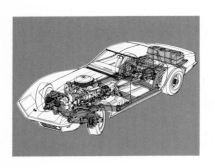

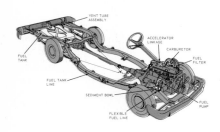

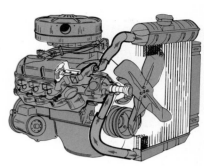
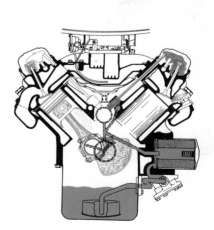

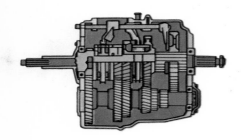

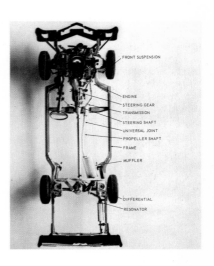

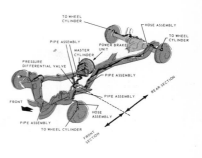

REMEMBERING WHAT YOU READ

When you are reading relatively unfamiliar subject matter, it is hard to remember what you read. We have all had the experience of reading a page with wandering mind, half convinced that everything is clear, and then suddenly realizing that nothing on that page has stuck with us. This is almost worse than not trying to read at all. For if you continue to do this, you form a bad habit that is hard to break. However, there is a way to break such a habit and to improve your reading skills so that you do remember what you read.

First, pause after every paragraph or even after every sentence and tell yourself just what you have read. Repeat the sense of it. That is, try to pick out the basic facts in the sentence or paragraph and tell yourself—out loud if you want to—what the facts are.

For example, suppose that you read, while studying about the engine, that "There are two openings, or ports, in the enclosed end of the engine cylinder." Now, what have you just read? Tell yourself the facts, but in your own words. You might say, for instance, "One end of the cylinder is closed except for two openings called ports."

See what you've done? You have taken the sentence and repeated the sense of it to yourself in your own words. You have intelligently thought about it. You have learned an important fact about engine cylinders. By now you will find it hard to forget that the enclosed end of the engine cylinder has two ports.

To learn a fact, therefore, think about it intelligently. Phrase it in your own words. That is the essence of studying. Just remember—and use—the procedure. It will be hard at first, but as you progress, it will become increasingly easier. Soon, if you continue to use the procedure, you will find that it has become second nature to you. Furthermore, the facts will stick with you. Your memory will improve.

1

The Automobile and Automotive Industry

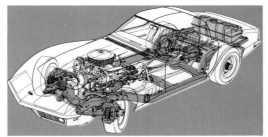

This chapter describes the history and development of the modern automobile. It is an introduction to the automobile itself.

§ 1–1. THE FIRST GASOLINE AUTOMOBILES

Perhaps the first "automobile" propelled by a gas engine was made in 1863. It had a one-cylinder engine using lighting gas (not liquid gasoline) as fuel. The French inventor, Lenoir, actually drove it 6 miles. Much experimental work went on during the next few years, both on engines and on the carriages, or bodies, in which they could be mounted. By 1855 Daimler and Benz, in Germany, had built vehicles that ran on liquid fuel similar to gasoline. In the early 1890's, the French firm of Daimler and Panhard began the manufacture of automobiles with the engine in front and with a

transmission and drive chain that carried the power to the rear wheels.

The first successful American car was built by the Duryea Brothers (Charles and Frank) in Massachusetts in 1893. Other American inventors were soon experimenting and building their own versions of the "horseless carriage." By 1896, Henry Ford, Ransom Olds, Alexander Winton, and Charles King had built automobiles that ran more or less successfully. Much of this work was done in and around Detroit, Michigan.

By 1900, several factories had been set up in Detroit and elsewhere to make automobiles. Two of

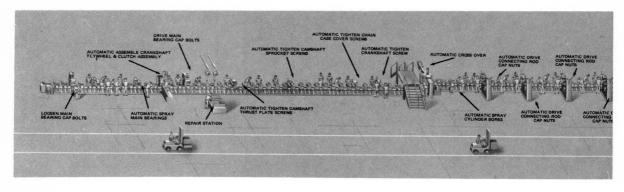

Fig. 1-1. Bird's-eye view of an automatic engine assembly line. Many of the operations being performed on this line are done by automatic machines. Engines move from left to right. *(The Cross Company)*

the most important ideas that these early inventors and manufacturers developed were interchangeability and mass production.

1. Interchangeability. Interchangeability of parts was a relatively new idea in 1900. Before then, many of the individual parts for machines were more or less handmade. Each was different from the others, and each part had to be hand-fitted to the machine. This was a long and costly process, and when a part wore out a new one had to be made by hand.

The new idea was to make parts identical to each other. Thus, all pistons and other parts for a particular type of engine were made to be as nearly alike as possible. Screws, nuts, washers, and other such parts were standardized. All this required precision machinery that could turn out thousands of identical parts. Then, when an engine was being assembled, it was not necessary to fit each part separately. Everything would go together with a minimum of special fitting work.

2. Mass production. Along with interchangeability came the idea of mass production. If all parts were made to be interchangeable, you would not have to stop to fit each part to the machine. The job of building an engine, for example, was simplified to the point of merely installing the parts onto or into the engine block. Later came the idea of having the assemblers stand in one place as the machine being assembled was moved along on a conveyor belt (Fig. 1-1). Henry Ford was the first automotive manufacturer to use the conveyor belt. In 1913, he developed an assembly line in which the automobile frame was pulled along on a conveyor

and workmen on both sides attached parts to it. These parts were fed to the workmen by secondary conveyors. This reduced assembly time for an automobile from a day and a half or two days to less than two hours. Futhermore, it now became possible for thousands of cars to come off the end of an assembly line every day.

In the years that followed, the techniques of mass production were further developed, just as the automobile itself was improved each year. At the same time, the road system in the United States was tremendously extended and improved.

By 1970, there were more than 100 million automobiles, trucks, and buses in the United States operating on nearly 4 million miles of streets and highways. Today, of course, the United States is a nation on wheels, and the automotive vehicle has become a basic necessity. Furthermore, the business of making and servicing automobiles has become one of the biggest businesses in the world, giving employment to about one out of every seven working men and women in the United States.

§ 1-2. THE AUTOMOTIVE INDUSTRY The automotive industry employs millions of men and women directly. Also, because of the enormous quantities of raw materials, such as steel, cloth, glass, and rubber, that the automotive industry uses, it provides jobs for millions of other people in related industries.

Each year the automotive industry of the United States produces more than seven million new cars, varying in price from less than $2,000 to more than $10,000. In addition, several hundred thousand

2

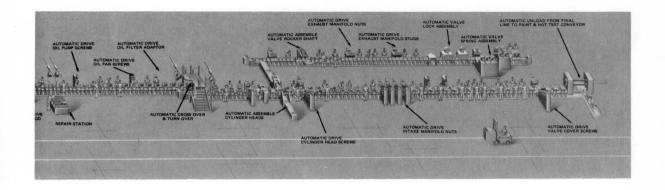

foreign-built cars are imported into the United States each year.

There are also millions of engine-powered machines built each year for agricultural, construction, and manufacturing operations. Every year more than six million small engines are built for lawn mowers, power saws, snow removers, and similar equipment.

One of the most important jobs in the world today is to keep all this powered equipment operating, and only trained people can do that. The need is urgent, and the opportunities are great. Men who have learned how to service and repair automotive equipment have taken a big step forward toward a satisfying career in the automotive industry.

§ 1–3. OPPORTUNITIES IN THE AUTOMOTIVE INDUSTRY

There are more than 12 million men and women working in the automotive industry. This means that there are many good job opportunities for you. You are making a good start by studying automotive mechanics. Most of the better-paying jobs require a knowledge of how the automobile operates and how it must be serviced and maintained.

What are some of the jobs you can look forward to?

First, of course, is the automotive mechanic. Today, he is a highly respected, skilled, and well-paid worker. His income compares favorably with that of men in other skilled professions. His services are always in demand.

For many men, a job as an automotive mechanic becomes a stepping stone to greater things. For the automotive mechanic can move up to become service manager, parts manager, or sales manager of an automotive shop or dealer agency. He might someday be able to open his own shop and have others work for him in his own business. A great majority of the independent service garages and service stations in the United States are owned and operated by good automotive mechanics who have moved up the ladder. There are about 30,000 automobile dealers, 100,000 independent garages, and 200,000 service stations. So you can see that there are big opportunities for the hard-working man who knows his business.

But that's not all. If a man knows automobiles and has a good personality, he might become an automotive jobber salesman or a field representative of one of the parts manufacturers. He might move on up to be a factory representative of an automobile manufacturer, working out of a zone office or out of the factory. Or perhaps he might be invited to come into the factory where he would have the opportunity to work his way up through the office or manufacturing departments.

It can happen. Take the case of one self-trained machinist who started at the bottom and worked his way up to become head of a giant corporation that now bears his name—Walter P. Chrysler! But this is only one example among thousands. Many men have started at the bottom and have moved up to positions of great responsibility in the automotive business.

These successful men had one thing in common—the ability to study and work hard. You can

3

Fig. 1–2. Partial cutaway view of a V-8 engine prepared for display at a show. Show engines are carefully cut away and painted so people can see how they are made. *(Chrysler Motors Corporation)*

succeed in the same way—by studying and working hard—by getting everything you can out of this book and out of the courses you are taking in school.

This book has been prepared with the assistance of experts in the automotive industry and, as you will note, has hundreds of illustrations supplied by the automotive manufacturers. The book has one major purpose—to prepare you for an interesting and well-paid job in the automotive field. This is your book to study to help you make your future successful.

§ 1–4. COMPONENTS OF THE AUTOMOBILE Basically, the automobile consists of four components (Fig. 1–12 shows three of these). They are:
1. The engine, or source of power.
2. The framework, or support for the engine and wheels, which includes the steering and braking systems.
3. The power train, or mechanism that carries the power from the engine to the car wheels.
4. The body.

To these might be added the car-body accessories, which include the heater, lights, radio, and other devices that contribute to the convenience and comfort of the car passengers.

§ 1–5. THE ENGINE The engine (Figs. 1–2 to 1–5) is the source of power that makes the wheels go around and the car move. The automobile engine is an internal-combustion engine because the fuel (gasoline) is burned inside it. (A steam engine is an external-combustion engine because the fuel is burned outside the engine.)

The burning of gasoline inside the engine produces high pressure in the engine combustion chambers. This high pressure forces pistons to move; the movement is carried by connecting rods to the engine crankshaft. The crankshaft is

Fig. 1–3. V-8 engine cut away and painted for display. *(Chrysler Motors Corporation)*

Fig. 1–4. Cutaway view of a slant-six engine. *(Chrysler Motors Corporation)*

thus made to rotate; the rotary motion is carried through the power train to the car wheels so that they rotate and the car moves.

On a later page, we shall describe these parts and go into full detail on how the engine is constructed and how it operates. For the moment, we can remember that the engine requires a fuel system to supply it with a mixture of air and fuel.

The fuel system does this by pumping liquid gasoline from a tank into the carburetor, a mixing device that mixes the gasoline with air. The mixture is delivered to the engine where it is burned. The engine also needs a cooling system; the combustion of the air-fuel mixture in the

Fig. 1–5. Cutaway view of a six-cylinder engine used in the Camaro. *(Chevrolet Motor Division of General Motors Corporation)*

engine creates a very high temperature (as high as 6000°F). The cooling system takes heat away from the engine by circulating a liquid coolant (water mixed with antifreeze) between the engine and a radiator. The coolant gets hot as it goes through the engine. It cools off as it goes through the radiator. Thus, it continually takes heat away from the engine, where it could do damage, and delivers it to the radiator. Air passing through the radiator takes heat away from the radiator. Thus, the heat goes from the engine to the radiator and then to the passing air.

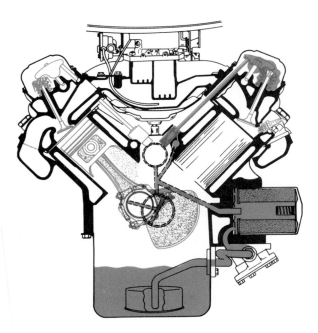

Fig. 1–6. Lubricating system of a V-8 engine in sectional view from the end.

The engine also includes a lubricating system (Fig. 1–6). The purpose of the lubricating system is to supply all moving parts inside the engine with lubricating oil; the oil keeps moving parts from wearing excessively. The engine requires a fourth system, the ignition system. The ignition system provides high-voltage electric sparks that ignite, or set fire to, the charges of air-fuel mixture in the engine combustion chambers.

These four systems are discussed briefly in following sections. Then, in later chapters, we shall describe them in detail.

§ 1–6. FUEL SYSTEM

The fuel system (Fig. 1–7) consists of a tank in which gasoline is stored, a pump which pumps gasoline from the tank, a carburetor which mixes the gasoline with air, and fuel lines (metal tubes) connecting the three.

1. Fuel pump. There are two types of fuel pump, mechanical and electric. The mechanical type is mounted on the engine. It contains an airtight, flexible diaphragm attached by linkage to a rocker arm. The rocker arm rests on an eccentric, or offset, section of the engine camshaft. When the engine operates, the eccentric forces the rocker arm to rock back and forth, causing the diaphragm to move up and down. This produces a pumping action that pumps gasoline from the fuel tank to the carburetor.

The electric fuel pump uses electricity from the battery or alternator to operate a plunger, bellows, diaphragm, or impeller. This action pumps fuel from the fuel tank to the carburetor.

One type of electric fuel pump is mounted inside the fuel tank. It contains a small electric motor that spins an impeller which pushes gasoline from the fuel tank to the carburetor.

2. Carburetor. The carburetor (Fig. 1–8) is essentially a mixing device which mixes liquid gasoline with air. In this process, it throws a fine spray of gasoline into air passing through the carburetor on its way to the engine. The gasoline vaporizes and mixes with the air to form a highly combustible mixture. This mixture then enters the engine combustion chambers, where it is ignited. It burns, causing the engine to produce power.

Carburetors have been made in a great variety of sizes and shapes. It is estimated that more than 500 models of carburetors have been used on American cars in the past five years alone. Actually, all carburetors are basically the same. They all have a reservoir (called the float bowl), in which gasoline from the fuel pump is stored, and gasoline

Fig. 1–6A. Cutaway view of a V-8 engine and transmission, specially prepared for show purposes. *(Chevrolet Motor Division of General Motors Corporation)*

passages through which the gasoline can flow to the discharge nozzles. Also, the carburetor has larger passages through which air can flow. The air first goes through an air cleaner (Fig. 1–9) on the carburetor, which filters out dirt and dust which would otherwise get into the engine and damage it.

As the air flows through the carburetor, it picks up gasoline that is flowing from the discharge nozzles. The mixture then leaves the carburetor and flows into the engine cylinders. On later pages, we will describe exactly what happens to the mixture in the engine cylinders. Briefly, however, you might like to know that the mixture is pressed into a smaller volume (compressed) and then set on fire. An explosion follows, and the pressure caused by this explosion causes mechanical parts to move in the engine so that the engine produces power.

Carburetors have a number of special devices to take care of different operating conditions. For example, when you "step on the gas" to speed up and go around another car, you push down on the accelerator pedal. This causes an extra squirt of gasoline to shoot out into the air passing through the carburetor. The extra gasoline then gives the engine the boost it needs to speed up. Carburetors also have high-speed circuits; these are special passages which allow extra gasoline to flow steadily into the passing air when the accelerator is mostly or fully open for high-speed driving.

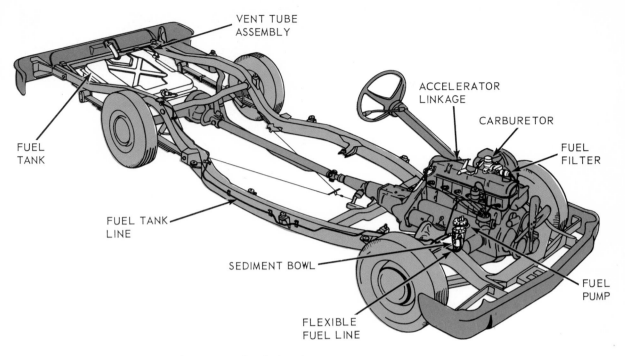

Fig. 1-7. Schematic drawing of an automotive fuel system.

And as you probably already know, when you try to start a cold engine, extra gasoline is needed. A device called the choke, which on most cars works automatically, causes the carburetor to deliver extra gasoline during cranking with the engine cold. All these devices, and others, are discussed in detail in the chapter on the fuel system.

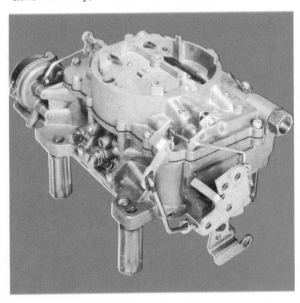

Fig. 1-8. External view of an automotive carburetor.

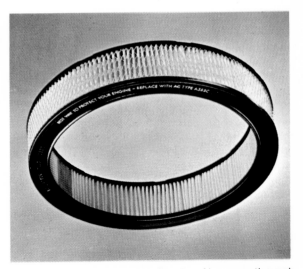

Fig. 1-9. Air cleaner for a carburetor. Air passes through this on the way to the engine and the filter removes dust from the air. *(AC Spark Plug Division of General Motors Corporation)*

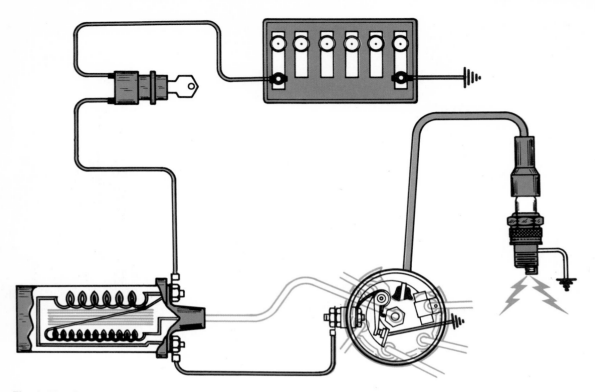

Fig. 1–10. Schematic drawing of an automotive ignition system.

§ 1–7. IGNITION SYSTEM The ignition system (Fig. 1–10) is part of the electric system of the automobile. Its purpose is to produce high-voltage surges (up to 20,000 volts) and to deliver them to the combustion chambers in the engine. These high-voltage surges then cause electric sparks in the combustion chambers. The sparks ignite, or set fire to, the air-fuel mixture in the combustion chambers so that it burns and causes the engine to operate.

The ignition system consists of three basic parts: the ignition distributor, the ignition coil, and the spark plugs, together with the connecting wires. When the engine is running, the ignition coil is repeatedly connected to and disconnected from the battery. Every time the coil is connected, it becomes loaded with electrical energy. Then, when it is disconnected, the "load" of electrical energy is released in a high-voltage surge. This surge flows through the wiring to the spark plug in the engine cylinder that is ready to fire. You must understand that all this takes place very rapidly. At high speed, the whole series of events happens in less than one three-hundredth of a second. That is, there will be as many as 300 of these events

every second that the engine is running at high speed.

§ 1–8. LUBRICATING SYSTEM There are a great many moving metal parts in the engine. These parts must be protected by lubricating oil so that there will be no actual metal-to-metal contact. The moving parts, in effect, float on films of oil.

The lubricating system is built into the engine (Fig. 1–6). An oil pump takes oil from the oil pan and forces it through holes drilled in the engine block and crankshaft. This oil thereby reaches the various bearings that support rotating shafts and the different moving parts in the engine. It covers the surfaces of the moving parts to prevent metal-to-metal contact and undue wear of the parts.

If the moving parts were in actual metal-to-metal contact, the parts would soon wear out and would then have to be replaced. Rub your hands together, hard, and feel how hot they become. Then wash your hands in soap and water and feel how easily they slip on each other. Much the same thing happens in the engine; the oil allows the parts to slip on each other easily, without undue heat and wear.

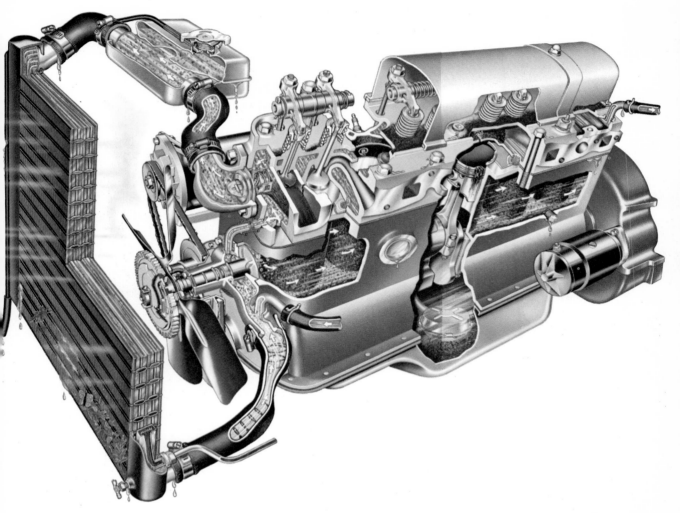

Fig. 1–11. Cooling system for an automotive engine. This illustration was especially prepared by the makers of Prestone antifreeze to show the various points in the cooling system where leakage of coolant can occur. *(Union Carbide Corporation)*

§ 1–9. COOLING SYSTEM A great deal of heat is produced in the engine by the burning of the air-fuel mixture. Some of this heat escapes from the engine through the exhaust gases (the hot gases left after the gasoline is burned). But enough remains in the engine to cause serious trouble unless removed by some other means. The cooling system (Fig. 1–11) takes care of this additional heat. The cooling system is built into the engine. There are hollow spaces around each engine cylinder and combustion chamber. These hollow spaces are called water jackets, since they are filled with water. When the engine is running, the water takes heat from the engine, becoming hot in the process. A water pump pumps the hot water from the engine water jackets into the radiator. The radiator has two sets of passages. One set carries water. The other set carries air (pulled through by car motion and the engine fan). As the hot water passes through, it gives up its heat to the air passing through. The cooled water then reenters the engine, where it can pick up more heat. In operation, water continuously circulates between the engine and radiator, carrying heat from the engine to the radiator. By this means, excessive engine temperatures are prevented.

Fig. 1–12. Automotive chassis showing many of the essential automotive parts normally hidden under the body. *(Oldsmobile Division of General Motors Corporation)*

§ 1–10. FRAME AND CHASSIS A frame is required to support the engine, car body, wheels, and other car components. Frames are made of channel, or U-shaped, sections, welded or riveted together. Cross bracing makes them rigid enough to withstand the shocks, blows, twists, and vibrations they meet in operation.

When the engine, wheels, power train, brakes, and steering system are installed on the frame, the assembly is then called the chassis (see Figs. 1–12 and 1–13).

In most cases, the engine is supported by the frame at three or four places. The supporting arrangement includes rubber pads, or washers, which are placed between the support lugs on the engine and the brackets on the frame. The rubber pads, or washers, prevent metal-to-metal contact. They thus absorb engine vibration and noise. They prevent this vibration and noise from being carried directly to the frame and consequently to the car body and passengers.

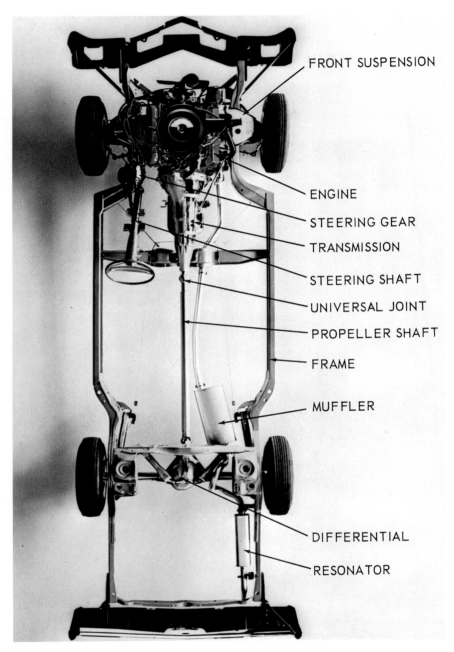

FRONT SUSPENSION

ENGINE

STEERING GEAR

TRANSMISSION

STEERING SHAFT

UNIVERSAL JOINT

PROPELLER SHAFT

FRAME

MUFFLER

DIFFERENTIAL

RESONATOR

Fig. 1–13. Another view of an automotive chassis, looking down from above. *(Oldsmobile Division of General Motors Corporation)*

§ 1–11. SPRINGS AND SHOCK ABSORBERS

The wheels are attached to the frame through springs (Figs. 1–12 to 1–17). The springs support the weight of the vehicle. They also allow the wheels to move up and down as the wheels meet holes or bumps in the road. Thus, little of this up-and-down movement is carried to the car frame, body, and passengers. Springs are of four types: coil, torsion bar, leaf, and air. All these are described and illustrated in later chapters.

Springs alone will not give a satisfactory ride; shock absorbers must be used with them. You can show why this is true with a small coil spring. Hang a weight on the spring. Lift the weight, and let it drop. It will move down, expanding the spring. Then the spring will rebound, pulling the weight up. The weight will move up and down (oscillate) for some time. On a car without shock absorbers, a similar action would take place. The repeated up-and-down movement of the springs and wheels would produce a very rough ride. Further, the driver would have great difficulty in controlling the car, particularly on curves.

To eliminate this excessive up-and-down movement of the springs and wheels, a shock absorber is placed at each wheel. Shock absorbers are filled with fluid. In operation, wheel movement causes the shock absorber to force this fluid through small openings (orifices). Since fluid can pass through restricted openings rather slowly, this puts a restraint on wheel and spring movement. The restraint imposed prevents excessive wheel movement. It also damps out the spring oscillations quickly after the hole or bump is passed.

Fig. 1–14. View of the front end of an automotive chassis, looking forward from the center of the car. *(Chevrolet Motor Division of General Motors Corporation)*

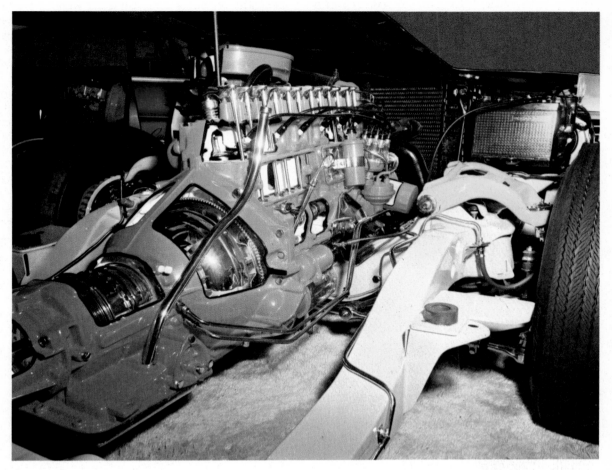

Fig. 1-15. Another view of the front end of an automotive chassis, looking forward from the center of the car. *(Chevrolet Motor Division of General Motors Corporation)*

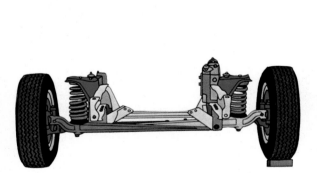

Fig. 1-16. "I-Beam" front suspension used on many Ford trucks. The right wheel is shown raised so that the I-Beam action can be seen. *(Ford Motor Company)*

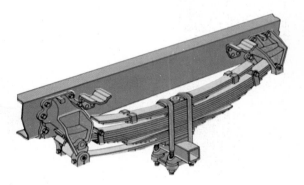

Fig. 1-17. Heavy-duty truck suspension system. *(Ford Motor Company)*

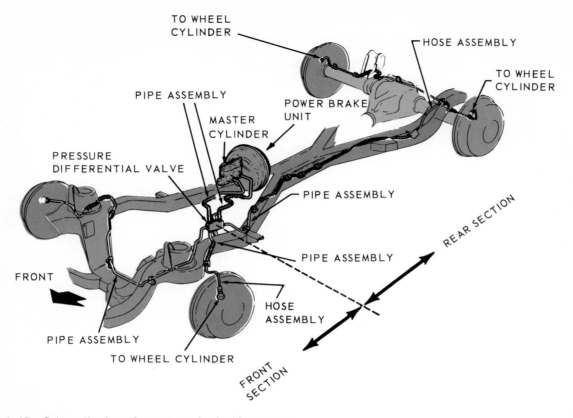

Fig. 1–18. Schematic view of an automotive braking system.

§ **1–12. STEERING SYSTEM** The steering system permits the front wheels to be pivoted on their supports to the right or left so that the car can be steered. The steering wheel is mounted on a steering shaft that extends into the steering gear. The bottom end of the shaft has a worm gear that rotates as the wheel is turned. A gear sector is meshed with the worm gear; rotation of the worm gear causes the gear sector to rotate. This movement causes the pitman arm, attached to the sector, to swing to the right or left. This action, in turn, pushes or pulls on the tie rods attached to the pitman arm. The steering-knuckle arms, attached to the front wheels, are therefore forced to swing the wheels to the right or left on their pivots.

§ **1–13. BRAKES** Brakes are necessary to slow or stop the car. Practically all cars use hydraulic brakes (which operate by applying pressure to a fluid). A typical hydraulic-brake system is shown in Fig. 1–18. In most modern brake systems, there is a fluid-filled cylinder, called the master cylinder, which contains two separate sections. There is a piston in each section and both pistons are connected to a brake pedal in the driver's compartment. When the brake pedal is pushed by the driver, the two pistons move in the two sections of the master cylinder. This forces brake fluid out and through the brake lines, or tubes, to the brake mechanisms at the wheels. In a typical system, the brake fluid from one section of the master cylinder goes to the two front-wheel brakes. The brake fluid from the other section goes to the two rear-wheel brakes. The purpose of this is that, if one section fails, the other section will still provide braking.

There are two different types of brake mechanisms at the wheels, the drum-and-shoe type, and the disk type. In the drum-and-shoe type, there is a wheel brake cylinder with two pistons. When brake fluid is forced into the brake cylinder by the action at the master cylinder, the two pistons are forced outward. This causes the curved brake shoes to move into contact with the brake drum. The brake shoes apply friction to the brake drum, forcing it and the wheel to slow or stop.

In the disk type, a rotating disk, attached to the wheel, is positioned between flat brake shoes. One or more pistons, actuated by the brake fluid from the master cylinder, force the shoes into contact with the rotating disk and this slows or stops the car.

§ 1-14. POWER TRAIN The power train (Figs. 1-19 and 1-20) contains several mechanisms which carry the engine power to the rear wheels. These are the clutch, transmission, propeller shaft, differential, and rear axles.

NOTE: Cars equipped with automatic transmissions normally do not have a clutch. On these, the transmission operates automatically so that the driver is not required to use a clutch or to shift gears.

The clutch is a friction-type uncoupling device. It is linked to a clutch pedal in the driver's compartment. When the driver pushes down on the clutch pedal, the linkage forces a flat disk, or plate, to move. This movement releases the pressure from a friction disk. With the pressure released, there is no friction at work in the clutch, and the

power flow is therefore interrupted. Then, the engine runs without transmitting power to the power train.

The transmission (Figs 1-21 to 1-24) provides different gear ratios between the engine and wheels. This is necessary with the gasoline engine, since the engine produces little power at low speed. Thus, for accelerating the car from a standing start, considerable power is required; the engine should be running at a fairly high speed. The driver, therefore, shifts the transmission gears into first; this gear position permits the engine to run at a fairly high speed while turning the rear wheels at a fairly low speed. A typical first-gear ratio would be that the engine shaft turns 12 times to turn the rear wheels once. Thus, the engine develops high power, and the car moves away from the curb and accelerates quickly. Next, the driver shifts to second (momentarily declutching to permit movement of the gears in the transmission). In second, the car accelerates to a higher speed. In second, a typical ratio would be 8:1 (8 to 1). Finally, the driver shifts to third. In this gear

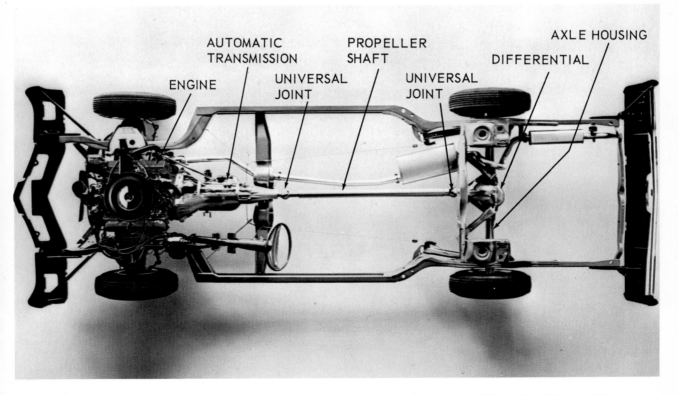

Fig. 1-19. Top view of an automotive chassis with power-train components named. *(Oldsmobile Division of General Motors Corporation)*

15

Fig. 1–20. View from the bottom of the Ford Bronco, showing the suspension parts in yellow and the power-train parts in light blue. This is a four-wheel drive vehicle, with propeller shafts connecting to differentials at both the rear and front wheels. *(Ford Motor Company)*

FRONT
DIFFERENTIAL

FRONT
PROPELLER
SHAFT

TRANSFER
CASE

REAR
PROPELLER
SHAFT

REAR
DIFFERENTIAL

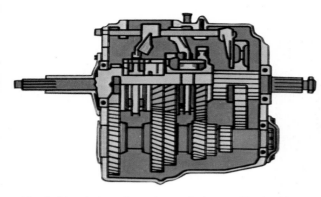

Fig. 1–21. Automotive transmission. *(Ford Motor Company)*

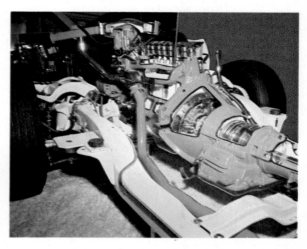

Fig. 1–23. Cutaway views of an automatic transmission and engine. *(Chevrolet Motor Division of General Motors Corporation)*

Fig. 1–22. Cutaway view of an automatic transmission used on the Chevrolet Camaro. *(Chevrolet Motor Division of General Motors Corporation)*

Fig. 1–24. Cutaway of an automatic transmission, especially prepared for display. *(Chevrolet Motor Division of General Motors Corporation)*

position, there is a direct drive through the transmission; the propeller shaft turns at the same speed as the engine crankshaft. In third, a typical ratio would be 4:1. There is another gear position, reverse. In this position, the propeller shaft is made to rotate in a reverse direction so that the car goes backwards.

The propeller shaft is a drive shaft to carry the power from the transmission to the rear-wheel axles. It contains two devices, a universal joint (or joints) and a slip joint. These joints permit the shaft to lengthen and shorten and, in effect, to bend. This shaft flexibility is necessary because the rear wheels move up and down as a result of spring actions at the rear of the car.

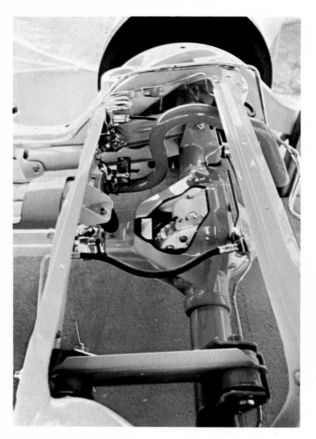

Fig. 1-25. A view from the side of an automotive chassis, showing the differential cut away. *(Chevrolet Motor Division of General Motors Corporation)*

Fig. 1-26. Close up view of cutaway differential. For show jobs such as this, the cutaway parts are protected by a plastic shield. *(Chevrolet Motor Division of General Motors Corporation)*

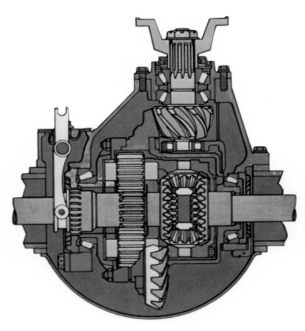

Fig. 1-27. Sectional view of a two-speed differential. This unit is for use on trucks. The driver can shift the differential up or down and thus double the number of gear ratios between the engine and the wheels. *(Ford Motor Company)*

§ 1-15. DIFFERENTIAL The differential (Figs. 1-25 to 1-27) contains gears that carry the driving power from the propeller shaft to the rear-wheel axles. A differential is necessary so that the two rear wheels can rotate different amounts when the car goes around a turn. As this happens, the outside wheel must turn more times that the inside wheel. The differential permits this action while still delivering power to both rear wheels.

All these power-train components, as well as the other components of the automobile, are covered in detail in following chapters.

Fig. 1-28. An automotive diagnostic line. As the car is moved along this line, the testing equipment checks the various components on the car. The customer can watch the proceedings through the show windows and can also read the meters showing the results of the tests. *(Bear Manufacturing Company)*

§ 1-16. AUTOMOTIVE SERVICE Servicing automobiles is a big business. With a hundred million cars, trucks, and buses running billions of miles a year, a tremendous amount of service is needed. By service, we mean periodic checking of all the various parts on the car (Fig. 1-28), making adjustments to the different mechanisms when necessary, replacing parts when they wear out, and, in general, restoring new-car performance.

This service work requires a great variety of activities. Sometimes you simply turn a nut or screw. Or it may be as simple as taking the battery caps off to give the battery some water. On the other hand, it may require removal of bolts so that parts can be lifted off and internal mechanisms exposed. Then, these internal parts can be adjusted, repaired, or replaced.

In the chapters that follow, we will discuss all the mechanisms on the automobile, from the engine, transmission, and differential, to the steering and suspension system. The earlier chapters describe how these components work. The later chapters tell you how to service them—that is, how to check, adjust, repair, or replace them.

Fig. 1–29. An automobile prepared for public display. The car is enclosed in a plastic bubble. The body is periodically raised so the chassis can be seen. *(Six Flags Over Georgia* and *Chevrolet Division of General Motors Corporation)*

MAKING NOTES IN YOUR NOTEBOOK

You will normally make notes in your notebook on two occasions: when you are studying and when you are working in the shop.

When you are studying your lesson in the textbook, have your notebook open. Start with a fresh notebook page at the beginning of the lesson. Write the lesson number or page numbers of your textbook at the top of the notebook page, along with the date (or perhaps your instructor has some instructions for you to follow). As you read your lesson, jot down the high spots.

In the shop you will use a different approach. You can't carry your notebook around with you all the time. Keep your notebook on your bench or in a drawer. After you complete a job, jot down the important points covered or special problems encountered. These notations are simply reminders. You can redo the page in the evening.

You can also make sketches in your notebook of various wiring diagrams, structural arrangements, machining methods, and so on, that are more easily drawn than described in words.

You can insert articles and illustrations you run across in technical publications that relate to your studies. For instance, you might come across the wiring circuit and description of a new ignition system. You could clip this out and insert it in the electrical section of your notebook.

Fig. 1-30. Cutaway view of a V-8 engine especially prepared for show. Note how the various parts have been painted to make them stand out. As you study the later chapters that describe engines, turn back to this and the other illustrations in this chapter and identify the different parts of the engine. *(Chrysler Motors Corporation)*

ORGANIZING YOUR NOTEBOOK

When you write something down in your notebook, you "write it down in your brain," too. This means that you can remember it more easily. But if it does become hazy in your mind, you can always refresh your memory by looking it up in your notebook.

The better you keep your notebook, the easier it will be to find the facts you have written down. For example, you can organize your notebook into sections (engines, electric systems, steering, and so on) or even keep separate notebooks on each topic. With a loose-leaf notebook, you can remove old pages and insert new ones. You can rearrange the pages to suit yourself. If you get a page dirty, you can redo it and throw the dirty page away.

As you develop your notebook, you will find that it becomes increasingly valuable as a storehouse of information. If it is properly organized, you will refer again and again to the material you have compiled in it. You will be proud of your notebook.

CHAPTER

2

Shop Practice

This chapter describes automotive-shop hand tools and explains how to use and take care of them. It discusses safety in the shop, that is, the safe way to work and to handle tools. It also discusses various fasteners, such as screws, bolts, nuts, studs, washers, and snap rings.

---

§ 2-1. SHOPWORK Work that is done in the automotive shop is quite varied. All automotive service jobs, however, are made up of a few basically simple steps:

1. Measuring. You have to measure to find out what service the automobile requires. In some cases, you measure length or thickness or diameter. In other cases, you measure vacuum or power or voltage or speed or pressure. Taking some sort of measurement is often the first step in an automotive service job.

2. Disassembly. You may have to do a disassembly job when the measurements show that something is wrong and repair work is needed.

3. Metalwork, or machining. Often, the repair job requires removal of metal from parts (as by filing, honing, drilling, and so on). When this is done by a machine (such as an electric drill or hone), the process is often called *machining*.

4. Installing new parts. Sometimes you find that old parts have worn out (such as piston rings, valves, bearings, and so on). So you must fit and install new parts. These actions usually require measuring and machining.

5. Reassembly. After the necessary work is done on the different parts of the mechanism being repaired, the parts must be put back together. The mechanism must be reassembled and reinstalled on the car.

6. Adjustments. Some of the mechanisms on the automobile must be adjusted after a repair job. This compensates for wear, restores the original specifications, and so on.

You will learn how all these jobs are done on the engine and other automobile components as you study this book. Just remember this: Some of the service jobs may appear complicated. But every one of them can be broken down into the six steps listed above. And each step is basically simple.

Thus, not one of the automotive service jobs is really complicated. They are all made up of a series of simple steps.

§ 2-2. SPECIFICATIONS In the automotive shop, you often hear the word "specifications," or "specs." The specifications give you the correct measurements. The engineers who design the car, the production men who build it, and the engineers who plan the proper ways to service it— all these men work out the proper measurements, or specifications, for the various parts of the car. They are listed in the automobile manufacturer's shop manual. Then, whenever the automotive mechanic is doing a service job, he goes to the shop manual to look up the specifications. In this way, he can compare the measurements he finds on the car with those which the factory specifies. The amount that the measurements are off tells him what he must do. For example, suppose that the mechanic measures the cylinders on the car and finds that they have worn to a larger size. If they are only slightly oversized, he can take care of the wear by installing new piston rings. But if the wear is considerable, the cylinders must be machined (honed or bored).

The specifications tell you what the measurements should be. When things are not "up to spec," then a repair or readjustment job may be required.

§ 2-3. FASTENERS Fasteners include screws, bolts, studs, nuts, cotter pins, lock washers, snap rings, keys, and rivets. Before we discuss these further, let us note the difference among screws, bolts, and studs. These are often confused.

1. Screws (Fig. 2-1). The term "machine screw" refers to the type of fastener which is driven, or turned, into drilled and threaded holes in metal parts. The screw is turned down into the threaded hole to hold another part in place. There are many varieties and types of screw.

2. Bolts (Fig. 2–1). Bolts require nuts. The bolt is put through holes in parts to be attached to each other, and the nut is then turned onto the bolt.

3. Studs (Fig. 2–1). Studs, or stud bolts, as they are often called, are like bolts or screws except that they have no heads and are threaded at both ends. One end goes into a threaded hole, and a nut is turned onto the other end.

§ 2–4. THREADS Screws, bolts, and studs have external threads. Nuts and threaded holes for screws, bolts, and studs have internal threads. Threads are made with taps and dies (see § 2–20). Threads (or *screw threads*, to use the full name) are designated in several ways. They are designated by size (by outside diameter or by a number), by the number of threads per inch (or *pitch*), by thread series (coarseness or fineness of thread), and by thread class (quality of finish and fit).

1. Size. Size means the diameter of the bolt or screw (Fig. 2–2); it is the outside diameter of the threads. Diameters above 1/4 inch are classified by the actual measurement in fractions of an inch (1/4, 5/16, 3/8, and so on). Diameters below 1/4 inch are classified by number (0, 1, 2, 3, and so on up to 12). The table (Fig. 2–3) shows sizes of some of the smaller screws or bolts.

2. Pitch. Pitch is the number of threads per inch (Fig. 2–2). You can determine the pitch of the threads of any bolt or screw by counting the number of threads in an inch (Fig. 2–2). Or you can use a regular thread-pitch gauge (Fig. 2–4). Note that the gauge has a number of blades and that each blade has a different number of teeth per inch. Each blade is marked with the number of teeth it has per inch. To determine the number of teeth per inch, or pitch, of a bolt, you try different blades until you find the one that fits the the threads.

3. Thread series. Generally speaking, the larger the diameter of a bolt, the coarser the thread. By "coarse" we mean largeness of the threads. A coarse thread is comparatively large, and there are relatively few threads per inch. The opposite of coarse is *fine*. A fine thread is comparatively small, and there are more threads per inch. There are six different series of threads, as indicated in the table (Fig. 2–3). The coarse-thread series (designated UNC, for Unified National Coarse,* or NC, for National Coarse) is for gray iron, soft metals, and plastics. A coarse thread shortens

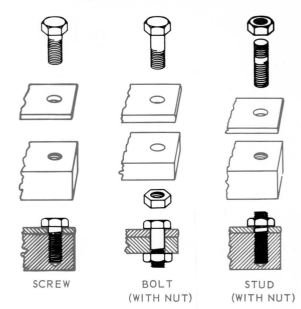

SCREW | BOLT (WITH NUT) | STUD (WITH NUT)

Fig. 2–1. A screw, a bolt, and a stud. The top views show the attaching parts separated but aligned in readiness for assembly. The bottom views are sectional views.

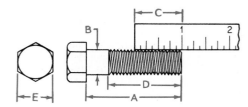

Fig. 2–2. A hex-head screw or bolt with parts named: *A*, length; *B*, diameter; *C*, pitch, or threads per inch; *D*, length of thread; *E*, size of wrench required for head.

disassembly and reassembly time, since a coarse-threaded bolt requires fewer turns to remove and install. The fine-thread series (designated UNF, for Unified National Fine,* or NF, for National Fine) is for applications where greater bolt strength and additional accuracy of assembly are required. The extra-fine-thread series (UNEF, for Unified National Extra Fine,* or NEF, for National Extra

---

* The term "Unified" refers to a thread form which is somewhat different from other thread forms. Before this thread form was designed, United States screw-thread standards did not conform with British and Canadian standards. Thus, British and Canadian screws did not always fit American machinery, and vice versa. However, in 1948, a standard for an interchangeable thread (Unified National Coarse and Unified National Fine) was adopted, and industry is changing over to it in the three countries.

Size	Diameter (decimal)	Threads per inch					
		Coarse (UNC or NC)	Fine (UNF or NF)	Extra fine (UNEF or NEF)	8 thread series	12 thread series	16 thread series
0	0.0600	...	80				
1	0.0730	64	72				
2	0.0860	56	64				
3	0.0990	48	56				
4	0.1120	40	48				
5	0.1250	40	44				
6	0.1380	32	40				
8	0.1640	32	36				
10	0.1900	24	32				
12	0.2160	24	28	32			
$\frac{1}{4}$	0.2500	20	28	32			
$\frac{5}{16}$	0.3125	18	24	32			
$\frac{3}{8}$	0.3750	16	24	32			
$\frac{7}{16}$	0.4375	14	20	28			
$\frac{1}{2}$	0.5000	13	20	28		12	
$\frac{9}{16}$	0.5625	12	18	24		12	
$\frac{5}{8}$	0.6250	11	18	24		12	
$\frac{3}{4}$	0.7500	10	16	20	...	12	16
$\frac{7}{8}$	0.8750	9	14	20	...	12	16
1	1.0000	8	12	20	8	12	16
$1\frac{1}{8}$	1.1250	7	12	18	8	12	16
$1\frac{1}{4}$	1.2500	7	12	18	8	12	16
$1\frac{3}{8}$	1.3750	6	12	18	8	12	16
$1\frac{1}{2}$	1.5000	6	12	18	8	12	16

Fig. 2–3. Screw thread sizes and pitches.

Fine) uses a thread that is still finer. There are also the 8 thread series, the 12 thread series, and the 16 thread series. These are for use in larger sizes of bolt. Each series has the same pitch regardless of bolt size. Thus, in the 16 thread series, there are 16 threads per inch on all sizes of bolt (or $\frac{3}{4}$ inch up to 6 inches). Refer to the table (Fig. 2–3) for information on various thread series and sizes.

4. Thread classes. There are a number of different thread classes; the difference among classes is one of accuracy, or tolerance. That is, in one class of thread, the internal threads (or nut) fit the external threads (or bolt) rather tightly. Another class of thread has a looser fit. The intermediate fit is most widely used; the classes having a tight fit and a loose fit are confined to special applications. Actually, there are two systems of classification, the new Unified thread-standard classification (see footnote on page 24 for the explanation of "Unified") and the traditional Ameri-

Fig. 2–4. Thread-pitch gauge.

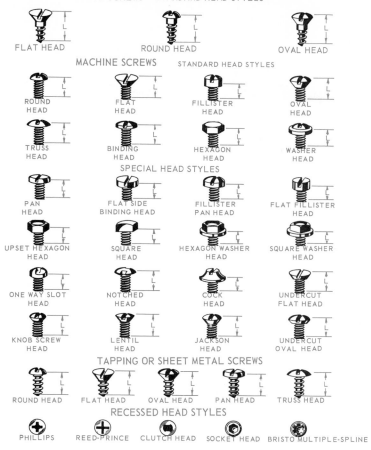

WOOD SCREWS STANDARD HEAD STYLES

FLAT HEAD ROUND HEAD OVAL HEAD

MACHINE SCREWS STANDARD HEAD STYLES

ROUND HEAD FLAT HEAD FILLISTER HEAD OVAL HEAD

TRUSS HEAD BINDING HEAD HEXAGON HEAD WASHER HEAD

SPECIAL HEAD STYLES

PAN HEAD FLAT SIDE BINDING HEAD FILLISTER PAN HEAD FLAT FILLISTER HEAD

UPSET HEXAGON HEAD SQUARE HEAD HEXAGON WASHER HEAD SQUARE WASHER HEAD

ONE WAY SLOT HEAD NOTCHED HEAD COCK HEAD UNDERCUT FLAT HEAD

KNOB SCREW HEAD LENTIL HEAD JACKSON HEAD UNDERCUT OVAL HEAD

TAPPING OR SHEET METAL SCREWS

ROUND HEAD FLAT HEAD OVAL HEAD PAN HEAD TRUSS HEAD

RECESSED HEAD STYLES

PHILLIPS REED-PRINCE CLUTCH HEAD SOCKET HEAD BRISTO MULTIPLE-SPLINE

METHOD OF MEASURING LENGTHS OF SCREWS INDICATED BY DISTANCE BETWEEN ARROWS-L: LENGTH

Fig. 2–5. Various types of screwheads. The recessed head styles require special screwdrivers as shown in Fig. 2-6. *(Detroit Power Screwdriver Company)*

can Standard. Ultimately, it is assumed that the American Standard will be dropped and the Unified classes used.

a. Unified classes. There are six Unified classes: 1A, 1B, 2A, 2B, 3A, and 3B. The letter A designates external threads (as on bolts, screws, and studs). The letter B designates internal threads (as in nuts). Classes 1A and 1B provide the loosest fit and permit easy and quick assembly even when the threads are dirty or somewhat battered. Classes 2A and 2B provide fairly tight fit and are used for most commercial products. For close tolerance and exceptionally uniform fit, classes 3A and 3B are used.

b. American Standard classes. There are two of these standards, 2 and 3. They correspond to some extent to the Unified classes 2A and 2B, and 3A and 3B.

5. Complete thread designation. As we noted at the start of this section, screw threads are designated in four ways: size, pitch, series, and class. For example, consider a $\frac{1}{4}$-20 UNC-2A thread. From this designation, we know that the diameter is $\frac{1}{4}$ inch, that there are 20 threads to an inch, that the thread is a Unified National Coarse, and that it is an external class 2 thread.

§ 2–5. SCREWS AND BOLTS As already noted (§ 2–3), screws, or machine screws, enter threaded holes, and bolts are used with nuts. However, as far as appearance is concerned, they may be very similar. Actually, a great variety of screws and bolts

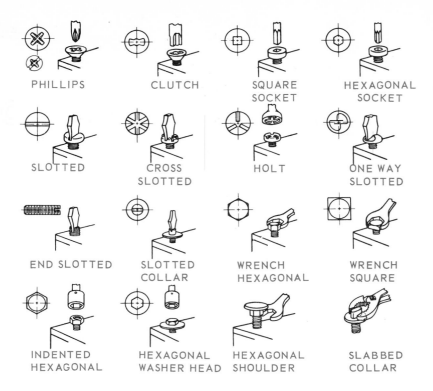

PHILLIPS   CLUTCH   SQUARE SOCKET   HEXAGONAL SOCKET

SLOTTED   CROSS SLOTTED   HOLT   ONE WAY SLOTTED

END SLOTTED   SLOTTED COLLAR   WRENCH HEXAGONAL   WRENCH SQUARE

INDENTED HEXAGONAL   HEXAGONAL WASHER HEAD   HEXAGONAL SHOULDER   SLABBED COLLAR

Fig. 2–6. Types of screwdrivers and wrenches required to drive the various types of screws.

are used on the automobile. Most bolts have hexagonal (six-sided) heads (Fig. 2–2). Screws may also have hexagonal (or "hex") heads, but they are also supplied with other provisions for driving (Fig. 2–5). Wrenches and screwdrivers to drive the various types of bolts and screws are illustrated in Fig. 2–6 and discussed on the following pages.

The setscrew is a special type of screw (Fig. 2–7). Its purpose is to fasten a collar, gear, or similar part to a shaft. The setscrew is turned down in a threaded hole in the collar or gear until the inner end contacts the shaft. The inner end, or point, of the setscrew "bites" into the shaft and holds the collar or gear in the set position. Figure 2–7 shows various types of setscrew points.

One special type of screw cuts its own threads; this is a *self-tapping* screw (Fig. 2–8). The end of the screw is somewhat smaller and may have one or more slots cut in it. These slots form cutting edges on the threads so that, when the screw is turned into the hole, threads are cut in the hole.

There is another special type of screw that not only cuts its own threads but also drills the hole (Fig. 2–9). The point of the screw is formed into a

FLAT POINT   CONE POINT   OVAL POINT   CUP POINT

Fig. 2–7. Types of setscrew points.

Fig. 2–8. Self-tapping screw.

drill and tempered. Thus, when this screw is used, only one operation is required, because it drills, taps the hole, and fastens.

§ 2–6. NUTS Nuts are of various shapes (Fig. 2–10). The slotted and castle (or castellated) nuts are used with a cotter pin (§ 2–7). Other nuts are used with lock washers (§ 2–8). Cotter pins and lock washers prevent the nuts from working loose and dropping off. Lock washers are also used under the heads of bolts and screws to keep them from loosening.

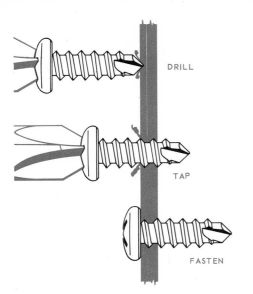

DRILL

TAP

FASTEN

Fig. 2–9. Drill-and-tap screw. *(Great Lakes Screw Division of U. S. Industries, Inc.)*

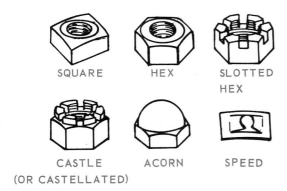

SQUARE HEX SLOTTED HEX

CASTLE ACORN SPEED
(OR CASTELLATED)

Fig. 2–10. Several common nuts.

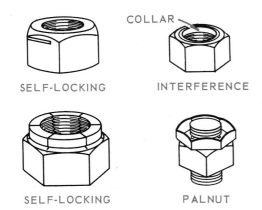

COLLAR

SELF-LOCKING INTERFERENCE

SELF-LOCKING PALNUT

Fig. 2–11. Self-locking nuts.

Fig. 2–12. Cotter pin before installation (top) and after installation through the hole in a bolt and the slots in a nut.

Another locking method uses two nuts. The second nut is turned down on and tightened against the first nut. The second nut, sometimes called a *jam nut*, locks the first nut in place and thereby keeps it from working loose.

The speed nut (Fig. 2–10) is formed from sheet metal. It is quickly installed by pressing it down into place on the stud or bolt.

Some nuts have a "built-in" locking feature (Fig. 2–11). The self-locking nut at the upper left in Fig. 2–11 has a slot cut in the side, and the upper threads are somewhat distorted. When the nut is turned down on a bolt, the separated sections of the nut are drawn slightly together. The spring effect produces friction on the threads that acts to prevent nut movement. The interference nut has a collar of fiber or soft metal. The bolt threads cut threads in the fiber or soft metal as the nut is turned on the bolt. The additional material jams in the bolt threads to keep the nut from loosening. The self-locking nut with the vertical slots (lower left) is made with the inner diameter of the upper section slightly smaller than the bolt diameter. Thus, the upper segments of the nut press against the bolt threads to hold the nut in position. The palnut is a single-thread lock nut.

§ 2–7. COTTER PINS Cotter pins (Fig. 2–12) are used with slotted and castle nuts. The bolt has a hole through which the cotter pin passes. To use the pin, the nut is tightened, and the nut slots are lined up with the hole in the bolt. Then the cotter pin is inserted and the two legs of the pin bent, as shown.

§ 2–8. LOCK WASHERS Lock washers (Fig. 2–13) are placed between the nut or screwhead and a flat washer (Fig. 2–13). The edges left by the split

PLAIN EXTERNAL INTERNAL EXTERNAL INTERNAL

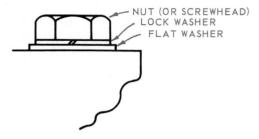

NUT (OR SCREWHEAD)
LOCK WASHER
FLAT WASHER

Fig. 2-13. Top, lock washers. Bottom, a plain lock washer installed between a flat washer and a nut (or screwhead).

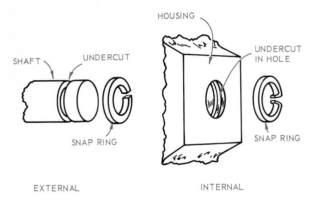

SHAFT UNDERCUT
SNAP RING
EXTERNAL

HOUSING
UNDERCUT IN HOLE
SNAP RING
INTERNAL

Fig. 2-14. Using snap or retaining rings.

OIL PASSAGES
SNAP RING
BEARING
SPROCKET

Fig. 2-15. Using snap-ring pliers to remove snap ring from a Turbo Hydra-Matic transmission subassembly. *(Cadillac Motor Car Division of General Motors Corporation)*

(in the plain lock washer) cut into the nut or screwhead and keep it from turning and loosening. The toothed lock washers provide many edges to improve the locking effect. In some assemblies, the flat washer is not used; the lock washer is placed between the nut or screwhead and the machine part.

§ 2-9. SNAP RINGS External snap or retaining rings (Fig. 2-14) are used on shafts to prevent the endwise movement of a gear or collar on the shaft. Internal snap or retaining rings are used in housings and similar machine parts to keep shafts or other components in position. The external snap ring must be expanded with special snap-ring pliers so that it slips over the shaft and into the undercut on the shaft. The internal snap ring must be contracted so that it can slip into the hole and into the undercut.

AXIAL ASSEMBLY		END-PLAY TAKE-UP	
INTERNAL	BASIC FOR HOUSINGS AND BORES	INTERNAL	BOWED FOR HOUSINGS AND BORES
EXTERNAL	BASIC FOR SHAFTS AND PINS	EXTERNAL	BOWED FOR SHAFTS AND PINS
INTERNAL	INVERTED FOR HOUSINGS AND BORES	INTERNAL	BEVELED FOR HOUSINGS AND BORES
EXTERNAL	INVERTED FOR SHAFTS AND PINS	EXTERNAL	BEVELED FOR SHAFTS AND PINS
EXTERNAL	HEAVY-DUTY FOR SHAFTS AND PINS	EXTERNAL	BOWED E-RING FOR SHAFTS AND PINS
EXTERNAL	HIGH-STRENGTH FOR SHAFTS AND PINS	EXTERNAL	PRONG-LOCK® FOR SHAFTS AND PINS

Fig. 2-16. Tru-Arc retaining rings. (Copyright 1958, 1965-1966, *Waldes Kohineer, Inc.* Reprinted with permission.)

Figure 2–15 shows snap-ring pliers being used to remove the snap ring from a subassembly of one model of the Turbo Hydra-Matic automatic transmission.

The Tru-Arc retaining ring (Fig. 2–16) is a special type of snap ring. It has two lips with holes into which the pin ends of the special snap-ring pliers fit (Fig. 2–17). Thus, there is less chance of the pliers slipping off the ring during removal or installation. These rings are made for both internal and external installation.

§ 2–10. KEYS AND SPLINES Keys and splines are used to lock gears, pulleys, collars, and other similar parts to shafts. Figure 2–18 shows a typical key installation. The key is a wedge-shaped piece of metal. It fits into slots (or keyways) cut into the shaft and collar (or pulley or gear) being installed on the shaft. The key thus locks the shaft and collar together.

Splines (Fig. 2–19) are internal and external teeth cut in both the shaft and the installed part. When the pinion, gear, pulley, or collar is installed, it is the same as having a great number of keys between

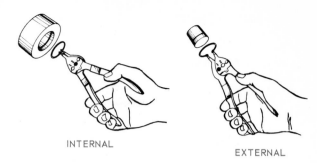

INTERNAL

EXTERNAL

Fig. 2–17. Tru-Arc retaining-ring pliers to install internal and external rings. (Copyright 1958, 1965-1966, *Waldes Kohineer, Inc.* Reprinted with permission.)

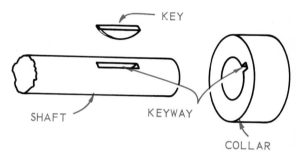

Fig. 2–18. Using a key.

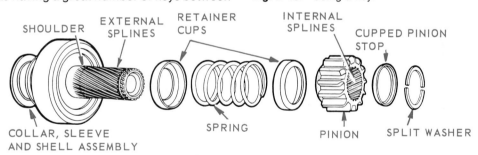

Fig. 2–19. Disassembled cranking-motor sprag clutch drive, showing internal and external splines. *(Delco-Remy Division of General Motors Corporation)*

it and the shaft. In many mechanisms, the splines fit loosely so that the gear or other part is free to move back and forth on the shaft. The splines, however, force both to rotate together.

§ 2–11. RIVETS Rivets (Fig. 2–20) are metal pins used to fasten two parts together more or less permanently. In the automobile, the rivets are installed cold (in construction work, they may be heated). One end of the rivet has a head. After the rivet is in place, a driver, or a hammer and rivet set, is used to form a head on the other end of the rivet.

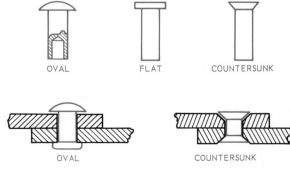

Fig. 2–20. Rivets before installation (top) and after installation (bottom).

§ 2–12. SCREWDRIVERS The screwdriver is used to drive, or turn, screws with slotted or recessed heads. The most common type is the driver for slotted screwheads (Figs. 2–6 and 2–21). Do not use a screwdriver as a pry bar or as a punch or chisel; you are likely to break it. Keep the tip properly ground (Fig. 2–22), with the sides prac-

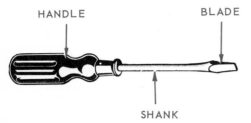

Fig. 2–21. Screwdriver.

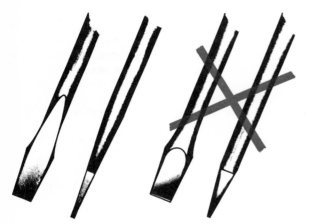

Fig. 2–22. Right and wrong ways to grind a screwdriver tip. *(General Motors Corporation)*

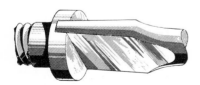

Fig. 2–23. Screwdriver tip must fit the screw slot.

Fig. 2–24. Offset screwdriver. *(General Motors Corporation)*

tically parallel at the end. If the sides are tapered, the tip tends to rise up out of the screw slot when it is turned. Always select the proper screwdriver for the job; the tip should fit snugly in the screw slot (Fig. 2–23). A screwdriver that is too large or too small is hard to use and may damage the screw or part being worked on.

The Phillips-head screw (Fig. 2–6) has two slots that cross at the center. It is widely used on automobile trim and molding; there is less chance that the screwdriver will slip out of the slots and damage the finish. Three sizes of Phillips-head screwdriver, 4-, 6-, and 8-inch, handle most automotive work.

Offset screwdrivers (Fig. 2–24) are handy for removing screws in places that are hard to get to. The two blades are at right angles; the ends can be reversed as a screw is tightened or loosened.

§ 2–13. HAMMERS The ball-peen hammer (Fig. 2–25) is the one most commonly used by mechanics. It should be gripped on the end, and the face should strike the object squarely, as shown in Fig. 2–25. Hammers for striking on easily marred sur-

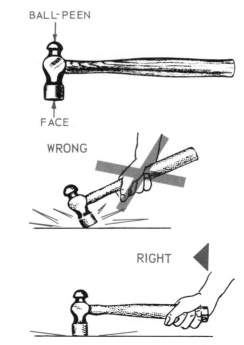

Fig. 2–25. Ball-peen hammer, showing the wrong and right ways to grip and use it. *(General Motors Corporation)*

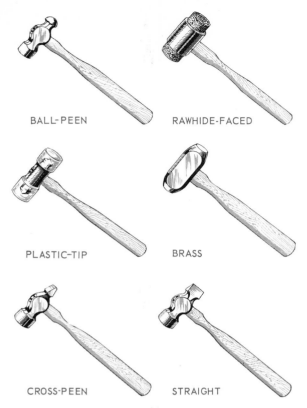

BALL-PEEN   RAWHIDE-FACED

PLASTIC-TIP   BRASS

CROSS-PEEN   STRAIGHT

Fig. 2-26. Various types of hammers.

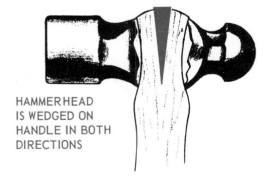

HAMMERHEAD
IS WEDGED ON
HANDLE IN BOTH
DIRECTIONS

Fig. 2-27. How a hammerhead is wedged on a handle. *(General Motors Corporation)*

faces are shown in Fig. 2-26. These include the rawhide-faced, plastic-tip, and brass hammers.

Check the hammerhead attachment to the handle occasionally. A wedge or screw is put into the head end of the handle (Fig. 2-27) to spread it and keep the head from coming loose. Make sure that the wedge or screw is tight each time you start to use the hammer. If the head flies off, it may injure someone.

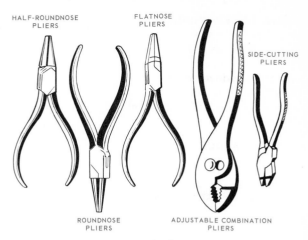

HALF-ROUNDNOSE PLIERS   FLATNOSE PLIERS   SIDE-CUTTING PLIERS

ROUNDNOSE PLIERS   ADJUSTABLE COMBINATION PLIERS

Fig. 2-28. Various types of pliers.

§ 2-14. PLIERS A few of the many kinds of cutting and gripping pliers are shown in Fig. 2-28. Do not use pliers to grip hardened-steel surfaces; this dulls the teeth in the plier jaws. Do not use standard pliers on nuts or bolts; this damages the nut or bolthead so that wrenches do not fit on them. Use wrenches or special pliers described below.

1. Channellock pliers. These pliers (Fig. 2-29) have a quick adjustment that permits the jaws to be widened or narrowed to accommodate various sizes of nuts and boltheads. There are interlocking tongues and grooves on the two parts of the pliers so that the two halves of the jaws can be moved closer together or farther apart.

2. Locking pliers. Self-adjustable, locking pliers are shown in Fig. 2-30. This device, called a LeverWrench ©, has a toggle and floating wedge arrangement that automatically adjusts the pliers the instant the jaws hit the object.

§ 2-15. WRENCHES Wrenches of many types are available, including open-end, box, combination open-end and box, socket, nut driver, torque, Allen, and adjustable. Each has its special use.

1. Open-end wrenches. Open-end wrenches are designed to tighten or loosen nuts and bolts (Fig. 2-31). The opening is usually at an angle to the body to permit turning a nut or bolt in a restricted space. After the nut or bolt is turned as far as the restricted space allows, the wrench can be turned over 180 degrees to permit further turning of the nut or bolt. By turning the wrench over

Fig. 2–29. Channellock pliers. *(Channellock, Inc.)*

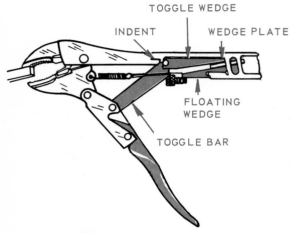

Fig. 2–30. Self-adjustable locking pliers. *(Leverage Tools, Inc.)*

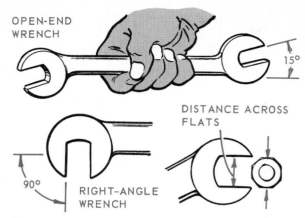

Fig. 2–31. Open-end wrenches.

after each swing, the nut or bolt can be loosened or tightened satisfactorily (Fig. 2–32). Pull on the wrench rather than push. If it is necessary to push, do so with the palm of the hand and keep the fingers out of the way so that, if the nut or bolt suddenly gives, the knuckles will not be hurt. Make sure that the wrench fits the nut or bolt-head snugly. If it fits loosely, excessive strain is thrown on the wrench and it may spring or break. The nut or bolthead may also be damaged. Do not use a pipe or another wrench on the end of the wrench to gain additional leverage. The wrench is designed to withstand the maximum leverage that a man can apply by hand on its end; gaining added leverage with a pipe or another wrench may cause the wrench to break. Never use a hammer to strike on a wrench except where the wrench has been specially designed to be used in this manner.

2. Box wrenches. Box wrenches (Fig. 2–33) serve the same purpose as open-end wrenches. However, the opening into which the nut or bolt-head fits completely surrounds, or boxes, the nut or bolthead. Box wrenches can be used in very restricted spaces because of the thinness of the metal in the wrench head (Fig. 2–34). The wrench

cannot slip off the nut. The 12-point box wrench, now almost universally used, has 12 notches in the head, so that a nut or bolt can be installed or removed even where there is a swing of only 15 degrees. Some box wrenches have the head at an angle of 15 degrees to the handle to provide added clearance for the hand (Fig. 2–35).

3. Combination open-end and box wrenches. These have a box wrench on one end and an open-end wrench on the other (Fig. 2–33). The box wrench is more convenient than the open-end wrench for the final tightening or breaking loose of a nut or a bolt but is less convenient for otherwise turning the nut or the bolt. The box must be lifted completely off the nut and then placed back on for each swing. On the other hand, the open-end wrench is less convenient for the final tightening or breaking loose of a nut or a bolt, since it is more likely to slip off; but it is more convenient for running a nut or a bolt off or on. Thus, the combination open-end and box wrench enables the mechanic to use one type and then the other by merely reversing the ends.

4. Socket wrenches. These wrenches are somewhat similar to box wrenches, except that the sockets are detachable (Fig. 2–36) and are used with special handles. Figure 2–37 illustrates a set of socket wrenches with several types of handle. The sockets fit into the handles, the proper type of handle being selected for the particular job.

5. Nut drivers. Nut drivers have handles like screwdrivers but have adaptors at the working end on which sockets can be installed. Nut drivers are used like screwdrivers after the proper size of socket has been put on the shank.

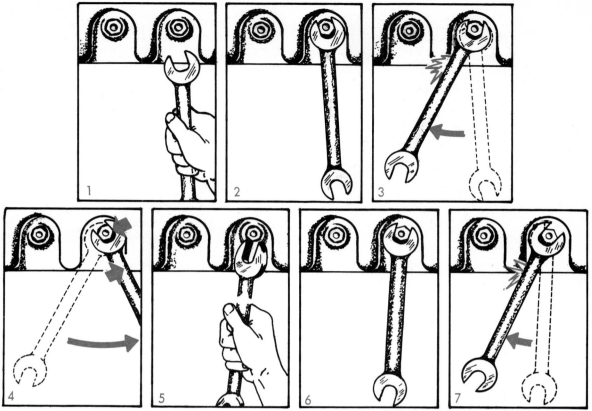

Fig. 2-32. How a wrench can be turned over to turn a nut in a restricted space. *(General Motors Corporation)*

Fig. 2-33. Box and combination wrenches.

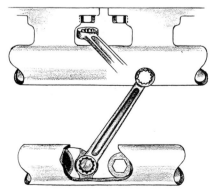

Fig. 2-34. The box wrench can be used in a restricted space. *(General Motors Corporation)*

6. Torque wrenches. A torque wrench (Fig. 2–38) is necessary for working on the modern automotive vehicle, since many nuts and bolts must be tightened the correct amount—not too little or too much (Fig. 2–39). Excessive tightening of nuts and bolts causes distortion of parts and danger of stripped threads or broken bolts, and insufficient tightening may permit the nut or the bolt to loosen. By using a torque wrench, the amount of torque being applied can be read on the dial to permit tightening within the specified limits.

7. Allen wrenches. These are used on Allen screws (Fig. 2–40). This type of screw is not widely used on automobiles, although the caster and camber adjustments on the front wheels of some cars are made by turning an Allen screw type of pivot pin.

Fig. 2-35. A 15-degree box wrench. *(General Motors Corporation)*

33

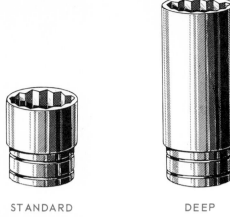

STANDARD   DEEP

Fig. 2–36. Sockets. The deep socket is for hard-to-get-at items, such as spark plugs.

8. Adjustable wrench. This wrench has an adjustable jaw so that it can be adjusted to fit nuts and boltheads of various sizes. Figure 2–41 shows the wrong way and the right way to use an adjustable wrench. Be sure that the wrench jaws are tightened on the nut or bolt flats.

§ 2–16. CHISELS Cold chisels come in different shapes (Fig. 2–42); all are for cutting metal by driving with a hammer. The chisel is normally held in the left hand. It should be held rather loosely so that, if the hammer does not strike squarely, the hand will give with the hammer blow and will be less subject to injury. For chipping with a chisel, goggles should be worn to prevent the possibility of chips flying into the eye. A chisel that has mushroomed on the end because of repeated hammer blows should not be used until the end has been dressed on a grinding wheel so that the turned-over metal is removed (Fig. 2–43).

§ 2–17. PUNCHES Punches are used to knock out rivets and pins, to align parts for assembly, and to mark locations of holes to be drilled. Punches for knocking out rivets and pins are of two kinds, the *starting* and the *pin punch* (Fig. 2–44). The starting punch is tapered and is used merely to break the rivet loose after the rivethead has been ground off or cut off with a chisel. The pin punch is then used to drive the rivet out.

The *center punch* (Fig. 2–45) is handy not only for marking hole locations for drilling but also for marking parts before they are disassembled so that they can be reassembled in the same relative location. Unless the hole location is marked

with a center punch before a hole is drilled, the drill may wander, or move around, on the surface of the piece through which the hole is to be drilled (Fig. 2–46). If the hole location is first center-punched, the drill will not do this.

§ 2–18. FILES Files are cutting tools with a large number of cutting edges, or teeth. Files have many uses, and consequently there are hundreds of types of file with many types of cut. A typical file with the various parts named is shown in Fig. 2–47. The term "cut" refers to the cuts that have been made across the face of the file to form the file teeth. When the cuts are relatively far apart, the file is termed a "rough" or "coarse-cut" file. When they are close together, the file is termed a "smooth" or "dead-smooth" file. The terms indicating coarseness or fineness are, in order, rough, coarse, bastard, second-cut, smooth-cut, and dead-smooth. Figure 2–48 illustrates four of these. The coarser the file, the more metal it removes with each file stroke.

When only one series of cuts has been taken across the face of the file, with all cuts parallel to one another, the file is known as a *single-cut file*, regardless of its coarseness. When the file has two series of cuts across its face in two different directions, it is known as a *double-cut file* (Fig. 2–49). Double-cutting a file produces a large number of small teeth, each little tooth being much like the point of a chisel.

Files are classified according to their shape. Files may be flat, triangular, square, half-round, or round, with or without taper from the heel to the top. Many special types of files are also available. Selection of the cut and shape of a file depends upon the work to be done. A few types of files are shown in Fig. 2–50.

A handle should be put on a file before it is used. Otherwise, you might accidentally drive the pointed tang into your hand. Handles are made in various sizes for various sizes of file. To install the handle, place the file tang into the hole in the handle, and tap the butt end of the handle on the bench (Fig. 2–51). Never hammer on the file to drive it into place. The file is brittle and may shatter.

If the file is not cutting, a file card should be used to clean the file teeth. The file card is a wire-bristled brush. Tapping the handle on the bench every few strokes during filing tends to keep the file clean, but the file card will also be required.

When a file is not in use, it should be put away carefully. If a file is thrown into a drawer with

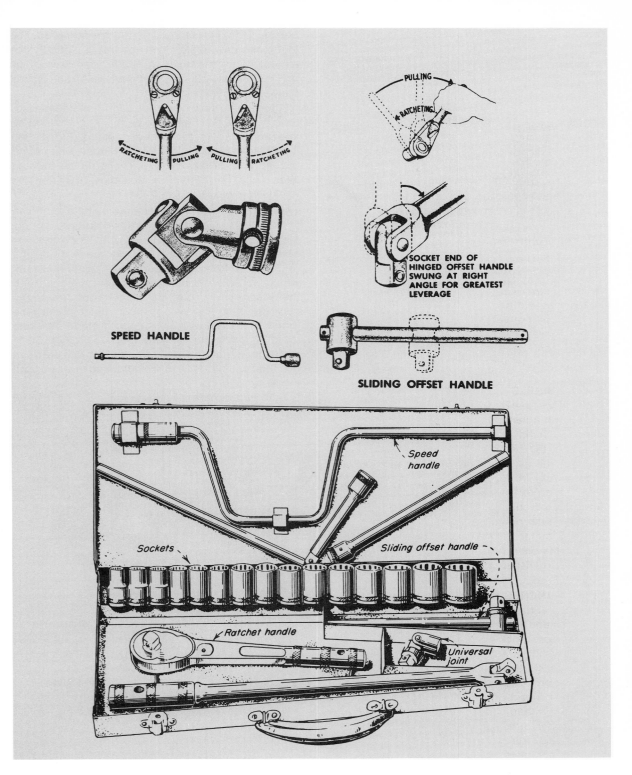

Fig. 2–37. Set of socket wrenches with handles. *(General Motors Corporation* and *New Britain Machine Company)*

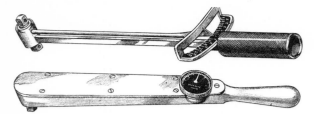

Fig. 2–38. Torque wrenches. *(General Motors Corporation)*

other tools, the file teeth will be chipped and dulled. They should be protected by putting the file in a file rack or by wrapping it. Also, files are subject to rusting and should therefore be kept away from moisture.

● **CAUTION:** Never attempt to use a file as a pry bar, and never hammer on it. The file is brittle and will break easily. If it is hit with a hammer, it is likely to shatter in a dangerous manner.

§ 2–19. HACKSAWS The hacksaw is a special type of saw for sawing metal (Fig. 2–52). The blades are replaceable, and the frame is adjustable for various blade lengths. It is very important that the correct type of the blade be selected for the work to be done. Blades are made with 14 to 32 teeth

per inch. Using a blade with the wrong number of teeth not only makes the job more difficult but also damages the blade or causes it to break. Figure 2–56 illustrates correct and incorrect blades for various jobs.

After the correct blade for a job has been selected, it should be placed in the hacksaw frame and tightened to the proper tension (Fig. 2–53). Insufficient tension causes the blade to bend and probably to break. The teeth should be pointed away from the handle so that they cut when the hacksaw is pushed (Fig. 2–54).

In using the hacksaw, it should be held as shown in Fig. 2–55. On the forward, or cutting, stroke, move the hacksaw evenly and with uniform pressure. Lift the blade slightly from the work on the return stroke to avoid wear on the back of the teeth, which would soon dull them. Never twist or bend the blade when cutting, since such treatment may break it. In sawing sheet metal, it may be found that even with the 32-tooth blade only one tooth is in contact with the metal. For such work, the sheet metal may be clamped in a vise between two blocks of wood and the cut taken through both the wood and the metal.

Take good care of the blades. Do not throw them into a toolbox with other tools and thus dull

Fig. 2–39. Using a torque wrench to tighten cylinder-head bolts on a V-8 engine. The numbers indicate the order in which the bolts should be tightened. *(Chrysler-Plymouth Division of Chrysler Motors Corporation)*

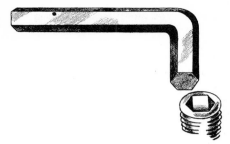

Fig. 2-40. Allen screw and wrench. *(General Motors Corporation)*

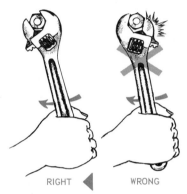

RIGHT ◀ WRONG

Fig. 2-41. When using an adjustable wrench, pull on the handle so that the major load is carried by the stationary jaw, as shown at the left. *(General Motors Corporation)*

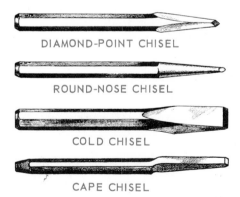

DIAMOND-POINT CHISEL

ROUND-NOSE CHISEL

COLD CHISEL

CAPE CHISEL

Fig. 2-42. Types of chisels. *(General Motors Corporation)*

BEFORE AND AFTER DRESSING

Fig. 2-43. How to dress, or grind, a chisel. *(General Motors Corporation)*

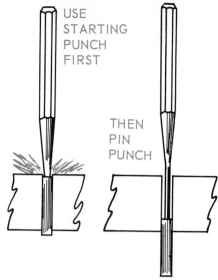

USE STARTING PUNCH FIRST

THEN PIN PUNCH

Fig. 2-44. Using starting and pin punches. *(General Motors Corporation)*

the teeth. Wipe the blades with an oily cloth occasionally to keep them from rusting.

§ 2-20. TAPS AND DIES Taps and dies are devices used for cutting inside and outside threads. (See § 2-4 for information on threads.)

Taps are made in several styles (Fig. 2-57). The taper tap is used to thread a hole completely through a piece of metal, the plug tap to thread a hole only part way, and the bottoming tap to thread a hole to the bottom when the hole does not go all the way through the metal.

The tap is held in a tap wrench (Fig. 2-58). The wrench jaws are adjustable and can be tightened to hold the tap securely. The tap should be started square in the hole and the wrench turned smoothly and evenly. A lubricant, such as lard, should be applied to the tap. Every time two complete turns of the tap have been made, the tap should be backed off about a quarter turn and lubricant applied.

Dies cut outside threads (Fig. 2-59). Dies are held in diestocks (Fig. 2-60) during the cutting operation. The procedure is similar to that required for tapping. The rod should be chamfered

Fig. 2-45. Center punch. *(General Motors Corporation)*

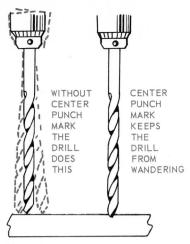

Fig. 2–46. How center-punching a hole location will keep the drill from wandering. *(General Motors Corporation)*

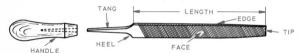

Fig. 2–47. Typical file, with its parts named. *(General Motors Corporation)*

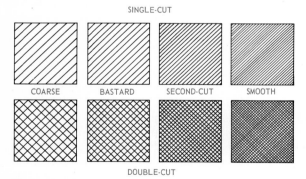

Fig. 2–48. File cuts. *(General Motors Corporation)*

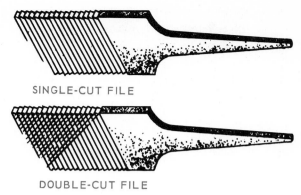

Fig. 2–49. Single-cut and double-cut files. *(General Motors Corporation)*

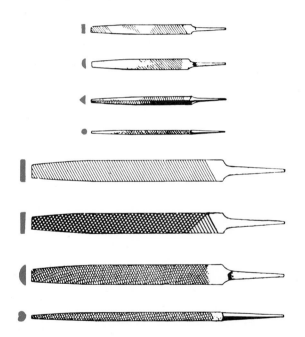

Fig. 2–50. Several types of files.

on the end so that the die starts easily. Every two complete turns, the die should be backed off a quarter turn and lubricant, such as lard, applied.

§ 2–21. MEASURING DEVICES The measuring of linear distances is one of the most important of all the jobs performed in an automotive service shop. In almost every step of automotive service, measurements are taken to determine size, fit, or clearance. And unless the measurements are properly taken, the service job will not be correct; improper operation or failure of the unit being serviced will result.

Almost everyone is familiar with the ruler, or scale, for measuring on flat surfaces (Fig. 2–61). To measure the diameter of a shaft or the thickness of a part, an outside caliper or micrometer is used. To measure the diameter of a hole, an inside caliper or micrometer is used. Special dial-indicator gauges are also available to take such measurements. The measurement of small clearances or gaps is required in brake work, setting valve tappets, fitting pistons, adjusting spark plugs, and so on. For such work, feeler gauges are used. The procedures for using these measuring devices are detailed in the following paragraphs.

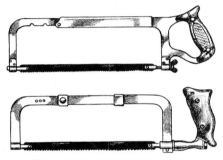

Fig. 2–51. Tapping the butt end of a file handle on the bench to tighten the file tang in the handle. *(General Motors Corporation)*

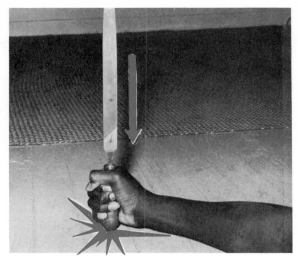

Fig. 2–52. Two types of hacksaws. *(General Motors Corporation)*

1. Feeler gauges. These gauges are essentially strips or blades of hardened and tempered steel or other metal, ground or rolled with extreme accuracy to the proper thickness. They are generally supplied in sets (Fig. 2–62), each blade marked with its thickness in thousandths of an inch. In Fig. 2–62, for example, the "3" means 0.003 inch, the "4" means 0.004 inch, and so on. Some feeler gauges have two steps, or thicknesses, and are called *stepped* feeler gauges (Fig. 2–63). The tip of the blade is somewhat thinner than the remainder of the blade. The blade marked "10–12" in Fig. 2–63, for example, is 0.010 inch thick at the tip and 0.012 inch thick on the thicker portion, which starts about ½ inch from the end of the blade. This type of feeler gauge is handy on certain jobs, such as valve-tappet-clearance adjustment where the specifications may call, for example, for a clearance of 0.006 to 0.008 inch.

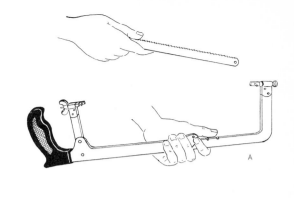

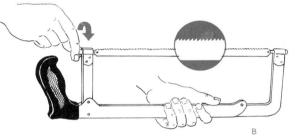

Fig. 2–53. (A) Inserting and (B) tightening a blade in a hacksaw.

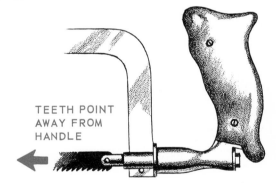

TEETH POINT AWAY FROM HANDLE

Fig. 2–54. The proper relationship between the teeth and the hacksaw handle. *(General Motors Corporation)*

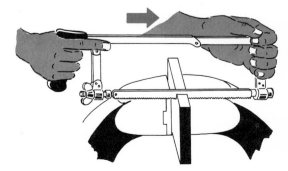

Fig. 2–55. Holding a hacksaw while sawing.

39

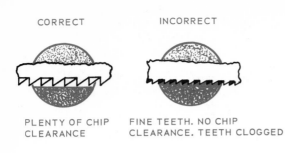

CORRECT   INCORRECT

PLENTY OF CHIP
CLEARANCE

FINE TEETH. NO CHIP
CLEARANCE. TEETH CLOGGED

PLENTY OF CHIP
CLEARANCE

FINE TEETH. NO CHIP
CLEARANCE. TEETH CLOGGED

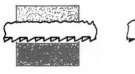 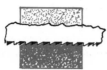

TWO TEETH AND MORE
ON SECTION

COARSE TEETH
STRADDLES WORK
STRIPPING TEETH

TWO OR MORE TEETH
ON SECTION

COARSE PITCH
STRADDLES WORK

Fig. 2-56. Correct and incorrect number of teeth for various jobs. The correct number is shown to the left for each job.

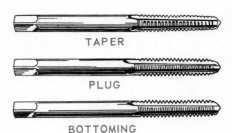

Fig. 2-57. Hand taps. *(Greenfield Tap and Die Corporation)*

TAPER

PLUG

BOTTOMING

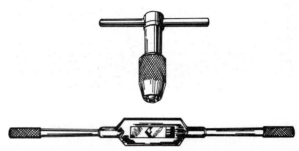

Fig. 2-58. Adjustable hand-tap wrenches. *(Greenfield Tap and Die Corporation)*

Fig. 2-59. Dies. *(Greenfield Tap and Die Corporation)*

By making the adjustment so that the 0.006-inch gauge fits and the 0.008-inch gauge does not, the specified clearance is obtained.

Wire feeler gauges (Fig. 2-64) are similar to flat feeler gauges except that the wire feelers are made of carefully calibrated steel wire of the proper diameter. They are useful in making spark-plug gap and similar checks.

Feeler gauges should never be forced into a space to be measured. They should not be allowed to become bent, torn, or battered. They should be wiped with a clean, oily cloth occasionally. With care, feeler gauges will last a long time without losing their accuracy.

2. Calipers. Calipers (Fig. 2-65) can be used to take a number of different measurements. Figure 2-66 illustrates the use of an outside caliper to measure the diameter of a shaft. The caliper should be adjusted to slip over the shaft easily of its own weight. It should not be forced, since this springs

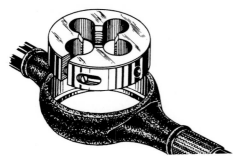

Fig. 2–60. A diestock with die above it ready to be put in place. *(Greenfield Tap and Die Corporation)*

Fig. 2–61. Ruler, or steel scale.

Fig. 2–62. Set of feeler gauges. *(General Motors Corporation)*

Fig. 2–63. Set of stepped feeler gauges. *(General Motors Corporation)*

Fig. 2–64. Set of wire feeler gauges.

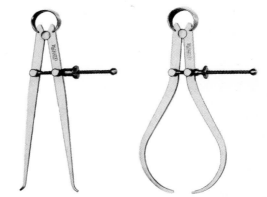

Fig. 2–65. (Left) Inside calipers. (Right) Outside calipers.

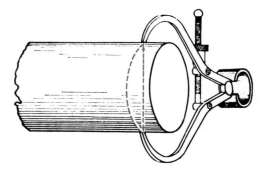

Fig. 2–66. Using an outside caliper to measure shaft diameter. *(South Bend Lathe Works)*

the caliper and prevents accurate measurement. After the caliper has been adjusted, it can be placed against a scale, as shown in Fig. 2–67, in order to determine the shaft diameter. One leg of the caliper should be held against the end of the scale and the reading on the scale at the other leg noted.

Inside calipers are used in a similar manner to measure the diameter of holes. Figure 2–68 illustrates an inside caliper in use. It should be entered in the hole at an angle, as shown by the dotted lines, and then slowly straightened. Adjust it until it slips into the hole with a slight drag. The caliper

must be held square across the diameter of the hole. After the caliper is adjusted, the measurement can be read from the scale, as shown in Fig. 2–69.

The micrometer (Fig. 2–70), or "mike," as it is often called, is a special type of caliper designed to measure in thousandths of an inch. It is a precision instrument and must be carefully treated. When the thimble is turned clockwise, the spindle moves toward the anvil; when the thimble is turned in the opposite direction, the spindle moves away from the anvil (Fig. 2–71). The hub, or barrel, of the micrometer is marked off in uniform spacings, each of which is 0.025 inch. The thimble is spaced

41

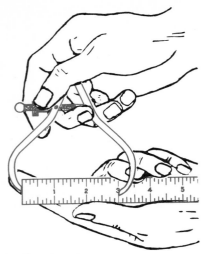

Fig. 2-67. Checking the measurement to which an outside caliper has been adjusted. *(South Bend Lathe Works)*

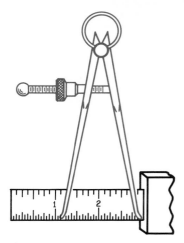

Fig. 2-69. Checking the measurement to which an inside caliper has been adjusted. *(South Bend Lathe Works)*

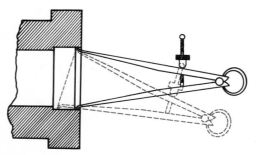

Fig. 2-68. Using an inside caliper to measure the diameter of a hole. *(South Bend Lathe Works)*

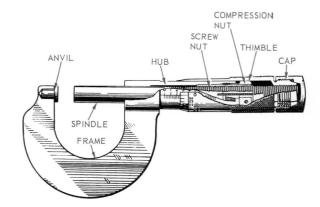

Fig. 2-70. Micrometer. *(General Motors Corporation)*

off into 25 graduations around its circumference, each graduation indicating 0.001 inch (Fig. 2-72). The internal threads of the thimble are such that every revolution of the thimble moves the thimble on the hub 0.025 inch. When the thimble has been turned to bring the spindle up against the anvil, the thimble will have been brought up to the "0" marking on the hub and the "0" marking on the thimble will have aligned with the lateral line on the hub. If the thimble is backed off to give 0.010-inch clearance between the anvil and the spindle, the "10" marking on the thimble will align with the lateral line on the hub; this indicates 0.010 inch. If the thimble is backed off four revolutions exactly, the thimble will clear the "1" marking on the hub, which indicates 0.10 inch, or four times 0.025. If the thimble were then turned back part of a revolution, say to the "12" marking, then the total dis-

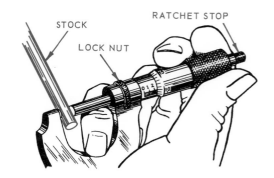

Fig. 2-71. Using a micrometer to measure the diameter of a rod.

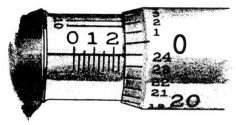

Fig. 2–72. Hub and thimble markings on a micrometer. *(General Motors Corporation)*

tance between the anvil and the spindle would be 0.10 inch plus 0.012 inch, or 0.112 inch. By thus adding the hub and thimble markings and remembering that each hub marking represents 0.025 inch and each spindle marking represents 0.001 inch, the measurement to which the micrometer has been adjusted can easily be read. Figure 2–73 shows examples of various micrometer settings. Once the reading has been taken, it can be translated from decimals to fractions, if desired, by reference to the decimal-equivalent table (Fig. 2–74).

Inside micrometers are also available for taking measurements of hole diameters (Fig. 2–75), as, for instance, the bore of an engine cylinder. Other special micrometers are found useful in automotive shops. The special micrometer shown in Fig. 19–3 has long anvil and spindle jaws which permit easy measurement of the crankshaft-journal diameter. Much of the precision machinery used in the automotive shop has micrometer adjustments; cylinder honing or boring equipment, other hones, machine lathes, crankshaft lathes, precision grinders—all have such adjustments.

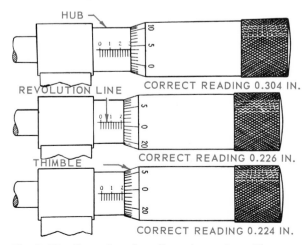

CORRECT READING 0.304 IN.

CORRECT READING 0.226 IN.

CORRECT READING 0.224 IN.

Fig. 2–73. Examples of reading micrometer settings.

$\frac{1}{64}$	.0156	$\frac{17}{64}$	.2656	$\frac{33}{64}$	.5156	$\frac{49}{64}$	.7656
$\frac{1}{32}$	.0312	$\frac{9}{32}$	.2812	$\frac{17}{32}$	.5312	$\frac{25}{32}$	.7812
$\frac{3}{64}$	.0468	$\frac{19}{64}$	.2969	$\frac{35}{64}$	.5469	$\frac{51}{64}$	.7969
$\frac{1}{16}$	.0625	$\frac{5}{16}$	.3125	$\frac{9}{16}$	.5625	$\frac{13}{16}$	.8125
$\frac{5}{64}$	.0781	$\frac{21}{64}$	.3281	$\frac{37}{64}$	.5781	$\frac{53}{64}$	.8281
$\frac{3}{32}$	.0937	$\frac{11}{32}$	.3437	$\frac{19}{32}$	.5937	$\frac{27}{32}$	.8437
$\frac{7}{64}$	.1094	$\frac{23}{64}$	.3594	$\frac{39}{64}$	.6094	$\frac{55}{64}$	.8594
$\frac{1}{8}$	.125	$\frac{3}{8}$	.375	$\frac{5}{8}$	.625	$\frac{7}{8}$	.875
$\frac{9}{64}$	.1406	$\frac{25}{64}$	.3906	$\frac{41}{64}$	.6406	$\frac{57}{64}$	.8906
$\frac{5}{32}$	.1562	$\frac{13}{32}$	.4062	$\frac{21}{32}$	.6562	$\frac{29}{32}$	.9062
$\frac{11}{64}$	.1719	$\frac{27}{64}$	.4219	$\frac{43}{64}$	.6719	$\frac{59}{64}$	.9219
$\frac{3}{16}$	.1875	$\frac{7}{16}$	.4375	$\frac{11}{16}$	.6875	$\frac{15}{16}$	.9375
$\frac{13}{64}$	.2031	$\frac{29}{64}$	.4531	$\frac{45}{64}$	.7031	$\frac{61}{64}$	.9531
$\frac{7}{32}$	.2187	$\frac{15}{32}$	.4687	$\frac{23}{32}$	.7187	$\frac{31}{32}$	.9687
$\frac{15}{64}$	.2344	$\frac{31}{64}$	.4844	$\frac{47}{64}$	.7344	$\frac{63}{64}$	.9843
$\frac{1}{4}$	.25	$\frac{1}{2}$	.5	$\frac{3}{4}$	.75	1	1.0

Fig. 2–74. Table of decimal equivalents.

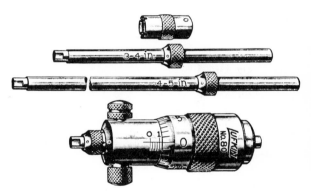

Fig. 2–75. Inside micrometer. *(General Motors Corporation)*

In the use of the micrometer, extreme care must be exercised to prevent damaging it. In particular, *it should never be clamped* on the piece to be measured. The micrometer should be tightened only enough to cause a slight drag as it is slid over the piece being measured. Clamping distorts the micrometer or ruins the screw threads.

3. Dial indicators. These are gauges that use a dial face and needle to register measurements. The needle is connected by gearing and linkage to a movable contact point. Movement of the contact point registers in thousandths of an inch on the dial face. Figure 2–76 shows a dial indicator in use checking the end play in the rear unit of the Turbo Hydra-Matic transmission. Figure 18–30 illustrates a dial indicator being used to check cylinder walls in an engine. There are numerous other pictures of dial indicators in the book.

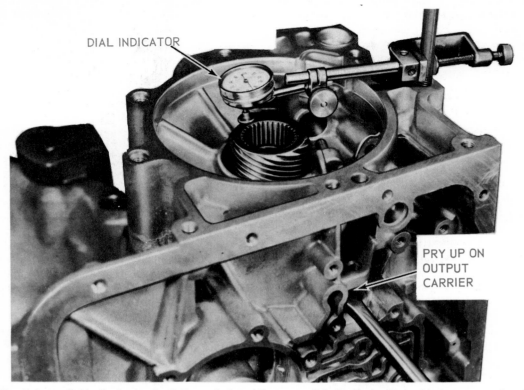

DIAL INDICATOR

PRY UP ON
OUTPUT
CARRIER

Fig. 2–76. Using a dial indicator to check the end play of the rear unit in the Turbo Hydra-Matic transmission. The dial indicator is held in place by a special clamp and fixture, and the output carrier is then pried up to see how much it will move. *(Cadillac Motor Car Division of General Motors Corporation)*

§ **2–22. DRILLS** Drills are tools for making holes. The type of material in which a hole is to be made determines the type of drill bit that must be used. The drill bit, or twist drill, is a cylindrical bar with helical grooves and a point (Fig. 2–77). The point is shaped so as to provide cutting edges to cut into material. The helical grooves provide passages through which the chips that have been cut can pass away from the working surface. The shape of the point varies with the material.

Twist drills have either a tapered or a straight shank, such as that shown in Fig. 2–77. The straight-shank drill is more commonly used in ordinary shopwork.

For most shopwork, electrically operated drills are used. These may be portable (Fig. 2–78) or permanently assembled into a floor- or bench-mounted press (Fig. 2–79). The drill must have good care and must be correctly used. It must be kept clean and must be oiled periodically according to the manufacturer's recommendations. Always turn off the drill before attempting to oil it.

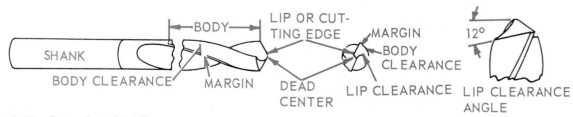

Fig. 2–77. Parts of a twist drill.

This is one of the fundamentals of safety practice in any shop. *Always turn off a machine before attempting to oil it.*

Never load a drill so much that it stalls. This is very damaging. Do not click the switch off and on in an attempt to start a stalled drill. This is likely to burn out the switch or the motor. Relieve the feed pressure to avoid stalling as the drill bit breaks through the finished work.

If a portable drill is used, do not drag it around by the cable, and do not leave it lying around on the floor so that the cable or the drill bit is stepped on or run over and damaged.

§ 2–23. REMOVING BROKEN STUDS Occasionally studs or bolts break off, and the removal of the broken part is necessary. If the break is above the surface, it may be possible to file flats on two sides of the stud or bolt so that a wrench can be used to back it out. Also, a slot may be cut so that a screwdriver can be used. If the break is below the surface, an extractor may be required. The first step in the removal of a stud broken off below the surface is to center-punch the stud and drill a small hole down into it. Follow this with a larger drill that makes a hole in the stud nearly as large as the small diameter of the threads, leaving only a thin shell. Then a screw extractor is used. One type, called the *Ezy-Out*, is tapered and has a coarse spiral thread with sharp edges. An extractor of the right size is selected, inserted into the hole in the stud, and turned counterclockwise with a wrench (Fig. 2–80). The thread edges bite into the sides of the hole in the stud so that the stud is screwed out.

A second type of extractor is driven into the hole in the stud so that the edges bite into the sides of the hole. A wrench is then used to turn the extractor and back out the stud. Another type of extractor is similar in construction except that it is not tapered and has three sharp splines instead of flutes. It is used in a similar manner.

If a stud extractor is not available, it is sometimes possible to tap a diamond-pointed chisel into the hole in the stud and turn the chisel to back out the stud (Fig. 2–81).

§ 2–24. HELI-COIL The use of aluminum for cylinder blocks and other automotive-engine com-

Fig. 2–78. Electric drill—hand-held type.

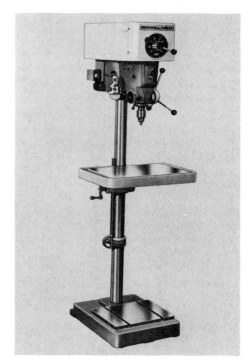

Fig. 2–79. Drill press. The electric drill is permanently mounted in the stand.

Fig. 2–80. Using a stud extractor to remove a broken stud. *(General Motors Corporation)*

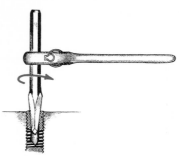

Fig. 2-81. Using a diamond-pointed chisel to remove a broken stud in an emergency. *(General Motors Corporation)*

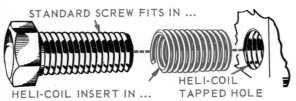

Fig. 2-82. Heli-Coil installation. *(Chrysler-Plymouth Division of Chrysler Motors Corporation)*

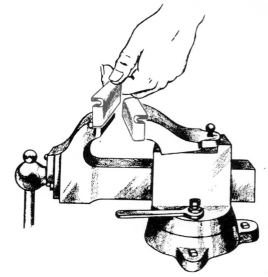

Fig. 2-83. Bench vise, showing soft jaws being put into place on the vise jaws.

Fig. 2-84. Arbor press.

ponents has brought with it the problem of stripped or worn threads. Aluminum, being softer than cast iron or steel, is more susceptible to thread wear and damage. To repair defective threads, the hole is drilled and then tapped with a special Heli-Coil tap. Finally, a Heli-Coil insert is installed to bring the hole back to its original thread size (Fig. 2-82).

§ 2-25. BENCH VISE The bench vise (Fig. 2-83) is used to hold a piece or part while it is being sawed, filed, chiseled, or otherwise worked on. When the handle is turned, a screw in the base of the vise moves the movable jaw toward or away from the stationary jaw. To avoid marring or otherwise damaging finished surfaces of parts that are to be clamped in the vise, caps of copper or similar soft metal are placed over the steel jaws of the vise. These are usually referred to as "soft" jaws.

§ 2-26. ARBOR PRESSES Arbor presses have many uses in the automobile shop. The simplest (Fig. 2-84) has a handle that rotates a gear which is meshed with a rack. This causes the rack to move down or up as required. The lower end of the rack has a tool- or arbor-holding device. A considerable amount of pressure can be exerted on the arbor through the handle, and this makes it relatively easy to remove or install bearings and bushings,

to burnish bushings, and to perform other similar jobs. The larger presses of this type may be operated hydraulically, that is, by liquid pressure acting in a cylinder.

§ 2-27. OILSTONE There are many types of oilstones, varying not only in shape and size but also in the fineness or coarseness of the abrasive dust that makes up the stone. Stones should always be moistened with oil when used, or they will become clogged or glazed and will no longer cut properly. If this happens the stone may be cleaned with solvent and then reoiled. Since stones are brittle, they should not be dropped or otherwise subjected to rough treatment.

§ 2–28. GRINDER The grinder (Fig. 2–85) has one or more grinding wheels made of abrasive material bonded together. When the wheel is rotated by the motor, objects held against the wheel are ground down. Thus, the grinder can be used to shape and sharpen tools.

The grinding wheels can be broken by hard blows, by heavy pressure, or by excessive tightening of the spindle nut. Thus, reasonable caution should be exercised in the use of the grinding wheel. Goggles should always be worn, and the safety shield should be in place when the wheel is used. In general, the purpose of using the grinding wheel is to restore the working edges of the tool to their original shape and sharpness. Overheating of the tool should be avoided, since this draws the temper of the steel. The tool should be dipped in water repeatedly during the grinding process to prevent it from becoming too hot.

§ 2–29. TAKING CARE OF YOURSELF IN THE SHOP Work quietly, and give your work your un-

Fig. 2–85. Pedestal grinder with two wheels.

divided attention. You should never indulge in horseplay or create an unnecessary disturbance. Such actions may distract someone and cause him to get hurt. Keep your tools and equipment under control. Don't scatter them about or lay them on operating machinery or equipment (Fig. 2–86). Keep them out of aisles and working spaces where someone may trip over them. Use special care to keep jack handles and creepers out of the way (Fig. 2–87); tripping over these is one of the most common causes of accidents in the automobile shop. Don't put sharp objects or tools into your pockets. You may cut your hand or get stabbed. Make sure that your clothing is suited to the job and that you do not have a dangling tie, loose sleeves, and so on, that could get caught in moving machinery (Fig. 2–88). Wipe excess oil and grease off your hands, because oil and grease make your hands slippery so that you cannot get a good grip on tools or parts. Do not use a compressed-air hose to blow dirt from your clothes. Never point the hose at another person. Particles of dirt may be blown at sufficient speed to penetrate the skin or eyes. Goggles or a face shield (Fig. 2–89) should be worn when the air hose is used, as well as during chipping, grinding, or any other job where there is danger to the eyes from flying particles. When using a car jack, make sure that it is centered so that it does not slip and allow the car to drop. Never jack up a car when someone is working under it. Use car stands or supports, properly placed, before going under a car (Fig. 2–90).

§ 2–30. TAKING CARE OF YOUR TOOLS Tools should be clean and in good condition, as noted in previous articles. Greasy and oily tools are hard to hold and use; wipe them off before trying to use them. Always use the proper tool for the job; using the wrong tool may damage the tool or the part being worked on, and it may lead to personal injury. Do not use a hardened hammer or punch on a hardened surface. Hardened steel is brittle, almost like glass, and may shatter from heavy blows. Slivers from the head of the hammer or from the punch may fly out and may become embedded in the hand or, worse, in the eye. Use a soft hammer or punch on hardened parts.

§ 2–31. USING POWER-DRIVEN EQUIPMENT A great variety of power-driven equipment is used in the automobile shop. The instructions for using any equipment should be studied carefully before

Fig. 2–86. Tools should not be scattered about. Always keep them within easy reach.

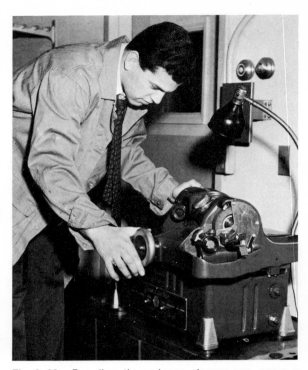

Fig. 2–88. Dangling tie or loose sleeves can cause a serious accident.

Fig. 2–87. Jack handle should be kept up and the creeper should be standing against the wall when it is not in use.

Fig. 2–89. Face shield or goggles and proper clothing should be worn when using any tool or power equipment that can throw chips or sparks.

the equipment is operated. Hands and clothes should be kept away from moving machinery, such as the engine flywheel, fan, and so on. Keep hands out of the way when using any cutting device, such as cylinder-boring equipment or a

drum lathe. Do not attempt to feel the finish while the machine is in operation, since there may be slivers of metal that will cut your hands badly. When using any honing or grinding equipment, keep hands away from rotating parts, and do not

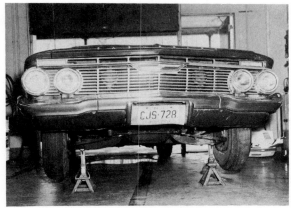

Fig. 2–90. Properly located car stands will hold the car safely.

Fig. 2–91. Gasoline and other flammable substances should be stored in safety containers.

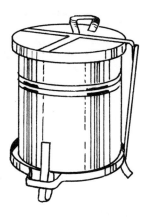

Fig. 2–92. Oily rags should be stored in special safety containers.

try to feel the finish with the machine in operation. When working on any device with compressed springs, such as clutches or valves, use great care to prevent the springs from slipping and jumping loose. If this happens, the spring may take off at high speed and hurt someone.

Never attempt to adjust or oil moving machinery unless the instructions specifically state that this should be done.

§ 2–32. FIRE PREVENTION The automobile requires gasoline to operate, and gasoline is a highly flammable substance (Fig. 2–91). Therefore, you should be particularly careful around the shop to avoid spilling gasoline. If gasoline is spilled, it should be wiped up at once and the rags put outside or in a safe place to dry. Naturally, smokers should be very careful, since open flames in the presence of gasoline vapors cause the vapors to explode. This is so great a danger that smoking is strictly prohibited in many automobile shops. Oily rags and waste are another potential source of fire, since they may ignite by spontaneous combustion, that is, by the oil on the rags (by chemical action) causing so much heat to develop that the rags catch fire. Oily rags and waste should be placed in covered metal containers provided for them (Fig. 2–92).

An engine that has a gasoline leak in the fuel line, tank, pump, or carburetor is extremely dangerous, since the gasoline may catch fire very easily. Before such an engine is started, the leak should be repaired and all gasoline wiped up. Care should be used to avoid shorts or grounds in the electric circuit that may cause sparks, especially around the carburetor or the fuel pump. In particular, the ground cable should be disconnected from the battery first when a battery is being removed from a car. This prevents the possibility of a ground when the cable clamp is being loosened from the insulated terminal. For the same reason, the ground cable should be reconnected *last* on reinstallation of the battery.

Review Questions

1. What are the six basic steps in automotive shopwork?
2. What are specifications, and how are they used in shopwork?
3. Name a few types of fastener.
4. Explain the difference among screws, bolts, and studs.
5. How are thread sizes designated?
6. What is meant by thread pitch? How is pitch measured?
7. What is meant by thread series?
8. What is meant by thread classes?
9. Name a few different kinds of nuts.
10. Explain the purpose of cotter pins.
11. Explain the purpose of lock washers.
12. Explain the purpose of snap rings.
13. What are some cautions to observe in using a screwdriver?
14. What types of screwdriver are there?
15. Describe the Phillips screwdriver. Where are Phillips-head screws used?
16. What are offset screwdrivers?
17. Describe the correct manner of using a hammer.
18. Name several types of wrench.
19. What is an open-end wrench?
20. What are box wrenches?
21. What are socket wrenches?
22. Name and describe the use of several types of socket-wrench handles.
23. What is a torque wrench, and why is it used?
24. Describe the proper method of using a chisel.
25. Name several uses of punches. What types of punch are there?
26. What is the purpose of a file?
27. What is a single-cut file? A double-cut file?
28. What terms designate the coarseness or fineness of a file?
29. Describe the procedure of using a file.
30. Describe the proper method of installing a blade in a hacksaw frame and the proper manner of using a hacksaw.
31. What is a tap? A die? Describe how they are used.
32. Name three styles of tap.
33. Describe the procedure of measuring a shaft with an outside caliper.
34. Describe the procedure of measuring the diameter of a hole with an inside caliper.
35. Describe the procedure of taking a measurement with a micrometer.
36. What are feeler gauges? Stepped feeler gauges?
37. Name the important points to watch in practicing safety procedures when working in the shop.
38. Name the important things to do in taking care of tools.
39. Name the important things to watch to prevent any fires from breaking out in the shop.

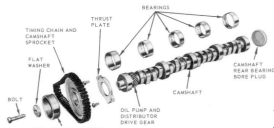

CHAPTER
3

Engine Operation

This chapter explains how engines are constructed and what makes them run. Following chapters discuss different types of automotive engines in detail.

THE BASIC FACTS ABOUT ATOMS

§ 3–1. ATOMS You might think it strange for us to start this chapter, on how engines operate, with an explanation of atoms. But an engine will not run until atoms start getting together inside the engine. Therefore, we should take a close look at atoms.

You could make a list a mile long of all the different things you see around you—this book, your chair, the window, the trees or buildings outside, the clouds, and so on. And all these things are made of metals, wood, paper, glass, cloth, leather, clay, water, air, and thousands of other materials. But amazingly enough, all these different things are made of only a few basic "building blocks" called *atoms.* Of course, atoms are not really "blocks", as we will learn when we study them. There are only about 100 different kinds of atoms. But these 100 kinds of atoms can be put together in millions of different ways to form millions of different substances. You can compare this with the 26 letters of our alphabet. These letters can be put together in many different ways to make up the several hundred thousand words in our language.

Now, about those 100 or so kinds of atoms. We have special names for each kind, such as copper, iron, carbon, oxygen, silver, gold, uranium, aluminum, and mercury. The silver in the dime in your pocket is made up of an almost countless number of one kind of atom. The oxygen in the air you breathe and in the water you drink is made up of a vast number of another kind of atom. Any substance made up of only one kind of atom is called an *element.* Silver is an element. So are oxygen, and hydrogen, and sodium, and all the others

listed in the table of elements on page 54. Actually, the table lists only a few of the more common elements.

§ 3–2. SIZE OF ATOMS Atoms are very small. In a single drop of water there are more than 100 billion billion atoms. This is about 30 billion atoms for every person living on the earth. If you tried to count your share—your 30 billion atoms—it would take you 1,000 years if you counted one atom every second, day and night. And this is only your share of just one drop of water.

Here is another comparison. Suppose that you started with a cubic inch of hydrogen gas (at 32°F and atmospheric pressure). This cube (Fig. 3–1) would contain about 880 billion billion atoms (880,000,000,000,000,000,000). Now suppose that we were able to expand this cubic inch until it was large enough to enclose the earth (Fig. 3–2). This means it would measure 8,000 miles on each edge.

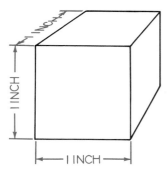

Fig. 3–1. One cubic inch of hydrogen gas at atmospheric pressure and at 32°F contains about 880 billion billion atoms.

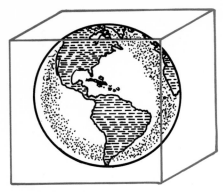

Fig. 3–2. If the cube of hydrogen were expanded until it were large enough to enclose the earth, each hydrogen atom would be about ten inches in diameter.

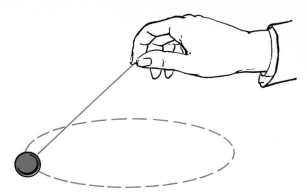

Fig. 3–3. The electron in a hydrogen atom circles the proton like a ball on a rubber band swung in a circle around the hand.

If the atoms were expanded in proportion, each hydrogen atom would measure about 10 inches in diameter. Yes, atoms are very small.

You might think that the atoms in a cubic inch of hydrogen would be packed closely together. This is not so. The distance between atoms is considerably greater than the diameter of the atoms themselves. In our greatly expanded cubic inch of hydrogen, where the hydrogen atoms are about 10 inches in diameter, the distance between atoms would average 2 or 3 feet.

§ 3–3. INSIDE THE ATOM Now let us, in our imagination, look inside atoms to see what they are made of. You are likely to be disappointed. For there is almost nothing inside the atoms. Take, for example, the hydrogen atom. It is made up of only two particles. One of these is at the center, or *nucleus*, of the atom. The other, a comparatively long distance away, is whirling in an orbit around the nucleus. The center particle is called a *proton*. The outside particle, in orbit around the proton, is called an *electron*.

Suppose that the proton were the size of a marble. If you laid this marble under the basket at one end of a standard high school basketball court (84 feet long), the electron would be as far away as the other basket. And there would be nothing in between. It is all just empty space.

The proton has a tiny charge of positive electricity (indicated by a plus [+] sign). The electron has a tiny charge of negative electricity (indicated by a minus [−] sign). Opposites attract. Minus attracts plus. Plus attracts minus. Thus, the negatively charged electron is pulled toward the positively charged proton. But balancing this inward-pulling

force is the outward pull of centrifugal force. This is somewhat like the balancing of forces you get when you whirl a ball on a rubber band in a circle around your hand (Fig. 3–3). The rubber band pulls the ball toward your hand. But the centrifugal force pushes the ball away. The result is that the ball moves in an orbit, or in a circle, around your hand.

§ 3–4. HELIUM The simplest atom is hydrogen. It has one proton and one electron. Next, as we go from the simplest to the more complex atoms, is helium, another gas. The helium atom has two protons (+ charges) in its nucleus and two electrons (− charges) circling the nucleus (Fig. 3–4). In addition, the nucleus has two other particles which are electrically neutral (have no charge) and are therefore called *neutrons*. The neutrons weigh almost the same as the protons. They seem to serve as a sort of nuclear "glue" to keep the two protons together in the nucleus. Like electrical

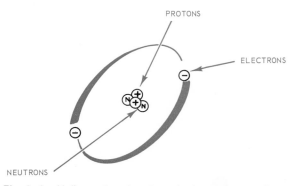

Fig. 3–4. Helium atom has two electrons, two protons, and two neutrons.

charges repel each other, and, without the neutrons, the protons would fly apart. But the presence of the neutrons in the nucleus seems to nullify this repulsive force between the protons so that they stay together inside the nucleus.

§ 3–5. MORE COMPLEX ATOMS

The next element after helium in complexity is lithium, a very light metal. The lithium atom (Fig. 3–5) has a nucleus with three protons and four neutrons. Three electrons, one for each proton, circle the nucleus.

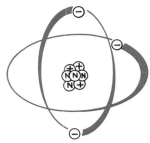

Fig. 3–5. Lithium atom.

Next is beryllium, another metal, with four protons, five neutrons, and four electrons; boron with five protons, five neutrons, and five electrons; carbon with six, six, and six; nitrogen with seven, seven, and seven; oxygen with eight, eight, and eight; and so on. Note that each atom normally has the same number of electrons as protons. This makes the atom electrically neutral, since negative charges equal positive charges. However, as we will soon learn, some kinds of atoms are not always able to hold on to all their electrons. These electrons therefore "wander" off, leaving electrically unbalanced atoms behind (with + charges). The ability of electrons to free themselves from atoms in this manner gives us the phenomenon of electricity, as we will learn later.

§ 3–6. THE SOLID-ATOM MYTH

A long time ago, many scientists guessed that atoms were round balls, more or less like tiny marbles. But as studies of the atom progressed and evidence accumulated, scientists learned that the atom was, in fact, nearly all empty space. We have mentioned this before. Consider, for example, the aluminum atom. It has 13 electrons circling its nucleus. These electrons circle in three orbits, or "shells," as scientists call them. The inner shell holds two electrons, the second shell eight electrons, the outer shell three electrons. The electrons are much lighter than the protons and neutrons in the nucleus and presumably much smaller. If an aluminum nucleus were the size of a marble (a "shooter," or "taw," or "glassie") and if it were placed on the 50-yard line of a football field, the outer electrons of the aluminum atom would be as far away as the goal posts. If you stood at a goal post, you couldn't even see the marble.

If this is so, and the atoms are really almost all empty space, why don't they all fall in on one another? The answer seems to be that the electrons circle the nucleus so rapidly that they present almost a continuous surface so that, in effect, atoms act like solid balls. There is more to it than this, however. The repulsive effect between electrons is also a factor. Electrons, being of like electrical charge, repel each other.

Under certain conditions, atoms are crushed together. Inside the sun and certain other stars, the force of gravity, or weight of material above, overcomes the electron effect. As a consequence, the material in the center of some of the stars is crushed so closely together that a cubic inch of the "stuff" would weigh hundreds of tons on earth.

§ 3–7. CHEMICAL REACTIONS

There is another very common situation which brings atoms close together. This occurs when two or more atoms link up, or combine, to form a *molecule*. The linking-up process is called *chemical reaction*. For example, two atoms of hydrogen and one atom of oxygen react to form one molecule of water (Fig. 3–6). Water has the chemical formula H_2O, which means each molecule has two atoms of hydrogen and one atom of oxygen. When one atom of sodium (chem-

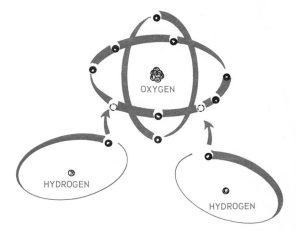

Fig. 3–6. One atom of oxygen uniting with two atoms of hydrogen to form a molecule of water, or H_2O.

TABLE OF ELEMENTS

Name	Symbol	Atomic number	Approximate atomic weight	Electron arrangement
Aluminum	Al	13	27	·2)8)3
Calcium	Ca	20	40	·2)8)8)2
Carbon	C	6	12	·2)4
Chlorine	Cl	17	35.5	·2)8)7
Copper	Cu	29	63.6	·2)8)18)1
Hydrogen	H	1	1	·1
Iron	Fe	26	56	·2)8)14)2
Magnesium	Mg	12	24	·2)8)2
Mercury	Hg	80	200	·2)8)18)32)18)2
Nitrogen	N	7	14	·2)5
Oxygen	O	8	16	·2)6
Phosphorus	P	15	31	·2)8)5
Potassium	K	19	39	·2)8)8)1
Silver	Ag	47	108	·2)8)18)18)1
Sodium	Na	11	23	·2)8)1
Sulfur	S	16	32	·2)8)6
Zinc	Zn	30	65	·2)8)18)2

ical symbol Na) unites with one atom of chlorine (chemical symbol Cl), a molecule of common table salt is formed (NaCl). Another example is sugar, each molecule of which has 12 atoms of carbon, 22 atoms of hydrogen, and 11 atoms of oxygen and the chemical formula $C_{12}H_{22}O_{11}$.

During a chemical reaction, one or more of the electrons in the outer shells of some of the atoms are shared with other atoms. This matter of sharing will become clearer as we discuss electron shells, or orbits.

§ 3–8. ELECTRON SHELLS According to atomic theory, electrons can occupy certain positions only as they orbit atomic nuclei. They are not scattered or darting about like insects flying around a light. Instead, they move in specific orbits, or positions. These positions are called shells, and you can think of them as hollow spheres, like basket balls, of varying sizes, one outside another. The smallest or innermost shell can hold only two electrons. The next larger, or second, shell can hold eight electrons. Think of these electrons as traveling slightly above, on, or below the surfaces of the shells. The third shell can hold 18 electrons and the fourth 32. The fifth shell can hold 28 electrons; the sixth, 9; the seventh, 2 or more.

A basic rule is that a shell must be filled up before the next shell can be started. There have to be two electrons in the inner shell before a second shell is started. Then the second shell has to have eight electrons before the third shell is started, and so on.

Another basic rule is that, during a chemical reaction, only the electrons in the outermost shell react. The inner electrons and the nucleus of the atom do not enter into the chemical reaction; that is, the outside electrons move from one atom to

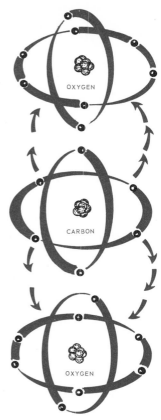

Fig. 3–7. Two atoms of oxygen uniting with one atom of carbon to form a molecule of carbon dioxide, or CO_2.

another or are shared by two atoms. Take the chemical reaction that produces water, during which two hydrogen atoms unite with one oxygen atom. Each hydrogen atom has only one electron. The oxygen atom has eight electrons, two in the inner shell and six in the second shell. The second shell can hold eight electrons, as we have already noted. In human terms, we could say that the second orbit is looking for two more electrons—it is greedy for the two additional electrons. Thus, oxygen is very active, chemically. It reacts with many other elements in its "eagerness" to fill the outer orbit of its atoms.

When oxygen reacts with hydrogen, the electrons of two hydrogen atoms enter the outer orbit of one oxygen atom (Fig. 3–6). The three atoms thus become linked together to form one molecule of water (H_2O).

Essentially, the atoms are held together by electrical attraction. The hydrogen atoms, having lost their electrons, each have a positive electric

charge. The oxygen atom, having acquired two electrons, has a double negative charge. The oxygen atom is thus able to attract and hold the two hydrogen atoms electrically.

§ 3–9. COMBUSTION Combustion, or fire, is a common chemical reaction in which the gas oxygen combines with other elements, such as hydrogen or carbon. One type of combustion occurs in the automobile engine. A mixture of air and gasoline vapor is compressed and then ignited, or set on fire. The air is about 20 percent oxygen. Gasoline is mostly hydrogen and carbon (and is thus called a *hydrocarbon*). The chemical reaction during combustion is between the three elements of oxygen, hydrogen, and carbon.

We have seen how one oxygen atom combines with two hydrogen atoms to form H_2O, or water. Similarly, one carbon atom combines with two oxygen atoms to form a molecule of CO_2, or carbon dioxide (Fig. 3–7). Carbon dioxide is a gas. The carbon atom has six electrons in two shells, two electrons in the inner shell and four in the outer shell. When an atom of carbon combines with two atoms of oxygen, each oxygen atom takes two of the carbon atom outer-shell electrons.

Thus, during the combustion process, oxygen in the air combines with the carbon and hydrogen in the gasoline to form carbon dioxide and water vapor. During the process, temperatures go as high as 6000°F. Both the water, in vapor form, and the carbon dioxide, a gas, leave the engine through the exhaust system.

NOTE: With ideal combustion, all the hydrogen and carbon are converted to H_2O and CO_2. In the engine, however, ideal combustion is not achieved, and some hydrocarbons are left over. Also, some carbon monoxide (CO) is produced instead of CO_2. These products contribute to the smog problem.

§ 3–10. HEAT We mentioned that combustion is accompanied by high temperatures. But what do we mean by "high temperature" or "heat"? From the scientific point of view, heat is simply the rapid motion of atoms or molecules in a substance.

This is not easy to understand. First, we must understand that the atoms and molecules of any substance are in rapid motion. Even though a piece of iron appears solid and motionless, the atoms and molecules in the iron are in rapid motion. The atoms in a piece of hot iron are moving faster than those in a piece of cold iron.

§ 3–11. CHANGE OF STATE Maybe we can clear up the matter by discussing change of state. If we put a pan of ice cubes over a fire, the ice cubes soon melt, or turn to water. Then, the water boils, or turns to vapor. Most substances can exist in any of three states—solid, liquid, or gas (or vapor). When a substance changes from one state to another, it undergoes a change of state.

A change in the speed of molecular motion, if great enough, results in a change of state. For example, in ice, the water molecules are moving slowly and in restricted paths. But as the temperature increases, the molecules move faster and faster. Soon, the molecules are moving so fast that they break out of their restricted paths. The ice turns to water (at 32°F). As molecular speed increases still more, the boiling point is reached (212°F at sea level). Now the molecules are moving so fast that great numbers of them fly clear out of the water. The water boils, or turns to vapor.

§ 3–12. PRODUCING CHANGE OF STATE But what makes the water molecules move faster? Here is a simple explanation. During combustion, oxygen unites with carbon or hydrogen atoms. The new molecules thus formed are set into extremely rapid motion. The rushing together of the atoms to satisfy the unbalance of electric charges can be said to produce this rapid motion. Now, the newly formed and rapidly moving molecules from the fire below the pan bombard the pan. This bombardment sets the molecules of metal in the pan into rapid motion (the pan becomes hot). The metal molecules, in turn, bombard the ice molecules. The ice melts and then turns to vapor.

§ 3–13. LIGHT AND HEAT RADIATIONS This is only a partial description of what takes place during combustion. In addition to the swiftly moving molecules, the fire also produces radiations. We can see these radiations as light and feel them as heat. They are produced by certain actions inside the atoms of fuel and oxygen. A partial explanation of these actions is that the inner electrons of the atoms are disturbed by the actions of the outer electrons as they move between atoms. The inner electrons jump between shells. Each jump is accompanied by a tiny flash of radiant energy.

§ 3–14. EXPANSION OF SOLIDS WITH HEAT When a piece of iron is heated, it expands. A steel rod that measures 10 feet in length at 100°F will measure 10.07 feet in length at 1000°F (Fig. 3–8).

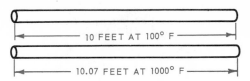

Fig. 3–8. Steel rod that measures 10 feet at 100°F will measure 10.07 feet at 1,000°F.

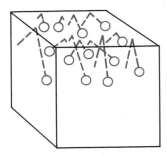

Fig. 3–9. Gas pressure in a container is the result of the ceaseless bombardment of the inner sides of the container by the fast-moving molecules of gas. This bombardment is shown on only one side of the container for simplicity. It actually takes place against all the inner sides. The molecules are shown tremendously enlarged. Also, of course, there are billions of molecules entering into the action, not just a few, as shown.

Here is the reason. As the rod is heated, the molecules in it move faster and faster. They need more room for this and therefore push adjacent molecules away so that the rod gets longer.

§ 3–15. EXPANSION OF LIQUIDS AND GASES Liquids and gases also expand when heated. A cubic foot of water at 39°F will become, when heated to 100°F, 1.01 cubic feet. A cubic foot of air at 32°F, heated to 100°F without a change of pressure, will become 1.14 cubic feet. These expansion effects result from more rapid molecular motion, which tends to push the molecules farther apart so that they spread out and take up more room.

§ 3–16. INCREASE OF PRESSURE A different sort of effect results if the volume is held constant while the cubic foot of air is heated from 32 to 100°F. If we start with a pressure of 15 psi (pounds per square inch), we find that the pressure increases to about 17 psi at 100°F. This can also be explained by the molecular theory of heat.

Gas pressure in a container is due entirely to the unending bombardment of the gas molecules against the inside of the container (Fig. 3–9). As

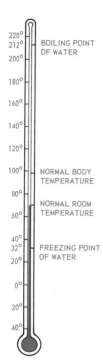

220°
212° — BOILING POINT OF WATER
200°

180°

160°

140°

120°

100° — NORMAL BODY TEMPERATURE
80°

60° — NORMAL ROOM TEMPERATURE

40°
32° — FREEZING POINT OF WATER
20°

0°

20°

40°

Fig. 3-10. Fahrenheit thermometer.

we have already said, gas molecules move about in all directions at high speeds. They are continually bumping into one another and into any solid that is in their way. Thus, the walls of the container are bumped by these countless billions of molecules. These "bumps" add up to a combined push, or pressure.

Fig. 3-11. Coil-type thermostat. The coil winds up or unwinds as the temperature goes up or down. The resulting motion can be used to operate a control.

As temperature increases, the molecules of gas move faster. They bump the walls of the container harder and more often. The result is higher pressure in the container.

Another way to increase pressure in a container is to compress the gas in the container into a smaller volume. This is what happens in engine cylinders. The mixture of air and gasoline vapor is squeezed to about one-ninth or one-tenth of its original volume. The molecules are moving much

faster, hitting the cylinder head and piston more often and faster. The pressure goes up.

Still greater pressure is then achieved in the engine cylinder by igniting the compressed air-fuel mixture. When this happens, the mixture burns, as has already been explained, and the temperature of the burning gas goes as high as 6000°F. This means that the gas molecules are moving at very high speed. They hit the top of the piston so hard and so often that a push, or pressure, of 2 to 3 tons may be registered on the piston. This pressure, or push, is due entirely to countless fast-moving molecules bombarding the piston.

§ 3-17. INCREASE OF TEMPERATURE Not only pressure but also temperature increases when a gas is compressed. Moving the molecules closer together causes them to bump into one another more often so that they are set into faster motion. Faster motion means a higher temperature. For example, in the diesel engine, air is compressed to as little as one-sixteenth of its original volume. This raises the temperature of the air to as much as 1000°F. Of course, the heat produced by the action soon escapes from the compressed air and its container into the surrounding air. Any hot object loses heat until its temperature falls to that of the surrounding medium.

§ 3-18. THE THERMOMETER The thermometer (Fig. 3-10) shows a familiar use of the expansion of liquids as temperature goes up. The liquid, usually mercury (a metal that is liquid at ordinary temperatures), is largely contained in the glass bulb at the bottom of the glass tube. As temperature increases, the mercury expands. Part of it is forced up through the hollow glass tube. The higher the temperature, the more the mercury expands and the higher it is forced up through the tube. The tube is marked off to indicate the temperature in degrees.

§ 3-19. THE THERMOSTAT Different metals expand at different rates with increasing temperatures. Aluminum expands about twice as much as iron as their temperatures go up. This difference in expansion rates is used in thermostats. Thermostats do numerous jobs in the automobile. One type is shown in Fig. 3-11. It consists of a coil made up of two strips of different metals, brass and steel, for example, welded together. When the coil is heated, one metal expands faster than the other, causing the coil to wind up or unwind.

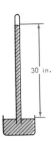

Fig. 3-12. Barometer. The mercury in the tube will stand at about 30 inches above the surface of the mercury in the dish at an atmospheric pressure of 15 psi.

§ 3-20. GRAVITY Gravity is the attractive force between all objects. When we release a stone from our hand, it falls to earth. When a car is driven up a hill, part of the engine power is being used to lift the car against gravity. Likewise, a car can coast down a hill with the engine turned off, because gravity pulls downward on the car.

Gravitational attraction is usually measured in terms of weight. We put an object on a scale and note that it weighs 10 pounds. What we mean is that the object has sufficient mass for the earth to register this much pull on it. Gravitational attraction gives any object its weight.

§ 3-21. ATMOSPHERIC PRESSURE The air is also an "object" that is pulled toward the earth by gravity. At sea level and average temperature, a cubic foot of air weighs about 0.08 pound, or about 1.25 ounce. This seems like very little. But the blanket of air—our atmosphere—surrounding the earth is many miles thick. This means that there are, in effect, many thousands of cubic feet of air piled on top of one another, all adding their

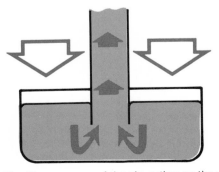

Fig. 3-13. The pressure of the air, acting on the surface of the mercury and through the mercury, holds the mercury up in the tube. If the air pressure increases, the mercury will be forced higher in the tube.

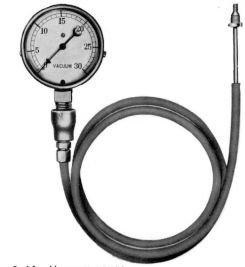

Fig. 3-14. Vacuum gauge.

weight. The total weight, or downward push, of this air amounts to about 15 psi at sea level. The pressure of all this air pushing downward is about 2,160 pounds on every square foot. Since the human body has a surface area of several square feet, it has a total pressure of several tons on it.

It would seem that this tremendous pressure would crush you. The reason that it does not is that the internal pressures inside the body balance the outside pressure. Fish have been found thousands of feet below the surface of the ocean, where pressures are more than 100,000 psi (or 700 tons per square foot). The fish can live because their internal pressures balance these immense outside pressures.

§ 3-22. VACUUM A vacuum is the absence of air or any other matter. Astronauts, on their way to the moon and the other planets, soon leave the blanket of air surrounding the earth and pass into the vast region of empty space. Out in space, there are only a few scattered atoms of air. This is a vacuum.

§ 3-23. PRODUCING A VACUUM There are many ways to produce a vacuum. The automobile engine, as it operates, produces a partial vacuum in the engine cylinders. The fuel pump works by producing a partial vacuum.

1. Barometer. The mercury barometer is another device that utilizes a vacuum. You can make a barometer by filling a long tube with mercury and

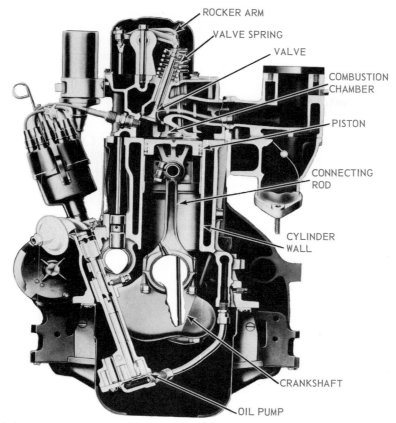

Fig. 3–15. Sectional view of an engine showing the piston in one of the cylinders.

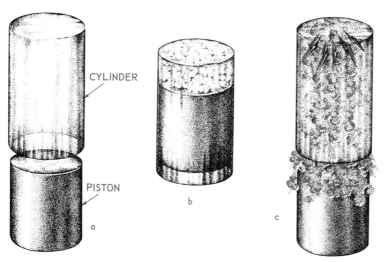

Fig. 3–16. Three views showing the actions in an engine cylinder (a). The piston is a metal plug that fits snugly into the engine cylinder (b). When the piston is pushed up into the cylinder, air is trapped and compressed. The cylinder is drawn as though it were transparent so that the piston can be seen (c). The increase of pressure as the gasoline vapor and air mixture is ignited pushes the piston out of the cylinder.

then closing the end. Next, turn the tube upside down, and put the end in a dish of mercury. Now, open the end. Some of the mercury will run down out of the tube, leaving the upper end of the tube empty (a vacuum). See Fig. 3–12.

The barometer is used to measure atmospheric pressure. When atmospheric pressure increases, the increased push on the mercury forces it higher in the tube (Fig. 3–13). When atmospheric pressure goes down, the mercury also goes down in the tube. The barometer is used to forecast weather. Before a storm, the atmospheric pressure usually drops. This is due to the heated and therefore lighter air accompanying a storm. Thus, when the mercury "falls" in the barometer, it indicates that a storm is coming.

2. Vacuum gauge. The vacuum gauge is really a pressure gauge. The type of vacuum gauge used in automotive service contains a bellows or diaphragm which is linked to an indicating needle on the dial face (Fig. 3–14). When the vacuum gauge is connected to the engine (to the intake manifold, as shown in Fig. 26–4), the vacuum produced by the engine causes the needle to move and register the amount of vacuum. This action results because the vacuum causes part of the air in the bellows or back of the diaphragm to pass into the engine. Then, air pressure causes the

bellows or diaphragm to move, thereby causing the needle to move. The amount that the needle moves depends on the amount of vacuum. The amount of vacuum that a running engine can produce is a measure of engine condition. The vacuum gauge is thus a good diagnostic tool to determine the actual condition of the engine. This is discussed in detail in a later chapter.

ENGINE OPERATION

§ 3–24. THE ENGINE CYLINDER Most automotive engines have six or eight cylinders. Since similar actions take place in all cylinders, let us concentrate on one cylinder to study engine operation. Figure 3–15 shows an end view of an engine, cut away so that the cylinder, piston, valve, and

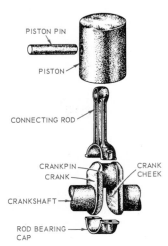

Fig. 3–18. Piston, connecting rod, piston pin, and crankpin on an engine crankshaft in disassembled view. The piston rings are not shown.

other parts can be seen. Essentially, the cylinder is nothing more than a cylindrical air pocket, closed at one end. A movable metal plug—the piston—fits snugly into the open end of the cylinder. The piston is made of aluminum or other suitable metal. It is a snug fit, but it is still loose enough to slide easily up and down in the cylinder.

Figure 3–16 shows this action. In Fig. 3–16*a*, the piston is below the cylinder. The cylinder is drawn as though it were transparent so that the actions inside it can be seen. Figure 3–16*b* shows the piston pushed up into the cylinder. This upward movement of the piston traps air in the cylinder and compresses it (pushes it into a smaller space).

Fig. 3–17. Typical piston with piston rings in place. When the piston is installed in the cylinder, the rings are compressed into the grooves in the piston.

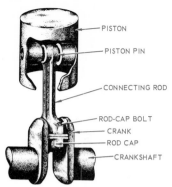

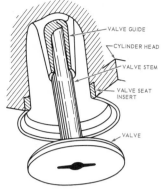

Fig. 3–19. Piston and connecting-rod assembly attached to the crankpin on a crankshaft. The piston rings are not shown. The piston is partly cut away to show how it is attached to the connecting rod.

Fig. 3–21. Valve and valve seat in a cylinder head. The cylinder head, valve-seat insert, and valve guide have been partly cut away so that the valve stem can be seen.

If we could now put some gasoline vapor into the compressed air, and if we were able to apply a lighted match or spark to the air-vapor mixture, it is obvious what would happen. The gasoline vapor would burn. High pressure would be created, and the piston would be blown out of the cylinder, as shown in Fig. 3–16c. This is about what happens in the engine cylinder. A mixture of gasoline vapor and air enters the cylinder, the piston moves up to compress it, the compressed mixture is ignited, and the resulting combustion pushes the piston downward.

§ 3–25. PISTON RINGS The piston must be a fairly loose fit in the cylinder. If it were a tight fit, then, as it became hot, it would expand and might stick in the cylinder. This, of course, could ruin the engine. On the other hand, if the piston fitted too loosely, excessive amounts of air-fuel mixture and combustion pressure would leak past. This loss would seriously reduce engine performance.

To provide a good sealing fit between the piston and cylinder, piston rings are used. The rings are split at one point and are fitted into grooves cut into the outside of the piston (Fig. 3–17). When

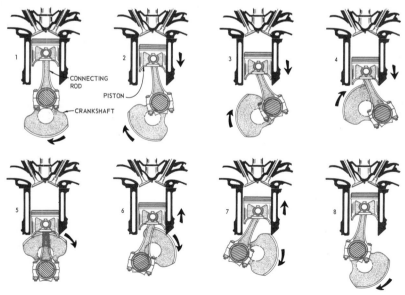

Fig. 3–20. Sequence of actions as the crankshaft completes one revolution and the piston moves from top to bottom to top again.

the piston is installed in the cylinder, these rings are compressed into the grooves so that the split ends almost come together. The rings fit tightly against the cylinder wall and against the sides of the groove so that there is a good seal between the cylinder wall and piston. Little combustion pressure can escape past the rings. Even with the good seal the piston and rings can still slide freely up and down in the cylinder.

§ 3–26. RECIPROCATING TO ROTARY MOTION

As we mentioned in § 3–24, the piston moves up and down in the cylinder. This up-and-down motion is called *reciprocating motion*. The piston moves in a straight line. This straight-line motion must be changed to rotary, or turning, motion in order for it to turn the car wheels. A crank and a connecting rod (Figs. 3–18 and 3–19) change reciprocating to rotary motion.

The crank is an offset section of the engine crankshaft. It swings around in a circle as the shaft rotates. The connecting rod connects the crankpin of the crank to the piston (Fig. 3–19). The crank end of the connecting rod is attached to the crankpin by the rod bearing cap. The cap is fastened to the connecting rod with the rod-cap bolts (Fig. 3–19). The cap and rod have bearings which permit the crankpin to rotate freely within the rod. The piston end of the rod is attached to the piston

by the *piston pin*, or *wrist pin*. The piston pin is held in two bearings in the piston. A bearing in the piston-pin end of the connecting rod (or bearings in the piston) permits the rod to swing back and forth on the piston pin.

NOTE: The crank end of the connecting rod is sometimes called the rod "big end," and the piston end is called the rod "small end."

Now, let us see what happens as the piston moves up and down in the cylinder (Fig. 3–20). As the piston starts down, the connecting rod tilts to one side so that the lower end can follow the circular path of the crankpin. If you follow the sequence of action as shown in Fig. 3–20 (steps numbered 1 to 8), you will note that the connecting rod tilts or swings back and forth on the piston pin while the lower end moves in a circle along with the crankpin.

§ 3–27. THE VALVES

There are two openings, or ports, in the enclosed end of the cylinder, one of which is shown in Fig. 3–15. One of the ports permits the mixture of air and gasoline vapor to enter the cylinder. The other port permits the burned gases, after combustion, to exhaust, or escape, from the cylinder.

The two ports have valves assembled into them. These valves close off one or the other port, or both ports, during the various stages of engine

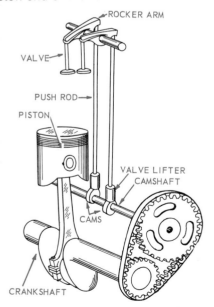

Fig. 3–22. Valve-operating mechanism for an I-head, or overhead-valve, engine. Only the essential moving parts for one cylinder are shown.

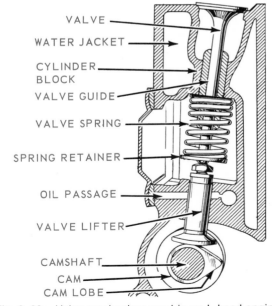

Fig. 3–23. Valve mechanism used in an L-head engine. The valve is raised off its seat with every camshaft rotation.

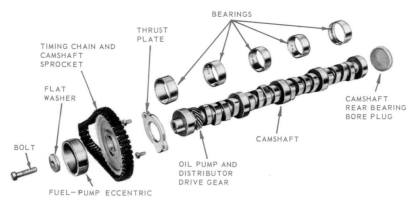

Fig. 3–24. Camshaft and related parts for an eight-cylinder (V-8) engine. *(Ford Division of Ford Motor Company)*

operation. The valves are nothing more than accurately machined metal plugs (on long stems) that close the openings when they are seated (have moved up into the openings). Figure 3–21 shows a valve and valve seat of the type generally used in automotive engines; the valve is shown pushed down off the valve seat so that it is opened. This type of valve is called a *poppet valve*.

When the valve closes, it moves up so that the outer edge rests on the seat. In this position, the valve port is closed so that air or gas cannot escape from the cylinder.

A spring on the valve stem (Fig. 3–23) tends to hold the valve on its seat (closed). The lower end of the spring rests against the cylinder head. The upper end rests against a flat washer, or spring retainer, which is attached to the valve stem by a retainer lock (also called a *keeper*). The spring is under *compression*, which means that it tries

to expand and therefore spring-loads the valve in the closed position.

A valve-opening mechanism opens the valve, or lifts it off its seat, at certain times. On most engines, this mechanism, called the *valve train*, includes a cam on the camshaft, a valve lifter, a push rod, and a rocker arm (Fig. 3–22). As the camshaft turns, the high spot (called the *cam lobe*) on the cam comes around under the valve lifter. This raises the lifter, which in turn pushes upward on the push rod. The push rod, as it is lifted, causes the end of the rocker arm to move up. The rocker arm pivots around its supporting shaft so that the valve end of the rocker arm is forced downward. This downward movement forces the valve to move downward off its seat so that it opens. After the cam lobe moves out from under the valve lifter, the valve spring forces the valve up onto its seat again.

Fig. 3–25. Intake stroke. The intake valve (at left) has opened, and the piston is moving downward, drawing air and gasoline vapor into the cylinder.

Fig. 3–26. Compression stroke. The intake valve has closed, and the piston is moving upward, compressing the mixture.

Fig. 3–27. Power stroke. The ignition system produces a spark that ignites the mixture. As it burns, high pressure is created, pushing the piston down.

Fig. 3–28. Exhaust stroke. The exhaust valve (right) has opened, and the piston is moving upward, forcing the burned gases from the cylinder.

Figure 3–23 shows a valve mechanism for an engine in which the valves are located in the cylinder block instead of the head. With this arrangement, the camshaft is directly below the valve lifter, and no push rods or rocker arms are necessary. Although the valve-in-block arrangement is a simpler design, most automotive engines are the valve-in-head type (Fig. 5–14). The valve-in-head engine has certain advantages.

Figure 3–24 shows a typical camshaft. It has a cam for each valve in the engine, or two cams per cylinder. The camshaft is driven by gears, or by a chain, from the crankshaft. It turns at one-half crankshaft speed. The cam lobes are so positioned on the camshaft as to cause the valves to open and close in the cylinders at the proper time with respect to the actions taking place in the cylinders.

§ 3–28 ACTION IN A CYLINDER The actions taking place in the engine cylinder can be divided into four stages, or strokes. "Stroke" refers to piston movement; a stroke occurs when the piston moves from one limiting position to the other. The upper limit of piston movement (position 1 in Fig. 3–20) is called TDC (top dead center). The lower limit of piston movement is called BDC (bottom dead center). A stroke is piston movement from TDC to BDC or from BDC to TDC. In other words, the piston completes a stroke each time it changes its direction of motion.

Where the entire cycle of events in the cylinder requires four strokes (or two crankshaft revolutions), the engine is called a *four-stroke-cycle engine*, or a *four-cycle engine*. The term "Otto cycle" is also applied to this type of engine (after Friedrich Otto, a German scientist of the nineteenth century). The four piston strokes are intake, compression, power, and exhaust. (Two-stroke-cycle engines are also in use; in these, the entire cycle of events is completed in two strokes, or one crankshaft revolution.)

There is sometimes some misunderstanding about the term "cycle." A cycle is simply a series of events that repeat themselves. The cycle of the seasons (spring, summer, fall, and winter) is one example. The cycle of the four piston strokes in the four-stroke-cycle engine is another.

NOTE: For the sake of simplicity in the following discussion, the valves are considered to open and close at TDC and BDC. Actually, they are not timed to open and close at these points, as is explained in a later chapter. Also, the illustrations showing the four strokes (Figs. 3–25 to 3–28) are much simplified. They show the intake and exhaust valves separated and placed on either side of the cylinder so that both can be seen.

1. *Intake* (Fig. 3–25). On the intake stroke, the intake valve has opened. The piston is moving down, and a mixture of air and vaporized gasoline is entering the cylinder through the valve port. The mixture of air and vaporized gasoline is delivered to the cylinder by the fuel system and carburetor (discussed in Chap. 9).

The reason that the air-fuel mixture enters the cylinder is as follows. As the piston moves down, a partial vacuum is produced in the cylinder, and atmospheric pressure (pressure of the air) outside the engine pushes air into the engine cylinder. This air passes through the carburetor, where it picks up a charge of gasoline vapor, and then through the intake manifold and intake-valve port.

2. *Compression* (Fig. 3–26). After the piston reaches BDC, or the lower limit of its travel, it begins to move upward. As this happens, the intake valve closes. The exhaust valve is also closed, so that the cylinder is sealed. As the piston moves upward (pushed now by the revolving crankshaft and connecting rod), the air-fuel mixture is compressed. By the time the piston reaches TDC, the mixture has been compressed to as little as one-tenth of its original volume, or even less. This compression of the air-fuel mixture increases the pressure in the cylinder. Or, to say it another way, the molecules that compose the air-fuel mixture have been pushed closer together. They therefore bump into the cylinder walls and piston head more often. The increasing frequency of the bumps means that a stronger push is registered on the walls and head; the pressure is higher. The molecules, being pushed closer together, also collide with one another more frequently. This, in turn, sets them into more rapid motion. We know that more rapid motion and increased temperature mean the same thing. Therefore, when the air-fuel mixture is compressed, not only does the pressure in the cylinder go up, but the temperature of the mixture also increases.

3. *Power* (Fig. 3–27). As the piston reaches TDC on the compression stroke, an electric spark is produced at the spark plug. The spark plug consists essentially of two wire electrodes, electrically insulated from each other. The ignition system (part of the electric system discussed in Chap. 15)

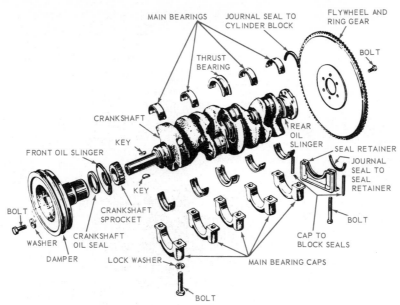

Fig. 3–29. Crankshaft and related parts used in an eight-cylinder V-type engine. *(Lincoln-Mercury Division of Ford Motor Company)*

delivers a high-voltage surge of electricity to the spark plug to produce the spark. The spark ignites, or sets fire to, the air-fuel mixture. It now begins to burn very rapidly, and the cylinder pressure increases to as much as 600 psi (pounds per square inch) or even more. This means that the hot gases are pushing against every square inch of the combustion chamber and the piston head with a pressure of 600 pounds or more. For example, a piston 3 inches in diameter with a head area of about 7 square inches would have a pressure on it of over 2 tons. This terrific push against the piston forces it downward, and a power impulse is transmitted through the connecting rod to the crankpin on the crankshaft. The crankshaft is rotated as the piston is pushed down by the pressure above it.

Let us take a look at the activities we have just described from the molecular point of view. That is, let us see how the increased pressure can be explained by considering the air-fuel mixture as a vast number of molecules. We have already noted, in the previous paragraph, that compressing the mixture increases both its temperature and its pressure. The molecules move faster (higher temperature) and bump the cylinder walls and piston head more often (higher pressure). Then, when combustion takes place, the hydrocarbon molecules of gasoline are violently split apart into hydrogen and carbon atoms. The hydro-

gen and carbon atoms then unite with oxygen atoms in the air (see § 3–9). All this sets the molecules into extremely rapid motion (still higher temperature, which may momentarily reach 6000°F). The molecules begin to bombard the cylinder walls and piston head much harder and more often. In other words, the pressure goes up much higher.

It may be a little difficult, at first, to visualize a 2-ton push on the piston head as resulting from the bombardment of molecules far too small to be seen. But remember that there are billions upon billions of molecules in the combustion chamber, all moving at speeds of many miles a second. Their combined hammering on the piston head adds up to the high pressure that is registered.

4. Exhaust (Fig. 3–28). As the piston reaches BDC again, the exhaust valve opens. Now, as the piston moves up on the exhaust stroke, it forces the burned gases out of the cylinder through the exhaust-valve port. Then, when the piston reaches TDC, the exhaust valve closes and the intake valve opens. Now, a fresh charge of air-fuel mixture will be drawn into the cylinder as the piston moves down again toward BDC. The above four strokes are continuously repeated.

§ 3–29. MULTIPLE-CYLINDER ENGINES A single-cylinder engine provides only one power impulse every two crankshaft revolutions and is delivering power only one-fourth of the time. To provide for a more continuous flow of power, modern engines use four, six, eight, or more cylinders. The power impulses are so arranged as to follow one another, or overlap (on six- and eight-cylinder engines). This gives a more nearly even flow of power from the engine.

§ 3–30. FLYWHEEL The power impulses in a multicylinder engine follow each other, or overlap, to provide a fairly even flow of power. However, additional leveling off of the power impulses is desirable. This makes the engine run still more smoothly. To achieve this, a flywheel is used (Fig. 3–29). The flywheel is a fairly heavy steel wheel, attached to the rear end of the crankshaft.

To get a better idea of how the flywheel does its job, let us look at a single-cylinder engine. This engine delivers power only one-fourth of the time —during the power stroke. During the other three strokes, it is absorbing power—to push out the exhaust gas, to produce a vacuum on the intake stroke, to compress the air-fuel mixture. Thus, during the power stroke, the engine tends to speed up. During the other strokes, it tends to slow down. Any rotating wheel, including the flywheel, resists any effort to change its speed of rotation (this is due to inertia). When the engine tends to speed up, the flywheel resists it. When the engine tends to slow down, the flywheel resists it. Of course, in the single-cylinder engine, there would still be some speedup and slowdown. But the flywheel minimizes it. In effect, the flywheel absorbs power from the engine during the power stroke (or speedup time) and then gives it back to the engine during the other three strokes (or slowdown time) of the cycle.

In the multicylinder engine, the flywheel acts in a similar manner to smooth out still more the peaks and valleys of power flow from the engine. In addition, the flywheel forms part of the clutch. The flywheel also has teeth on its outer edge that mesh with the electric cranking-motor drive pinion when the engine is being cranked to start it.

Review Questions

1. What are molecules?
2. What are atoms?
3. What is a chemical reaction?
4. What is combustion?
5. What does the term "change of state" mean?
6. Describe combustion in the engine.
7. Explain what heat is in terms of molecular activity.
8. Explain gas pressure in terms of molecular actions.
9. Why does the gas pressure in a container increase with increasing temperature?
10. What is vacuum?
11. What are the four stages, or strokes, of engine operation?
12. Describe the actions in the cylinder during each of the four strokes.
13. Explain how the reciprocating motion of the piston is changed to rotary motion.
14. Describe the construction and operation of the valves.
15. Explain why a flywheel is used.

Study Questions

1. Make a sketch of a cylinder with valve ports, spark plug, piston, piston rings, connecting rod, and crankshaft.
2. Make sketches which show the four strokes, or stages, of engine operation, and write a brief explanation of the actions which take place in the cylinder during each stroke of the cycle.

CHAPTER 4

Engine Measurements and Performance

This chapter describes various ways in which engines and engine performance are measured. These include not only physical measurements, such as cylinder diameter, length of piston stroke, and so on, but also engine performance measurements, such as torque and horsepower.

§ 4–1. **WORK** Work is the moving of an object against an opposing force. The object is moved by a push, a pull, or a lift. For example, when a weight is lifted, it is moved upward against the pull of gravity. Work is done on the weight. Also, when a coil spring is compressed, work is done on the spring (Fig. 4–1).

Work is measured in terms of distance and force. If a 5-pound weight is lifted off the ground 1 foot, the work done on the weight is 5 foot-pounds (ft-lb), or 1 times 5. If the 5-pound weight is lifted 2 feet, the work done is 10 ft-lb:

Distance times force equals work.

Fig. 4–1. When a spring is compressed, work is done on that spring, and energy is stored in it.

§ 4–2. **ENERGY** Energy is the ability, or capacity, to do work. When work is done on an object, energy is stored in that object. Lift a 20-pound weight 4 feet and you have stored up energy in the weight. The weight can do 80 ft-lb of work. If a spring is compressed, energy is stored in it, and it can do work (Fig. 4–2).

§ 4–3. **POWER** Work can be done slowly, or it can be done rapidly. The rate at which work is done is measured in terms of power. A machine that can do a great deal of work in a short time is called a *high-powered* machine:

Power is the rate, or speed, at which work is done.

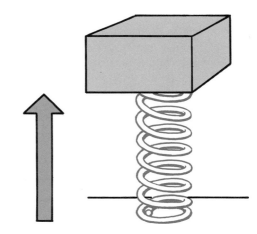

Fig. 4–2. When the spring is released, it can do work on another body, lifting a weight against the force of gravity, for instance.

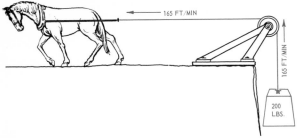

165 FT/MIN

165 FT/MIN

200 LBS.

Fig. 4–3. One horse can do 33,000 ft-lb of work a minute.

§ 4–4. HORSEPOWER A horsepower (hp) is the power of one horse, or a measure of the rate at which a horse can work. A 10-hp engine, for example, can do the work of 10 horses.

A horsepower is 33,000 ft-lb per minute (Fig. 4–3). In the illustration, the horse walks 165 feet in 1 minute, lifting the 200-pound weight. The amount of work involved is 33,000 ft-lb (165 feet × 200 pounds). The time is 1 minute. If the horse did this work in 2 minutes, then it would be only "half" working; it would be putting out only ½ hp. The formula for horsepower is

$$hp = \frac{\text{ft-lb per min}}{33,000} = \frac{L \times W}{33,000 \times t}$$

where hp = horsepower
  L = length, in feet, through which W is exerted
  W = force, in pounds, exerted through distance L
  t = time, in minutes, required to move W through L

Problem

You have a heavy box loaded with sand that you must drag across a level lot for 500 feet in 2 minutes. It requires a pull of 2,000 pounds to pull the box. What horsepower is required?

Solution: Substituting in the formula,

$$hp = \frac{L \times W}{33,000 \times t} = \frac{500 \times 2000}{33,000 \times 2} = 15.15 \text{ hp}$$

Problem

You must select a gasoline engine capable of raising a coal-mine elevator, which weighs 12,000 pounds loaded, 200 feet per minute. Ignoring friction and other power losses, what would be the minimum horsepower you could select?

Solution: Substituting in the formula,

$$hp = \frac{L \times W}{33,000 \times t} = \frac{200 \times 12,000}{33,000 \times 1} = 72.72 \text{ hp}$$

§ 4–5. TORQUE Torque is twisting, or turning, effort. You apply torque to the top of a screw-top jar when you loosen it (Fig. 4–4). You apply torque to the steering wheel when you take a car around a turn. The engine applies torque to the wheels to make them rotate.

Fig. 4–4. Torque, or twisting effort, must be applied to loosen and remove the top from a screw-top jar.

Torque, however, must not be confused with power. Torque is turning effort which *may or may not result in motion.* Power is something else again. It is the rate at which work is being done, and this means that something must be moving.

Torque is measured in pound-feet (or lb-ft, not to be confused with ft-lb of work). For example, if you pushed on a windlass crank with a 20-pound push and if the crank were 1½ feet long (from center to handle), you would be applying 30 lb-ft of torque to the crank (Fig. 4–5). You would be applying this torque regardless of whether or not the crank was turning, just so long as you continued to apply the 20-pound push to the crank handle.

Fig. 4–5. Torque is measured in pound-feet (lb-ft) and is calculated by multiplying the push by the crank offset, or the distance of the push from the rotating shaft.

§ 4-6. FRICTION Friction is the resistance to motion between two objects in contact with each other. If you put this book on a table and then pushed the book, you would find that it took a certain amount of push (Fig. 4-6). If you put a second book on top of the book, you would find that you had to push harder to move the two books on the table top (Fig. 4-7). Thus, friction, or resistance to motion, increases with the load. The higher the load, the greater the friction. There are three classes of friction: dry, greasy, and viscous.

1. Dry friction. This is the resistance to relative motion between two dry objects, for instance, a board being dragged across a floor.

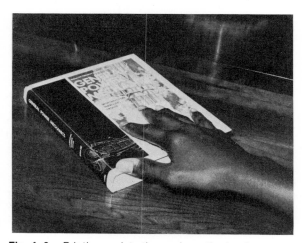

Fig. 4-6. Friction resists the push on the book.

Fig. 4-7. Increasing the weight, or load, increases the friction.

2. Greasy friction. This is the friction between two objects thinly coated with oil or grease. In an automobile engine, greasy friction may occur in an engine on first starting. Most of the lubricating oil may have drained away from the bearing surfaces and from the cylinder walls, and piston rings. When the engine is started, only the small amount of oil remaining on these surfaces protects them from undue wear. Of course, the lubricating system quickly supplies additional oil, but before this happens, greasy friction exists on the moving surfaces. The lubrication between the surfaces where greasy friction exists is not sufficient to prevent wear. This is the reason why automotive engineers say that initial starting and warm-up of the engine is hardest on the engine and wears it the most.

3. Viscous friction. "Viscosity" is a term that refers to the tendency of liquids, such as oil, to resist flowing. A heavy oil is more viscous than a light oil and flows more slowly (has a higher viscosity, or higher resistance to flowing). Viscous friction is the friction, or resistance to relative motion, between adjacent layers of liquid. In an engine bearing supplied with sufficient oil, layers of oil adhere to the bearing and shaft surfaces. In effect, layers of oil clinging to the shaft are carried around by the rotating shaft. They wedge between the shaft and the bearing (Fig. 4-8). The wedging action lifts the shaft so that the oil itself supports the weight, or load. Now, since the shaft is supported ("floats") on layers of oil, there is no metal-to-metal contact. However, the layers of oil must move over each other,

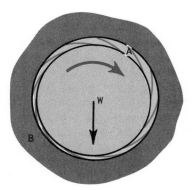

Fig. 4-8. Shaft rotation causes layers of clinging oil to be dragged around with it. The oil moves from the wide clearance A and is wedged into the narrow clearance B, thereby supporting the shaft weight W on an oil film. The clearances are exaggerated in the illustration.

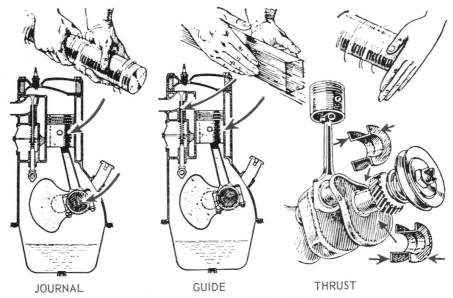

JOURNAL   GUIDE   THRUST

Fig. 4-9. Three types of friction-bearing surfaces in an automobile engine.

and it does require some energy to make them do so. The resistance to motion between these oil layers is called *viscous friction*.

4. Bushings and bearings. In the engine, as in almost all machinery, the moving parts are lubricated with oil. The surfaces that move against each other are thus protected against damaging dry friction. These surfaces are of special mate-

rials, specially prepared. The cylinder walls, for example, against which the pistons and piston rings slide, are of smooth gray iron or other metal with good wearing qualities. The cylinder walls in some small engines are chrome-plated to improve their resistance to wear. The piston rings (§ 7–3) are also made of material that gives long life. Shafts are supported by bushings or bear-

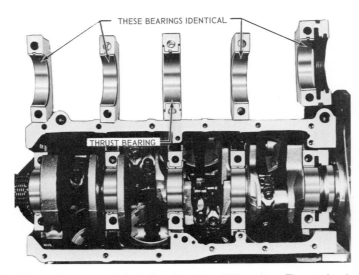

THESE BEARINGS IDENTICAL

THRUST BEARING

Fig. 4-10. Arrangement of the main, or crankshaft, bearings in a V-8 engine. The engine is shown from the bottom. The bearing caps, with bearings, have been removed and placed above the engine. *(Buick Motor Division of General Motors Corporation)*

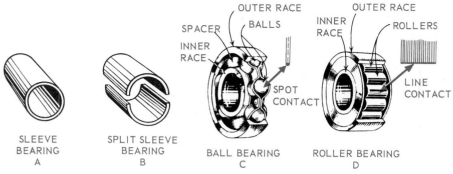

Fig. 4-11. Sleeve, ball, and roller bearings.

ings. Three types of bearing surfaces found in engines are shown in Fig. 4-9.

Figure 3-29 shows the main bearings which support the crankshaft in the engine. Figure 4-10 is a bottom view of an engine with the oil pan and the bearings and bearing caps removed. The bearings are of the split type and consist of two matching halves. Each half has a steel back to which a relatively soft bearing material has been added. Details of engine-bearing construction will be found in a following chapter.

Some engines use ball and roller bearings (Fig. 4-11). These bearings provide rolling friction, which is lower than the sliding friction of the types discussed in the previous paragraph. Ball and roller bearings can be sealed with their lubricant already in place; such bearings require no other lubrication. Figure 5-30 illustrates an engine in which the crankshaft is supported on four sealed ball bearings. The bearings at the two ends of the connecting rod are roller bearings.

§ 4-7. BORE AND STROKE The size of an engine cylinder is referred to in terms of the bore and stroke. The *bore* is the diameter of the cylinder. The *stroke* is the distance the piston travels from BDC (bottom dead center) to TDC (top dead center). (See Fig. 4-12.) The bore is always mentioned first. For example, in a 4- by 3½-inch cylinder, the diameter, or bore, is 4 inches, and the stroke is 3½ inches. These measurements are used to figure the piston displacement.

Before about 1955, most engines were built with a relatively long stroke and small bore, like, for instance, a 3 by 4 engine. More recently, however, engines have been designed with a relatively short stroke and large bore, as, for example, one 1968 350-hp Chevrolet engine has a 4-inch bore and a

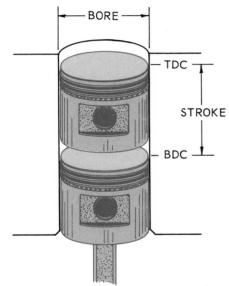

Fig. 4-12. Bore and stroke of an engine cylinder.

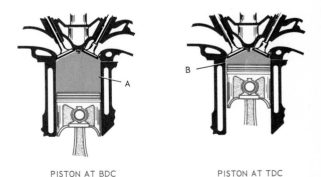

PISTON AT BDC　　　　PISTON AT TDC

Fig. 4-13. Compression ratio is the volume in a cylinder with the piston at BDC divided by its volume with the piston at TDC, or A divided by B.

71

$3\frac{1}{4}$-inch stroke. Such engines are called "oversquare." A "square" engine has a bore and stroke of equal measurements.

There are several reasons for the swing to the oversquare engine. With the shorter piston stroke, there is less friction loss (§ 4–14). Also, the shorter stroke reduces inertia and centrifugal loads on the engine bearings. In addition, the shorter stroke permits a reduction of engine height and, thus, a lower hood line.

§ 4–8. PISTON DISPLACEMENT

Piston displacement is the volume that the piston displaces as it moves from BDC to TDC. Piston displacement of a 4- by $3\frac{1}{2}$-inch cylinder, for example, would be the volume of a cylinder 4 inches in diameter and $3\frac{1}{2}$ inches long, or

$$\frac{\pi \times D^2 \times L}{4} = \frac{3.1416 \times 4^2 \times 3\frac{1}{2}}{4}$$

$$= \frac{3.1416 \times 16 \times 3\frac{1}{2}}{4} = 43.98 \text{ cu in.}$$

If the engine has eight cylinders, the total displacement would be 43.98 times 8, or 351.84 cubic inches.

§ 4–9. COMPRESSION RATIO

The compression ratio of an engine is a measurement of how much the air-fuel charges are compressed in the engine cylinders. It is calculated by dividing the air volume in one cylinder with the piston at BDC by the air volume with the piston at TDC (Fig. 4–13).

NOTE: The air volume with the piston at TDC is called the *clearance volume*, since it is the clearance that remains above the piston at TDC.

For example, the engine of one popular car has a cylinder volume of 42.35 cubic inches at BDC (*A* in Fig. 4–13). It has a clearance volume of 4.45 cubic inches (*B* in Fig. 4–13). The compression ratio, therefore, is 42.35 divided by 4.45, or 9.5/1 (that is, 9.5:1). In other words, during the compression stroke, the air-fuel mixture is compressed from a volume of 42.35 cubic inches to 4.45 cubic inches, or to 1/9.5 of its original volume.

§ 4–10. INCREASING COMPRESSION RATIO

In recent years, the compression ratios of automotive engines have been repeatedly increased. This increase offers several advantages. The power and

economy of an engine increase as the compression ratio goes up (within limits) without a comparable increase in engine size or weight. In effect, an engine with a higher compression ratio "squeezes" the air-fuel mixture harder (compresses it more). This causes the air-fuel mixture to produce more power on the power stroke. Here is the reason: A higher compression ratio means a higher initial pressure at the end of the compression stroke. This means that, when the power stroke starts, higher combustion pressures will be attained; a harder push will be registered on the piston. The burning gases will also expand to a greater volume during the power stroke. It all adds up to this: There is more push on the piston for a larger part of the power stroke. More power is obtained from each power stroke.

Increasing the compression ratio does, however, bring up special problems. For one thing, as the compression ratio goes up, the problem of detonation, or knocking, becomes more acute. There is a detailed discussion of knocking and its prevention in Chap. 10.

§ 4–11. VOLUMETRIC EFFICIENCY

The amount of air-fuel mixture taken into the cylinder on the intake stroke is a measure of the engine's volumetric efficiency. If the mixture were drawn into the cylinder very slowly, a full measure could get in. But the mixture must pass very rapidly through a series of restricting openings and bends in the carburetor and intake manifold. In addition, the mixture is heated (from engine heat); it therefore expands. The two conditions, rapid movement and heating, reduce the amount of mixture that can get into the cylinder. A full charge of air-fuel mixture cannot enter, because the time is too short and because the air becomes heated.

Volumetric efficiency is the ratio between the amount of air-fuel mixture that actually enters the cylinder and the amount that could enter under ideal conditions. For example, a certain cylinder has an air volume (*A* in Fig. 4–13) of 47 cubic inches. If the cylinder were allowed to completely "fill up," it would take in 0.034 ounce of air. However, suppose that the engine were running at a fair speed, so that only 0.027 ounce of air could enter during each intake stroke. This means that volumetric efficiency would be only about 80 percent (0.027 is 80 percent of 0.034). Actually, 80 percent is a good volumetric efficiency for an engine running at fairly high speed. Volumetric efficiency of some engines may drop to as low as 50 percent at high speeds. This is another way of saying that the cylinders are only "half-filled" at high speeds.

This is one reason why engine speed and output cannot continue to increase indefinitely. At higher speed, the engine has a harder time "breathing," or drawing in air. It is "starved" for air and cannot produce any further increase in power output.

To improve volumetric efficiency, intake valves can be made larger. Also, the intake-manifold passages can be made larger and as straight and short as possible. Carburetors are often equipped with extra circuits, or air passages (additional barrels, as noted in Chap. 9), which open at high speed to improve engine breathing. All these help the engine to produce more power at higher speeds.

§ 4–12. BRAKE HORSEPOWER The horsepower output of engines is measured in terms of *brake horsepower* (bhp) because a braking device is used to hold the engine speed down while horsepower is measured. When an engine is rated at 300 horsepower, for example, it is actually brake horsepower that is meant. This is the amount of power the engine can produce at a particular speed at wide-open throttle.

The usual way to rate an engine is with a *dynamometer* (Fig. 4–14). This device has a dynamo, or generator, that is driven by the engine. The amount of electric current the generator produces is a measure of the amount of horsepower the engine is developing.

Some dynamometers are used to test engines that have been removed from cars (Fig. 4–14). The dynamometer used in the service shop checks the engine *in* the car. This type of unit is called a *chassis dynamometer* (Figs. 4–15 and 4–16). On these, the rear wheels of the car are placed on rollers. Then, the engine drives the wheels, and the wheels drive the rollers. The rollers can be loaded varying amounts so that engine output can be measured. The use of the chassis dynamometer is becoming more common in the automotive servicing field, since it can give a very

Fig. 4–15. Chassis dynamometer of the flush-floor type. The rollers are set at floor level. *(Clayton Manufacturing Company)*

Fig. 4–16. Automobile in place on a chassis dynamometer. The rear wheels drive the dynamometer rollers, which are flush with the floor, and instruments on the test panel measure car speed, engine power output, engine vacuum, fuel ratio, and so on. *(Clayton Manufacturing Company)*

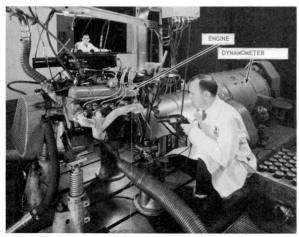

Fig. 4–14. Dynamometer used for testing engines and measuring their power output. *(General Motors Corporation)*

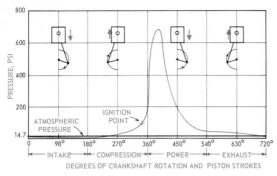

Fig. 4–17. Pressures in an engine cylinder during the four piston strokes. The four strokes require two crankshaft revolutions (360 degrees each), a total of 720 degrees of rotation. This curve is for a particular engine operating at one definite speed and throttle opening. Changing the speed and throttle opening would change the curve (particularly the power curve).

quick report on engine conditions (by measuring output at various speeds and loads). This type of dynamometer is also valuable in testing and adjusting automatic transmissions, since checks and adjustments can be made in the shop; no road testing is necessary.

§ 4–13. INDICATED HORSEPOWER The engine may also be evaluated in terms of ihp (indicated horsepower). Indicated horsepower is based on the power actually developed inside the engine cylinders by the combustion processes. A special indicating device (an oscilloscope) is required to determine ihp. This device measures the pressure continuously throughout the four piston strokes (intake, compression, power, exhaust). A graph of the cylinder pressures taken during a typical test of engine ihp is shown in Fig. 4–17. The four small drawings show the crank, rod, and piston positions as well as directions of motion during the four strokes. Note that the pressure in the cylinder is about atmospheric at the beginning of the intake stroke. Then it falls a little below atmospheric as the delivery of the air-fuel mixture to the cylinder lags behind piston movement (that is, volumetric efficiency is less than 100 percent). When the compression stroke begins, the pressure starts to increase as the piston moves upward in the cylinder. A little before the piston reaches TDC, ignition takes place. Now the air-fuel mixture burns, and pressure goes up very rapidly. It reaches a peak of around 680 psi at about 25 degrees past TDC on the power stroke. Pressure then falls off rapidly as the power stroke continues.

But there is still a pressure of around 50 psi at the end of the power stroke. When the exhaust stroke begins, the pressure falls off and drops to about atmospheric at the end of the stroke.

A graph such as the one shown in Fig. 4–17 supplies the information needed to determine ihp. This is because ihp is based on the average pressure during the power stroke minus the average pressures during the other three strokes.

Some of the power developed in the engine cylinders (or ihp) is used in overcoming friction in the engine. Thus, ihp is always greater than bhp (or power delivered by engine). § 4–15 explains how bhp and ihp are related.

§ 4–14. FRICTION HORSEPOWER Friction losses in an engine are sometimes referred to in terms of fhp (friction horsepower). This expression means the amount of horsepower used up in the engine to overcome friction. Friction horsepower is determined by driving the engine with an elec-

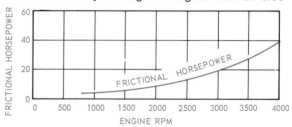

Fig. 4–18. Friction-horsepower curve, showing the relationship between fhp and engine speed.

tric motor to measure the horsepower required to drive it. During this test, the engine is at operating temperature, but there is no fuel in the carburetor, and the throttle is held wide open. At low speed, friction is relatively low. But as engine speed increases, fhp goes up rapidly. The graph (Fig. 4–18) shows fhp in a typical engine at different speeds. At 1,000 rpm, the fhp is only about 4 hp. But, at 2,000 rpm, it is nearly 10 hp. At 3,000 rpm, it is up to 21 hp, and, at 4,000 rpm, it is about 40 hp.

One of the major causes of frictional loss (or fhp) in an engine is piston-ring friction. Under some conditions, the friction of the rings on the cylinder walls accounts for 75 percent of all friction losses in the engine. For example, Fig. 4–18 shows an fhp of 40 hp at 4,000 rpm. It could be that 75 percent, or 30 hp, is due to friction between the rings and cylinder walls. Understanding this fact makes us more fully aware of the difficult job the rings have in the engine. It also points up one advantage of the short-stroke, over-square engine. With a short stroke, the piston rings do not have as far to slide on the cylinder walls, and thus ring friction is reduced. This lowers frictional losses in the engine.

§ 4-15. RELATING BHP, IHP, AND FHP

Brake horsepower is the power delivered, ihp is the power developed in the engine, and fhp is the power lost owing to friction. The relationship among the three is

$$bhp = ihp - fhp$$

That is, the horsepower delivered by the engine (bhp) is equal to the horsepower developed (ihp) minus the power lost owing to friction (fhp).

§ 4-16. SAE HORSEPOWER

The SAE (Society of Automotive Engineers) horsepower rating of engines is used to compare engines on the basis of the number and diameter of the cylinders (usually for tax purposes), as follows:

$$SAE\ hp = \frac{D^2 \times N}{2.5}$$

where D = diameter of cylinder, or bore
N = number of cylinders

This formula does not take into consideration such factors as length of stroke, rpm, and so forth.

§ 4-17. ENGINE TORQUE

Torque is turning effort. When the piston is moving down on the power stroke, it is applying torque to the engine crankshaft (through the connecting rod). The harder the push on the piston, the greater the torque applied. Thus, the higher the combustion pressures, the greater the amount of torque.

The dynamometer is normally used to check engine torque. Torque can be measured along with horsepower on the dynamometer.

§ 4-18. BRAKE HORSEPOWER VS. TORQUE

The torque that an engine can develop changes with engine speed (see Fig. 4-19). During intermediate speeds, volumetric efficiency is high (there is sufficient time for the cylinders to become fairly well "filled up"). This means that, with a fairly full charge of air-fuel mixture, higher combustion pressures will develop. With higher combustion pressures, the engine torque is higher.

But, at higher speed, volumetric efficiency drops off (there is not enough time for the cylinders to become filled up with air-fuel mixture). Since there

is less air-fuel mixture to burn, the combustion pressures will not go so high. There will be less push on the pistons, and thus engine torque will be lower. Note, in the graph (Fig. 4-19), how the torque drops off as engine speed increases.

The bhp curve of an engine is considerably different from the torque curve. Figure 4-20 is the bhp of the same engine for which the torque curve is shown in Fig. 4-19. It starts low at low speed and increases steadily with speed until a high engine speed is reached. Then, as still higher engine speeds are attained, bhp drops off.

The drop-off of bhp is due not only to reduced torque at higher speed but also to increased fhp at the higher speed. Figure 4-21 compares the curves of these three factors, torque, bhp, and fhp, of an engine.

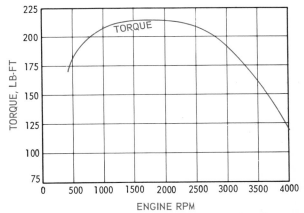

Fig. 4-19 Torque curve of an engine, showing the relationship between torque and speed.

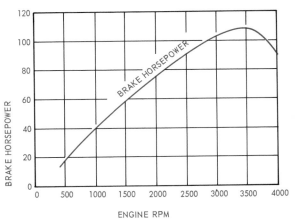

Fig. 4-20. Curve showing the relationship between bhp and engine speed.

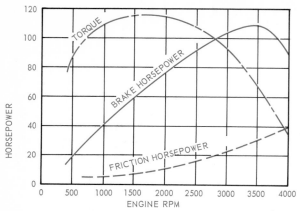

Fig. 4–21. Torque-bhp-fhp curves of an engine.

NOTE: The curves (Figs. 4–18 to 4–21) are for one particular engine only. Different engines have different torque, bhp, and fhp curves. Peaks may be at higher or lower speeds, and the relationships may not be as indicated in the curves shown.

§ 4–19. ENGINE EFFICIENCY The term "efficiency" means the relationship between the effort exerted and the results obtained. As applied to engines, efficiency is the relationship between the power delivered and the power that could be obtained if the engine operated without any power loss. Engine efficiency can be computed in two ways, as *mechanical* efficiency and as *thermal* efficiency.

1. Mechanical efficiency. This is the relationship between bhp and ihp, or

$$\text{Mechanical efficiency} = \frac{\text{bhp}}{\text{ihp}}$$

EXAMPLE: At a certain speed, the bhp of an engine is 116, and its ihp is 135. Mechanical efficiency is thus bhp/ihp = 116/135 = 0.86, or 86 percent. That is, 86 percent of the power developed in the cylinders is delivered by the engine. The remaining 14 percent, or 19 hp, is consumed as fhp.

2. Thermal efficiency. "Thermal" means of or pertaining to heat. The thermal efficiency of the engine is the relationship between the power output and the energy in the fuel burned to produce this output.

Some of the heat produced by the combustion process is carried away by the engine cooling system. Some of it is lost in the exhaust gases, since they are still hot as they leave the cylinder. These are heat (thermal) losses that reduce the thermal

efficiency of the engine. They do not add to the power output of the engine. The remainder of the heat, in causing the gases to expand and produce high pressure, forces the pistons down so that the engine develops power. Because there is a

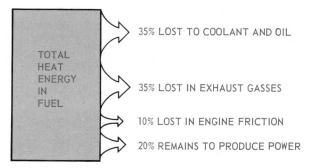

Fig. 4–22. Energy loss from cylinders to wheels.

great deal of heat lost during engine operation, thermal efficiencies of the gasoline may be as low as 20 percent and are seldom higher than 25 percent.

§ 4–20. OVERALL EFFICIENCY The gasoline enters the engine with a certain energy content, a certain ability to do work. At every step in the process, from the burning of the gasoline in the cylinders to the rotation of the car wheels, energy is lost. Figure 4–22 illustrates these losses as determined for one engine and car during a test run. Note that as little as 15 percent of the energy in the gasoline remains to actually propel the car. This energy is used to overcome rolling resistance, air resistance, power-train resistance, and to accelerate the car.

1. Rolling resistance. This results from irregularities in the road over which the wheels ride, as well as the flexing of the tires as the weight of the car is brought to bear on the various portions of the tire in turn.

2. Air resistance. Air resistance is the resistance the air offers to the passage of the car body through it. As car speed increases, so does the air resistance. At 90 mph (miles per hour), tests show that as much as 75 percent of the power the engine is delivering is used up in overcoming air resistance. Streamlining the car body reduces this power loss from air resistance.

3. Acceleration. Power is required to increase car speed. The power applied to accelerate the car overcomes the inertia of the car. Energy in the form of car speed is stored in the car.

Review Questions

1. Define work. In what terms is it measured?
2. Define energy.
3. Define power.
4. Define a horsepower.
5. An engine raises 16,500 pounds 10 feet in 30 seconds. What horsepower is the engine delivering?
6. Define inertia.
7. Define torque. Explain the difference between torque and work.
8. Define friction. What are the three classes of friction?
9. What are the bore and stroke of an engine?
10. What is piston displacement? What is the piston displacement of an engine with a 4-inch bore and a 4-inch stroke?
11. Explain what the term "compression ratio" means.
12. The clearance volume in an engine is 6 inches, and the cylinder volume at BDC is 51 inches. What is the compression ratio of this engine?
13. What are some advantages of increasing compression ratio? What are some disadvantages?
14. Define volumetric efficiency.
15. Define brake horsepower.
16. Define indicated horsepower.
17. Define friction horsepower.
18. What is the relationship among bhp, ihp, and fhp?
19. How can you use bhp and ihp to find the mechanical efficiency of an engine?
20. Define thermal efficiency.

Study Questions

1. Give the reasons in terms of inertia why quick stops and starts in driving a car waste gasoline.
2. If you were told to measure the piston displacement of an engine, how would you do so?
3. If you were told to measure the compression ratio of an engine, how would you do so?
4. As volumetric efficiency of an engine increases, does the engine tend to deliver more or less torque? Explain the reason for your answer.
5. Find the operating instructions for a chassis dynamometer. Read them and write a brief explanation of how to use a dynamometer.
6. Explain how to determine ihp.
7. Can you think of a way to measure the thermal efficiency of an engine?

CHAPTER

5

Engine Types

This chapter discusses various classifications of engines. All automotive engines are of the internal-combustion type (except for some experimental external-combustion, or steam, engines). However, they can be classified according to: 1, Number of cylinders; 2, Arrangement of cylinders; 3, Arrangement of valves; 4, Type of cooling; 5, Number of cycles (two or four); 6, Type of fuel burned; 7, Type of cycle (Otto, diesel, rotating combustion, etc.).

There are also a number of automotive power plants that cannot be classified in the above manner because of their unorthodox design. These include turbines and the Sterling, Wankel, and steam engines. They are discussed separately at the end of the chapter.

---

§ 5–1. NUMBER AND ARRANGEMENT OF CYL-INDERS American passenger-car engines have four, six, or eight cylinders. Imported cars offer a greater variety, as there are models with engines of two, three, four, six, eight, and twelve cylinders. Engines with two, three, four, six, and eight cylinders are described and illustrated in the following articles. Cylinders can be arranged in several ways: in a row (in line), in two rows or banks set at an angle (V type), in two rows opposing each other (flat, or pancake), or like spokes on a wheel (radial airplane type). Figure 5–1 shows various cylinder arrangements.

§ 5–2. TWO-CYLINDER ENGINES The cylinders of two-cylinder engines can be arranged in three ways: in-line, opposed, and V. A cutaway view of an in-line two-cylinder engine, used in a small German automobile, is shown in Fig. 5–2. Figure 5–3 is a cutaway view of an opposed-cylinder, or flat, two-cylinder engine. This engine, used in the DAF of Holland car (Fig. 5–4), is air-cooled (see § 5–12), and the two cylinders oppose each other. The crankshaft and camshaft are positioned between the two cylinders. The valves are in the cylinder heads (I-head arrangement, as explained in a later article).

§ 5–3. THREE-CYLINDER ENGINES Three-cylinder engines are in-line. Figure 5–5 is a cutaway view of a three-cylinder in-line engine. This is a

two-stroke-cycle engine (not a four-stroke-cycle), as explained in a following section. Briefly, the crankcase in this engine serves as an intake and precompression chamber. Each cylinder has its own sealed-off section of the crankcase. Thus, the main bearings that support the crankshaft are of the sealed type so that the crankcase is, in effect, divided into three separate compartments, one for each cylinder.

Figure 5–5 also shows the details of the transmission. This engine is used on a front-drive car, and the differential is located between the engine and the transmission. The mounting arrangement of a similar engine is shown in Fig. 5–6.

§ 5–4. FOUR-CYLINDER ENGINES The cylinders of a four-cylinder engine can be arranged in any of three ways: in-line, V, or opposed. In the V type, the cylinders are in two banks or rows of two cylinders each, and the two rows are set at an angle to each other. In the opposed type, the cylinders are in two banks or rows of two cylinders each, set opposite each other.

1. *In-line engines.* Figure 5–7 is a cutaway view of a four-cylinder in-line engine. The cylinders are arranged in one row, or line. A very similar engine is shown in Fig. 5–8. In this engine, the cylinders are slanted to one side to permit a lower hood line. In a sense, this engine is just one-half of a V-8 engine. There are relatively few slant-four engines produced in the United States.

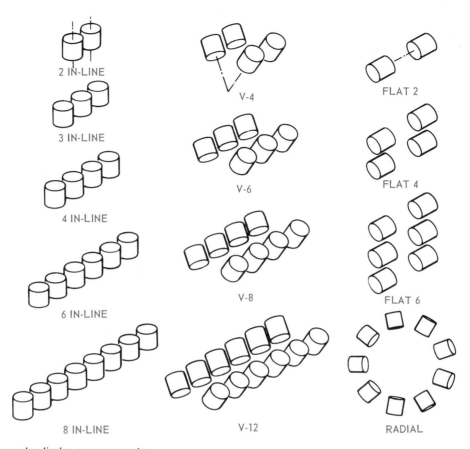

Fig. 5-1. Several cylinder arrangements.

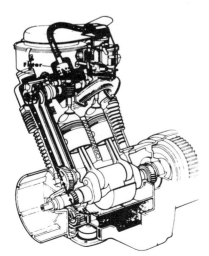

Fig. 5-2. Cutaway view of the two-cylinder, in-line, air-cooled NSU Prinz engine. The arrows show the action of the crankcase ventilator. *(NSU of Germany)*

Fig. 5-3. Cutaway view of a two-cylinder, air-cooled engine with cylinders opposing each other. *(DAF of Holland)*

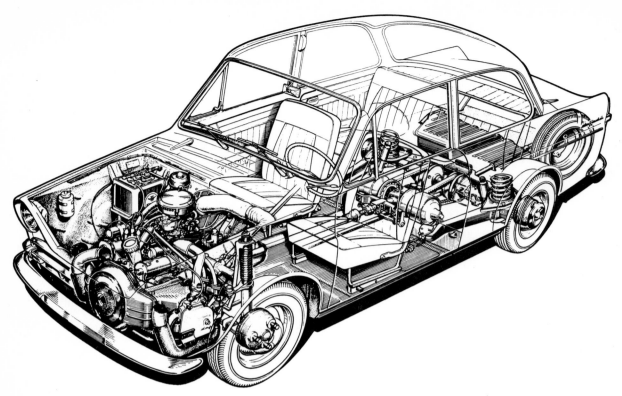

Fig. 5–4. Cutaway view of the Daffodil car, which uses the two-opposed-cylinder engine shown in the previous illustration. *(DAF of Holland)*

Fig. 5–5. Cutaway view of a three-cylinder, two-stroke-cycle, in-line engine. *(SAAB of Sweden)*

Fig. 5-6. Mounting arrangement of a three-cylinder, two-stroke-cycle, in-line engine. Note that the automobile is front drive and that inboard disk brakes are used. *(Mercedes-Benz)*

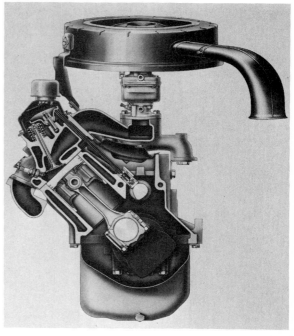

Fig. 5-8. Sectional view, from end, of a four-cylinder, in-line, overhead-valve engine. The cylinders are slanted to one side to permit a lower hood line. *(Pontiac Motor Division of General Motors Corporation)*

Fig. 5-7. Partial cutaway view of a four-cylinder, in-line, overhead-valve engine. *(Chevrolet Motor Division of General Motors Corporation)*

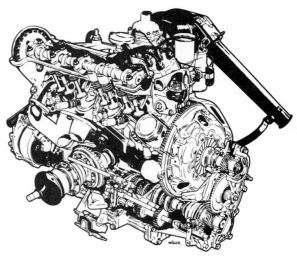

Fig. 5-9. Slant-four-cylinder OHC engine with integrated clutch and transmission. *(SAAB of Sweden)*

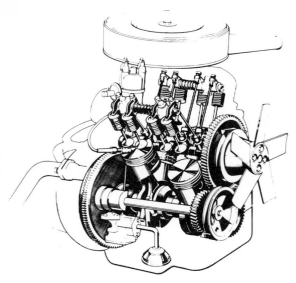

Fig. 5-10. Phantom view of V-4 engine showing major moving parts in engine. *(Ford Motor Company of Germany)*

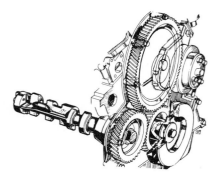

Fig. 5-11. Balance shaft used in V-4 engine to counteract rocking tendency in engine. *(Ford of Britain)*

Another slant-four engine, with overhead camshaft (OHC) and integrated clutch, transmission, and differential, is shown in Fig. 5–9. This engine is especially interesting because of its overhead camshaft. Other engines previously described have the camshaft in the lower part of the engine, with the valves being operated by lifters, push rods, and rocker arms (see Figs. 3–22, 5–3, 5–7, etc.). However, with the camshaft located in the cylinder head, as shown in Fig. 5–9, there is no need for push rods or, in some engines, rocker arms or lifters. This has certain advantages, as will be explained on a later page.

2. *V-4 engines.* The V-4 engine has two rows of two cylinders each, set at an angle, or a V, to each other. The crankshaft has only two cranks, with connecting rods from opposing cylinders in the two banks being attached to the same crankpin. Each crankpin has two connecting rods attached to it. Figure 5–10 is a phantom view of a V-4 engine with the internal moving parts emphasized. This type of engine is rather difficult to balance with counterweights on the crankshaft (see § 6–8), and the engine illustrated achieves balance by using a balance shaft that turns in a direction opposite to the crankshaft (Fig. 5–11).

3. *Flat four-cylinder engines.* Figure 5–12 shows the flat four-cylinder engine used by Volkswagen. The two banks, or rows, of cylinders oppose each other. The flat design, sometimes called a *pancake* engine, requires very little head room so that the engine compartment can be very compact. The Volkswagen engine is air-cooled and is mounted at the rear of the car (Fig. 5–13).

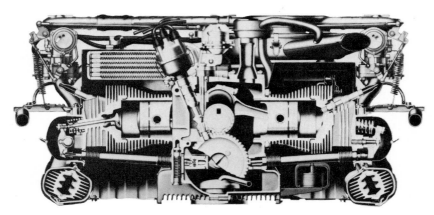

Fig. 5-12. Flat-four-cylinder engine with two banks, of two cylinders each, opposing each other. This is an air-cooled engine. *(Volkswagen)*

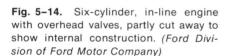

Fig. 5-13. Mounting arrangement of the flat-four-cylinder engine at the rear of the automobile. *(Volkswagen)*

Fig. 5-14. Six-cylinder, in-line engine with overhead valves, partly cut away to show internal construction. *(Ford Division of Ford Motor Company)*

§ 5-5. SIX-CYLINDER ENGINES Most six-cylinder engines are in-line, although there are V-6 and flat-six engines. This compares with the four-cylinder engines (§ 5-4), which can also be either in-line, V-type, or flat.

1. In-line engines. Figure 5-14 shows a six-cylinder in-line engine partly cut away so that the internal construction can be seen. The valves are overhead; this is an I-head engine. In this engine, the crankshaft is supported by seven main bearings. Thus, there is a bearing on each side of every crank for additional support and rigidity.

Figure 5-15 shows a slant-six overhead-valve engine. This engine is similar to other six-cylinder

in-line engines except that the cylinders are slanted to one side, similar to the four-cylinder engine shown in Fig. 5-8, so that the hood line can be lowered. This engine is also interesting because it has been supplied with either a cast-iron or a die-cast-aluminum cylinder block. This feature will be discussed in a following article, where cast-iron blocks are compared with aluminum blocks.

Figure 5-16 is a partial cutaway view of a six-cylinder in-line OHC (overhead camshaft) engine with the camshaft being driven by a neoprene belt reenforced with fiber-glass cords. The belt has a facing of woven nylon fabric on the tooth

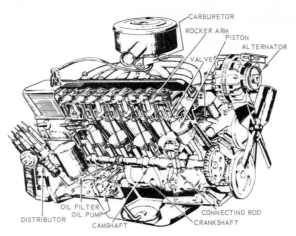

CARBURETOR
ROCKER ARM
PISTON
ALTERNATOR
VALVE
OIL FILTER
OIL PUMP
DISTRIBUTOR
CAMSHAFT
CONNECTING ROD
CRANKSHAFT

Fig. 5–15. Slant-six, in-line, overhead-valve engine, cut away to show internal parts. Cylinders are slanted to permit a lower hood line. *(Dodge Division of Chrysler Motors Corporation)*

side. The teeth on the belt fit teeth molded into the outer diameters of the drive and driven pulleys. This is very similar to the metal chain-and-sprocket arrangement used in chain-driven camshafts. However, the neoprene belt is said to be quieter and does not require lubrication.

2. V-6 engines. Several V-6 engines have been built. This design uses two three-cylinder banks that are set at an angle, or V, to each other. The crankshaft has only three cranks, with connecting rods from opposing cylinders in the two banks

being attached to the same crankpin. Each crankpin has two connecting rods attached to it. Figure 5–17 illustrates one version of this design.

3. Flat-six engines. Figure 5–18 shows the flat-six engine used in the Chevrolet Corvair. This engine is air-cooled and mounted at the rear of the vehicle.

§ 5–6. EIGHT-CYLINDER ENGINES At one time the eight-cylinder in-line engine was widely used, but it has been replaced by the V-8 engine (Fig.

Fig. 5–16. Partial cutaway view of a six-cylinder engine with overhead camshaft driven by a toothed neoprene belt. *(Pontiac Motor Division of General Motors Corporation)*

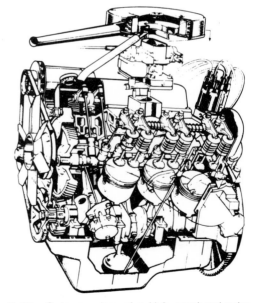

Fig. 5–17. Cutaway view of a V-6, overhead-valve engine. *(Ford Motor Company of Germany)*

5–19). In the V-8, the cylinders are arranged in two rows, or banks, of four cylinders each, with the two rows being set at an angle to each other. In effect, this engine is much like two four-cylinder in-line engines mounted on the same crankcase and working to a single crankshaft. The crankshaft in the V-8 has four cranks, with connecting rods from opposing cylinders in the two rows being attached to a single crankpin. Thus, two rods are attached to each crankpin, and two pistons work to each crankpin. The crankshaft is usually supported on five bearings.

The V-8 engine shown in Fig. 5–19 has overhead valves operated by valve lifters, push rods, and rocker arms from a single camshaft located between the two cylinder banks. Some high-performance engines have overhead camshafts, with the camshafts located in the cylinder heads.

One version of this design has a single overhead camshaft in each cylinder head. Another version has two overhead camshafts in each cylinder head, one for the intake valves, the other for the exhaust valves. This is a total of four camshafts in the engine. An engine of this type is shown in Fig. 5–20. Advantages of the overhead camshaft will be discussed on a later page.

§ 5–7. TWELVE- AND SIXTEEN-CYLINDER ENGINES Twelve- and sixteen-cylinder engines have been used in passenger cars, buses, trucks and industrial installations. The cylinders are usually arranged in two banks (V type or pancake type), three banks (W type), or four banks (X type). The pancake engine is similar to a V engine except that the two banks are arranged in a plane, but

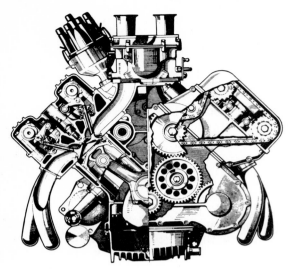

Fig. 5–20. Sectional view from the end of a V-8 engine with four overhead camshafts. Right bank has been cut away to show the camshaft drive arrangement. Left bank has been cut away to show the internal construction of the engine and locations of the valves and other components. *(Renault)*

opposing; the cylinders work to the same crankshaft. The only passenger car now being made with a twelve-cylinder engine is the Ferrari.

§ 5–8. RADIAL ENGINE The radial engine, largely used in aircraft, has the cylinders radiating from a common center like the spokes of a wheel. All connecting rods work to a common crankpin. The radial engine is air-cooled (§ 5–12).

§ 5–9. V-TYPE COMPARED WITH IN-LINE ENGINES Although in-line eight-cylinder engines were once widely used in automobiles, they have been superseded by V-8 engines. Engineers mention several advantages of the V-8 engine. It permits a shorter but lighter and more rigid engine. The arrangement permits the use of intake manifolding that assures relatively even distribution of the air-fuel mixture to all cylinders (since all cylinders are relatively close together). This contrasts with the in-line engine, where end cylinders could be fuel-starved while the center cylinders would be getting adequate fuel. Some eight-cylinder in-line engines used two carburetors to help this situation.

The more rigid engine permits higher running speeds and higher combustion pressures (higher power outputs) with less difficulty from flexing, or bending, of the cylinder block and crankshaft.

Flexing throws the engine out of line, increases frictional losses and wear, and may also set up internal vibrations.

The shorter engine makes possible more passenger space on the same wheel base, or a shorter wheel-base car. In addition, the V-8 permits a lowering of the hood line and thus a lower car profile. This is because the carburetor and other parts can be nested between the two rows of cylinders so they do not take up headroom above the cylinders.

§ 5–10. FIRING ORDER The firing order, or order in which the cylinders deliver their power strokes, is selected as part of the engine design so as to give a well-distributed pattern along the crankshaft. In other words, having two cylinders at one end of the crankshaft fire one after another is avoided insofar as possible. In in-line engines, cylinders are numbered from the front to the back of the engine, (1, 2, 3, 4, for example, in a four-cylinder engine). The two firing orders used in four-cylinder in-line engines are 1–3–4–2 or 1–2–4–3.

Two firing orders used in six-cylinder in-line engines are 1–5–3–6–2–4 or 1–4–2–6–3–5. The firing order on the V-6 engine used in some Buick cars is 1–6–5–4–3–2. The cylinders in the two banks, or rows, are numbered from front to back as follows:

> Right bank 2–4–6
> Left bank   1–3–5

The right bank is the right-hand row as seen from the driver's seat.

In one V-8 engine, the firing order is 1–8–4–3–6–5–7–2, and the cylinders are numbered:

> Right bank 2–4–6–8
> Left bank   1–3–5–7

Different V-8 manufacturers number their cylinders differently, and thus firing-order numbering systems are different. Knowledge of the firing order of an engine is important whenever any service work, particularly ignition work, is being done on it.

§ 5–11. VALVE ARRANGEMENTS The intake and exhaust valves in the engine can be arranged in various positions in the cylinder head or block. These arrangements are termed "L," "I," "F," and "T." Remember the word "lift," and it will be easy to recall the four valve arrangements

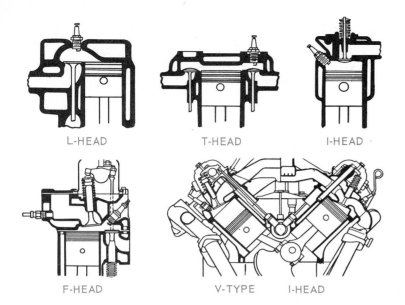

L-HEAD   T-HEAD   I-HEAD

F-HEAD   V-TYPE   I-HEAD

Fig. 5–21. Valve arrangements. Compare these line drawings with the sectional and cutaway views of various engines shown elsewhere in the book. The T-head arrangement is shown for comparison only. It is not in use today.

(Fig. 5–21). The I-head design is by far the most common.

1. L-head engine. In the L-head arrangement (Figs. 5–21 and 5–22), the combustion chamber and cylinder form an inverted L. The intake and exhaust valves are located side by side, with all valves for the engine arranged in one line (except for V-8 L-head engines, in which they are in two lines, as shown in Fig. 5–22). This arrangement permits the use of a single camshaft to operate all valves. Since the valve mechanisms are in the block, removal of the cylinder head for major overhaul of the engine is relatively easy. However, in the opinion of automotive engineers, the L-head engine, although rugged and dependable, is not particularly adapted to higher-compression engines. One reason is that the valves require a certain minimum space to move up into when they open. This space, plus the minimum clearance required above the top of the piston, determines the minimum possible clearance volume [volume with piston at TDC (top dead center)]. Since the clearance volume cannot be decreased below this minimum, there is a limit to how much the compression ratio of this engine can be increased. [Remember that the compression ratio is the ratio between volume at BDC (bottom dead center) and clearance volume, or volume at TDC.] On the other hand, the overhead-valve (I-head) engine is more adaptable to higher compression ratios, as explained in following paragraphs.

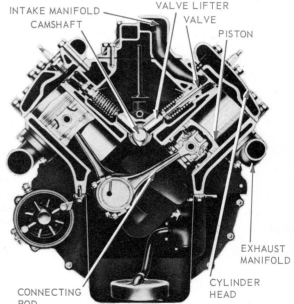

INTAKE MANIFOLD
CAMSHAFT
VALVE LIFTER
VALVE
PISTON
EXHAUST MANIFOLD
CYLINDER HEAD
CONNECTING ROD

Fig. 5–22. Sectional view from the end of a V-8 engine with L heads. This engine has not been manufactured since 1953, when Ford changed over to the I-head engine. *(Ford Motor Company)*

2. I-head engine. In the I-head, or overhead-valve, engine, the valves are carried in the cylinder head (Fig. 5–21). In in-line engines, the valves are usually in a single row, as shown in Figs. 5–7 and 5–15. In V-8 engines, the valves may be arranged in a single row in each bank (Fig. 5–19), or they may be placed in a double row in each bank (Fig. 5–23). Regardless of arrangement, a single camshaft actuates all valves, with valve lifters, push rods, and rocker arms carrying the motion from the cams to the valves (Fig. 3–22).

The overhead-valve arrangement has come into widespread use in recent years, since it is more adaptable to the higher-compression-ratio engines. In an engine with overhead valves, it is practical to reduce the clearance volume a proportionally greater amount than in an L-head engine. If you study the illustrations of the various L-head and I-head engines in the book, you will see that the method of grouping the valves directly above the piston permits a smaller clearance volume. In some I-head engines, there are pockets in the piston heads into which the valves can move when the valves are open with the piston at TDC. In some engines, the clearances between the pistons and valves are only a few thousandths of an inch.

3. *Overhead camshafts.* As already noted, the I-head engine, in its most common version, uses push rods and rocker arms to operate the valves. This design is often referred to as a *push-rod* engine. The push rods and rocker arms impose some inertia, however, that tends to affect valve action. That is, the push rods and rocker arms have to be moved before the valve moves. This slows the valve action somewhat. At lower speeds, this does not matter. But as speed increases, the inertia effect also increases, causing a lag in valve action. This tends to limit top engine speed. However, with the overhead camshaft, the cams work directly on the rocker arms or valve lifters. This results

in quicker valve response so that higher engine speeds are possible. The single-overhead-camshaft engine (one camshaft in each cylinder head) is called an SOHC engine. The double-overhead-camshaft engine is a DOHC engine.

Figures 5–9, 5–16, and 5–20 show various OHC engines. In most engines, the overhead camshaft (or camshafts) is driven by a metal chain and sprockets. But in one, the camshaft is driven by a neoprene belt (Fig. 5–16).

4. *F-head engine.* This engine is, in a sense, a combination L-head and I-head engine (Figs. 5–21 and 5–24). The intake valves are in the head, and the exhaust valves are in the block. Both sets are driven from the same camshaft.

5. *V-type and pancake engine valve arrangements.* V-type and pancake engines can use L heads or I heads. Most engines, however, use the I-head arrangement for the reasons already noted in previous paragraphs. All the newer high-output engines use I heads.

§ 5–12. CLASSIFICATION BY COOLING Engines are classified as liquid-cooled or air-cooled. Most present-day American automobile engines are liquid-cooled. The Corvair, Volkswagen, and some other automobile engines are air-cooled. (See Figs. 5–12 and 5–18.) Also, the small one- and two-cylinder engines used on power mowers and other garden equipment are air-cooled. In air-cooled engines, the cylinder barrels are usually separate and are equipped with metal fins which give a large radiating surface. This permits engine heat to radiate from the cylinders. Many air-cooled

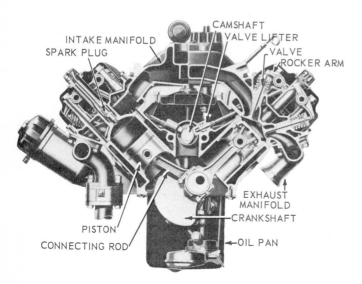

INTAKE MANIFOLD
SPARK PLUG
CAMSHAFT
VALVE LIFTER
VALVE
ROCKER ARM
EXHAUST
MANIFOLD
CRANKSHAFT
PISTON
CONNECTING ROD
OIL PAN

Fig. 5–23. Sectional view from the end of a V-8 engine with overhead valves. *(Dodge Division of Chrysler Motors Corporation)*

Fig. 5–24. Cutaway view of an F-head engine. *(Rolls-Royce Limited)*

Fig. 5–25. Six-cylinder, in-line engine partly cut away to show engine cooling system. Arrows indicate direction of water flow in the engine water jackets. Radiator is not shown. *(Oldsmobile Division of General Motors Corporation)*

engines are equipped with metal shrouds which direct the airflow around the cylinders for improved cooling.

Liquid-cooled engines use a liquid (water with an antifreeze compound added) to serve as the cooling medium. They have water jackets surrounding the cylinders and the combustion chambers in the cylinder block and head (Fig. 5–25). Water can circulate freely through these jackets. The water enters from the bottom of the engine radiator and circulates through the engine, where it absorbs heat and thus becomes quite hot. It then exits from the engine water jackets and pours into the radiator upper tank. From there, it passes

down through the radiator to the lower tank. The radiator has two sets of passages, water passages from top to bottom and air passages from front to back. The air passing through (pulled through by the engine fan and the forward motion of the car) picks up the heat from the hot water passing down through the radiator. The result is that the water entering the lower tank is cool and ready for another trip through the engine. This constant circulation is kept going by the water pump, which is mounted on the front end of the engine and is driven by the fan belt. The fan is usually mounted on the water-pump pulley so that both turn together. Chapter twelve contains detailed descriptions of the two basic types of cooling system, air-cooled and liquid-cooled.

§ 5–13. CLASSIFICATION BY CYCLES

Engines can be classified as either two-stroke-cycle or four-stroke-cycle. In the four-stroke-cycle engine (usually called a four-cycle engine), already discussed (in § 3–28), the complete cycle of events requires four piston strokes (intake, compression, power, and exhaust). In the two-stroke-cycle, or two-cycle, engine, the intake and compression strokes and the power and exhaust strokes are in a sense combined. This permits the engine to produce a power stroke every two piston strokes, or every crankshaft rotation.

In the two-cycle engine, the piston acts as a valve, clearing valve ports in the cylinder wall as it nears BDC. A fresh air-fuel charge enters through the intake port, and the burned gases exit through the exhaust port. The complete cycle of operation is as follows: As the piston nears TDC, ignition takes place (Fig. 5–26). The high combustion pressures drive the piston down, and the thrust through the connecting rod turns the crankshaft. As the piston nears BDC, it passes the intake and exhaust

Fig. 5–27. As the piston approaches BDC, it uncovers the intake and exhaust ports. Burned gases stream out through the exhaust port, and a fresh charge of air-fuel mixture enters the cylinder, as shown by the arrows. *(Johnson Motors)*

ports in the cylinder wall (Fig. 5–27). Burned gases, still under some pressure, begin to stream out through the exhaust port. At the same time, the intake port, now cleared by the piston, begins to deliver air-fuel mixture, under pressure, to the cylinder. The top of the piston is shaped to give the incoming mixture an upward movement. This helps to sweep the burned gases ahead and out through the exhaust port.

After the piston has passed through BDC and starts up again, it passes both ports, thus sealing them off (Fig. 5–28). Now the fresh air-fuel charge above the piston is compressed and ignited. The same series of events takes place again and continues as long as the engine runs.

We mentioned that the air-fuel mixture is delivered to the cylinder under pressure. In most engines, this pressure is put on the mixture in the crankcase. The crankcase is sealed except for a leaf, or reed, valve at the bottom. The reed valve is a flexible, flat metal plate that rests snugly against the floor of the crankcase. There are holes under the reed valve that connect to the engine carburetor. When the piston is moving up, a partial vacuum is produced in the sealed crankcase. Atmospheric pressure lifts the reed valve off the holes, and air-fuel mixture enters the crankcase (Fig. 5–26). After the piston passes TDC and starts down again, pressure begins to build up in the crankcase. This

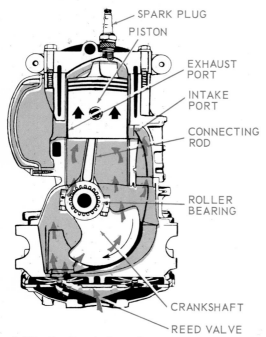

SPARK PLUG
PISTON
EXHAUST PORT
INTAKE PORT
CONNECTING ROD
ROLLER BEARING
CRANKSHAFT
REED VALVE

Fig. 5–26. Sectional view of a two-cycle engine with the piston nearing TDC. Ignition of the compressed air-fuel mixture occurs approximately at this point. *(Johnson Motors)*

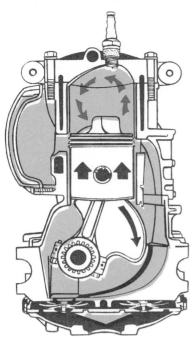

Fig. 5–28. After the piston passes BDC and moves up again, it covers the intake and exhaust ports. Further upward movement of the piston traps and compresses the air-fuel mixture. *(Johnson Motors)*

pressure closes the reed valve so that further downward movement of the piston compresses the trapped air-fuel mixture in the crankcase. The pressure which is built up on the air-fuel mixture then causes it to flow up through the intake port into the engine cylinder when the piston moves down far enough to clear the intake port (Fig. 5–27).

Instead of using a reed valve in the crankcase, some engines have a third, or transfer, port in the cylinder (Fig. 5–29). In this type of engine, the in-

take port is cleared by the piston as it approaches TDC. When this happens, the air-fuel mixture pours into the crankcase to fill the partial vacuum left by the upward movement of the piston. Then, as the piston moves down, the intake port is cut off by the piston. The air-fuel mixture in the crankcase is compressed, and the other actions then take place as already described.

An engine with a transfer port is shown in Fig. 5–30. This is a three-cylinder two-cycle engine of a somewhat different construction. The crankshaft is supported on four sealed ball bearings, and roller bearings are used at both ends of the connecting rod (at crankpin and piston pin). The crankpins are 120 degrees apart. The crankcase is separated into three compartments, one for each cylinder, so as to utilize the crankcase pressure as the piston moves down to transfer the air-fuel mixture from the crankcase to the cylinder.

Another type of two-cycle engine uses valves in the cylinder head to exhaust the burned gases (Fig. 5–31). As the piston moves down past the intake ports (note that there is a ring of them around the cylinder) the exhaust valves open. Now the incoming air can efficiently clear the cylinder of exhaust gases. The engine shown in Fig. 5–31 is a diesel engine, and only air enters through the intake ports. Section 5–15 discusses diesel engines.

Note that the two-cycle engine produces a power stroke every crankshaft revolution. The four-cycle engine requires two crankshaft revolutions for each power stroke per cylinder. You might conclude from this that a two-cycle engine could produce twice as much horsepower as a four-cycle engine of the same size, running at the same speed. However, this is not true. In the two-cycle engine, when the intake and exhaust ports have been cleared by the piston, there is always some

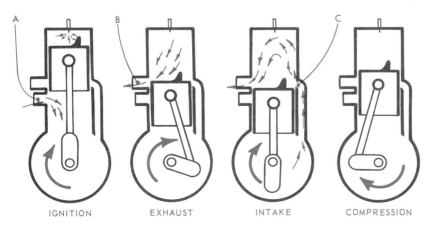

IGNITION　　EXHAUST　　INTAKE　　COMPRESSION

Fig. 5–29. Actions in a three-port, two-cycle engine. Note the intake port (A), exhaust port (B), and transfer port (C).

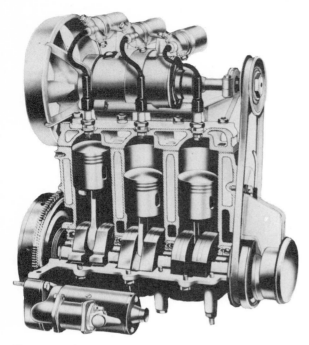

Fig. 5-30. Sectional view of a three-cylinder, two-cycle engine. *(Daimler-Benz)*

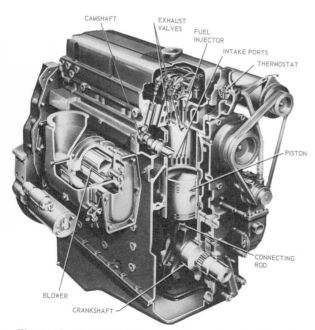

CAMSHAFT

EXHAUST VALVES

FUEL INJECTOR

INTAKE PORTS

THERMOSTAT

PISTON

CONNECTING ROD

BLOWER

CRANKSHAFT

Fig. 5-31. Cutaway view of a two-cycle diesel engine which uses exhaust valves in the cylinder head. *(Detroit Diesel Engine Division of General Motors Corporation)*

mixing of the fresh charge and the burned gases. Not all the burned gases get out, and this prevents a fuller fresh charge from entering. Therefore, the power stroke that follows is not so powerful as it could be if all the burned gases were exhausted and a full charge of air-fuel mixture entered. In the four-cycle engine, nearly all the burned gases are forced from the combustion chamber by the upward-moving piston. And a comparatively full charge of air-fuel mixture can enter because a complete piston stroke is devoted to the intake of the mixture (contrasted with only part of a stroke on the two-cycle engine). Therefore, the power stroke produces more power.

§ 5-14. CLASSIFICATION BY FUEL Internal-combustion engines can be classified according to the type of fuel they use. Automotive engines, in general, use gasoline. Some bus and truck engines use LPG (liquefied petroleum gas): these are essentially gasoline engines adapted for LPG. Diesel engines use diesel fuel oil. Chapter 10 describes these fuels in detail.

§ 5-15. DIESEL ENGINES In the diesel engine, air alone enters the cylinder on the intake stroke, and air alone is compressed on the compression stroke. At the end of the compression stroke, the fuel is injected, or sprayed, into the combustion chamber. In diesel engines the compression ratios are as high as 21:1, and this produces pressures of about 500 psi (pounds per square inch) at the end of the compression stroke. When air is rapidly compressed to this pressure, it will be heated to a temperature of about 1000°F. This temperature is high enough to ignite fuel oil sprayed into the heated air. Thus, no separate ignition system is required; the oil is ignited by the heat resulting from the compression of the air.

The four-stroke-cycle diesel engine requires four piston strokes for the complete cycle of actions, just as in the gasoline engine. These are intake, compression, power, and exhaust. In many two-cycle diesel engines, a blower or rotary type of pump is used to produce the initial pressure on the ingoing air. The piston serves as a valve, or valves, clearing ports as it nears BDC. Fresh air enters the intake ports, and the burned gases exhaust through the exhaust ports. The type shown in Figs. 5-31 to 5-33 has exhaust valves at the top of the cylinder. The burned gases are forced through this exhaust-valve port as the valve opens and the piston moves down to clear the intake

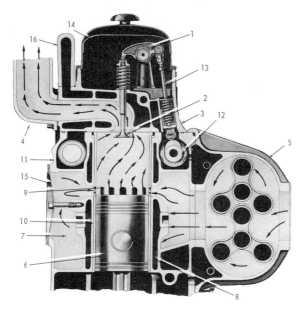

Fig. 5–32. Two-stroke-cycle, diesel engine with exhaust valves in the top of the cylinder. Arrows show the flow of air from the blower, through the cylinder, and out the exhaust manifold.

1. Exhaust-valve rocker	9. Port admitting air to cylinder
2. Exhaust valve	10. Cylinder liner
3. Cylinder head	11. Cylinder block
4. Exhaust manifold	12. Camshaft
5. Blower	13. Push rod
6. Piston	14. Rocker cover
7. Air box	15. Hand-hole cover
8. Cooling-water passage	16. Water manifold

(*Detroit Diesel Engine Division of General Motors Corporation*)

ports. Then, as the piston moves up, it closes off the intake ports. At the same time, the exhaust valve closes. Now, the air is trapped and compressed. The sequence of actions in a two-stroke-cycle engine is shown in Fig. 5–33.

§ 5–16. DIESEL-ENGINE APPLICATIONS

Diesel engines have been made in a great variety of sizes and outputs, from a few to 5,000 horsepower. They are used in passenger cars, trucks, buses, farm and construction machinery, ships, electric power plants (up to about 5,000 kilowatts), and other mobile and stationary applications.

Diesel engines are used in only one passenger car manufactured in the United States, but they are common in trucks, buses, and other commercial equipment. However, in Europe, passenger cars equipped with diesel engines are rather common. For example, Mercedes-Benz has produced about half a million diesel-powered automobiles since 1950. Many of these have been imported to the United States. Figure 5–34 is a sectional view of their four-cylinder in-line diesel engine for passenger cars. This engine has 121 cubic inches displacement and a compression ratio of 21:1. It peaks at 60 hp at 4,200 rpm.

For heavy-duty applications, some diesel engines have four valves per cylinder—two intake and two exhaust valves (Fig. 5–35). The additional valves improve engine breathing and thus increase engine output, particularly at the higher speeds.

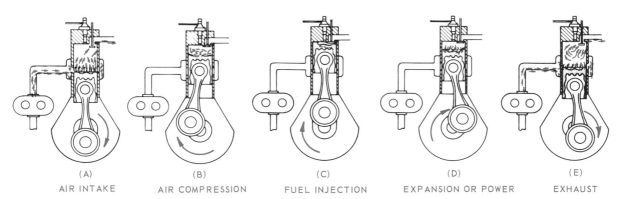

(A)	(B)	(C)	(D)	(E)
AIR INTAKE	AIR COMPRESSION	FUEL INJECTION	EXPANSION OR POWER	EXHAUST

Fig. 5–33. Sequence of events in the two-stroke-cycle diesel engine. (*Detroit Diesel Engine Division of General Motors Corporation*)

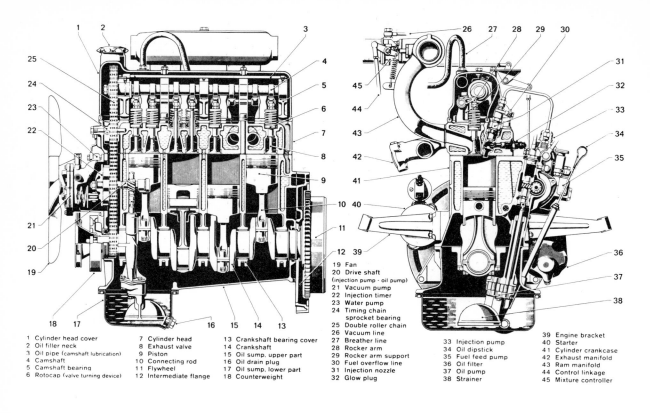

Fig. 5-34. Sectional views of a four-cylinder diesel engine for passenger cars. *(Mercedes-Benz)*

19 Fan		
20 Drive shaft		
(injection pump · oil pump)		
21 Vacuum pump		
22 Injection timer		
23 Water pump		
24 Timing chain		
sprocket bearing		
25 Double roller chain		
26 Vacuum line		
27 Breather line		
28 Rocker arm		
29 Rocker arm support		
30 Fuel overflow line		
31 Injection nozzle		
32 Glow plug		

1 Cylinder head cover	7 Cylinder head	13 Crankshaft bearing cover
2 Oil filler neck	8 Exhaust valve	14 Crankshaft
3 Oil pipe (camshaft lubrication)	9 Piston	15 Oil sump, upper part
4 Camshaft	10 Connecting rod	16 Oil drain plug
5 Camshaft bearing	11 Flywheel	17 Oil sump, lower part
6 Rotocap (valve turning device)	12 Intermediate flange	18 Counterweight

33 Injection pump	39 Engine bracket	
34 Oil dipstick	40 Starter	
35 Fuel feed pump	41 Cylinder crankcase	
36 Oil filter	42 Exhaust manifold	
37 Oil pump	43 Ram manifold	
38 Strainer	44 Control linkage	
	45 Mixture controller	

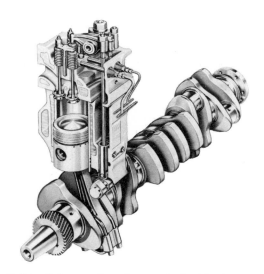

Fig. 5-35. Cutaway view of one cylinder of a four-cycle diesel engine using two intake and two exhaust valves in each cylinder. *(Cummins Engine Company, Incorporated)*

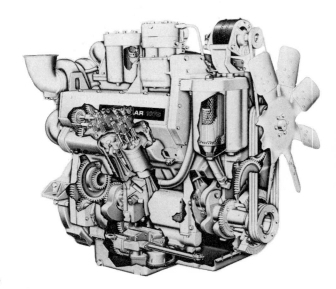

Fig. 5-36. Partial cutaway of a V-8, diesel engine using overhead camshafts. *(Caterpillar Tractor Co.)*

Figure 5–36 shows another diesel engine which has four valves per cylinder and also overhead camshafts.

Another application is shown in Fig. 5–37, which is a three-cylinder four-cycle diesel engine for marine use.

§ 5–17. GAS TURBINE The gas turbine, now making its appearance as an automotive power plant, consists, in essence, of two sections, a gasifier section and a power section. Figure 5–38 is a simplified sectional view of a turbine, and Fig. 5–39 is a cutaway view of an actual unit. The compressor in the gasifier has a rotor with a series of blades around its outer edge. As it rotates, air between the blades is carried around and thrown out by centrifugal force. This action supplies the burner with air at relatively high pressure. Fuel is sprayed into the compressed air. The fuel used can be gasoline, kerosene, or oil. As the fuel burns, a further increase in pressure results. The high-pressure, high-temperature gas then passes through the gasifier nozzle diaphragm. A series of stationary blades directs this high-pressure gas against a series of curved blades on the outer edge of the gasifier turbine rotor. The resulting high pressure against the curved blades causes the gasifier turbine rotor to spin a high speed. Since the gasifier turbine rotor and the compressor rotor are mounted on the same shaft, the compressor

rotor is also spun at high speed. This action continues to supply the burner with an ample amount of compressed air. The action continues as long as fuel is supplied to the burner.

After the high-pressure, high-temperature gas leaves the gasifier section, it enters the power turbine. Here, it strikes another series of stationary curved blades which directs it against a series

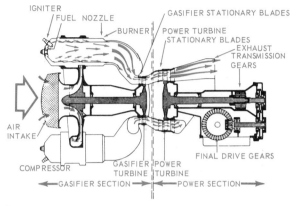

Fig. 5–38. Experimental gas turbine for automotive vehicles. The gasifier section burns fuel in a burner and delivers the resulting gas to the power section, where it spins the power turbine. The power turbine then turns the vehicle wheels through a series of gears. *(General Motors Corporation)*

Fig. 5–37. Three-cylinder diesel engine for inboard-outboard motor boat. The propeller drive is to the right. *(Perkins Engines, Limited)*

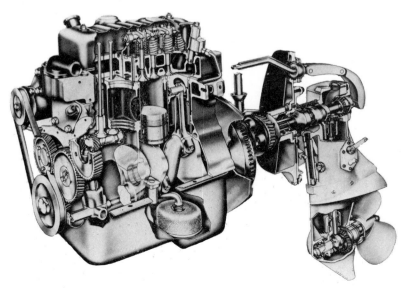

Fig. 5–39. Cutaway view of a gas turbine. *(Caterpillar Tractor Co.)*

of curved blades on the outer edge of the power turbine rotor. The resulting high pressure against these rotor blades spins the rotor at high speed. In some models, the turbine may turn up to 50,000 rpm. This high rpm is reduced by a series of transmission gears before the power is applied to the vehicle wheels.

§ 5–18. OTHER ENGINE TYPES Several other types of internal-combustion engines have been proposed or are being tested for use as automotive power plants. These include the free-piston engine and the Wankel and Sterling engines.

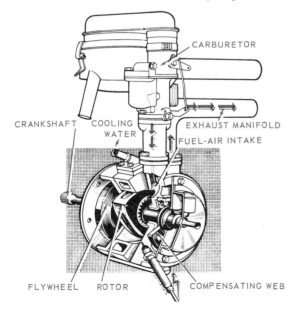

Fig. 5–40. Cutaway view of a Wankel engine.

§ 5–19. WANKEL ENGINE This engine makes use of a three-lobe rotor that rotates eccentrically in an oval chamber (Fig. 5–40). The rotor is mounted on the crankshaft through external and internal gears. The four cycles of intake, compression, power, and exhaust are going on simultaneously around the rotor when the engine is running. Figure 5–41 will give you an idea of how the engine works. The rotor lobes (A, B, and C) are sealed tightly against the side of the oval chamber. The rotor has oval-shaped depressions on its three faces between the lobes. These are shown in dashed lines in Fig. 5–41. Let us follow the rotor around as it goes through the four cycles. At I, upper left, lobe A has passed the intake port, and the air-fuel mixture (1) is ready to enter. At II, upper right, lobe A has moved on around so that the space between lobes A and C and the chamber wall (2) is increasing and the air-fuel mixture is entering. At III, lower right, the intake is continuing as the combustion space (3) continues to increase. The intake has reached its maximum at IV (4).

To see what happens to the air-fuel mixture, let us go back to I, upper left, again. Here, an air-fuel charge has been trapped between lobes A and B (5) as lobe A passes the intake port. Further rotation of the rotor reduces the combustion space (6), as shown at II. Then, at III, the combustion space (7) is at a minimum, so that the mixture reaches maximum compression. At this instant, the spark plug fires and ignites the mixture. Now the power cycle begins. At IV, the expanding gases (8) force the rotor around, and this action is shown continuing in I (9) and II (10). With further rotation of the rotor, the leading lobe clears the exhaust port, and the burned gases are forced out, as shown at III (11) and IV (12). There are three power cycles for each rotor revolution, and the engine is delivering power almost continuously.

Although the Wankel engine has not been adopted for use in any American car, it is being used in a German BMW sedan and the NSU Spider, a two-seat sports car also manufactured in Germany (Fig. 5–42). Several companies around the world have been licensed to manufacture the engine, including Curtis-Wright in the U.S., Daimler-Benz and others in Germany, Perkins in England, and Kogyo in Japan. Therefore, these engines are now in production. Mercedes-Benz is working on a 4-rotor Wankel engine said to develop 400 hp.

§ 5–20. STERLING ENGINE This engine makes use of the fact that the pressure in a container of

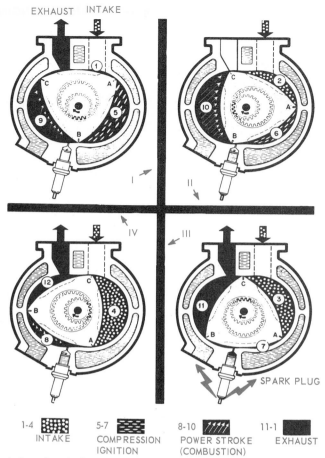

EXHAUST　INTAKE

I　II　III　IV

SPARK PLUG

| 1-4 INTAKE | 5-7 COMPRESSION IGNITION | 8-10 POWER STROKE (COMBUSTION) | 11-1 EXHAUST |

Fig. 5–41. Actions in a Wankel engine during one complete rotation of the rotor.

gas goes up when the gas is heated and goes down when the gas is cooled. A specific amount of gas is sealed in the engine, and it is alternately heated and cooled. When it is heated, its increasing pressure pushes a power piston down. When it is cooled, its lowered pressure, in effect, pulls the power piston up.

Figure 5–43 is a simplified drawing of a Sterling engine. The upper, or displacer, piston does not produce power but simply causes the air to move between the heater and the cooler sections of the engine. The power piston moves up and down between the power chamber and the buffer space. The two pistons are linked by a rhombic drive to a pair of synchronizing gears which, in turn, drive the output shaft. The name "rhombic" comes from the fact that the four links form a rhombus, which is is a geometric figure of four parallel sides.

Let us follow the engine through a complete cycle of events and see how it operates. We will start with the pistons in the position shown in Fig. 5–43. The working gas has been heated, and therefore its pressure has gone up. This increase of pressure, applied to the head of the power piston, forces the piston to move down. Note that the working gas expands during this action.

The power piston, in moving down, pushes downward through its two connecting links against the two gears. The gears therefore rotate and turn the engine output shaft. In the meantime, the rotation of the gears causes the two links to the displacer piston to pull the displacer piston down. This increases the hot space above the displacer piston so that some of the working gas can flow from the power chamber toward this space. As it moves through the cooler on the way to this upper space, the gas is cooled and its pressure drops.

Note that there is a buffer space below the power piston. This buffer space contains a specific

Fig. 5–42. Cutaway view of a two-rotor Wankel engine with attached torque converter and transmission. This engine is the same as the single rotor unit in the previous illustrations except that there are two rotors on a single shaft. Each rotor turns in its own chamber. *(NSU of Germany)*

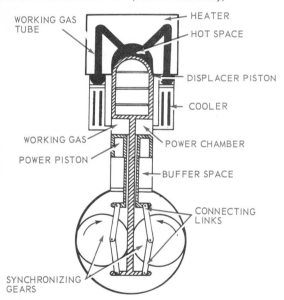

Fig. 5–43. Schematic drawing of a Sterling engine.

amount of gas. When the power piston moves down, this gas is compressed, and its pressure goes up. Now, after the power piston has reached BDC, the pressure of this buffer gas becomes higher than the pressure of the working gas. Remember that the working gas has been cooled, so that its pressure has dropped. Now, with the buffer gas at a higher pressure than the working gas, the power piston is pushed up. This motion is transmitted through the two links to the gears, rotating them on around to the position shown in Fig. 5–43.

In the meantime, the working gas that has flowed into the hot space becomes heated. The heating effect results from the continuous combustion of a fuel such as kerosene or oil. Heating the working gas causes its pressure to increase, and once again the power piston is forced down by the increasing pressure.

The action, therefore, results from the repeated heating and cooling of the working gas. When the working gas is heated, it drives the power piston down. When it cools, the buffer-gas pressure forces the piston up. You might think that this heating and cooling would take considerable time and would result in an awkward, slow, and inefficient engine. However, recent experimental engines, using helium as the working gas, at an average pressure of 1,500 psi, have operated at 3,000 rpm with an efficiency of 30 percent, which is as good as, or better than, most automotive engines.

Some engineers have proposed the Sterling engine for such small-engine applications as lawnmowers. They are very easy to start, silent in operation, and simple in basic design. Other engineers believe that they will appear first for large stationary applications, as, for instance, for remote electric power plants or pumping stations. One possibility is that they will be used to power space satellites and space stations. In space, no source of heat other than the sun would be needed. With a large reflector to gather heat from the sun and a large radiator to radiate the heat away, a Sterling engine would operate without any fuel at all.

Review Questions

1. What are seven ways in which engines are classified?
2. What are four-cylinder arrangements?
3. Compare the V-type with the in-line engine, and explain the advantages of each.
4. What are three valve arrangements?
5. Compare the L-head and I-head valve arrangements. Explain the advantages of each.
6. What do SOHC and DOHC mean?
7. Describe the actions in a two-cycle engine.
8. Explain the differences between gasoline and diesel engines.
9. Describe the action in a diesel engine.
10. Name some diesel-engine applications.
11. Describe the operation of a gas turbine.
12. Describe the operation of a free-piston engine.
13. Describe the operation of a Wankel engine.
14. Describe the operation of a Sterling engine.
15. What are the advantages of an overhead-camshaft engine?

Study Questions

1. What are some advantages of a diesel engine in a passenger car? Some disadvantages?
2. Do you think diesel engines will ever come into wide use in passenger cars? Why?
3. If you want further information on diesel engines, get a book on them from your library. Make a list of the different types and the different applications of diesel engines.

CHAPTER

6

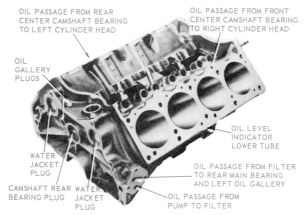

Counterweights

Engine Construction— Block, Crankshaft, and Bearings

This and the following two chapters describe the construction of automotive engines and supply you with the background information you need to move on into the engine trouble-diagnosis and servicing sections of the book.

§ 6–1. THE ENGINE   Thus far the engine has been considered from the viewpoint of its operation. We have seen how the mixture of air and fuel is delivered by the fuel system to the engine cylinder, where it is compressed, ignited, and burned. We have noted that this combustion produces a high pressure that pushes the piston down so that the crankshaft is rotated. Now let us examine the various parts of the engine in detail.

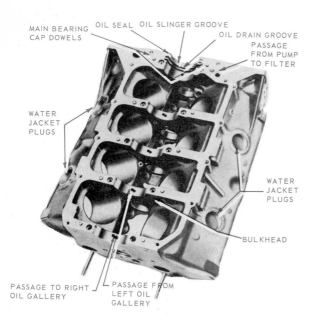

MAIN BEARING CAP DOWELS — OIL SEAL — OIL SLINGER GROOVE — OIL DRAIN GROOVE — PASSAGE FROM PUMP TO FILTER

WATER JACKET PLUGS

WATER JACKET PLUGS

BULKHEAD

PASSAGE TO RIGHT OIL GALLERY — PASSAGE FROM LEFT OIL GALLERY

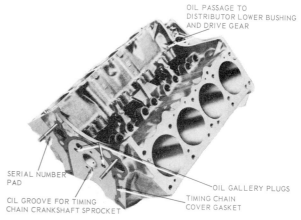

OIL PASSAGE FROM REAR CENTER CAMSHAFT BEARING TO LEFT CYLINDER HEAD

OIL PASSAGE FROM FRONT CENTER CAMSHAFT BEARING TO RIGHT CYLINDER HEAD

OIL GALLERY PLUGS

WATER JACKET PLUG

CAMSHAFT REAR BEARING PLUG

WATER JACKET PLUG

OIL LEVEL INDICATOR LOWER TUBE

OIL PASSAGE FROM FILTER TO REAR MAIN BEARING AND LEFT OIL GALLERY

OIL PASSAGE FROM PUMP TO FILTER

OIL PASSAGE TO DISTRIBUTOR LOWER BUSHING AND DRIVE GEAR

SERIAL NUMBER PAD

CIL GROOVE FOR TIMING CHAIN CRANKSHAFT SPROCKET

OIL GALLERY PLUGS

TIMING CHAIN COVER GASKET

Fig. 6–1.   Three views of a cylinder block from a V-8, overhead-valve, liquid-cooled engine, showing locations of water and oil passages and plugs. *(Pontiac Motor Division of General Motors Corporation)*

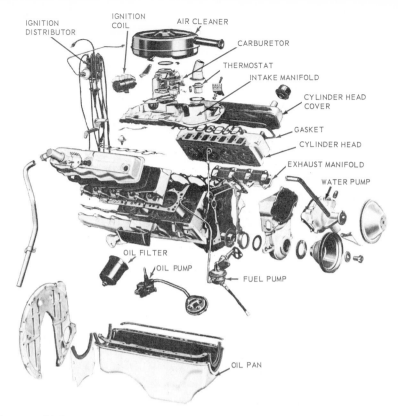

Fig. 6-2. External parts which are attached to engine block when engine is assembled. *(Chrysler-Plymouth Division of Chrysler Motors Corporation)*

§ 6-2. ENGINE CYLINDER BLOCK The cylinder block of liquid-cooled engines (Fig. 6-1) forms the basic framework of the engine. (In air-cooled engines, the cylinders are often separate parts. See Fig. 6-6.) Other parts are attached to the cylinder block or are assembled in it (Figs. 6-2 and 6-3). The block is cast in one piece from gray iron or iron alloyed with other metals, such as nickel or chromium. Some blocks are cast from aluminum. The engine shown in Fig. 5-15, for example, has been supplied with either a die-cast-aluminum or a cast-iron block. The block contains not only the cylinders but also the water jackets that surround them. In aluminum blocks, cast-iron or steel cylinder sleeves (also called *bore liners*) are used. These metals have better wearing qualities than aluminum and can better withstand the wearing effect of the pistons and rings moving up and down in the cylinders. In the engine shown in Fig. 5-15, the aluminum block has iron cylinder bore

liners cast into the die-cast block. For most engines, cast iron has been found to be a satisfactory cylinder-wall material. However, in some small engines, the cylinder walls are plated with chromium, a very hard metal, to reduce wall wear and lengthen their service life.

L-head engine blocks contain openings for the valves and valve ports (Figs. 5-21 and 5-22). On both L-head and I-head engines, the bottom of the block supports the crankshaft (with main bearings and bearing caps) and also the oil pan. Figure 6-4 shows a crankshaft for a six-cylinder engine with bearing halves and caps. From this picture, you can visualize how the crankshaft is hung from the bottom of the block by the bearings and caps.

On most engines, the camshaft is supported in the cylinder block by bushings that fit into machined holes in the block (Figs. 3-24 and 5-15). (On a few engines, the camshaft is located on the cylinder head, as shown in Figs. 5-16 and 5-20).

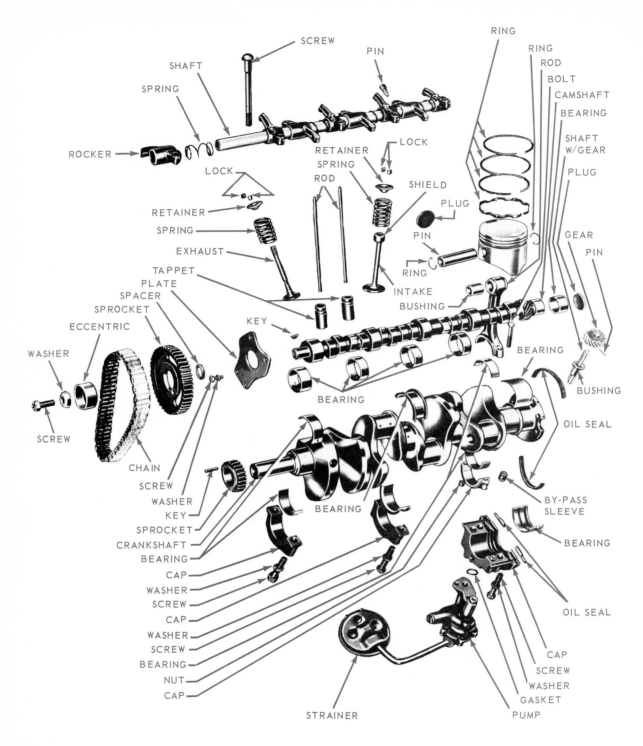

Fig. 6-3. Internal parts from the cylinder block and head of a V-8 engine. *(Chrysler-Plymouth Division of Chrysler Motors Corporation)*

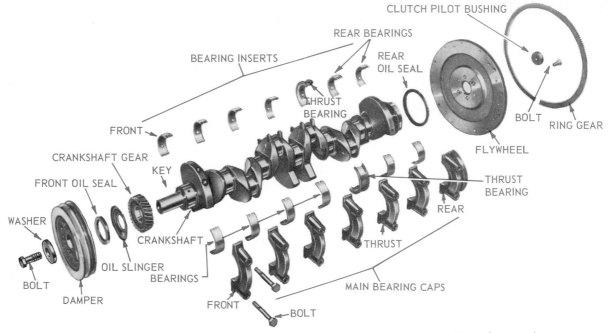

Fig. 6–4. Crankshaft and related parts for a six-cylinder engine. *(Ford Division of Ford Motor Company)*

The intake and exhaust manifolds are attached to the side of the cylinder block on L-head in-line engines (Fig. 6–5). On L-head V-8 engines, the intake manifold is located between the two banks of cylinders. In this engine, there are two exhaust manifolds, one on the outside of each bank (Fig. 5–22). On I-head engines, the manifolds are attached to cylinder head (Figs. 5–7 and 6–2).

Other parts attached to the block include the water pump (attached at the front, as shown in Fig. 6–2), the timing gear or timing chain cover (at front), the flywheel and clutch housing (at rear), the ignition distributor, and the fuel pump. The cylinder head is mounted on top of the block.

The various parts are attached to the cylinder block with sealing gaskets. The gaskets (§ 6–4)

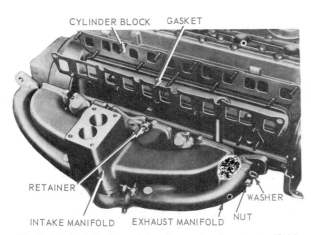

Fig. 6–5. Installation of intake and exhaust manifolds on the cylinder block of a typical L-head engine.

Fig. 6–6. Piston, connecting rod, cylinder, and related parts from a six-cylinder, air-cooled, pancake engine.

1. Cylinder	4. Oil ring	7. Connecting-rod bolt
2. Cylinder gasket	5. Piston	8. Connecting-rod bearing
3. Compression rings	6. Connecting rod	9. Connecting-rod cap

(Chevrolet Motor Division of General Motors Corporation)

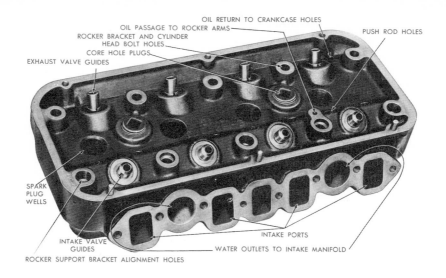

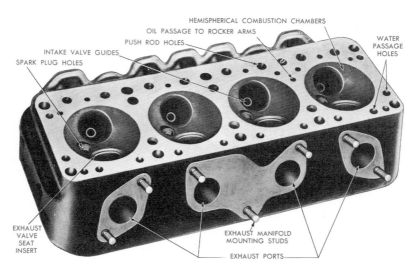

Fig. 6-7. Top and bottom views of cylinder head from a V-8, overhead-valve engine. *(Dodge Division of Chrysler Motors Corporation)*

are placed between the part and the block. Then, tightening the attaching bolts or nuts flattens the gasket to provide a good seal which prevents leakage (of water, oil, or gas).

Some parts are attached with bolts, others with nuts and studs. Studs are threaded at both ends; one end is tightened into a threaded hole in the block, the part to be attached is put into place, and a nut is tightened on the other end of the stud to hold the part in position. In some places, retaining or lock washers are put under the nuts or boltheads (see §§ 2-3 to 2-8).

A cylinder from the air-cooled Chevrolet Corvair engine is shown in Fig. 6-6, along with the piston and related parts. The cylinders are installed on the crankcase, and the cylinder head is installed on top of the cylinders. Figures 5-12 and 5-18 show air-cooled engines.

§ 6-3. CYLINDER HEAD The cylinder head is usually cast in one piece from iron, from iron alloyed with other metals, or from aluminum alloy. Aluminum has the advantage of combining lightness with high heat conductivity. That is, an alu-

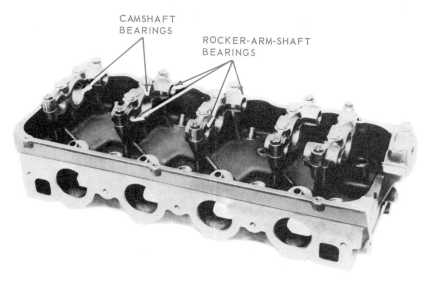

Fig. 6–8. Cylinder head for an overhead-camshaft engine, showing bearings to support the camshaft and the rocker-arm-shaft bearings. *(Ford Division of Ford Motor Company)*

minum head tends to run cooler, other factors being equal. There are two types of head, L head and I head.

1. L head. The L head, or flat head, is comparatively simple (Figs. 5–21 and 5–22). It contains water jackets for cooling; in the assembled engine, these water jackets are connected through openings to the cylinder-block water jackets. Spark-plug holes are provided, along with pockets into which the valves can move as they open.

2. I head. This head is somewhat more complex, since it must include, along with the other items noted for the L head, the valves and valve-operating mechanisms (Figs. 5–21 and 6–7). Examine the various illustrations of I-head engines in the book to see how the valves are carried in the head. Later pages describe the valve-operating mechanisms.

3. Head for overhead-camshaft engine. The cylinder head for an OHC engine has the additional job of supporting the camshaft. A variety of arrangements are used, as you will note if you examine the illustrations of OHC engines in the book. See Fig. 6–8, for example.

4. Head for air-cooled engines. Figures 6–9 and 6–10 illustrate cylinder heads for air-cooled engines. Both of these engines are of the opposed-cylinder, or pancake, type. (See Figs. 5–12 and 5–18.) Thus, these engines require two cylinder heads each. The heads carry the valves and rocker arms, just as in other I-head engines (Fig. 6–10).

§ 6–4. GASKETS The joint between the cylinder block and the head must be tight and able to withstand the pressure and heat developed in the combustion chambers. The block and head cannot be machined flat and smooth enough to provide an adequate seal. Thus, gaskets are used (Figs. 6–2 and 6–11). Head gaskets are made of thin sheets of soft metal or of asbestos and metal. All cylinder, water, valve, and head-bolt openings are cut out. When the gasket is placed on the block and the head installed, tightening of the head bolts (or nuts) squeezes the soft metal so that the joint is effectively sealed. Gaskets are also used to seal joints between other parts, such as between the oil pan, manifolds, or water pump and the block.

§ 6–5. OIL PAN The oil pan is usually formed of pressed steel (Fig. 6–12). It usually holds 4 to 9 quarts of oil, depending on the engine design. The oil pan and the lower part of the cylinder block together are called the *crankcase*; they enclose, or encase, the crankshaft. The oil pump in the lubricating system draws oil from the oil pan and sends it to all working parts in the engine. The oil drains off and runs down into the pan. Thus, there is constant circulation of oil between the pan and the working parts of the engine. (See Chap. 11 for details of engine lubricating systems.)

105

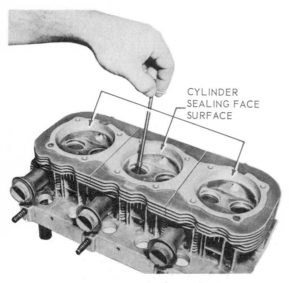

Fig. 6–9. One of the two cylinder heads used on a six-cylinder, air-cooled, pancake engine. The tool is being used to clean the valve-guide bores. *(Chevrolet Motor Division of General Motors Corporation)*

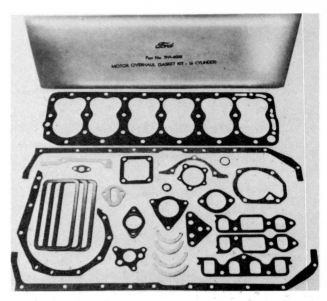

Fig. 6–11. Motor-overhaul gasket kit for a six-cylinder engine, showing the various gaskets used in the engine. *(Ford Motor Company)*

Fig. 6–10. One of the two cylinder-head assemblies used in a four-cylinder, air-cooled, pancake engine. *(Volkswagen)*

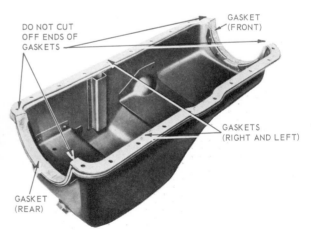

Fig. 6–12. Oil pan with gaskets in place, ready for pan replacement. *(Chrysler-Plymouth Division of Chrysler Motors Corporation)*

§ 6–6. EXHAUST MANIFOLD The exhaust manifold (Fig. 6–13) is essentially a tube for carrying the burned gases away from the engine cylinders.

The exhaust manifold is attached to the side of the block on L-head engines and to the side of the cylinder head of I-head engines. On V-8 engines, there are two exhaust manifolds, one for

each bank of cylinders. On some V-8 engines, they are connected by a crossover pipe and exhaust through a common muffler and tail pipe (Fig. 9–2). On others, each manifold is connected to a separate exhaust pipe, muffler, and tail pipe (Fig. 6–14). Refer to §§ 9–44 and 9–45 for details of the muffler and exhaust system.

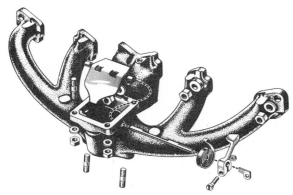

Fig. 6-13. Exhaust manifold for a six-cylinder, in-line engine with heat-control valve and parts in disassembled view.

§ 6-7. INTAKE MANIFOLD   The intake manifold (Figs. 6-15 and 6-16) is essentially a tube, or tubes, for carrying the air-fuel mixture from the carburetor to the engine intake-valve ports. The carburetor is mounted on the intake manifold. The intake manifold is mounted on the side of the cylinder block in L-head engines and on the side of the cylinder head in I-head engines. On V-8 engines, the intake manifold is situated between the two cylinder banks. Figure 6-16 shows the intake manifold for a V-8 engine. A two-barrel carburetor is used on this engine. The two-barrel carburetor is, in effect, two separate carburetors assembled together. Each barrel feeds four cylinders, as shown by the arrows. Chapter 9 discusses various carburetors in detail.

§ 6-8. CRANKSHAFT   The crankshaft is a one-piece casting or forging of heat-treated alloy steel of considerable mechanical strength (Figs. 6-4 and 6-17). The crankshaft must be strong enough to take the downward thrusts of the pistons during the power strokes without excessive distortion. In addition, the crankshaft must be carefully balanced to eliminate undue vibration resulting from the weight of the offset cranks. To provide balance, crankshafts have counterweights opposite the cranks. Crankshafts have drilled oil passages (Fig. 6-17) through which oil can flow from the main to the connecting-rod bearings (see § 6-11).

The flow of power from the engine cylinders is not smooth. Although the power impulses overlap (on six- and eight-cylinder engines), there are times when more power is being delivered than at other times (Fig. 6-18). This tends to make the crankshaft speed up and then slow down. However, the flywheel combats this tendency. The

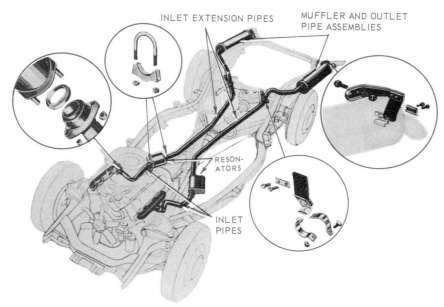

INLET EXTENSION PIPES

MUFFLER AND OUTLET PIPE ASSEMBLIES

RESONATORS

INLET PIPES

Fig. 6-14. Dual exhaust system for a V-8 engine. Each bank of cylinders has its own exhaust system. The circles show details of assembly and attachment. *(Lincoln-Mercury Division of Ford Motor Company)*

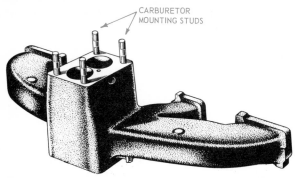

Fig. 6-15. Intake manifold for an in-line, six-cylinder engine.

Fig. 6-16. Intake manifold for an I-head, V-8 engine. The arrows show the air-fuel mixture flow from the two barrels of the carburetor to the eight cylinders in the engine. The central passage connects between the two exhaust manifolds; exhaust gas flows through this passage during engine warm-up. *(Pontiac Motor Division of General Motors Corporation)*

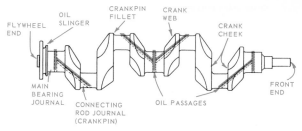

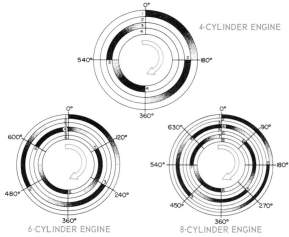

Fig. 6-17. Line drawing of a typical crankshaft, showing the names of the parts, and a cutaway view of a crankshaft for a V-8 engine. Note the oil passages drilled to the crankpins for lubricating rod bearings. *(Johnson Bronze Company* and *Ford Division of Ford Motor Company)*

Fig. 6-18. Power impulse in four-, six-, and eight-cylinder engines during two crankshaft revolutions. The complete circle represents two crankshaft revolutions, or 720 degrees. Less power is delivered toward the end of the power stroke, as indicated by lightening of the shaded areas that show power impulses. Note the power overlap on six- and eight-cylinder engines.

flywheel is a comparatively heavy wheel bolted to the rear end of the crankshaft (Fig. 6-4). The inertia of the flywheel tends to keep it turning at constant speed. Thus, the flywheel absorbs energy as the crankshaft tries to speed up and gives back energy as the crankshaft tries to slow down (see § 3-30).

In addition to this function, the flywheel also has gear teeth around its outer rim (a ring gear) that mesh with the cranking-motor drive pinion

for cranking the engine. The rear face of the flywheel also serves as the driving member of the clutch (on engines so equipped).

The front end of the crankshaft carries three devices, the gear or sprocket that drives the camshaft, the vibration damper (§ 6-9), and the fan-

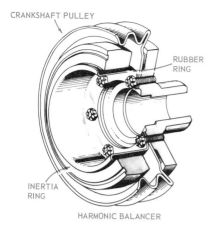

CRANKSHAFT PULLEY

RUBBER RING

INERTIA RING

HARMONIC BALANCER

Fig. 6–19. Partial cutaway view of a torsional vibration damper. *(Pontiac Motor Division of General Motors Corporation)*

belt pulley. The pulley drives the engine fan, water pump, and generator with a V belt.

§ 6–9. VIBRATION DAMPER The power impulses tend to set up torsional vibration in the crankshaft. When a piston moves down on its power stroke, it thrusts, through the connecting rod, against a crankpin with a force that may exceed 3 tons. This force tends to twist the crank ahead of the rest of the crankshaft. Then, a moment later, the force against the crank is relieved. The crank then tends to untwist, or move back into its original relationship with the rest of the crankshaft. This twist-untwist, repeated with every power impulse, tends to set up an oscillating motion in the crankshaft. This is torsional vibration; if it were not controlled, it would cause the oscillations to build up so much that the crankshaft might actually break at certain speeds. To control torsional vibration, devices called *vibration dampers*, or *harmonic balancers*, are used. They are usually mounted on the front end of the crankshaft (Fig. 6–4) and the fan-belt pulley is incorporated into them.

A typical damper consists of two parts, a small damper flywheel and the pulley, bonded to each other by a rubber insert about ¼ inch thick (Fig. 6–19). The pulley is mounted to the front end of the crankshaft. As the crankshaft tends to speed up or slow down, the damper flywheel imposes a dragging effect (because of its inertia). This effect, which slightly flexes the rubber insert, tends to hold the pulley and crankshaft to a constant speed. The action tends to check the twist-

untwist, or torsional vibration, of the crankshaft. This relieves the stresses in the crankshaft.

§ 6–10. ENGINE BEARINGS Bearings are installed in all the various places in the engine where there is relative motion between the engine's component parts (Fig. 6–20). These engine bearings are called *sleeve bearings* because they are in the shape of a sleeve that fits around the rotating journal, or shaft. Connecting-rod and crankshaft (also called *main*) bearings are of the split, or half, type (Fig. 6–21). On these main bearings, the upper bearing half is installed in the counterbore in the cylinder block. The lower bearing half is held in place by the bearing cap (Fig. 6–4). On connecting-rod big-end (or crankshaft) bearings, the upper bearing half is installed in the rod, and the lower half is placed in the rod cap (Fig. 7–1). The small-end (or piston-pin) bearing in the connecting rod is of the full-round, or *bushing*, type (7 in Fig. 7–1).

The main bearings in most engines do not have the oil-distributing grooves shown in Fig. 6–21. They may or may not have the annular grooves; many engines do not have these grooves. On other engines, only the upper halves of the main bearings have them. On still other engines, both the upper and lower main-bearing halves have the annular grooves. Connecting-rod big-end bearings usually do not have oil grooves.

NOTE: Some engines use ball bearings to support the crankshaft and roller bearings at the crankpin and piston-pin ends of the connecting rod (Fig. 5–30). The engines in American cars, and in most imports, however, use the type of bearing described in this section.

The typical bearing half is made of a steel or bronze back to which one to three linings of bearing material are applied (Fig. 6–22). The bearing material is relatively soft. Thus, if wear takes place, it will be the bearing that wears rather than the more expensive engine part. Then, the bearing, rather than the engine part, can be replaced when wear has progressed to the replacement point.

§ 6–11. BEARING LUBRICATION As we have already noted, viscous friction causes the rotating journal to carry oil around the bearing; the journal load is supported by layers of oil (§ 4–6). The journal must be smaller in diameter than the bearing (Fig. 6–23) so that there will be clearance (called *oil clearance*) between the two. In the

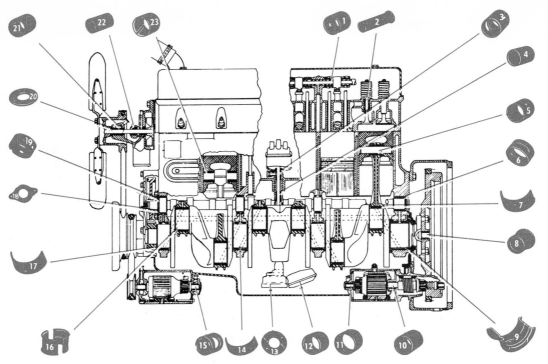

Fig. 6-20. Various bearings and bushings used in a typical engine.

1. Rocker-arm bushing
2. Valve-guide bushing
3. Distributor bushing, upper
4. Distributor bushing, lower
5. Piston-pin bushing
6. Camshaft bushing
7. Connecting-rod bearing
8. Clutch pilot bushing
9. Flanged main bearing
10. Cranking-motor bushing, drive end
11. Cranking-motor bushing, commutator end
12. Oil-pump bushing
13. Distributor thrust plate
14. Intermediate main bearing
15. Generator bushing
16. Connecting-rod bearing, floating type
17. Front main bearing
18. Camshaft thrust plate
19. Camshaft bushing
20. Fan thrust plate
21. Water-pump bushing, front
22. Water-pump bushing, rear
23. Piston-pin bushing

(Johnson Bronze Company)

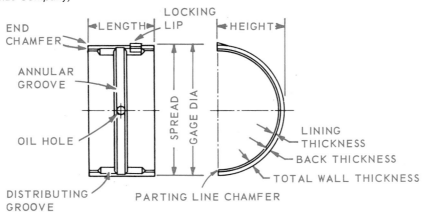

Fig. 6-21. Typical sleeve-type bearing half with parts named. Many bearings do not have annular and distributing grooves. *(Federal-Mogul-Bower Bearings, Inc.)*

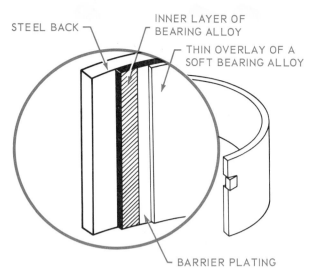

Fig. 6-22. Construction of a three-layer bearing. Some bearings have three layers, as shown. Others have two layers. *(Federal-Mogul-Bower Bearings, Inc.)*

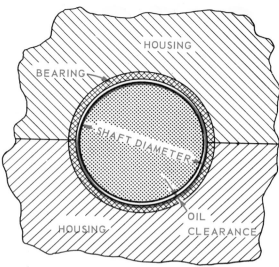

Fig. 6-23. Oil clearance between bearing and shaft journal.

engine, oil circulates through this clearance. The lubricating system constantly feeds oil to the bearing. It enters through the oilhole (Fig. 6-21), and the rotating journal carries it around to all parts of the bearing. The oil works its way to the outer edges of the bearing. From there, it is thrown off and drops back into the oil pan. The oil thrown off helps lubricate other engine parts, such as the cylinder walls, pistons, and piston rings.

As the oil moves across the faces of the bearings, it not only lubricates them but also helps to cool them. The oil is relatively cool as it leaves the oil pan. It picks up heat in its passage through the bearing. This heat is then carried down to the oil pan and released to the air passing around the oil pan. The oil also flushes and cleans the bearings. It tends to flush out particles of grit and dirt that may have worked into the bearing. The particles are carried back to the oil pan by the circulating oil. They then tend to drop to the bottom of the oil pan or are removed from the oil by the oil screen or filter.

§ 6-12. BEARING OIL CLEARANCES The greater the oil clearance (Fig. 6-23), the faster oil flows through the bearing. Proper clearance varies somewhat with different engines, but 0.0015 inch would be a typical clearance. As the clearance becomes greater (owing to bearing wear, for instance), the amount of oil flowing through and being thrown

off increases. With a 0.003-inch clearance (only twice 0.0015 inch), the oil throwoff increases as much as five times. A 0.006-inch clearance allows twenty-five times as much oil to flow through and be thrown off.

Thus, as bearings wear, more and more oil is thrown onto the cylinder walls. The piston rings cannot handle these excessive amounts of oil; part of it works up into the combustion chambers, where it burns and forms carbon. Resulting carbon accumulations in the combustion chambers reduce engine power and cause other engine troubles (see Chap. 26). Excessive bearing oil clearances can also cause some bearings to fail from oil starvation. Here's the reason: The oil pump can deliver only so much oil. If the oil clearances are excessive, most of the oil will pass through the nearest bearings. There won't be enough for the more distant bearings; these bearings will probably fail from lack of oil. An engine with excessive bearing oil clearances usually has low oil pressure; the oil pump cannot build up normal pressure because of the excessive oil clearances in the bearings.

On the other hand, if oil clearances are not sufficiently great, there will be metal-to-metal contact between the bearing and shaft journal. Extremely rapid wear and quick failure will result. Also, there will not be enough oil throwoff for adequate lubrication of cylinder walls, pistons, and rings.

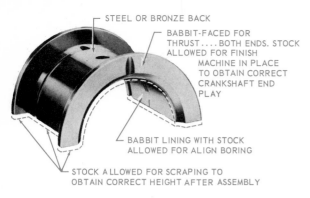

STEEL OR BRONZE BACK

BABBIT-FACED FOR THRUST.... BOTH ENDS. STOCK ALLOWED FOR FINISH MACHINE IN PLACE TO OBTAIN CORRECT CRANKSHAFT END PLAY

BABBIT LINING WITH STOCK ALLOWED FOR ALIGN BORING

STOCK ALLOWED FOR SCRAPING TO OBTAIN CORRECT HEIGHT AFTER ASSEMBLY

Fig. 6–24. Crankshaft thrust bearing of the semifitted type. *(Federal-Mogul-Bower Bearings, Inc.)*

§ **6–13. ENGINE BEARING TYPES** Early engines and some late-model heavy-duty engines use poured bearings. This bearing is prepared by fitting a journal-sized jig or mold into the counterbore and pouring molten bearing material into the opening. The resulting bearing is then scraped and smoothed to provide the final fit and clearance.

In modern automotive engines, *precision-insert* bearings are used. These bearings are so precisely made that they can be installed without any machining or fitting. In many engines, it is possible to replace the main bearings without removing the crankshaft (see § 19–5).

Some engines use *semifitted* bearings (Fig. 6–24). These have a few thousandths of an inch of extra bearing material that must be removed after the bearings are installed so as to establish the final fit. This procedure is described in § 19–7.

§ **6–14. BEARING REQUIREMENTS** Bearings must be able to do other things besides carry the loads imposed on them, as noted below.

1. Load-carrying capacity. Modern engines are lighter and more powerful. They have higher compression ratios and thus impose greater bearing loads. Only a few years ago, bearing loads were around 1,600 to 1,800 psi (pounds per square inch). Today, connecting-rod bearing loads of 6,000 psi are not uncommon.

2. Fatigue resistance. When a piece of metal is repeatedly stressed so that it flexes or bends, it tends to harden and ultimately breaks. This is called *fatigue failure.* Repeatedly bending a piece of wire or sheet metal will demonstrate fatigue failure. Bearings are subjected to varying loads and are thus repeatedly stressed. The bearing

material must be able to withstand these varying loads without failing from fatigue.

3. Embeddability. This term refers to the ability of a bearing to permit foreign particles to embed in it. Dirt and dust particles enter the engine despite the air cleaner and oil filter. Some of them work onto the bearings and are not flushed away by the oil. A bearing protects itself by permitting such particles to sink into, or embed in, the bearing lining material. If the bearing were too hard to allow this, the particles would simply lie on the surface. They would scratch the shaft journal and probably gouge out the bearing. This, in turn, would cause overheating and rapid bearing failure. Thus, the bearing material must be soft enough for adequate embeddability.

4. Conformability. This is associated with embeddability. It refers to the ability of the bearing material to conform to variations in shaft alignment and journal shape. For example, suppose that a shaft journal is slightly tapered. The bearing under the larger diameter will be more heavily loaded. If the bearing material has high conformability, it will "flow" slightly away from the heavily loaded areas to the lightly loaded areas. This redistributes the bearing material so that the bearing is more uniformly loaded. A similar action takes place when foreign particles embed in the bearing. As they embed, they displace bearing material, thus producing local high spots (Fig. 18–18). However, with high conformability, the material flows away from the high spots. This tends to prevent local heavy loading that could cause bearing failure.

5. Corrosion resistance. The bearing materials must be resistant to corrosion, since some of the by-products of combustion may form corrosive substances.

6. Wear rate. The bearing material must be so hard and tough that it will not wear too fast. At the same time, it must be soft enough to permit good embeddability and conformability.

§ **6–15. BEARING MATERIALS** The bearing back is usually of steel. The lining material is a combination of several metals, mixed, or alloyed, to provide the combination of desired characteristics. Such metals as copper, lead, tin, mercury, antimony, cadmium, aluminum, and silver are used. Many combinations are possible. Each ingredient, or metal, supplies certain characteristics. The engine designer selects the combination of ingredients that will best suit his engine.

Review Questions

1. What part forms the basic framework of the engine?
2. Describe briefly how the cylinder block is made.
3. Name six items that are attached to the cylinder block.
4. What is the purpose of a gasket? Name several places where gaskets are used in the engine.
5. What is the purpose of the oil pan?
6. Explain the major differences between a liquid-cooled and an air-cooled engine.
7. Explain the major differences between the L head and the I head.
8. What function does the intake manifold perform? What function does the exhaust manifold perform?
9. What is the purpose of the crankshaft vibration damper?
10. What is the main purpose of the flywheel? What are the two other duties the flywheel often has?
11. What are some of the characteristics of a good bearing?
12. What is the common name of the bearings that support the crankshaft? Describe the manner in which they support the crankshaft.

Study Questions

1. What advantage might there be in making an engine with separate cylinders, instead of making the cylinder block in one casting? What disadvantages?
2. Which is more important to the operation of the engine, the intake manifold or the exhaust manifold? Why?
3. Is the following statement true? "The more cylinders an engine has, the larger the flywheel must be." Give the reason for your answer.
4. Define torsional vibration.
5. How does the vibration damper on the crankshaft operate?
6. Can you think of any advantages the precision-insert bearing might have over other types of bearings? Can you think of any disadvantages?

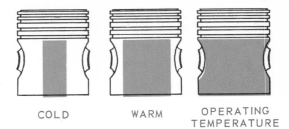

COLD WARM OPERATING TEMPERATURE

Engine Construction — Pistons and Rods

This chapter continues the discussion of engine construction and describes various types of pistons, rings, and connecting rods.

§ 7–1. **CONNECTING ROD** The connecting rod (Fig. 7–1) is attached at one end to a crankpin on the crankshaft and at the other end to a piston, through a piston pin or wrist pin. The connecting rod must be very strong and rigid and also as light as possible. The connecting rod carries the power thrusts from the piston to the crankpin. At the same time, the rod is in eccentric motion (Fig. 3–20). To minimize vibration and bearing loads, the rod must be light in weight.

The crankpin end of the rod (rod big end) is

attached to the crankpin by the rod cap and bolts (Fig. 7–1). A split-style bearing is installed between the crankpin and the rod and rod cap.

The piston end of the rod (rod small end) is attached to the piston by means of a piston pin. The pin passes through bearings in both the piston and the connecting rod. There are three methods of attaching the rod and piston with the piston pin (Figs. 7–2 to 7–4). One type locks the pin to the piston with a lock bolt (Fig. 7–2); the connecting rod has a sleeve bearing that permits the rod to rock back and forth on the pin.

A second design provides a press fit of the piston pin in the connecting rod. The press fit is tight enough to prevent the piston pin from moving out of position. This is a commonly used design

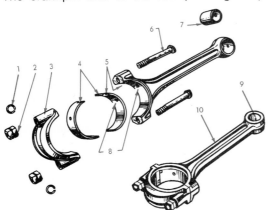

Fig. 7–1. Connecting rod with bearings and bearing cap in disassembled view (top) and assembled view (bottom).

1. Cap-bolt-nut lock washer
2. Cap-bolt nut
3. Cap
4. Rod bearings
5. Tongue and groove
6. Cap bolt
7. Piston-pin bearing
8. Oilholes
9. Oilhole
10. Assembled rod

(Chrysler-Plymouth Division of Chrysler Motors Corporation)

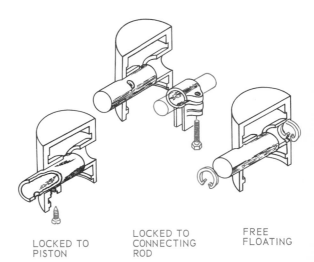

LOCKED TO PISTON

LOCKED TO CONNECTING ROD

FREE FLOATING

Fig. 7–2. Three piston-pin arrangements.

in American car engines. A variation of this design (Fig. 7–3), used in some imported cars, locks the connecting rod to the piston pin by means of a clamp screw. With either variation of this design, sleeve bearings in the piston permit the pin to turn back and forth.

The third design has sleeve bearings in both the rod and piston; the pin is not locked to either. The pin is kept from moving out and scoring the cylinder wall by a pair of lock rings that fit into undercuts in the piston (Fig. 7–4).

To provide piston-pin lubrication, many connecting rods have an oil-passage hole drilled from the crankpin-journal bearing to the piston-pin bearing. Oil reaches the piston-pin bearing

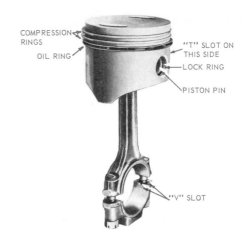

Fig. 7–4. Piston and connecting-rod assembly of the type having lock rings to hold the piston pin in position in the piston and connecting rod. *(Dodge Division of Chrysler Motors Corporation)*

by traveling the following path: from the oil pump to oil lines in the cylinder block; from these oil lines to the main bearings; from the main bearings through oil passages drilled in the crankshaft (Fig. 6–17); from the crankshaft oil passages to the connecting-rod bearings; from the connecting-rod bearings through the rod oil passages to the piston-pin bearings.

On many V-8 engines, cylinder walls and piston pins are lubricated by oil jets from opposing connecting rods. That is, each rod has a groove or hole that indexes with an oil-passage hole in the crank journal every crankshaft revolution. When this happens, a jet of oil spurts into the opposing cylinder in the other cylinder bank.

To maintain good engine balance, connecting rods and caps are carefully matched in sets for engines. All rods in an engine must be of equal weight; if they are not, noticeable vibration may result. In original assembly, rods and caps are individually matched to each other and usually carry identifying numbers so they will not be mixed if the engine is disassembled for service. They must not be mixed during any service job, since this could result in poor bearing fit and bearing failure.

§ 7–2. PISTONS AND PISTON RINGS As already noted (in § 3–24), the piston is essentially a cylindrical plug that moves up and down in the engine cylinder. It is equipped with piston rings to provide a good seal between the cylinder wall and piston. Although the piston appears to be a

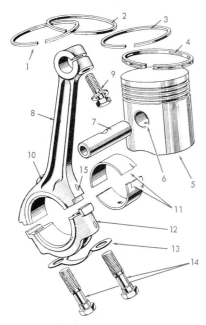

Fig. 7–3. Connecting-rod and piston assembly in disassembled view. Note the clamping screw to clamp the rod on the piston pin.

1–3. Piston rings
4. Piston oil ring
5. Piston
6. Piston-pin lubricating hole
7. Piston pin
8. Connecting rod
9. Clamping screw and washer

10. Cylinder-wall oil-spit hole
11. Connecting-rod bearing
12. Connecting-rod cap
13. Lock washer
14. Cap bolts
15. Connecting-rod and cap marking

(MG Car Company, Limited)

115

simple part, it is actually quite complex from the design standpoint. But before we discuss pistons, let us examine piston rings.

§ 7–3. PISTON RINGS A good seal must be maintained between the piston and cylinder wall to prevent blow-by. "Blow-by" is the name that describes the escape of burned gases from the combustion chamber, past the piston, and into the crankcase. In other words, these gases "blow by" the piston. It is not practical to fit the piston to the cylinder closely enough to prevent blow-by. Thus, piston rings must be used to provide the necessary seal.

The rings are installed in grooves in the piston, as shown in Fig. 7–4. Actually, there are two types of ring, compression rings and oil-control rings. The compression rings seal in the air-fuel mixture as it is compressed and also the combustion pressures as the mixture burns. The oil-control rings scrape off excessive oil from the cylinder wall and return it to the oil pan. Figure 7–5 shows typical compression and oil-control rings. The rings have joints (they are split) so that they can be expanded and slipped over the piston head and into the recessed grooves cut in the piston. Rings for automotive engines usually have butt joints, but in some heavy-duty engines, the joints may be angled, lapped, or of the sealed type.

The rings are somewhat larger in diameter than they will be when in the cylinder. Then, when they are installed, they are compressed so that the joints are nearly closed. Compressing the rings gives them an initial tension; they press tightly against the cylinder wall.

§ 7–4. COMPRESSION RINGS Compression rings are made of cast iron. Typical compression rings are shown in Fig. 7–8.

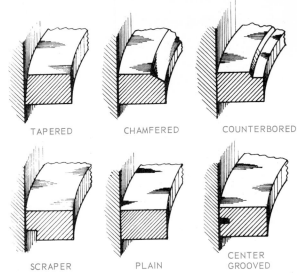
Fig. 7–6. Compression-ring shapes. *(Muskegon Piston Company)*

1. Counterbored and scraper rings. Counterbored and scraper compression rings are used in many engines for top and second compression rings. Figure 7–7 shows the action of these rings during the intake stroke. Internal forces produced by cutting away a corner of the rings cause them to twist slightly, as shown. Thus, as they move down on the intake stroke, they produce a scraping action that scrapes off oil that might have been left on the cylinder wall by the oil-control rings. Then, on the exhaust and compression strokes, when the rings are moving upward, they tend to "skate" over the film of oil on the cylinder wall. Less oil is carried up into the combustion chamber. Wear is minimized.

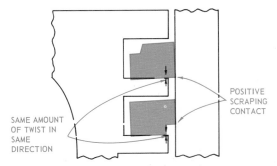
Fig. 7–7. Action of counterbored and scraper compression rings during the intake stroke. Internal forces of rings tend to twist them so that a positive scraping contact is established between rings and cylinder wall. This helps to remove any excessive oil that has worked past the oil-control rings. *(Perfect Circle Company)*

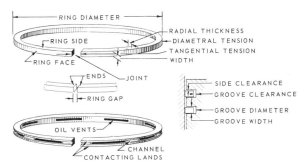
Fig. 7–5. A compression ring (top) and an oil-control ring (bottom) with various parts named. *(Sealed Power Company)*

116

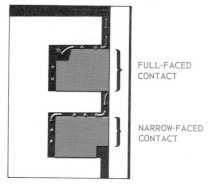

FULL-FACED CONTACT

NARROW-FACED CONTACT

Fig. 7–8. Action of counterbored and scraper compression rings during a power stroke. The combustion pressure presses the rings against the cylinder wall with full-face contact, thus forming a good seal. *(Perfect Circle Company)*

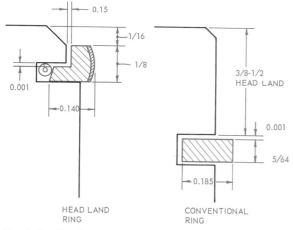

HEAD LAND RING   CONVENTIONAL RING

Fig. 7–9. Headland piston ring installation compared with conventional ring. Note that the headland ring is located nearer the top of the piston, thus eliminating the space between the piston and cylinder wall found in the conventional design. *(Sealed Power Corporation)*

On the power stroke, combustion pressures press down on top of and back of the rings. This overcomes the internal tensions and causes them to untwist and thus present full-face contact with the cylinder walls for effective sealing (Fig. 7–8).

2. Headland rings. This ring has a modified L-shaped cross section (Figs. 7–9 and 7–10). Its name comes from the fact that the ring covers, or shields, the headland area of the piston. This is the area of the piston between the top ring groove and the head, or top, of the piston. Note that the piston is of a special type, with the piston being chamfered at the top. The combination largely eliminates the space between the piston and cylinder wall above the top ring. This space, in other piston and ring combinations, holds a certain amount of air-fuel mixture that does not burn. The cylinder wall and piston cool this air-fuel mixture below the combustion point. The result is that the unburned gasoline vapor passes out of the engine and can produce smog (§9–46). However, with the headland rings and special pistons this space is eliminated so that the amount of unburned gasoline exhausted from the cylinders is reduced.

A second advantage claimed for the headland ring is that it reacts more swiftly to the buildup of combustion pressure. As combustion starts, the increasing pressure acts quickly on the upper lip of the ring, forcing it out and into good sealing contact with the cylinder wall. This reduces blow-by and thus simplifies the requirements of the closed-crankcase ventilating system (§ 9–46).

Because of the more complete combustion of the air-fuel mixture in the cylinder, and the reduction of blow-by, the new ring is claimed to increase available horsepower up to 10 percent.

3. Ring coatings. Various coatings are used on compression rings as an aid to effective wear-in and to prevent rapid wear. By "wear-in" we mean this: When new, the rings and cylinder wall have certain irregularites and do not fit perfectly; however, after a time, these irregularities are worn away so that a much better fit results. Relatively soft substances such as phosphate, graphite, and iron oxide, which wear rapidly, are often used to coat the rings and thus help this wear-in. These coatings also have good oil-absorbing properties. They "soak up" some oil, and this improves ring lubrication. These coatings also tend to pre-

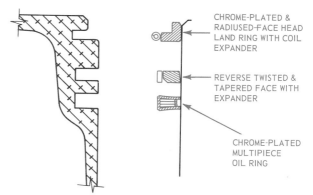

CHROME-PLATED & RADIUSED-FACE HEAD LAND RING WITH COIL EXPANDER

REVERSE TWISTED & TAPERED FACE WITH EXPANDER

CHROME-PLATED MULTIPIECE OIL RING

Fig. 7–10. Sectional view of piston and rings showing, at top, the headland compression ring. *(Sealed Power Corporation)*

vent ring *scuffing*. Scuffing results from metal-to-metal contact, high local temperatures, and actual small-area welding of the ring and cylinder-wall metal. The welds, of course, break with further ring movement. But scuffed places, or scratches and gouges, are left. The coatings tend to prevent scuffing, since a weld cannot take place unless there is actual iron-to-iron contact.

Although most ring coatings are relatively soft, as noted above, there is one coating, coming into widespread use, that is extremely hard. This is a chromium plate, or coating. You might think that a chromium-plated ring would cause rapid cylinder-wall wear. But actually the use of such rings reduces cylinder-wall wear, according to many tests. The reason is this: The chromium plate is lapped to a very smooth finish. One manufacturer, for instance, specifies that surface irregularities must be no greater than 0.0001 inch (one ten-thousandth) in the finished ring. With this extreme smoothness, wear-producing "high spots" are at a minimum; cylinder-wall wear is therefore low. Further, since chromium will not normally weld to cast iron, welding and scuffing of the rings are not apt to occur.

§ 7–5. WHY TWO RINGS? Two compression rings are used to reduce the pressure drop across each one. At the start of the power stroke, pressures in the combustion chamber may go as high as 1,000 psi. Pressure in the crankcase is about atmospheric. Thus, the pressure differential could be around a thousand pounds per square inch. It would be difficult for a single compression ring to hold this much pressure. However, with the second ring, the pressure is, in effect, divided between the two. Not only does this reduce blowby, or loss of pressure past the upper ring, but it also reduces the load on the upper ring so that it does not press quite so hard on the cylinder wall. Ring friction and cylinder and ring wear are thus reduced.

§ 7–6. OIL-CONTROL RINGS The oil-control ring or rings have the job of preventing excessive amounts of oil from working up into the combustion chamber. As already mentioned, oil throwoff from the bearings lubricates the cylinder walls, pistons, and rings. Some connecting rods have an oil-spit hole (Fig. 7–3) which spits oil onto the cylinder wall every time it indexes with the oilhole in the crankpin. Under most circumstances, there is far more oil thrown onto the cylinder walls than

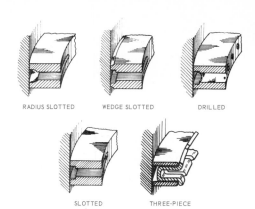

Fig. 7–11. Types of integral, or one-piece, oil-control rings compared with a three-piece type. *(Muskegon Piston Ring Company)*

is needed. Most of it must be scraped off and returned to the oil pan. If too much oil is left on the cylinder walls, it will work its way up into the combustion chamber, where it will burn. This would increase oil consumption so that the engine would require the addition of oil at frequent intervals. Also, the burned oil would foul the spark plug, hamper the action of the compression rings, and increase the possibility of engine knock (see § 10–11).

The oil that is scraped off the cylinder walls does several things. It carries away particles of carbon, dust, and dirt. These particles are then removed by the oil screen or filter. The oil also provides some cooling effect. In addition, the oil on the rings helps provide a seal between the rings and the cylinder wall. Thus, the oil, as it circulates, lubricates and also cleans, cools, and seals.

There are three general types of oil-control rings: the one-piece slotted cast-iron type, the one-piece pressed-steel type, and the three-piece

Fig. 7–12. One-piece, pressed-steel, oil-control piston ring. The segmental construction of this ring, with its three-way spring effect, provides pressure against the upper and lower sides of the ring groove as well as against the cylinder wall. *(Muskegon Piston Ring Company)*

steel rail type with expander (Figs. 7–11 and 7–12). The one-piece types of rings have holes or slots between the upper and lower faces, or surfaces, that bear on the cylinder wall. Oil scraped off the cylinder wall passes through these openings and through holes or slots in the back of the oil-ring grooves in the piston. From there, the oil returns to the oil pan. The slots in the ring also tend to distribute the oil all around the cylinder wall so that no area will be oil-starved.

Some rings of the one-piece type are installed with expander rings (one is shown below the oil-control ring in Fig. 7–17). The expander spring increases the pressure of the ring on the cylinder wall and thus improves the oil-scraping effect.

In recent years, the one-piece cast-iron oil-control ring has given way largely to the one-piece pressed-steel and the dual-rail and expander spacer types (Figs. 7–12 to 7–15). In the latter type, the expander spacer (or spring) forces the rails not only outward into contact with the cylinder wall but also upward and downward against the upper and lower sides of the ring groove in the piston. This provides a more effective seal at these three vital points to provide effective oil control. In contrast, the one-piece cast-iron ring can seal against only one side of the ring groove in the piston at a time, thus leaving open a path through which oil can pass upward toward the combustion chamber. The one-piece pressed-steel type of oil-control ring is favored for use in engines with worn cylinder walls (see §7–9).

§ 7–7. WHY ONLY ONE RING? On earlier passenger-car engines, pistons with relatively long skirts were used, with four piston rings installed on them. Pistons of this type are shown in Figs. 7–16, 7–19, and 7–20. The lower two rings

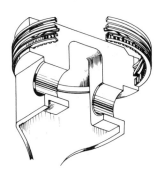

Fig. 7–13. Cutaway views of rings and piston to show construction. The second compression ring has an inner tension ring. The oil ring consists of an expander spacer and two rails. *(Thompson, Ramo, Wooldridge, Inc.)*

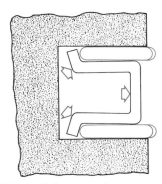

Fig. 7–14. Action of the expander spacer, as shown by arrows, forcing rails out against the cylinder wall and up and down against the sides of the ring grooves. *(Perfect Circle Corporation)*

Fig. 7–15. Piston and connecting-rod assembly, disassembled so the various parts can be seen. The oil-control ring is of the three-piece type. The piston is the slipper type with the skirt partly cut away. *(Ford Division of Ford Motor Company)*

119

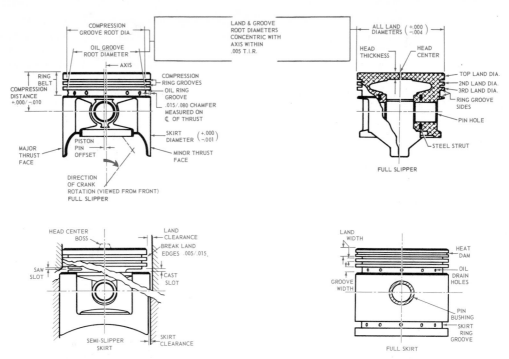

Fig. 7–16. Full-skirt, semi-slipper, and full-slipper pistons with parts named.

were customarily oil-control rings. However, the trend toward lower hood lines and thus squatter engines made it necessary to shorten the piston and reduce the number of rings to three, only one of which was an oil-control ring. It was possible to do this because of many engineering and manufacturing improvements and the more effective action of the modern oil-control ring such as the three-piece type. Article 7–9 discusses the effectiveness of the rings in controlling oil in modern engines.

§ 7–8. EFFECT OF SPEED ON OIL CONTROL
As engine speed increases, the oil-control rings have a harder time controlling the oil and preventing excessive amounts from passing them. There are several reasons for this. The engine and engine oil are hotter. Hot oil is thinner and can pass the rings more easily. More oil is pumped at high speed, so that more oil is thrown onto the cylinder walls. This means the oil-control rings have a harder job to do. And they have less time to do it. Thus, at high speed, more oil gets past the rings and is burned in the combustion chamber. This increases oil consumption considerably. An engine may use two or three times as much oil at

high speed as at low speed. Much, but not all, of this is due to the reduced effectiveness of the rings at high speed in controlling the oil.

§ 7–9. REPLACEMENT RINGS
As mileage piles up, the rings and cylinders (among other parts) wear. Cylinders wear tapered and out of round (Fig. 19–14). This means that the rings become less and less effective in controlling oil and holding compression. There comes a time when the engine is losing so much power and is burning so much oil that repair is required. Then, when the engine is torn down, the first step is to decide whether the cylinder is so badly tapered that it must be honed or bored (§§ 19–10 to 19–18) or whether new replacement rings will make a satisfactory repair. If taper wear is not too great, satisfactory repair can often be made by installing a set of special rings. Figure 18–36 illustrates such a set of rings.

The lower of the two compression rings (2 in Fig. 18–36) has a *ring expander* behind it. The ring expander is a steel spring in the shape of a wavy or humped ring (one is shown below the oil-control ring in Fig. 7–17). It adds tension, or cylinder-wall pressure, to the compression or oil-control ring. With the ring expander, the ring is made somewhat thinner (from back to front) so that it is more flexible. The ring expander then more than makes up for any loss of tension from the reduced thickness. The combination offers high flexibility with high tension. In a tapered or out-of-round bore, the ring must expand and contract—it must change shape—as it moves up and down. The combination (piston ring plus ring expander) gives the ring a better chance to conform to the changing shape of the bore as the ring moves up and down in the cylinder.

NOTE: Some engines use expanders under the oil-control rings. These engines use only one oil-control ring per piston (see Fig. 7–17). The oil-control rings are of the one-piece slotted cast-iron type, and the additional assistance of the expander is desirable in achieving adequate oil control.

The oil-control rings in the replacement set shown in Fig. 18–36 are of two types. The upper ring (3) is of the slotted cast-iron type. It uses a ring expander. The lower one (4) is of the dual-rail and expander spacer type (see also Fig. 7–14).

§ 7–10. PISTONS Pistons have been made in a variety of shapes and designs. Pistons for the older-style, long-stroke, small-bore engine were

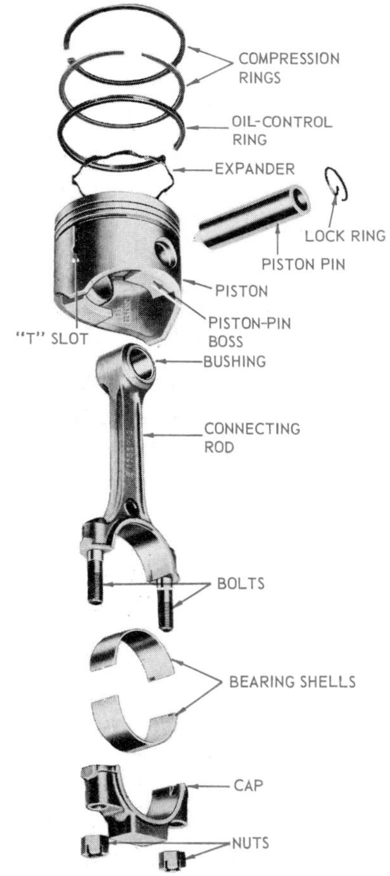

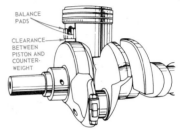

Fig. 7–18. Modern slipper piston and connecting rod assembled to crankshaft. Note the small amount of clearance between the piston and counterweights on the crankshaft. *(Chevrolet Motor Division of General Motors Corporation)*

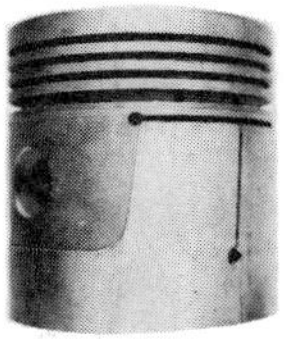

Fig. 7–19. Full-skirt piston with horizontal and vertical slots cut in the skirt. The horizontal slot reduces the path for heat travel, and the vertical slot allows for expansion without an increase of piston diameter.

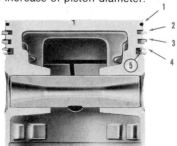

Fig. 7–20. Piston with rings in sectional view, showing heat dam and ring shapes: (1) heat dam; (2) upper compression ring; (3) lower compression ring; (4) oil ring; (5) ring expander. *(Studebaker Corporation)*

Fig. 7–17. Slipper-type piston and connecting-rod assembly, disassembled so that the internal construction of the piston can be seen. Note that the piston skirt is short under the piston-pin bosses. This allows clearance between the piston and crankshaft counterweights when the piston is at BDC. The arrangement permits a lower and more compact engine construction. *(Dodge Division of Chrysler Motors Corporation)*

Fig. 7–21. Cam-ground piston viewed from bottom. When the piston is cold, its diameter at A (the piston-pin holes) may be 0.002 to 0.003 inch less than at B. *(Chrysler-Plymouth Division of Chrysler Motors Corporation)*

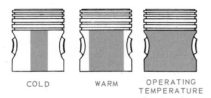

COLD   WARM   OPERATING TEMPERATURE

Fig. 7–22. As the cam-ground piston warms up, the expansion of the skirt distorts the piston from an elliptical to a round shape so that the area of normal clearance between the piston and the cylinder wall is increased.

BELT

STRUT

Fig. 7–23. Pistons with cast-in belt and cast-in strut to provide expansion control. *(Thompson, Ramo, Wooldridge, Inc.)*

Fig. 7–24. Pistons for modern internal-combustion engines.

generally of the full-skirt type (Fig. 7–16). Then, as lower hood lines and oversquare engines (see § 4–7) became popular, the semislipper and full-slipper pistons came into use. On these pistons, the number of piston rings was reduced to three, two compression and one oil-control, as already noted (§ 7–7). One reason for the slipper piston is that, on the short-stroke, oversquare engine, the piston skirt had to be cut away to make room for the counterweights on the crankshaft (Figs. 7–17 and 7–18). Also, the slipper piston, being shorter and having part of its skirt cut away, is lighter. This reduces the inertia load on the engine bearings and, in addition, makes for a more responsive engine.

Inertia is a property of all material objects. Any object in motion resists, in effect, any effort to change its speed or direction. The piston is continuously accelerating, decelerating, and changing direction as it moves up and down in the cylinder. The inertia of the piston must be overcome to produce this, and overcoming the inertia places a load on the rod bearings. The lighter the piston, the less the bearing load and the longer the bearings will last.

Another way to lighten the piston is to make it of light metal. Thus, most automotive-engine pistons today are made of aluminum, which is less than half as heavy as iron. Iron pistons were common in the earlier engines. Aluminum expands more rapidly than iron with increasing temperature, however, and since the cylinder block is of iron, special provisions must be made to maintain proper piston clearance at operating temperatures.

§ 7–11. PISTON CLEARANCE Piston clearance is the distance between the piston and the cylinder wall. Proper clearance varies with different engines, but it is generally in the neighborhood of 0.001 to 0.004 inch. In operation, this clearance is filled with oil so that the piston and rings move on films of oil.

If the clearance is too small, there will be loss of power from excessive friction, severe wear, and possible seizure of the piston in the cylinder. Seizure would cause complete engine failure. On the other hand, if clearances are excessive, *piston slap* will result. Piston slap is caused by the sudden tilting of the piston in the cylinder as the piston starts down on the power stroke. The piston shifts from one side of the cylinder to the other with sufficient force to produce a distinct noise. Usually, piston slap is a problem only in older engines with worn cylinder walls and worn or collapsed piston skirts, any of which produce excessive clearance.

Pistons run many degrees hotter than the adjacent cylinder walls and therefore expand more. This expansion must be controlled in order to avoid loss of adequate piston clearance. Such a loss could lead to serious engine trouble. The problem is more acute with aluminum pistons, because aluminum expands more rapidly than iron with increasing temperature.

§ 7–12. EXPANSION CONTROL IN PISTONS

There are several ways of controlling the expansion of piston skirts. One method is to keep heat away from the lower part of the piston as much as possible. One way of doing this, in the old-style full-skirt piston, is to cut horizontal slots in the piston just below the lower oil-control ring groove (Fig. 7–19). These slots reduce the path for the heat traveling from the cylinder head to the skirt. Thus, the skirt does not become so hot and does not expand so much. In addition, some full-skirt pistons had vertical slots cut in the skirt (Fig. 7–19) which would allow metal expansion in the skirt without appreciable increase of the piston diameter.

Another method of reducing heat travel to the piston skirt makes use of a *heat dam* (Fig. 7–20). The dam consists of a groove cut near the top of the piston. This reduces the size of the path the heat can travel from the piston head to the skirt. The skirt therefore runs cooler and does not expand so much.

Many pistons today are finished so that they have a slightly oval shape when cold. These pistons are called *cam-ground* pistons (Fig. 7–21) because they are finish-ground on a machine that uses a cam to move the piston toward and away from the grinding wheel as the piston is revolved. When a cam-ground piston warms up, it assumes a round shape. Its area of contact with the cylinder wall therefore increases (Fig. 7–22). "Contact" here does not mean actual metal-to-metal contact. There must be clearance between the piston and cylinder wall, as previously noted. What is meant is that, when cold, the oval shape of the piston permits normal clearance in only a small area (there being excessive clearance elsewhere). But as the piston warms up, this area of normal clearance increases. The effect comes about as follows. The head of the piston expands uniformly in all directions, but the relatively stiff piston-pin

bosses are more effective in transmitting this outward thrust. Thus, these bosses move outward, causing the piston to assume a more round shape.

Another method of controlling piston expansion is to use struts, bands, or belts cast into the piston (Fig. 7–23). These cause the outward thrust of the expanding piston head to be carried more toward the piston-pin bosses than toward the thrust faces so that the effect is similar to that of the cam-ground pistons.

§ 7–13. PISTON-HEAD SHAPE

The simplest piston head is the flat head (Fig. 7–18). However, the demand for higher-compression engines has made it necessary to reduce the clearance volume (the volume above the piston at TDC). A limiting factor here is that the valves must have room to open without striking the piston head. A solution is to provide notches in the piston head for adequate valve clearance when the piston is at TDC. Also, some piston heads must have a trough, or be dished, to improve the turbulence or swirling of the air-fuel mixture (Fig. 7–24). Such turbulence improves the combustion process.

§ 7–14. PISTON-PIN OFFSET

In some engines, the piston pin is offset from the centerline of the piston toward the major thrust face. This is the face that bears most heavily against the cylinder wall during the power stroke (Fig. 7–25). If the pin is centered, the minor thrust face will remain in contact with the cylinder wall until the end of the compression stroke. Then, as the power stroke starts, the rod angle changes from left to right (in Fig. 7–25). This causes a sudden shift of the side thrust on the piston from the minor thrust face to

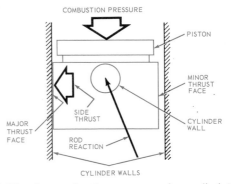

Fig. 7–25. As combustion pressure is applied to the piston head, and the connecting-rod angle changes from left to right, side thrust on the piston will cause it to shift abruptly toward the major thrust face.

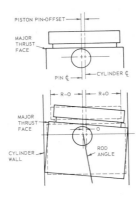

Fig. 7–26. If the piston pin is offset toward the major thrust face, combustion pressure will cause the piston to tilt to the right, as shown, to reduce piston slap. R = radius of piston. O = offset of piston pin. *(Bohn Aluminum and Brass Company, Division of Universal American Corporation)*

Fig. 7–27. Piston with top-ring-groove cast-in fortification. *(Thompson, Ramo, Wooldridge, Inc.)*

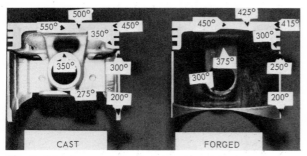

Fig. 7–28. Cast and forged pistons, cut in half to show the operating temperatures at comparable points in the two pistons. *(Thompson, Ramo, Wooldridge, Inc.)*

Fig. 7–29. Forged aluminum piston, cut in half and etched to bring out the grain flow. The etched lines show the directions that the metal flowed during the forging process. *(Thompson, Ramo, Wooldridge, Inc.)*

the major thrust face. If there is any appreciable clearance, piston slap will result.

However, if the piston pin is offset (Fig. 7–26), the combustion pressure will cause the piston to tilt as the piston nears TDC, as shown, so that the lower end of the major thrust face will first make contact with the cylinder wall. Then, after the piston passes TDC and the reversal of side thrust occurs, full major-thrust-face contact is made with less tendency for piston slap to occur.

The tilting action occurs because there is more combustion pressure on the right-hand part of the piston (which measures R + O, or piston radius plus offset) than on the left-hand side of the piston (which measures R − O).

§ 7–15. RING-GROOVE FORTIFICATION The compression rings are in periodic motion relative to the ring grooves. At the beginning of the power stroke, as the piston goes up over TDC and starts down again, the top compression ring is forced down hard against the lower side of the ring groove. The increasing combustion pressures produce this action. Then, during the intake stroke, the vacuum in the cylinder causes the top compression ring to move up and into contact with the upper side of the ring groove. Thus, the ring is repeatedly striking the upper and lower sides of the ring groove.

In high-performance engines, these repeated impacts can cause rapid ring-groove wear. It is the top ring groove that is most critical, because it receives the greater part of the combustion pressures. To combat this wear, pistons for some high-performance engines have top-ring-groove fortification. The fortification consists of a ring of cast iron or nickel-iron alloy which is cast into the piston (Fig. 7–27). For cast pistons in medium duty, the inserts are stamped from steel sheets. In forged pistons, inserts cannot be used. Instead, if ring fortification is required, it is accomplished by spraying the groove area with molten metal having the proper wear resistance. Then, the groove is machined to the proper dimensions.

§ 7–16. HIGH-PERFORMANCE PISTONS Aluminum pistons can be either cast or forged. Cast pistons are made by pouring molten aluminum into molds. Forged pistons are made from slugs of aluminum alloy which, when subjected to high forging pressure, flows, or extrudes, into the dies to form pistons. Both must be heat-treated.

The forged piston is denser and forms a better heat path to allow the heat to get away from the piston head (Fig. 7–28). The flags indicate the temperatures at comparable points with both pistons operating under the same conditions.

The forged piston also has a grain flow that improves its wearing ability. Figure 7–29 shows the grain flow in a forged piston. Note that the flow is vertical in the skirt, that is, in the direction that the piston moves in the cylinder.

The forged piston is also lighter and thus produces lower inertial forces as it accelerates and decelerates in the cylinder. Taking all these factors together, it can be seen that the forged piston is the preferred piston for high-performance engines.

Some high-performance pistons also have special skirt configurations for added strength. The oval skirt (Fig. 7–30) and the undulated skirt (Fig. 7–31) are designed to provide high strength. They are for use in high-performance automobiles but they are strong enough for competition engines. The outboard piston-pin boss piston (Fig. 7–32) is designed for maximum strength and is for competition engines. Note that the piston-pin bosses are outside the walls of the piston and also that the thrust faces of this piston are relatively small.

Fig. 7–30. Piston with oval skirt. *(Thompson, Ramo, Wooldridge, Inc.)*

Fig. 7–31. Piston with undulated skirt. *(Thompson, Ramo, Wooldridge, Inc.)*

Fig. 7–32. Piston with outboard piston-pin bosses. *(Thompson, Ramo, Wooldridge, Inc.)*

Review Questions

1. What is the purpose of the connecting rod?
2. What three methods of attaching the piston and connecting rod with the piston pin are in common use?
3. In what ways is the piston pin lubricated?
4. What two functions must piston rings perform?
5. What is the purpose of the coatings on piston rings?
6. Why are two compression rings used?
7. Describe two late-type oil-control rings.
8. What is the effect of engine speed on oil control?
9. Describe a ring expander, and explain its purpose.
10. Describe a slipper piston. Why is this type of piston replacing the full-skirt type?
11. What is meant by piston clearance?
12. What is happening in the cylinder when piston slap is heard?
13. What is blow-by?
14. What is meant by expansion control as applied to pistons. Describe four ways to achieve it.
15. Describe the action of cam-ground pistons as they warm up in operation.
16. What is the purpose of offsetting the piston pin?
17. What is the purpose of ring-groove fortification?
18. Describe several high-performance pistons.

Study Questions

1. Explain in writing what is meant by ring wear-in.
2. Make drawings of several types of compression rings.
3. Make a drawing of a typical piston and name the various parts.
4. Make drawings of several types of oil-control rings.

HORSE SHOE   PIN TYPE   CONICAL TYPE

CHAPTER

Engine Construction — Valves and Valve Trains

This chapter continues the discussion of engine construction and describes valves and various types of valve mechanisms.

§ 8–1. CAMS AND CAMSHAFT A cam is a device that can change rotary motion into linear, or straight-line, motion. The cam has a high spot, or lobe; a follower riding on the cam will move away from or toward the camshaft as the cam rotates (Fig. 8–1).

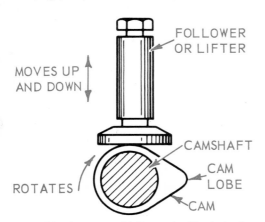

Fig. 8–1. Simple cam and follower (or lifter). As the cam revolves, the follower follows the cam surface by moving up and down.

In the engine, cams on the camshaft cause the intake and exhaust valves to open. Figures 5–22 and 5–23 show the valve mechanisms (or *valve trains*) on L-head and I-head engines. There is a cam on the camshaft for each valve, or two cams per cylinder. In addition, the camshaft has an eccentric to operate the fuel pump and a gear to drive the ignition distributor and oil pump. The camshaft is driven from the crankshaft by sprock-

Fig. 8–2. Crankshaft and camshaft sprockets with chain drive for a six-cylinder engine, showing timing marks on sprockets: (1) camshaft-sprocket mark; (2) crankshaft-sprocket mark; (3) center line of shafts. Note that the larger of the two sprockets is on the camshaft so that it turns at one-half crankshaft speed. *(Chrysler-Plymouth Division of Chrysler Motors Corporation)*

ets and chain (Figs. 8–2 and 8–3) or by two gears (Fig. 8–4). The camshaft sprocket or gear has twice as many teeth as the sprocket or gear on the crankshaft. This gives a 1:2 gear ratio; the camshaft turns at half the speed of the crankshaft. Thus, every two revolutions of the crankshaft

Fig. 8-3. Crankshaft and camshaft sprockets with chain drive for a V-8 engine. *(Chrysler-Plymouth Division of Chrysler Motors Corporation)*

produce one revolution of the camshaft and one opening and closing of each valve (in the four-cycle engine).

The camshaft is mounted in bearings in the lower part of the cylinder block in most in-line engines. It is located between the two banks of cylinders in V-8 engines (Fig. 5–23). In a few engines, the camshaft is located on the cylinder head (Figs. 5–16 and 5–20).

Fig. 8-4. Crankshaft and camshaft gears for a six-cylinder engine. Note timing marks on gears. *(Buick Motor Division of General Motors Corporation)*

§ **8-2. VALVES** As already noted, each cylinder has two valves, an intake valve and an exhaust valve. The cam lobes on the camshaft are so related to the crankshaft crankpins (through the gears or sprockets and chain) as to cause the valves to open and close with the correct relationship to the piston strokes (see § 8–15).

Various types of valves have been used in the past, among them sliding-sleeve and rotary. But the valve in general use today is the mushroom, or poppet, valve (Figs. 8–5 and 8–6). The valve is normally held closed and firmly seated by one or more heavy springs and by pressures in the combustion chamber. The manner in which springs are attached to the valves is described in § 8–6.

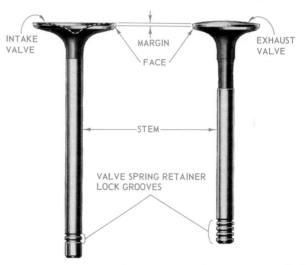

Fig. 8-5. Typical poppet valves. *(Chrysler-Plymouth Division of Chrysler Motors Corporation)*

§ **8-3. VALVE COOLING** The intake valve runs relatively cool, since it passes only air-fuel mixture. But the exhaust valve must pass the very hot burned gases. The exhaust valve may actually become red hot in operation. Figure 8–7 shows a typical temperature pattern of an exhaust valve. Note that the valve stem is coolest, the part near the valve face being next coolest. This is because the valve stem passes heat to the valve guide, and this helps keep the valve stem cool. Likewise, the valve face passes heat to the valve seat, and this helps keep the valve face cool. It is obvious that the valve seat and guide must be cooled, in turn. To provide adequate cooling of these parts, the cylinder head must be carefully designed so as to permit good water circulation around the

127

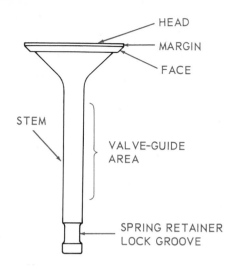

Fig. 8-6. Valve with its parts named.

HEAD
MARGIN
FACE
STEM
VALVE-GUIDE AREA
SPRING RETAINER LOCK GROOVE

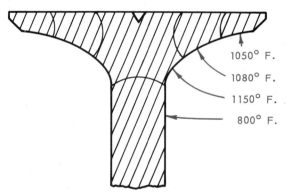

1050° F.
1080° F.
1150° F.
800° F.

Fig. 8-7. Temperatures in an exhaust valve. Valve is shown in sectional view. *(Eaton Manufacturing Company)*

critical areas. In some L-head engines, water-distributing tubes were used to force additional water to circulate around the valve seat. Some I-head engines include water nozzles for the same purpose. In one late-model six-cylinder I-head engine, a series of deflectors in the head improved circulation around the valve seats (Fig. 8-8).

Figure 8-7 emphasizes the importance of proper valve seating. If the valve face and valve seat do not mate properly or are rough or worn, then full-face contact will not take place. This means that there is a smaller area of contact through which heat transfer (and valve-face cooling) can take place. At the same time, uneven contact may mean that hot exhaust gases will leak between the valve face and seat in some spots. These spots will naturally run hotter. Actually, a poor seat may

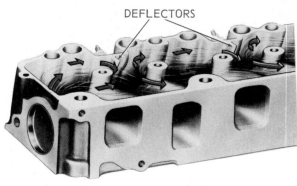

DEFLECTORS

Fig. 8-8. Water circulation in the cylinder head of a late-model, six-cylinder, I-head engine. Arrows show direction of water flow. Note effect of deflectors. *(Ford Division of Ford Motor Company)*

cause a valve to run several hundred degrees hotter than normal; there might be local hot spots at even higher temperatures. Naturally, these higher temperatures greatly shorten valve life: The hot spots wear or burn away more rapidly.

§ 8-4. SODIUM-COOLED VALVE To aid valve cooling and thus increase valve life, many heavy-duty engines use sodium-cooled valves. This valve has a hollow stem partly filled with metallic sodium (Fig. 8-9). Sodium melts at 208°F. Thus, at operating temperatures, the sodium is liquid. As the valve moves up and down, the sodium is thrown upward into the hotter part of the valve. It absorbs heat, which it then gives up to the cooler stem as it falls down into the stem again. This circulation cools the valve head. The valve therefore runs cooler. A sodium-cooled valve will run as much as 200°F cooler than a solid-stem valve of similar design. This means, other factors being equal, longer valve life.

● **CAUTION:** Sodium is a highly reactive element. If a piece of sodium is dropped into water, it will burst into flame with almost explosive violence. If it gets on the skin, it will cause deep and serious burns. Of course, as long as it is safely sealed in the valve stem, there is no danger. But if the hollow stem of a sodium-cooled valve is cracked or broken, then it is potentially dangerous. Old or damaged sodium valves should be disposed of in a safe manner. Some manufacturers recommend burying them deep underground. Not all sodium valves are marked, but they can usually be recognized by their oversize stems.

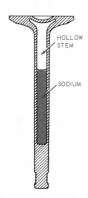

Fig. 8-9. Sectional view of a sodium-cooled valve.

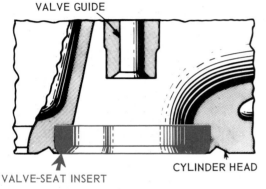

Fig. 8-10. Cutaway view of a valve-seat insert. The insert is indicated by the arrow. *(Chrysler-Plymouth Division of Chrysler Motors Corporation)*

§ 8-5. VALVE SEAT The exhaust-valve seat is also subjected to the extremely high temperatures of the burned gases. For this reason, the exhaust-valve seats in some engines are made of special heat-resistant steel-alloy insert rings (Fig. 8-10). These rings hold up better than the block or head materials. Also, when they do become worn so much that they connot be refinished with a valve-seat grinder, they can be replaced.

There are drawbacks to the use of valve-seat inserts. For one thing, they complicate engine manufacture. For another, the interface between the insert and the cylinder head interferes with the flow of heat so that the seat runs hotter. This means that the valve itself runs hotter and wears more rapidly. Thus, engine designers prefer, if possible, to use the integral type of valve seat, that is, the type which is part of the cylinder head itself. For severe service, the valve seats may be hardened by a special electric-induction process (Fig. 8-11). For some heavy-duty engines, however, seat inserts are required.

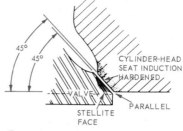

Fig. 8-11. For severe service, the valve seat can be hardened by a special electric-induction process. This process induces local heating by induction coils. The valve shown here is stellite-faced. Stellite is extremely resistant to heat and wear. Note that the faces of the valve seat and valve are shown as being parallel. *(Chevrolet Motor Division of General Motors Corporation)*

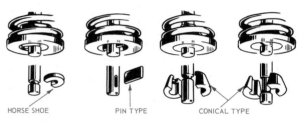

Fig. 8-12. Types of valve-spring-retainer locks; or keepers.

§ 8-6. L-HEAD VALVE TRAIN The L-head-engine valve train (Fig. 3-23) consists of the camshaft, valve lifter, valve spring, and valve. The valve spring is compressed between the cylinder block and a spring retainer. The spring retainer is attached to the end of the valve stem with a retainer lock (Fig. 8-12). The retainer holds the lock in place in the undercut or slot in the valve stem. The valve rides in the valve guide; this is essentially nothing more than a hollow steel tube, carefully dimensioned to be a tight fit in the block and to have a close clearance fit with the valve stem.

There are two types of valve lifter, the solid or mechanical lifter and the hydraulic lifter (§ 8-13). The solid lifter is essentially a cylinder with an adjustment screw that can be turned in or out to attain the correct clearance between the screw-head and valve stem. This clearance, called *tappet clearance* or *valve lash,* is included to assure valve seating. If there were no clearance, then dimension changes due to temperature changes might so lengthen the valve stem as to keep it from closing. This could lead to quick valve failure. The valve lifter is free to rotate in its mounting; this rotation distributes the wear from the cam over the face of the lifter.

Fig. 8–13. One type of rocker arm used in overhead-valve engines. *(Chevrolet Motor Division of General Motors Corporation)*

§ 8–7. I-HEAD VALVE TRAIN In the I-head, or overhead-valve, engine, a push rod and rocker arm are required, in addition to the parts used in the valve train of the L-head engine (see Figs. 5–14 and 5–15). There are several types of rocker arm. In one type, the rocker arm has an adjustment screw (Fig. 8–13). This type of rocker arm is shown assembled in an engine in Fig. 5–15. Note that the rocker arms are lined up on the rocker-arm shaft with the adjustment-screw ends resting on the push rods. The push rods extend through openings in the cylinder head and block to the valve lifters above the cams. On some engines, the rocker arms are made of cast iron (Fig. 8–13), and on others they are made of steel stampings (Fig. 5–15).

A different type of rocker arm and support is shown in Fig. 8–14. This rocker arm is a heavy steel stamping. Each T-shaped rocker-arm support supports two rocker arms, as shown. The rocker-arm supports are positioned on the cylinder head by the rocker-arm retainer, as shown. Each retainer positions two rocker-arm supports. Clips on the rocker-arm retainer hold the rocker arms on their supports and prevent them from slipping off.

Fig. 8–17. Rocker arm of the type using a ball pivot, with associated parts. *(Chevrolet Motor Division of General Motors Corporation)*

A still different design of rocker arm is shown in Fig. 8–17, with the rocker arm shown in sectional view in Fig. 8–18. This rocker arm is a heavy steel stamping, shaped as shown. The push-rod end is formed into a socket in which the end of the push rod rides. The rocker arm is supported by a ball pivot mounted on a stud. The stud is hollow and opens into an oil gallery in the head. Oil feeds through the stud to the ball pivot for lubrication. Also, the push rod is hollow and feeds oil from the valve lifter to the contact area between the push rod and the rocker arm. Adequate lubrication of the moving parts of the valve train is thus assured. The valve clearance on this design is

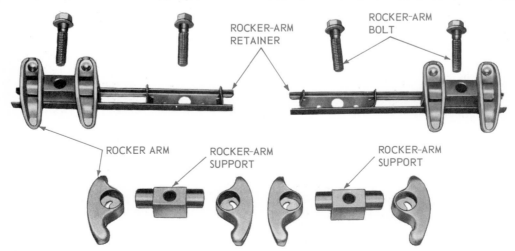

Fig. 8–14. Rocker arms, supports, and retainers. *(Cadillac Motor Car Division of General Motors Corporation)*

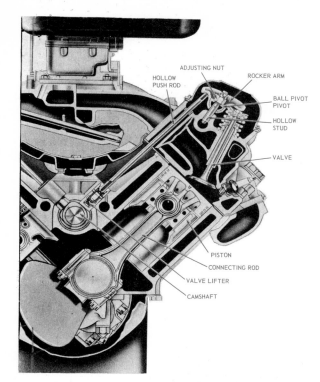

Fig. 8–18. Sectional view of one bank of a V-8 engine using ball-pivoted valve rocker arms. *(Pontiac Motor Division of General Motors Corporation)*

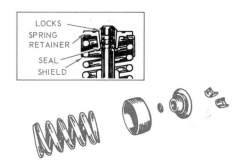

Fig. 8–19. Disassembled and sectional assembled views of valve and spring assembly with oil seal and shield. *(Chevrolet Motor Division of General Motors Corporation)*

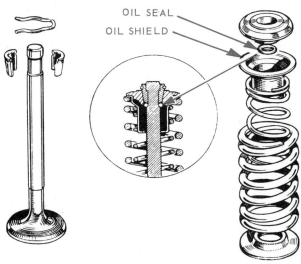

Fig. 8–20. Disassembled and sectional assembled views of a valve and spring assembly with oil seal and shield. *(MG Car Company, Limited)*

measured between the rocker arm and valve stem, as with the other design. However, on this design, adjustment is made by turning the adjustment nut above the ball pivot up or down on the mounting stud. This raises or lowers the rocker arm to increase or decrease valve clearance.

NOTE: In some engines using hydraulic valve lifters (§ 8–13), there is no provision for adjusting valve lash, since the lifters hydraulically take up any clearance when the valve is closed. On this type of engine, some manufacturers specify that, if valves and valve seats are ground, then the valve stems should be shortened by grinding off the tips. This restores the proper linkage dimensions (see § 17–9). Other engines with hydraulic valve lifters do have provisions for adjustment, as explained on following pages.

In many I heads, the valves are carried in replaceable valve guides. In other I heads, the guides are part of the head. That is, they are holes bored in the head and are not separate parts. On these, if the guides become worn, they can be reamed to a larger size and valves with oversize stems installed.

In many late-model I-head engines, special provision is made to prevent oil seepage past the valve stems into the combustion chamber. Figure 8–19 shows one type of seal and shield, or "shedder," as it is also called. The seal, which is a rubberlike ring, fits between the spring retainer skirt and an undercut in the valve stem. The shield covers the top two turns of the spring. The seal prevents oil from seeping down the valve stem past the locks and retainer. The shield prevents undue amounts of oil from being thrown through the spring onto the valve stem. A variation of this design is shown in Fig. 8–20. Here, the shield is on the inside of the valve springs rather than on the outside. The purpose of the shield is the same,

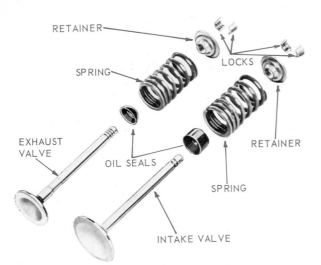

Fig. 8-21. Disassembled view of valves, springs, oil seals, and related parts. *(Dodge Division of Chrysler Motors Corporation)*

however: to shield the valve stem from excessive oil.

Another type of seal to prevent oil seepage past the valve stem is shown in Figs. 8–21 and 8–22. This type of oil seal fits down against the cylinder head and around the valve stem as shown in Fig. 8–22.

§ 8-8. F-HEAD VALVE TRAINS In the F-head engine, one valve is in the head, and the other valve is in the block. The exhaust valve is located in the block (see Fig. 5–24). Thus, this engine is a combination L-head and I-head engine and has valve trains as described in the previous two articles.

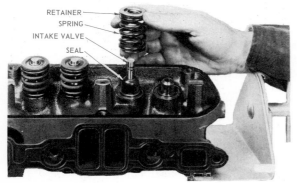

Fig. 8-22. Installation of valve, spring, oil seal, and related parts. *(Dodge Division of Chrysler Motors Corporation)*

§ 8-9. VALVE ROTATION If the exhaust valve were to rotate a little each time it opened, many valve troubles would be minimized. For example, one common cause of valve burning is deposits on the valve face. These deposits, which are products of combustion, tend to prevent normal valve seating so that the valve overheats and burns. Another valve trouble is sticking. This condition usually results from accumulations of carbon (from burned oil) on the valve stem. These deposits work into the clearance between the valve stem and valve guide; the valve sticks, or "hangs up," in the guide and does not close. Then the valve overheats and burns.

If the valve rotates as it opens and closes, there will be less chance of valve-stem accumulations causing the valve to stick. Further, there will be a wiping action between the valve face and seat; this tends to prevent any build-up of face deposits. In addition, valve rotation results in more uniform valve-head temperatures for this reason: Some parts of the valve seat may be hotter than others; actual hot spots may develop. If the same part of the valve face continued to seat on the hot spot, a corresponding hot spot would develop on the valve face. The hot spot on the valve face would wear or burn away faster. But if the valve rotates, no one part of the face will be continuously subjected to the higher temperature. Thus, longer valve life will result.

§ 8-10. VALVE ROTATORS There are several types of valve rotators. In the free type, the valve is relieved of all spring pressure so that it is free to rotate. Engine vibration then causes it to rotate. Another type assures positive rotation of the valve by imposing a rotating force on the valve stem each time the valve opens.

§ 8-11. FREE-TYPE VALVE ROTATOR Figure 8–23 shows the details of a free-type valve rotator. Instead of the usual spring-retainer lock, this design uses a split washer lock and a tip cup. As the valve lifter moves up, the adjustment screw pushes up on the tip cup. The tip cup then carries the motion to the lock and valve retainer. The retainer is lifted, thereby taking up the valve-spring pressure. Note that the spring pressure is taken off the valve stem; the valve is free. Since it is free, it can rotate when it is open.

§ 8-12. POSITIVE-TYPE VALVE ROTATOR Figure 8–24 shows the details of one positive-type

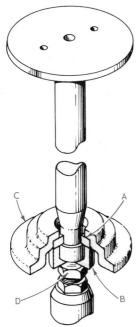

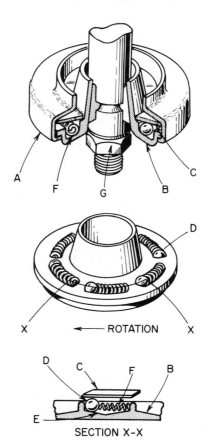

Fig. 8–23. Construction of "free-type" valve rotator: (A) spring-retainer lock; (B) tip cup; (C) spring retainer; (D) lifter adjustment screw. *(Thompson Products, Inc.)*

valve rotator. This design applies a rotating force on the valve stem each time it opens, thus assuring positive rotation of the valve. A seating collar (*A*) is spun over the outer lip of the spring retainer (*B*). The valve spring rests on the seating collar. The collar encloses a flexible washer (*C*) placed above a series of spring-loaded balls (*D*). The middle view shows how the balls and springs are positioned in grooves in the spring retainer. The bottoms of the grooves (races) are inclined as shown in the bottom view (*E*), which is a section (*X-X*) cut from the middle view. When the lifter is raised, the adjustment screw (*G*) lifts the valve and applies an increasing pressure on the seating collar. This flattens the flexible washer (*C*) so that the washer applies the spring load on the balls (*D*). As the balls receive this load, they roll down the inclined races. This causes the retainer to turn a few degrees and thus turn the valve a few degrees. When the valve closes, the spring pressure is reduced so that the balls return to their original positions, ready for the next valve motion.

§ 8–13. HYDRAULIC VALVE LIFTER This type of lifter, now used in many engines, is very quiet in operation, because it assures zero tappet clearance (or valve lash). Also, this lifter usually requires

Fig. 8–24. Construction of positive-rotation type of valve rotation: (A) seating collar; (B) spring retainer; (C) flexible washer; (D) balls; (E) lifter adjustment screw. *(Thompson Products, Inc.)*

no adjustment in normal service; variations due to temperature changes or to wear are taken care of hydraulically.

Figure 8–25 shows the details of a hydraulic valve lifter as used in a V-8 I-head engine. Figure 8–26 shows the operation of a similar valve lifter. Oil is fed into the valve lifter from the oil pump and through an oil gallery that runs the length of the engine. When the valve is closed, oil from the pump is forced into the valve lifter through the oilholes in the lifter body and plunger. The oil forces the ball-check valve in the plunger to open. Oil then passes the ball-check valve and enters the space under the plunger. The plunger is therefore forced upward until it comes into contact with the valve push rod (or valve stem in L-head engines). This takes up any clearance in the system.

ARRANGEMENT OF VALVES AND VALVE LIFTERS

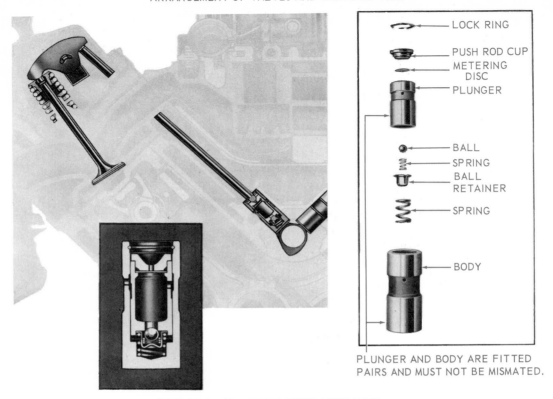

LOCK RING
PUSH ROD CUP
METERING DISC
PLUNGER

BALL
SPRING
BALL RETAINER
SPRING

BODY

PLUNGER AND BODY ARE FITTED
PAIRS AND MUST NOT BE MISMATED.

OPERATION OF VALVE LIFTER MECHANISM

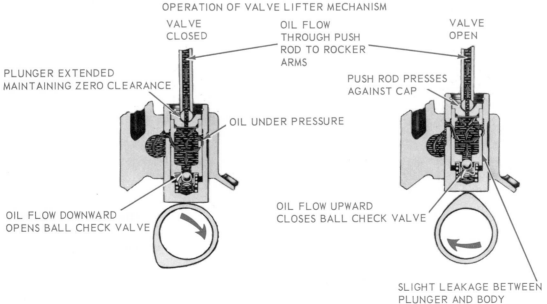

VALVE CLOSED

OIL FLOW THROUGH PUSH ROD TO ROCKER ARMS

VALVE OPEN

PLUNGER EXTENDED
MAINTAINING ZERO CLEARANCE

PUSH ROD PRESSES
AGAINST CAP

OIL UNDER PRESSURE

OIL FLOW DOWNWARD
OPENS BALL CHECK VALVE

OIL FLOW UPWARD
CLOSES BALL CHECK VALVE

SLIGHT LEAKAGE BETWEEN
PLUNGER AND BODY

Fig. 8–25. Sectional view of a V-8, I-head engine, showing location of the hydraulic valve lifter in the valve train. The inserts show the construction and operation of the lifter. *(Cadillac Motor Car Division of General Motors Corporation)*

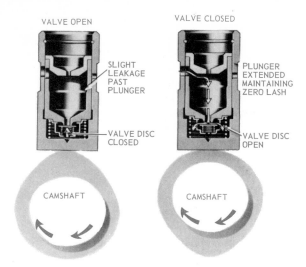

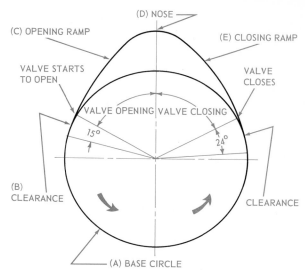

Fig. 8–26. Two positions of the hydraulic valve lifter, with valve open and closed. *(Lincoln-Mercury Division of Ford Motor Company)*

Fig. 8–27. Cam for a mechanical valve lifter.

Now, when the cam lobe moves around under the lifter body, the lifter is raised. Since there is no clearance, there is no tappet noise. Raising of the lifter and the valve produces a sudden increase in pressure in the body chamber under the plunger. This causes the ball-check valve to close. Oil is therefore trapped in the chamber, and the lifter acts like a simple one-piece lifter. It moves up as an assembly and causes the valve to open. Then, when the valve closes, the lifter moves down and the pressure on the plunger is relieved. If any oil has been lost from the chamber under the plunger, oil from the engine oil pump can cause the ball-check valve to open so that engine oil can refill the chamber, as noted above.

§ 8–14. CAMS FOR MECHANICAL AND HYDRAULIC LIFTERS Cam shapes for hydraulic and mechanical lifters differ. The mechanical lifter requires a cam (Fig. 8–27) that will provide clearance (*B*) when the valve is closed. The cam must rotate a few degrees off the base circle to take up this clearance. Then, the valve begins to open. The opening ramp (*C*) has curvature. This reduces the acceleration on the valve-train parts. After the nose (*D*) has passed under the lifter, the valve starts closing. The closing ramp also has curvature to "let down" the valve gradually so that it does not pound the valve seat too hard. Clearance reappears as the base circle (*A*) passes under the lifter.

The hydraulic valve lifter requires no clearance. Also, the ramps are shorter, permitting the valves

to open and close faster with less overlap (overlap occurs when both the intake and the exhaust valves are open at the same time—see § 8–15). The nose is more rounded because of this ramp curvature.

§ 8–15. VALVE TIMING In previous discussions of valve action, it was assumed that the intake and exhaust valves were opening and closing at TDC and BDC. Actually, as can be seen from Fig. 8–28, the valves are not timed in this manner. In the valve-timing diagram shown, the exhaust valve starts to open at 47 degrees before BDC on the power stroke and stays open until 21 degrees after TDC on the intake stroke. This additional time that the exhaust valve is opened gives more time for the exhaust gases to leave the cylinder. By the time the piston reaches 47 degrees before BDC on the power stroke, the combustion pressures have dropped considerably (see Fig. 4–17). Little power is lost by giving the exhaust gases this extra time to exhaust from the cylinder.

In a similar manner, leaving the intake valve open for 56 degrees past BDC after the intake stroke gives additional time for air-fuel mixture to flow into the cylinder. As you will recall from our discussions of volumetric efficiency (§ 4–11), delivery of adequate amounts of air-fuel mixture to the engine cylinders is a critical item in engine operation. Actually, the cylinders are never quite "filled up" when the intake valve closes (volumetric efficiency is well below 100 percent).

Leaving the intake valve open for a number of degrees past BDC after the intake stroke does increase volumetric efficiency, however.

Timing of the valves is due to the shape of the lobe on the cam and the relationship between the gears or sprockets and chain on the camshaft and crankshaft. Changing the relationship between the driving and driven gears or sprockets changes the timing at which the valves open and close. For example, if the camshaft gear were de-meshed and moved ahead one tooth and then re-meshed, the valves would open and close earlier. Suppose this moved the valve action ahead 15 degrees. Then the exhaust valve would open at 62 degrees before BDC on the power stroke and close at only 6 degrees before TDC on the exhaust stroke (in the example shown in Fig. 8–28). The intake-valve actions would likewise be moved ahead. These valve-action advances would seriously reduce engine performance. Also, in the newer engines, which use very small clearances between the valves and piston heads, there would be danger of the pistons striking the valve heads. This, of course, could severely damage the engine. To prevent such troubles, the gears or sprockets are marked so that they can be properly aligned (see Figs. 8–2 to 8–4).

§ 8–16. HIGH-PERFORMANCE CAMS
For high-performance engines, such as those used in racing and drag-strip cars, the cams are contoured to give a longer duration of valve opening and also to reduce the time required for the valves to open and close. This means higher accelerations and decelerations of the valve-train parts.

Figure 8–29 shows valve timing for a road-and-drag cam. Note that the intake valve opens 30 degrees before TDC and that the exhaust valve does not close until 27 degrees after TDC, giving an overlap of 57 degrees. The exhaust valve opens at 68 degrees before BDC and the exhaust valve does not close until 68 degrees after BDC. The long duration of valve opening gives the engine a better chance to breathe at high speeds. However, low-speed and idling characteristics become very poor because of the great overlap. Thus, to eliminate rough idle, the idling speed must be increased considerably. All this means that the engine will have very poor fuel economy.

Another method of improving high-speed performance is to use high-lift cams, that is, cams that will increase the amount the valves open.

As an example, in one engine the standard camshaft produced a lift, or valve opening, of about 0.400 inch. The high-performance cam for this engine produces a lift of 0.450 inch. The additional 0.050-inch opening allows a greater amount of gas to pass in a given time and thus improves engine breathing and high-speed performance. However, there is a limit to the amount of lift that cams can provide because of the close clearances between valves, when open, and the pistons at TDC. If the lift is too great, the piston will strike the valve and cause severe damage. Carbon build-up would be critical here, too.

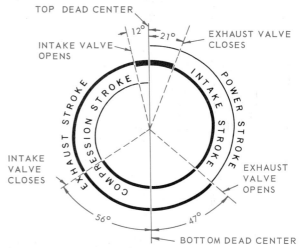

Fig. 8–28. Intake- and exhaust-valve timing. The complete cycle of events is shown as a 720-degree spiral, which represents two complete crankshaft revolutions. Timing of valves differs for different engines.

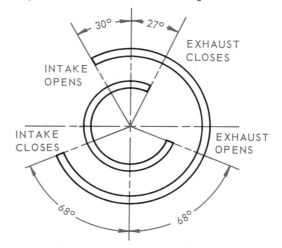

Fig. 8–29. Intake- and exhaust-valve timing for cams of a "road-and-drag" high performance camshaft.

Review Questions

1. Does the camshaft turn at the same, at one-half, or at twice crankshaft speed?
2. Describe the action of an intake valve; an exhaust valve.
3. Describe the action of a sodium-cooled valve.
4. What are the advantages of valve rotation? Describe two types of valve rotators.
5. Describe the operation of a hydraulic valve lifter.
6. What does the term "valve timing" mean?
7. What are exhaust-valve seat inserts, and why are they used?
8. Describe the action of the silent-lash rocker arm.
9. Explain the difference between the cams for solid valve lifters and cams for hydraulic valve lifters.
10. In Fig. 8–28, for how many degrees of crankshaft rotation is the exhaust valve open? For how many degrees of crankshaft rotation is the intake valve open?
11. What are high-performance cams? Explain the difference between these cams and standard cams.

Study Questions

1. Make a sketch of the valve-operating mechanism for an L-head engine, starting with the camshaft and ending with the valve seat.
2. Make a sketch of the valve-operating mechanism for an I-head engine, starting with the camshaft and ending with the valve seat.
3. If an engine is operating at 2,150 rpm, how many times would the exhaust valve in cylinder 1 open in 1 minute?
4. Draw a valve-timing chart in which the intake valve opens at TDC and closes at 30 degrees after BDC, and the exhaust valve opens at 30 degrees before BDC and closes at 5 degrees after TDC.

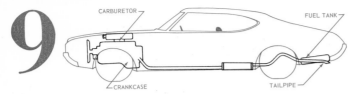

9

Automotive Fuel Systems and Fuels

This chapter describes the operation of automotive-engine fuel systems and dicusses various types of fuel pumps, carburetors, and other components used in fuel systems. The major part of the chapter is concerned with gasoline-fuel systems with carburetors, since this type of system is by far the most commonly used automotive-engine fuel system.

§ 9–1. PURPOSE OF THE FUEL SYSTEM The fuel system has the job of supplying a combustible mixture of air and fuel to the engine. The fuel system must vary the proportions of air and fuel to suit different operating conditions. When the engine is cold, for example, then the mixture must be rich (have a high proportion of fuel). The reason for this is that the fuel does not vaporize readily at low temperatures. Therefore, extra fuel must be added to the mixture so that there will be enough vaporized fuel to form a combustible mixture (see § 9–19).

§ 9–2. FUEL-SYSTEM COMPONENTS The fuel system consists of the fuel tank, fuel pump, fuel filter, carburetor, intake manifold, and fuel lines, or tubes, connecting the tank, pump, and carburetor (Figs. 9–1 and 9–2). Some gasoline engines use a fuel-injection system; in this system, a fuel-injection pump replaces the carburetor. Details of these components are discussed in following articles.

§ 9–3. FUEL TANK The fuel tank (Fig. 9–3) is normally located at the rear of the vehicle. It is made of sheet metal and is attached to the frame. The filler opening of the tank is closed by a cap. The tank end of the fuel line is attached at or near the bottom of the tank. In some tanks, there is a filtering element at the fuel-line connection. The tank also contains the sending unit of the fuel gauge. The tank may also have a vent pipe which allows air to escape when the tank is being filled (Fig. 9–2).

The free escape of vaporized gasoline from the fuel tank through the vent pipe is considered

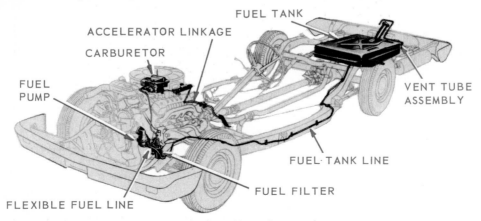

Fig. 9–1. Fuel system for a car with a V-8 engine. *(Ford Motor Company)*

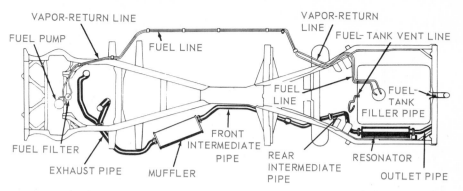

Fig. 9–2. Fuel and exhaust systems in place on a car frame. The carburetor and the engine are not shown. (*Cadillac Motor Car Division of General Motors Corporation*)

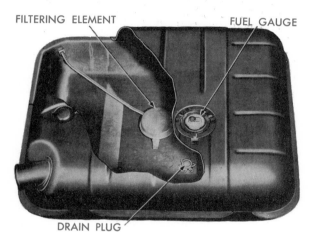

Fig. 9–3. Fuel tank, partly cut away to show the filtering element and the drain plug. (*Chrysler-Plymouth Division of Chrysler Motors Corporation*)

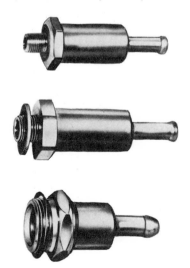

Fig. 9–4. In-line fuel filters. (*Ford Division of Ford Motor Company*)

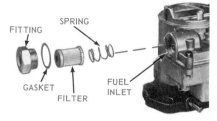

Fig. 9–5. Fuel filter located in the carburetor. (*Buick Motor Division of General Motors Corporation*)

objectionable because it contributes to the formation of smog (see § 9–46). Thus, cars manufactured since 1970 have been equipped with a vehicle vapor recovery system (VVR system). In this system, the fuel-tank vent pipe is connected to a trap, or condenser, which contains the vapor and prevents its escape into the air (§ 9–46).

§ 9–4. FUEL FILTERS AND SCREENS Fuel systems have filters and screens to prevent dirt in the fuel from entering the fuel pump or carburetor. Dirt could, of course, prevent normal operation of these units and cause poor engine performance. One type of filter is incorporated in the fuel pump (Fig. 9–8). It may also be a separate unit connected into the fuel line between the tank and fuel pump or between the fuel pump and carburetor (Fig. 9–1). Or it may be in or on the carburetor itself. Figure 9–4 shows the type that is outside the carburetor but mounted on it. The screw threads enter a tapped hole in the carburetor. The fuel line fits on the opposite end of the filter. Figure 9–5 shows the type that is installed in the carburetor itself. This filter has an element made of pleated paper.

§ 9–5. FUEL GAUGES There are two types of fuel gauge, *balancing coil* and *thermostatic.* Each has a tank unit and a dash unit.

1. *Balancing coil* (Fig. 9–6). The tank unit in this fuel gauge contains a sliding contact that slides back and forth on a resistance as the float moves up and down in the fuel tank. This changes the amount of electric resistance the tank unit offers. Thus, as the tank empties, the float drops and the sliding contact moves to reduce the resistance. The dash unit contains two coils, as shown in Fig. 9–6. When the ignition switch is turned on, current from the battery flows through the two coils. This produces a magnetic pattern that acts on the armature to which the pointer is attached. When the resistance of the tank unit is high (tank filled and float up), then the current flowing through the E (empty) coil also flows through the F (full) coil. Thus the armature is pulled to the right so that the pointer indicates on the F, or "full," side of the dial. But when the tank begins to empty, the resistance of the tank unit drops. Thus, more of the current flowing through the empty coil passes through the tank unit. Since less is flowing through the full coil, its magnetic field is weaker. As a result, the empty coil pulls the armature toward it, and the pointer swings around to indicate toward the E (empty) side of the dial.

2. *Thermostatic* (Fig. 9–7). This gauge has a pair of thermostat blades, each with a heating coil. The coils are connected in series through the ignition switch to the battery. The tank unit also has a float that actuates a cam. The cam, in turning, imposes more or less bending on the tank thermostat blade. When the tank is full, the float is up and the cam puts a considerable bend in the blade.

Then, when the ignition switch is turned on, current flows through the heater coils. When the tank blade is hot enough, it bends farther so that the contacts separate. Then the blade cools, and the points reopen. This action continues as long as the ignition switch is on. Meanwhile, the blade in the dash unit is heated and bends a like amount. Movement of this blade is carried through linkage to the pointer, which then moves to indicate on the "full" side of the dial. However, if the tank is nearly empty, then the float is down and the cam bends the tank thermostat blade only a little. As a result, only a small amount of heating is enough to bend the blade farther and open the contacts. Thus, the dash-unit blade bends only a little, and the pointer indicates toward the "empty" side.

§ 9–6. FUEL PUMPS   The fuel system uses a fuel pump to deliver fuel from the tank to the carburetor. There are two general types of fuel pump, mechanical and electric. Electric fuel pumps are discussed in § 9–9. Mechanical fuel pumps are operated by an eccentric (an off-center section) on the engine camshaft as explained below. The mechanical fuel pump is mounted on the side of the cylinder block in in-line engines. In some V-8 engines, the pump is mounted between the two cylinder banks. Most modern V-8 engines have the fuel pump mounted on the side of the cylinder block, at the front of the engine.

The mechanical fuel pump has a rocker arm, the end of which rests on the camshaft eccentric. Many V-8 engines also use a push rod extending from the eccentric to the rocker arm.

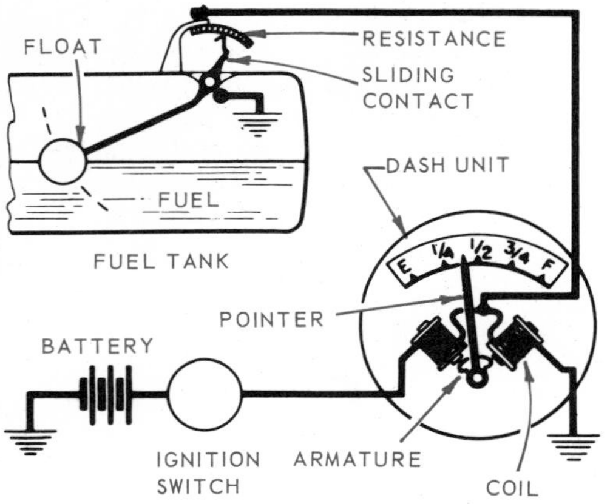

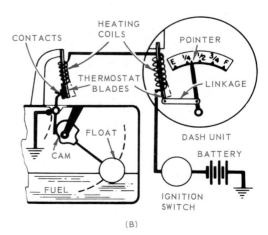

(A)

(B)

Fig. 9–6. Schematic wiring circuit of a balancing-coil fuel-gauge indicating system.

Fig. 9–7. Schematic wiring circuit of a thermostatic fuel-gauge indicating system.

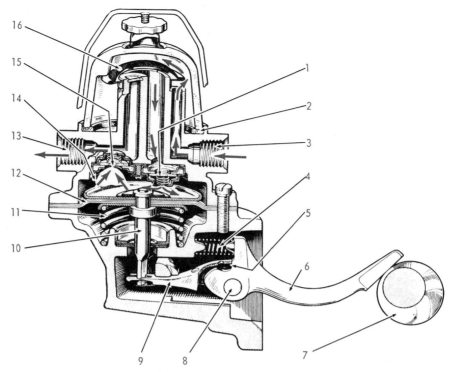

Fig. 9–8. Sectional view of a fuel pump.

1. Inlet valve
2. Joint under cover bowl
3. Fuel inlet
4. Operating-arm return spring
5. Abutment on operating arm
6. Rocker arm
7. Eccentric on camshaft
8. Pivot
9. Connecting link
10. Pull rod
11. Diaphragm return spring
12. Diaphragm
13. Fuel outlet
14. Pump chamber
15. Outlet valve
16. Gauze filter

(Hillman Motor Car Company, Limited)

As the camshaft rotates, the eccentric causes the rocker arm to rock back and forth. The inner end of the rocker arm is linked to a flexible diaphragm which is clamped between the upper and lower pump housings (Fig. 9–8). There is a spring under the diaphragm that maintains tension on the diaphragm. As the rocker arm rocks, it pulls the diaphragm down and then releases it. The spring then forces the diaphragm up. Thus, the diaphragm moves up and down as the rocker arm rocks.

This diaphragm movement alternately produces a partial vacuum and pressure in the space above the diaphragm. When the diaphragm moves down, a partial vacuum is produced. Then, atmospheric pressure, acting on the fuel in the tank, forces fuel through the fuel line and into the pump. The inlet valve in the pump opens to admit fuel, as shown by the arrows in Fig. 9–8. Note that the

fuel first passes through a filter bowl and screen.

When the diaphragm is released by the return movement of the rocker arm, the spring forces the diaphragm upward, producing pressure in the space above the diaphragm. This pressure closes the inlet valve and opens the outlet valve. Now fuel is forced from the fuel pump through the fuel line to the carburetor.

The actions in the pump as the eccentric rotates are shown in Figs. 9–9 and 9–10. The fuel from the fuel pump enters the carburetor past a needle valve in the float bowl. If the bowl is full, the needle valve closes so that no fuel can enter. When this happens, the fuel pump cannot deliver fuel to the carburetor. In this case, the rocker arm continues to rock. However, the diaphragm remains at or near its lower limit of travel; its spring cannot force the diaphragm upward so long as the carburetor float bowl will not accept further fuel.

141

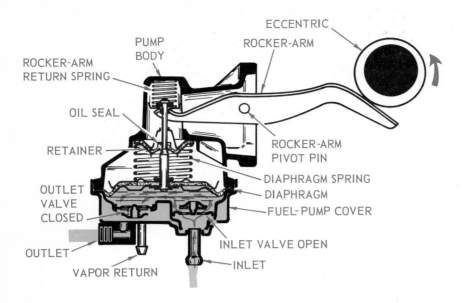

ECCENTRIC

Fig. 9–9. When the eccentric rotates so as to push the rocker arm down, the arm pulls the diaphragm up. The inlet valve opens to admit fuel into the space under the diaphragm.

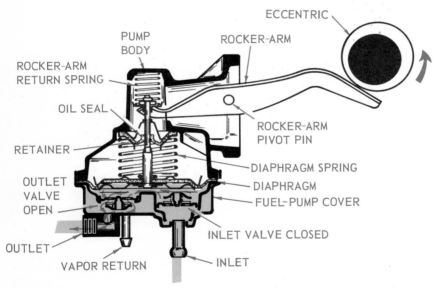

ECCENTRIC

Fig. 9–10. When the eccentric rotates so as to allow the rocker arm to move up under it, the diaphragm is released so it can move down, producing pressure under it. This pressure closes the inlet valve and opens the outlet valve so fuel flows to the carburetor.

However, as the carburetor uses up fuel, the needle valve opens to admit fuel to the float bowl. Now the diaphragm can move up (on the rocker-arm return stroke) to force fuel into the carburetor float bowl.

§ 9–7. VAPOR-RETURN LINE Note that the fuel system shown in Fig. 9–2 has a vapor-return line running from the fuel pump to the fuel tank. This line is installed on many cars having air conditioning. With air conditioning, under-the-hood temperatures are likely to be higher. The air-condi-

tioning condenser delivers more heat under the hood. Also, during idle the engine cooling system is relatively inefficient, and this allows under-the-hood temperatures to increase. The higher temperatures tend to cause vapor to form in the fuel pump.

To understand why vapor can form in the fuel pump, let us note first that the pump alternately produces vacuum and pressure. During the vacuum phase, the boiling, or vaporizing, temperature of the fuel goes down. The lower the pressure, the lower the temperature at which any liquid

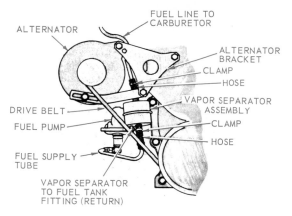

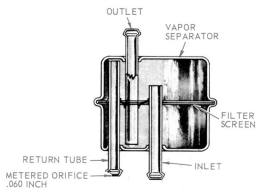

Fig. 9–11. Top, location of the fuel vapor separator, in line between the fuel pump and the carburetor, on V-8 engine. Bottom, enlarged sectional view of fuel vapor separator. *(Chrysler-Plymouth Division of Chrysler Motors Corporation)*

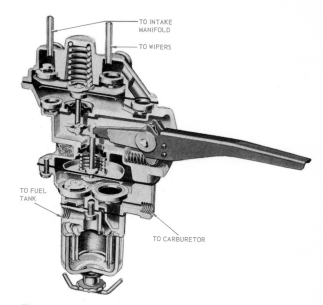

Fig. 9–12. Cutaway view of a fuel and vacuum pump. The vacuum unit is at the top; the fuel pump is at the bottom. *(Lincoln-Mercury Division of Ford Motor Company)*

vaporizes. For example, water boils at 212°F at sea level—atmospheric pressure 14.7 psi (pounds per square inch)—see § 3–22. But at 16,000 feet above sea level, where the pressure is around 7 psi, water boils at 185°F.

The combination of increased temperature and partial vacuum in the fuel pump can cause fuel to vaporize. This produces vapor lock, a condition that prevents normal delivery of fuel to the carburetor so that the engine stalls.

The vapor-return line, which is connected to a special outlet in the fuel pump, allows the vapor to return to the fuel tank. At the same time, the vapor-return line permits excess fuel being pumped by the fuel pump to return to the fuel tank. This additional fuel, in constant circulation, helps to keep the fuel pump cool and thus prevent vapor from forming.

Some cars have a vapor separator connected between the fuel pump and the carburetor (Fig. 9–11). It consists of a sealed can, a filter screen, an inlet and outlet fitting, and a metered orifice for the return line to the fuel tank. Any fuel vapor that the fuel pump produces enters the vapor separator (as bubbles) along with fuel. These bubbles of vapor rise to the top of the vapor separator, and the vapor then is forced, by fuel-pump pressure, to pass through the fuel-return line and back to the fuel tank, where it then condenses back into liquid fuel.

§ 9–8. COMBINATION PUMPS These pumps contain not only a fuel pump, such as has been described above, but also a vacuum pump (Fig. 9–12). The vacuum pump provides a vacuum to operate vacuum-type windshield wipers. The vacuum pump is similar in construction and action to the fuel pump. It has a pair of valves and a spring-loaded diaphragm. However, it pumps air instead of fuel, producing a vacuum as it does so.

§ 9–9. ELECTRIC FUEL PUMPS There are various types of electric fuel pumps. One of the latest types is mounted in the fuel tank (Fig. 9–13). It contains an impeller which is driven by an electric motor (Fig. 9–14). This pushes fuel through the fuel line to the carburetor. Other types of

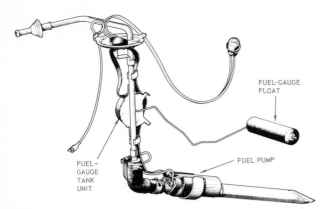

Fig. 9-13. Location of electric fuel pump in fuel tank. It is mounted on the same support as the fuel-gauge tank unit. *(Buick Motor Division of General Motors Corporation)*

electric fuel pumps are mounted in the engine compartment. One design is shown in Fig. 9-15. It contains a flexible metal bellows that is operated by an electromagnet. When the electromagnet is connected to the battery (by turning on the ignition switch), it pulls down the armature and thereby extends the bellows. This produces a vacuum in the bellows; fuel from the fuel tank enters the bellows through the inlet valve. Then, as the armature reaches its lower limit of travel, it opens a set of contact points. This disconnects the electromagnet from the battery. The return spring therefore pushes the armature up and collapses the bellows. This forces fuel from the bellows through the outlet valve and to the carburetor. As the armature reaches the upper limit

of its travel, it closes the contacts so that the electromagnet is again energized and pulls the armature down once more. This series of actions is repeated as long as the ignition switch is turned on.

§ 9-10. AIR CLEANERS As already noted, the fuel system mixes air and fuel to produce a combustible mixture. A great deal of air passes through the carburetor and engine—as much as 100,000 cubic feet of air every 1,000 car miles. This is a great volume of air, and it is likely to contain a great amount of floating dust and grit. The grit and dust could, if they entered the engine, cause serious engine damage. Therefore an air cleaner is mounted on the air horn, or air entrance, of the carburetor to keep out the dirt (Fig. 9-16). All air entering the engine through the carburetor must first pass through the air cleaner. The upper part of the air cleaner contains a ring of filter material (fine-mesh metal threads or ribbons, special paper, cellulose fiber, or polyurethane) through which the air must pass. This material provides a fine maze that traps most of the dust particles. Some air cleaners have an oil bath. This is a reservoir of oil past which the incoming air must flow. The moving air picks up particles of oil and carries them up into the filter. There the oil washes accumulated dust back down into the oil reservoir. The oiliness of the filter material also improves the filtering action.

The air cleaner also muffles the noise resulting from the intake of air through the carburetor, muffler, and valve ports. This noise would be quite

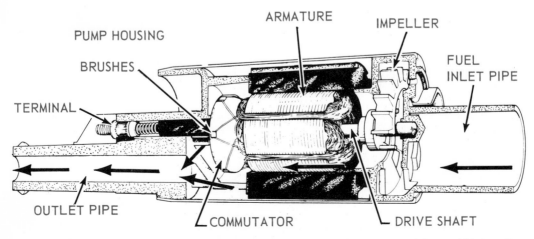

Fig. 9-14. Cutaway view of tank-mounted electric fuel pump. *(Buick Motor Division of General Motors Corporation)*

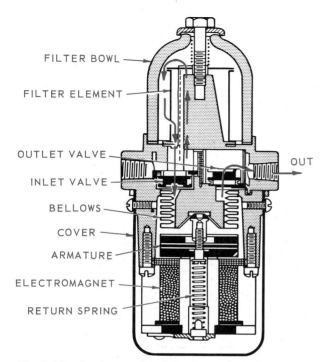

FILTER BOWL

FILTER ELEMENT

OUTLET VALVE

INLET VALVE

BELLOWS

COVER

ARMATURE

ELECTROMAGNET

RETURN SPRING

OUT

Fig. 9–15. Sectional view of an electric fuel pump.

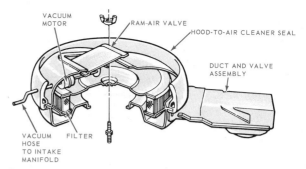

VACUUM
MOTOR

RAM-AIR VALVE

HOOD-TO-AIR CLEANER SEAL

DUCT AND VALVE
ASSEMBLY

VACUUM
HOSE
TO INTAKE
MANIFOLD

FILTER

Fig. 9–17. Ram-air air cleaner with ram-air valve shown open. *(Ford Motor Company)*

noticeable if it were not for the air cleaner. In addition, the air cleaner acts as a flame arrester in case the engine backfires through the carburetor. Backfiring may occur at certain times as a result of ignition of the air-fuel mixture in the cylinder before the intake valve closes. When this happens, there is a momentary flashback through the carburetor. The air cleaner prevents this flame from erupting from the carburetor and possibly igniting gasoline fumes outside the engine.

Some late-model cars have a ram-air air cleaner (Fig. 9–17). It allows additional air to be forced into the air cleaner during open throttle or heavy-

load operation. Under these conditions, a vacuum motor, connected to the intake manifold by a vacuum hose, operates to open a ram-air valve, as shown in Fig. 9–17. This valve is in line with the air scoop on the engine hood, and when it opens, extra air from the air scoop is forced into the carburetor. This improves engine performance under these conditions. At other times, the manifold vacuum is great enough to hold the ram-air valve closed, and air enters the filter through the snorkel tube or duct and valve assembly (see § 9–11) in the normal manner.

§ 9–11. THERMOSTATICALLY CONTROLLED AIR CLEANER

The thermostatically controlled air cleaner is part of a controlled combustion system (CCS) or an improved combustion system (IMCO) used on many late-model cars. The CCS and IMCO are explained in § 9–46. The CCS and IMCO include leaner carburetor calibration at idle and part throttle plus leaner choke calibration. These leaner calibrations could cause reduced engine performance at low air temperatures. To correct for this condition, the thermostatically controlled air cleaner is used. This is also called the heated air system (HAS) by General Motors because it injects heat into the air going into the carburetor during cold weather when the engine is cold (Fig. 9–18). This improves engine performance after a cold start and during engine warm-up. Thus, the leaner calibrations, which reduce the amount of smog-causing unburned fuel in the exhaust, can be used without sacrificing cold-engine performance.

One air cleaner of this type is shown in Fig. 9–19. It contains a sensing spring which reacts to the temperature of the air entering the carburetor through the air cleaner. This spring controls an air-bleed valve (see Fig. 9–20). When the

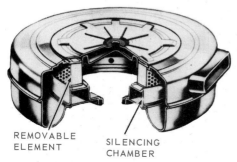

REMOVABLE
ELEMENT

SILENCING
CHAMBER

Fig. 9–16. Typical air cleaner, partly cut away to show the filter element. *(Ford Motor Company)*

145

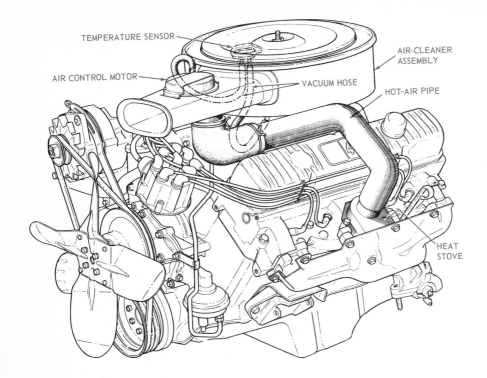

TEMPERATURE SENSOR

AIR-CLEANER ASSEMBLY

AIR CONTROL MOTOR

VACUUM HOSE

HOT-AIR PIPE

HEAT STOVE

Fig. 9–18. Heated air system installed on a V-8 engine. *(Buick Motor Division of General Motors Corporation)*

entering air is cold, the sensing spring holds the bleed valve closed. Now, intake-manifold vacuum is applied to the vacuum chamber so that the diaphragm is pushed upward by atmospheric pressure and the diaphragm spring is compressed. In this position, linkage from the diaphragm raises the control-damper assembly so that the snorkel

tube is blocked off. All air now has to enter from the hot-air pipe. This pipe is connected to the heat stove on the exhaust manifold. Therefore, as soon as the engine starts and the exhaust manifold begins to warm up, hot air is delivered to the carburetor and engine. This improves cold and warm-up operation.

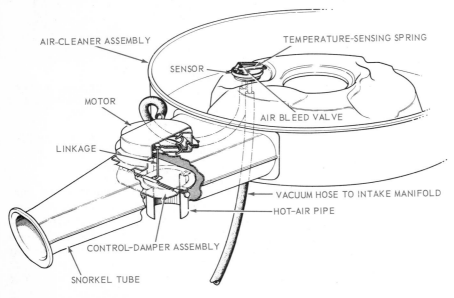

AIR-CLEANER ASSEMBLY

TEMPERATURE-SENSING SPRING

SENSOR

MOTOR

AIR BLEED VALVE

LINKAGE

VACUUM HOSE TO INTAKE MANIFOLD

HOT-AIR PIPE

CONTROL-DAMPER ASSEMBLY

SNORKEL TUBE

Fig. 9–19. Air cleaner with thermostatic control. *(Chevrolet Motor Division of General Motors Corporation)*

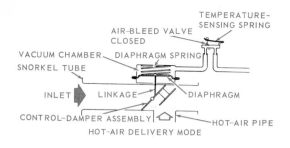

TEMPERATURE-SENSING SPRING

AIR-BLEED VALVE CLOSED

VACUUM CHAMBER — DIAPHRAGM SPRING
SNORKEL TUBE

INLET   LINKAGE   DIAPHRAGM

CONTROL-DAMPER ASSEMBLY   HOT-AIR PIPE

HOT-AIR DELIVERY MODE

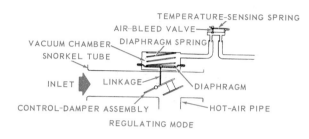

TEMPERATURE-SENSING SPRING

AIR-BLEED VALVE
VACUUM CHAMBER — DIAPHRAGM SPRING
SNORKEL TUBE

INLET   LINKAGE   DIAPHRAGM

CONTROL-DAMPER ASSEMBLY   HOT-AIR PIPE

REGULATING MODE

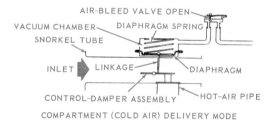

AIR-BLEED VALVE OPEN
VACUUM CHAMBER — DIAPHRAGM SPRING
SNORKEL TUBE

INLET   LINKAGE   DIAPHRAGM

CONTROL-DAMPER ASSEMBLY   HOT-AIR PIPE

COMPARTMENT (COLD AIR) DELIVERY MODE

Fig. 9–20. Operational modes for air cleaner with thermostatic control. *(Chevrolet Motor Division of General Motors Corporation)*

As the engine begins to warm up, the ingoing air during the hot-air delivery mode (see top, Fig. 9–20) goes above 100°F. This causes the temperature-sensing spring to raise the air bleed partly. Now, some air can bleed into the line to the intake manifold, and this reduces the vacuum at the diaphragm. The spring therefore pushes the diaphragm part of the way down so that the control damper moves away from the closed-snorkel position. It assumes a position that permits some cold air from the engine compartment to mix with the hot air from the heat stove (center, Fig. 9–20). The combination is of the correct proportions to provide an air temperature of about 100°F.

As the engine compartment heats up and reaches a temperature of 100°F or above, the air bleed is opened wide by the temperature-sensing spring. This reduces the vacuum above the diaphragm so much that the diaphragm spring can push the con-

trol damper all the way down, as shown at the bottom in Fig. 9–20. Now, all air entering the air cleaner and carburetor is taken from the engine compartment.

A similar thermostatically controlled air cleaner is shown in Figs. 9–21 and 9–22. This design, however, has a thermostatic bulb that acts directly on the valve plate. When the engine is cold, the thermostatic bulb has positioned the valve plate as shown in Fig. 9–22 so that all ingoing air must come from the hot-air duct which is connected to a shroud around the exhaust manifold. As the engine warms up, the hotter air from the shroud causes the thermostatic bulb to start moving the valve plate. Thus, some air begins to enter from the engine compartment. With further increases of temperature, the valve plate moves farther so that more compartment air enters. When the engine compartment becomes hot, then most or all ingoing air comes from the engine compartment.

The design shown in Figs. 9–21 and 9–22 includes a vacuum override motor. This motor operates on intake-manifold vacuum. During cold-engine acceleration, when additional air is needed, the motor overrides the thermostatic control to open the system to both engine compartment and heated air so that adequate air is delivered to the carburetor.

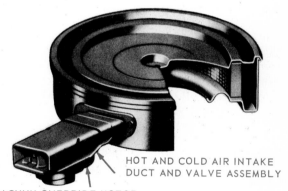

HOT AND COLD AIR INTAKE DUCT AND VALVE ASSEMBLY

VACUUM OVERRIDE MOTOR

Fig. 9–21. Air cleaner with thermostatic control. *(Ford Division of Ford Motor Company)*

§ 9–12. CARBURETION Carburetion is the mixing of the gasoline fuel with air so that a combustible mixture is obtained. The carburetor performs this job, supplying a combustible mixture of varying degrees of richness to suit engine operating conditions. The mixture must be rich (have a higher percentage of fuel) for starting, acceleration, and

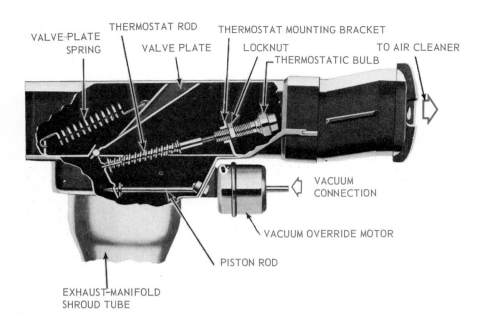

VALVE-PLATE SPRING — THERMOSTAT ROD — THERMOSTAT MOUNTING BRACKET — VALVE PLATE — LOCKNUT — TO AIR CLEANER — THERMOSTATIC BULB — VACUUM CONNECTION — VACUUM OVERRIDE MOTOR — PISTON ROD — EXHAUST-MANIFOLD SHROUD TUBE

Fig. 9–22. Cutaway view of hot- and cold-air intake ducts and valve assembly used with air cleaner in previous illustration. *(Ford Division of Ford Motor Company)*

high-speed operation. And it should lean out (become less rich) for operation at intermediate speed with a warm engine. The carburetor has several different *circuits*, or passages, through which fuel and air-fuel mixture flow under different operating conditions to produce the varying richness of the air-fuel mixture. All this is explained in the following articles.

§ 9–13. VAPORIZATION When a liquid changes to a vapor (undergoes a *change of state*), it is said to evaporate. Water placed in an open pan will evaporate: it changes from a liquid to a vapor. Clothes hung on a line will dry: the water in the clothes turns to vapor. When the clothes are well spread out, they will dry more rapidly than when they are bunched together. This illustrates an important fact about evaporation. The greater the surface exposed, the more rapidly evaporation takes place. A pint of water in a tall glass will take quite a while to evaporate. But a pint of water in a shallow pan will evaporate much more quickly (Fig. 9–23).

§ 9–14. ATOMIZATION In order to produce very quick vaporization of the liquid gasoline, it is sprayed into the air passing through the carburetor. Spraying the liquid turns it into many fine droplets. This effect is called *atomization* because the liquid is broken up into small droplets (but not actually broken up into atoms, as the name implies). Each droplet is exposed to air on all

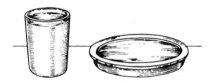

Fig. 9–23. Water will evaporate from the shallow pan faster than from the glass: the greater the area exposed to air, the faster the evaporation.

sides so that it vaporizes very quickly. Thus, during normal running of the engine, the gasoline sprayed into the air passing through the carburetor turns to vapor, or vaporizes, almost instantly.

§ 9–15. CARBURETOR FUNDAMENTALS A simple carburetor could be made from a round cylinder with a constricted section, a fuel nozzle, and a round disk, or valve (Fig. 9–24). The round cylinder is called the *air horn*, the constricted section the *venturi*, and the valve the *throttle valve*. The throttle valve can be tilted more or less to open or close the air horn (Fig. 9–25). When the throttle is turned to the horizontal position, it shuts off, or *throttles*, the air flow through the air horn. When the throttle is turned away from this position, air can flow through the air horn.

§ 9–16. VENTURI EFFECT As air flows through the constriction, or venturi, a partial vacuum is produced at the venturi. This vacuum then causes

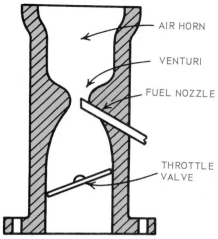

Fig. 9-24. Simple carburetor consisting of an air horn, a fuel nozzle, and a throttle valve.

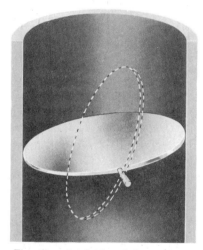

Fig. 9-25. Throttle valve in the air horn of a carburetor. When the throttle is closed, as shown, little air can pass through. But when the throttle is opened, as shown dashed, there is little throttling effect.

the fuel nozzle to deliver a spray of gasoline into the passing air stream. The venturi effect (of producing a vacuum) can be illustrated with the setup shown in Fig. 9-26. Here, three dishes of mercury (a very heavy metallic liquid) are connected by tubes to an air horn with a venturi. The greater the vacuum, the higher the mercury is pushed up in the tube by atmospheric pressure. Note that the greatest vacuum is right at the venturi. Also, it should be remembered that the faster the air flows through, the greater the vacuum.

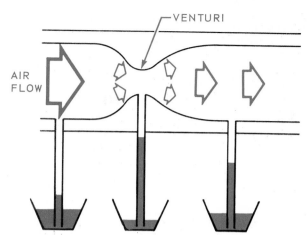

Fig. 9-26. Three dishes of mercury and tubes connected to an air horn show differences in vacuum by the distance the mercury rises in the tubes. The venturi has the highest vacuum.

You can visualize the reason for the vacuum in the venturi if you remember that the air is made up of countless molecules. A simple explanation of the cause might be as follows: As air moves into the top of the air horn, all the air molecules are moving at the same speed. But if all are to get through the venturi, they must speed up and move through faster. For instance, let us see what happens to two molecules, one behind the other. As the first molecule enters the venturi, it speeds up, tending to leave the second molecule behind. The second molecule, as it enters the venturi, also speeds up. But the first molecule has, in effect, a head start. Thus, the two molecules are farther apart in the venturi than they were before they entered it: Now visualize a great number of particles going through the same action. Note that as they pass through the venturi, they are farther apart than before they entered. This is just another way of saying that a partial vacuum exists in the venturi. A partial vacuum is a thinning out of the air, a more than normal distance between air molecules.

§ 9-17. FUEL-NOZZLE ACTION The partial vacuum occurs in the venturi, just where the end of the fuel nozzle is located. The other end of the fuel nozzle is in a fuel reservoir (the float bowl), as shown in Fig. 9-27. With the vacuum at the upper end of the nozzle, atmospheric pressure (working through a vent in the float-bowl cover) pushes fuel up through the nozzle and out into the passing air stream. The fuel enters the air

149

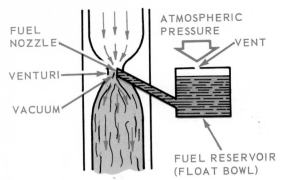

Fig. 9-27. Venturi, or constriction, causes a vacuum to develop in the air stream just below the constriction. Then atmospheric pressure pushes fuel up and out the fuel nozzle.

stream as a fine spray which quickly turns into vapor as the droplets of fuel evaporate. The more air that flows through the air horn, the greater the vacuum in the venturi and the more fuel delivered.

§ 9-18. THROTTLE-VALVE ACTION As already mentioned, the throttle valve can be tilted in the air horn to allow more or less air to flow through (Fig. 9-25). When it is tilted to allow more air to flow through, then larger amounts of air-fuel mixture are delivered to the engine. The engine develops more power and tends to run faster. But if the throttle valve is tilted so as to throttle off most of the air, then only small amounts of air-fuel mixture are delivered, and the engine produces less power and tends to slow down. Linkage between the throttle valve and an accelerator pedal in the driver's compartment permits the driver to position the throttle valve to suit operating requirements (Fig. 9-28).

§ 9-19. AIR-FUEL RATIO REQUIREMENTS As already noted, the fuel system must vary the air-fuel ratio to suit different operating requirements. The mixture must be rich (have a high proportion of fuel) for starting but must be relatively lean

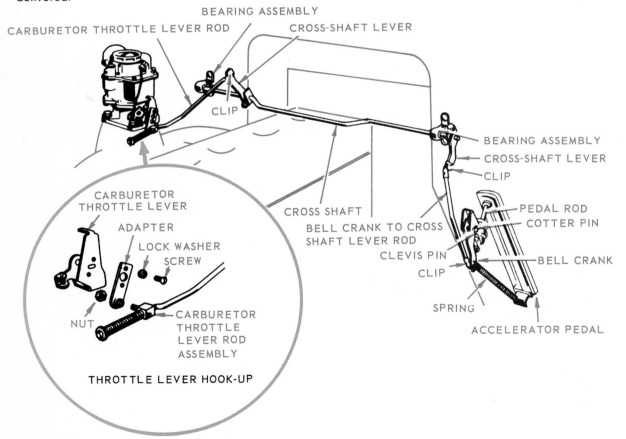

Fig. 9-28. Linkage between the accelerator pedal and the carburetor throttle valve.

(have a lower proportion of fuel) for part-throttle intermediate-speed operation. Figure 9–29 is a graph showing typical air-fuel ratios as related to various car speeds. Ratios and speeds at which they are obtained vary with different cars. In the example shown, a rich mixture of about 9:1 (9 pounds of air for each pound of fuel) is supplied for initial starting. Then, during idle, the mixture leans out to about 12:1. At intermediate speeds, the mixture further leans out to about 15:1. But at higher speeds, with a wide-open throttle, the mixture is enriched to about 13:1. Opening of the throttle at any speed for acceleration causes a momentary enrichment of the mixture. Two examples of this are shown in Fig. 9–29 [at about 20 mph (miles per hour) and at about 30 mph].

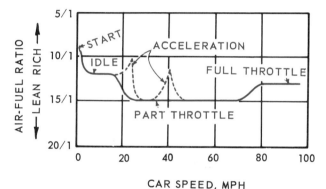

CAR SPEED, MPH

Fig. 9–29. Graph of air-fuel ratios for different car speeds. The graph is typical, but car speeds at which the various ratios are obtained may vary with different cars. Also, there may be some variation in the ratios.

It would appear, from the above discussion, that the engine itself demands a greatly varying air-fuel ratio for the different operating conditions. This is not quite true. For example, the mixture must be very rich for initial start, because the fuel vaporizes very poorly under this condition. The engine and carburetor are cold, the air speed is low, and much of the fuel does not vaporize. Thus, an extra amount of fuel must be delivered by the carburetor so that enough will vaporize for starting. Likewise, sudden opening of the throttle for acceleration allows a sudden inrush of air. Extra fuel must enter at the same time (that is, the mixture must be enriched), because only part of the fuel vaporizes and mixes with the ingoing air to provide the proper proportions of air and fuel to the engine.

The following articles describe the various cir-

cuits in carburetors that supply the required air-fuel mixture for different operating conditions.

§ 9–20. CARBURETOR CIRCUITS The various circuits in the carburetor are:

1. Float circuit
2. Idling- and low-speed circuit
3. High-speed part-load circuit
4. High-speed full-power circuit
5. Accelerator-pump circuit
6. Choke

The following articles discuss each of these in detail.

§ 9–21. FLOAT CIRCUIT The float circuit includes the float bowl and a float and needle-valve arrangement. The float and the needle valve operate to maintain a constant level of fuel in the float bowl. If the level is too high, then too much fuel will feed from the fuel nozzle. If it is too low, too little fuel will feed. In either event, poor engine performance will result. Figure 9–30 is a simplified drawing of the float system. If fuel enters the float bowl faster than it is withdrawn, the fuel level will rise. This will cause the float to move up and push the needle valve into the valve seat.

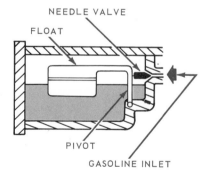

Fig. 9–30. Simplified drawing of a carburetor float system.

This, in turn, shuts off the fuel inlet so that no fuel can enter. Then, if the fuel level drops, the float moves down and releases the needle so that the fuel inlet is opened. Now fuel can enter. In actual operation, the fuel is maintained at a practically constant level. The float tends to hold the needle valve partly closed so that the incoming fuel just balances the fuel being withdrawn.

Figure 9–31 shows an actual carburetor with a dual float assembly partly cut away so that the

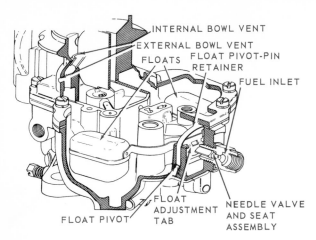

INTERNAL BOWL VENT
EXTERNAL BOWL VENT
FLOATS
FLOAT PIVOT-PIN RETAINER
FUEL INLET
FLOAT PIVOT
FLOAT ADJUSTMENT TAB
NEEDLE VALVE AND SEAT ASSEMBLY

Fig. 9-31. Carburetor partly cut away to show the float circuit. *(American Motors Corporation)*

two floats can be seen. The carburetor has a float bowl that partly surrounds the carburetor air horn. The two floats are attached by a U-shaped lever and operate a single needle valve. Figure 9-32 shows the float circuit for a four-barrel carburetor. This carburetor is, in effect, two two-barrel carburetors. The primary barrels supply the engine during most operating conditions, but the secondary barrels come into operation for improved acceleration and high-speed performance. Note that this carburetor has two separate float circuits, each with its own double-float assembly. The two float bowls are connected by a balance passage to assure equal fuel levels and air pressures in the two bowls.

§ 9-22. FLOAT-BOWL VENTS The float bowls of many carburetors are vented into the carburetor

air horn at a point above the choke valve. The carburetor shown in Fig. 9-32 is vented in this manner. The purpose of this arrangement is to equalize the effect of a clogged air cleaner. For example, suppose that the air cleaner has become clogged with dirt so that the passage of air through it is restricted. This means that a partial vacuum will develop in the carburetor air horn. As a result, a somewhat greater vacuum is applied to the fuel nozzle (since this vacuum is added to the venturi vacuum). If the float-bowl vent opens externally to the atmosphere (as shown in Fig. 9-27), the atmospheric pressure will then cause greater amounts of fuel to be delivered. The mixture will be too rich.

However, if the float bowl is vented internally into the carburetor air horn, then there will be a balance between the float bowl and air horn; air pressure will be the same in both. The effect of a clogged air cleaner is eliminated. Carburetors vented in this manner are called *balanced* carburetors. Carburetors with float bowls vented to the atmosphere are *unbalanced* carburetors.

Some carburetors are equipped with a special mechanical valve which permits either external or internal venting to suit different operating conditions. When a hot engine is idling or operating at low speeds, under-the-hood temperatures go up excessively. This causes gasoline vapors to form in the float bowl. An internally vented bowl would feed these vapors to the carburetor air horn and could unduly enrich the mixture, causing poor engine performance. The carburetor shown in Fig. 9-33 has a special valve, linked to the throttle-valve shaft, which vents the float bowl externally (as shown in the circle) when the throttle is closed. This allows any fuel vapors that form in the

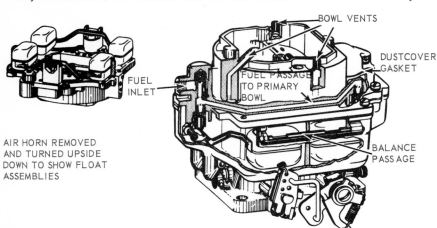

BOWL VENTS
DUSTCOVER GASKET
FUEL INLET
FUEL PASSAGE TO PRIMARY BOWL
BALANCE PASSAGE

AIR HORN REMOVED AND TURNED UPSIDE DOWN TO SHOW FLOAT ASSEMBLIES

Fig. 9-32. Float system of a four-barrel carburetor. *(Oldsmobile Division of General Motors Corporation)*

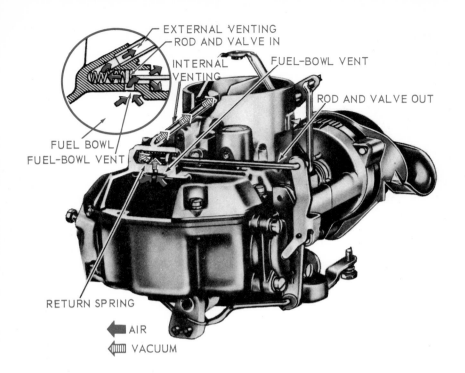

EXTERNAL VENTING
ROD AND VALVE IN

INTERNAL VENTING

FUEL-BOWL VENT

ROD AND VALVE OUT

FUEL BOWL
FUEL-BOWL VENT

RETURN SPRING

AIR

VACUUM

Fig. 9–33. Mechanically operated float-bowl venting system. *(Lincoln-Mercury Division of Ford Motor Company)*

bowl during hot idle to vent into the atmosphere, where they cannot cause an overrich mixture. Then, when the throttle is opened, the valve is pulled out past the float-bowl vent so the float bowl becomes vented internally to the carburetor air horn, as shown to the right in Fig. 9–33.

Another method of taking care of the excessive enriching of the mixture as a result of high idle temperatures is to use a thermostatic valve to admit additional air (Fig. 9–34). When under-the-hood temperatures are high, the thermostatic blade warps and lifts the valve off its seat. Now, air can flow through a special air passage to the intake manifold, thus compensating for the increased richness of the air-fuel mixture from the idle circuit. This valve is also called an *idle compensator*.

Some carburetors are vented both internally and externally by a combination vent (Fig. 9–31). This assures proper air pressure above the fuel under all operating conditions. At the same time, venting the bowl with the small external vent will improve hot-idle and low-speed operation by permitting fuel vapors that form in the float bowl to vent into the atmosphere.

§ 9–23. IDLE AND LOW-SPEED CIRCUITS

When the throttle is closed or only slightly opened, only a small amount of air can pass through the air

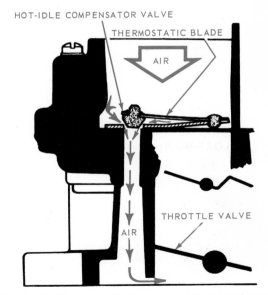

HOT-IDLE COMPENSATOR VALVE

THERMOSTATIC BLADE

AIR

AIR

THROTTLE VALVE

Fig. 9–34. Thermostatically operated float-bowl venting system, using a hot-idle air valve. *(Pontiac Motor Division of General Motors Corporation)*

horn. The air speed is low, and practically no vacuum develops in the venturi. This means that the fuel nozzle will not feed fuel. Thus, the carburetor must have another circuit to supply fuel

153

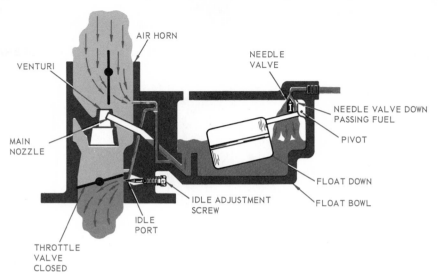

Fig. 9–35. Idle and low-speed circuit in a carburetor. The throttle valve is closed so that only a small amount of air can get past it, and all fuel is being fed past the idle adjustment screw. The dark color is fuel; the light color is air.

during operation with a closed or slightly opened throttle.

This circuit, called the *idle and low-speed circuit,* is shown in operation in a typical carburetor in Fig. 9–35. It consists of passages through which air and fuel can flow. With the throttle closed as shown, there is a high vacuum below the throttle valve from the intake manifold. Atmospheric pressure pushes air and fuel through the passages as shown. They mix and flow past the tapered point of the idle adjustment screw. The mixture has a

high proportion of fuel (is very rich). It leans out somewhat as it mixes with the small amount of air that gets past the closed throttle valve. But the final mixture is still satisfactorily rich (see Fig. 9–29) for good idling. The mixture richness can be adjusted by turning the idle adjustment screw in or out to permit less or more air-fuel mixture to flow past the screw.

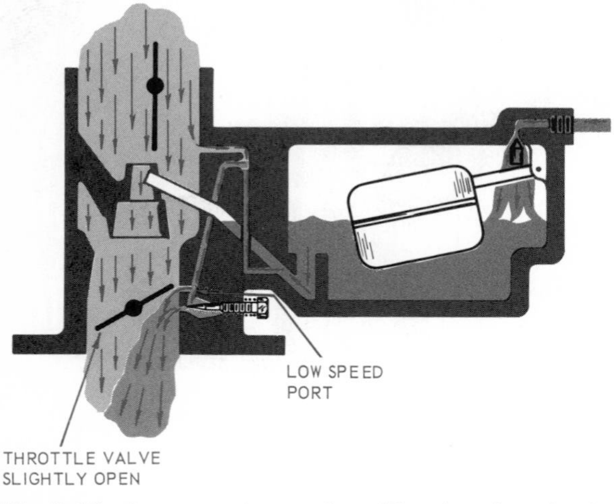

§ 9–24. LOW-SPEED OPERATION When the throttle is opened slightly, as shown in Fig. 9–36, the edge of the throttle valve moves past the low-speed port in the side of the air horn. This port is a vertical slot or a series of small holes one above the other. Additional fuel is thus fed into the intake manifold through the low-speed port. This fuel mixes with the additional air moving past the slightly opened throttle valve to provide sufficient mixture richness for part-throttle low-speed operation.

Some air bleeds around the throttle plate through the low-speed port when the edge of the throttle is only part way past this port. This air improves the atomization of the fuel discharging from the low-speed port.

§ 9–25. OTHER IDLE AND LOW-SPEED CIRCUITS There are many varieties of idle and low-speed circuits in addition to the one shown in Figs. 9–35 and 9–36. In two-barrel carburetors, each barrel has its own idle and low-speed circuit. In many

Fig. 9–36. Low-speed operation. The throttle valve is slightly open and fuel is being fed through the low-speed port as well as through the idle port. The dark color is fuel; the light color is air.

four-barrel carburetors, only the primary barrels have idle and low-speed circuits (§ 9–39).

§ 9–26. HIGH-SPEED PART-LOAD CIRCUIT

When the throttle valve is opened sufficiently so that its edge moves well past the low-speed port, there is little difference in vacuum between the upper and lower part of the air horn. Thus, little air-fuel mixture will discharge from the low-speed port. However, under this condition, enough air is moving through the air horn to produce an appreciable vacuum in the venturi. As a result, the fuel nozzle centered in the venturi (called the *main nozzle* or the *high-speed nozzle*) begins to discharge fuel (as explained in § 9–17). The main nozzle supplies the fuel during operation with the throttle partly to fully opened. Figure 9–37 shows this action. The circuit from the float bowl to the main nozzle is called the *high-speed circuit*.

The wider the throttle is opened and the faster the air flows through the air horn, the greater the vacuum in the venturi. This means that additional fuel will be discharged from the main nozzle (because of the greater vacuum). As a result, a nearly constant air-fuel ratio is maintained by the high-speed circuit from part- to wide-open throttle.

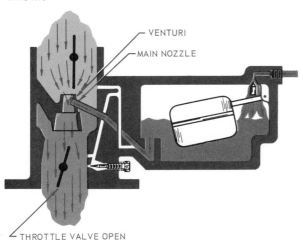

Fig. 9–37. High-speed circuit in carburetor. The throttle valve is open, and fuel is being fed through the high-speed, or main, nozzle. The dark color is fuel; the light color is air.

§ 9–27. FULL-POWER CIRCUIT

For high-speed full-power wide-open-throttle operation, the air-fuel mixture must be enriched (see Fig. 9–29). Additional devices are incorporated in the carburetor to provide this enriched mixture during high-speed full-power operation. They are operated mechanically or by intake-manifold vacuum.

§ 9–28. MECHANICALLY OPERATED FULL-POWER CIRCUIT

This circuit includes a metering-rod jet (a carefully calibrated orifice) and metering rod with two or more steps of different diameters (Fig. 9–38). The metering rod is attached to the throttle linkage (Fig. 9–39). When the throttle is opened, the metering rod is lifted. But when the throttle is partly closed, then the larger diameter of the metering rod is in the metering-rod jet. This somewhat restricts fuel flow to the main nozzle. However, adequate amounts of fuel do flow for normal part-throttle operation. When the throttle is opened wide, the rod is lifted enough to cause the smaller diameter, or step, to move up into the metering-rod jet. Now, the jet is less restricted, and more fuel can flow. The main nozzle

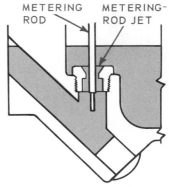

Fig. 9–38. Metering rod and metering-rod jet, for better performance at full throttle.

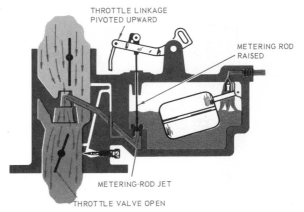

Fig. 9–39. Mechanically operated, full-power circuit. When the throttle is opened, as shown, the metering rod is raised so the smaller diameter of the rod clears the jet, allowing additional fuel to flow.

155

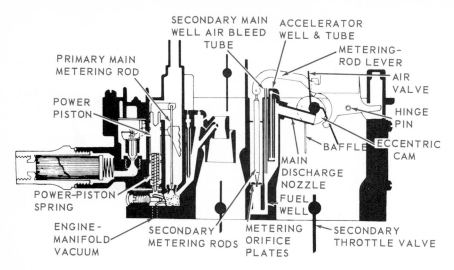

Primary main metering rod, Power piston, Power piston spring, Engine-manifold vacuum, Secondary metering rods, Secondary main well air bleed tube, Accelerator well & tube, Metering-rod lever, Air valve, Hinge pin, Eccentric cam, Baffle, Main discharge nozzle, Fuel well, Metering orifice plates, Secondary throttle valve

Fig. 9–40. Sectional view of a carburetor using a power piston actuated by intake-manifold vacuum to control the position of the metering rod. *(Buick Motor Division of General Motors Corporation)*

is therefore supplied with more fuel, and the resulting air-fuel mixture is richer.

§ 9–29. VACUUM-OPERATED FULL-POWER CIRCUIT
This circuit is operated by intake-manifold vacuum. It includes a vacuum piston or diaphragm linked to a valve or a metering rod similar to the one shown in Fig. 9–38. One design is shown in Fig. 9–40. During part-throttle operation, the piston is held in the lower position by intake-manifold vacuum. However, when the throttle is opened wide, manifold vacuum is reduced, and this allows the spring under the vacuum piston to push the

piston upward. This motion raises the metering rod so that the smaller diameter of the rod clears the jet. Now, more fuel can flow to handle the full-power requirements of the engine.

A carburetor using a spring-loaded diaphragm to control the position of the metering rod is shown in Fig. 9–41. The action is similar to that of the carburetor using a spring-loaded piston. When the throttle is opened so that intake-manifold vacuum is reduced, the spring raises the diaphragm, and this allows the metering rod to be lifted so that its smaller diameter clears the jet, thus allowing more fuel to flow.

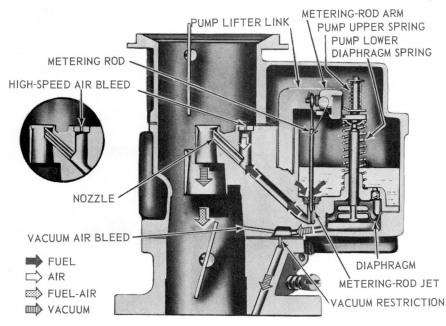

Metering rod, High-speed air bleed, Pump lifter link, Metering-rod arm, Pump upper spring, Pump lower spring, Diaphragm spring, Nozzle, Vacuum air bleed, Diaphragm, Metering-rod jet, Vacuum restriction

FUEL, AIR, FUEL-AIR, VACUUM

Fig. 9–41. Sectional view of a carburetor using a spring-loaded diaphragm actuated by intake-manifold vacuum to control the position of the metering rod. *(Ford Division of Ford Motor Company)*

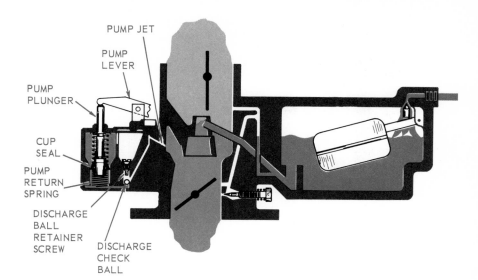

Fig. 9-42. Accelerator-pump circuit in a carburetor of the type using a pump plunger.

PUMP JET

PUMP LEVER

PUMP PLUNGER

CUP SEAL

PUMP RETURN SPRING

DISCHARGE BALL RETAINER SCREW

DISCHARGE CHECK BALL

§ 9-30. COMBINATION FULL-POWER CIRCUITS

In some carburetors, a combination full-power circuit is used that is operated both mechanically and by vacuum from the intake manifold. In one such carburetor, there is a metering rod that is linked to a vacuum diaphragm as well as to the throttle linkage (Fig. 9-41). Thus, mechanical movement of the throttle to "full open" lifts the metering rod to enrich the mixture. Or loss of intake-manifold vacuum (as during a hard pull up a hill or during acceleration) will cause the vacuum-diaphragm spring to raise the metering rod for an enriched mixture.

§ 9-31. ACCELERATOR-PUMP CIRCUIT
For acceleration, the carburetor must deliver additional

fuel (see § 9-19). Rapid opening of the throttle allows a sudden inrush of air. Consequently there is a sudden demand for additional fuel. Carburetors have accelerator-pump circuits to provide this extra fuel. Figure 9-42 shows one type. It includes a pump plunger which is forced downward by a pump lever that is linked to the throttle. When the throttle is opened, the pump lever pushes the pump plunger down, and this forces fuel to flow through the accelerator-pump circuit and out the pump jet (Fig. 9-43). This fuel enters the air passing through the carburetor to supply the additional fuel needed.

Note that the attachment between the pump plunger and the pump and seal is through a spring. This spring applies pressure to the pump so that

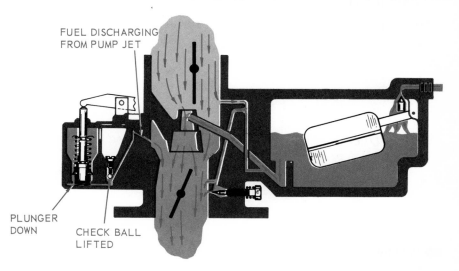

Fig. 9-43. When the throttle is opened, the pump lever pushes the pump plunger down, forcing fuel to flow through the accelerator-pump circuit and out the jet.

FUEL DISCHARGING FROM PUMP JET

PLUNGER DOWN

CHECK BALL LIFTED

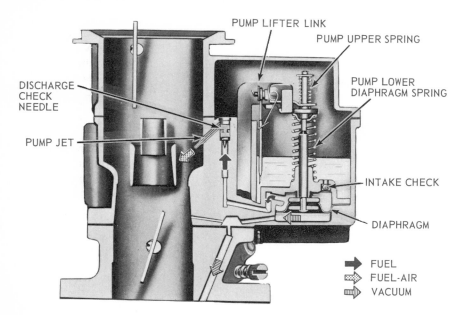

Fig. 9-44. Accelerator-pump circuit of the type using a spring-loaded diaphragm. Opening of the throttle allows the lower diaphragm spring to lift the diaphragm and force fuel through the accelerator-pump circuit and out through the jet.

the accelerator-pump circuit immediately begins discharging fuel through the jet. The spring maintains this pressure all the time that the throttle is held open until the pump is all the way down, as shown in Fig. 9-43. This arrangement allows the accelerator-pump circuit to discharge fuel for several seconds, or until the full-power circuit can take over. It therefore permits smooth acceleration.

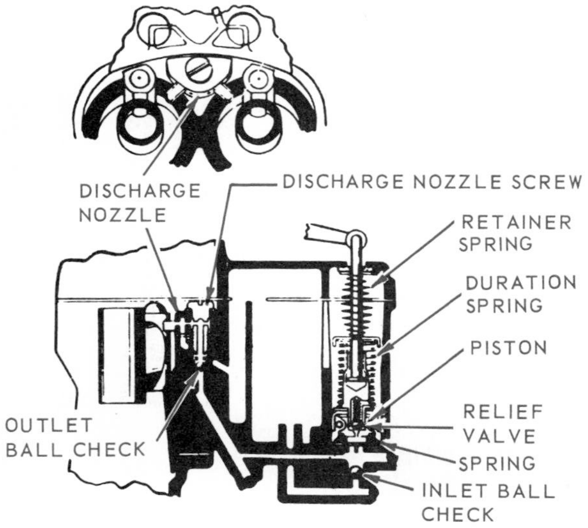

One type of accelerator-pump circuit that uses a diaphragm instead of a plunger is shown in Fig. 9-44. When the throttle is opened, the pump lower diaphragm spring lifts the diaphragm, and this forces additional fuel from the chamber above the diaphragm through the accelerator-pump circuit and out the pump jet.

An accelerator-pump circuit for a dual carburetor is shown in Fig. 9-45. This carburetor has two barrels; there is a discharge nozzle for each. The fuel flow from the accelerator pump is split between the two barrels.

§ 9-32. CHOKE When the engine is being cranked for starting, the carburetor must deliver a very rich mixture to the intake manifold. With the engine and carburetor cold, only part of the fuel vaporizes, and thus extra fuel must be delivered. In this way, enough evaporates to make a combustible mixture that permits the engine to start.

During cranking, air speed through the carburetor air horn is very low. Vacuum from the venturi action and vacuum below the throttle would be insufficient to produce adequate fuel flow for starting. Thus, to produce sufficient fuel flow during cranking, the carburetor has a choke (Fig. 9-46). The choke consists of a valve in the top of the air horn controlled mechanically or by an automatic device. When the choke valve is closed, only a small amount of air can get past it (the valve "chokes off" the air flow). Then, when the engine is cranked, a fairly high vacuum

Fig. 9-45. Accelerator-pump system and location of the discharge nozzles in a dual carburetor.

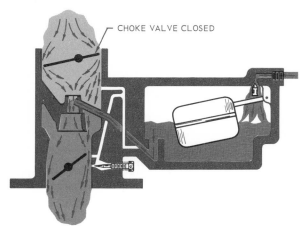

CHOKE VALVE CLOSED

Fig. 9–46. With the choke valve closed, intake-manifold vacuum is introduced into the carburetor air horn, causing the main nozzle to discharge fuel.

develops in the air horn. This vacuum causes the main nozzle to discharge a heavy stream of fuel. The quantity delivered is sufficient to produce the correct air-fuel mixture needed for starting the engine.

As soon as the engine starts, its speed increases from a cranking speed of around 100 rpm (revolutions per minute) to over 400 rpm. Now, more air and a somewhat leaner mixture are required. One method of satisfying this requirement is to mount the choke valve off center and to have a spring arrangement in the choke linkage. With this arrangement, the additional air the engine requires causes the valve to partly open against the spring pressure. Another arrangement is to include a small spring-loaded section in the valve; this section opens to admit the additional air.

§ 9–33. AUTOMATIC CHOKES Mechanically controlled chokes are operated by a pull rod on the dash. The pull rod is linked to the choke valve; when it is pulled out, the choke valve is closed. With this arrangement, the driver must remember to push the control rod in to the dechoked position as soon as the engine begins to warm up. If he does not, the carburetor will continue to supply a very rich mixture to the engine. This excessive richness will cause poor engine performance and carboned valves, piston rings, and spark plugs.

To prevent such troubles, most cars now have an automatic choke. Most automatic chokes operate on exhaust-manifold temperature and intake-manifold vacuum. Figure 9–47 shows an automatic choke on a carburetor. It includes a thermostatic spring and a vacuum piston, both linked to the choke valve. The thermostatic spring is made up of two different metal strips welded together and formed into a spiral. Owing to differences in expansion rates of the two metals, the thermostatic

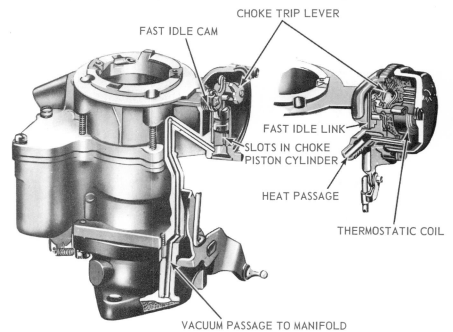

CHOKE TRIP LEVER

FAST IDLE CAM

FAST IDLE LINK

SLOTS IN CHOKE PISTON CYLINDER

HEAT PASSAGE

THERMOSTATIC COIL

VACUUM PASSAGE TO MANIFOLD

Fig. 9–47. Automatic choke system on a carburetor. (*Ford Division of Ford Motor Company*)

spring tends to wind up or unwind with changing temperature. When the engine is cold, the spring has wound up enough to close the choke valve and spring-load it in the closed position. Now, when the engine is cranked, a rich mixture is delivered to the intake manifold. As the engine starts, air movement through the air horn causes the choke valve to open slightly (working against the thermostatic-spring tension). In addition, the vacuum piston is pulled outward by intake-manifold vacuum to produce some further opening of the choke valve.

The choke valve is thus positioned properly to permit the carburetor to supply the rather rich mixture required for cold-engine idling operation. When the throttle is opened, the mixture must be enriched. The accelerator pump provides some additional fuel, but still more fuel is required when the engine is cold. This additional fuel is secured by the action of the vacuum piston. When the throttle is opened, intake-manifold vacuum is lost. The vacuum piston releases and is pulled inward by the thermostatic-spring tension. The choke valve therefore moves toward the "closed" position and causes the mixture to be enriched. During the first few moments of operation, the choke valve is controlled by the vacuum piston.

However, the thermostatic spring begins to take over as the engine warms up. The thermostatic spring is in a housing that is connected to the exhaust manifold through a small tube. Heat passes through this tube and enters the thermostatic-spring housing. Soon, the thermostat begins to warm up. As it warms up, the spring unwinds. This causes the choke valve to move toward the "opened" position. When operating temperature is reached, the thermostatic spring has unwound enough to fully open the choke valve. No further choking takes place.

When the engine is stopped and cools, the thermostatic spring again winds up, as noted above, to close the choke valve and spring-load it in the "closed" position.

Figure 9-47 shows a carburetor partly cut away so that the construction of the automatic choke can be seen. The vacuum passage to the vacuum piston is shown, but the heat tube to the exhaust manifold is not. The heat tube introduces heat from the exhaust manifold into the thermostatic-spring housing.

In many engines, the thermostat is located in a well in the exhaust manifold where it can quickly react to the manifold heat as the engine starts (see Fig. 9-54). The thermostat is connected by a link to the carburetor. Some carburetors using this arrangement have vacuum pistons. Others have vacuum diaphragms. Both cooperate with the thermostat as previously noted to control the choke-valve position during warm-up.

Some carburetors pick up heat to operate the thermostat from the engine cooling water. That is, the thermostat housing has a passage through which the cooling water flows (Fig. 9-48). The action is similar to other automatic chokes previously discussed.

Instead of a vacuum piston, many automatic chokes now use a vacuum-operated diaphragm (Fig. 9-49). The operation is quite similar. However, the diaphragm provides considerably more force to break loose the choke valve in case it has stuck. The linkage from the diaphragm to the choke-valve lever rides freely in a slot in the lever. During certain phases of warm-up operation, the changing vacuum causes the linkage to ride to

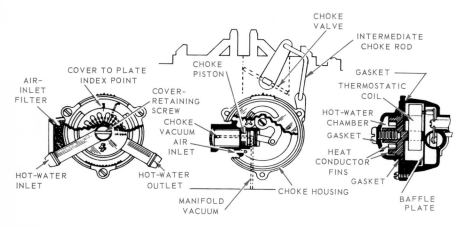

Fig. 9-48. Water-heated choke in cutaway views to show the construction. (*Buick Motor Division of General Motors Corporation*)

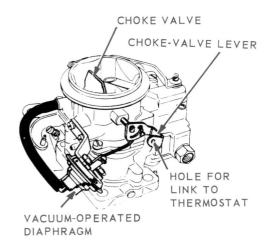

CHOKE VALVE

CHOKE-VALVE LEVER

HOLE FOR LINK TO THERMOSTAT

VACUUM-OPERATED DIAPHRAGM

Fig. 9–49. Automatic choke using a vacuum-operated diaphragm. *(Chrysler-Plymouth Division of Chrysler Motors Corporation)*

the end of the slot in the choke lever and move the choke valve. For example, when the throttle is opened during cold-engine operation, loss of intake-manifold vacuum causes the diaphragm to move; this movement carries the choke-valve lever around so that the choke valve is moved toward the "closed" position. This action provides a richer mixture for good acceleration.

§ 9–34. MANIFOLD HEAT CONTROL
During initial warm-up of the engine, just after starting, vaporization of the gasoline in the air-fuel mixture entering the engine is relatively poor. Gasoline vaporizes more slowly when it is cold (see § 10–2). In order to improve fuel vaporization and therefore cold-engine operation, a device is provided to heat the intake manifold when it is cold. This device, called the *manifold heat-control valve*, is built into the exhaust and intake manifolds. Two arrangements are used, one for in-line engines, another for V-8 engines.

1. In-line engines. In these engines, the exhaust manifold is located under the intake manifold. At a central point, there is an opening from the exhaust manifold into a chamber, or oven, surrounding the intake manifold (Figs. 9–50 and 9–51). A butterfly valve is situated in this opening (see Fig. 6–13). When the valve is turned one way, the opening is closed off. The position of the valve is controlled by a thermostat. When the engine is cold, the thermostatic spring unwinds and moves the valve to the "closed" position (left in Fig. 9–51). Now, when the engine is started, the hot exhaust gases must pass through the opening and circulate through the oven around the intake manifold (Figs. 9–50 and 9–51). Heat from the exhaust gas quickly warms the intake manifold and helps the fuel to vaporize. Thus, cold-engine operation is improved. As the engine warms up, the thermostatic spring winds up and moves the valve to the "opened" position (right in Fig. 9–51). Now, the exhaust gases pass directly into the exhaust pipe and no longer circulate in the oven around the intake manifold.

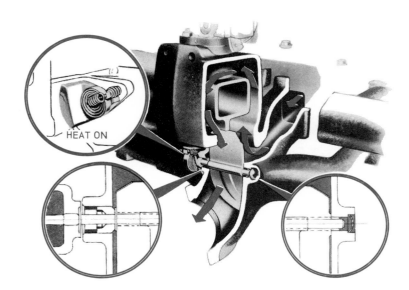

HEAT ON

Fig. 9–50. Intake and exhaust manifolds of a six-cylinder, in-line engine, cut away so the location and the action of the manifold heat control can be seen. The heat-control valve is in the "heat on" position, directing hot exhaust gases up and around the intake manifold, as shown by the arrows. *(Ford Motor Company)*

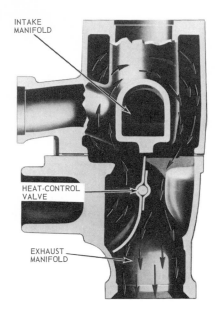
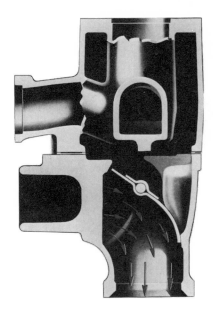

Fig. 9–51. Two extreme positions in the exhaust manifold of the manifold heat-control valve, which controls the flow of exhaust gases through the intake-manifold jacket. *(Chevrolet Motor Division of General Motors Corporation)*

2. *V-8 engines.* In V-8 engines, the intake manifold between the two banks of cylinders has a special passage (Figs. 6–16 and 9–52) through which exhaust gases can pass. One of the exhaust manifolds has a thermostatically controlled valve that closes when the engine is cold. This causes the exhaust gases to pass from one exhaust manifold through the special passage in the intake manifold and enter the other exhaust manifold. Heat from the exhaust gases then heats the air-fuel

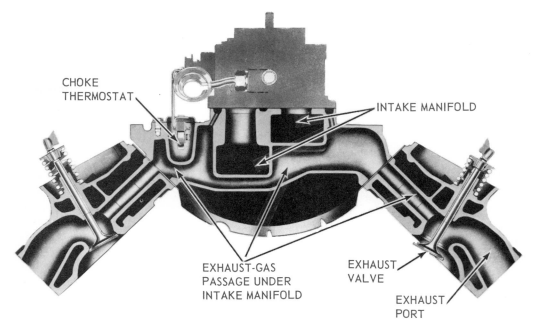

Fig. 9–52. Exhaust-gas passage under the intake manifold in a V-8 engine. Note the well in which the carburetor choke thermostat is located. *(Buick Motor Division of General Motors Corporation)*

162

mixture in the intake manifold for improved cold-engine operation. As the engine warms up, the thermostatically controlled valve opens. Then, the exhaust gases from both exhaust manifolds pass directly into the exhaust pipes.

§ 9–35. ANTI-ICING

When fuel is sprayed into the air passing through the air horn, it evaporates, or turns to vapor. During evaporation, the fuel takes on heat. That is, it takes heat from the surrounding air and metal parts. This is the same effect you get when you pour alcohol on your hand. Your hand feels cold. If you blow on your hand, thus causing the alcohol to evaporate faster, your hand will feel still colder. The faster evaporation takes heat away from your hand, the cooler your hand feels.

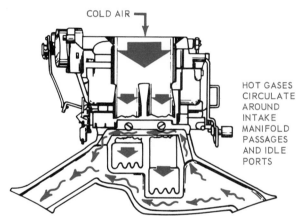

COLD AIR

HOT GASES CIRCULATE AROUND INTAKE MANIFOLD PASSAGES AND IDLE PORTS

Fig. 9–53. Intake manifold and carburetor idle ports heating passages. Hot exhaust gases heat these areas as soon as the engine starts. *(Cadillac Motor Car Division of General Motors Corporation)*

Now, let us see how this affects the carburetor. Spraying and evaporation of the fuel "rob" the surrounding air and carburetor of heat. Under certain conditions, the surrounding metal parts are so cooled that any moisture in the air will condense and actually freeze on the metal parts. The ice can build up sufficiently, if conditions are right, to cause the engine to stall. The condition is most apt to occur during the warm-up period following the first start-up of the day, with air temperatures in the range of 40 to 60°F and the air fairly humid.

To prevent such icing, many carburetors have special anti-icing circuits. One arrangement for a V-8 engine is shown in Fig. 9–53. During the warm-up period, the manifold-heat control valve shunts hot exhaust gases from one exhaust manifold to the other (see § 9–34). Part of this hot exhaust gas circulates around the carburetor idle ports and near the throttle-valve shaft. This adds enough heat to guard against ice formation. Another carburetor has water passages in the carburetor. The water comes from the engine cooling system; a small amount of the cooling water bypasses through a special water manifold in the carburetor throttle body. This adds enough heat to the carburetor to prevent icing.

§ 9–36. FAST IDLE

When the engine is cold, some throttle opening must be maintained so that the engine will idle faster than it would when warm. Otherwise, the slow idle with the engine cold might cause the engine to stall. With fast idle, enough air-fuel mixture gets through, and air speeds are great enough, to produce adequate vaporization and a sufficiently rich mixture. Fast idle is obtained by a fast-idle cam which is linked to the choke valve (Fig. 9–54). When the engine is cold, the automatic choke holds the choke valve closed. In this position, the linkage has revolved the fast-idle cam so that the adjusting screw rests on the high point of the cam. The adjusting screw therefore prevents the throttle valve from moving to the "fully closed" position. The throttle valve is held partly open for fast idle. As the engine warms up, the choke valve opens. This rotates the fast-idle cam so that the high point moves from under the adjusting screw. The throttle valve closes for normal hot-engine slow idle.

§ 9–37. AIR BLEED AND ANTISIPHON CIRCUITS

In the high-speed circuits of various carburetors, small openings are incorporated to permit air to enter, or *bleed* into, the circuit. This action produces some premixing of the air and fuel so that better atomization and vaporization are attained. The action also helps to maintain a more uniform air-fuel ratio. At higher speeds, a proportionately larger amount of fuel tends to discharge from the main nozzle. But at the same time the faster fuel movement through the high-speed circuit causes more air to bleed into the circuit. Thus, the air-bleed holes tend to equalize the air-fuel ratio.

Air-bleed passages are also used in low-speed and idle circuits to permit some air to bypass the closed throttle valve and mix with the fuel feeding through the idle circuit (Fig. 9–35). These passages are also sometimes called *antisiphon* cir-

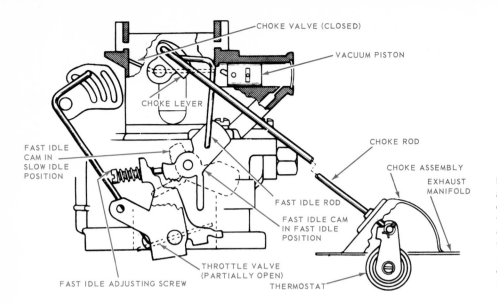

Fig. 9-54. Vacuum- and thermostatically operated choke with the thermostat located in the exhaust manifold. Note two positions of the fast idle cam. *(Chrysler-Plymouth Division of Chrysler Motors Corporation)*

cuits, since they act as air vents to prevent the siphoning of fuel from the float bowl at intermediate engine speeds.

If air-bleed passages become plugged, they may cause the float bowl to be emptied after the engine shuts off. When the engine is shut off, the intake manifold cools down and a slight vacuum forms as a result. With open air bleeds, air can move through the bleeds to satisfy the vacuum. But if the air bleeds are plugged, then the vacuum will cause the float bowl to empty through the idle circuit.

§ 9-38. SPECIAL CARBURETOR DEVICES Other special devices in carburetors include:

1. Vacuum circuits to control the ignition-distributor spark advance (see § 15-6).
2. Throttle-return checks and magnetically controlled dashpots to retard throttle closing (on cars with automatic transmissions).
3. Electric kick-down switches (on some cars equipped with automatic transmissions).
4. Governors to control or limit top engine speed.
5. Solenoid throttle modulator which allows the throttle plate to close completely when the ignition is turned off.

Figure 9-55 shows a throttle-return check on a carburetor. The throttle-return check contains a spring-loaded diaphragm which traps air behind it when the throttle is opened. Then, when the throttle is released, the return check slows the

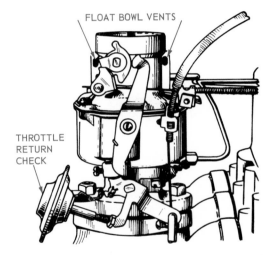

Fig. 9-55. Throttle-return check on a carburetor. *(Chevrolet Motor Division of General Motors Corporation)*

throttle movement so that it closes slowly. This guards against sudden throttle closing that might cause the engine to stall. The electric kick-down switch, used on some cars with automatic transmissions, provides an electrical means of downshifting the transmission into a lower gear when the throttle is opened wide (under certain conditions). Use of governors is largely confined to heavy-duty vehicles; they prevent over speeding and rapid wear of the engine. In one type, control is directly on the throttle valve; it tends to close the valve as rated speed is reached. Another type

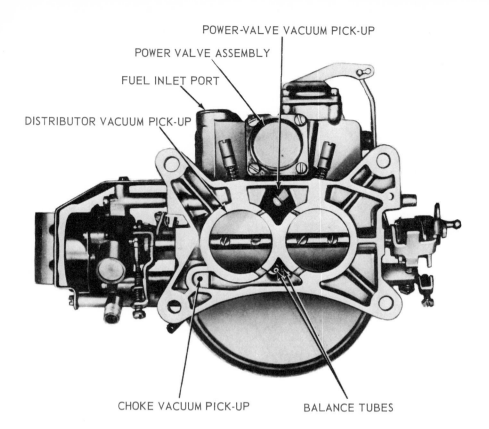

POWER-VALVE VACUUM PICK-UP

POWER VALVE ASSEMBLY

FUEL INLET PORT

DISTRIBUTOR VACUUM PICK-UP

CHOKE VACUUM PICK-UP   BALANCE TUBES

Fig. 9–56. Bottom view of a dual carburetor. *(Ford Division of Ford Motor Company)*

interposes a throttle plate between the carburetor throttle valve and the intake manifold. The throttle plate moves toward the "closed" position as rated speed is reached to prevent delivery of additional amounts of air-fuel mixture and any further increase in engine speed.

§ **9–39. DUAL AND QUAD CARBURETORS** Carburetors with more than a single barrel are used on many engines. Thus, many carburetors have two barrels (dual carburetors), and others have four barrels (quad carburetors). The purpose of the additional barrels is to improve engine "breathing," particularly at high speeds. That is, the extra barrels permit more air and fuel to enter the engine. Of course, if air were the only consideration, then a single large-diameter barrel could be used. But with only a single large barrel, venturi action would be poor, and proper air-fuel ratios would be hard to achieve under varying operating conditions.

1. Dual carburetor. The dual carburetor is essentially two single-barrel carburetors in a single assembly (Fig. 9–56). Each barrel handles the air-fuel requirements of half the engine cylinders. For example, Fig. 6–16 shows the air-fuel delivery pattern in a V-8 engine. One carburetor barrel supplies cylinders 2, 3, 5, and 8. The other barrel supplies cylinders 1, 4, 6, and 7. The arrows indicate the pattern in Fig. 6–16. Each barrel has a complete set of circuits; the throttle valves are fastened to a single throttle shaft, so that both valves open and close together.

2. Quad (four-barrel) carburetor. The four-barrel carburetor (Figs. 9–32 and 9–57) consists essentially of two dual carburetors combined in a single assembly. The carburetor has four barrels and four main nozzles and thus is often called a *quadrijet,* or *quad, carburetor.* One pair of barrels makes up the primary side, the other pair the secondary side (Fig. 9–57). Under most operating conditions, the primary side alone takes care of engine requirements. However, when the throttle is moved toward the "wide-open" position for acceleration or full-power operation, the secondary side comes into operation. It supplies additional amounts of air-fuel mixture. Thus, engine breathing improves. That is, the engine receives more air-fuel mixture,

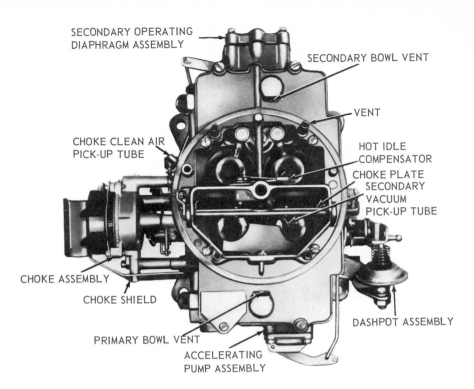

SECONDARY OPERATING
DIAPHRAGM ASSEMBLY

SECONDARY BOWL VENT

VENT

HOT IDLE
COMPENSATOR

CHOKE PLATE
SECONDARY
VACUUM
PICK-UP TUBE

CHOKE CLEAN AIR
PICK-UP TUBE

CHOKE ASSEMBLY

CHOKE SHIELD

DASHPOT ASSEMBLY

PRIMARY BOWL VENT

ACCELERATING
PUMP ASSEMBLY

Fig. 9–57. Top view of a four-barrel, or quad, carburetor. *(Ford Division of Ford Motor Company)*

volumetric efficiency (§ 4–11) is higher, and the engine produces more horsepower.

§ 9–40. MULTIPLE CARBURETORS To achieve still better engine "breathing," some high-performance engines are equipped with more than one carburetor. The additional carburetors supply more air and fuel and thus improve high-speed, full-power engine performance. The ultimate in this is to equip each engine cylinder with its own carburetor, and many racing and drag-strip or hot-rod cars are equipped in this manner; an eight-cylinder engine would have eight carburetors.

Figure 9–58 shows a three-carburetor installation. The three carburetors are linked together to the accelerator pedal.

§ 9–41. SUPERCHARGER In some engines, power is boosted through the use of a *supercharger*, which increases the amount of air-fuel mixture delivered to the engine. One system, used on the Chevrolet Corvair flat-six air-cooled engine, is shown in Fig. 9–59. The supercharger contains a compressor and a turbine, linked together by a common shaft. The turbine contains a rotor with a series of blades against which exhaust gas is directed. This spins the rotor at high speed, and

the compressor rotor is thus turned at high speed. The compressor rotor therefore compresses the air-fuel mixture being delivered from the carburetor and sends it on its way to the engine cylinders. In operation, the supercharger may compress the mixture to a pressure of as much as 6 pounds per square inch (above atmospheric pressure).

Because the supercharger or compressor rotor is driven by a turbine, the assembly is sometimes called a *turbo supercharger*, or a *turbo charger*. On some engines, the supercharger is driven by a belt or gears from the engine instead of by an exhaust-gas turbine.

§ 9–42. FUEL INJECTION The fuel-injection system uses, instead of a carburetor, a series of injection nozzles and a high-pressure fuel pump to spray the fuel into the air entering the engine cylinders. The end effect is the same: A properly proportioned mixture of air and fuel enters the cylinders. Some engineers, however, consider the fuel-injection system to be more responsive and more desirable for high-performance engines.

The layout of one fuel-injection system is shown in Fig. 9–60. The major parts include an air-intake and air-meter assembly, a fuel pump and meter,

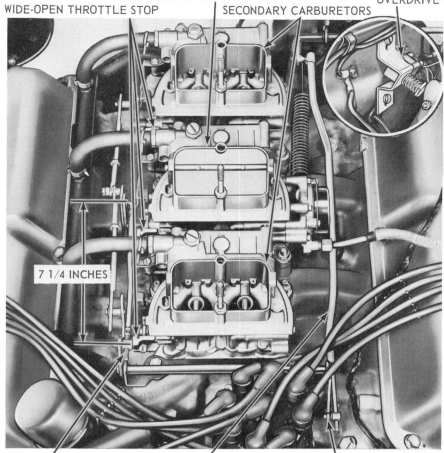

PRIMARY CARBURETOR

SECONDARY CARBURETORS

OVERDRIVE KICKDOWN SWITCH

7 1/4 INCHES

PRIMARY THROTTLE LEVER   ACCELERATOR-TO-BELLCRANK ROD   BELLCRANK LEVER

Fig. 9–58. Three-carburetor installation on a V-8 engine. *(Ford Division of Ford Motor Company)*

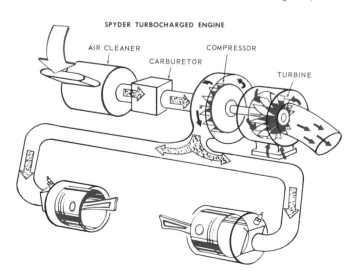

SPYDER TURBOCHARGED ENGINE

AIR CLEANER

CARBURETOR

COMPRESSOR

TURBINE

Fig. 9–59. Schematic layout of a turbo-super-charger system on a flat, six-cylinder engine. *(Chevrolet Motor Division of General Motors Corporation)*

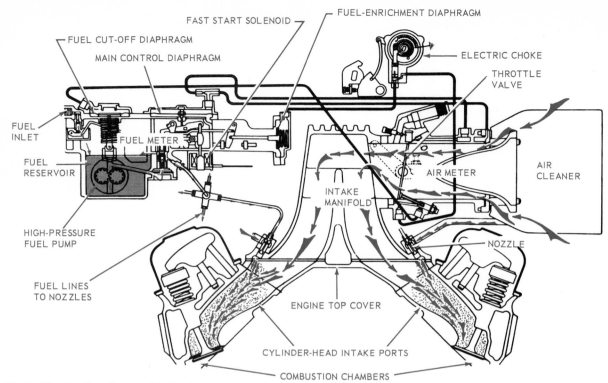

Fig. 9–60. Sectional view of fuel-injection system used on a V-8 engine. *(Chevrolet Motor Division of General Motors Corporation)*

and an intake manifold with eight fuel nozzles (one for each cylinder). The air-intake assembly has a throttle valve which is linked to the accelerator pedal. When the driver depresses the accelerator pedal, more air is admitted to the intake manifold. Interconnected controls then actuate the fuel meter so that more fuel is sprayed from the fuel nozzles into the manifold.

Fuel is delivered to the reservoir by a standard fuel pump, just as in other fuel systems. The high-pressure fuel pump in the reservoir, driven off the ignition distributor, delivers fuel to the metering chamber. From there, it can pass on to the fuel nozzles or flow back into the reservoir. The amount that is delivered to the fuel nozzles depends on the requirements of the engine, that is, on the engine operating conditions. For instance, if the engine is cold, a choke system comes into operation to enrich the mixture for cold starting and initial running. Likewise, the mixture is enriched for acceleration and high-speed performance. The controls to accomplish this are based on the vacuum in the air-meter venturi, which actuates a diaphragm in the fuel meter. This diaphragm posi-

tions the plunger in the metering chamber so that there is a change in the amount of fuel which is delivered to the injection nozzles in accordance with the engine and operating requirements.

Figure 9–61 is a schematic view of another fuel-injection system that differs in many respects from the system illustrated in Fig. 9–60. This system has a two-plunger pump, each plunger feeding three cylinders through a metering unit. Fuel is injected into the intake ports of the cylinders. The metering units are controlled by a linkage to the accelerator pedal, and the amount of fuel delivered by the pump is controlled by a centrifugal governor. Other controls are included to increase the richness of the air-fuel mixture for starting, cold operation, and high-speed full-power running. There are also pressure cells built into the diaphragms of the injection pump which alter the amount of fuel delivered in accordance with the altitude and the density of the air. At higher altitudes, the air is less dense and therefore less fuel is required to achieve the normal air-fuel-mixture ratio. The pressure cells take care of this adjustment automatically.

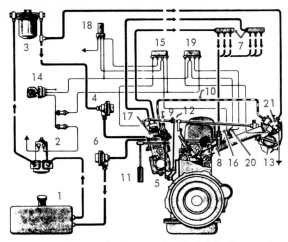

Fig. 9–61. Schematic layout of a fuel-injection system used on a six-cylinder engine.

1. Fuel tank
2. Fuel feed pump
3. Fuel filter
4. Damper container (inlet)
5. Injection pump
6. Damper container (outlet)
7. Fuel metering units
8. Injection valves
9. Cooling-water thermostat
10. Additional air duct
11. Accelerator pedal
12. Control linkage
13. Throttle connector
14. Ignition starter switch
15. Relay
16. Thermo switch in cooling-water circuit
17. Magnetic switch for mixture control
18. Time switch
19. Relay
20. Thermo time switch in cooling-water circuit
21. Electromagnetic starter valve with atomizing jet

(Mercedes-Benz, Daimler-Benz Aktiengesellschaft)

§ 9–43. ELECTRONIC FUEL-INJECTION SYSTEM

A fuel-injection system that is controlled by electronic means is illustrated in Figs. 9–62 to 9–64. This system was especially designed for the Volkswagen flat-four, air-cooled engine (Fig. 5–12). A major reason for developing this system was to improve the combustion process and reduce the amount of smog-producing substances in the exhaust (§ 9–46 discusses smog). The fuel is injected into the intake manifolds behind the intake valves, and the injection is timed to coincide with valve opening by triggering contacts in the ignition distributor. The amount of fuel injected is controlled by the length of time the fuel injectors are open. This, in turn, is determined by a number of sensors which send electrical signals to the transistorized control unit, as shown in Fig. 9–62. Figure 9–63

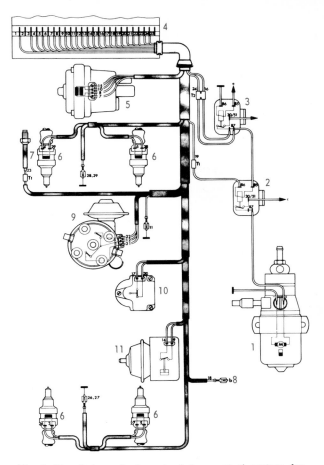

Fig. 9–62. Schematic layout of the control system for the Volkswagen electronic fuel-injection system. The electronic control unit (4) receives signals from various sensors and integrates them to determine the amount of fuel to be injected.

1. Fuel pump
2. Pump relay
3. Main relay
4. Control unit
5. Intake-manifold pressure sensor
6. Injector
7. Cylinder-head temperature sensor
8. Crankcase sensor
9. Ignition distributor
10. Throttle switch
11. Full-load pressure switch

(Volkswagen)

illustrates the air-supply system and its controls. Figure 9–64 illustrates the fuel-supply system.

§ 9–44. EXHAUST SYSTEM
The exhaust system includes the exhaust manifold, exhaust pipe, muffler, and tail pipe (Figs. 6–14 and 9–2). Some V-8 engines use a crossover pipe to connect their two exhaust manifolds. Other cars with V-8 engines use two separate exhaust systems, one for each

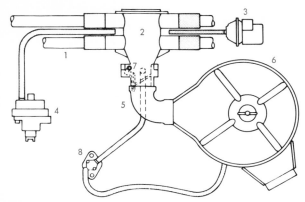

Fig. 9–63. Air-supply control for Volkswagen electronic fuel-injection system.

1. Air pipes to cylinders
2. Air distributor
3. Pressure switch
4. Pressure sensor

5. Idling circuit
6. Air cleaner
7. Adjusting screw

(Volkswagen)

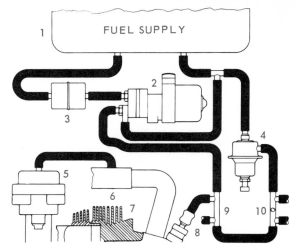

Fig. 9–64. Fuel supply system for Volkswagen electronic fuel-injection system.

1. Fuel tank
2. Electric fuel pump
3. Filter
4. Pressure regulator
5. Intake-manifold pressure sensor

6. Air pipe
7. Cylinder head
8. Fuel injector
9. and 10. Distribution pipes to injectors.

(Volkswagen)

cylinder bank (Fig. 6–14). This improves the "breathing" ability of the engine, allowing it to exhaust more freely and thus increase power output to some extent.

§ 9–45. MUFFLER The muffler (Fig. 9–65) contains a series of holes, passages, and resonance chambers to absorb and damp out the high-pressure surges introduced into the exhaust system as the exhaust valves open. This quiets the exhaust. Some new exhaust-system designs do not use a muffler. Instead, the exhaust pipe has a series of scientifically shaped restrictions that

damp out the exhaust noises without unduly restricting the flow of exhaust gases.

§ 9–46. ATMOSPHERIC POLLUTION AND SMOG The automobile engine and fuel system release to the atmosphere a variety of gaseous compounds, including unburned hydrocarbons and carbon monoxide. These compounds contribute

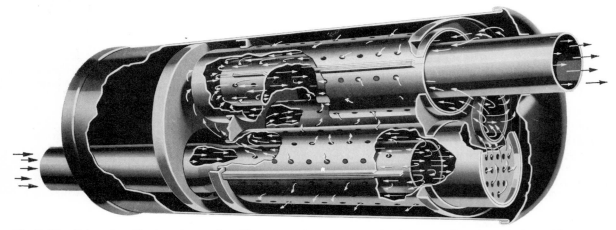

Fig. 9–65. Exhaust muffler in cutaway view. The arrows show the path of exhaust-gas flow through the muffler. *(Chevrolet Motor Division of General Motors Corporation)*

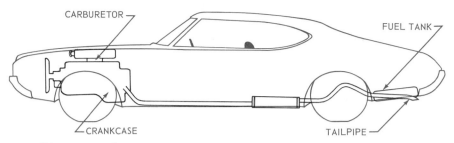

Fig. 9–66. Four possible sources of atmospheric pollutants from the automobile.

to the formation of smog which often hangs over our larger cities. Because smog is a threat to health, automotive manufacturers have introduced certain devices and have changed designs to minimize these smog-causing substances. Actually, there are four possible sources of these substances in the automobile: crankcase, carburetor, fuel tank, and exhaust system (Fig. 9–66).

1. Crankcase ventilator. Air must circulate through the crankcase when the engine is running. The reason for this is that water and liquid fuel appear in the crankcase during certain phases of engine operation. Also, there is some blow-by on power strokes, during which combustion gases enter the crankcase. The water appears as a product of combustion (§ 3–9). When the engine is cold, some of the water condenses on the cylinder walls and drops down into the crankcase. Likewise, some of the fuel condenses on the cylinder walls and enters the crankcase. Unless these liquids are removed, they will combine with the engine oil to form sludge (see § 11–3). In normal operation, as the engine warms up, these liquids vaporize and are removed by the crankcase ventilating system.

In earlier engines, the crankcase was ventilated by an opening at the front of the engine and a vent tube at the back of the engine. The forward movement of the car plus the rotation of the crankshaft in the crankcase caused air to pass through the crankcase and remove the water and fuel vapors, discharging them into the atmosphere.

To prevent this pollution of the atmosphere, modern engines have closed or positive crankcase ventilating (PCV) systems which send the crankcase ventilating air up to the intake manifold so that it re-enters the engine cylinders. There, any unburned fuel is burned. Figures 9–67 and 9–68 show closed crankcase ventilating systems for a six-cylinder and a V-8 engine.

In the six-cylinder engine (Fig. 9–67), filtered air from the carburetor air cleaner enters the oil filler

cap and passes down into the valve rocker-arm chamber above the cylinder head. From there it goes through the push-rod holes and through the oil drain holes into the crankcase. Then it flows back up to the valve rocker-arm chamber and out through a connecting hose at the back of the rocker-arm cover and into the intake manifold. A slight vacuum is maintained in the engine crankcase because of a slight restriction in the oil filler cap. A crankcase ventilating regulator valve (Fig. 9–69) is located in the line between the rocker-arm cover and the intake manifold. This valve, known as a PCV valve, is open most of the operating time to permit good circulation through the crankcase.

Fig. 9–67. Closed-crankcase ventilating system on a six-cylinder engine. *(Ford Division of Ford Motor Company)*

171

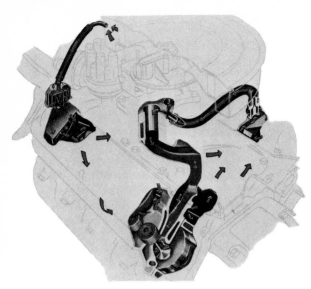

Fig. 9–68. Closed-crankcase ventilating system on a V-8 engine. *(Ford Division of Ford Motor Company)*

However, during idle, when the intake manifold vacuum is high, the high vacuum causes the valve to move to the closed position. Then, there is only a small passage which greatly reduces air flow. Without this valve, excessive air would flow during idle, and this would upset the idle air-fuel mixture and cause poor idling.

In the V-8 system (Fig. 9–68), the filtered air from the carburetor air cleaner enters one valve rocker-arm through the oil filler cap, flows down through the crankcase and up to the other valve rocker-arm chamber in the other cylinder bank. From there it

```
FROM
CRANKCASE
AND/OR                    TO
ROCKER                    INTAKE
ARM COVER                 MANIFOLD

    LOW SPEED OPERATION—
    HIGH MANIFOLD VACUUM
    HIGH SPEED OPERATION—
    LOW MANIFOLD VACUUM

FROM
CRANKCASE
AND/OR                    TO
ROCKER                    INTAKE
ARM COVER                 MANIFOLD
```

Fig. 9–69. Operation of closed-crankcase ventilating regulator valve. *(Ford Division of Ford Motor Company)*

flows through the regulator valve into the intake manifold.

2. Exhaust system. Combustion in the engine is never quite complete so that unburned fuel (hydrocarbons) and carbon monoxide escape in the exhaust gases. There are two ways to reduce these undesirable, smog-causing pollutants. One way is to inject extra fresh air into the hot exhaust gases in the exhaust manifold to complete the combustion; the other is to alter the engine design sufficiently to improve combustion within the engine cylinders.

a. Air injection. The air-injection, or Thermactor, system is illustrated in Fig. 9–70. In this system, an engine-driven air pump sends air through an air bypass valve to an air manifold assembly mounted on the side of the exhaust manifold. As the hot exhaust gases exit from the engine cylinder, they are met with a blast of fresh air that completes the combustion process. The check valve prevents a back-flow of exhaust gases to the air pump when the exhaust-gas pressure exceeds the air-pump pressure. The air bypass valve (Fig. 9–71) operates during engine deceleration (when intake-manifold vacuum is high) to momentarily shunt the air from the air pump to atmosphere instead of to the exhaust manifolds.

b. Engine design. In recent years, a series of changes have been made in engines and in fuel and ignition systems which have resulted in a marked reduction in the undesirable contaminants released in the exhaust gas. Various names have been applied to these changes. Chrysler calls their changes the *cleaner air package* (CAP). Ford uses the term *improved combustion* (IMCO). General Motors uses *controlled combustion system* (CCS).

The Chrysler CAP is illustrated in Fig. 9–72. It uses leaner calibrations on the carburetors, a modified choke calibration, retarded distributor advance at idle, and a vacuum-operated sensing valve. This valve advances the ignition timing during closed-throttle deceleration and during acceleration. This gets the combustion started sooner in the engine cylinders.

The Ford IMCO system also includes leaner carburetors and choke calibrations, and modification of the distributor so as to advance the ignition timing during deceleration. This improves combustion during this time. In addition, the stroke has been lengthened on some engines. For example, one 1969 Ford six-cylinder engine has a stroke of 3.91 inches compared with 3.13 inches in the previous year. This longer stroke provides more

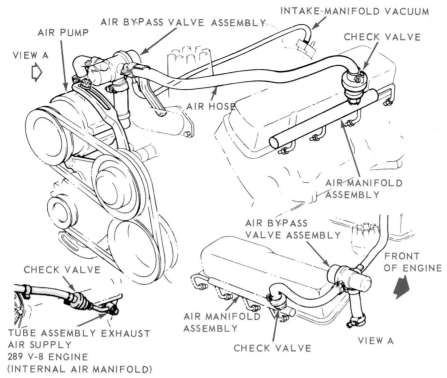

Fig. 9–70. Thermactor system on a V-8 engine. *(Ford Division of Ford Motor Company)*

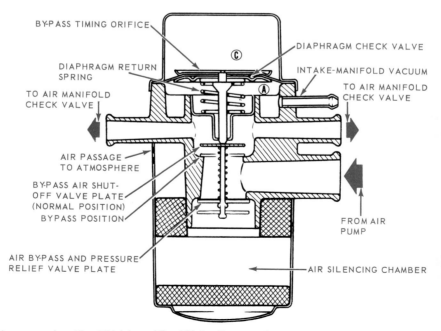

Fig. 9–71. Air by-pass valve. *(Ford Division of Ford Motor Company)*

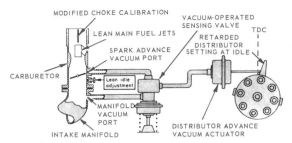

Fig. 9–72. Schematic drawing of the Chrysler CAP, or cleaner air package. *(Chrysler Motors Corporation)*

burning time for better combustion. The lean carburetor settings, which could reduce engine performance after a cold start in cold weather, were compensated for, as already explained, by use of a thermostatically controlled air cleaner (§ 9–11).

The General Motors CCS also has lean carburetor settings and distributor modifications, as already noted. Their thermostatically controlled air cleaner is similar to the Ford unit (§ 9–11).

Another design change that reduces exhaust contaminants is the use of the headland piston ring and special piston (see § 7–4). This ring eliminates the cool space found in other designs between the piston and the cylinder wall, above the top compression ring. This space traps air-fuel mixture that is unable to burn because of the cool adjacent surfaces. The headland ring, in eliminating this space, reduces exhaust contaminants.

3. Carburetor and fuel tank. As the temperature changes, the fuel tank "breathes." That is, as the tank heats up, the air inside it expands, and part of it passes out through the tank vent tube (or the vent in the tank cap). Then, when the tank cools, the air inside it contracts, and air enters the tank. This breathing causes a loss of fuel, because any air that leaves the tank contains gasoline vapor.

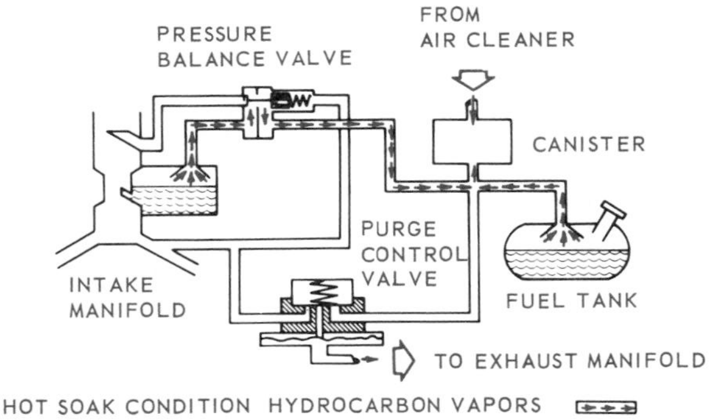

The carburetor also loses fuel from its float bowl in a similar manner. When the engine is shut off, the float bowl is full. The heat from the engine then causes part or all of this fuel to vaporize and pass out of the engine though the carburetor and air cleaner.

To prevent these losses, a closed system that will store and condense these vapors is necessary. Such systems are called FEC (fuel evaporation control) or VVR (vehicle vapor recovery) systems. One system is shown in Fig. 9–73. The canister is filled with activated charcoal. Just after the engine is shut off and heat is entering the carburetor, the gasoline vapors from the float bowl pass through the canister and are adsorbed by the charcoal. Then, when the engine starts, air passes through the canister in the opposite direction, picking up the adsorbed gasoline and carrying it to the intake manifold. Note that the vapors from the fuel tank are also captured in the same manner. The pressure balance valve closes off the vents from the float bowl to the outside so that no gasoline vapor can exit to the atmosphere. But when the engine starts, the pressure balance valve opens the vents for normal carburetor actions. The purge control valve, operating from exhaust-gas pressure, opens to allow air to pass from the canister to the intake manifold when the engine is running.

An evaporative control engineered by Chevrolet is shown in Fig. 9–74. The purge line is connected into the line from the positive-crankcase-ventilation valve to the carburetor. The carburetor is protected from engine heat by insulation and an aluminum heat dissipater.

§ 9–47. DIESEL-ENGINE FUEL SYSTEM In the diesel engine, air alone is compressed. Then, at the end of the compression stroke, the fuel sys-

Fig. 9–73. Fuel evaporation control system. *(Esso Research and Engineering Company)*

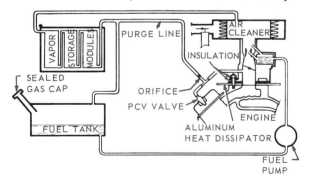

Fig. 9–74. Fuel evaporation control system. *(Chevrolet Motor Division of General Motors Corporation)*

tem injects fuel oil (§ 5–15). A typical diesel-engine fuel system is shown in Fig. 9–75. The fuel pump delivers fuel oil at a comparatively low pressure to the injector (there is an injector in each cylinder). The injector contains a plunger that is operated and forced downward by a rocker arm. The rocker arm is actuated by a push rod and cam on the camshaft (the arrangement is much like the overhead-valve train). When the plunger is forced down, oil is forced from the spray tip at high pressure; it sprays into the compressed air in the cylinder and ignites from the heat of compression (§ 5–15). Power output from the engine is changed by altering the effective length of the plunger stroke. If the effective length is short, then only a small amount of fuel will be sprayed into the cylinder, and the engine will produce relatively little power and run slowly. But as the effective length of the plunger stroke is increased, more oil is injected and power output increases.

§ 9–48. LPG FUEL SYSTEM Liquefied petroleum gas (LPG) is a fuel that is liquid only under pressure (see Chap. 10). When the pressure is reduced,

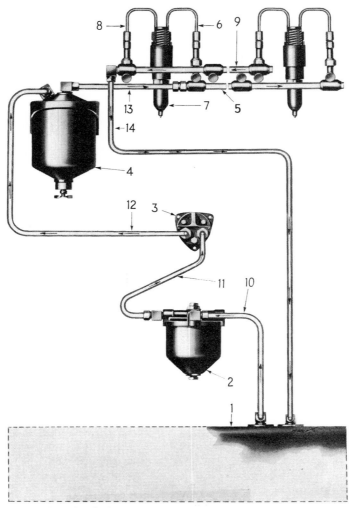

Fig. 9–75. General Motors diesel-engine fuel system.

1. Fuel tank
2. Primary filter
3. Fuel pump
4. Secondary filter
5. Lower (inlet) fuel manifold
6. Inlet tube to injector
7. Injector
8. Outlet tube from injector
9. Upper (outlet) fuel manifold
10.–14. Fuel lines

(Detroit Diesel Engine Division of General Motors Corporation)

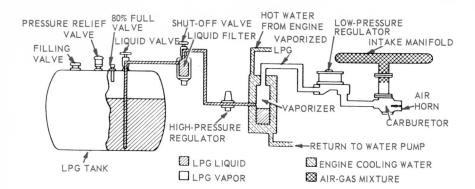

PRESSURE RELIEF VALVE
80% FULL VALVE
FILLING VALVE
LIQUID VALVE
SHUT-OFF VALVE
LIQUID FILTER
HOT WATER FROM ENGINE
VAPORIZED LPG
LOW-PRESSURE REGULATOR
INTAKE MANIFOLD
AIR HORN
CARBURETOR
VAPORIZER
HIGH-PRESSURE REGULATOR
LPG TANK
RETURN TO WATER PUMP

▨ LPG LIQUID
☐ LPG VAPOR
▨ ENGINE COOLING WATER
▨ AIR-GAS MIXTURE

Fig. 9-76. Fuel system for LPG fuel system shown schematically.

the fuel vaporizes. Thus, the LPG fuel system must have a pressure-tight fuel tank in which to store the fuel at adequate pressures. A typical LPG fuel system is shown in Fig. 9-76. Pressure in the tank forces fuel through the filter, high-pressure regulator, and vaporizer. The high-pressure regulator reduces the pressure so that the fuel starts to turn to vapor. This vaporizing process is completed in the vaporizer. The vaporizer has an inner tank surrounded by a water jacket through which water from the cooling system passes. The water adds heat to the fuel so that it is effectively vaporized. It then passes through the low-pressure regulator, where the pressure on it is further reduced (to slightly below atmospheric). It then enters the car-

buretor. The carburetor is essentially a mixing valve; it mixes the vaporized fuel and air in the proportions required by the engine. The low-pressure regulator reduces the pressure on the vaporized fuel to slightly *below* atmospheric pressure to prevent it from flowing into the carburetor when the engine is off. Fuel will flow only when the engine is running and there is a vacuum in the carburetor venturi (or air horn).

LPG fuel systems have been used on some trucks and buses and also for fork-lift and platform trucks of the type used inside factory buildings. This system is well suited for such applications because the fuel burns clean and the exhaust gases contain very little contaminants.

*R*eview *Questions*

1. What is the purpose of the fuel system?
2. What are the components of the fuel system?
3. Describe a fuel tank.
4. Is the fuel tank airtight? Explain the reason for your answer.
5. How does the balancing-coil type of fuel gauge work?
6. How does the bimetal-thermostat type of fuel gauge work?
7. What is the purpose of the fuel pump? Describe briefly how the fuel pump operates.
8. What is a combination fuel pump? Why is this type of pump used?
9. Describe the construction and operation of a tank-mounted fuel pump.
10. What is the purpose of the vapor-return line?
11. What is the purpose of the vapor separator?
12. What is the purpose of the air cleaner?
13. What is a ram-air air cleaner, and how does it work?
14. What is a thermostatically controlled air cleaner, and how does it work?
15. When the piston moves down on the intake stroke in the engine, what causes air to pass through the carburetor and intake-valve port into the cylinder?
16. What is vaporization?
17. What is volatility?
18. Describe the venturi effect.
19. What is atomization?
20. Describe the operation of the carburetor float system.
21. Describe the operation of the carburetor idling and low-speed circuits.

176

22. Describe the operation of the carburetor high-speed part-load circuit.
23. Describe the operation of the carburetor high-speed full-power circuit that is mechanically operated. Vacuum-operated. Operated by combined vacuum and mechanical action.
24. What is the difference between an updraft and a downdraft carburetor?
25. Why is an accelerator-pump system required in a carburetor?
26. How does the accelerator-pump system operate?
27. What is the purpose of the choke?
28. Describe the operation of a typical choke.
29. What is the purpose of the air bleed in carburetors?
30. Which fuel system is more complicated, the one used on a gasoline engine or the one used on a diesel engine?
31. What three jobs must the diesel-engine fuel system perform in delivering the fuel oil to the engine cylinder?
32. Describe the construction and operation of an LPG fuel system.
33. Define smog.
34. In what ways does the automobile engine contribute to the formation of smog?
35. Describe a positive crankcase ventilating system and explain how it works.
36. Describe the Thermactor system.
37. Describe some changes in engine design which have reduced the smog problem.
38. What is the CAP? The IMCO system? The CCS?
39. Explain how an FEC or VVR system works.

Study Questions

1. Make a sketch of a gasoline-engine fuel system, naming the units, and write a brief essay describing how the system operates.
2. Make a sketch of the electric circuit of the balancing-coil type of fuel-gauge system.
3. Make a sketch of the electric circuit of the bimetal-thermostat type of fuel-gauge system.
4. One gallon equals 0.134 cubic foot. If a cubic foot of air weighs 0.08 pound and a gallon of gasoline weighs 6.4 pounds, how many gallons of air would be used with 1 gallon of gasoline with a mixture ratio of 15:1 (15 pounds of air for 1 pound of fuel)?
5. Make a sketch of a simple carburetor, showing the float system and the idling circuit.
6. Make a sketch of a simple carburetor, showing the same parts as in the previous question, plus the venturi and high-speed circuit.
7. Write a sequence story describing the action of the automatic choke, starting with "1. Engine is cold; thermostatic spring has wound up and closed the choke valve."
8. Describe what takes place when a liquid is "atomized," and explain why this action helps to vaporize the liquid.
9. Thousands of miles out in space from the earth's surface, there is no atmosphere. Explain why a gasoline engine would not operate at such a distance from the earth without special apparatus. What special apparatus would be required to make it operate?

CHAPTER 10

QUENCH AND SQUISH AREA

WEDGE HEMISPHERIC

Automotive-engine Fuels

This chapter discusses the origin and characteristics of various fuels used in automotive-type engines, including gasoline, LPG (liquefied petroleum gas), and diesel-engine fuel oil.

§ 10–1. GASOLINE Gasoline is a hydrocarbon (made up of hydrogen and carbon compounds). These compounds split into hydrogen and carbon atoms when gasoline burns; these atoms then unite with oxygen atoms. Gasoline is produced by a complex refining process from crude oil, or petroleum. No one knows exactly how petroleum originated. It is found in "pools," or reservoirs, underground. When a well is drilled down to a reservoir, the underground pressure forces the petroleum up and out of the well. The petroleum must then be put through an intricate refining process; the resulting products include gasoline, many grades and kinds of lubricating oil and fuel oil, and many other products.

§ 10–2. VOLATILITY OF GASOLINE Actually, gasoline is not a simple substance. It is a mixture of a number of different hydrocarbons; each has its own characteristics. Aside from its combustibility, one of the important properties of gasoline is *volatility.*

Volatility refers to the ease with which a liquid vaporizes. The volatility of a simple compound like water or alcohol is determined by increasing its temperature until it boils, or vaporizes. A liquid that vaporizes at a relatively low temperature has a high volatility; it is highly volatile. If its boiling point is high, its volatility is low. A certain heavy oil with a boiling point of 600° F has a very low volatility. Water has a relatively high volatility; it boils at 212° F at atmospheric pressure.

Gasoline is blended from different hydrocarbon compounds, each having a different volatility, or boiling point. The proportions of high-volatility and low-volatility hydrocarbons must be correct for the operating conditions, as noted below.

1. Easy starting. For easy starting with a cold engine, gasoline must be highly volatile so that it will vaporize readily at a low temperature. Thus, a percentage of the gasoline must be highly volatile. For the colder Northern states, the percentage must be higher than for the South.

2. Freedom from vapor lock. If the gasoline is too volatile, engine heat will cause it to vaporize in the fuel pump. This can cause vapor lock, which prevents normal fuel delivery to the carburetor and would probably produce stalling of the engine. Thus, the percentage of highly volatile gasoline must be kept low to prevent vapor lock. The use of a vapor-return line to return vaporized fuel from the fuel pump to the fuel tank, and also to circulate extra fuel through the fuel pump to keep it cool, is discussed in § 9–7.

3. Quick warm-up. The speed with which the engine warms up depends in part on the percentage of gasoline that will vaporize immediately after the engine starts and thus contribute to engine operation. Volatility for this purpose does not have to be quite so high as for easy starting. But, all the same, it must be fairly high.

4. Smooth acceleration. When the throttle is opened for acceleration, there is a sudden increase in the amount of air passing through the throttle valve. At the same time, the accelerator pump delivers an extra amount of gasoline. If this gasoline does not vaporize quickly, there will be a momentary interval during which the air-fuel mixture will be too lean. This will cause the engine to hesitate, or stutter. Immediately after, as the gasoline begins to evaporate, the mixture will become temporarily too rich. Here again there will be poor combustion and a tendency for the engine to hesitate. A sufficient proportion of the gasoline must be sufficiently volatile to assure adequate vaporization for smooth acceleration.

5. *Good economy.* For good economy, or maximum miles per gallon, the fuel must have a high heat content, or energy, and low volatility. High overall volatility tends to reduce economy, since it may produce an overrich mixture under many operating conditions. On the other hand, the lower-volatility fuels tend to burn more efficiently and have a higher heat content. However, the lower-volatility fuels increase starting difficulty, reduce speed of warm-up, and do not give quite as good acceleration. Thus, only a limited percentage of the gasoline can be of low volatility.

6. *Freedom from crankcase dilution.* Crankcase dilution results when part of the gasoline enters the engine cylinders in an unvaporized condition. It does not burn but runs down the cylinder walls and enters the oil pan, where it dilutes the oil. This process washes lubricating oil from the cylinder walls (thus increasing wear of walls, rings, and pistons). Also, the diluted oil is less able to provide lubrication for other engine parts, such as the bearings. To avoid damage from crankcase dilution, the gasoline must be sufficiently volatile so that little enters the cylinders in liquid form.

7. *The volatility blend.* As can be seen from the discussion above, no one volatility would satisfy all engine operating requirements. On the one hand, the fuel must be of high volatility for easy starting and good acceleration. But it must also be of low volatility to give good fuel economy and combat vapor lock. Thus, gasoline must be blended from various amounts of different hydrocarbons having different volatilities. Such a blend satisfies the various operating requirements.

§ 10-3. ANTIKNOCK VALUE During normal combustion in the engine cylinder, an even increase of pressure occurs. Under some conditions, the last part of the compressed air-fuel mixture explodes to produce a sudden and sharp pressure increase. This may cause a rapping or knocking noise that sounds almost as though the piston head had been struck a hard hammer blow. Actually, the sudden pressure increase does impose a sudden heavy load on the piston that is almost like a hammer blow. This can be very damaging to the engine, wearing moving parts rapidly and perhaps even causing parts to break. Also, some of the energy in the gasoline is wasted, since the sudden pressure increase does not permit best utilization of the fuel energy.

Some types of gasoline are much more knock-producing than others. Because knocking is such an undesirable characteristic, gasoline producers improve their fuels to reduce the knocking tendencies. Also certain chemicals have been found to reduce knocking tendency when added to the gasoline. The actual rating of the antiknock tendencies of gasolines are given in terms of *octane number,* or the ONR (octane number rating).

§ 10-4. HEAT OF COMPRESSION To understand why knocking occurs, we should remember what happens to air or any other gas when it is compressed. We noted (§ 5-15) that the diesel engine compresses air to about one-fifteenth of its original volume and that this increases air temperature to about 1000°F. Articles 3-16 and 3-17 contain an explanation of why this temperature increase occurs (it is due to crowding the air molecules closely together). The temperature rise is called *heat of compression.* Let us see how heat of compression affects knocking.

§ 10-5. CAUSE OF KNOCKING During normal burning of fuel in the combustion chamber, the spark at the spark plug starts the burning process. A wall of flame spreads out in all directions from the spark (moving outward almost like a rubber balloon being blown up). The wall of flame travels rapidly outward through the compressed mixture until all the charge is burned. The speed with which the flame travels is called the *rate of flame propagation.* The movement of the flame wall through the combustion chamber during normal combustion is shown in the row of pictures to the left in Fig. 10-1. During combustion, the pressure increases to several hundred psi (pounds per square inch). It may exceed 1,000 psi in modern high-compression engines.

Under certain conditions, the last part of the compressed air-fuel mixture, or end gas, explodes before the flame front reaches it (Fig. 10-1, right). Remember that the end gas is being subjected to increasing pressure as the flame progresses through the air-fuel mixture. This increases the temperature of the end gas (because of heat of compression and also radiated heat from the combustion process). If the temperature reaches the critical point, this end gas will explode, as previously noted, before the flame front arrives. The effect is almost the same as if the piston head had been struck a heavy hammer blow. In fact, it sounds as though this had happened. The sudden

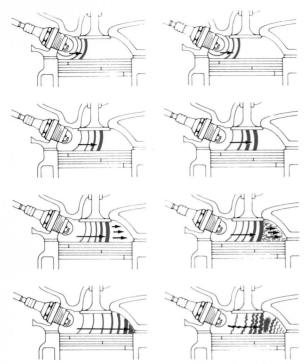

Fig. 10-1. Normal combustion without knocking is shown in the vertical row to the left. The fuel charge burns smoothly from beginning to end, providing an even, powerful thrust to the piston. Knocking is shown in the vertical row to the right. The last part of the fuel explodes, or burns, almost instantaneously, to produce detonation, or knocking. *(General Motors Corporation)*

shock load due to detonation of the last part of the charge increases wear on bearings and may actually break engine parts if the knocking is severe enough.

§ 10-6. COMPRESSION RATIO VS. KNOCKING
As compression ratios of engines have gone up (see §§ 4-9 and 4-10), so has the tendency for engines to knock. Here is the reason. With a higher compression ratio, the mixture, at TDC (top dead center), is more highly compressed and *is at a higher initial temperature.* With higher initial pressure and temperature, the temperature at which detonation occurs is reached sooner. Thus, high-compression engines have a greater tendency to knock. However, special fuels have been developed for use with the higher-compression engines, as explained below. These special fuels have a greater resistance to being set off suddenly by heat of compression. They are less apt to explode

suddenly, and they depend for their ignition on the wall of flame traveling through the air-fuel mixture.

§ 10-7. MEASURING ANTIKNOCK VALUES
There are several methods of measuring the anti-knock value of fuels. The rating is made in terms of octane number. This rating is called the ONR. A high-octane gasoline is highly resistant to knock. A low-octane fuel knocks rather easily. For example, there is one fuel called *iso-octane* that is very resistant to knocking; it is given an octane rating of 100. Another fuel, called *heptane,* knocks very easily; it is given a rating of zero. A mixture of half iso-octane and half heptane (by volume) would have a 50 ONR. A mixture of 90 percent iso-octane and 10 percent heptane would have an ONR of 90.

Actually, iso-octane and heptane are reference fuels, used only to test and rate unknown fuels. The test is made approximately as follows: The fuel to be tested is used in an engine under various conditions and compression ratios and its tolerance to knocking noted. Then the two reference fuels are mixed in varying proportions and used to run the engine under identical conditions. For example, suppose that a mixture of 88 percent iso-octane and 12 percent heptane is found to produce the same knocking characteristics as the fuel being tested. Then the reference fuel and the fuel being tested are considered to have the same 88 ONR. There are two basic methods for testing fuels, laboratory and road.

1. Laboratory method. A special test engine is used which has an adjustable head. With this engine, the compression ratio can be changed. The fuel to be tested is used to operate the engine, and the compression ratio is increased until a certain intensity of knocking is obtained. Then, without changing the compression ratio, the engine is switched to a mixture of iso-octane and heptane. The proportion of iso-octane is decreased until the same intensity of knocking is noted. Since the proportion of iso-octane of the reference-fuel mixture is known, the octane rating of the fuel being rated is also known.

2. Road-test methods. Road testing of fuels gives results that are more closely related to actual highway operation. One road test, the Cooperative Fuel Research (CFR) Modified Uniontown road test, rates fuels for knock intensity at wide-open throttle at various speeds. Octane is assigned by comparing knocking of the fuel being tested

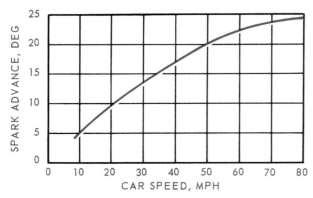

Fig. 10-2. Borderline knock curve. The fuel being tested will knock if the ignition spark is advanced to any value above the curve at any speed.

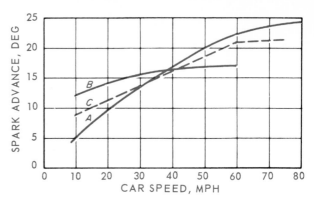

Fig. 10-3. Comparison of borderline knock curves of two fuels, A and B. Curve C is the spark advance actually provided by the ignition distributor on the engine.

to reference fuels (iso-octane and heptane) of known octane values.

Another road test, called the Modified Borderline procedure, rates the fuel at various speeds and is considered to give more information on fuel performance. This test is made by running the car at various speeds and then determining the amount of ignition spark advance the fuel can tolerate at each speed without knocking. If the spark is advanced too much at any particular speed, knocking will occur. Thus, the test results give a curve that shows, at every speed, the knock characteristics of the fuel being tested (Fig. 10-2). Any spark advance above the curve causes knock.

It must be noted, however, that some fuels knock at high speeds and others knock at low speeds. For example, refer to Fig. 10-3. This shows the curves of two fuels, A and B. Curve C is the amount of spark advance the distributor provides on the engine used in the test (see § 15-6 for a discussion of spark-advance mechanisms). If, at any particular speed, the distributor advances the spark more than the fuel can tolerate, the fuel will knock. Thus, at low speed, fuel A will knock, since the spark advance is more than the fuel can tolerate (that is, curve C is above curve A at low speed). On the other hand, fuel A will not knock at high speed, since the spark advance is not up to the amount the fuel can tolerate at high speed. But fuel B shows a different picture. It will not knock at low speed but will knock at high speed with the spark-advance curve shown. These curves, which apply only to fuels A and B, emphasize the fact that different fuels act differently at different speeds and in different engines.

§ 10-8. DETONATION VS. PREIGNITION Thus far, we have discussed the type of knocking that results from detonation, or sudden explosion, of the last part of the fuel charge. This type of knocking is usually regular in character and is most noticeable when the engine is accelerated or is under heavy load, as when climbing a hill. Under these conditions, the accelerator is nearly or fully wide-open, and the engine is taking in a full air-fuel charge on every intake stroke. This means the compression pressures reached are at the maximum; detonation pressures are more likely to be reached after the mixture is ignited.

There are other types of abnormal combustion, however, including surface ignition, preignition, and rumble. Surface ignition can originate from hot spots in the combustion chamber, such as on a hot exhaust valve or spark plug, or from combustion-chamber deposits. In some cases the deposits may break loose so that particles float free and become hot enough to produce ignition. Surface ignition can occur before (preignition) or after the spark occurs at the spark plug. Also, it can cause engine rumble and rough operation, or mild to severe knocking. In some cases, the hot spots act as substitutes for the spark plugs so that the engine continues to run even after the ignition switch is turned off. This condition can cause serious engine damage.

Preignition, surface ignition, and rumble are usually considered to be service problems, resulting from inadequate servicing of the engine, from the installation of the wrong spark plugs (which run too hot), and from the use of incorrect fuels and lubricating oils for the engine and type of operation. With incorrect fuel or oil, engine deposits may occur which will lead to surface ignition and rumble. The engine deposits not only can cause surface ignition, but they also increase the compression ratio so that the engine becomes more susceptible to knock.

§ 10-9. CHEMICAL CONTROL OF KNOCKING
Several chemicals have been found that, added to gasoline, tend to prevent detonation of the last part of the fuel charge during combustion. One theory regarding this is that the chemical tends to increase the reaction time of the fuel. That is, it increases the time required for the end gas to explode. This increased time gives the flame front time to reach the end gas so that it enters into the normal combustion process instead of exploding. One of the compounds most successful in preventing knocking is tetraethyl lead, commonly called *ethyl* or *tel*. A small amount added to gasoline thus raises the ONR of the gasoline.

To prevent the combustion products of the lead from depositing in the combustion chambers (on plugs, valves, walls, and pistons), special scavengers are also added. These compounds (ethylene dibromide and ethylene dichloride, for example) tend to change the lead compounds into forms which will vaporize and exit with the exhaust gases.

§ 10-10. MECHANICAL FACTORS AFFECTING KNOCKING
The shape of the combustion chamber has a great effect on the tendency of the engine to knock. The combustion chamber of an I-head engine is bounded at the top by the cylinder head, intake and exhaust valves, and the spark plug. It is bounded at the bottom by the piston head and top compression ring (Fig. 10-4). There are two general shapes, wedge and hemispheric (Fig. 10-5). Figures 5-8 and 5-23 illustrate engines with these two types of combustion chambers. The shape determines turbulence, squish,

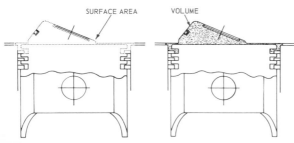

Fig. 10-4. Combustion chamber. The surface area is shown by the dotted line.

and quench, and these three factors affect knock.

1. Turbulence. When you stir your coffee, you impart turbulence to it so that the cream and sugar mix with the coffee. In a like manner, imparting turbulence to the air-fuel mixture entering the combustion chamber assures more uniform mixing so that the combustion is more uniform. Turbulence also reduces the time required for the flame front to sweep through the compressed mixture.

2. Squish. Squish refers to the way the piston, in some combustion chambers, squishes, or squeezes, a part of the air-fuel mixture at the end of the compression stroke. Figure 10-6 shows the squish area in a combustion chamber. As the piston nears TDC, the mixture is squished, or pushed, out of the squish area. As it squirts out, it promotes turbulence and thus further mixing of the air-fuel mixture.

3. Quench. We mentioned that knocking results when the end-gas temperature goes too high and the end gas explodes before the flame front reaches it. However, if some heat is extracted from the end gas, then its temperature will not reach the detonation point. In the arrangement shown in

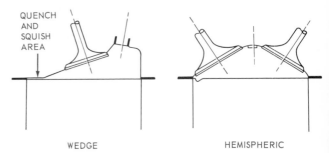

Fig. 10-5. Wedge and hemispheric combustion chambers. *(General Motors Corporation)*

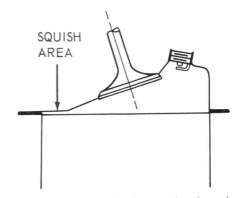

Fig. 10-6. Squish area in the combustion chamber.

Fig. 10–6, the squish area is also a quench area. The closeness of the cylinder head to the piston and the relative coolness of these metallic surfaces cause heat to be extracted from the end gas so that the tendency for detonation to occur is quenched.

4. The hemispheric combustion chamber. With the hemispheric combustion chamber, the spark plug can be located near the center of the dome (Fig. 5–23). Then, when combustion starts, the flame front has a relatively short distance to travel. There are no distant pockets of end gas to detonate. The chamber has no squish or quench areas. However, there is relatively little turbulence.

5. The wedge combustion chamber. With the wedge combustion chamber, the spark plug is located to one side, and the flame front must travel a greater distance to reach the end of the wedge (Fig. 5–8). The end of the wedge has a squish and quench area which cools the end gas to prevent detonation and at the same time imparts turbulence to the mixture.

6. Smog. The shape of the combustion chamber also influences the amount of contaminants that will appear in the exhaust gases. The relatively cool metal surfaces of the cylinder head and piston top retard combustion. Therefore, the layers of air-fuel mixture next to these metal surfaces do not burn completely. Thus, the wedge combustion chamber, with its larger surface area, produces a greater percentage of contaminants per power stroke than the hemispheric combustion chamber. See § 9–46 for additional information on smog.

§ 10–11. OTHER FACTORS AFFECTING KNOCKING
Many operating conditions in an engine affect knocking. For example, higher air temperatures increase the tendency to knock, higher humidity (or damper air) as well as higher altitudes (or lower density air) reduce the tendency to knock, engine deposits (carbon in combustion chamber) increase knock tendency, advancing the spark increases the tendency to knock, and leaning the mixture increases the tendency of the engine to knock.

All these factors point up the need for good maintenance of the modern high-compression engine. Accumulations of scale in the cooling system, which reduce cooling efficiency; clogged fuel lines or nozzles in the carburetor, which lean out the mixture; improper ignition timing; engine deposits—all these increase knocking tendencies of the engine.

§ 10–12. OTHER GASOLINE ADDITIVES
In addition to the antiknock compounds and their related lead-compound-vaporizing substances which are put into gasoline to raise its ONR (§ 10–9), many other additives are used. Major types include:

1. Oxidation inhibitors to help prevent the formation of gum while the gasoline is in storage.

2. Metal deactivators to protect the gasoline from the harmful effects of certain metals picked up in the refining process or in the vehicle fuel system.

3. Antirust agents to protect the vehicle fuel system.

4. Anti-icers to combat carburetor icing and fuel-line freeze.

5. Detergents to keep the carburetor clean.

6. Phosphorus compounds to combat surface ignition and spark-plug fouling.

7. Dye for identification.

In addition to all these, the refining process is very carefully controlled so as to keep to a minimum sulfur compounds and gum-forming substances. Sulfur compounds, in excess, will form sulfur acids which could seriously damage metal parts and bearings. Gum-forming substances, in excessive amounts, will form deposits in carburetor circuits and intake manifolds and on valves, pistons, and rings. Proper refining techniques minimize the amount of these harmful substances.

§ 10–13. CHEMISTRY OF COMBUSTION
We have already noted (in § 3–9) that gasoline, in burning, forms water, or H_2O, and carbon dioxide, or CO_2. *This occurs when enough oxygen is present to take care of all the hydrogen and carbon atoms.* However, in the gasoline engine, sufficient amounts of oxygen are not usually present. As a result, the carbon does not usually attain complete combustion. Some atoms of carbon are able to unite with only one atom of oxygen (instead of two). This produces carbon monoxide, or CO. Carbon monoxide is a dangerously poisonous gas. It has no color, is tasteless, and has practically no odor. But 15 parts of carbon monoxide in 10,000 parts of air makes the air dangerous to breathe. Higher concentrations may cause quick paralysis and death. For this reason, an engine should never be operated in a closed space, such as a garage, without some means of exhausting the gas into the outside air. Remember this fact:

Enough carbon monoxide can be produced in 3 minutes by an automobile engine running in a closed one-car garage to cause paralysis and death. *Never operate an engine with the garage doors closed!*

Another effect of incomplete combustion is the appearance in the exhaust gases of various unburned hydrocarbons. As already mentioned (§ 9–46), these compounds contribute to smog, which is considered to be a health hazard in many populous places. Automotive companies are working on exhaust-system devices that will convert these compounds to harmless gases. Also, new cars are being equipped with closed-crankcase ventilating systems to prevent the escape of blow-by gases from the engine (§ 9–46). Of course, with perfect combustion, there would be no problem. At least one automotive company is working on the problem from this angle, trying to so improve combustion that harmful compounds in the exhaust gases will be eliminated.

§ 10–14. DIESEL-ENGINE FUELS
Diesel engines use fuel oil. The fuel oil is sprayed into the compressed air in the combustion chamber at the end of the compression stroke. Heat of compression ignites the fuel oil, and the combustion stroke follows (see § 5–15). Diesel oil is light, with a low viscosity and high cetane number.

§ 10–15. DIESEL-FUEL VISCOSITY
Viscosity refers to the tendency of a liquid to resist flowing. Water has a low viscosity; it flows easily. A light oil is more viscous than water, but it still flows easily and has a relatively low viscosity. Heavy oil has a high viscosity; it flows slowly. The fuel oil used in diesel engines must have a relatively low viscosity so that it flows easily through the fuel-pumping system. But it must have sufficient viscosity to provide lubrication for the moving parts in the pumping system. However, if the viscosity is too high, the fuel will not spray, or atomize, easily and thus will not burn well.

§ 10–16. CETANE NUMBER OF DIESEL FUEL
The cetane number of diesel fuel refers to the ease with which the fuel ignites. With a high cetane number, the fuel ignites with relative ease (or at a relatively low temperature). The lower the cetane number, the higher the temperature must go to ignite the fuel. The lower the cetane number, the more likely the fuel is to knock. The fuel being sprayed into the cylinder will not ignite quickly so that it tends to accumulate. Then, when ignition does take place, there will be a combustion knock as the fuel present suddenly burns. On the other hand, if the cetane number is sufficiently high, the fuel will ignite and begin to burn as soon as the injection spray starts. There will thus be an even combustion-pressure rise and no knock.

§ 10–17. LIQUEFIED PETROLEUM GAS (LPG)
This fuel requires a special fuel system (§ 9–48). There are actually two types of LPG that have been used for automotive-engine fuel, *propane and butane.* Of these, propane is the more widely used. Sometimes, small amounts of butane are added. Propane boils at −44°F (at atmospheric pressure). Thus, it can be used in any climate where temperatures below this are not reached. Butane cannot be used in any place where temperatures below 32°F are reached, since it is liquid below that temperature. If it remains liquid, it will not vaporize in the fuel system and will thus never reach the engine.

Review Questions

1. What is the meaning of the term "hydro-carbon"?
2. Define volatility.
3. What is meant by volatility blend?
4. Define heat of compression.
5. Explain what causes knocking in an engine cylinder.
6. Explain how the antiknock values of gaso-lines are determined.
7. What is the difference between detonation and preignition?
8. What is surface ignition? Preignition? Rumble?
9. What are some mechanical factors affecting knocking?
10. What does squish mean? Quench?
11. Explain the difference between the hemisphe-ric and the wedge combustion chambers.
12. What factors affect knocking in a cylinder?
13. Name seven gasoline additives and explain their purpose.
14. Can you tell by the odor whether or not carbon monoxide is present in a room? Is there any danger in breathing carbon monoxide? Why?
15. What does cetane number in diesel fuel mean?

Study Questions

1. Write an essay on the volatility blend in gaso-line, explaining why the blend must be made from fuels of different volatilities.
2. Describe in detail the actions that produce knocking in the engine cylinder.
3. Describe the different tests used to octane-rate gasoline.
4. Make a list of the various gasoline additives and describe the various jobs that these addi-tives do.

CHAPTER

11

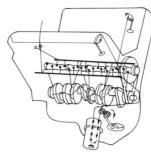

Engine Lubricating Systems

This chapter describes various types of engine lubricating systems and discusses the operation of their component parts. In addition, the purpose and properties of lubricating oil are described. We have already discussed friction (§ 4–6), engine bearings (§§ 6–10 to 6–15), and the action of the piston rings in controlling oil on the cylinder walls (§§ 7–3 to 7–9). If the facts outlined in these sections are not clear in your mind, we suggest that you reread them. They are closely related to the material on lubricating systems contained in the following pages.

---

§ 11–1. PURPOSE OF LUBRICATING SYSTEM

We normally think of lubricating oil as a substance that makes possible minimum wear or low frictional loss between adjacent moving surfaces. However, the lubricating oil circulating through the engine to all moving parts requiring lubrication performs other jobs. The lubricating oil must:

1. Lubricate moving parts to minimize wear.
2. Lubricate moving parts to minimize power loss from friction.
3. Remove heat from engine parts by acting as a cooling agent.
4. Absorb shocks between bearings and other engine parts, thus reducing engine noise and extending engine life.
5. Form a good seal between piston rings and cylinder walls.
6. Act as a cleaning agent.

1 and 2. Minimizing wear and power loss from friction. Friction has been discussed in some detail (§ 4–6). The type of friction encountered in the engine is normally viscous friction, that is, the friction between adjacent moving layers of oil. If the lubricating system does not function properly, sufficient oil will not be supplied to moving parts, and greasy or even dry friction will result between moving surfaces. This would cause, at least, considerable power loss, since power would be used in overcoming these types of friction. At most, major damage would occur to engine parts as greasy or dry friction developed. Bearings would wear with extreme rapidity; the heat resulting from

dry or greasy friction would cause bearing disintegration and failure, so that connecting rods and other parts would be broken. Insufficient lubrication of cylinder walls would cause rapid wear and scoring of walls, rings, and pistons. A properly operating engine lubricating system supplies all moving parts with sufficient oil so that only viscous friction is obtained.

3. Removing heat from engine parts. The engine oil is in rapid circulation throughout the engine lubrication system. All bearings and moving parts are bathed in streams of oil. In addition to providing lubrication, the oil absorbs heat from engine parts and carries it back into the oil pan. The oil pan in turn absorbs heat from the oil, transferring it to the surrounding air. The oil thus acts as a cooling agent.

4. Absorbing shocks between bearings and other engine parts. As the piston approaches the end of the compression stroke and the mixture in the cylinder is ignited, pressure in the cylinder suddenly increases many times. A load of as much as 3 tons is suddenly imposed on the top of a 3-inch piston as combustion takes place. This sudden increase in pressure causes the piston to thrust down hard through the piston-pin bearing, connecting rod, and connecting-rod bearing. There is always some space, or clearance, between bearings and journals; this space is filled with oil. When the load suddenly increases as described above, the layers of oil between bearings and journals must act as cushions, resisting penetration or "squeezing out," and must continue to interpose a film of oil between the adjacent metal surfaces. In thus absorbing and cushioning the hammerlike effect of the suddenly imposed loads, the oil quiets the engine and reduces wear of parts.

5. Forming a seal between piston rings and cylinder walls. Piston rings must form a gastight seal with the cylinder walls, and the lubricating oil that is delivered to the cylinder walls helps the piston rings to accomplish this. The oil film on the cylinder walls compensates for microscopic irregularities in the fit between the rings and walls and fills in any gaps through which gas might escape. The oil film also provides lubrication of the rings, so that they can move easily in the ring grooves and on the cylinder walls.

6. Acting as a cleaning agent. The oil, as it circulates through the engine, tends to wash off and carry away dirt, particles of carbon, and other foreign matter. As the oil picks up this material, it carries it back to the crankcase. There, larger particles drop to the bottom of the oil pan.

§ 11–2. **PROPERTIES OF OIL** A satisfactory engine lubricating oil must have certain characteristics, or properties. It must have proper viscosity (body and fluidity) and must resist oxidation, carbon formation, corrosion, rust, extreme pressures, and foaming. Also, it must act as a good cleaning agent, must pour at low temperatures, and must have good viscosity at extremes of high and low temperature.

Any mineral oil, by itself, does not have all these properties. Lubricating-oil manufacturers therefore put a number of additives into the oil during the manufacturing process. An oil for severe service may have many additives, as follows:

1. Usually a viscosity-index improver
2. Pour-point depressants
3. Oxidation inhibitors
4. Corrosion inhibitors
5. Rust inhibitors
6. Foam inhibitors
7. Detergent-dispersants
8. Extreme-pressure agents

These are discussed below.

1. Viscosity (body and fluidity). Primarily, viscosity is the most important characteristic of lubricating oil. Viscosity refers to the tendency of oil to resist flowing. In a bearing and journal, layers of oil adhere to the bearing and journal surfaces.

These layers must move, or slip, with respect to each other, and the viscosity of the oil determines the ease with which this slipping can take place. Viscosity may be divided for discussion into two parts, body and fluidity. Body has to do with the resistance to oil-film puncture, or penetration, during the application of heavy loads. When the power stroke begins, for example, bearing loads sharply increase. Oil body prevents the load from squeezing out the film of oil between the journal and the bearing. This property cushions shock loads, helps maintain a good seal between piston rings and cylinder walls, and maintains an adequate oil film on all bearing surfaces under load.

Fluidity has to do with the ease with which the oil flows through oil lines and spreads over bearing surfaces. In some respects, fluidity and body are opposing characteristics, since the more fluid an oil is, the less body it has. The oil used in any particular engine must have sufficient body to perform as explained in the previous paragraph and yet must have sufficient fluidity to flow freely through all oil lines and spread effectively over all bearing surfaces. Late types of engines have more closely fitted bearings with smaller clearances and consequently require oils of greater fluidity that will flow readily into the spaces between bearings and journals.

Temperature influences viscosity. Increasing temperature reduces viscosity. That is, it causes oil to lose body and gain fluidity. Decreasing temperature causes oil viscosity to increase. The oil gains body and loses fluidity. Since engine temperatures range several hundred degrees from cold-weather starting to operating temperature, a lubricating oil must have adequate fluidity at low temperatures so that it will flow. At the same time, it must have sufficient body for high-temperature operation.

2. Viscosity ratings. Viscosity of oil is determined by use of a *viscosimeter*, a device that determines the length of time required for a definite amount of oil to flow through an opening of a definite diameter. Temperature is taken into consideration during this test, since high temperature decreases viscosity, while low temperature increases viscosity. In referring to viscosity, the lower numbers refer to oils of lower viscosity (thinner). The Society of Automotive Engineers (SAE) rates oil viscosity in two different ways, for winter and for other than winter. Winter-grade oils are tested at $0°$ and $210°$ F. There are three grades, SAE5W, SAE10W, and SAE20W, the "W" indicating winter grade. For other than winter use, the grades are SAE20, SAE30, SAE40, and SAE50, all without the "W" suffix. Some oils have multiple ratings, which means they are equivalent, in viscosity, to several single-rating oils. An SAE10W-30 oil, for example, is comparable to SAE10W, SAE20W, and SAE30 oils.

3. Viscosity index. When oil is cold, it is thicker and runs more slowly than when it is hot. In other words, it becomes more viscous when it is cooled. On the other hand, it becomes less viscous when it is heated. In normal automotive-engine operation, we do not have to be too concerned about this change of oil viscosity with changing temperature. We recognize that the engine is harder to start at low temperature because the oil is thicker, or more viscous. But until the engine is cooled to many degrees below zero, we do not have to take any special steps to start it.

Some oils change viscosity a great deal with temperature change. Other oils show a much smaller change of viscosity with temperature change. In order to have an accurate measure of how much any particular oil will change in viscosity with temperature change, the viscosity-index scale was adopted. Originally, the scale ran from 0 to 100. The higher the number, the less the oil viscosity changes with temperature changes. Thus, an oil with a VI (viscosity index) of 100 will change less in viscosity with temperature changes than an oil with a VI of 10. In recent years, special VI-improving additives have been developed which step up viscosity indexes to as much as 300. Such an oil shows relatively little change in viscosity from very low to relatively high temperature.

You could especially appreciate the significance of VI if you were operating automotive equipment in a very cold climate (say, in northern Alaska). You would have to start engines at temperatures as much as 60° below zero (92° below freezing). But, once started, the engines would soon reach operating temperatures that heat the oil to several hundred degrees. If you could select an oil of a relatively high VI, then it would be fluid enough to permit starting but would not thin out (or lose viscosity) so much that lubricating effectiveness would be lost. On the other hand, an oil with a low VI would probably be so thick at low temperatures that it might actually prevent starting. But if you could start, it might then thin out too much as it warmed up.

Oil companies make sure that their oils have a sufficiently high VI to operate satisfactorily in the variations of temperatures they will meet. Also, they supply oil with multiple-viscosity ratings. For example, an oil may be designated SAE10W-30, which indicates that it is comparable to SAE10W, SAE20W, and SAE30 oils.

4. Pour-point depressants. At low temperatures, some oils become so thick that they will not pour at all. Certain additives can be put into oil which will depress, or lower, the temperature point at which the oil will become too thick to flow. Such additives keep the oil fluid at low temperatures for adequate engine lubrication during cold-weather starting and initial operation.

5. Resistance to carbon formation. Cylinder walls, pistons, and rings operate at temperatures of several hundred degrees. This temperature, acting on the oil films covering walls, rings, and pistons, tends to cause the oil to break down or burn so that carbon is produced. Carbon formation can cause poor engine performance and damage to the engine. Carbon may pack in around the piston rings, causing them to stick in the ring grooves. This prevents proper piston-ring operation, so that blow-by, poor compression, excessive oil consumption, and scoring of cylinder walls may result. Carbon may build up on the piston head and in the cylinder head. This fouls spark plugs, excessively increases compression so that knocking occurs, and reduces engine performance. Carbon may form on the underside of the piston to such an extent that heat transfer will be hindered and the piston will overheat. Pieces of carbon may break off and drop into the oil pan, where they may be picked up by the lubrication system. They could then clog oil channels and lines so that the flow of lubricating oil to engine parts would be dangerously reduced. A good lubricating oil must be sufficiently resistant to the heat and operating conditions in the engine to exhibit a minimum amount of carbon formation.

6. Oxidation inhibitors. When oil is heated to fairly high temperatures and then agitated so that considerable air is mixed with it, the oxygen in the air tends to combine with oil, oxidizing it. Since this is the treatment that engine oil undergoes (that is, it is heated and agitated with or sprayed into the air in the crankcase), some oil oxidation is bound to occur. A slight amount of oxidation will do no particular harm; but if oxidation becomes excessive, serious troubles may occur in the engine. As the oil is oxidized, it breaks down to form various harmful substances.

Some of the products of oil oxidation coat engine parts with an extremely sticky, tarlike material. This material may clog oil channels and tend to restrict the action of piston rings and valves. A somewhat different form of oil oxidation coats engine parts with a varnishlike substance that has a similar damaging effect on the engine. Even if these substances do not form, oil oxidation may produce corrosive materials in the oil that will corrode bearings and other surfaces, causing bearing failures and damage to other parts. Oil chemists and refineries control the refining processes and may add certain chemicals known as *oxidation inhibitors* so that engine lubricating oils resist oxidation.

7. Corrosion and rust inhibitors. At high temperatures, acids may form in the oil which can corrode engine parts, especially bearings. Corrosion inhibitors are added to the oil to inhibit this corrosion. Also, rust inhibitors are added. These displace water from metal surfaces so that oil coats them. Also, they have an alkaline reaction to neutralize combustion acids.

8. Foaming resistance. The churning action in the engine crankcase also tends to cause the engine oil to foam, just as an egg beater causes an egg white to form a frothy foam. As the oil foams up, it tends to overflow, or to be lost through the crankcase ventilator (§ 9–46). In addition, the foaming oil is not able to provide normal lubrication of bearings and other moving parts. Foaming oil in hydraulic valve lifters will cause them to function poorly, work noisily, wear rapidly, and possibly break. To prevent foaming, antifoaming additives are mixed with the oil.

9. Detergents-dispersants. Despite the filters and screens at the carburetor and crankcase ventilator (§ 9–46), dirt does get into the engine. In addition, as the engine runs, the combustion processes leave deposits of carbon on piston rings, valves, and other parts. Also, some oil oxidation may take place, resulting in still other deposits. Then, too, metal wear in the engine puts particles of metal into the oil. As a result of these various conditions, deposits tend to build up on and in engine parts. The deposits gradually reduce the performance of the engine and speed up wear of parts. To prevent or slow down the formation of these deposits, some engine oils contain a detergent additive.

The detergent acts much like ordinary hand soap. When you wash your hands with soap, the soap surrounds the particles of dirt on your hands,

causing them to become detached so that the water can rinse them away. In a similar manner, the detergent in the oil loosens and detaches the deposits of carbon, gum, and dirt. The oil then carries the loosened material away. The larger particles drop to the bottom of the crankcase, but smaller particles tend to remain suspended in the oil. These impurities, or contaminants, are flushed out when the oil is changed.

To prevent the particles from clotting, and to keep them in a finely divided state, a dispersant is added to the oil. Without the dispersant, the particles would tend to collect and form large particles. These large particles might then block the oil filter and reduce its effectiveness. They could also build up in oil passages and plug them, thus depriving bearing and other engine parts of oil. The dispersant prevents this and thus greatly increases the amount of contaminants the oil can carry and still function effectively.

Lubricating-oil manufacturers now place more emphasis on the dispersant qualities of the additive than on its detergent qualities. If the contaminants can be kept suspended in the oil as small particles, they will not deposit on engine parts and there is less need of detergent action.

10. Extreme-pressure resistance. The modern automotive engine subjects the lubricating oil to very high pressures, not only in the bearings, but also in the valve train. Modern valve trains have heavy valve springs and high-lift cams. This means that the valves must move farther against heavier spring opposition. To prevent the oil from squeezing out, extreme-pressure additives are put into the oil. They react chemically with metal surfaces to form very strong, slippery films which may be only a molecule or so thick. Thus, they supplement the oil by providing protection during moments of extreme pressure.

§ 11–3. WATER-SLUDGE FORMATION
Water sludge is a thick, creamy, black substance that often forms in the crankcase. It clogs oil screens and oil lines, preventing normal circulation of lubricating oil to engine parts. This can result in engine failure from oil starvation.

1. How sludge forms. Water collects in the crankcase in two ways. First, water is formed as a product of combustion (§ 3–9). Second, the crankcase ventilating system (described in § 9–46) carries air, with moisture in it, through the crankcase. If the engine parts are cold, the water condenses and drops into the crankcase. There, it is churned up with the lubricating oil by the action of the crankshaft. The crankshaft acts much like a giant egg beater and whips the oil and water into the thick, black, mayonnaiselike "goo" known as *water sludge.* The black color comes from dirt and carbon.

2. Why sludge forms. If a car is driven for long distances each time it is started, the water that collects in the crankcase while the engine is cold quickly evaporates. The crankcase ventilating system then removes the water vapor. Thus, no sludge will form. However, if the engine is operated when cold most of the time, then sludge will form. For example, the home-to-shop-to-home sort of driving, each trip being only a few miles, is sludge-forming. When a car is used for short-trip start-and-stop driving, the engine never has a chance to warm up enough to get rid of the water. The water accumulates and forms sludge.

3. Preventing sludge. To prevent sludge, the car must be driven long enough, after being started, for the engine to heat up and get rid of the water in the crankcase. If this is impractical, then the oil must be changed frequently. Naturally, during cold weather, it takes longer for the engine to warm up. Thus, in cold weather, the trips must be still longer, or oil must be changed still more frequently, to prevent water accumulation and sludge formation.

§ 11–4. SERVICE RATINGS OF OIL We have already mentioned that lubricating oil is rated as to its viscosity by number. Lubricating oil is also rated in another way, by what is called *service* designation. That is, it is rated according to the type of service for which it is best suited. There are five service ratings: MS, MM, and ML for gasoline or other spark-ignition engines, and DG and DS for diesel engines. The oils differ in their characteristics and in the additives they contain.

1. MS oil. This oil is for severe service and unfavorable operating conditions. It is to be used where there are special lubricating requirements for bearing-corrosion and engine-deposit control because of operating conditions or engine design. This includes:
   a. Low operating temperature and short-trip start-stop driving conditions.
   b. High-speed highway driving, where oil will become unusually hot, as during a summer-vacation trip.
   c. Heavy-load operation, such as is typical of highway truck service.

2. MM oil. This oil is for medium service, such as:
   a. High-speed but fairly short trips.
   b. Continuous high-temperature and heavy-load conditions.
   c. Operation at moderate cold-air temperatures where the car is used for both long and short trips.

3. ML oil. This oil is for comparatively light service where most of the trips are longer than 10 miles and where no extremes of air temperature are encountered.

● **CAUTION:** Do not confuse *viscosity* and *service* ratings of oil. Some people think that a high-viscosity oil is a "heavy-duty" oil. This is not necessarily so. Viscosity ratings refer to the thickness of the oil; thickness is not a measure of heavy-duty quality. Remember that there are two ratings, viscosity and service. Thus, an SAE 10 oil can be an MS, MM, or ML oil. Likewise, an oil of any other viscosity rating can have any one of the three service ratings (MS, MM, or ML).

4. DS oil. This is an oil for lubricating diesel engines operating under the most severe service conditions, such as:
   a. Continuous low temperatures and light loads.
   b. Continuous high-temperature and heavy-load conditions.
   c. Operation on fuels of high sulfur content or abnormal volatility.

5. DG oil. This is an oil for lubricating diesel engines operating under comparatively light to normal conditions, such as are typical of most trucking and farm-tractor operations.

§ 11–5. OIL CHANGES From the day that fresh oil is put into the engine crankcase, it begins to lose its effectiveness as an engine lubricant. This gradual loss of effectiveness is largely due to the accumulation of various contaminating substances. For instance, water sludge may accumulate, as already noted (§ 11–3). In addition, during engine operation, carbon tends to form in the combustion chamber. Some of this carbon gets into the oil. Gum, acids, and certain lacquerlike substances may also be left by the combustion of the fuel or may be produced in the oil itself by the high engine temperatures. In addition, the air that enters the engine (in the air-fuel mixture) carries with it a certain amount of dust. Even though the air filter is operating efficiently, it will not remove all the dust. Then, too, the engine releases fine metal particles as it wears. All these substances tend to circulate with the oil. As the mileage piles up, the oil accumulates more and more of these contaminants. Even though the engine has an oil filter, some of these contaminants will remain in the oil. Finally, after many miles of operation, the oil will be so loaded with contaminants that it is not safe to use. Unless it is drained and clean oil put in, engine wear will increase rapidly.

Modern engine oils are compounded to fight contamination. They contain certain chemicals (called *additives*) which deter corrosion and foaming and help to keep the engine clean by detergent action. Yet they cannot keep the oil in good condition indefinitely. After many miles of service, the oil is bound to become contaminated, and it should be changed.

Up until about 1960, the recommendations were these: For dusty or cold-weather start-and-stop driving, the oil should be changed every 500 miles or 60 days. For "average" operation, that is, short-run start-and-stop service on paved roads with moderate temperatures, mixed with longer trips, the oil should be changed every 1,000 miles. For open-highway driving on paved roads, oil should be changed every 2,000 miles.

With the development of improved lubricating oils and more efficient oil and air filters, automotive manufacturers have liberalized their recommendations as follows: With favorable operating conditions some manufacturers recommend that the oil should be changed every two months or 4,000 miles of operation, whichever occurs first. Other manufacturers put the change intervals at every two months or 6,000 miles, whichever occurs first. All recommend that for more adverse driving conditions, such as start-and-stop, cold-weather, or dusty conditions, the oil should be changed more frequently.

NOTE: Automobile manufacturers recommend that the oil be changed (along with the oil filter) and the air filter cleaned whenever the car has been subjected to a spell of dusty driving or has encountered a dust storm. When dusty conditions are encountered in driving, the air and oil filters are likely to become clogged with dust rather quickly. This means that the oil takes on an excessive amount of dust. This dust must be removed from the engine by draining the oil, cleaning the air filters, and replacing the oil filter.

§ 11–6. OIL CONSUMPTION Oil is lost from the engine in three ways: by burning in the combustion chambers, by leakage in liquid form, and by passing out of the crankcase in the form of a mist (which, in the closed-crankcase ventilating system, will also be burned in the combustion chambers. See § 9–46). Two main factors affect oil consumption, *engine speed* and *the amount that engine parts have worn.* High speed produces high temperature. This, in turn, lowers the viscosity of the oil so that it can more readily work past the piston rings into the combustion chamber, where it is burned. In addition, the high speed exerts a centrifugal effect on the oil that is feeding through the oil lines drilled in the crankshaft to the connecting-rod journals. Thus, more oil is fed to the bearings and subsequently thrown on the cylinder walls. Also, high speeds cause "ring shimmy." With this condition, the oil-control rings cannot function effectively. Crankcase ventilation (§ 9–46) causes more air to pass through the crankcase at high speed. This causes oil to be lost in the form of mist.

As engine parts wear, oil consumption increases. Worn bearings tend to throw more oil onto the cylinder walls. Tapered and worn cylinder walls prevent normal oil-control-ring action. The rings cannot change shape rapidly enough to conform with the worn cylinder walls as the rings move up and down. More oil consequently gets into the combustion chamber, where it burns and fouls spark plugs, valves, rings, and pistons. Carbon formation aggravates the condition, since it further reduces the effectiveness of the oil-control rings. Where cylinder-wall wear is not excessive, installation of special oil-control rings reduces oil consumption by improving the wiping action so that less oil can move past the rings. After cylinder-wall wear has progressed beyond a certain point, the cylinders must be machined and new rings installed to bring oil consumption down.

Worn intake-valve guides will also increase oil consumption because oil will leak past the valve stems and will be pulled into the combustion chamber along with the air-fuel mixture every time the intake valves open. Installation of new valve guides, reaming of guides and installation of valves with oversize stems, or installation of valve-stem seals, will reduce oil consumption from this cause.

Another cause of excessive oil consumption is a cracked vacuum-pump diaphragm, which passes oil into the intake manifold and from there into the engine cylinders, where it is burned (see § 26–14).

§ 11–7. TYPES OF LUBRICATING SYSTEMS Two types of lubricating systems have been used on four-cycle automotive engines, splash and combination splash and pressure feed. In addition, there are various lubrication methods for two-cycle engines.

1. Splash. In the splash lubricating system, oil is splashed up from the oil pan or oil trays in the lower part of the crankcase. The oil is thrown upward as droplets or fine mist and provides adequate lubrication to valve mechanisms, piston pins, cylinder walls, and piston rings (Fig. 11–1). The straight splash lubrication system is not used on many automotive engines today, having been largely replaced by the pressure-feed system (explained below). Even in the pressure-feed system, however, many moving engine parts are lubricated by splashing oil. The splash system is

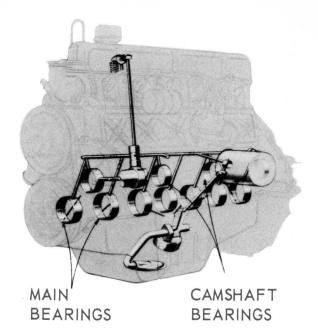

MAIN BEARINGS   CAMSHAFT BEARINGS

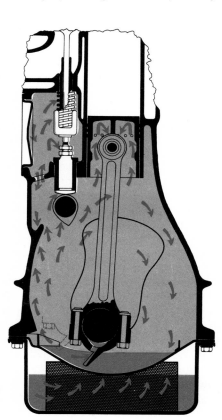

Fig. 11–1. Splash lubricating system used on an in-line engine. An oil pump maintains the proper level of oil in the tray under the connecting rods.

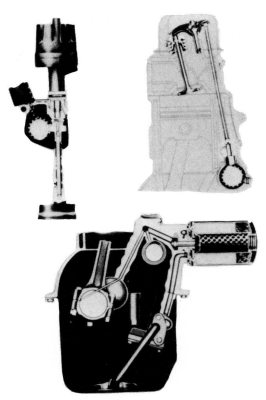

Fig. 11–2. Lubrication system of a six-cylinder, overhead-valve engine with seven main bearings. *(Ford Division of Ford Motor Company)*

widely used in small four-cycle engines for lawn-mowers, outboard marine operation, and so on.

In the engine shown in Fig. 11–1, dippers on the connecting-rod bearing caps enter oil trays in the oil pan with each crankshaft revolution to produce the oil splash. An oil pump delivers oil from the oil pan to the trays. Note that this is an L-head engine. A splash lubricating system would not be satisfactory for an I-head engine, because there would be no way for the oil splash to reach the valve mechanisms in the head.

2. Combination splash and pressure feed. In this lubricating system, many of the engine parts are lubricated by oil fed to them under pressure from the oil pump (Figs. 11–2 to 11–4). The oil from the pump enters an oil line (or a drilled header, or channel, or gallery, as it is variously called). From the oil line, it flows to the main bearings and camshaft bearings. The main bearings have oil-feed holes or grooves that feed oil into drilled passages in the crankshaft. The oil flows through these passages to the connecting-rod bearings. From there, on some engines, it flows through holes drilled in the connecting rods to the piston-pin bearings.

In I-head engines, oil is fed under pressure to the valve mechanisms in the head. For example, on some engines having the rocker arms mounted on shafts, the shafts are hollow and feed oil to the rocker arms. On engines that have independently mounted rocker arms (Fig. 8–17), the mount-

ing studs are hollow and feed oil from an oil gallery in the head to the rocker-arm ball pivots. The oil spills off the rocker arms and provides lubrication for the valve stems and push-rod and valve-stem tips so that all valve-mechanism parts are adequately lubricated.

Cylinder walls are lubricated by splashing oil thrown off from the connecting-rod bearings. Some engines have oil-spit holes or grooves in the connecting rods that index with drilled holes in the crankpin journals with each revolution. As this happens, a stream of oil is spit, or thrown, onto the cylinder walls (Fig. 11–5). On many V-8 engines, the oil-spit holes or grooves are so arranged that they deliver their jets of oil into opposing cylinders in the other cylinder bank. That is, the spit holes in the connecting rods in the right-hand bank lubricate the cylinder walls in the left-hand bank and vice versa. In many engines, the piston pins are lubricated with oil scraped off the cylinder walls by the piston rings. The piston has grooves, holes, or slots to feed oil from the oil-control-ring groove, or from oil scoops on the piston, to the piston-pin bushings.

3. Two-cycle engines. In the two-cycle engine, the air-fuel mixture passes through the crankcase on its way from the carburetor to the engine cylinders (§ 5–13). For this reason it is not possible to maintain a reservoir of oil in the crankcase; the oil would be picked up by the passing air-fuel mixture, carried to the engine cylinders, and burned. Therefore, to provide lubrication of two-cycle engine parts, the oil is mixed with the fuel. As the air and oil-fuel mixture enters the crankcase, the fuel, being more volatile, evaporates and passes on to the engine as an air-fuel mixture. Some of the oil is carried along with the air-fuel mixture and is burned. But enough oil is left behind to keep the moving engine parts coated with oil and thus adequately lubricated.

With most two-cycle engines, the oil is poured into the fuel tank along with the gasoline. The engine shown in Fig. 5–30 has a special oil-metering system which feeds oil from a reserve oil tank to the carburetor, and the mixing takes place in the carburetor air horn.

§ 11–8. OIL PUMPS The two general types of oil pumps used in pressure-feed lubricating systems are shown in Figs. 11–6 and 11–7. The gear-type pump uses a pair of meshing gears. As the gears rotate, the spaces between the gear teeth are filled with oil from the oil inlet. Then, as the

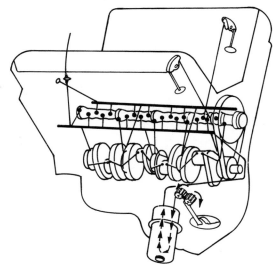

Fig. 11–3. Simplified drawing of lubricating system for a V-8 engine. *(Cadillac Motor Car Division of General Motors Corporation)*

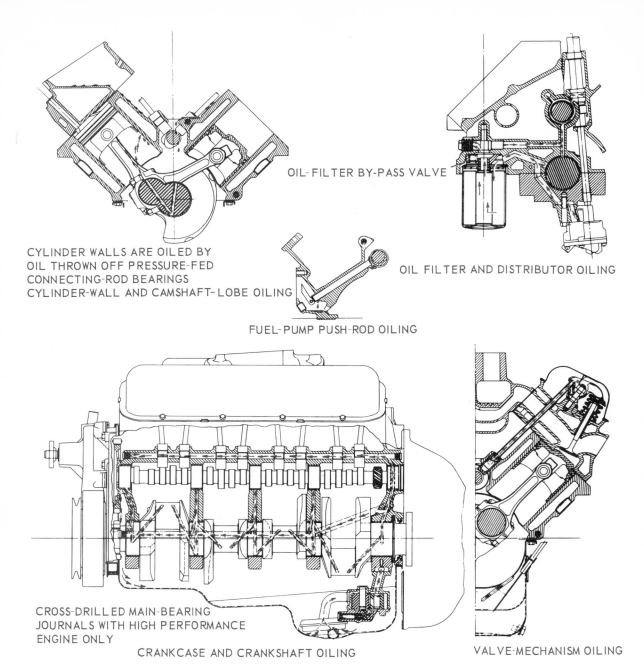

OIL-FILTER BY-PASS VALVE

CYLINDER WALLS ARE OILED BY
OIL THROWN OFF PRESSURE-FED
CONNECTING-ROD BEARINGS
CYLINDER-WALL AND CAMSHAFT-LOBE OILING

OIL FILTER AND DISTRIBUTOR OILING

FUEL-PUMP PUSH-ROD OILING

CROSS-DRILLED MAIN-BEARING
JOURNALS WITH HIGH PERFORMANCE
ENGINE ONLY

CRANKCASE AND CRANKSHAFT OILING

VALVE-MECHANISM OILING

Fig. 11-4. Lubrication system of a V-8, overhead-valve engine. Arrows show flow of oil to the moving parts in the engine. *(Chevrolet Motor Division of General Motors Corporation)*

teeth mesh, the oil is forced out through the oil outlet. The rotor-type pump uses an inner rotor and an outer rotor. The inner rotor is driven and causes the outer rotor to turn with it. As this happens, the spaces between the rotor lobes become filled with oil. Then, when the lobes of the inner rotor move into the spaces in the outer rotor, the oil is squeezed out through the outlet. Oil pumps are usually driven from the engine camshaft, from the same spiral gear that drives the ignition distributor (Fig. 11-8). The oil intake for the oil pump is attached to a float in many engines. This float-

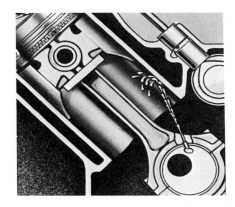

Fig. 11–5. When a hole in the connecting rod aligns with a hole in the crankpin, oil is sprayed onto the cylinder wall, as shown, providing lubrication of the piston and rings. *(Lincoln-Mercury Division of Ford Motor Company)*

ing intake then takes oil from the top of the oil in the oil pan. Since dirt particles sink, the top oil is cleanest.

§ 11–9. RELIEF VALVE To keep the oil pump from building up excessive pressures, a relief valve is included in the lubricating system. The valve consists of a spring-loaded ball (Fig. 11–6) or a spring-loaded plunger. When the pressure reaches the preset value, the ball or plunger is moved against its spring to open a port through which oil can flow back to the oil pan. Thus, enough of the oil flows past the relief valve to prevent excessive pressure. The oil pump can normally deliver much more oil than the engine requires. This is a safety factor that assures adequate delivery of oil under extreme operating conditions.

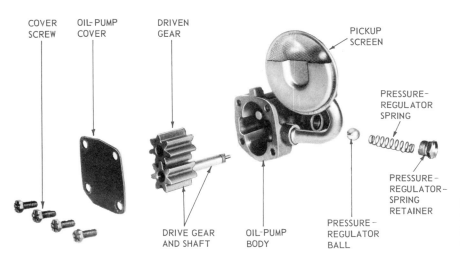

Fig. 11–6. Disassembled view of a gear-type oil pump. *(Pontiac Motor Division of General Motors Corporation)*

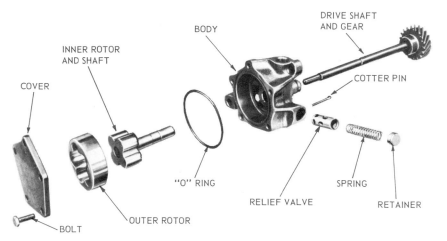

Fig. 11–7. Disassembled view of a rotor-type oil pump. *(Dodge Division of Chrysler Motors Corporation)*

195

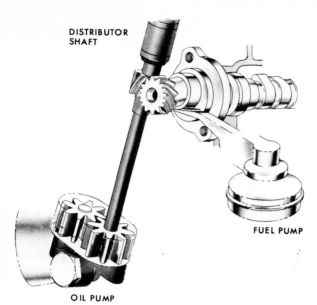

DISTRIBUTOR SHAFT

FUEL PUMP

OIL PUMP

Fig. 11–8. Oil pump, distributor, and fuel pump drives. The oil pump is the gear type. A gear on the end of the camshaft drives the ignition distributor and an extension of the distributor shaft drives the oil pump. The fuel pump is driven by an eccentric on the camshaft. *(Buick Motor Division of General Motors Corporation)*

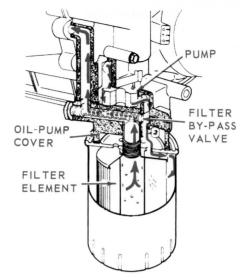

PUMP

OIL-PUMP COVER

FILTER BY-PASS VALVE

FILTER ELEMENT

Fig. 11–9. Cutaway view of a full-flow oil filter with by-pass valve. *(Buick Motor Division of General Motors Corporation)*

§ 11–10. OIL FILTERS Most lubricating systems have an oil filter. Some or all of the oil from the oil pump circulates through this filter. In the filter is a cartridge of filtering material that traps particles of foreign matter. The filter thus helps to keep the oil clean and prevents the particles from entering the engine, where they might damage bearings or other engine parts. Filters are of two types, those which filter part of the oil from the oil pump (called *by-pass* filters), and those which filter all the oil in circulation through the system (called *full-flow* filters). The full-flow filter includes a spring-loaded bypass valve that serves as a protection against oil starvation in case the filter becomes clogged with contaminants. When this happens, the valve is opened by the increased pressure from the pump trying to push oil through. With the valve opened, oil bypasses the filter; the engine is thus assured of sufficient oil. However, the filter element should be replaced periodically so that the filter will maintain filtering efficiency. Figure 11–9 is a cutaway view of a filter.

§ 11–11. OIL-PRESSURE INDICATORS The oil-pressure indicator tells the driver what the oil pressure is in the engine. This gives warning if

some stoppage occurs in the lubrication system that prevents delivery of oil to vital parts. Oil-pressure indicators are of three general types, pressure-expansion, electric-resistance, and indicator light. The latter two are the more commonly used.

1. Pressure-expansion. The pressure-expansion indicator uses a hollow Bourdon (curved) tube that is fastened at one end and free at the other. The oil pressure is applied to the curved tube through an oil line from the engine and causes the tube to straighten out somewhat as pressure increases. This movement is transmitted to a needle by linkage and gears from the end of the tube. The needle moves across the face of a dial and registers the amount of oil pressure.

2. Electric. Electrically operated oil-pressure indicators are of two types, the balancing-coil type and the bimetal-thermostat type. The balancing-coil type makes use of two separate units, the engine unit and the indicating unit (Fig. 11–10). The engine unit consists of a variable resistance and a movable contact that moves from one end of the resistance to the other in accordance with varying oil pressure against a diaphragm. As pressure increases, the diaphragm moves inward, causing the contact to move along the resistance so that more resistance is placed in the circuit between the engine and indicating units. This reduces the amount of current that can flow in

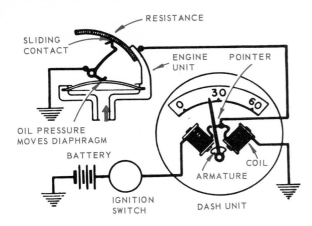

Fig. 11-10. Electric circuit of electric-resistance oil-pressure indicator.

the circuit. The indicating unit consists of two coils that balance each other in a manner similar to electrically operated fuel gauges (§ 9–5). In fact, this type of indicator operates in the same manner as the fuel indicator, the only difference being that the fuel indicator uses a float that moves up or down as the gasoline level changes in the gasoline tank, but, in the oil-pressure indicator, changing oil pressure operates a diaphragm that causes the resistance change.[Refer to the discussion on the operation of the fuel-indicator gauge (§ 9–5).]

The bimetal-thermostat-type oil-pressure indicator is similar to the bimetal-thermostat fuel gauge (§ 9–5). The dash units are practically identical. The engine unit of the oil-pressure indicator, although somewhat different in appearance from the tank unit of the fuel gauge, operates in a similar manner. Varying oil pressure on a diaphragm distorts the engine-unit thermostat blade varying amounts, and this distortion produces a like distortion in the dash-unit thermostat blade, causing the oil pressure to be registered on the dash unit.

3. Indicator light. Instead of a gauge, many vehicles have an oil-pressure indicator light. The light comes on when the ignition is turned on and the oil pressure is low. Normally, after the engine has started and oil pressure has built up, the light goes off. If it does not, then the engine and lubricating system should be checked at once to find the cause of low oil pressure. The light is connected to a pressure switch in the engine which is closed except when oil pressure increases to normal values. The indicator light and the pressure switch are connected in series to the battery through the ignition switch. When the ignition switch is turned on, the indicator light comes on and stays on until the engine starts and the oil pressure builds up enough to open the pressure switch.

§ 11–12. OIL-LEVEL INDICATORS To determine the level of the oil in the oil pan, an oil-level stick, or "dipstick," is used. The dipstick is so placed that it protrudes down into the oil. It can be withdrawn to determine the oil level by noting how high the oil rises on the dipstick. In the closed or positive crankcase ventilating system (PCV), the dipstick tube is sealed at the top when the dipstick is in place. This keeps unfiltered air from entering the crankcase and crankcase gases from escaping.

Review Questions

1. Name the six jobs that the engine lubrication oil must perform.
2. How does the engine oil remove heat from the engine?
3. What are the main characteristics that a satisfactory engine lubricating oil must have?
4. What is viscosity?
5. What are the two properties into which viscosity may be divided?
6. What is oil body?
7. What is oil fluidity?
8. Does temperature influence the viscosity of oil? In what way?
9. Why must engine oil be resistant to carbon formation?
10. Why is oil oxidation harmful to the engine?
11. What is viscosity index?
12. What is water-sludge formation? Is this most likely to form during long drives or during short drives with frequent stops during which the engine is turned off?
13. In what three principal ways is oil lost from the engine?
14. What are the two main types of lubrication system?

15. Describe the actions that produce lubrication of engine parts in a splash lubrication system.
16. Describe the actions that produce lubrication of engine parts in a pressure-feed lubrication system.
17. What is the purpose of an oil pump?
18. What is the purpose of the relief valve in a pressure-feed lubrication system? How does the relief valve operate?
19. What are the two types of oil filters? Describe briefly how each operates.
20. What is a floating oil intake? How does it operate?
21. Name two types of oil-pressure indicators.
22. What is crankcase ventilation, and why is it desirable on the gasoline engine?
23. Describe the closed-crankcase ventilating system.
24. Why is it important to keep the crankcase ventilator valve in good operating condition?
25. How can you determine the oil level in the oil pan of an engine?

Study Questions

1. In modern engines, the tendency has been to provide closer fits of bearings. On such engines, must the oil viscosity be greater or less? Explain the reason for your answer.
2. If you were driving a car, would you rather have the fuel gauge or the oil-pressure gauge stick?
3. Can you think of a design for an automatic gauge that would automatically indicate the level of the oil in the engine oil pan?
4. As engine bearings and cylinder walls wear, it is sometimes the practice to use a lubricating oil of a different viscosity. Is the viscosity less or greater than the viscosity of the oil used in a new engine? Explain your reasoning.
5. Make a sketch of a pressure-expansion-type oil-pressure indicator, and write a brief explanation of how it operates.
6. Make a sketch of a balancing-coil-type oil-pressure indicator, and write a brief explanation of how it operates.
7. Make a sketch of a bimetal-thermostat-type oil-pressure indicator, and write a brief explanation of how it operates.

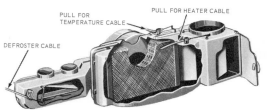

CHAPTER

12

Engine Cooling Systems

DEFROSTER CABLE

PULL FOR
TEMPERATURE CABLE

PULL FOR HEATER CABLE

This chapter discusses the construction and operation of automotive-engine cooling systems. As previously noted, the cylinder block and cylinder head have water jackets (§§ 6–2 and 6–3) through which cooling water can circulate. It is this circulation of water between the water jackets and the radiator that makes the cooling system effective.

§ 12–1. PURPOSE OF COOLING SYSTEM The purpose of the cooling system is to keep the engine at its most efficient operating temperature at all engine speeds and all driving conditions. During the combustion of the air-fuel mixture in the engine cylinders, temperatures as high as 4500°F may be reached by the burning gases. Some of this heat is absorbed by the cylinder walls, cylinder heads, and pistons. They, in turn, must be provided with some means of cooling, so that their temperatures will not reach excessive values. Cylinder-wall temperature must not increase beyond about 400 or 500°F. Temperatures higher than this will cause the lubricating-oil film to break down and lose its lubricating properties. But it is desirable to operate the engine at temperatures as close to the limits imposed by oil properties as possible. Removing too much heat through the cylinder walls and head would lower engine thermal efficiency (§ 4–19). Cooling systems are designed to remove about 30 to 35 percent of the heat produced in the combustion chambers by the burning of the air-fuel mixture.

Since the engine is quite inefficient when cold, the cooling system includes devices that prevent normal cooling action during engine warm-up. These devices allow the working parts to reach operating temperatures more quickly and shorten the inefficient cold-operating time. Then, when the engine reaches operating temperatures, the cooling system begins to function. Thus, the cooling system cools rapidly when the engine is hot, and it cools slowly or not at all when the engine is warming up or cold.

Two general types of cooling systems are used, air cooling and liquid cooling. Most automotive

engines now employ liquid cooling, although engines for airplanes, motorcycles, power lawn mowers, and so forth, are all air-cooled. Air-cooled engines have metal fins on the heads and cylinders to help radiate the heat from the engine. Cylinders are usually partly or completely separated to improve air circulation around them. Special shrouds and blowers are used on many air-cooled engines to improve air circulation around the cylinders and heads. Figures 5–12 and 5–18 illustrate air-cooled engines.

The liquid cooling systems usually employ a water pump to maintain circulation in the system. Figures 5–25 and 12–1 show cooling systems for V-8 engines. The water pump, driven by a belt from the engine crankshaft, circulates the cooling liquid between the radiator and engine water jackets, as shown. The cooling liquid is water. Antifreeze compounds are added to the water during the winter. Following articles describe the cooling-system components in detail.

§ 12–2. WATER JACKETS Just as we might put on a sweater or a jacket to keep warm on a cool day, so are water jackets placed around the engine cylinders. There is this difference: Water jackets are designed to keep the cylinders cool. The water jackets are cast into the cylinder blocks and heads (§§ 6–2 and 6–3).

§ 12–3. WATER PUMPS Water pumps are usually of the impeller type and are mounted at the front end of the cylinder block between the block and the radiator (Figs. 5–25 and 12–1). The pump (Figs. 12–2 and 12–3) consists of a housing, with a water inlet and outlet, and an impeller. The impeller is

199

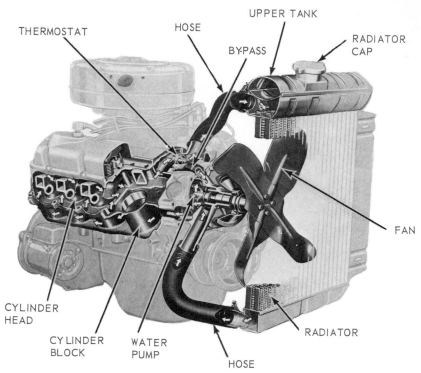

Fig. 12-1. Cutaway view of a V-8 engine showing its cooling system. (Ford Motor Company)

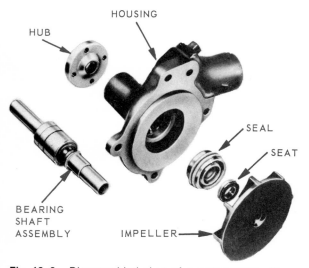

Fig. 12-2. Disassembled view of a water pump. (Pontiac Motor Division of General Motors Corporation)

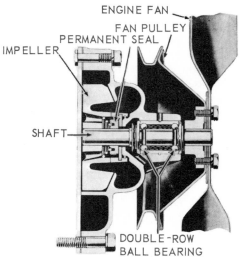

Fig. 12-3. Sectional view of a water pump, showing the manner of supporting a shaft on double-row ball bearing and the method of mounting the fan and the pulley on the shaft.

a flat plate mounted on the pump shaft with a series of flat or curved blades, or vanes. When the impeller rotates, the water between the blades is thrown outward by centrifugal force and is forced through the pump outlet and into the cyl-

inder block. The pump inlet is connected by a hose to the bottom of the radiator, and water from the radiator is drawn into the pump to replace the water forced through the outlet.

The impeller shaft is supported on one or more

bearings; a seal prevents water from leaking out around the bearing. The pump is driven by a belt to the drive pulley, mounted on the front end of the engine crankshaft.

§ 12-4. ENGINE FAN The engine fan is usually mounted on the water-pump shaft and is driven by the same belt that drives the pump and the generator (Fig. 12–3). The purpose of the fan is to provide a powerful draft of air through the radiator. Some applications are equipped with a fan shroud that improves fan performance. The shroud increases the efficiency of the fan, since it assures that all air pulled back by the fan must first pass through the radiator.

1. Fan belt. The belts are of the V type. Friction between the sides of the belt and the sides of the grooves in the pulleys causes the driving power to be transmitted through the belt from one pulley to the other. The V-type belt provides a substantial area of contact, so that considerable power may be transmitted; the wedging action of the belt as it curves into the pulley grooves aids in preventing belt slippage.

2. Variable-speed fan drive. Many engines use a variable-speed fan drive which reduces fan speed to conserve horsepower at high engine speed and also when cooling requirements are low. At high speeds, a typical engine fan might use up several horsepower and, in addition, might produce some noise. The variable-speed fan drive (Fig. 12–4) contains a small fluid coupling partly filled with a special silicone oil. When engine cooling requirements are severe, as during high-temperature,

high-speed operation, more oil is injected into the fluid coupling, and this causes more power to pass through the coupling. Fan speed therefore goes up. When cooling requirements are low, as during cool-weather, intermediate-speed operation, oil is withdrawn from the fluid coupling so that less power passes through and fan speed drops off.

The amount of oil in the fluid coupling, and thus fan speed, is controlled by a thermostatic strip (Fig. 12–4) which is held at its two ends by clips to the face of the fan drive. The strip bows outward with increasing under-the-hood temperatures, and this motion allows a control piston centered in the fan drive to move outward. The outward-moving piston causes more oil to flow into the fluid coupling, and this speeds up the fan for improved cooling. As the under-the-hood temperatures drop, the thermostatic strip straightens, forcing the control piston in. This action causes oil to leave the fluid coupling so that fan speed drops.

3. Flex fan. Another system of reducing power requirements to drive the fan and fan noise at high speed is to use a fan with flexible blades (Fig. 12–5). With this design, the pitch of the blades decreases as fan speed increases, owing to centrifugal force. The result is that each blade pushes less air, and thus power needs and noise are less at higher speeds.

§ 12-5. RADIATOR The radiator (Fig. 12–1) is a device for holding a large volume of water in close contact with a large volume of air so that heat

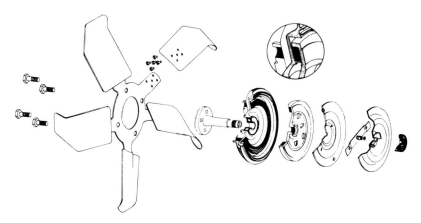

Fig. 12–4. Fan drive assembly. The fan drive contains a small fluid coupling which varies fan speed according to cooling requirements. *(Ford Division of Ford Motor Company)*

Fig. 12-5. Flexible-blade engine-cooling-system fan. (*Ford Division of Ford Motor Company*)

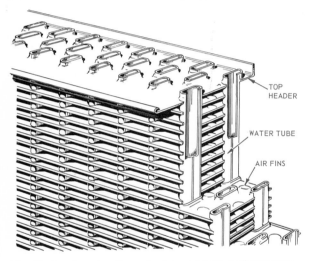

Fig. 12-6. Construction of a tube-and-fin radiator core.

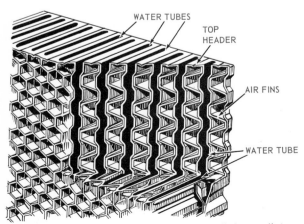

Fig. 12-7. Construction of a ribbon-cellular radiator core.

will transfer from the water to the air. The radiator core is divided into two separate and intricate compartments; water passes through one, and air passes through the other. There are several types of radiator core. Two of the more commonly used types are the tube-and-fin (Fig. 12-6) and the ribbon-cellular (Fig. 12-7). The tube-and-fin type consists of a series of long tubes extending from the top to the bottom of the radiator (or from upper to lower tank). Fins are placed around the tubes to improve heat transfer. Air passes around the outside of the tubes, between the fins, absorbing heat from the water in passing.

The ribbon-cellular radiator core (Fig. 12-7) is made up of a large number of narrow water passages formed by pairs of thin metal ribbons soldered together along their edges, running from the upper to the lower tank. The edges of the water passages, which are soldered together, form the front and back surfaces of the radiator core. The water passages are separated by air fins of metal ribbon, which provide air passages between the water passages. Air moves through these passages from front to back, absorbing heat from the fins. The fins, in turn, absorb heat from the water moving downward through the water passages. As a consequence, the water is cooled.

Radiators can be classified in another way, according to the direction that the water flows through them. In some, the water flows from top to bottom (down-flow type). In others, the water flows horizontally from an input tank on one side to another tank on the other side (cross-flow type).

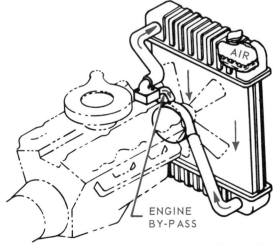

Fig. 12-8. Cooling system using a down-flow radiator. (*Harrison Radiator Division of General Motors Corporation*)

202

These two types are shown in Figs. 12–8 and 12–9.

The water tank above or to the side of the radiator serves two purposes. It provides a reserve supply of water, and it also provides a place where the water can be separated from any air that might be circulating in the system. The tank has a filler cap which can be removed for addition of water as necessary.

Many systems have a separate supply tank (Figs. 12–10 and 12–11). The separate supply tank reduces the height of the radiator itself, and it also can be placed for easier filling when additional water is required.

Radiator grills, which add to the streamlined appearance of the car, place some added load on cooling systems, since they tend to restrict the flow of air through the radiator. However, where they are used, the cooling system is designed to meet all cooling requirements adequately.

§ 12–6. HOT-WATER CAR HEATER Many automobiles are equipped with car heaters of the hot-water type (Figs. 12–12 and 12–13). This device might be considered a secondary radiator that transfers heat from the cooling system to the passenger compartment of the automobile instead of to the air passing through the main radiator. Hot water from the engine is circulated through the heater radiator, and a small electric motor drives a fan that forces air through the radiator section of the heater. The air absorbs heat from the heater radiator.

Figure 12–13 shows a cutaway view of the heater core and the heater and defroster controls. The cables are connected to control knobs in the

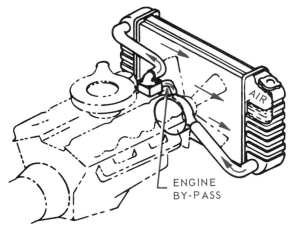

Fig. 12–9. Cooling system using a cross-flow radiator. *(Harrison Radiator Division of General Motors Corporation)*

Fig. 12–10. Cooling system using a down-flow radiator and a separate supply tank. Although the supply tank is shown above the radiator, it can be placed to one side or wherever it is convenient. *(Harrison Radiator Division of General Motors Corporation)*

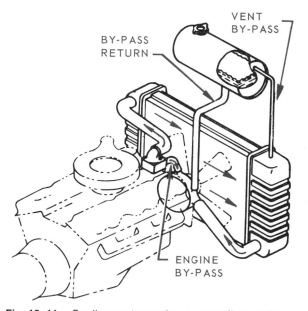

Fig. 12–11. Cooling system using a cross-flow radiator and a separate supply tank. The supply tank can be placed anywhere that is convenient in relation to the radiator. *(Harrison Radiator Division of General Motors Corporation)*

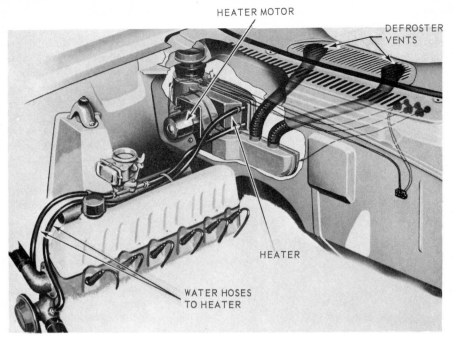

Fig. 12–12. Car heater system. Hot water from the engine cooling system circulates through a small radiator. The fan blows air through the radiator. *(Ford Division of Ford Motor Company)*

driver's compartment so that he can choose the amount of warm air he wishes to be directed against the windshield and into the car.

§ 12–7. THERMOSTAT The thermostat is placed in the water passage between the cylinder head and the top of the radiator (Fig. 12–1). Its purpose is to close off this passage when the engine is cold, so that water circulation is restricted, causing the engine to reach operating temperature more quickly. The thermostat consists of a thermostatic device and a valve (Fig. 12–14). Various valve arrangements and thermostatic devices have been used. The bellows type contains a liquid that evaporates with increasing temperature so that the internal pressure causes the bellows to expand and raise the valve off its seat. This permits water to circulate between the engine and radiator. Instead of a liquid, most thermostats are now powered by a wax pellet which expands with in-

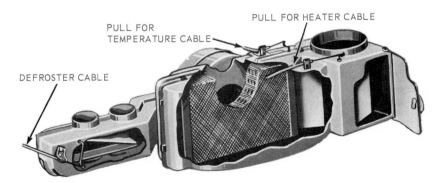

Fig. 12–13. Heater-system controls. Operating the controls changes the positions of the valves so that more or less warm air can be sent through the defroster vents. *(Ford Division of Ford Motor Company)*

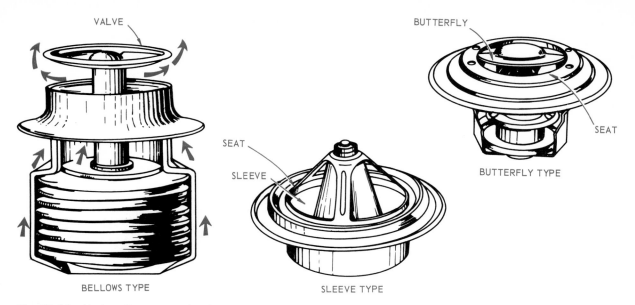

Fig. 12–14. Various thermostats for the engine cooling system. The bellows type is shown open with arrows indicating water flow past the valve. *(Chrysler-Plymouth Division of Chrysler Motors Corporation)*

creasing temperature to open a valve. The sleeve and the butterfly thermostats shown in Fig. 12–14 both use the wax pellet.

Thermostats are designed to open at specific temperatures. For example, a thermostat designated as a 180°F unit will start to open between 177° and 182°F and will be fully open at 202°F. A 160°F thermostat will operate at 20° below these figures. Thermostats of the proper characteristics are selected to suit the operating requirements of the engine as well as the kind of antifreeze used. For example, with permanent-type (glycol) antifreeze, a 180°F thermostat is recommended by the automotive manufacturers. With alcohol-type antifreeze, a 160°F thermostat is recommended.

With the engine cold and the thermostatic valve consequently closed, the water cannot pass between the engine and radiator. Instead, it recirculates through the cylinder block and head. Restriction of water circulation in this manner prevents the removal of any appreciable amount of heat from the engine by the cooling system. The engine consequently reaches operating temperatures more rapidly. When the engine reaches operating temperature, the thermostatic valve begins to open. Then, water can circulate through the radiator, and operation of the cooling system proceeds in a normal manner, as already described.

A by-pass is required to permit water to circulate within the engine itself when the engine is cold.

However, when the engine warms up, the by-pass must close or become restricted. Otherwise, the water would continue to circulate within the engine itself and too little would go to the radiator for cooling.

One by-pass system uses a small, spring-loaded valve which is forced open by the water pressure from the pump when the thermostat is closed. As the thermostat opens, the water pressure drops within the engine, and the by-pass valve closes.

Another widely used system has a blocking by-pass thermostat (Fig. 12–15). This thermostat operates like others already described, but it also has a secondary valve. When the primary valve is closed, the circulation to the radiator is shut off. However, the secondary valve is open, permitting water to circulate through the by-pass. But when the primary valve opens, permitting water to flow to the radiator, the secondary valve closes, thus blocking off the engine by-pass.

§ 12–8. RADIATOR PRESSURE CAP To improve cooling efficiency and prevent evaporation and surge losses, many late automobiles use a pressure cap on the radiator (Fig. 12–16). At sea level, where atmospheric pressure is about 15 psi (pounds per square inch), water boils at 212°F. At higher altitudes, where atmospheric pressure is less, water boils at lower temperatures. Higher pressures increase the temperature required to

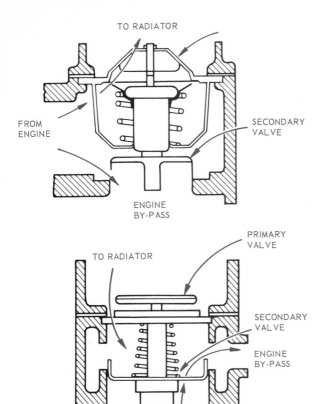

Fig. 12-15. Blocking by-pass thermostats. *(Harrison Radiator Division of General Motors Corporation)*

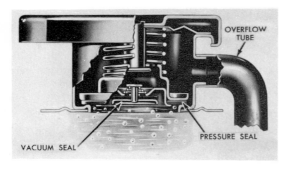

Fig. 12-16. Radiator pressure cap.

boil water. Each added pound per square inch increases the boiling point of water about 3¼°F. The use of a pressure cap on the radiator increases the air pressure within the cooling system several pounds per square inch. Thus, the water may be circulated at higher temperatures without boiling. The water therefore enters the radiator at a higher temperature, and the difference in temperature

between the air and the water is greater. Heat then is more quickly transferred from the water to the air, improving cooling efficiency. Evaporation of water is reduced by the higher pressure, inasmuch as the boiling point of the water is higher. The pressure cap also prevents loss of water due to surging when the car is quickly braked to a stop.

The pressure cap fits over the radiator filler tube and seals tightly around the edges. The cap contains two valves, the blowoff valve and the vacuum valve. The blowoff valve consists of a valve held against a valve seat by a calibrated spring. The spring holds the valve closed so that pressure is produced in the cooling system. If pressure rises above that for which the system is designed, the blowoff valve is raised off its seat, relieving the excessive pressure. Pressure caps are designed to provide as much as 15 pounds of pressure per square inch in the cooling system; this increases the boiling point of the water to almost 250°F.

The vacuum valve is designed to prevent the formation of a vacuum in the cooling system when the engine has been shut off and begins to cool. If a vacuum forms, atmospheric pressure from the outside causes the small vacuum valve to open, admitting air into the radiator. Without a vacuum valve, the pressure within the radiator might drop so low that atmospheric pressure would collapse it.

§ 12-9. CLOSED AND SEALED COOLING SYSTEMS
The cooling systems on some imported cars, such as the Volvo and Fiat, are sealed and do not normally require the addition of any water. The sealed cooling system used by Volvo is shown in Fig. 12-17. The cover of the expansion tank has a valve which opens when the pressure in the system increases to the predetermined value. When the engine cools and a partial vacuum develops, a vacuum valve opens to admit air into the expansion tank. The cushion of air in the expansion tank permits the coolant to expand as it gets warm without any loss of coolant. Without the expansion tank, coolant would be lost through the filler cap. Even though there should be no loss, Volvo recommends that the cooling system and expansion tank be drained and flushed out with clean water once a year. The expansion tank is translucent so that it is not necessary to remove the filler cap to determine whether or not more water is needed.

A closed, but not sealed, cooling system is shown in Fig. 12-18. The translucent plastic

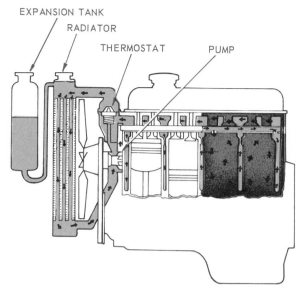

Fig. 12-17. Sealed cooling system used in Volvo. *(A. B. Volvo)*

As the engine warms up, the coolant expands, and part of it is forced into the reservoir. If the coolant temperature approaches the boiling point, the vent valve in the radiator cap closes. Now, pressure increases in the cooling system to prevent boiling. When the engine cools and the coolant contracts, the vent valve opens to permit coolant to flow back from the reservoir into the tank.

§ 12-10. ANTIFREEZE SOLUTIONS Antifreeze solutions are required to prevent freezing of the water when temperatures drop below 32°F. When water freezes in the engine, the resulting expanding force is often sufficient to crack the cylinder block and the radiator. Antifreeze solutions added to and mixed with the water prevent freezing of the mixture. A good antifreeze material must mix readily with water, prevent freezing of the mixture at the lowest temperatures encountered, and circulate freely. It must not damage the cooling system by corrosive action or lose its antifreezing properties after extended use. The most commonly used antifreeze materials are either alcohol (or alcohol-base) or ethylene glycol. The alcohol-base materials make only temporary antifreeze solutions, since they evaporate at temperatures below the boiling point of water and thus are gradually lost. Such materials require periodic additions to maintain an antifreeze solution of adequate strength.

reservoir is marked on the side to indicate whether or not more coolant should be added. It has an overflow pipe which is vented to the atmosphere so that the system can operate at atmospheric pressure when the engine is comparatively cool.

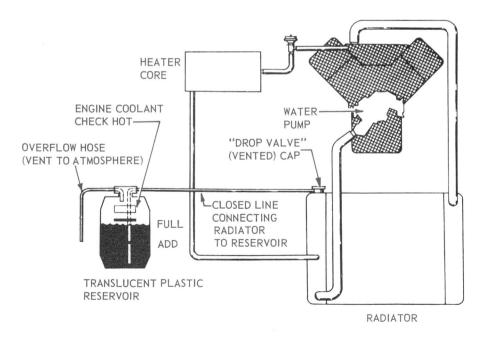

Fig. 12-18. Closed cooling system. *(Cadillac Motor Car Division of General Motors Corporation)*

The ethylene glycol antifreeze materials are of the so-called "permanent" type, since they remain liquid at the boiling point of water. Permanent-type antifreezes must be used with air-conditioned cars because, in these, under-the-hood temperatures are higher. The antifreezes with the lower boiling points would soon boil away.

Antifreeze materials are mixed with water in various proportions according to the expected temperature. The lower the temperature, the higher the percentage of antifreeze material.

§ 12–11. TEMPERATURE INDICATORS In order that the operator will know at all times the water temperature in the cooling system, a temperature indicator is installed in the car. An abnormal heat rise is a warning of abnormal conditions in the engine. The indicator thus warns the operator to stop the engine before serious damage is done. Temperature indicators are of three general types, vapor-pressure, electric, and indicator light.

1. Vapor-pressure. The vapor-pressure temperature indicator consists of an indicator bulb and a tube connecting the bulb to the indicator unit. The indicator unit contains a curved, or Bourdon, tube, one end of which is linked to the indicator needle. The other end is open and is connected through a tube to the bulb. The indicator bulb, usually placed in the water jacket of the engine, is filled with a liquid that evaporates at fairly low temperature. As the engine temperature increases, the liquid in the bulb begins to evaporate, creating pressure that is conveyed through the connecting tube to the Bourdon tube in the indicating unit. The pressure tends to straighten out the tube; the resulting movement causes the indicating needle to move across the dial face and indicate the temperature in the water jacket.

2. Electric indicators. Electrically operated temperature indicators are of two types, the balancing-coil type and the bimetal-thermostat type. The balancing-coil-type oil-pressure indicator (§ 11–11), fuel gauge (§ 9–5), and temperature indicator all operate in a similar manner. The dash indicating units are, in fact, practically identical, consisting of two coils and an armature to which a needle is attached (Fig. 12–19). The engine unit changes resistance with temperature in such a way that at higher temperatures it has less resistance and thus passes more current. When this happens, more current passes through the right-hand coil in the indicating unit, so that the armature to which the needle is attached is attracted by the

increased magnetic field. The armature and the needle move around so that the needle indicates a higher temperature.

The bimetal-thermostat-type temperature indica-

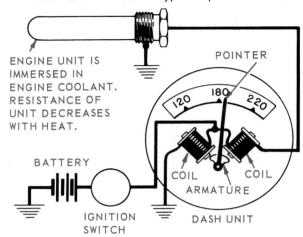

Fig. 12–19. Circuit diagram of electric-resistance temperature-indicator system.

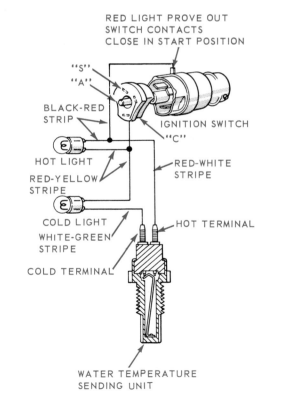

Fig. 12–20. Temperature indicating system using COLD and HOT indicating lights. *(Ford Division of Ford Motor Company)*

tor is similar to the bimetal-thermostat fuel gauge (§ 9–5). The dash units are practically identical. The engine unit of the temperature indicator, while slightly different in appearance from the tank unit of the fuel gauge, operates in a somewhat similar manner. In the temperature indicator, the temperature of the cooling liquid is directly imposed on the engine-unit thermostatic blade. When the temperature is low, most of the blade heating must come from electric current. More current flows, and the dash unit distorts a considerable amount to indicate a low temperature. As temperature increases, less heat from current flow is required to bring the engine-unit blade up to operating temperature. Less current flows, and the dash unit indicates a higher temperature. Instead of a temperature indicator, some cars are using two indicator lights which come on to indicate normal and high engine temperatures.

3. Indicator-light. One indicator-light system is shown in Fig. 12–20. This system has a water tem-perature sending unit mounted on the engine so that it is exposed to the cooling-system water. The sending unit is connected to two light bulbs and the battery through the ignition switch. When the ignition switch is first turned on, to start a cold engine, the sending-unit thermostatic blade is in the proper position to connect the COLD light to the battery. It comes on. The COLD light, which appears in blue on the instrument panel, remains on until the engine approaches operating temperature. As this happens, the thermostatic blade in the sending unit is bent by the increasing temperature. The blade therefore moves off the cold terminal, disconnecting the COLD light so that it turns off. If the engine overheats, the thermostat will warp further so that it moves under the hot terminal. This connects the HOT bulb to the battery so that it glows and appears in red on the instrument panel. This is a signal to the driver that the engine has overheated and that it should be stopped before damage results.

Review Questions

1. What is the purpose of the engine cooling system?
2. What are the two general types of cooling systems?
3. Give three examples of air-cooled engines.
4. What are water jackets?
5. What is the purpose of water-distributing tubes?
6. What function does the water pump perform?
7. Where are water pumps usually mounted? How are they usually driven?
8. What is the purpose of the engine fan? Where is it located, and how is it usually driven?
9. What is a V belt?
10. Describe a radiator, and explain how it operates.
11. Classify radiators according to the direction water flows through them.
12. What is the purpose of the thermostat? How does it operate?
13. Explain how a blocking bypass thermostat works.
14. What is the purpose of the pressure-type radiator cap?
15. Describe a closed or sealed cooling system.
16. Why are antifreeze solutions used? Give the characteristics of a good antifreeze solution.
17. Into what two classifications are the most commonly used antifreeze solutions divided?
18. Name the three general types of engine temperature indicator.
19. Describe how the vapor-pressure temperature indicator operates.
20. Describe how the balancing-coil-type temperature indicator operates. The bimetal-thermostat-type.
21. Describe how a pressure-type radiator cap operates.
22. Explain how the indicator-light system described in the book works.

*S*tudy Questions

1. What advantages might an air-cooled engine have over a liquid-cooled engine?
2. What might happen if the water-distributing tubes were left out of an engine?
3. Would a forced-circulation cooling system stop functioning completely if the water pump stopped operating?
4. Can you think of any reasons for not using a flat belt in place of the V belt?

5. Make a sketch of a vapor-pressure temperature-indicator system, and write a brief explanation of how it operates.
6. Make a sketch of a balancing-coil-type temperature-indicator system, and write a brief explanation of how it operates.
7. Make a sketch of a bimetal-thermostat-type temperature-indicator system, and write a brief explanation of how it operates.

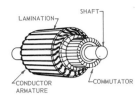

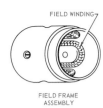

13

The Electric System —
Battery and
Cranking Motor

This and the following three chapters discuss electric systems used in automobiles (Fig. 13-1). The electric system does several jobs. It cranks the engine for starting. It supplies the high-voltage surges that ignite the compressed air-fuel mixture in the combustion chambers. It includes the battery, cranking motor, generator, regulator, ignition system, radio, lights, heater motor, indicating gauges, and so on. All these are discussed in the pages that follow.

STORAGE BATTERY

§ 13-1. PURPOSE OF BATTERY The battery (Fig. 13-2) supplies current for operation of the cranking motor and the ignition system when the engine is being cranked for starting. It also supplies current for light, radio, and other electrical accessories at times when the generator is not operating fast enough to handle the electrical load. The amount of current the battery can supply is strictly limited by the "capacity" of the battery, which in turn depends on the amount of chemicals it contains.

§ 13-2. CHEMICALS IN BATTERY The chemicals used in the battery are sponge lead, a solid; lead oxide, a paste; and sulfuric acid, a liquid. These three substances are brought together in such a way that they can react chemically to produce a flow of current. The lead oxide and sponge lead are held in plate grids to form positive and negative plates.

The plate grid (Fig. 13-3) consists of a framework of antimony-lead alloy with interlocking horizontal and vertical bars. The plate grids are made into plates (Fig. 13-4) by the application of lead oxide pastes; the horizontal and vertical bars serve to hold the pastes in the plate.

After the plates are assembled into the battery, the battery is given an initial "forming" charge; this changes the lead oxide paste in the negative, or minus, plate to sponge lead and changes the lead oxide paste in the positive, or plus, plate to lead peroxide.

§ 13-3. BATTERY CONSTRUCTION In making the battery, several similar plates are properly spaced and welded, or *lead-burned*, to a strap to form a plate group (Fig. 13-5). Plates of two types are used, one for the positive plate group, the other for the negative plate group. A positive plate group is nested with a negative plate group, with separators placed between the plates to form an element (Fig. 13-6). Separators (Fig. 13-7) are designed to hold the plates apart so that they do not touch, and at the same time they must be porous enough to permit liquid to circulate between the plates. Wooden sheets, spun glass matted into sheets, and porous sponge-rubber sheets have been used as separator material. Late-model batteries have separators made of polyvinal chloride or polyethelyne-saturated cellulose.

The elements are placed in cells in the battery case. Covers are then put on and sealed around the edges with sealing compound. Then, terminals are built up through the covers from the positive- and negative-group plate straps (Fig. 13-2). Adjacent negative and positive terminals are connected by connector straps. Each cover has an opening through which liquid can be added when the filler cap or vent plug is unscrewed. After the liquid has been added and the battery given an initial charge, it is ready for operation.

Another method of connecting between cells, used on many late-model batteries, is shown in Figs. 13-2 and 13-8. Here, the battery has a one-piece cover that covers all cells. The plate straps of adjacent cells are connected by a connector

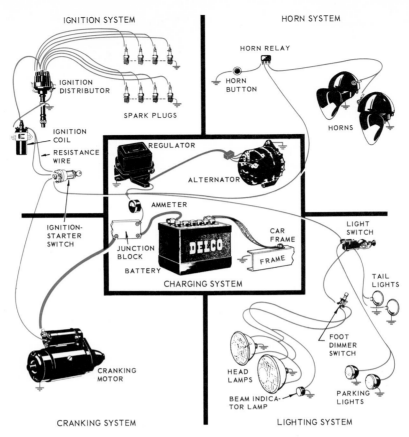

Fig. 13–1. Typical car electric system, illustrating the electric units and the connections between them. The symbol ⏚ means ground, or the car frame. By using the car frame as the return circuit, only half as much wiring is required. *(Delco-Remy Division of General Motors Corporation)*

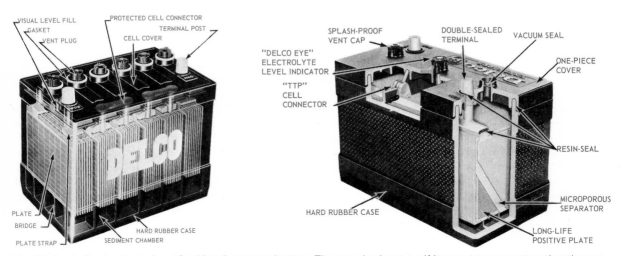

Fig. 13–2. Left, phantom view of a 12-volt storage battery. The case is shown as if it were transparent so that the construction of the cells can be seen. Right, cutaway view of a six-volt storage battery with TTP (through the partition) connectors. *(Delco-Remy Division of General Motors Corporation)*

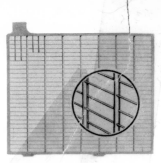

Fig. 13-3. Battery plate grid.

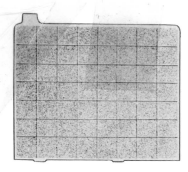

Fig. 13-4. Battery plate. Lead oxide paste has been applied to the plate grid, and the plate is ready to be attached to the plate strap. The plate is attached by lead-burning the lug *(to upper left)* to the plate strap.

Fig. 13-5. Battery plate group.

that passes through the partitions between the cells, as shown. This close connection between cells reduces battery resistance and thus improves battery performance.

§ 13-4. CHEMICAL ACTIVITIES IN BATTERY

The liquid, called the *electrolyte,* is made up of about 40 percent sulfuric acid and about 60 percent water. When sulfuric acid is placed between

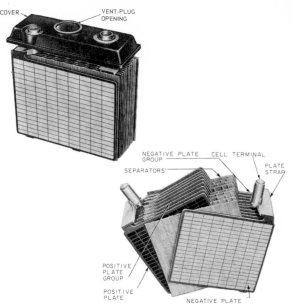

Fig. 13-6. Battery element, assembled and partly assembled.

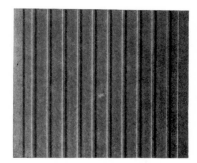

Fig. 13-7. Battery separator.

the plates, chemical actions take place that remove electrons from one group of plates and mass them at the other. This transfer of electrons is carried on by chemical activity until there is sufficient imbalance of electrons to create a 2-volt pressure between the two groups of plates. This results in a pressure of 2 volts between the two terminals of the battery cell. If the two terminals are not connected by any circuit, no further appreciable chemical activity takes place. However, when the two terminals do become connected by an electric circuit, electrons (current) will flow. They flow from the terminal where chemical activity has massed them, through the circuit, to the other terminal where the chemical activity has taken them away. Chemical activities now begin again;

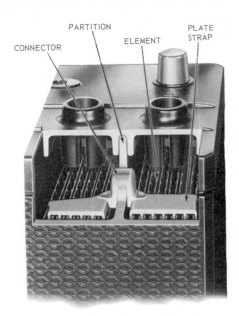

CONNECTOR PARTITION ELEMENT PLATE STRAP

Fig. 13-8. Cutaway view of two cells in a battery which has a one-piece cover and cell connectors that pass through the partitions between the cells. *(Delco-Remy Division of General Motors Corporation)*

so the 2-volt pressure is maintained, and the current flow continues. The chemical actions "use up" the sponge lead, lead peroxide, and sulfuric acid. Thus, after a certain amount of current has been withdrawn, the battery is *discharged* (or "run down," or "dead") and is not capable of delivering any additional current. When the battery has reached this state, it may then be *recharged*. This is done by supplying it with a flow of current from some external source, such as a generator, which forces current through the battery in a reverse direction. This reverses the chemical activities in the battery. Thus, the plates are restored to their original composition, and the battery becomes recharged. It is then ready to deliver additional current.

The chemical actions that take place are rather complicated and are not fully understood. The sponge lead (negative plate) and lead peroxide (positive plate) change to *lead sulfate* during the discharge process. The sulfate comes from the sulfuric acid; the electrolyte loses acid and gains water as the sulfate goes into the plates. Thus, discharging the battery changes the two different chemicals in the battery plates to a third chemical, lead sulfate. Recharging the battery causes the lead sulfate to change back to sponge lead in the negative plates and lead peroxide in the posi-

tive plates. Meantime, the sulfuric acid reappears in the electrolyte of the battery.

§ 13-5. CONNECTING CELLS Automotive batteries are usually either 6-volt or 12-volt units. There are three cells in the 6-volt battery; the three cells are connected in series. In series connections, the voltages add. There are six cells in the 12-volt battery, the cells being connected in series. Some special applications use 24-volt batteries; these special-purpose batteries have 12 cells.

§ 13-6. BATTERY RATINGS The amount of current that a battery can deliver depends on total area and volume of active plate material and the amount and strength of electrolyte. Batteries are rated in several ways.

1. Twenty-hour rate. The 20-hour rate represents the amount of current a battery can deliver for 20 hours without cell voltage dropping below 1.75 volts, starting with a temperature of 80°F. A battery delivering 5 amperes for 20 hours would be rated as a 100-ampere-hour battery (5 × 20).

2. Twenty-five-ampere rate. The 25-ampere rate measures battery performance at a moderate constant-current output at 80°F to a final limiting voltage of 1.75 volts per cell. This figure indicates the ability of the battery to carry the electrical operating load (lights, ignition, etc.) when the generator is not operating.

3. Cold rate. This rating indicates the number of minutes a battery can deliver 300 amperes at 0°F before the cell voltage drops below 1.0 volt. It gives an indication of the cold-weather starting ability of the battery. A typical rating applying to a 100-ampere-hour battery is that the battery will supply 300 amperes for about 3.6 minutes at 0°F before cell voltages drop to 1.0 volt.

§ 13-7. BATTERY EFFICIENCY The ability of the battery to deliver current varies within wide limits, depending on temperature and rate of discharge. At low temperature, chemical activities are greatly reduced; the sulfuric acid cannot work so actively on the plates, and thus the battery is less efficient and cannot supply as much current for as long a time. High rates of discharge will not produce as many ampere-hours as low rates of discharge because the chemical activities take place only on the surfaces of the plates; the chemical activities do not have time to penetrate the plates and utilize the materials that have formed below the plate surfaces.

§ 13-8. VARIATIONS IN TERMINAL VOLTAGE

Because the battery produces voltage by chemical means, the voltage varies according to a number of conditions. These conditions and their effect on battery voltage may be summed up as follows:

1. Terminal voltage, battery being *charged,* increases with:
   a. Increasing charging rate. To increase charging rate (amperes input), the terminal voltage must go up.
   b. Increasing state of charge. As state of charge goes up, voltage must go up to maintain charging rate.
   c. Decreasing temperature. Lower battery temperatures require a higher voltage to maintain charging rate.
2. Terminal voltage, battery being discharged, decreases with:
   a. Increasing discharge rate. As the rate of discharge goes up, chemical activities increase and cannot penetrate plates so effectively; therefore, voltage is reduced.
   b. Decreasing state of charge. With less active materials and sulfuric acid available, less chemical activity takes place, and voltage drops.
   c. Decreasing temperature. With lower temperature, the chemical activities cannot go on so effectively, and the voltage drops.

CRANKING MOTOR

§ 13-9. FUNCTION OF CRANKING MOTOR The cranking, or starting, motor electrically cranks the engine for starting. It is a special direct-current motor operating on battery voltage and is mounted on the engine flywheel housing. Let us consider the basic principles of motors.

§ 13-10. BASIC MOTOR PRINCIPLES When current moves through a conductor, a magnetic field builds up around that conductor. If the conductor is held in a magnetic field, as from a horseshoe magnet, force will be exerted on the conductor. Figure 13-9 illustrates the conductor held in a magnetic field. Figure 13-10 shows the conductor in end view with the resulting magnetic field indicated. The cross in the center of the conductor indicates that the current is flowing away from the reader. This causes the magnetic field from this current flow to circle the conductor in a counterclockwise direction. The circular magnetic field to the left of the con-

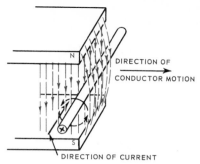

Fig. 13-9. Conductor held in a magnetic field from a magnet. The direction of the current flow and the encircling magnetic field around the conductor are shown by arrows.

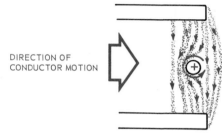

Fig. 13-10. End view of the conductor shown in Fig. 13-9.

ductor is in the same direction as the straight-line magnetic field from the magnet. To the right of the conductor, it is in the opposite direction. This weakens the magnetic field to the right of, and strengthens the magnetic field to the left of the conductor, causing the resulting magnetic field to distort around the conductor, as shown in Fig. 13-10.

Magnetic lines of force have a rubber-band characteristic of trying to shorten up to a minimum length. Thus the magnetic-field pattern shown in Fig. 13-10 will cause a push toward the right to be exerted on the conductor as the bent lines of force try to straighten out. The more current flowing, the more the lines of force will be distorted around the conductor, and the stronger will be the push. Increasing the straight-line magnetic field will have a similar result.

§ 13-11. MOTOR CONSTRUCTION If we bend the conductor into a U and connect the two ends to the two halves of a split copper ring, we shall have the elements of an electric motor (Fig. 13-11). Stationary brushes, connected to a battery and resting on the split ring, and two poles of a magnet complete the elementary motor. The U-shaped

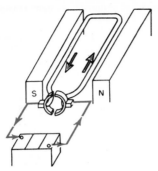

Fig. 13-11. Simple electric motor with a two-segment commutator.

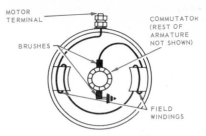

Fig. 13-13. Wiring circuit of a cranking motor.

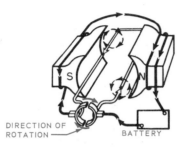

Fig. 13-14. Schematic drawing of a cranking motor. The heavy arrows show direction of current flow, and the light circular arrows indicate the direction of the magnetic field around the conductors. Compare this with Fig. 13-11.

conductor loop and the split ring (which is called the *commutator*) are so designed as to be able to rotate together. Current flows from the battery, through the right-hand brush and segment of the commutator, through the conductor and left-hand segment and brush, back to the battery, as shown. This causes the left-hand part of the conductor to be pushed upward and the right-hand part to be pushed downward (see Fig. 13-10). Thus the loop rotates in a clockwise direction. As the two sides of the loop reverse positions, the direction of the current flow through the two sides reverses. The force thus continues to rotate the loop clockwise.

The cranking motor must use more than one loop to develop any appreciable power. Actually, many loops or conductors are used, as shown in Fig. 13-12, which illustrates a cranking-motor armature. The ends of the conductors are connected to the commutator segments.

To obtain sufficient magnetic-field strength for powerful cranking-motor action, the natural magnetic strength of the magnetic poles is aided by field windings. Current flows through the field windings in such a direction as to aid the magnetic field between the two poles. Figure 13-13 illustrates a simple wiring diagram of a cranking

motor. Current enters the motor and passes through the two field windings, then through the armature, and back to the battery. If the battery connections were reversed, the current would flow through the armature first, as shown in Fig. 13-14, which illustrates schematically a simple motor. This type of motor is called a *series-wound,* or *series,* motor, since the armature and field windings are connected in series.

The wiring diagram illustrated in Fig. 13-13 is

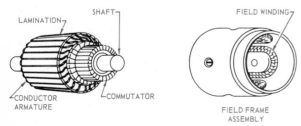

Fig. 13-12. Two major parts of a cranking motor: the armature and the field assembly. *(Delco-Remy Division of General Motors Corporation)*

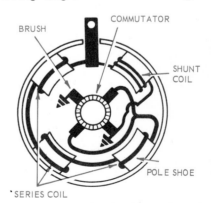

Fig. 13-15. Wiring circuit of a four-pole series-shunt, or compound, cranking motor. *(Delco-Remy Division of General Motors Corporation)*

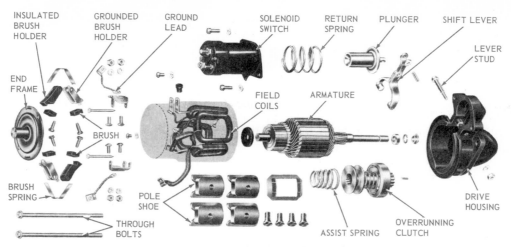

Fig. 13-16. Disassembled view of a cranking motor. *(Delco-Remy Division of General Motors Corporation)*

of a two-pole two-brush cranking motor. Many cranking motors have four brushes and four poles. Some also have one or two shunt windings (and are called *series-shunt*, or *compound*, units). The shunt windings prevent overspeeding (see Fig. 13–15).

A typical cranking motor with the main parts disassembled is shown in Fig. 13–16. The cranking motor consists of the commutator end head, holding the brushes; the field frame, into which the field windings are assembled around pole shoes; the drive housing, which houses the drive assembly and supports the motor on the engine flywheel housing; the armature; and the drive assembly. Some cranking motors also have a solenoid that operates the shift lever (§ 13–15).

§ 13–12. DRIVE ARRANGEMENT The drive assembly contains a small pinion that, in operation, meshes with teeth cut in the flywheel (Fig. 13–17). This provides considerable gear reduction, so that the armature must rotate about fifteen times to cause the flywheel to rotate once. The cranking motor thus requires only about one-fifteenth as much power as would an electric motor directly coupled to the crankshaft, since the armature turns fifteen times for each flywheel revolution. The armature may revolve about 2,000 to 3,000 rpm (revolutions per minute) when the cranking motor is operated, thus causing the flywheel to spin at speeds as high as 200 rpm. This is ample for starting the engine.

After the engine starts, it may increase in speed to 3,000 rpm or more. If the cranking-motor drive

pinion remained in mesh with the flywheel, it would be spun at 45,000 rpm because of the 15:1 gear ratio. This means that the armature would be spun at this terrific speed, and centrifugal force would cause the conductors and commutator segments to be thrown out of the armature, ruining it. To prevent such damage, automatic meshing and de-meshing devices are used. For passenger cars they are of two general types, inertia and overrunning clutch.

§ 13–13. INERTIA DRIVE The inertia drive depends on the inertia of the drive pinion to produce meshing. Inertia is the property that all things have that resists any change in motion. When the drive pinion is not rotating, it resists any force that attempts to set it into motion. Two types of inertia drive are discussed below, the Bendix and the Folo-Thru.

1. Bendix drive. In the Bendix drive (Fig. 13–17), the drive pinion is mounted loosely on a sleeve that has screw threads matching internal threads in the pinion. When the cranking motor is at rest, the drive pinion is not meshed with the flywheel teeth. As the cranking-motor switch is closed, the armature begins to rotate. This causes the sleeve to rotate also, since the sleeve is fastened to the armature shaft through the heavy spiral Bendix spring. Inertia prevents the pinion from instantly picking up speed with the sleeve. The sleeve thus turns within the pinion, just as a screw would turn in a nut held stationary. This forces the pinion endwise along the sleeve so that it goes into mesh with the flywheel teeth. As the

217

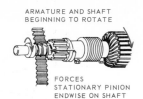
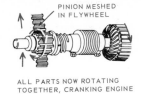
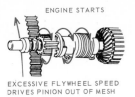

ARMATURE AND SHAFT
BEGINNING TO ROTATE

FORCES
STATIONARY PINION
ENDWISE ON SHAFT

PINION MESHED
IN FLYWHEEL

ALL PARTS NOW ROTATING
TOGETHER, CRANKING ENGINE

ENGINE STARTS

EXCESSIVE FLYWHEEL SPEED
DRIVES PINION OUT OF MESH

Fig. 13-17. Operation of a Bendix drive. *(Delco-Remy Division of General Motors Corporation)*

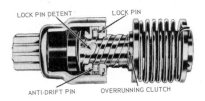

LOCK PIN DETENT   LOCK PIN

ANTI-DRIFT PIN   OVERRUNNING CLUTCH

Fig. 13-18. Folo-Thru cranking-motor drive. The skirt of the pinion has been cut away so that the lock and the anti-drift pins can be seen. *(Ford Motor Company)*

pinion reaches the pinion stop, the endwise movement stops. The pinion must now turn with the armature, causing the engine to be cranked. The spiral spring takes up the shock of meshing.

After the engine begins to run and increase in speed, the flywheel rotates the drive pinion faster than the armature is turning. This causes the pinion to be spun back out of mesh from the flywheel. That is, the pinion turns on the sleeve, and the screw threads on the pinion and sleeve cause the pinion to be backed out of mesh from the flywheel.

2. Folo-Thru drive. This drive (Fig. 13-18) is very similar in many respects to the Bendix drive. It has a sleeve attached through a spiral spring to the armature shaft. The sleeve has threads

which match internal threads in the pinion base. Also included in the pinion base are two small spring-loaded pins. One is an antidrift pin that prevents the pinion from drifting into mesh with the flywheel when the engine is running. It imposes a frictional drag that holds the pinion in the de-meshed position. The other pin is a lock pin that drops into a detent in the sleeve thread as the pinion moves out to the cranking position. This holds the pinion in mesh with the engine flywheel during cranking. It prevents the pinion from being kicked out of mesh by a false start (during which the engine might fire a few times and then die). The pinion is thus held in mesh, and cranking continues until the engine really gets started. Then, as the engine speed increases to around 400 rpm, centrifugal force on the lock pin moves it out of the detent, and the pinion de-meshes from the flywheel in the same manner as in the Bendix drive.

§ 13-14. OVERRUNNING CLUTCH The overrunning clutch (Fig. 13-19) is operated by a shift lever that causes the drive pinion to be moved along the armature shaft and into mesh with the flywheel teeth. As the shift lever completes its travel, it closes the cranking-motor switch so that

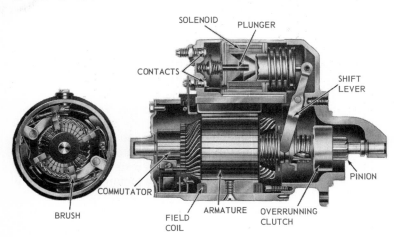

SOLENOID   PLUNGER

CONTACTS

SHIFT
LEVER

BRUSH

COMMUTATOR

FIELD
COIL

ARMATURE

OVERRUNNING
CLUTCH

PINION

Fig. 13-19. Sectional view of an enclosed shift-lever cranking motor. *(Delco-Remy Division of General Motors Corporation)*

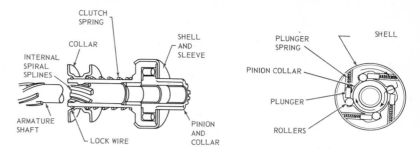

Fig. 13–20. Cutaway and end sectional views of an overrunning clutch. *(Delco-Remy Division of General Motors Corporation)*

cranking takes place. Straight or spiral splines cut in the armature shaft and the clutch sleeve cause both to rotate together. A spiral spring is placed between the clutch housing and the shift-lever collar. This spring compresses if the pinion and the flywheel teeth should happen to butt instead of mesh. Then, after the cranking-motor switch is closed and the armature starts to rotate, meshing is completed by the spring pressure, so that cranking can take place.

The clutch (Fig. 13–20) consists of the outer shell, which has four hardened steel rollers fitted into four notches, and the pinion and collar assembly. The notches are not concentric but are smaller in the end opposite to the plunger springs (Fig. 13–20). When the armature and the shell begin to rotate, the pinion is momentarily stationary. This causes the rollers to rotate into the smaller sections of the notches, where they jam tight. The pinion must now rotate with the armature, cranking the engine. After the engine starts, it spins the pinion faster than the armature is turning, so that the rollers are rotated into the larger sections of the notches, where they are

free. This allows the pinion to spin independently of, or *overrun*, the remainder of the clutch. A spring on the shift lever pulls the pinion back out of mesh when the shift lever is released.

Gear reduction. The cranking motor shown in Fig. 13–21 has a gear reduction which increases cranking torque. The shift lever (or fork) is enclosed. When it is actuated by the solenoid, it not only shifts the overrunning-clutch pinion into mesh with the flywheel, it also shifts the large driven gear on the clutch shaft into mesh with the smaller gear on the armature shaft. The gear ratio between the armature and the flywheel, due to the extra gears in the cranking motor, is 45:1. That is, the armature turns 45 times to turn the flywheel, and the engine crankshaft, once. This provides a high cranking torque for starting.

§ 13–15. CRANKING - MOTOR CONTROLS Cranking-motor controls have varied from a simple foot-operated pedal to automatic devices that close the cranking-motor circuit when the accelerator pedal is depressed. The present system that has been almost universally adopted for pas-

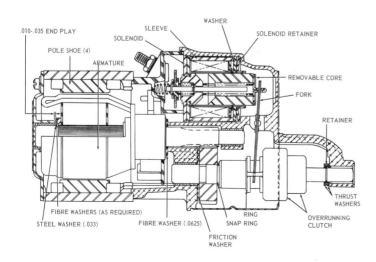

Fig. 13–21. Sectional view of a gear-reduction, overrunning-clutch cranking motor. *(Chrysler-Plymouth Division of Chrysler Motors Corporation)*

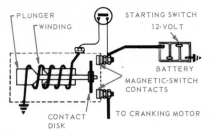

Fig. 13-22. Magnetic-switch schematic wiring circuit.

senger cars and many other vehicles has starting contacts in the ignition switch. When the ignition key is turned against spring pressure past the ON position to START, the starting contacts close. This connects the cranking-motor solenoid or magnetic switch to the battery. After the engine starts and the ignition key is released, spring pressure returns it to the ON position.

Bendix-type cranking motors use a magnetic switch (Fig. 13-22). When the starting contacts in the ignition switch are closed, the magnetic-switch

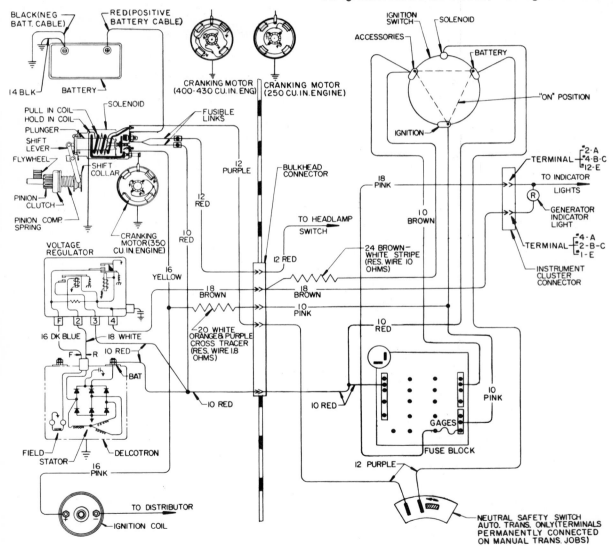

PART OF ENGINE WIRING HARNESS   PART OF INSTRUMENT WIRING HARNESS

Fig. 13-23. Wiring circuit of starting, charging, and ignition systems in an automobile. *(Buick Motor Division of General Motors Corporation)*

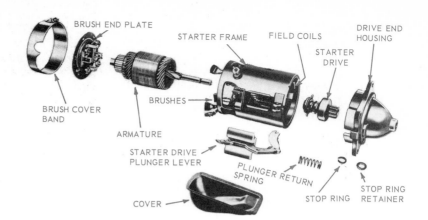

Fig. 13-24. Cranking motor with a sliding pole shoe to actuate the shift lever in disassembled view. *(Ford Motor Company)*

winding is connected to the battery. The magnetism produced in the winding pulls the plunger in, forcing the contact disk against the magnetic-switch contacts. Now, current can flow through the contacts and disk to the cranking motor to operate the cranking motor. After the engine starts and the driver takes his hand off the ignition key, the key is returned by spring action to the ON position. This opens the magnetic-switch winding circuit so that a spring moves the plunger and contact away from the magnetic-switch contacts. Now, the cranking-motor circuit is opened and the cranking motor stops operating.

On cranking motors with overrunning clutches, a solenoid is commonly used, mounted on, or in, the cranking motor. The solenoid not only closes the cranking-motor circuit but also shifts the overrunning-clutch pinion into mesh with the flywheel (Fig. 13–23). Although the solenoid is similar in operation to the magnetic switch, it has two windings, a pull-in winding and a hold-in winding. They work together to pull the core in, meshing the pinion and closing the cranking-motor circuit. As the switch contacts close, the pull-in winding is shorted out, since it is connected between the two solenoid terminals. By this combination of windings, the magnetic strength is considerably increased. This provides sufficient pulling power to accomplish the twofold job of meshing the pinion and closing the switch. After the pinion is meshed and the switch is closed, less magnetism is required to hold the core in. Consequently, the pull-in winding becomes shorted out to reduce the drain on the battery during the cranking operation.

On the Ford cranking motor illustrated in Fig. 13–24, there is no separate solenoid. Instead, the cranking-motor field windings serve the dual

purpose of producing the magnetic field which causes the shifting action and also causes the armature to rotate. The magnetic field causes the pole shoe to slide in the frame. This action moves the shift lever so that the drive pinion is forced into mesh with the flywheel teeth. Figure 13–25 is a wiring diagram of the control circuit for the cranking motor. When the ignition switch is turned to START and the automatic-transmission neutral safety switch is closed, the magnetic-switch winding is connected to the battery. This causes the magnetic switch (starter relay) to close its contacts to directly connect the cranking motor (called *starter* in the illustration) to the battery.

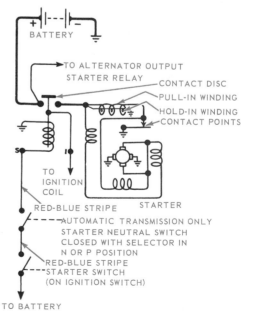

Fig. 13-25. Wiring circuit of a starting system. *(Ford Motor Company)*

221

One of the field windings acts as the winding to move the pole shoe. It has two parts, as shown, a pull-in winding and a hold-in winding. As the magnetic switch closes its contacts, these two windings are connected directly across the battery (through the contact points), thus producing maximum magnetic strength. The other three field windings are connected in series with the armature. The magnetic field of the pole-shoe actuating windings moves the pole shoe and shifts the drive pinion into mesh. At the same time, the armature begins to turn so that the engine is cranked. As the pole shoe and shift lever move, they cause the contact points to open. Now, the pull-in winding is connected in series with the armature and its magnetism drops. At the same time, however, the hold-in winding retains its full magnetism so that the pole-shoe is retained in the cranking position. As soon as the ignition switch is released so that it returns to the ON position, the magnetic-switch winding is disconnected from the battery. It opens its contacts to disconnect the cranking motor from the battery so that cranking stops. The drive pinion is demeshed from the flywheel by the return spring.

1. Automatic transmissions. On cars equipped with automatic transmissions, a special switch is connected to the circuit to prevent starting while the car is in gear. As shown in Fig. 13–23, the switch (neutral safety switch) is connected between the ignition switch and the solenoid. This switch is open at all transmission-lever positions except neutral (and park, in some cars).

2. Ignition resistance. The system shown in Fig. 13–23 includes a resistance wire in the wiring harness labeled "20 white, orange, and purple cross tracer (res. wire 1.8 ohms)." The resistance is in series with the ignition-coil primary when the engine is running. This protects the ignition contact points from excessive current. However, during cranking, the ignition switch shorts out the resistance (when the key is turned to START). Now, full battery voltage is imposed on the ignition coil for good performance during cranking. The resistance is also called a *ballast* resistance. On some cars, the resistance is a separately mounted part. But most cars have the resistance in the wiring harness.

3. Other controls. A considerable variety of other controls has been used in the past to prevent cranking-motor operation at all times except when starting. Vacuum switches, which are mounted on the intake manifold or mounted in the carburetor, have been used extensively. This type of vacuum switch will close its contacts when the engine is not running but will open them when the engine starts and a vacuum builds up in the intake manifold. Vacuum switches were usually linked to the throttle so that, at part to full throttle, the contacts were opened. This was an added safeguard against cranking-motor operation while the engine was running. Some applications used a solenoid relay. This was a small relay with a single winding and a pair of contacts. When the control switch or circuit was closed, it would connect the relay winding to the battery. Then, the relay would close its contacts to connect the solenoid windings to the battery so that the solenoid would operate as described above. On some heavy-duty applications, a two-step control has been used. This control first imposes a relatively low voltage on the cranking motor so as to get the armature started. Then, full voltage is imposed to crank the engine. A still different heavy-duty system uses a series-parallel switch with two 12-volt batteries. During normal operation with the engine running, the two batteries are connected in parallel and the system is 12-volt throughout. But for starting, the two batteries are connected in series to supply the cranking motor with 24 volts. This higher voltage causes the cranking motor to develop a higher cranking torque.

Review Questions

1. Name several jobs that the electric current performs on the automobile.
2. Name the main components of the electric system.
3. What is the purpose of the storage battery?
4. What is the purpose of the cranking motor? Where is it mounted on the engine?
5. Does a storage battery actually store electricity?
6. When a battery is being discharged, does the sulfuric acid in the electrolyte increase or decrease?
7. What are three common methods of rating batteries? Which rating is most commonly used in referring to battery capacity?
8. When a battery is being charged, does increasing battery temperature require a higher or a lower charging voltage to maintain the same charging rate?
9. Why must the cranking-motor drive pinion be de-meshed from the engine flywheel after the engine starts?
10. Describe briefly the operation of the Bendix drive. Of the Folo-Thru drive.
11. Describe briefly the operation of the overrunning-clutch drive.
12. Describe briefly the operation of the solenoid in the cranking-motor control circuit.
13. What is the purpose of the resistance wire in the ignition primary circuit?
14. Explain the operation of the cranking motor with the sliding pole shoe.

Study Questions

1. Draw the symbol for ground, and explain what this term means.
2. Find out the locations of the battery on various automobiles.
3. Where is the regulator usually mounted on the automobile?
4. Lay a flat piece of cardboard on top of a bar or horseshoe magnet, and sprinkle some iron filings on the cardboard just over the magnet. Tap the cardboard lightly, and the iron filings will form in lines that indicate the magnetic lines of force. Make a sketch of these lines of force.
5. Describe briefly the construction of a battery.
6. Name the principal parts of a cranking motor.
7. Describe the operation of a cranking motor.

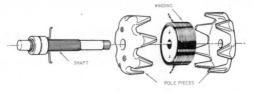

The Electric System— The Charging Circuit

This chapter continues the discussion of the electric system and describes the construction and operation of the generators and regulators which form part of the charging circuit. The battery, also part of the charging circuit, was discussed in the previous chapter.

GENERATOR

§ 14–1. **FUNCTION OF GENERATOR** The generator is a device that converts mechanical energy from the automobile engine into a flow of electric current. The generator replaces in the battery the current used in starting the engine and also supplies current for operation of electrical devices, such as the ignition system, lights, radio, and so on. The generator is usually mounted on the side of the engine block. It is driven by the engine fan belt.

For many years, all automotive generators were direct-current (d-c) units. In recent years, alternating-current (a-c) generators, or alternators, as they are also called, have come into widespread use. Direct current flows in one direction only. Alternating current flows first in one direction and then in the other.

§ 14–2. **GENERATOR PRINCIPLES (D-C TYPE)** When a conductor is moved through a magnetic field, current will be induced to move or flow through the conductor. If a conductor is held in a magnetic field and moved as shown in Fig. 14–1, a flow of current will be induced in the conductor in the direction shown, that is, toward the reader. This is indicated by the dot in the end of the conductor. Figure 14–2 illustrates the distortion of the magnetic field produced as the conductor moves through it. The magnetic lines of force tend to pile up ahead of the conductor and wrap around it, circling the conductor in a clockwise direction. Use of the "left-hand rule" indicates the direction of the current flow. If the left hand is placed around the conductor with the fingers pointing in the direction of the lines of force cir-

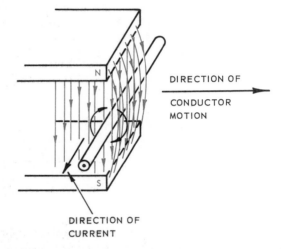

DIRECTION OF

CONDUCTOR MOTION

DIRECTION OF CURRENT

Fig. 14–1. Conductor, moving through a magnetic field, as shown, will have a flow of current induced in it, as indicated.

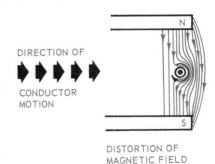

DIRECTION OF

CONDUCTOR MOTION

DISTORTION OF MAGNETIC FIELD

Fig. 14–2. Distortion of a magnetic field as a conductor is moved through it and as current flows in the conductor.

cling the conductor, the thumb will point in the direction of the current flow. The conductor must move across the magnetic field so that it cuts through lines of force. If the conductor moved parallel to the lines of force (for instance, from the top to the bottom of Fig. 14-2), no lines of force would be cut and no current would be induced in the conductor. The rate at which lines of force are cut determines the amount of current (or number of electrons) that will flow in the conductor. Thus, if the conductor is moved more rapidly through the magnetic field, more lines of force per second will be cut and more current will flow through the conductor. Likewise, if the magnetic

field is strengthened (number of lines of force increased), the current flow will be increased as the conductor moves through the magnetic field.

§ 14-3. D-C GENERATOR CONSTRUCTION

If the conductor is bent into the shape of a U and the two ends connected to the two halves of a split copper ring, we have the elements of a generator (Fig. 14-3). Stationary brushes, connected to the "load" (an electric light or other current-consuming device) and resting on the split ring, and two poles of a magnet with windings around them complete the elementary generator. The U-shaped conductor and the split ring (called the *commutator*) are designed to rotate together. When they rotate in a clockwise direction, as shown, current is induced in them, as indicated by the arrows. The current flows toward the reader in the left-hand half of the loop and away from the reader in the right-hand half. The current flows out through the left-hand brush, most of it flowing first to the load, then to the right-hand brush, and finally back into the loop. Part of the current induced in the conductor flows through the two field windings assembled around the two magnetic poles. This current flow strengthens the magnetic field between the poles, thus increasing the amount of current induced in the conductor as it moves through the magnetic field. The left-hand rule can be used to check the direction of the magnetic field produced by the two field windings. Place the left hand around the winding with the fingers pointing in the direction in which the current flows. The thumb will point in the direction of

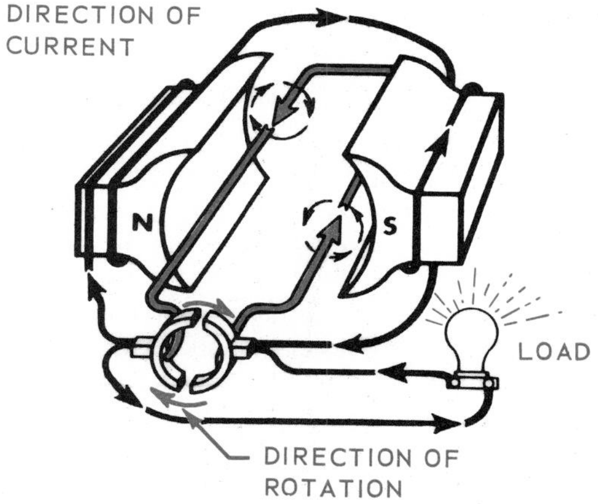

Fig. 14-3. Simplified schematic diagram of a generator. The heavy arrows show the direction of current flow, and the light circular arrows show the direction of magnetic fields around the conductors.

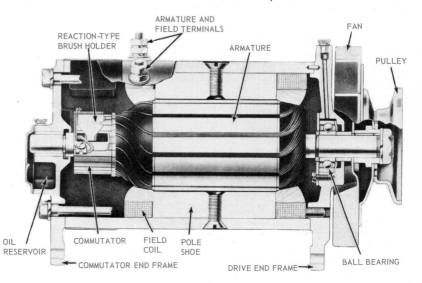

Fig. 14-4. Sectional view of a passenger-car, d-c generator. (*Delco-Remy Division of General Motors Corporation*)

225

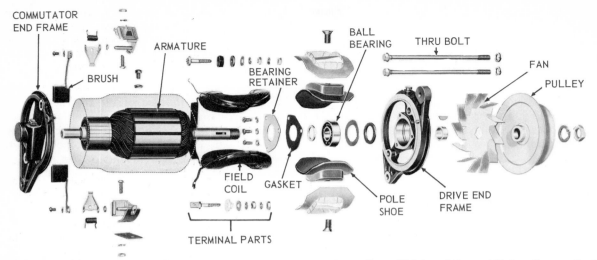

Fig. 14–5. Disassembled view of a passenger-car, d-c generator. *(Delco-Remy Division of General Motors Corporation)*

the magnetic lines of force. In the generator assembly (Fig. 14–4), the magnetic poles (called *pole shoes*) are placed on the opposite sides of an iron field frame. The field frame forms the return magnetic circuit for the lines of force from the south to the north pole.

The commutator is designed to allow the generator to produce a flow of direct current; that is, the current continues to flow in the same direction. As the two sides of the loop (Fig. 14–3) rotate and change positions with respect to each other, the two segments of the commutator also change positions so that the current continues to be fed to the left-hand brush in the same direction.

The generator must use many rotating loops in order to produce an appreciable amount of current. These loops, or conductors, are assembled into the armature (Fig. 14–4) and are connected to the segments of the commutator. To obtain a strong magnetic field, the field windings are made of many turns of wire. The field windings are connected in series, as shown in Fig. 14–3, and shunted across the two brushes.

Figure 14–4 illustrates a sectional view of a typical generator, and Fig. 14–5 shows an exploded view of a similar unit. The generator consists of a field frame, into which the field windings are assembled; the armature, which contains the moving conductors; brushes, which rest on the armature commutator; the two end heads, which support the armature in bearings; and the drive pulley, assembled to the armature shaft for driving the generator.

§ 14–4. ALTERNATOR (A-C GENERATOR) PRINCIPLES The d-c generator rotates the conductors in a stationary magnetic field. The a-c generator rotates a magnetic field so that stationary conductors cut the moving magnetic lines of force.

Let us look at a simple a-c generator (Fig. 14–6). In the simple, one-loop unit shown, the rotating bar magnet furnishes the moving field. At the top, as the north pole of the bar magnet passes the upper leg of the loop, and as the south pole passes the lower leg of the loop, current (electron flow) is induced in the loop in the direction shown by the arrows. At the bottom, the magnet has rotated half a turn so that its south pole is passing the

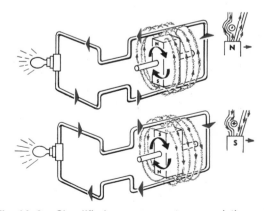

Fig. 14–6. Simplified a-c generator consisting of a single stationary loop of wire and a rotating bar magnet. The distortion of moving lines of force around a leg of the loop (conductor) and the direction of current (electron) flow are shown at the right.

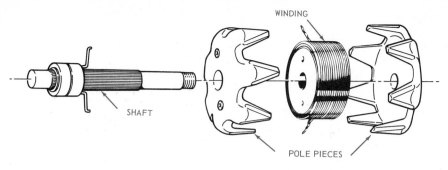

Fig. 14-7. Rotor of an a-c generator, in partly disassembled view. *(Delco-Remy Division of General Motors Corporation)*

upper leg of the loop and its north pole is passing the lower leg. Now, magnetic lines of force are being cut by the two legs in the opposite direction, and current (electron flow), of course, is induced in the loop in the opposite direction. Thus, as the magnet spins and the two poles alternately pass the two legs of the loop, electrons are pushed first in one direction and then in the other in the loop. In other words, the electrons alternate in direction; alternating current flows.

Two things will increase the strength of the current (number of electrons) moving in the loop: increasing the strength of the magnetic field, and increasing the speed with which the magnetic field moves past the two legs of the loop. A third method of increasing the current can also be used—increasing the number of loops.

In the actual a-c generator, or alternator, both the strength of the magnetic field and the number of loops are increased. Instead of a simple bar magnet, the rotating part of the a-c generator is made up of two or more pole pieces assembled on a shaft over an electromagnetic winding. The

electromagnet is made up of many turns of wire. When current flows in the electromagnetic winding, a strong magnetic field is created so that the pointed ends of the two pole pieces become, alternately, north and south poles (Fig. 14-7). The winding is connected to the battery through a pair of insulated rings that rotate with the shaft and a pair of stationary brushes that ride on the rings. The two ends of the winding are attached to the rings, and the brushes make continuous sliding (or slipping) contact with the slip rings (Fig. 14-8).

Figure 14-9 shows the stationary loops of an a-c generator assembled into a frame. The assembly is called a *stator*. The loops are interconnected as explained below so that the current produced in all loops adds together. Since this current is alternating, it must be treated in such a way as to rectify it, or convert it into direct current.

§ 14-5. ALTERNATOR The a-c generator, or alternator, produces alternating current. The battery, ignition system, and other electrical components

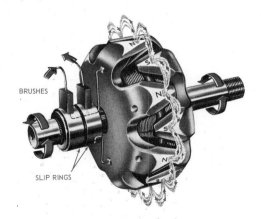

Fig. 14-8. Rotor of an a-c generator, showing brushes in place on slip rings. *(Delco-Remy Division of General Motors Corporation)*

Fig. 14-9. Stator of an a-c generator. *(Delco-Remy Division of General Motors Corporation)*

227

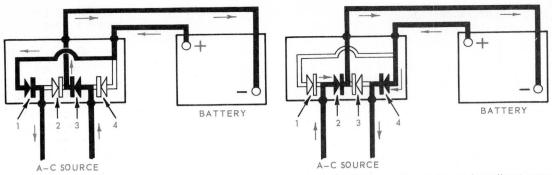

Fig. 14–10. Four diodes connected to an a-c source to rectify the alternating current and change it to direct current to charge a battery.

on the automobile cannot use ac, however; they are all d-c units. The a-c output must therefore be rectified, or changed to dc.

1. Rectifying ac. Most automotive a-c generators have built-in diode rectifiers. The *diode* is an electronic device that permits current to flow through it in one direction only. Figure 14–10 illustrates how four diodes can be used to change ac to dc. The four diodes are numbered 1 to 4 in the illustration. To the left, the current from the a-c source follows the conductors shown solid. Diodes 1 and 3 permit the current to flow through, but diodes 2 and 4 will not, since the current is flowing in the wrong direction from them. However, when the direction of the current has reversed, as shown to the right in Fig. 14–10, diodes 2 and 4 will pass the current but diodes 1 and 3 will not.

2. Three-phase. The circuit shown in Fig. 14–10 is termed *single-phase,* since there is only a single a-c source. Such a source would result in a pulsating current, much as a single-cylinder engine does not provide a smooth flow of power but rather a series of peaks between which no power is delivered. To provide a much smoother flow of current, a-c generators are built with three stator circuits which, in effect, give overlapping pulses of ac. When these are rectified, a comparatively smooth flow of dc is obtained.

The three stator circuits can be interconnected in either of two ways, with "Y" connections or with "delta" connections (Figs. 14–11 and 14–12). Both operate in a similar manner and are serviced in a similar way. The ac generated in the three legs of the stator passes through the six diodes and thereby is converted into dc.

3. Diode heat sinks. Diodes are usually mounted in the slip-ring end of the generator, in a metal bracket called a *heat sink.* The heat sink absorbs heat from the diodes, which become rather hot in

operation. The shape of the heat sink, with large radiating surfaces, allows this heat to be radiated into the air surrounding the generator. The diodes, therefore, do not overheat.

4. Types of a-c generator. Several types of a-c

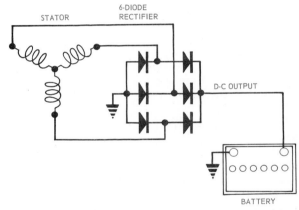

Fig. 14–11. Wiring circuit of an a-c generator with a six-diode rectifier and a Y-connected stator.

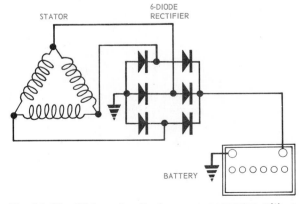

Fig. 14–12. Wiring circuit of an a-c generator with a six-diode rectifier and a delta-connected stator.

228

Fig. 14-13. Alternator installed on an engine in a car. *(Chrysler Motors Corporation)*

generator are in use. Figure 14-13 shows an a-c generator, or alternator, of the type used in Chrysler-built cars, mounted on an engine. Figure 14-14 illustrates another type.

§ 14-6. GENERATOR REGULATION Both a-c and d-c generators require regulation, and both achieve regulation in a similar manner: by limiting the amount of current flowing in the generator field winding (or windings). By "regulation" we mean preventing the generator from producing exces-

sive voltage and current. Without regulation, a generator would continue to increase its output as speed went up until it would be producing so much current that it would overheat and burn up.

To understand how a generator can overload itself by producing too much current, refer to the simplified diagram of a shunt generator (Fig. 14-3). As generator armature speed increases, the generator produces increasing voltage and more current. This is because the conductors are cutting more lines of force per second. The increased voltage not only sends more current to the load but it also sends more current through the generator field windings. This, in turn, causes the magnetic field to become stronger. The stronger magnetic field, providing more lines of force, further increases the number of lines of force the conductors cut per second. This sends the voltage still higher, so that there is a futher increase in generator output and field current. The voltage and current would continue to rise with increasing generator speed until so much current would be produced that the resulting heat would quickly destroy the generator. In addition, if the generator were connected to an automotive electric circuit, the battery would be greatly overcharged and the electrical devices turned on would be badly damaged or ruined. Consequently, some means of limiting the generator voltage and output must be used so that overheating of the generator and damage to the electrical equipment will not occur.

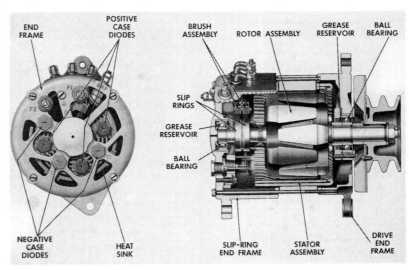

Fig. 14-14. End and sectional views of an a-c generator with built-in diode rectifiers. *(Delco-Remy Division of General Motors Corporation)*

§ 14-7. D-C GENERATOR REGULATION

The d-c generator uses an external resistance to control generator voltage and amperage output. Figure 14-15 illustrates one system of connecting this resistance. The regulator switch, a pair of points, remains closed so long as voltage or output is not excessive. This directly connects the external end of the field circuit to ground. When voltage, or output, increases to maximum values, the regulator switch is caused to open in the manner explained below. This inserts resistance into the field circuit. This resistance reduces the amount of current flowing in the field windings, which in turn weakens the magnetic field. Thus, the generator output, or voltage, is reduced or kept from increasing beyond safe values. The manner of connecting the resistance shown in Fig. 14-15 is used in some systems. Other systems use the connections shown in Fig. 14-16. In the first system, the resistance is inserted between the field windings and ground, and the field circuit is connected to the insulated brush inside the generator. The second system (Fig. 14-16) grounds the field circuit to the grounded brush inside the generator, and the resistance is connected into the field circuit between the insulated brush and the field windings. It is necessary to bear in mind these two systems of connecting the field circuit in any analysis of generators; testing procedures are different for the two systems.

§ 14-8. A-C GENERATOR REGULATION

A variety of regulating devices are used to regulate a-c generators. Essentially, regulation is accomplished in the same way as for d-c generators: by placing resistance in the generator field circuit. There are some peculiarities of a-c circuits, however, that merit special attention. A-c generator stators remain permanently connected to the battery,

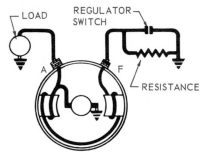

Fig. 14-15. D-c generator with an externally grounded field circuit.

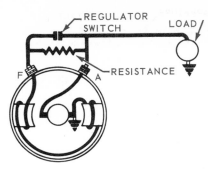

Fig. 14-16. D-c generator with an internally grounded field circuit.

through the diodes, so that no cutout relay is needed. The diodes prevent the battery from discharging back through the stator windings when the engine is not running. Some systems use only a voltage regulator for generator control. Some regulators use transistors. All these are covered in more detail in following articles.

Most automotive a-c generators do not require a current regulator. The generators are so designed and constructed that they have a built-in current-limiting action. As the current increases in strength it produces stronger magnetic fields in the stator windings. And as the magnetic field becomes stronger it effectively counteracts the rotating field. Thus, when the limiting current value is reached, the stator and rotating fields are in a sort of balance that prevents higher output.

CUTOUT RELAY

§ 14-9. CUTOUT RELAY

The d-c generator is connected to the battery through two separate devices, a cutout relay (or *circuit breaker*) and, on many cars, an *ammeter* (§ 14-13). The cutout relay closes the circuit between the generator and the battery when the generator is producing current. Also, it opens this circuit so that the battery cannot discharge back through the generator when the generator slows or stops. The cutout relay is a magnetic switch, operating on the same principles that cause the various regulating devices to operate. Thus an understanding of the cutout relay will be helpful in understanding regulators.

The cutout relay (Fig. 14-17) consists of two windings assembled around a core and a flat steel armature mounted on a hinge above the core. A contact point on the armature is placed just above a stationary point that is connected to the battery. When the generator is not operating, a spring on

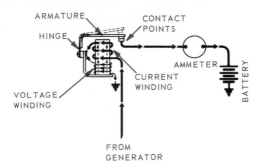

Fig. 14–17. Schematic wiring circuit of a cutout relay.

the armature holds the two points apart. This keeps the circuit between the generator and the battery open. The two windings consist of a current, or series, winding of a few turns of heavy wire and a voltage, or shunt, winding of many turns of fine wire. When the generator begins to operate, its voltage builds up, imposing voltage on the two windings. This creates a magnetic field that attracts the flat steel armature. Increasing generator voltage increases the magnetic attraction until operating voltage is reached. At this point, the attraction is strong enough to overcome the armature spring tension and pull the armature toward the winding core. This causes the two contact points to come together so that the generator is connected to the battery. Current flows from the generator to the battery. As it does so, it passes through the current, or series, winding in the right direction to add to the magnetic pull holding the points closed. Note the application of the left-hand rule to the two windings in the illustration.

When the generator stops, current begins to flow from the battery to the generator. A reversal in the direction of the current flow in the current winding takes place, causing its magnetic field to reverse. This means that the magnetic fields of the two windings no longer aid but buck each other. The result is that the magnetic field is so weakened that it can no longer hold the armature down. The armature spring tension pulls the armature up, separating the contact points. This opens the circuit between the battery and the generator.

REGULATORS

§ 14–10. REGULATORS FOR D-C GENERATORS
These regulators consist of a cutout relay (§ 14–9), a voltage regulator, and a current regulator (Fig. 14–18).

1. Voltage regulator. The voltage regulator (Fig. 14–19) prevents the circuit voltage from exceeding a predetermined safe maximum. A practically constant voltage is maintained in the system. This causes the generator to provide a charging rate in reverse ratio to the state of charge of the battery. That is, when the battery is low, it is supplied current at a high charging rate, and when it is charged, the charging rate tapers off to a few amperes.

The voltage regulator consists of a shunt winding and a flat steel armature mounted on a hinge above the winding core. When the battery is in a low state of charge, the regulator does not operate. Thus generator output increases to a value determined by speed and battery condition. As the battery approaches a charged condition, its voltage increases. There is then an increasing magnetic pull from the shunt winding on the armature. When the regulating voltage is reached, the magnetic pull is sufficient to overcome the spring tension holding the armature away from the winding core. The armature is pulled down, causing the points to separate. This inserts resistance into the generator field circuit so that the generator output and voltage are reduced. Reduction of generator voltage reduces the magnetic strength of the shunt winding. The armature, consequently, is pulled up by the armature spring tension, the points close, and generator output and voltage increase. The entire sequence is repeated many times a second, causing the resistance to be inserted into and removed from the generator field circuit as many as 200 times a

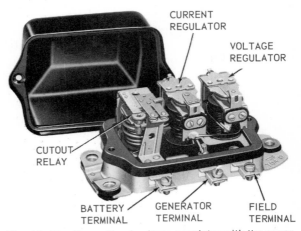

Fig. 14–18. Current and voltage regulator with the cover removed. *(Delco-Remy Division of General Motors Corporation)*

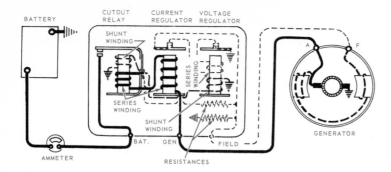

Fig. 14-19. Wiring circuit of the regulator shown in Fig. 14-18. *(Delco-Remy Division of General Motors Corporation)*

second. This action provides, in effect, a variable resistance that increases or decreases the effective resistance in the generator field circuit, according to the state of charge of the battery and the connected electrical load. When the battery is fully charged and there are no electrical devices connected to the generator, the points vibrate in such a way that the resistance remains in the generator field circuit most of the time. It is as if a high resistance were inserted into the generator field circuit. The generator output consequently drops to a low value. When the battery becomes partly discharged or electrical devices are turned on, the points vibrate in such a way as to keep the resistance in the field only a small part of the time. This allows a higher generator output. Thus the generator output varies within wide limits. The action of the voltage regulator allows the generator to produce the correct amount of current for every condition of operation up to the limits imposed by generator speed. When full generator output is required, the voltage regulator does not operate, and output is limited by the current regulator.

Some voltage regulators have more than one winding. One type uses a field-current winding through which the generator field current flows when the contact points are closed. When the points open, current stops flowing in this winding. Such action speeds up the operation of the regulator armature, causing the regulator to provide a more even voltage with less fluctuation.

2. Current regulator. The current regulator is constructed in a manner similar to the voltage regulator, except that the winding consists of a few turns of heavy wire through which full generator output passes. When the generator output reaches rated maximum, the current passing through the regulator winding is sufficient to overcome the armature spring tension and separate the regulator points. This inserts the resist-

ance into the generator field circuit, causing the generator output to drop off. As soon as the generator output is reduced, the magnetic pull of the regulator winding is reduced also, so that it can no longer hold the points open. They close, the generator field circuit is directly grounded, and the output increases. This cycle is repeated very rapidly, causing the current regulator to limit the current output of the generator to the value for which the generator is rated.

Some designs of current regulators use more than one winding. As with the voltage regulator, the added windings cause the points to vibrate more rapidly, producing a more even output.

3. Combined action. Either the voltage regulator on the current regulator operates at any one time; they never operate simultaneously. When the load requirements are high and the battery is low, the current regulator operates to prevent the generator output from exceeding its safe maximum. The voltage is not sufficient to cause the voltage regulator to operate. But if the load requirements are reduced or if the battery begins to come up to charge, the line voltage will increase to a value sufficient to cause the voltage regulator to operate. When this happens, the generator output is reduced; it falls below the value required to cause the current regulator to operate. All regulation is then dependent on the voltage regulator.

§ 14-11. TEMPERATURE COMPENSATION Most voltage regulators and some current regulators are temperature-compensated. This means that they will have higher settings when cold than when hot. As previously explained (§ 13-8), low battery temperatures make it necessary to apply higher voltages to obtain current input to the battery. Temperature compensation of the voltage regulator allows this increase of voltage with low temperature. Some current regulators are temperature-compensated to permit a higher generator output when the current regulator is cold than when it is hot, the generator output decreasing as the temperature of the current regulator increases. This safely allows generator output to remain high, if required, until the current regulator reaches operating temperature. Then, the output is reduced to a value in line with the safe hot-generator output.

Temperature compensation can be achieved in either of two ways. One design makes use of a bimetal thermostatic hinge on the regulator armature. The hinge adds tension at low temperatures, so that a higher voltage (or current, on current regulators) is required to open the regulator points. As temperature increases, the hinge loses tension, so that less voltage (or current) is required.

The second design makes use of a magnetic by-pass. This passes more magnetism at low temperatures; thus less magnetism is left over to attract the regulator armature. The voltage (or current) must go higher to cause regulator operation. As temperature increases, less magnetism is bypassed and the regulator setting is, in effect, reduced.

§ 14-12. REGULATOR FOR A-C GENERATORS

A considerable variety of a-c generator regulators have been developed in recent years. Some of these look, operate, and are adjusted much like the regulators used with d-c generators. Others

have no cutout relays (the rectifying diodes prevent reverse current or discharge of the battery through the generator stator windings). Still others make use of transistors which work with vibrating contact points to control generator field current and output. Another type has no moving parts at all, using transistors only for control. The latest types are discussed below.

1. Voltage regulator. Figure 14–20 shows the wiring circuit of a voltage regulator and ac generator. Figure 14–21 shows the regulator unit with the cover removed. In this system, the only regulation required is of the voltage, and thus the unit used is a voltage regulator. It works much like the voltage regulators of d-c generator regulators. That is, as voltage reaches the preset value, the regulator contact points open to insert resistance into the generator field circuit and thus prevent excessive voltage. The regulator contact points vibrate to maintain a steady voltage.

This regulator has two sets of contact points, a lower set and an upper set. At intermediate speeds, the lower contact points open and close, or vibrate, to control generator voltage. This action inserts and removes the resistance in the generator field circuit. At higher speed, however, the higher voltage generated causes the upper contacts to begin to vibrate. With the upper contact points closed, the generator field winding is shorted (both ends are connected to ground) so

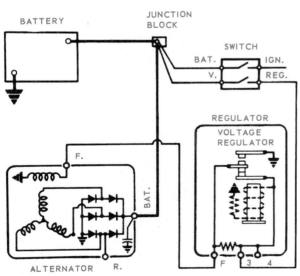

Fig. 14–20. Wiring circuit of a one-unit voltage regulator and a-c generator (alternator). *(Pontiac Motor Division of General Motors Corporation)*

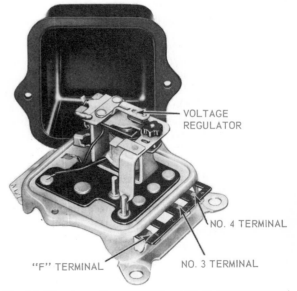

Fig. 14–21. A-c voltage regulator with its cover removed so that the unit can be seen. *(Pontiac Motor Division of General Motors Corporation)*

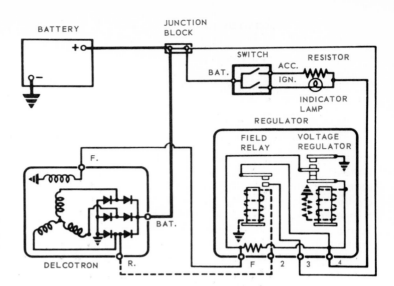

Fig. 14–22. Wiring diagram of an alternator with a two-unit regulator using a voltage regulator and a field relay. *(Chevrolet Motor Division of General Motors Corporation)*

that further voltage regulation is obtained. This combination of two sets of contact points provides proper voltage regulation throughout the full range of generator operating speed.

No current regulator is needed in this system. Neither is a cutout relay required. The diodes permit current to flow in only one direction, which is the direction required to charge the battery. When the generator slows or stops, the battery cannot discharge back through the generator, even though the two still remain connected to each other. The diodes prevent this reverse, or discharge, current from flowing.

Note that the generator-field windings are connected through the ignition switch to the battery (through regulator terminals 3 and F). When the ignition switch is turned off, the field is disconnected from the battery to prevent any drain on the battery when the engine is not running.

2. Voltage regulator with field relay. The wiring diagram of this regulator is shown in Fig. 14–22, and the regulator with cover removed is shown in Fig. 14–23. The regulator terminals are of the slip-connection type; a connector body on the vehicle wiring harness is keyed to mating slots in the regulator base to assure proper connections. There is a latch on the regulator base which holds the connector body in place on the terminals.

The voltage regulator works in the same way as the unit described above and illustrated in Figs. 14–20 and 14–21. The purpose of the field relay is to connect the alternator field to the battery when the ignition switch is closed and to disconnect it when the ignition switch is opened to

turn the engine off. It also operates the charge indicator lamp.

When the ignition switch is closed, and before the engine starts, the indicator lamp comes on to indicate that the alternator is not charging. With this condition, the current is flowing from the battery to the BAT. terminal of the ignition switch, through the resistor and indicator lamp which are in parallel, and then through the regulator

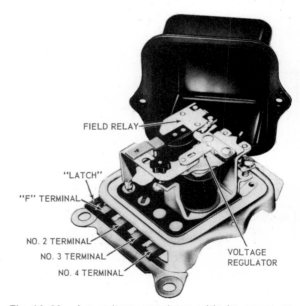

Fig. 14–23. A-c voltage regulator with its cover removed. This regulator includes a voltage-regulator unit and a field relay. *(Oldsmobile Division of General Motors Corporation)*

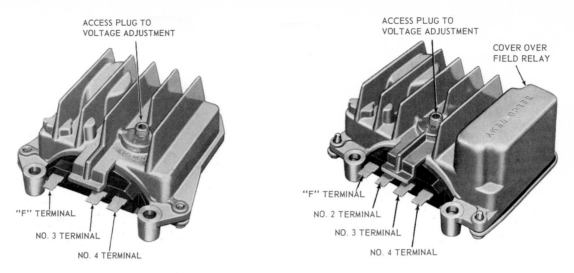

Fig. 14–24. Typical transistor voltage regulators. Left, the type without a field relay. Right, the type with a field relay. *(Delco-Remy Division of General Motors Corporation)*

lower contact points (via terminal 4). From there it flows through the alternator field winding to ground, and then back to the battery grounded terminal. This current flowing through the alternator field winding is great enough to produce a strong magnetic field. Then, when the engine starts and the alternator rotor begins to turn, the magnetic field rotates to produce voltage in the stator windings.

This voltage causes charging current to flow to the battery. At the same time, the voltage is applied to the winding of the field relay (via the R terminal on the alternator and terminal 2 on the regulator). The relay contacts therefore close, connecting terminal 4 of the regulator directly to the battery (through terminal 3). Now, both sides of the indicator lamp are connected to the same battery terminal, and there is no voltage on it. Therefore, this lamp goes out to indicate that the alternator is charging. Field current for the alternator now flows from terminal 4, through the voltage regulator lower contact points, and through terminal F to the F terminal on the alternator.

The alternator voltage is controlled by the action of the voltage regulator, as already noted.

3. Transistorized voltage regulator with field relay. Figures 14–24 and 14–25 are wiring diagrams and external views of this unit. The field relay operates in much the same way as the unit already described in previous paragraphs. The voltage regulator contains no moving parts; its

action depends entirely on transistors. The transistor is an electronic device that has an amplifying effect, much like a vacuum tube in a radio or TV set. When a small amount of current is supplied to the transistor base, a large current flows through the transistor.

The voltage regulator has two transistors and several resistors, as well as other electronic parts. In operation, the transistors limit the current flow to the alternator field windings so as to prevent excessive alternator voltage. If the voltage tends to exceed the specified maximum, the transistors

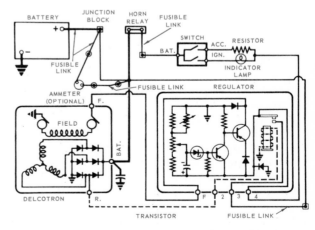

Fig. 14–25. Wiring diagram of a transistor voltage regulator with a field relay. *(Chevrolet Motor Division of General Motors Corporation)*

235

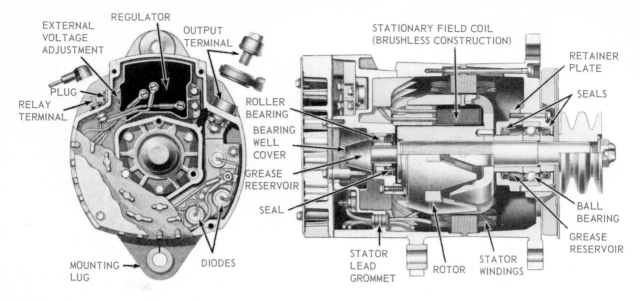

Fig. 14-26. Alternator with a built-in voltage regulator. *(Delco-Remy Division of General Motors Corporation)*

shut off the field current so that the voltage drops. Then, the transistors allow field current to flow again. This action is repeated with extreme rapidity so that the alternator charging voltage remains constant.

4. Integral voltage regulator. Some alternators now have built-in voltage regulators (Fig. 14-26). These regulators are transistorized and operate in the same way as the units already discussed.

§ 14-13. AMMETER Many charging circuits use an indicator lamp to indicate whether or not the alternator is charging the battery (§ 14-12). However, an ammeter is used on many cars. It provides a better idea to the driver of what is happening in the charging circuit. The ammeter shows in a general way how much current is flowing to the battery during charge, and how much is flowing from the battery if the alternator is not charging the battery.

The ammeter is connected between the battery and alternator. The typical ammeter is shown in Fig. 14-27. It includes a pivoted vane to which a needle is attached, a permanent magnet, and a heavy conductor. When no current flows to or from the battery, the pivoted vane is held between the two poles of the permanent magnet. In this position, the needle indicates zero. When current does flow, it passes through the conductor.

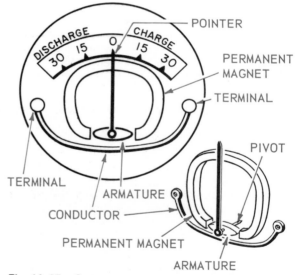

Fig. 14-27. Car ammeter, or charge indicator.

The magnetic field forces the vane to move. The stronger the current, the farther the vane moves. The needle, therefore, swings around to register the amount of current flowing through. If the current is flowing to the battery, the needle swings to the "charge" side. If the current is flowing from the battery, the needle swings to the "discharge" side.

Review Questions

1. Describe the major differences between d-c and a-c generators.
2. Why does the a-c generator require diodes?
3. What do diodes do?
4. What is the purpose of a generator output control?
5. What would happen to a d-c generator if it were not controlled as it increased in speed?
6. What are the two systems of connecting the d-c generator field circuit when an external regulating device is used?
7. What is the purpose of the cutout relay? What other name does this device have?
8. What is the essential difference between the d-c voltage regulator and the d-c current regulator, insofar as the physical construction is concerned? Insofar as the operation is concerned?
9. What is temperature compensation in the regulator? In what two general ways is temperature compensation obtained?
10. Describe the operation of the a-c voltage regulator.
11. Why is it that the alternator does not require a cutout relay?
12. What is the purpose of the field relay and how does it work?
13. Explain how a transistorized voltage regulator works.
14. Describe the operation of a car ammeter.

Study Questions

1. Describe the operation of a d-c generator.
2. Name the main parts of a d-c generator.
3. Make a wiring diagram of a cutout relay, and name the windings.
4. Make a wiring diagram of a d-c current and voltage regulator, and name the windings.
5. Make a wiring diagram of an a-c generator-regulator system, and then name each of the parts.
6. Describe the operation of a typical a-c generator.
7. Describe the different types of a-c regulator.

CHAPTER
15

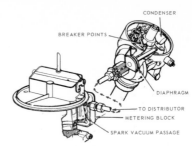

CONDENSER
BREAKER POINTS
DIAPHRAGM
TO DISTRIBUTOR
METERING BLOCK
SPARK VACUUM PASSAGE

The Electric System — The Ignition System

This chapter continues the description of the various components of the electric system and discusses the ignition system.

§ 15–1. FUNCTION OF IGNITION SYSTEM The ignition system supplies high-voltage surges (of as much as 30,000 volts) of current to the spark plugs in the engine cylinders. These surges produce the electric sparks at the spark-plug gaps that ignite, or set fire to, the compressed air-fuel mixture in the combustion chamber. Each spark is timed to appear at the plug gap just as the piston approaches top dead center on the compression stroke when the engine is idling. At higher speed or during part-throttle operation, the spark is advanced so that it occurs somewhat earlier in the cycle; the mixture thus has ample time to burn and deliver its power (§ 15–6). The ignition system consists of the battery, switch, ignition distributor, ignition coil, spark plugs, and wiring (Fig. 15–1).

Some systems use transistors to reduce the load on the distributor contact points. Other systems do not have contact points but use instead a combination of transistors and a magnetic pick-up in the distributor. These are explained in the following article.

§ 15–2. IGNITION DISTRIBUTOR The ignition distributor has two jobs. First, it closes and opens the circuit between the battery and the ignition coil. When the circuit closes, current flows in the ignition coil and builds up a magnetic field. When the circuit opens, the magnetic field in the coil collapses, and a high-voltage surge of current is produced by the coil. The distributor's second job is to distribute each high-voltage surge to the correct spark plug at the correct instant by means of the distributor rotor and cap and secondary wiring.

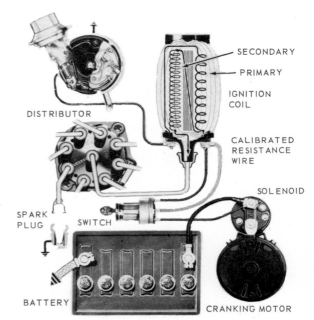

SECONDARY
PRIMARY
IGNITION COIL
CALIBRATED RESISTANCE WIRE
SOLENOID
DISTRIBUTOR
SPARK PLUG
SWITCH
BATTERY
CRANKING MOTOR

Fig. 15–1. Typical ignition system. It consists of the battery (source of power), ignition switch, ignition coil (shown schematically), distributor (shown in top view with its cap removed and placed below it), spark plugs (one shown in sectional view), and wiring. The coil is shown schematically with magnetic lines of force indicated. *(Delco-Remy Division of General Motors Corporation)*

There are two basic types of distributor: (1) the type using contact points to close and open the coil primary circuit; (2) the type using a magnetic pick-up and a transistor control unit to interrupt the current flow of the coil primary circuit.

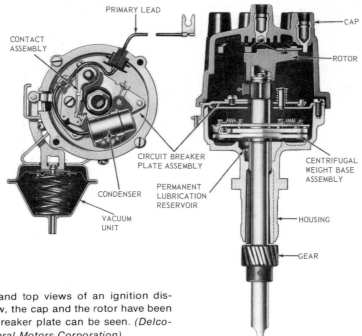

Fig. 15-2. Sectional and top views of an ignition distributor. In the top view, the cap and the rotor have been removed so that the breaker plate can be seen. (*Delco-Remy Division of General Motors Corporation*)

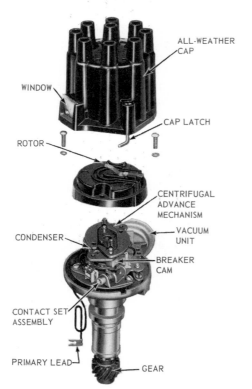

Fig. 15-3. Partly disassembled distributor. (*Delco-Remy Division of General Motors Corporation*)

1. Distributor with contact points. This distributor (Figs. 15-2 and 15-3) consists of a housing, a drive shaft with breaker cam, an advance mechanism, a breaker plate with contact points and a condenser, a rotor, and a cap. The shaft is usually driven by the engine camshaft through spiral gears (Fig. 3-24), and it rotates at one-half crankshaft speed. Usually, the distributor drive shaft is coupled with a shaft that drives the oil pump.

Rotation of the shaft and breaker cam causes the distributor contact points to open and close. The breaker cam usually has the same number of lobes as there are cylinders in the engine.* It rotates at half crankshaft speed, and the contact points close and open once for each cylinder with every breaker-cam rotation. Thus one high-voltage surge is produced by the coil for each cylinder every two crankshaft revolutions. This ignites the air-fuel mixture compressed in each cylinder every other crankshaft revolution.

---

* On some applications, the breaker cam has only one-half as many lobes as engine cylinders, but there are two sets of contact points that are arranged to close and open alternately. This produces the same effect as the breaker-cam and contact-point arrangement discussed above.

The rotor rotates with the breaker cam on which it is mounted. As it does so, a metal spring and segment on the rotor connect the center terminal of the cap with each outside terminal in turn, so that the high-voltage surges from the coil are directed first to one spark plug and then to another, and so on, according to the firing order.

2. *Distributor with magnetic pickup.* With the cap on, this distributor looks the same as the distributor using contact points. However, when the caps are removed, the difference between the two is apparent. Figure 15–4 shows the magnetic-pick-up distributor with the cap and rotor removed. Figure 15–5 is a schematic diagram of the ignition circuit. The transistor control unit is connected between the ignition-coil primary and the battery (through the ignition switch). It permits battery current to flow to the coil primary winding, and it interrupts this flow, on signals from the distributor. This action is similar to what happens when the points close and open in the contact-point distributor.

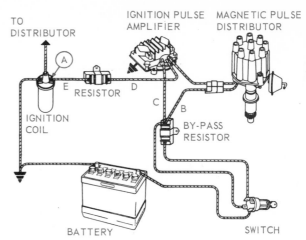

Fig. 15–5. Schematic diagram of an ignition system using a magnetic-pick-up distributor. *(Delco-Remy Division of General Motors Corporation)*

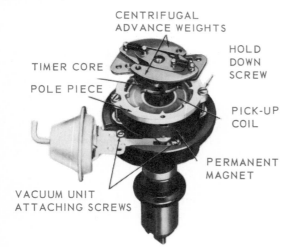

Fig. 15–4. Magnetic-pick-up distributor with cap and rotor removed. *(Delco-Remy Division of General Motors Corporation)*

The distributor is mounted and driven in the same manner as other distributors. The magnetic pick-up (Fig. 15–4) which provides the signals to the control unit contains a permanent ring magnet on top of which is mounted a pole piece. The pole piece has a series of teeth pointing inward. There are the same number of teeth as there are cylinders in the engine. Inside the permanent magnet is a pick-up coil containing many turns of wire. All these parts are assembled together over the

main bearing of the distributor housing, and the assembly is attached to a vacuum unit which provides vacuum advance (§ 15–6).

The timer core, made of iron, is assembled on the distributor shaft through the centrifugal advance mechanism and rotates with the shaft. It has the same number of teeth as there are cylinders in the engine. When the engine is operating and the distributor is rotating, the timer-core teeth and the pole-piece teeth align eight times for every shaft rotation (for an eight-cylinder engine). This compares with the eight times the points open (on an eight-cylinder engine) for every shaft revolution in the contact-point distributor. Each time the teeth align, a magnetic path is established through the pick-up coil. That is, magnetic lines of force from the permanent magnet cut through the turns of wire in the pick-up coil. Then, further shaft rotation moves the teeth apart so that the magnetic path is opened and the magnetic field quickly collapses. When this happens, a voltage is induced in the coil, and this sends a signal, or pulse of current, to the control unit. This produces the same effect in the primary circuit as the opening of contact points.

Before the pick-up coil sends its signal to the control unit, the conditions are as shown in Fig. 15–6 in the circuit. That is, current is flowing from the battery, through resistor R–6, and through the control unit (via R–1 and transistor TR–1) to the ignition coil primary winding.

But when the signal arrives in the control unit from the pick-up coil, it causes transistor TR–3 to

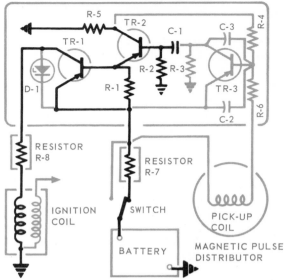

Fig. 15-6. Conditions in the ignition control circuit when current is flowing from the battery through the ignition-coil primary winding. *(Delco-Remy Division of General Motors Corporation)*

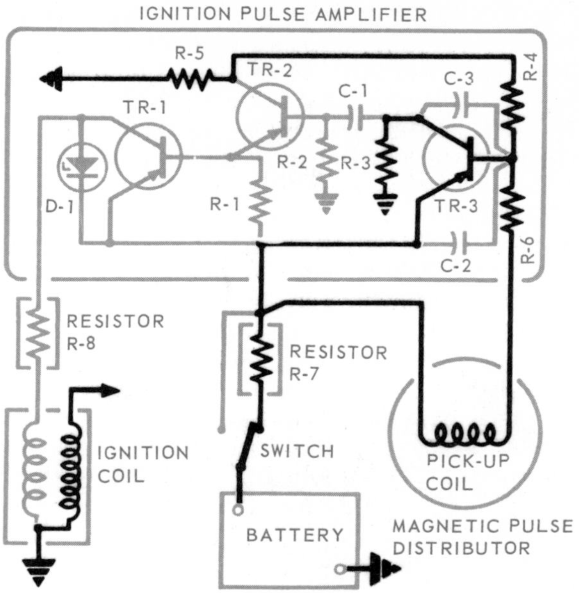

Fig. 15-7. Conditions when the pick-up coil in the distributor sends a signal to the control unit. *(Delco-Remy Division of General Motors Corporation)*

become conductive. The reason for this is that the pulse of current from the pick-up coil supplies the TR-3 transistor base with a small amount of current. When this happens, current flows as shown in Fig. 15-7. With TR-3 conductive, current is drained away from the base of TR-2 so that TR-2 becomes a nonconductor. Now, with no current flowing through TR-2, there is a reduced voltage drop across resistor R-1, and the base of TR-1 becomes approximately the same voltage as the lower TR-1 connection. Thus, there is no current flow at the TR-1 base—the TR-1 transistor now becomes, in effect, a diode—and current stops flowing from the battery through TR-1 to the coil primary winding.

With the sudden stoppage of current to the ignition-coil primary winding, the magnetic field in the ignition coil collapses, inducing a high voltage in the ignition-coil secondary winding. This high-voltage surge is delivered to the correct spark plug (the one ready to fire), by the distributor rotor and cap and secondary wiring, exactly as for the distributor with contact points.

3. Distributor with contact points and transistorized system. The wiring circuit of a distributor with contact points used with a transistorized ignition system is shown in Fig. 15-8. The contact points are connected between the transistor base

and the grounded side of the circuit. When the points are closed, the base is electrically connected to ground. Now, current carriers can appear at the base, and current can flow through the coil primary winding. A magnetic field builds up. When the contacts are opened, current carriers no longer are available at the transistor base. Current stops flowing through the transistor, the magnetic field in the coil collapses, and a spark appears at a spark-plug gap. Note that only a small current flows through the contact points. The points therefore last a long time, since they are not required to break the coil primary circuit—the transistor does that.

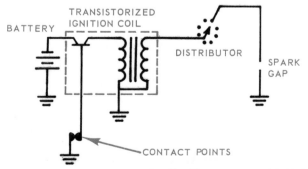

Fig. 15-8. Wiring circuit of an ignition system using a distributor with contact points and a transistor control.

§ 15–3. SPARK PLUGS The spark plug (Fig. 15–9) consists of a metal shell in which is fastened a porcelain insulator and an electrode extending through the center of the insulator. The metal shell has a short electrode attached to one side and bent in toward the center electrode. There are threads on the metal shell that allow it to be screwed into a tapped hole in the cylinder head. The two electrodes are of special heavy wire, and there is a gap of up to 0.040 inch between them. The electric spark jumps this gap to ignite the air-fuel mixture in the combustion chamber, passing from the center, or insulated, electrode to the grounded, or outer, electrode. The seals between the metal base, porcelain, and center electrode, as well as the porcelain itself, must be able to withstand the high pressure and temperature created in the combustion chamber during the power stroke.

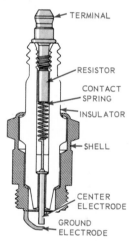

Fig. 15–9. Sectional view of a resistor-type spark plug. *(Ford Motor Company)*

Some spark plugs have been supplied with a built-in resistor (Fig. 15–9) which forms part of the center electrode. The purpose of this resistor is to reduce radio and television interference from the ignition system as well as to reduce spark-plug-electrode erosion caused by excessively long sparking. We have been talking of the high-voltage surge from the ignition-coil secondary as though it were a single powerful surge that almost instantly caused the spark to jump across the spark-plug gap. Actually, the action is more complex than that. There may be a whole series of preliminary surges before a full-fledged spark forms. At the end of the sparking cycle the spark may be

quenched and may reform several times. All this takes place in only a few ten-thousandths of a second. The effect is that the ignition wiring acts like a radio transmitting antenna; the surges of high voltage send out static that causes radio and television interference. However, the resistors in the spark plugs tend to concentrate the surges in each sparking cycle, reduce their number, and thus reduce the interference and also the erosive effect on the plug electrodes.

§ 15–4. SECONDARY WIRING The secondary wiring consists of the high-tension cables connected between the distributor cap, the spark plugs, and the high-tension terminal of the ignition coil. These cables carry the high-voltage surges that produce the sparks at the plug gaps. Thus, they must be heavily insulated to contain the high voltage, and the insulation must be able to withstand the effects of high temperature and oil as well as of high voltage.

Before 1961, the cores of the cables were of copper or aluminum wire. However, in 1961, automotive manufacturers in the United States began to install cables which had carbon-impregnated linen cores. The carbon-impregnated linen forms a resistance path for the high-voltage surges, producing the same effect as the resistors in the spark plugs mentioned above. These cables thus do an effective job of preventing the ignition system from interfering with radio and television.

In 1963, many cars began using cables with graphite-saturated fiber-glass cores. These operate in the same manner as the carbon-impregnated linen-core cables. However, it is claimed that they are less susceptible to breakage when pulled off spark plugs and have less tendency to char from high temperatures.

§ 15–5. IGNITION COIL The ignition coil transforms, or steps up, the 6 or 12 volts of the battery to the high voltage required to make the current jump the spark-plug gap. A high voltage is required because the air-fuel mixture between the two electrodes presents a high resistance to the passage of current. The voltage (pressure) must go very high in order to push current (electrons) from the center to the outside electrode. Let us consider in detail the actions in the ignition coil that enables it to produce high-voltage surges.

The ignition coil has two circuits through it, a primary circuit and a secondary circuit (Fig. 15–1). The secondary circuit is made up of a winding of

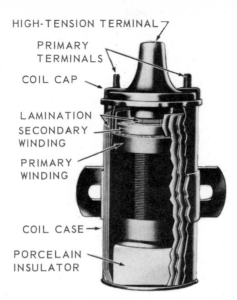

HIGH-TENSION TERMINAL

PRIMARY TERMINALS

COIL CAP

LAMINATION
SECONDARY WINDING

PRIMARY WINDING

COIL CASE

PORCELAIN INSULATOR

Fig. 15–10. Ignition coil with its case cut away to show how the primary winding is wound around the outside of the secondary winding. *(Delco-Remy Division of General Motors Corporation)*

Fig. 15–11. Magnetic fields surrounding two adjacent turns of wire in a winding through which current is passing.

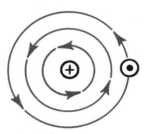

Fig. 15–12. Effect on an adjacent wire of an increasing magnetic field from one wire.

many thousands of turns of a fine wire. The primary circuit is made up of a winding of a few hundred turns of relatively heavy wire, wrapped or wound around the outside of the secondary winding, as shown in Fig. 15–10. When the distributor contact points close and current flows in the primary circuit, a magnetic field builds up. When the distributor contact points open and current stops flowing, the magnetic field collapses. The collapsing magnetic field induces high voltage in the secondary winding. This creates the high-voltage surge that is conducted through the distributor rotor and cap to a spark plug.

1. Creating the magnetic field. Current flowing through a winding causes a magnetic field. The magnetic field does not, however, spring up instantly when the circuit is closed to the battery. It takes a small fraction of a second (called the *buildup time*) for this to occur. The reason for this lies in the fact that the winding has self-induction. This term expresses the action that each turn of wire in the winding has on adjacent turns. Figure 15–11 illustrates the magnetic fields surrounding two adjacent turns of wire in the winding, seen in end view, as current flows in them. The current is flowing away from the reader as indicated by the crosses. When the current first starts to flow, the encircling magnetic fields begin to move outward from the wires in a manner somewhat like

the ripples on a pool of water moving out from where a stone has been dropped. Figure 15–12 illustrates the effect of this action on the right-hand wire. The increasing magnetic field cuts across the right-hand wire. It thus attempts to induce in that wire a flow of current in the opposite direction. This is indicated by the dot, which means the current is flowing toward the reader. To understand how current can be induced in the wire, consider the generator.

The generator causes a flow of current by moving conductors through a stationary magnetic field. However, if the conductors are held stationary and the magnetic field is moved, a flow of current also will be induced. This is the effect illustrated in Fig. 15–12. The turns of wire are stationary, but the expanding magnetic field from the left-hand wire moves across the right-hand wire. And since the magnetic field distorts around the right-hand wire in a clockwise direction, a flow of current is induced in a direction toward the reader. The left-hand rule will confirm this.

Actually, the current could not flow in this direction in the right-hand wire, because the battery is already forcing current through the winding and every turn of wire in the opposite direction, as shown in Fig. 15–11. But there is a tendency for a flow of current to be induced in the reverse direction in every turn of wire. The tendency is brought

243

about by the expanding magnetic fields from adjacent turns of wire. The result is that this tendency combats any increase in current flow through the winding. It takes a fraction of a second for the battery voltage to overcome this tendency and build up the magnetic field in the winding.

2. Effect on primary winding of collapsing the magnetic field. When the distributor contact points open, the current stops flowing, and the magnetic field from the primary winding begins to collapse. This means that the magnetic field surrounding each turn of wire begins to collapse back toward the wire. Thus, instead of the field's moving to the right, as shown in Fig. 15–12, the field moves to the left. This attempts to induce a flow of current in the right-hand wire in a direction opposite to that shown, or in the direction in which it flowed when the winding was connected to the battery. Such action, again, is self-induction.

3. Condenser effect. As the contact points separate in the distributor, the flow of current from the battery through the primary winding of the coil is interrupted. Instantly, the magnetic field begins to collapse, and this collapse attempts to reestablish the flow of current. If it were not for the condenser (also called a *capacitor*), the flow of current would be reestablished. This means a heavy electric arc would take place across the separating contact points. The points would burn, and the energy stored in the ignition coil as magnetism would be consumed by the arc. The condenser prevents this, however, because it momentarily provides a place for the current to flow as the points begin to move apart.

The condenser (or *capacitor*) is made up of two thin metallic plates separated by an insulator. The plates are two long, narrow strips of lead or aluminum foil, insulated from each other by special condenser paper and wrapped on an arbor to form a winding. The winding is then installed in a container. A condenser is shown in Fig. 15–13. The two plates provide a large surface area onto which the electrons (flow of current) can move during the first instant that the contact points separate. As will be remembered, it is the massing of electrons in one place in a circuit that causes them to move and produce what we know as a flow of current. Since the condenser provides a large surface area, many electrons can flow onto this large surface area without producing an excessive massing of electrons in one spot.

The number of electrons the condenser can accept is, however, limited, and it quickly becomes

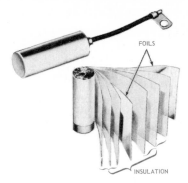

Fig. 15–13. Condenser assembled and with the winding partly unwound.

charged. But, by this time, the contact points are sufficiently far apart to prevent an arc from forming between them. In effect, the condenser acts as a reservoir into which electrons can flow during the first instant that the points begin to separate. By the time the reservoir is filled, the points are too far apart for the electrons to jump across them. The electrons, or current, consequently must stop flowing in the primary circuit. Since it is a current flow that sustains the magnetic field, the quick stoppage of the current causes the magnetic field to collapse rapidly. It is this rapid collapse that induces the high voltage in the secondary winding of the ignition coil.

4. Effect on secondary winding of magnetic-field collapse. The rapid collapse of the magnetic field causes the magnetic lines of force to move rapidly across the thousands of turns of wire in the secondary winding. This means that each turn will have voltage induced in it. Since all turns are connected in series so that the total voltage induced is the sum of the voltage of all the turns, the winding will supply a high voltage during the magnetic-field collapse. One end of the secondary winding is connected through ground to the side electrode in the spark plug. The other end of the secondary winding is connected through the cap and the rotor of the distributor and through the wiring to the center electrode in the spark plug. This high voltage, suddenly imposed on the spark plug, causes electrons (current) to jump across the gap, producing an electric spark. The instant that the spark is timed to occur is controlled by the spark-advance mechanisms located in the distributor (§ 15–6).

5. Summary. Let us review briefly the action taking place in the ignition system. As the piston in one of the engine cylinders starts up on the com-

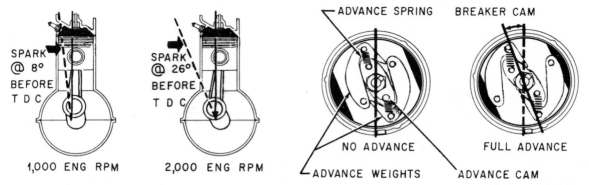

Fig. 15–14. Centrifugal-advance mechanism in no-advance and full-advance positions. In the typical example shown, the ignition is timed at 8° before top dead center on idle. There is no centrifugal advance at 1,000 engine rpm, but there is 26° total advance (18° centrifugal plus 8° due to original timing) at 2,000 engine rpm. *(Delco-Remy Division of General Motors Corporation)*

pression stroke, one of the distributor breaker-cam lobes moves away from the contact-point breaker arm. The contact points close, current flows through the primary winding of the ignition coil, and a magnetic field builds up. At the instant that the piston reaches the position in the cylinder at which ignition of the compressed air-fuel mixture should take place, the next cam lobe has moved around to where it strikes against the contact-point breaker arm so that the contact points separate. The current stops flowing in the primary circuit; the magnetic field collapses. This induces high voltage in the secondary winding. The rotor on top of the breaker cam, in the meantime, has moved into position opposite the outside distributor-cap terminal connected to the cylinder spark plug. The spark plug is thus connected to the secondary winding of the ignition coil through the cap and rotor at the instant that the high voltage is induced, and a spark therefore occurs at the spark-plug gap.

6. Ignition-coil resistor. In many passenger cars with 12-volt systems, there is a resistance wire in the ignition-coil primary circuit (see Figs. 13–23 and 15–1). This wire is shorted out by the ignition switch when it is turned to START. Now, full battery voltage is imposed on the ignition coil for good performance during cranking. After the engine is started and the ignition switch is turned to ON, the resistance is in the ignition primary circuit, thus protecting the contact points from excessive current.

§ 15–6. SPARK-ADVANCE MECHANISMS There are two general types of spark-advance mechanisms, centrifugal and vacuum. These mechanisms vary the spark timing for different engine-operating conditions, as explained in the following paragraphs.

1. Centrifugal. When the engine is idling, the spark is timed to occur just before the piston reaches top dead center on the compression stroke. At higher speeds, it is necessary to deliver the spark to the combustion chamber somewhat earlier. This will give the mixture ample time to burn and deliver its power to the piston. To provide this advance, a centrifugal advance mechanism is used (Fig. 15–14). It consists of two weights that throw out against spring tension as engine speed increases. This movement is transmitted through a toggle arrangement to the breaker cam (or to the timer core of magnetic-pick-up distributors). This causes the cam (or timer core) to advance, or move ahead, with respect to the distributor drive shaft. On the contact-point distributor, this advance causes the cam to open and close the contact points earlier in the compression stroke at high speeds. On the magnetic-pick-up distributor, the timer core is advanced so that the pick-up coil advances the timing of its signals to the transistor control unit. Since the rotor, too, is advanced, it comes into position earlier in the cycle, also. The timing of the spark to the cylinder consequently varies from no advance at low speed to full advance at high speed when the weights have reached the outer limits of their travel. Maximum advance may be as much as 45 degrees of crankshaft rotation before the piston reaches top dead center; it varies considerably with different makes of engines. The toggle arrangement and springs are designed to give the correct advance for maximum engine performance.

2. *Vacuum.* Under part throttle, a partial vacuum develops in the intake manifold. This means that less air and fuel will be admitted to the cylinder (volumetric efficiency is lowered). Thus, the mixture will be less highly compressed. The mixture will burn more slowly when ignited, and, in order to realize full power from it, the spark should be somewhat advanced. To secure this advance of the spark, a vacuum advance mechanism is used.

Figure 15–15 illustrates one type of vacuum advance mechanism used on contact-point distributors. It contains a spring-loaded and airtight diaphragm connected by a linkage, or lever, to the breaker plate. The breaker plate is supported on a bearing so that it can turn with respect to the distributor housing. It actually turns only a few degrees, since the linkage to the spring-loaded diaphragm prevents any greater rotation than this.

The spring-loaded side of the diaphragm is connected through a vacuum line to an opening in the carburetor (Fig. 15–16). This opening is on the atmospheric side of the throttle valve when the throttle is in the idling position. There is no vacuum advance in this position.

As soon as the throttle is opened, however, it swings past the opening of the vacuum passage. The intake-manifold vacuum can then draw air

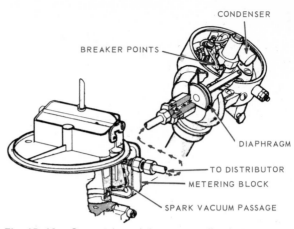

Fig. 15–16. Connection of the vacuum line between the carburetor and the vacuum-advance mechanism on the distributor. *(Ford Motor Company)*

from the vacuum line and the airtight chamber in the vacuum advance mechanism. This causes the diaphragm to move against the spring. The linkage to the breaker plate then rotates the breaker plate. This movement carries the contact points around so that the cam, as it rotates, closes and opens the points earlier in the cycle. The spark consequently appears at the spark-plug gap earlier in the compression stroke. As the throttle is opened wider, there will be less vacuum in the intake manifold and less vacuum advance. At wide-open throttle, there will be no vacuum advance at all. The spark advance under this condition will be provided entirely by the centrifugal advance mechanism.

On the magnetic-pick-up distributor, the vacuum advance mechanism is attached to the magnetic-pick-up assembly (Fig. 15–4) so that this assembly is rotated to provide the vacuum advance.

3. Combination of centrifugal and vacuum advances. At any particular engine speed, there will be a certain definite centrifugal advance due to engine speed plus a possible additional spark advance due to the operation of the vacuum advance mechanism. Figure 15–17 illustrates this. At 40 mph (miles per hour), the centrifugal advance mechanism provides 15 degrees spark advance on this particular application. The vacuum mechanism will supply up to 15 degrees additional advance under part-throttle conditions. However, if the engine is operated at wide-open throttle, this added vacuum advance will not be obtained. The advance in the usual application will vary somewhat between the straight line (centrifugal ad-

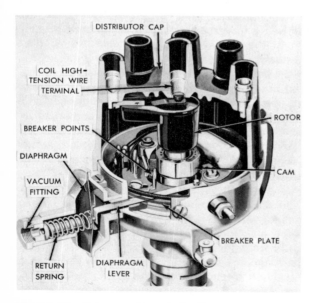

Fig. 15–15. Cutaway view of distributor, showing the construction of the vacuum-advance mechanism. *(Ford Division of Ford Motor Company)*

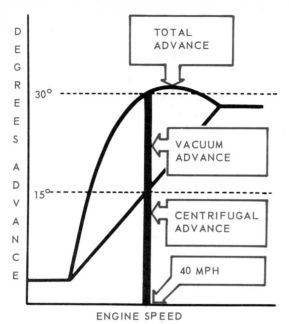

Fig. 15-17. Centrifugal- and vacuum-advance curves for one particular application.

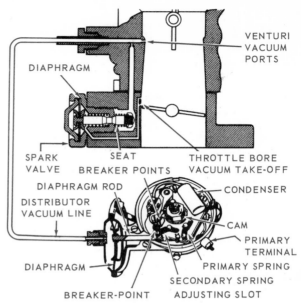

Fig. 15-18. Vacuum-line connections between a carburetor and a distributor having full vacuum control. *(Ford Division of Ford Motor Company)*

vance) and the curved line (centrifugal advance plus total possible vacuum advance) as the throttle is closed and opened.

4. Full vacuum control. The distributor illustrated in Fig. 15–18 does not contain a centrifugal advance mechanism. Instead, it utilizes vacuum from the carburetor venturi and intake manifold to produce the proper advance. Full control by vacuum means alone is possible because air speed through the carburetor air horn, and thus the vacuum in the venturi, is directly related to engine speed. Let us see how the system functions.

In the carburetor shown in Fig. 15–18, there are two vacuum openings in the air horn, one at the venturi and the other just above the throttle when it is closed. The lower, or throttle, vacuum takeoff opening may have two ports on some models, as shown in Fig. 15–18. These openings are connected by vacuum passages to each other and to the distributor vacuum advance mechanism by a

vacuum line. Vacuum imposed on the diaphragm in the vacuum advance mechanism causes the breaker-plate assembly to rotate. This is very similar to the action of other vacuum advance devices discussed in previous paragraphs. Rotation of the breaker-plate assembly causes an advance of the spark.

As engine speed increases, the vacuum at the venturi in the carburetor increases, owing to the increase of air speed through the venturi. This causes an increasing spark advance which is related to engine speed. At the same time, under part-throttle operating conditions, there will be a vacuum in the intake manifold; and this acts at the throttle vacuum ports in the carburetor to produce a further vacuum advance. Thus, the interrelation of the vacuum conditions at the two points in the carburetor produces, in effect, a combined speed advance (as with a centrifugal device) and vacuum advance.

Review Questions

1. What two jobs does the ignition distributor have?
2. What is the purpose of the spark plugs?
3. What is the purpose of the ignition coil?
4. Explain the difference between the contact-point and the magnetic-pick-up distributors.
5. What two types of spark advance are incorporated in many ignition distributors?
6. What is the purpose of the resistor in some spark plugs?
7. Name several indicating devices that can be read from the driver's compartment.

Study Questions

1. Make a wiring diagram of an ignition system, naming all the parts and describing the function of each of the parts.
2. Describe the operation of an ignition distributor with contact points. With a magnetic pick-up.

CHAPTER

16

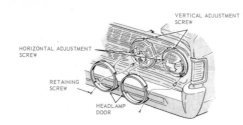

VERTICAL ADJUSTMENT SCREW

HORIZONTAL ADJUSTMENT SCREW

RETAINING SCREW

HEADLAMP DOOR

Other Electrical Devices

This chapter concludes the description of the various components in the electric system and discusses wiring circuits, lighting systems, power seat and window adjusters, horns, and other electrical accessories.

§ 16–1. **WIRING CIRCUITS** With the increasing number of electrically operated devices in the modern automobile, the wiring circuits have become rather complex. Figure 16–1 shows, for example, the engine-compartment wiring circuit for one model automobile. The wires between components are bound together into harnesses. Each wire is marked by means of special colors in the insulation; for example, light green, dark green, blue, red, black with a white tracer, and so on. These markings permit identification of the various wires in the harnesses.

The circuits between the engine-compartment components and the instrument panel are completed through connector plugs and receptacles. Figure 16–2 shows how the wiring harnesses are positioned and how the various connections are made. In this illustration, the instrument-panel cluster is shown as having been removed and laid down so that the back of it can be seen. As many as a dozen separate wires are gathered together and connected to a receptacle. Then the matching wires are connected to the matching plug. It becomes a simple matter, then, to push the plug into the receptacle to complete many connections at one time. Matching tangs and holes complete the connections between the wires. The plugs and receptacles have locking devices that prevent their coming loose in operation.

§ 16–2. **LIGHTS** The lighting system in a typical automobile includes the headlights, parking lights, direction-signal lights, side marker lights, stoplights, backup lights, tail lights, and the interior lights. The interior lights include instrument-panel lights, various warning, indicator, and courtesy lights which turn on when a car door is opened.

Figure 16–3 illustrates the wiring circuits for the headlights, tail lights, and backup lights. When the light switch is pulled out, the circuit from the battery to the headlights is completed. This circuit is through the foot selector switch. This switch has two positions, low beam and driving beam. These are also called passing beam and high beam.

Headlights are of two types, called type 1 and type 2, and are identified by the number (1 or 2) molded into the glass at the top of the lens. Type 1 has only one filament. Type 2 has two filaments, an upper beam and a lower beam. Cars with only one pair of headlights use type 2 headlights. Cars with two pairs of headlights use one pair of type 1 and one pair of type 2. The arrangements for the four-headlight system are shown in Fig. 16–4. Figure 16–5 shows the method of mounting and adjusting the headlights in one model car.

When the headlight switch is turned on and the foot selector switch is in the passing or low-beam position, one of the filaments in the type 2 light is on. When the foot selector switch is operated to switch to high beam, the other filament of the type 2 lights comes on along with the single filament of the type 1 lights. On cars with a single pair of headlights, type 2 headlights are used. The foot selector switch will then select either the upper-beam filament or the lower-beam filament.

The backup lights come on when the driver shifts into reverse. This closes a switch linked to the selector lever which connects the backup lights to the battery.

Blinker lights are installed on many cars to provide a means of signaling when a car is stalled on the highway or has pulled off to the side. The

249

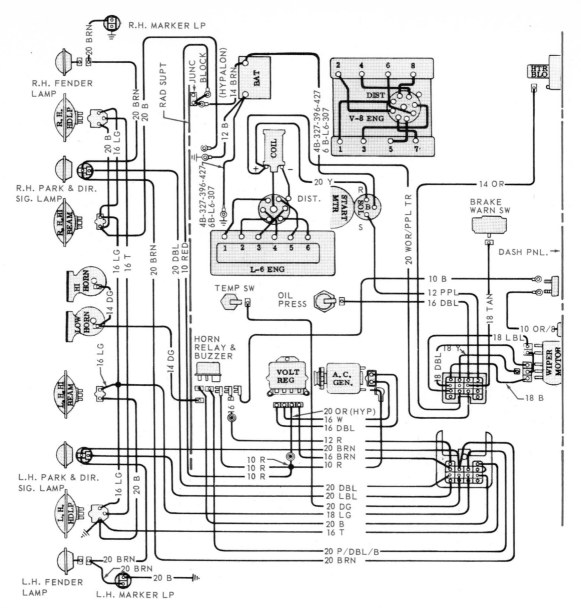

Fig. 16–1. Engine-compartment wiring circuit for a late-model Chevrolet. *(Chevrolet Motor Division of General Motors Corporation)*

blinking is much more noticeable than a steady light and provides a warning to approaching cars.

§ 16–3. HEADLIGHT COVER Some cars have vacuum-operated headlight covers that move upward to expose the headlights when they are turned on. The system lowers the covers when the headlights are turned off. Figure 16–6 shows one such system. There is a separate vacuum motor, or actuator, at each headlight, linked to a cover (Fig. 16–7). In operation, pulling out the light switch all the way to turn on the headlights operates a distribution valve that is mounted on the back end of the light switch. This valve then directs vacuum to the two vacuum motors. Vacuum thus applied to the diaphragms in the motors causes them to move and thus lift the headlight covers. The distribution valve also has an opening through which the atmo-

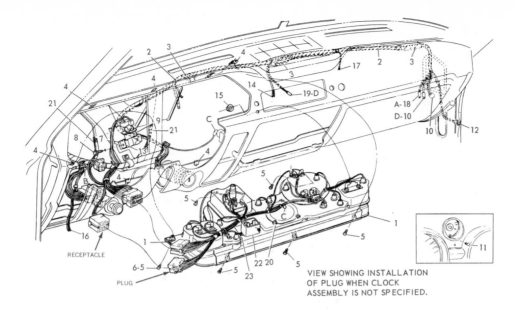

1. 10849 CLUSTER ASSY.
2. PART OF 14401 WIRING ASSY.
3. LOCATORS PART OF 14401 WIRING ASSY.
4. 382151-S2 SPRING NUT
5. 382144-S2 SCREW
6. 53049-S13
7. C1TF-13351- A BRACKET
8. 55906-S2 SCREW
9. C8ZB-13350-B FLASHER ASSY. EMERG. WARNING
10. TO 14405 WIRING ASSY.
11. C6GF-10C864-A PLUG INSTR. CLUSTER LENS OPENING
12. 13713 JAMB SWITCH (2-REQD.) R.H. SHOWN
    L.H. SYMM. OPPOSITE
13. 381863-S2 "J" NUT

14. TO BLOWER MOTOR
15. 375575-S STAMPED NUT
16. TO HEATER CONTROL SWITCH
17. TO HEATER RESISTOR
18. TO COURTESY LAMPS
19. TO GLOVE BOX LAMP
20. 55902-S8 SCREW
21. C5GB-62208A26-A FASTENER
22. C8ZB-17A553-A1-A2 SWITCH ASSY.-W/WIPER
23. 52724-S2 SCREW

A. 53C-D BLACK-BLUE STRIPE
B. 14A BLACK
C. 40 BLUE-WHITE STRIPE
D. 54D-E-G GREEN-YELLOW STRIPE

Fig. 16–2. Instrument-panel wiring for a late model Mustang. *(Ford Motor Company)*

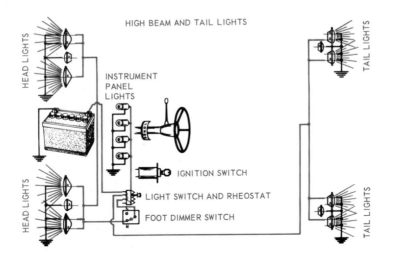

Fig. 16–3. Typical headlight wiring system.

Fig. 16–4. Two arrangements for dual headlamps.

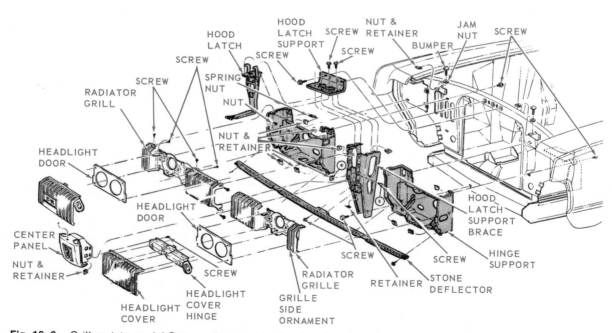

VERTICAL ADJUSTMENT SCREW

HORIZONTAL ADJUSTMENT SCREW

RETAINING SCREW

HEADLAMP DOOR

Fig. 16–5. Left front headlamps with the doors removed so the adjustment screws can be seen. *(Ford Motor Company)*

sphere side of the motor diaphragms are vented. Thus, atmospheric pressure is always applied to this side of the diaphragms.

When the headlights are turned off, the distribution valve allows atmospheric pressure to enter the vacuum side of the vacuum motors. Now, springs on the headlight covers cause them to drop down to cover the headlights.

There is a vacuum reservoir which holds sufficient vacuum for several cover operations if the headlights are turned on and off when the engine is not running. Also, the headlight covers can be

HOOD LATCH
HOOD LATCH SUPPORT
SCREW
NUT & RETAINER
JAM NUT
SCREW
SCREW
BUMPER
SCREW
HOOD LATCH
SCREW
SPRING NUT
NUT
RADIATOR GRILL
SCREW
NUT & RETAINER
HEADLIGHT DOOR
HEADLIGHT DOOR
HOOD LATCH SUPPORT BRACE
CENTER PANEL
NUT & RETAINER
SCREW
HEADLIGHT COVER HINGE
HEADLIGHT COVER
RADIATOR GRILLE
GRILLE SIDE ORNAMENT
SCREW
RETAINER
SCREW
STONE DEFLECTOR
HINGE SUPPORT

Fig. 16–6. Grill on late model Cougar disassembled to show location of various parts, including the headlight covers (to left). *(Ford Motor Company)*

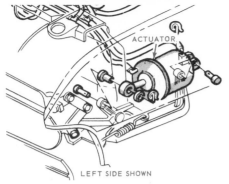

Fig. 16–7. Headlight cover actuator (vacuum motor) on a late model Chevrolet. *(Chevrolet Motor Division of General Motors Corporation)*

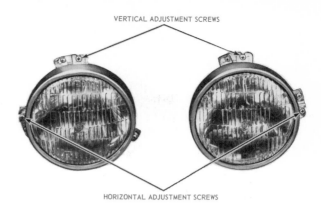

Fig. 16–8. Locations of headlight adjustment screws. *(Chrysler-Plymouth Division of Chrysler Motors Corporation)*

operated manually in case the vacuum system fails. This is done by turning on the headlights and then lifting the covers by hand.

§ 16–4. HEADLIGHT AIMING It is important for the headlights to be aimed correctly. If they are aimed too high or to the left, they might blind an oncoming driver and cause a serious accident. Incorrect aiming can also reduce the driver's ability to see the road properly and this could lead to an accident.

Most American cars have four headlamps. Figure 16–5 shows the two headlamps on the left side of a car. The four headlamps are either in a row, two on the left and two on the right, or else they are stacked, an upper and lower headlamp on each side. Commonly, there are two distinct types of headlamp, the one filament and the two filament. The two filament type is always placed outside or above the one filament lamp (Fig. 16–4). Headlights have three aiming buttons on the front lens. The adjustments are made by turning spring-loaded screws. There is one spring-

loaded screw at the top for up-and-down adjustment, and one at the side for left-to-right adjustment (Fig. 16–8).

There are several methods of checking the aiming of the headlights. The simplest uses a screen set 25 feet in front of the vehicle and a perfectly level floor. With the car aligned perpendicular to the screen, the low beam and high beam are checked separately (Fig. 16–9). Note that line 3 is the centerline of the lights and that line 5 is the centerline of the car. Lines 4 and 6 are the hot-spot (or high-intensity zone) reference lines. The low beams are adjusted so that the hot spot is 2 inches to the right of the reference lines and the high beams are adjusted so that their centers are 2 inches below line 3.

NOTE: Some manufacturers, in their aiming instructions, call for a full fuel tank and an empty car. Others call for a partly full tank and two people in the front seat. Tires must be inflated to the specified pressure. Just before checking the aim, after the car has been positioned, bounce each

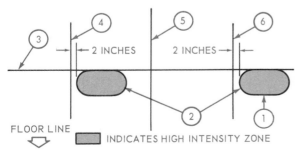
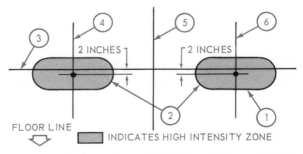

Fig. 16–9. Headlight patterns for low beam (left) and high beam (right). *(Chrysler-Plymouth Division of Chrysler Motors Corporation)*

Fig. 16-10. Headlight aimer. *(Chevrolet Motor Division of General Motors Corporation)*

corner of the car a couple of times to equalize the suspension system.

An instrument check with a Guide-Lamp tester is made as follows (Figs. 16-10 to 16-12).

1. Remove bezels, or doors, (Fig. 16-5) to expose adjustment screws (Fig. 16-8).

2. Mount the headlight aimers on either the No. 1 or No. 2 pair of lamps. The buttons or points on the headlamps should rest against the inner ring of the aimers. The aimers are held on the head-

HORIZONTAL
AIMING
SCREW

CENTER STRING OVER
"2R" ON AIMER ARM

Fig. 16-11. Headlamp horizontal adjustment. *(Chevrolet Motor Division of General Motors Corporation).*

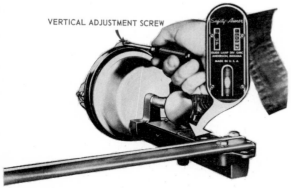

VERTICAL ADJUSTMENT SCREW

Fig. 16-12. Headlamp vertical adjustment. *(Chevrolet Motor Division of General Motors Corporation)*

lamps by suction cups. Moistening the cups will improve their hold.

3. Attach elastic string between the two aimer arms, hooking the knots in the slots provided (Fig. 16-11). Rotate the aimers so that the string just clears the points on the crossarms.

4. Turn the horizontal aiming screw on the left-hand lamp until the string is in position over the crossarm centerline. Turn the screw clockwise in making the final adjustment in order to take up any lash in the screw.

5. Repeat the procedure for the right-hand lamp.

6. Now start the vertical adjustment by first loosening the knob at the underside of each aimer arm and sliding the arm back and forth until the numeral 2 appears at the DOWN window in each aimer (Fig. 16-12).

NOTE: This setting gives the 2-inch drop in the high beams as noted above (see Fig. 16-9).

7. Turn the headlamp vertical adjustment screw on left-hand lamp counterclockwise until the bubble is at the inner end of the glass tube. Then turn the screw clockwise until the bubble is centered in the tube.

8. Repeat the procedure on the right-hand lamp.

9. Recheck the string at the ends of each crossarm for correct setting and the bubbles in the aimers for proper position.

10. Replace doors.

§ 16-5. STOPLIGHT SWITCH Until the introduction of the dual-braking system (see Chap. 40), stoplight switches were hydraulic. They contained a small diaphragm that was moved by hydraulic pressure when the brakes were applied. This action closed a switch which connected the stoplights to the battery.

When the dual-braking system came on the scene, however, the hydraulic switch could no longer be used. With this system, there are two separate hydraulic systems, one for the front wheels and one for the rear wheels. If the hydraulic switch were connected into one system and if it failed, then the car would have no stoplights, even though the other system would still be working and stopping the car.

Thus, the mechanical switch came into use. Figures 16-13 and 16-14 illustrate one design. When the pedal is pushed for braking, it carries the switch contacts with it (to left in Fig. 16-14). This

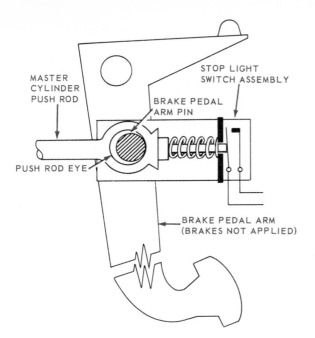

Fig. 16-13. Mechanical stoplight switch, shown open, with brakes not applied. *(Ford Motor Company)*

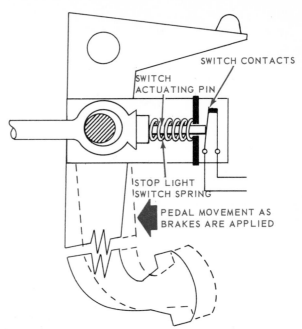

Fig. 16-14. Mechanical stoplight switch, shown closed, with brakes applied. *(Ford Motor Company)*

brings the switch contacts together so that the stoplights come on.

§ 16-6. SEAT ADJUSTERS Electric seat adjusters are used on front seats to adjust the seat height, position, and tilt (on some models). The adjuster that moves the seat up and down and from front to rear is called a four-way adjuster. This can also include a tilt feature which will provide tilt forward and tilt backward. The latter arrangement is called a six-way adjuster (Fig.

16-15). The adjuster includes a drive motor, a transmission, drive cables, jack screws, slides, tracks, and supports.

In operation, the closing of one of the switches starts the motor and also, in the transmission, operates one of the solenoids. A four-way adjuster has two solenoids, a six-way adjuster has three solenoids. Let us take a typical four-way adjuster, for example, and see what happens when the up-down switch is pushed up to raise the seat. The motor starts to turn and, at the same time, the up-

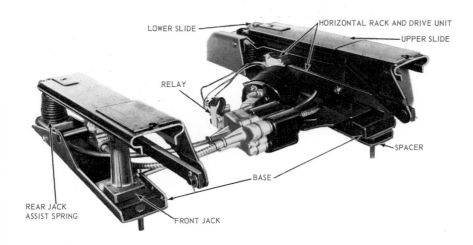

Fig. 16-15. Six-way power seat adjuster. *(Chrysler-Plymouth Division of Chrysler Motors Corporation)*

down solenoid is actuated to throw the up-down gears into mesh. (Actually not mesh—the solenoid pushes a driving dog into the side of the up-down gears.) The up-down gear turns in the proper direction to raise the seat. (If the switch were pushed down, the motor, and gear, would turn in the opposite direction.)

The drive is carried through drive cables to screw jacks on the lifting mechanism at the two sides of the seat. The screw jacks turn to raise the seat.

To move the seat back or forward, the back-or-forward switch is operated and this actuates the horizontal movement solenoid so that it causes the horizontal movement gear to turn. This carries the drive through drive cables to drive pinions to move the seat forward or back. The drive pinions turn on horizontal racks to produce the movement.

The six-way adjuster has a third solenoid, gear, and drive cables to produce the forward or backward tilt.

§ 16-7. WINDOW REGULATORS

A power window regulator has an electric motor which is mounted in the lower part of the door (Fig. 16-16). It drives a rack and lever, or levers, which raise or lower the window. Figure 16-16 shows one type which uses a single lever. The type using a pair of levers (one an equalizer arm) is shown in Fig. 16-17.

§ 16-8. WINDSHIELD WIPERS

The windshield-wiper blades are moved back and forth across the

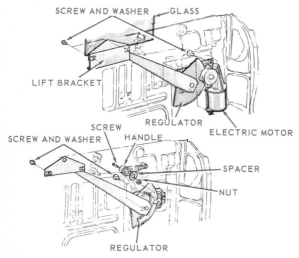

Fig. 16-16. Window regulators. Mechanical (at bottom) and electric (at top). (*Chrysler-Plymouth Division of Chrysler Motors Corporation*)

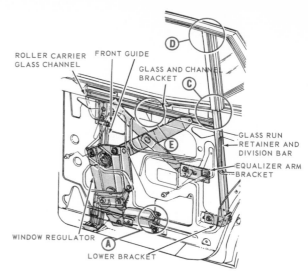

Fig. 16-17. Electric window regulator of the type using a pair of levers. (*Ford Motor Company*)

windshield by an electric motor that drives linkage through reduction gears (Fig. 16-18). The linkage is connected to a drive crank and pin to the motor. As the motor turns, the linkage is moved back and forth, causing the two pivots, to which the blades are attached, to turn back and forth.

§ 16-9. HORN AND RELAY

The horn is a vibrating-type device which has a diaphragm and a winding and a pair of contact points connected in series. When the horn winding is connected to the battery, the magnetism produced by the winding pulls the diaphragm down, creating a loud click. The diaphragm movement opens the contacts so that the diaphragm is released. This closes the contacts to reconnect the winding to the battery so that the cycle is rapidly repeated. The rapid movement of the diaphragm produces a distinctive noise. The tone and pitch of the horn are determined by the size and shape of the diaphragm as well as the path through which the sound must travel.

Most systems use a relay so as to avoid carrying the heavy current required by the horn up through the steering column and back. When the horn contacts on the steering wheel or column are closed by the driver, the relay winding is connected to the battery. The relay therefore closes its contacts to connect the horn to the battery.

On some cars, the horn relay serves a second purpose—as a warning that the ignition key has been left in the ignition switch when a car door

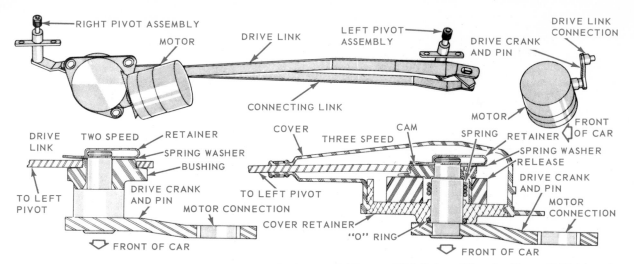

Fig. 16–18. Electric windshield-wiper arrangement for late-model Fury and V. I. P. cars. *(Chrysler-Plymouth Division of Chrysler Motors Corporation)*

is opened. Figure 16–19 shows the circuit. When the ignition key is in the ignition switch, a special set of contacts are closed. Now, if a car door is opened, the door switch will complete the circuit through the buzzer (upper) contacts and winding of the relay to the battery. The winding becomes energized and pulls the armature down. This opens

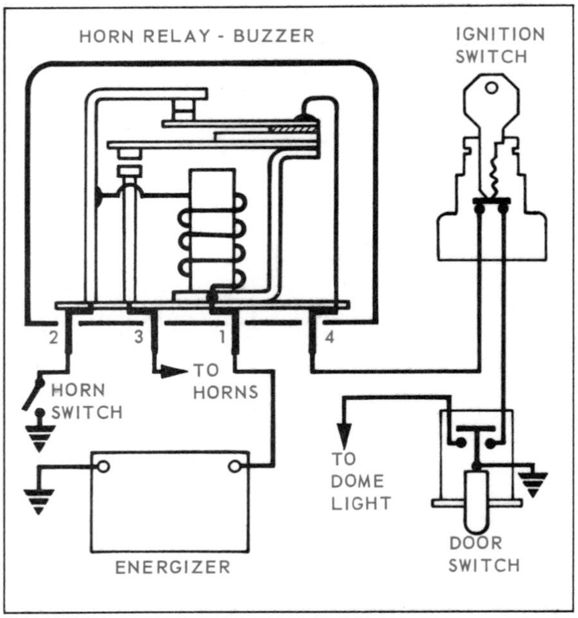

the contacts and the winding loses its magnetism so that the spring closes the contacts again. This cycle is repeated rapidly so that the relay emits a buzzing sound to warn the driver that he has forgotten his ignition key. Since many of the car thefts in this country are caused by the driver leaving his ignition key in the switch, this warning system serves as a deterrent to car theft.

§ 16–10. ELECTRIC FUEL-PUMP CONTROL SYSTEM

The tank-mounted electric fuel pump, described in § 9–9, is connected through a hydraulic switch to the ignition switch. The hydraulic switch is operated by pressure in the engine lubricating system. This switch has two pairs of contacts. When first starting, the first set of contacts is closed, and current is fed through these contacts from the solenoid on the cranking motor. This current flows to the fuel pump so that it operates. These connections continue as long as the engine is being cranked. As soon as the engine starts, the solenoid is disconnected from the battery so that this source of current is cut off. However, as soon as the engine starts, the oil pressure builds up and this causes the control switch to open the first set of contacts and close the second set of contacts. Now, current is fed to the fuel pump through the ignition switch and the second set of contacts in the control switch.

If the engine stalls during operation, the pressure will become too low to keep the second set of contacts in the control switch closed. They will open and the fuel pump will stop. If the engine

Fig. 16–19. Horn relay wiring system, which includes a buzzer reminder that the ignition key is still in the ignition switch when the car door is opened. *(Chevrolet Motor Division of General Motors Corporation)*

should suddenly lose oil pressure, the second set of contacts in the control switch will open so that the fuel pump stops. Now, the engine will run only until the fuel in the carburetor float bowl is used up. This protects the engine against serious damage from operating without oil pressure. The fuel pump will also stop when the ignition switch is turned off.

§ 16–11. OTHER ELECTRICAL DEVICES There are numerous other electrically operated devices used on various cars, including the radio, a seat warmer to warm the seat before the car heater brings the car interior up to a comfortable temperature, electric door locks that snap the door locks down at the touch of a button (Fig. 16–20), rear window defogger, station-wagon tailgate window washer, windshield washers, electric eye to shift the headlights from high beam to low beam when approaching another car, and so on. If you are interested in finding out more about these specialized devices, refer to the car-shop manuals or to specialized books on the subject, such as *Automotive Electrical Equipment* (McGraw-Hill).

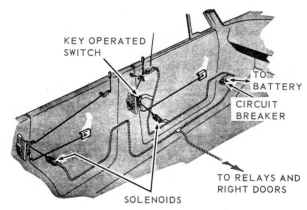

Fig. 16–20. Electric door lock system. *(Chrysler-Plymouth Division of Chrysler Motors Corporation)*

Review Questions

1. Explain how receptacles and plugs are used in car wiring.
2. What are the two types of headlights? How many filaments does each have?
3. Explain how the foot selector switch works.
4. Describe a headlight cover system and explain how it works.
5. Describe the procedure of aiming headlights with a screen. Of aiming headlights with the Guide-Lamp tester.
6. Explain how the two types of stoplight switches work.
7. Explain how a four-way seat adjuster works. A six-way seat adjuster.
8. Describe the operation of a power window regulator.
9. Describe the operation of an electric windshield wiper.
10. Describe the operation of a horn. Of the horn relay with warning buzzer.
11. Explain how the electric fuel-pump control described in the book works.
12. What are some other electrical devices on the modern car?

Study Questions

1. Look at the wiring diagrams in a late-model shop manual and trace out various circuits.
2. In a shop manual, read the detailed instructions for adjusting headlights. Write down the basic points on a piece of paper.
3. Draw a horn and horn-relay circuit.
4. Draw a typical headlight wiring circuit, including the stop and backup lights.

17

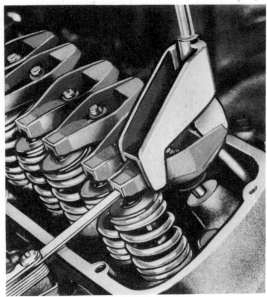

This chapter and the following two describe various engine services and explain how various troubles in the engine are corrected. Later chapters discuss servicing of the fuel, lubricating, cooling, and electric systems. You will notice, in the discussions of various engine-servicing jobs, that the time to do the job is often given. These figures are included to give you some idea of the size of the job and must not be considered accurate enough for cost-estimating service jobs. The procedures discussed in the three engine-service chapters are aimed at correcting specific troubles. There is another method of engine service called engine rebuilding. Some companies set up special engine disassembly and rebuilding lines. They bring in old, worn engines, disassemble them completely, repair or replace all worn parts, and then completely rebuild the engine, using only the old parts that are still in good condition. A good rebuilder can turn out rebuilt engines that are considered almost "as good as new."

Engine Service — Valves and Valve Mechanisms

---

§ 17-1. CLEANLINESS The major enemy of good service work is dirt. A trace of dirt left on a bearing or cylinder wall could ruin an otherwise good service job. Thus, you must be absolutely sure that you do not leave dirt or abrasive in the engine or on engine parts when you finish a service job.

Before any major service job, the block should be cleaned. Electrical units should be removed or covered if the engine is steam-cleaned so that moisture does not get into them.

VALVES AND VALVE TRAINS

§ 17-2. VALVE TROUBLES Valves must be properly timed. They must seat tightly and operate without lag. Valve-tappet clearance, as well as the clearance between the valve stems and guides, must be correct. Failure to meet any of these requirements means valve and engine trouble.

As an example, suppose that the clearance between valve stems and guides is excessive. This means that, on every intake stroke, oil will be pulled past the intake-valve stem and into the combustion chamber, where it will be burned. This, in turn, can lead to excessive oil consumption, engine deposits, preignition, clogged piston rings, and fouled spark plugs. Valve action may be hindered by carbon buildup on the valves and stems. This further reduces engine performance and may lead to valve burning. Thus, it can be seen that an apparently minor fault like excessive valve-stem clearance can cause serious engine trouble. This emphasizes the importance of performing every engine service correctly. Being slightly "off" on one measurement could cause serious engine trouble.

Types of trouble. Valve troubles include sticking, burning, breakage, wear, and deposits. The following articles supply information on the various valve services.

§ 17-3. **VALVE STICKING** Gum or carbon deposits on the valve stem (§ 17-7) will cause valve sticking (Fig. 17-1). Excessive valve-stem clearance speeds up valve deposits. Another cause of valve sticking is warped stems. This could result from overheating, an eccentric seat (which throws side pressure on the valve), or from a cocked spring or retainer (which tends to bend the stem). Insufficient oil would also cause valve sticking. Sometimes valves will stick when cold but will work free as the engine warms up.

NOTE: When valves and piston rings are badly clogged with deposits, an engine overhaul is usually required. However, there are certain compounds that can be put in the fuel or oil which will help to free rings and valves. One of these comes in a pressure can and is sprayed into the running engine through the carburetor (air cleaner off). When parts are not too badly worn and the major trouble seems to be from deposits, use of these compounds often postpones engine overhaul.

Fig. 17-1. Gummed intake valve. Note deposits under valve head. *(Clayton Manufacturing Company)*

§ 17-4. **VALVE BURNING** This is usually an exhaust-valve problem. Any condition that prevents normal exhaust-valve seating may lead to valve burning (Figs. 17-2 to 17-4). The poor seating prevents normal valve cooling through the valve seat. It also allows hot gases to blow by, further heating the valve. A worn guide also prevents normal valve cooling. If water circulation around the valve seat is impeded—by clogged distribution

Fig. 17-2. Valve burning due to seat distortion. The valve fails to seat in one area and hot exhaust-gas leakage in this area burns the valve. *(TRW Valve Division, Thompson, Ramo, Wooldridge, Inc.)*

Fig. 17-3. Valve burning due to failure of the valve to fully seat. Note that the valve is uniformly burned all the way around its face. *(TRW Valve Division, Thompson, Ramo, Wooldridge, Inc.)*

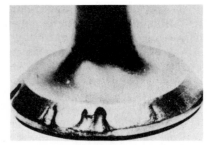

Fig. 17-4. Valve burning due to guttering. This is caused by accumulations of deposits on the valve face and seat. Parts of the deposits break off to form a path through which exhaust gas can pass when the valve is closed. This soon burns channels in the valve face, as shown. *(TRW Valve Division, Thompson, Ramo, Wooldridge, Inc.)*

tubes or jackets, for example—local hot spots may develop. This could cause seat distortion, poor seating, and overheated valves. Seat distortion can also result from improper cylinder-head-bolt tightening. Other conditions that could prevent normal seating include a weak or cocked valve spring and insufficient valve-tappet clearance.

Engine overloading or overheating will cause hot valves. A lean air-fuel mixture may cause valve burning; in this case, the fuel system should be serviced. Preignition and detonation, which produce high combustion pressures and temperatures, are hard on valves as well as other engine parts. Correction is to clean out carbon, retime the ignition, and use higher-octane fuel.

In some persistent cases of seat leakage (especially where deposits on the valve seat and face prevent normal seating), the use of an "interference angle" has proved helpful. The valve is faced at an angle 1/4 to 1 degree flatter than the seat angle (Fig. 17–5). This produces greater pressure at the outer edge of the valve seat; the valve-seat edge thus tends to cut through any deposits that have formed and thereby establish a good seal.

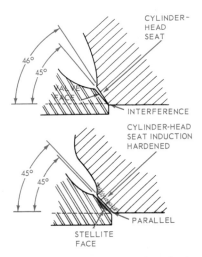

Fig. 17–5. Valve and valve-seat angles. At the top, the interference angle recommended for many intake and exhaust valves and seats. At the bottom, the parallel faces recommended for stellite-faced exhaust valves and induction-hardened exhaust-valve seats. *(Chevrolet Motor Division of General Motors Corporation)*

Figure 17–5 illustrates one manufacturer's recommendations for the valve and seat angles to get interference. Note that this manufacturer does not recommend interference on stellite-faced exhaust valves and induction-hardened exhaust-valve seats. These surfaces are so hard that no appreciable improvement in seating would be obtained by interference.

Sometimes valve stems will stretch, owing to overheating and to heavy valve springs. Lighter springs and elimination of overheating (§ 26–10) are the remedy here.

§ 17–5. VALVE BREAKAGE Any condition that causes the valve to overheat (§ 17–4) or to be subjected to heavy pounding (as from excessive tappet clearance or from detonation) may cause valves to break. Excessive tappet clearance permits heavy impact seating. If the seat is eccentric to the stem or if the valve spring or retainer is cocked, then the valve will be subjected to side movement or pressure every time it seats. Ultimately, this may cause it to fatigue and break. If the stem has been scratched during cleaning, the scratch may serve as a starting point for a crack and a break in the stem.

§ 17–6. VALVE-FACE WEAR In addition to the conditions discussed in § 17–4 (valve burning), excessive tappet clearance or dirt on the valve face or seat could cause valve-face wear. Excessive tappet clearance causes heavy impact seating that is wearing on the valve and may cause valve breakage (§ 17–5). Dirt may cause valve-face wear if the engine operates in dusty conditions or if the carburetor air cleaner is not functioning properly. The dust enters the engine with the air-fuel mixture, and some of it settles on the valve seat. The dust will also cause bearing, cylinder-wall, and piston and ring wear.

§ 17–7. VALVE DEPOSITS If the fuel has excessive amounts of gum in it, some of this gum may be deposited on the intake valve as the air-fuel mixture passes the valve on the way to the engine cylinder. Carbon deposits may form because of an excessively rich mixture or because of oil passing a worn valve guide (in the intake valve). Improper combustion, due to a rich mixture, defective ignition system, loss of compression in the engine, a cold engine, and so forth, will result in carbon deposits on the exhaust valves. Dirty or improper oil will cause deposits to form on the valves.

§ 17–8. VALVE SERVICE Valve service includes adjusting valve-tappet clearances (also called *adjusting valve lash*), grinding valves and valve seats, installing new seat inserts, cleaning or replacing valve guides, servicing the camshaft and camshaft bearings, and timing the valves. A complete valve service job, including grinding valves and seats, checking springs, cleaning guides, and tuning the engine, requires from about five hours (for an overhead-valve six-cylinder engine) to about eight hours (for an eight-cylinder L-head engine). Replacing the camshaft requires about eight hours; four additional hours are required for replacing camshaft bearings.

§ 17-9. VALVE-TAPPET CLEARANCE Checking and adjusting valve-tappet (or valve-lifter) clearance requires different procedures in different types and models of engines. Some engines with hydraulic valve lifters normally require no tappet-clearance adjustment, as noted below. Others require checking and adjustment whenever valve service work has been performed. The following procedures are typical.

● CAUTION: If a pressure-type radiator cap is used (§ 12-8), it should be removed during the adjusting procedure to prevent excessive engine temperatures.

1. *L-head engine with solid valve lifters.* Remove the valve-cover plates, and use a feeler gauge to measure the clearance between the valve stem and the adjusting screw in the valve lifter (Fig. 17-6). A two-step "go no-go" feeler gauge of the specified thicknesses can be used. Adjustment is correct when the "go" step fits the clearance but the "no-go" step does not.

Some specifications call for checking the clearance with the engine cold. With others, the engine should be warmed up and idling.* If the clearance is not correct, the adjusting screw must be turned in or out as necessary to correct it. Some tappet-adjusting screws are self-locking; others have a locking nut. On the second type, the locking nut must be loosened. This requires two wrenches, one to hold the screw, the other to turn the nut. Then, on both types, one wrench must be used to hold the valve lifter while a second wrench is used to turn the adjusting screw. Adjustment is correct when the feeler gauge can be moved between the screw and valve stem with some drag when the valve is closed. When a locking nut is used, it should be tightened after the adjustment is made and the clearance again checked. After the adjustment is completed, replace the cover plates, using new gaskets.

---

* On some engines, measurement is made with the engine cold and not running; the engine is turned over until the valve lifter is on the low point of the cam, and the clearance is then checked.

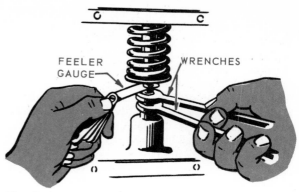

Fig. 17-6. Adjusting valve-tappet clearance, or valve lash, on an L-head engine.

2. *I-head engine with solid valve lifters.* On the overhead-valve engine, the valve cover must be removed and the clearance measured with a feeler gauge between the valve stem and the rocker arm. The engine must be warmed up and running at fast idle. Adjustment varies according to engine construction. Many rocker arms have an adjusting screw and locking nut. This type of rocker arm is mounted on a rocker-arm shaft. Adjustment is made on these by loosening the locking nut and turning the adjusting screw (Fig. 17-7). On other engines, the rocker arms are individually supported by studs, ball seats, and nuts (Fig. 17-8). On these, adjustment is made by turning the self-locking rocker-arm-stud nut until the specified clearance between the valve stem and rocker arm is attained.

3. *Free-type valve rotator.* Free-rotator valves

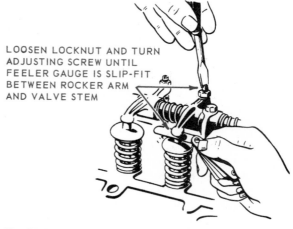

LOOSEN LOCKNUT AND TURN ADJUSTING SCREW UNTIL FEELER GAUGE IS SLIP-FIT BETWEEN ROCKER ARM AND VALVE STEM

Fig. 17-7. Adjusting valve-tappet clearance, or valve lash, on an overhead-valve engine.

Fig. 17-8. Adjusting valve-tappet clearance on an engine with rocker arms independently mounted on ball studs. Backing the stud nut out increases clearance. *(Chevrolet Motor Division of General Motors Corporation)*

(§ 8–11) are checked as for the solid lifter type; the clearance is checked between the tip cup on the valve stem and the adjusting screw in the valve lifter rather than between the valve stem and the screw.

4. Hydraulic valve lifters. On some engines with hydraulic valve lifters, no adjustment is provided in the valve train. In normal service, no adjustment is necessary. However, if valves and valve seats are ground, or if unusual and severe wear of the push-rod ends, rocker arm, or valve stem occurs, then some correction may be required to reestablish the correct valve-train length. Typical checking and correcting procedures follow.

a. *Ford.* Ford engines use two types of rocker arm, the shaft-mounted (Fig. 17–11) and the ball-stud-mounted (Fig. 17–12). On both types, the clearance in the valve train is checked with the valve lifter bled down so that the valve-lifter plunger is bottomed. First, the crankshaft must be turned so that the lifter is on the base circle or low part of the cam (rather than on the lobe). This is done by setting the piston in number one cylinder on TDC at the end of the compression stroke and then checking both valves in number one cylinder. The crankshaft can then be rotated as necessary to put other lifters on the base circles of their cams so that they can be checked. To make the check, a special tool is used to apply slow pressure on the rocker arm (Fig. 17–11 and

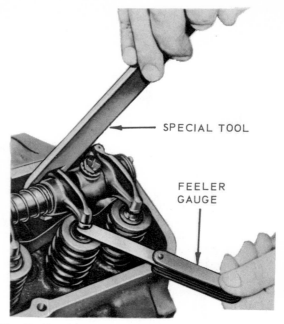

Fig. 17-11. Checking valve-train clearance on shaft-mounted rocker arm after the hydraulic valve lifter has been bled down with pressure from special tool. *(Ford Division of Ford Motor Company)*

Fig. 17-12. Checking valve-train clearance on ball-stud mounted rocker arm after the hydraulic valve lifter has been bled down with pressure from a special tool. *(Ford Division of Ford Motor Company)*

17-12) and gradually force oil out of the valve lifter so that the plunger bottoms. Then, the clearance gauge is used to check the clearance between the valve stem and rocker arm. If the clearance is too small, as it might be if valves and seats have been ground, then a shorter push rod should be installed. If it is excessive, either a short push rod has been incorrectly installed or there is excessive wear in the valve train (push-rod ends, valve stem, and rocker arm), and the worn parts must be replaced.

b. *Plymouth.* The procedure for setting Plymouth valves, which is typical of the Chrysler-manufactured engines, is necessary only when valves and valve seats have been ground. When this happens, the increased height of the valve stem above the cylinder head should be checked (Fig. 17–13). With the valve seated, place a special gauge tool over the valve stem. If the height is excessive, the end of the valve stem must be ground off to reduce the height to within limits. This assures that the hydraulic valve-lifter plunger will be working near its center position rather than near the bottom, as it would with an excessively high valve stem.

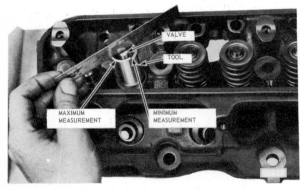

Fig. 17–13. Measuring valve-stem length with a special tool after the valve is installed in the head. *(Chrysler-Plymouth Division of Chrysler Motors Corporation)*

c. *Chevrolet.* The procedure for the Chevrolet engine is typical of the General Motors engines using the ball-pivot type of rocker arm (Fig. 17–14). With the valve lifter on the base circle of the cam, back off the adjusting nut until the push rod is loose. Then slowly turn the adjusting nut down until all side play, or looseness, is gone. Turn the adjusting nut down one additional full turn.

Fig. 17–14. Adjusting valve rocker-arm-stud nut to properly position the plunger of the hydraulic valve lifter. *(Chevrolet Motor Division of General Motors Corporation)*

This places the plunger of the valve lifter in its center position.

5. *F-head engine.* This engine (Fig. 5–24) requires a combined L-head and I-head adjustment procedure. The in-block valves are checked and adjusted as in an L-head engine. The in-head valves are checked and adjusted as in an I-head engine.

§ 17–10. BALL-STUD SERVICE If a ball stud is loose in the cylinder head or has damaged threads, it should be replaced. The old stud is removed with a special puller tool (Fig. 17–15). An oversize stud should then be installed. This requires reaming of the stud hole to take the oversize stud (Fig. 17–16). The size of stud to be installed determines the size of the reamer. For example, Chevrolet supplies studs 0.003 and 0.013 inch oversize. If the 0.003-inch oversize stud is to be installed, the special 0.003-inch oversize reamer should be used.

● **CAUTION:** The stud hole must always be reamed before an oversize stud is installed. Otherwise, the head may be cracked.

To install the new stud, use the special tool, as shown in Fig. 17–17, and drive the stud into place.

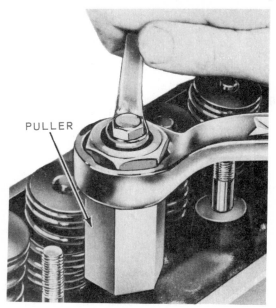

PULLER

Fig. 17-15. Removing rocker-arm stud with a special puller. As the sleeve is held stationary and the puller turned, the screw-thread action pulls the stud out of the head. *(Ford Division of Ford Motor Company)*

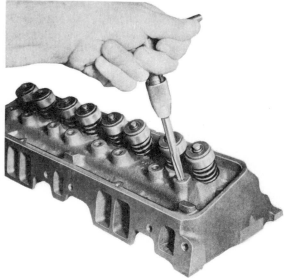

Fig. 17-16. Reaming stud hole for oversize ball stud. *(Chevrolet Motor Division of General Motors Corporation)*

When the tool is driven firmly down to the cylinder head, the stud is in the correct position.

§ 17-11. THE COMPLETE VALVE JOB A complete valve job requires the steps tabulated below.

Fig. 17-17. Installing ball stud. *(Ford Division of Ford Motor Company)*

Valve and valve-seat servicing are described in detail in following articles.

1. Drain cooling system and disconnect upper radiator hose from engine.

2. Remove air cleaner and disconnect accelerator rod, fuel line, air and vacuum hoses from carburetor.

3. Remove or move aside lines and hoses as necessary to get at the cylinder head.

4. Disconnect spark-plug wires and temperature sending unit wire.

5. Remove crankcase ventilating system and, on air-injection systems, disconnect the air hose at the check valve. Then remove the air-supply-tube assembly.

6. On many in-line engines, it is not necessary to remove manifolds. But in V-8 engines, the carburetor and intake manifold must be removed.

7. Remove rocker-arm cover or covers.

8. On engines with ball-stud-supported rocker arms, the rocker arms and push rods can be removed at this time. If they are left on, the nuts should be loosened so that the rocker arms can be moved aside and the push rods removed. Push rods should be placed in a rack in proper sequence so that they can be put back into the same spot from which they were removed.

9. On the engine with the rocker arms supported on shafts, remove the shaft assembly or assemblies (§ 17-16), and then remove the push rods in sequence.

10. Remove head bolts and take head off engine.

11. Remove valves and springs from head (keeping them in proper sequence so that they can be put back in the same spots from which they were removed).

12. Check valves and valve seats. Grind seats and reface valves as necessary. Check valve seating. Touch up valve-stem ends if necessary.

13. Check valve guides for wear. Clean, replace or ream for larger guide as necessary.

14. Replace valves and springs in head.

15. Install head, push rods, rocker arms, rocker-arm cover, and other parts removed during head removal.

§ 17–12. VALVE REMOVAL Before removing the valves, the cylinder head must be taken off (§ 17–15). Valves and valve parts must not be interchanged; each valve, with its own spring, retainer, and lock, must be replaced in the same valve port from which it was removed. Likewise, each push rod must be replaced in the same hole from which it was taken. Different valve-removing procedures are outlined below.

1. L-head engines. If the manifolds interfere with valve removal, they must be taken off the engine (§ 17–18). Then, a valve-spring compressor or lifter can be used to compress the valve spring. This releases the retainer lock, or keeper, so that it can be removed from the valve stem. Do not allow the lock to fall down into the crank-case; it could jam into moving parts and cause serious damage. Close openings through which the lock could drop with clean cloths, or use a magnet to hold the lock as it is released. With the lock off, the valve may be removed from the top of the block. Then the spring can be taken out.

2. Overhead-valve engines. The cylinder-head assembly, with valves and springs, is removed as a unit (§ 17–11). Figure 17–18 shows one type of spring compressor being used to compress a valve spring so that the valve retainer lock can be removed. Another type of valve-spring compressor, as well as a stand on which the head can be mounted for repair, is shown in Fig. 17–19. After the retainer lock is taken off the valve stem, the valve and spring can be removed from the head. Valve-stem seals or shields (Figs. 8–19 to 8–22) should be carefully inspected and replaced if worn or damaged. Many engine manufacturers recommend installation of new seals or shields whenever valves or valve springs are removed.

To replace a single valve spring, stem seal, or shield, it is not necessary to remove the head on many models. For instance, on the engine using the ball-pivot-type rocker arm, a special spring compressor can be installed in place of the rocker arm to compress the spring. To hold up the valve while the spring is being compressed, compressed air from the shop air supply is introduced into the cylinder through the spark-plug hole (Fig.

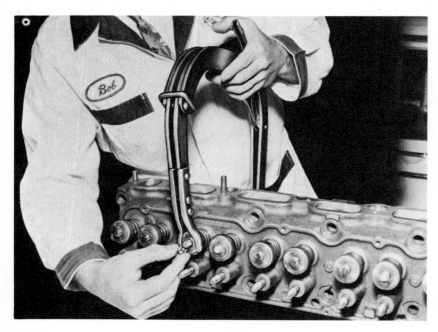

Fig. 17–18. Using a valve-spring compressor on the valve assemblies in a cylinder head. *(Chevrolet Motor Division of General Motors Corporation)*

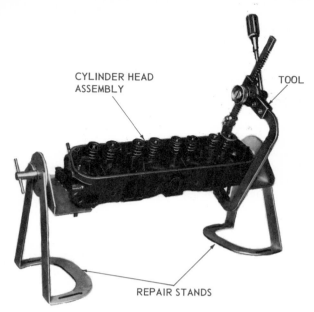

Fig. 17-19. Cylinder head mounted in a repair stand with a spring compressor tool in place. *(Chrysler-Plymouth Division of Chrysler Motors Corporation)*

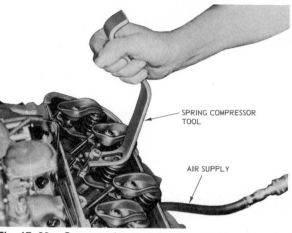

Fig. 17-20. Compressing valve spring while valve is being held closed with air pressure. *(Chevrolet Motor Division of General Motors Corporation)*

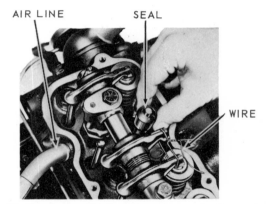

Fig. 17-21. Removal of a valve-stem seal after rocker arm has been wired out of the way. *(Ford Division of Ford Motor Company)*

17-20). A special air-hose adaptor is required for this which can be screwed into the spark-plug hole. The pressure will hold the valve closed while the spring is compressed. If the air pressure does not hold the valve closed, then the valve is stuck or damaged and the head will have to come off for a closer look.

NOTE: The air pressure may push the piston to BDC.

On some engines which have the rocker arms mounted on a shaft, it is possible to bleed down the hydraulic valve lifter with pressure applied with a special tool (Fig. 17-11), remove the push rod, and move the rocker arm to one side. With the rocker arm wired out of the way (Fig. 17-21), a valve-spring compressor can be used to compress the spring to remove the retainer, spring, and seal. Air pressure must be applied to the cylinder as explained in the previous paragraph to hold the valve on its seat when the spring is compressed.

§ 17-13. TESTING VALVE SPRINGS Valve springs should be tested for proper tension and for squareness. Special fixtures, such as the one shown in Fig. 17-22, are required to test for tension. The pressure required to compress the spring

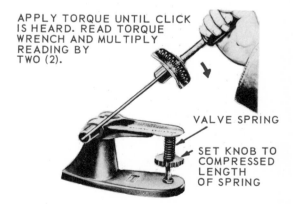

Fig. 17-22. Testing a valve spring for the proper tension in a special fixture. *(Ford Division of Ford Motor Company)*

to the proper length should be measured. To check for squareness, stand the spring, closed-coil end down, next to a steel square on a surface plate (Fig. 17–23). It should be rotated slowly to see if the top coil moves away from the square more than 5/64 inch (Ford). If the spring is more than 5/64 inch out of square or if it does not have the proper tension at the specified length, discard it. Such springs could cause faulty valve and engine performance.

§ 17–14. VALVE INSTALLATION After valves, valve seats, and valve guides have been serviced as noted in the following articles, they should be reinstalled in the block or head. The installation procedure is just the reverse of removal. The valve-assembly sequence for an overhead-valve

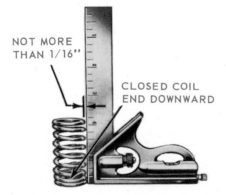

NOT MORE THAN 1/16″

CLOSED COIL END DOWNWARD

Fig. 17–23. Checking spring squareness. *(Ford Division of Ford Motor Company)*

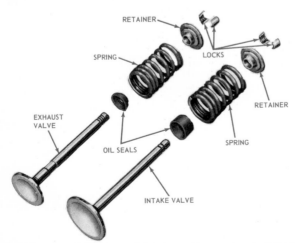

RETAINER

SPRING

LOCKS

RETAINER

EXHAUST VALVE

SPRING

OIL SEALS

INTAKE VALVE

Fig. 17–24. Exhaust and intake valves and associated parts in proper assembly relationship. *(Chrysler-Plymouth Division of Chrysler Motors Corporation)*

engine is shown in Fig. 17–24. Note that both valves use oil seals. New seals or shields should be installed if the old ones are worn or defective or if the manufacturer recommends new seals or shields as a part of valve or valve-spring service.

Some engine manufacturers want to make sure that the stem seals really seal, and to check this, they recommend the use of a special tool (Fig. 17–25). The tool has a suction cup which is placed over the end of the stem seal after it is installed. If suction can be held by the cup, then the seal is good. Figure 8–19 shows the construction of the seal being checked in Fig. 17–25.

Fig. 17–25. Use of a special tool to check the seal of the valve-stem seal. *(Pontiac Motor Division of General Motors Corporation)*

On I heads, after the valves with springs and seals or shields are reinstalled, the installed spring height should be measured, either with a scale or with a pair of dividers (Fig. 17–26). If the height is excessive (as it might be after valve and valve-seat grinding), then spring shims or spacers must be installed between the spring and the head. Do not install spacers that will reduce the spring height below the specified minimum. To do this would cause excessive spring pressure in the valve train and rapid wear of cams, push rods, rocker arms, and valves.

Be sure to install the valve springs in the proper position. For instance, many valve springs are different at each end and must not be installed upside down. Also, where a damper spring is used, it must be placed inside the valve spring with an exact relationship between the spring coils. One typical example is that the coil end of the damper

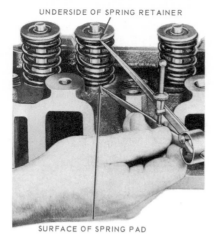

UNDERSIDE OF SPRING RETAINER

SURFACE OF SPRING PAD

Fig. 17–26. Measuring the assembled height of a valve spring. *(Ford Division of Ford Motor Company)*

spring should be 135 degrees (counterclockwise) from the coil end of the valve spring.

When installing free valves (§ 8–11), put tip cups and retainer locks back on the same valves from which they were removed. Worn sides of the locks should contact the tip cups. If the locks are badly worn, replace the locks and the tip cups. After free valves are installed, check them for freeness. Turn the engine over to open the valve, and then see if the valve can be turned. If the valve cannot be turned easily, it is probably binding against the tip cup. Grind a few thousandths of an inch off the valve stem. There should be a clearance of less than 0.004 inch between the valve stem and tip cup with the valve open. This clearance can be checked by mounting a dial indicator on the block so that the up-and-down movement of the valve can be measured as it is moved by hand. If the clearance is too great, grind a few thousandths of an inch off the upper edge of the tip cup. This is done by laying a piece of fine emery cloth on a flat surface, moving the tip cup back and forth on the emery cloth in a figure 8 pattern.

§ 17–15. REMOVING AND REPLACING HEADS
On some cars, the manifolds must be removed before the cylinder heads can be taken off. On the other cars, the manifolds can be left in place.

1. Removing cylinder heads. Follow the general instructions in § 17–11 to remove the cylinder heads. Do not pry the head off; this could put nicks in the head or block that would result in gasket leaks. Clean the head and block of carbon and gasket particles (§ 17–19).

2. Inspecting cylinder heads. After they are cleaned (§ 17–19), cylinder heads should be checked for cracks, warpage, or rough gasket surfaces. To check for cracks, moisten the surface of the head with kerosene, tap the head with a hammer, wipe the surface, and tap the head again. Cracks will be shown up by lines of kerosene appearing along the cracks. Warpage can be detected by laying a long straightedge against the sealing surfaces of the head.

On I heads, check the valve seats and valve guides as described in § 17–21 and § 17–22.

3. Replacing cylinder heads. After gasket surfaces on the head and block have been cleaned (§ 17–19), inspect them for roughness. File off any rough spots with a fine-cut mill file. Use a new gasket. If it is the lacquered type, handle it carefully to avoid chipping the lacquer. When the block has stud bolts, put the gasket into position, right side up. Use a gasket sealer only if it is specified by the manufacturer. For example, Chevrolet specifies that sealer should be used on the steel gaskets, but *not* on composition steel-asbestos gaskets.

If the block does not have stud bolts, use two pilot pins screwed into two boltholes to assure gasket alignment. Then lower the head into position, and run on the nuts or bolts finger-tight. Substitute bolts for pilot pins (if used).

● **CAUTION:** Make sure that all boltholes have been cleaned out. If they are not clean, the bolts may bottom against the foreign material and the head will not be tight.

Use a torque wrench to tighten the nuts or bolts. They must be tightened in the proper sequence and to the proper tension; if they are not, head or block distortion, gasket leakage, or bolt failure may occur. Refer to the sequence chart of the engine being serviced, and note the torque called for. Figure 17–27 shows the sequence for one head of a V-8 engine. Each nut or bolt should be tightened in several steps; that is, the complete circuit of all should be made at least twice, with each bolt or nut being drawn down little by little. When all are tightened to the correct tension, the engine should be run until it warms up and the tensions checked once again. Specifications for some engines using aluminum heads call for rechecking the tension after the engine has been turned off and has cooled.

269

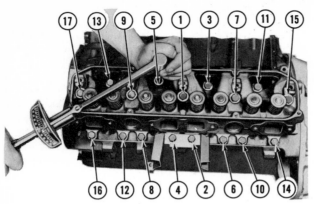

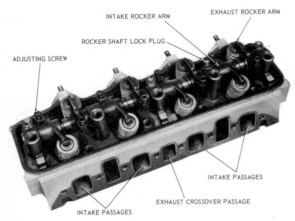

Fig. 17-27. Sequence chart for tightening cylinder-head bolts on a V-8 engine. *(Chrysler-Plymouth Division of Chrysler Motors Corporation)*

INTAKE ROCKER ARM

EXHAUST ROCKER ARM

ROCKER SHAFT LOCK PLUG

ADJUSTING SCREW

INTAKE PASSAGES

EXHAUST CROSSOVER PASSAGE

INTAKE PASSAGES

Fig. 17-28. Cylinder-head assembly *(Chrysler-Plymouth Division of Chrysler Motors Corporation)*

● **CAUTION:** Use great care and proceed slowly in tightening bolts so as to give the hydraulic valve lifters time to bleed down to their operating length. If the bolts are tightened too speedily, excessive pressure will be put on the lifters and they will be damaged. Also, the push rods might be bent.

● **CAUTION:** On I heads being installed with the rocker arm and shaft in place, make sure that push rods are in position and that the lower ends of the rods are in the valve-lifter sockets.

§ 17-16. SERVICING ROCKER-ARM ASSEMBLIES
Two methods of attaching the rocker arms to the cylinder head are used. With one, the rocker arms are mounted on a common shaft. With the other, the rocker arms are mounted individually on separate studs and move on ball pivots instead of a shaft.

There are several variations of the shaft-mounting arrangement. Figure 17-28 shows one of these. With this design the rocker arms are removed by taking out the shaft-locking plug and sliding the shaft out from the five supporting shaft struts on the head. In the design shown in Fig. 17-29, the shaft is removed, with the rocker arms on it, by removing the five bolts that hold the five shaft support brackets and shaft to the head. The rocker arms, brackets, and spacers can then be slipped off the shaft. A similar design is shown in Fig. 17-30, one difference being that this design has four shaft supports and the end rocker arms are held in place by washers and cotter pins.

ROCKER ARMS – RIGHT

ROCKER ARMS – LEFT

Fig. 17-29. Cylinder-head assemblies installed on the block of a V-8 engine. *(Chrysler-Plymouth Division of Chrysler Motors Corporation)*

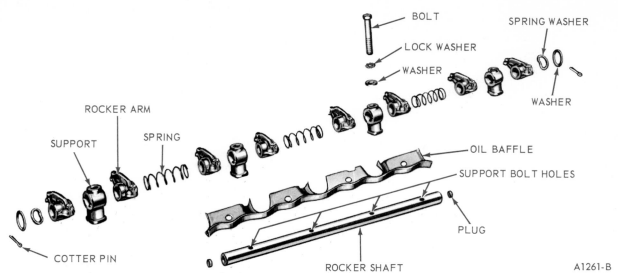

Fig. 17–30. Rocker-arm shaft, rocker arms, and associated parts in disassembled view. *(Ford Division of Ford Motor Company)*

Several other variations will be found on different engines.

On engines with independently mounted ball-pivot rocker arms (Fig. 8–17), rocker arms are removed by taking off the adjusting nuts. The rocker-arm studs can be replaced in the head if they have become loose or if the stud threads are damaged (§ 17–10).

After rocker arms are removed, they should be inspected for wear or damage. Rocker arms with bushings can be rebushed if the old bushing is worn. On some rocker arms, the valve ends, if worn, can be ground down on the valve-refacing machine. Excessively worn rocker arms should be discarded.

The silent-lash rocker arm (Fig. 8–15) can be disassembled by removing the eccentric retaining pin. If more than one rocker arm is being disassembled, do not mix the parts, but make sure all parts go back into the rocker arms from which they were taken. When reassembling a rocker arm, make sure the eccentric is installed so that the recessed dot (which is on the side with the smaller radius) is next to the plunger.

When reinstalling rocker arms and shafts on the cylinder head, make sure that the oilholes (in shafts so equipped) are on the underside so that they will feed oil to the rocker arms. Be sure that all springs and rocker arms are restored to their original positions as the shafts are reattached to the head.

§ 17–17. PUSH-ROD SERVICE Push rods should be inspected for wear at the ends and for straightness. Replace defective rods. Rods on some engines have one tip hardened and are so designated by a color stripe. The push rod should be installed so that the hardened end is toward the rocker arm. Always make sure that the lower end of the push rod is seated in the valve-lifter socket.

Special short-length push rods are available for some engines for possible use after valves and valve seats have been reground. Regrinding may result in excessive lengthening of the valve train (since the valve stem rises higher out of the cylinder head) so that the plunger may almost bottom in the hydraulic valve lifter. Using a shorter push rod corrects this condition (see § 17–9, 5, a). Some engine manufacturers recommend grinding off the end of the valve stem to bring the valve train length back to normal after a valve and valve-seat grinding job (§ 17–9, 5, b).

§ 17–18. REMOVING AND REPLACING MANIFOLDS Take the carburetor off the intake manifold. Handle it with care to avoid damaging it or spilling gasoline from the float bowl. Disconnect the vacuum lines, exhaust pipes, and, on air-injection engines, the air hose at the check valve. Then remove the air-supply-tube assembly. Remove nuts or bolts and take the manifolds off.

When reinstalling the manifolds, use new gaskets. Make sure that all trace of the old gaskets

Fig. 17-31. Sequence chart for tightening the intake-manifold attaching bolts on a V-8 engine. *(Chevrolet Motor Division of General Motors Corporation)*

has been removed from the head or block and manifolds. Tighten attaching nuts or bolts to the proper tension and in the proper sequence, using a torque wrench (see Fig. 17-31). Note that the center bolts are tightened first and that you work out from the center to the two ends.

§ 17-19. CLEANING CYLINDER HEAD After all parts are off the cylinder head, clean carbon from combustion chambers and valve ports with a wire brush driven by an electric drill (Fig. 17-32). Keep the wire brush away from valve seats, because it could scratch the seating surfaces. Scratched valve seats could cause poor valve seating and serious engine trouble. Blow out dust with an air hose.

Fig. 17-32. Cleaning combustion chamber and valve ports with wire brush. *(Chevrolet Motor Division of General Motors Corporation)*

● **CAUTION:** Always wear goggles when using a wire brush or similar equipment and also when using compressed air. They will protect the eyes from flying particles.

Clean all sludge and dirt from cylinder head. Clean valve guides thoroughly (§ 17-22).

Clean gasket surfaces with a flat scraper, being exceedingly careful to avoid scratching gasket surfaces. All traces of gasket material and sealer should be removed.

Inspect the cylinder head as explained in § 17-15.

§ 17-20. SERVICING VALVES First, clean the carbon off the valves. This may be done with a wire brush or buffing wheel (wear goggles when using the wheel so that particles of metal or dirt will not fly into your eyes). Valve stems should be cleaned with fine abrasive cloth. One method of doing this is to rotate the valve in a lathe or an electric drill while a strip of abrasive cloth is held wrapped partly around the stem. The valve can also be clamped in the soft jaws of a vise while the abrasive cloth, wrapped around the stem, is pulled back and forth. Do not cut metal from the valve stem, since this would cause excessive clearance at the valve guide.

Examine the valves as you clean them, discarding the valves that are cracked, badly pitted, burned, worn, or bent. Small pits or burns in the valve face can be removed as noted below. Do not mix the valves; after they are serviced, they must be returned to the valve ports from which they were taken.

Figure 17-33 shows specific parts of the valve to be inspected. Some engine manufacturers recommend the use of a run-out gauge (Fig. 17-34) to check the run-out, or eccentricity, of the valve

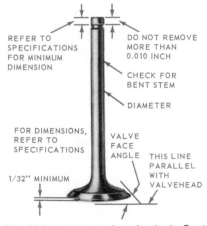

Fig. 17-33. Valve parts to be checked. On the valve shown, the stem is hardened on the end; therefore, not more than 0.010 inch should be removed. *(Ford Division of Ford Motor Company)*

272

Fig. 17–34. Use of a run-out gauge to check for valve-face eccentricity. *(Ford Division of Ford Motor Company)*

face. If the run-out is excessive as the valve is rotated in the gauge, the valve should be discarded. After valves are cleaned up, they should be temporarily replaced in their valve guides to check for valve-guide wear (§ 17–22). If guides are excessively worn, they must either be replaced or else reamed out to a larger size and valves with oversized stems installed.

● **CAUTION:** Sodium-cooled valves must be handled with special care, since the element sodium is highly reactive. See the Caution note at the end of § 8–4.

1. Refacing or grinding valves. * The valve stem is clamped in the chuck of the valve-refacing machine (Fig. 17–35). Then, the seating face of the valve is brought into contact with the rotating grinding wheel. The chuck is set at the proper angle to give the correct angle to the seating face. This angle must just match the valve-seat angle, or else there should be an interference angle of 1/4 to 1 degree (see Fig. 17–5).

At the start of the operation, the first cut should be a light one. If this cut removes metal from only one-third or one-half of the face, the valve may not be centered in the chuck or else the valve stem is bent. If bent, the valve should be discarded. On subsequent cuts, only sufficient metal

---

* At one time, it was common practice to lap valves instead of grinding them. In lapping, the valve and seat are covered with abrasive compound, and the valve is turned back and forth on the valve seat. This method is no longer recommended. However, some engine manufacturers recommended a light final lapping after valve grinding to perfect the valve-to-seat fit.

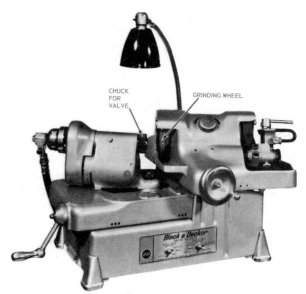

Fig. 17–35. Valve-refacing machine. *(Black and Decker Manufacturing Company)*

should be removed to true up the surface and remove pits. Do not take heavy cuts. If so much metal must be removed that the margin is lost (see Fig. 17–33), the outer edge will be sharp. This would cause the valve to run hot; it should be discarded. If new valves are required, reface them lightly to assure proper seating angles.

NOTE: Follow the operating instructions issued by the refacer manufacturer. In particular, dress the grinding wheel as necessary with the diamond-tipped dressing tool. As the diamond is moved across the rotating face of the wheel, it cleans and aligns the grinding face.

2. Valve-stem-tip refacing. If the tip ends of the valve stems are rough or worn unevenly, they can be ground lightly with the special attachment furnished with the valve-refacing machine.

● **CAUTION:** The ends of some valve stems are hardened and should have no more than a few thousandths of an inch ground off. Excessive grinding will expose soft metal so that the stem would wear rapidly in service.

§ 17–21. VALVE SEATS For effective valve seating and sealing, the valve face must be concentric with the valve stem, and the valve guide must be concentric with the valve face. Also, the valve-face angle must match the valve-seat angle (or have an interference angle). Thus, as a first step in valve-seat service, the valve guides must be cleaned and serviced (§ 17–22).

Valve seats are of two types, the integral type, which is actually the cylinder block or head, and the insert type, which is a ring of special metal set into the block or head (Fig. 8–10). Replacing seat inserts and grinding seats are described below.

1. Replacing valve-seat inserts. When a valve-seat insert is badly worn or has been ground down on previous occasions so that there is insufficient metal for another grind, it must be replaced. The old seat must be removed with a special puller. If a puller is not available, the insert should be punch-marked on two opposite sides and an electric drill used to drill holes almost through the insert. Then, a chisel and hammer can be used to break the insert into halves so that it can be removed. Care must be used so that the counterbore is not damaged. If the new insert fits too loosely, the counterbore must be rebored oversize and an oversize insert installed. The new insert should be chilled in dry ice for 15 minutes to shrink it so that it can be driven into place. Then, the valve seat should be ground.

2. Grinding valve seats. * Two general types of valve-seat grinders are used, the concentric grinder and the eccentric grinder. The concentric grinder rotates a grinding stone of the proper shape on the valve seat (Fig. 17–36). The stone is kept concentric with the valve seat by a pilot installed in the valve guide (Fig. 17–37). This means that the valve guide must be cleaned and serviced (§ 17–22) before the seat is ground. In the unit shown in Fig. 17–36, the stone is automatically lifted about once a revolution. This permits the stone to clear itself of grit and dust by centrifugal force. After the seat is ground, it will be too wide. It must be narrowed by using upper and lower grinding stones to grind away the upper and lower edges of the seat. A typical seat is shown in Fig. 17–38, and a gauge to measure the seat width is shown in Fig. 17–39.

The eccentric valve-seat grinder (Fig. 17–40) uses an eccentric grinding mechanism in which the grinding stone is offset from the center of the

---

* A method of servicing valve seats, no longer in wide use, requires valve-seat reamers or cutters. These tools have a series of teeth that cut material off the seat when they are turned on the seat. Use of a grinder is the preferred method for servicing valve seats.

Fig. 17–36. Concentric valve-seat grinder of the type using the patented Vibrocentric principle. The stone is rotated at high speed, and about once every revolution it is automatically lifted off the valve seat so that it can throw off loosened grit and grindings. *(Black and Decker Manufacturing Company)*

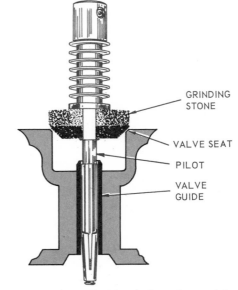

Fig. 17–37. Pilot on which grinding stone rotates. The pilot keeps the stone concentric with the valve seat. *(Black and Decker Manufacturing Company)*

valve seat. It makes only line contact with the valve seat. As the stone revolves, its center rotates slowly on an eccentric shaft. This permits the

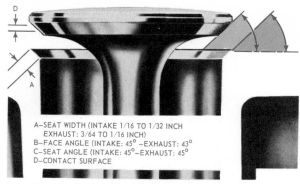

A—SEAT WIDTH (INTAKE 1/16 TO 1/32 INCH
    EXHAUST: 3/64 TO 1/16 INCH)
B—FACE ANGLE (INTAKE: 45° —EXHAUST: 43°
C—SEAT ANGLE (INTAKE: 45°—EXHAUST: 45°
D—CONTACT SURFACE

Fig. 17–38. Angles to which the valve seat and upper and lower cuts must be ground on one engine. The dimensions and angles vary among different engines. *(Chrysler Motors Corporation)*

SEAT WIDTH SCALE

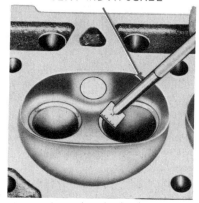

Fig. 17–39. Checking valve-seat width with a special tool. *(Ford Division of Ford Motor Company)*

line contact at which grinding is taking place to progress evenly around the entire valve seat. This valve-seat grinder also pilots the valve guide.

● **CAUTION:** Be sure to follow instructions furnished by the grinder manufacturer. Note that the grinding stone must be dressed frequently with the diamond-tipped dressing tool. Also, make sure that cuttings do not get into the block if the engine (L-head type) has not been completely torn down. To protect bearings and cylinders in L-head engines, cover cylinders with masking tape.

3. *Checking valve seats for concentricity.* After the valve guides are serviced and valve seats ground, the concentricity of the two can be checked with a valve-seat dial gauge (Fig. 17–41).

Fig. 17–40. Eccentric valve-seat grinder installed on a cylinder block, ready to grind a valve seat. The micrometer feed permits accurate feeding of the grinding wheel into the valve seat. *(Hall Manufacturing Company)*

Fig. 17–41. Valve-seat dial gauge. The unit shown is mounted in the valve guide. *(Oldsmobile Division of General Motors Corporation)*

The gauge is mounted in the valve guide and is rotated so that the indicator finger sweeps round the valve seat. Any eccentricity (or run-out) of the seat is thus registered on the gauge dial.

4. Testing valve seating. Contact between the valve face and seat may be tested by marking lines with a soft pencil about ¼ inch apart around the entire valve face. Then the valve should be put into place and, with light pressure, rotated half a turn to the left and then half a turn to the right. If this removes the pencil marks, the seating is good. The seating can also be checked with prussian blue. Coat the valve face lightly with prussian blue, put the valve on its seat, and turn it with light pressure. If blue appears all the way around the valve seat, the valve seat and guide are concentric with each other. Now, check concentricity of valve face with valve stem by removing prussian blue from valve and seat, lightly coating the seat with prussian blue, and then lightly rotating valve on seat. If blue transfers all the way around the valve face, the valve face and stem are concentric. This is a check similar to the run-out check (Fig. 17–34).

§ **17–22. VALVE-GUIDE SERVICE** As we have mentioned, the valve guide must be clean and in good condition for normal valve seating. A wire brush or adjustable-blade cleaner can be used to clean the guide (Fig. 17–42). If the guide is worn, it will require servicing. The servicing procedure required depends on whether the valve guide is of the integral or the replaceable type. If the valve guide is of the integral type (that is, bored directly

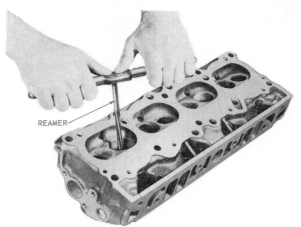

Fig. 17–43. Reaming valve guide. *(Pontiac Motor Division of General Motors Corporation)*

in the head), it must be reamed to a larger size (Fig. 17–43) and a valve with an oversize stem installed. If the worn guide is of the replaceable type, it should be removed and a new guide installed. Checking valve guides for wear is discussed below. In addition, the removal and installation of the replaceable type of valve guide are described.

1. Testing guide for wear. Clean the guide, and wipe it with a strip of cloth dampened with cleaning solvent. Pull the cloth through by hooking it to a piece of wire stuck through the guide.

One method of testing the guide makes use of a dial indicator (Fig. 17–44). With the valve in place, the camshaft is turned to raise the valve off its seat (on L-head engines). On I-head engines,

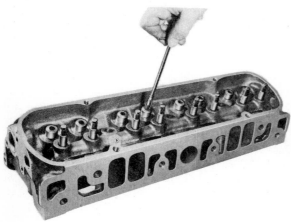

Fig. 17–42. Cleaning valve guide with adjustable-blade cleaner. *(Pontiac Motor Division of General Motors Corporation)*

Fig. 17–44. Dial indicator set up to measure valve-guide wear. *(Chrysler-Plymouth Division of Chrysler Motors Corporation)*

Fig. 17–45. Using a tool on a valve stem to hold the valve off its seat in the cylinder head. *(Chrysler-Plymouth Division of Chrysler Motors Corporation)*

use a special tool on the valve stem (Fig. 17–45) to hold the valve off its seat. The dial indicator is then installed on the block or head with the indicating button touching the edge of the valve head. Then, the valve can be moved sideways to determine the wear as indicated by the amount of movement. On some I-head engines, the recommendation is to check valve movement from the stem end with the valve seated (Fig. 17–46).

Fig. 17–46. Valve-stem clearance in valve guide being checked from the stem end of the valve. *(Ford Division of Ford Motor Company)*

Another checking method is to insert a tapered pilot into the guide until it is tight. Then, pencilmark the pilot at the top of the guide, remove it, and measure the pilot diameter ½ inch below

the pencil mark. This gives the guide diameter, which can then be compared with the valve-stem diameter.

Neither of the two above methods will accurately show up valve-guide eccentricity and bellmouthing. The valve guide is apt to wear oval-shaped or bellmouthed owing to the tendency for the valve to wobble as it opens and closes. The bellmouth wear shown in Fig. 17–47 is exaggerated. A small-hole gauge, shown in Fig. 17–47, will detect oval or bellmouth wear. It is used as shown: the split ball is adjusted until it is a light drag fit at the point being checked. Then, the split ball is measured with a micrometer. By checking the guide at various points, any eccentricity will be detected.

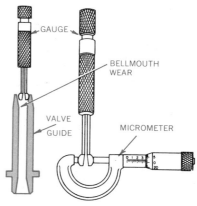

Fig. 17–47. Small-hole gauge is the most accurate device to check for valve-guide wear. The gauge is adjusted so that the split ball is a drag fit in the guide (left); then the split ball can be measured with a micrometer, as shown (right).

2. Removing valve guide (replaceable type). A guide puller (Fig. 17–48) is handy for removing the old valve guide. As the nut is turned on the screw, the guide is pulled out. On some L-head engines, the guide can be driven down into the valve-spring compartment. On I-head engines, the valve guide can be pressed out of the head with an arbor press.

3. Installing valve guide (replaceable type). New valve guides should be installed with a special driver, or replacer (Fig. 17–49). Guides can be installed in I heads with an arbor press. Guides must be installed to the proper depth in the block or head. Then, they must be reamed to size. This is usually done in two steps, a rough ream and then a second, or final, finishing ream. Figure 17–50 illustrates both the depth of assembly of

277

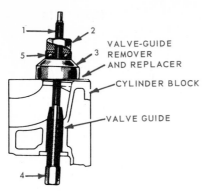

Fig. 17–48. Valve guide is removed from the cylinder block with a special puller: screw (1), nut (2), spacer (3), nut (4), bearing (5).

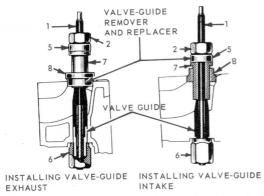

Fig. 17–49. Valve guide is installed in the cylinder block with a special replacer: screw (1), nut (2), spacer (5), recessed nut (6), sleeve (7), collar (8).

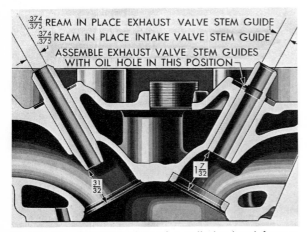

Fig. 17–50. Sectional view of a cylinder head from a V-8, overhead-valve engine, showing the reaming dimensions and the correct locations of intake and exhaust valve-stem guides. *(Chrysler-Plymouth Division of Chrysler Motors Corporation)*

valve guides and the reaming dimensions on one engine.

4. Checking concentricity with seat. After the guide is installed and reamed, its concentricity with the valve seat must be checked and correction made (by grinding the seat), if necessary (§ 17–21).

§ 17–23. CAMSHAFT Camshaft removal varies somewhat from engine to engine. The general procedure is as follows: Remove the radiator. Take the dynamic balancer or pulley from the crankshaft, and remove the gear or timing-chain cover. Detach the camshaft thrust plate (where present), and take off the camshaft sprocket and chain (where used). The distributor or oil pump (whichever has the driven gear) must be removed so that the gear will not interfere with the camshaft removal.

Next, on L-head engines, raise and block up the valves and valve lifters. This keeps the lifters from falling down behind the cams and jamming. On overhead-valve engines, the rocker-arm assemblies and push rods must be removed. Then the lifters must either be removed or else be lifted and held up out of the way by spring-type clothes pins as on the L-head engine. Now, the camshaft is free and can be pulled forward and out. Be very careful to keep the journals and cams from scratching the camshaft bearings. Support the rear of the camshaft as it is pulled so that journals and cams do not hit the bearings.

1. Checking camshaft. Check for alignment by rotating the camshaft in V blocks and using a dial indicator to check for eccentricity (Fig. 17–51).

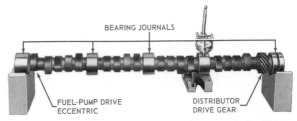

Fig. 17–51. Checking alignment of a camshaft. *(Chevrolet Motor Division of General Motors Corporation)*

A bent camshaft may sometimes be straightened in a hydraulic press. Journal diameters should be checked with a micrometer and the bearings with a telescope gauge. The two dimensions can then be compared to determine whether bearings are worn. If they are, they should be replaced.

2. Checking for cam wear. Figure 17–52 shows

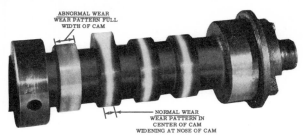

Fig. 17-52. Normal and abnormal cam wear. *(Oldsmobile Division of General Motors Corporation)*

normal and abnormal cam wear. If wear shows across the full width of the cam, it means excessive wear has taken place and a new camshaft should be installed (and the lifter should also be checked as explained in § 17-24, 4). The cam lobe lift can be checked with the camshaft in the engine. The height of the lobe can also be measured with a micrometer with the camshaft removed from the engine. Figure 17-53 shows the lobe-lift check on one engine. With the rocker-arm-shaft assembly removed and the dial indicator positioned as shown, turn the engine over slowly until the valve lifter is on the base circle of the cam. Set the indicator at zero and then rotate the engine until the lifter is on the point of the lobe. Note the indicator reading, which is the lobe lift.

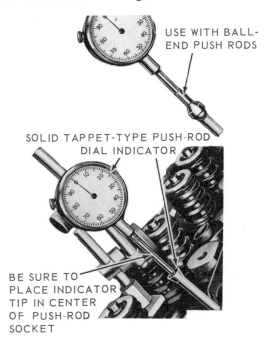

USE WITH BALL-END PUSH RODS

SOLID TAPPET-TYPE PUSH-ROD DIAL INDICATOR

BE SURE TO PLACE INDICATOR TIP IN CENTER OF PUSH-ROD SOCKET

Fig. 17-53. Cam lobe-lift check on one engine. *(Ford Division of Ford Motor Company)*

This check can also be made on some engines by moving a rocker arm to one side or taking off a single rocker arm instead of removing the entire rocker-arm-shaft assembly.

3. Replacing camshaft bearings. A special bearing remover and replacer bar is required to do this job. On some engines, the puller bar is threaded and a nut is turned to remove the bearings. On others, a hammer is used to drive against the bar and force the bearings out. Figure 17-54 shows a screw-type puller being used to remove center bearings in a V-8 and an in-line engine.

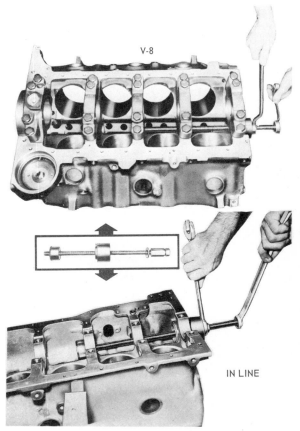

V-8

IN LINE

Fig. 17-54. Screw-type camshaft bearing remover and replacer, in use on a V-8 and an in-line engine. *(Chevrolet Motor Division of General Motors Corporation)*

You have to work from one end of the block and then the other when using this puller. The two end bearings are removed with a different sort of tool (Fig. 17-55) which is used to drive the end bearings inward so that they can be forced into the block and then taken out. In reinstalling the bearings on these engines, the end bearings must

279

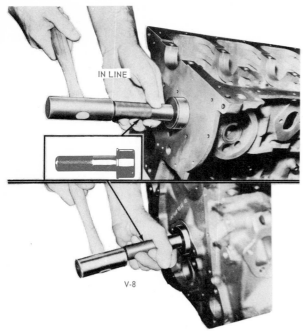

IN LINE

V-8

be driven in first (Fig. 17–55). These bearings serve as pilots to pull the new bearings into place with the screw-type puller.

Some engine manufacturers recommend a driver type of remover and replacer bar. The bar is put into position (Fig. 17–56) and a hammer used to drive out the bearings, one at a time. The same tool is used to drive the new bearings into place (Fig. 17–57). Oilholes in the new bearings

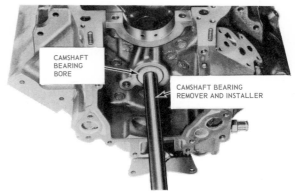

CAMSHAFT BEARING BORE

CAMSHAFT BEARING REMOVER AND INSTALLER

Fig. 17–55. Driver-type camshaft bearing remover and replacer, in use on the end camshaft bearings of an inline and a V-8 engine. *(Chevrolet Motor Division of General Motors Corporation)*

Fig. 17–56. Using a driver-type camshaft-bearing remover and replacer tool to remove camshaft bearings. *(Cadillac Motor Car Division of General Motors Corporation)*

REMOVER AND INSTALLER

BEARING

OIL HOLE

SCRIBE MARK

Fig. 17–57. Using a special tool to replace the camshaft bearings. Note the scribe marks on the faces of the bores to assure the proper alignment of the bearing oil holes with the oil holes in the cylinder block. *(Cadillac Motor Car Division of General Motors Corporation)*

280

should align with the oilholes in the block. Also, new bearings should be staked in place if the old bearings were staked. If the new bearings are not of the precision type, they will require reaming to establish the proper fit.

4. Timing the valves. The timing gears, or sprockets, and chain are marked to establish the proper positions and correct valve timing (Figs. 8–2 and 8–3). To get to these markings, however, the front of the car has to be partly torn down. Thus, some engines have another marking system for checking valve timing. This marking is on the flywheel or vibration damper, near the ignition-timing markings. When this marking is visible or registers with a pointer, a certain designated valve should be just opening or should have opened a specified amount. Valve action is observed by removing the valve cover.

When the flywheel or vibration damper is not marked, piston position can be measured with a special gauge inserted through a special hole in the head; the relationship of the piston with the valves can therefore be established.

5. Timing gear and chain. Gear run-out can be checked by mounting a dial indicator on the block, with the indicating finger resting on the side of the gear (Fig. 17–58). Run-out will then be indicated as the gear is rotated. Gear backlash is measured by inserting a narrow feeler gauge

Fig. 17–58. Checking the timing gear runout, or eccentricity, with a dial indicator. *(Buick Motor Division of General Motors Corporation)*

between the meshing teeth. Excessive run-out or backlash requires gear replacement. Excessive slack in the timing chain indicates a worn chain, and possibly worn sprockets.

§ 17–24. VALVE LIFTERS The solid and the hydraulic valve lifters require different servicing procedures.

1. Solid lifter. Solid lifters are removed from the camshaft side on some engines. This requires camshaft removal as a first step (§ 17–23). In most engines, lifters are removed from the valve or push-rod side. Lifters should be kept in order so that they can be restored to the bores from which they were removed. If the face of the adjusting screw in the lifter is worn, it may be smoothed on the valve-refacing machine. Oversize valve lifters may be installed on many engines if the lifter bores have become worn. Before this is done, the lifter bores must be reamed oversize.

2. Hydraulic valve lifter. On some engines, a "leak-down" test is used to determine the condition of the hydraulic valve lifters. One way in which this test is made is to insert a feeler gauge between the rocker arm and valve stem. Then, the time it takes for the valve lifter to leak enough oil to allow the valve to seat is noted. As the valve seats, the feeler gauge becomes loose and this indicates the end of the test. If the leak-down time is too short, the valve lifter is defective.

A more accurate leak-down test is made with the lifter out of the engine and installed in a special tester (Fig. 17–59). With this tester, the time required for a uniform pressure (from the weight on the end of the lever) to force the lifter plunger to bottom is measured. If it is too short, the lifter is defective.

To remove the hydraulic valve lifters from some engines, the push-rod cover and rocker-arm assembly must first be removed and the push rod taken out. On some engines with shaft-mounted rocker arms, the rocker arm can be moved by compressing the spring so that the push rod can be removed. Thus, the rocker-arm assembly does not have to be taken off.

The use of one lifter-removing tool is shown in Fig. 17–60. The tool is inserted through the push-rod opening in the block and is seated firmly on the end of the lifter. The lifter is then removed through the push-rod opening.

3. Servicing hydraulic valve lifters. The lifters should be disassembled and all parts cleaned in solvent. If any part is defective, the lifter should

Fig. 17–59. Checking the leak-down rate of a hydraulic valve lifter removed from an engine. *(Pontiac Motor Division of General Motors Corporation)*

MAGNET

Fig. 17–60. Removing a valve lifter with a special magnetic tool. *(Ford Division of Ford Motor Company)*

be replaced. On reassembly, fill the lifter with clean, light engine oil.

Work on only one lifter at a time so that you do not mix parts between lifters. Also, make sure each lifter goes back into the bore from which it was removed.

● CAUTION: Be extremely careful to keep everything clean when servicing and handling

hydraulic valve lifters. It takes only one tiny particle of dirt to cause a lifter to malfunction.

4. Checking lifter foot. The bottom, or cam side, of the lifter should be flat. It can be checked by placing a straightedge across the lifter bottom. If light can be seen between the straightedge and lifter, the lifter should be discarded. Also, the camshaft cams should be checked for excessive wear (§ 17–23).

*R*eview *Questions*

1. What is the first step to be taken before any engine service is performed?
2. Describe the operating characteristics of valves in good condition.
3. Describe various valve troubles.
4. What could cause valve sticking?
5. What could cause valve burning?
6. What could cause valve breakage?
7. What are the basic steps in a complete valve job?
8. Explain how to check and adjust valve-tappet

clearance in an L-head engine.
9. Describe the procedure of checking and adjusting the valve-tappet clearance on an overhead-valve engine with solid lifters.
10. Explain how to adjust the silent valve mechanism.
11. Explain two ways in which valve-train length can be adjusted in engines using hydraulic valve lifters.
12. Why is it desirable to use a valve rack when valves are removed from the engine?

13. Describe the procedure of removing the valves from an L-head engine. From an overhead-valve engine.
14. How are valve springs tested?
15. Explain how to remove, inspect, and replace cylinder heads.
16. Explain how to clean carbon from the head and block.
17. Describe the procedure of refacing valves.
18. When are new valve-seat inserts required?
19. Describe the procedure of concentric valve-seat grinding.
20. Describe the procedure of eccentric valve-seat grinding.
21. What is one of the greatest hazards in valve-seat grinding in L-head engines where pistons are not removed from the engine?
22. What is meant by valve-seat width, and how is the proper width secured?
23. How are valves and seats tested?
24. What services are required on valve guides?
25. How is a valve guide tested for wear?
26. In what two ways should a camshaft be tested after its removal from the engine?
27. How is the cam lobe lift measured?
28. Explain how to replace camshaft bearings.
29. What is meant by valve timing?
30. Explain how a hydraulic valve lifter is tested.

*S*tudy *Questions*

1. List various valve troubles, their causes, and cures.
2. Make a list of the steps required to adjust valve-tappet clearance in an L-head engine. In an overhead-valve engine.
3. Write a sequence story on the procedure of removing valves from an L-head engine. From an overhead-valve engine.
4. List the steps required to remove a cylinder head from an L-head engine and clean it and the block of carbon. Do the same for an overhead-valve engine.
5. List the steps required to check and service valves. Valve seats.
6. List the steps required to check and service valve guides.
7. Write a sequence story on how to check a camshaft.
8. Write a sequence story on how to clean and check a hydraulic valve lifter.

18

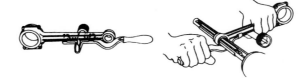

Engine Service — Pistons and Rods

This chapter continues the discussion of engine service and describes the servicing of connecting rods, rod bearings, pistons, and piston rings.

CONNECTING RODS AND ROD BEARINGS

§ 18-1. BEARING OIL-LEAK DETECTOR On many engines, the connecting-rod and main bearings (crankshaft bearings) can be checked for wear with an oil-leak detector (Fig. 18-1) before the engine is torn down. To use the detector, the oil pan is removed (§ 18-4), and the detector hose is connected to the pressure side of the engine lubricating system (at the oil filter, for example). Then, with the detector filled with SAE 30 oil, an air pressure of 25 psi (pounds per square inch) is applied to the detector tank. This pressure forces oil through the engine lubricating system. If bearings are worn, considerable oil will leak from them. Worn bearings greatly increase engine oil consumption because they pass more oil (see § 26-14). The detector manufacturer states that

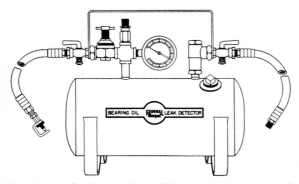

Fig. 18-1. Engine-bearing oil-leak detector to check main and connecting-rod bearings for wear. *(Federal-Mogul Service Division of Federal-Mogul-Bower Bearings, Incorporated)*

a normal bearing will leak between 20 and 150 drops of oil a minute. If it leaks more, the bearing is worn. If it leaks less than 20 drops per minute, then either the bearing clearance is too small or else the oil line to the bearing is stopped up.

NOTE: When oil-passage holes in the crankshaft and bearing align, considerable oil will be forced through the bearing, giving the appearance of excessive wear. In such a case, the crankshaft should be rotated somewhat to move the oilholes out of register.

§ 18-2. PREPARING TO REMOVE RODS Connecting rods and pistons are removed as an assembly from the engine. Removing, servicing, and replacing connecting rods requires about 5 to 8 hours, according to the type of engine. About 3 additional hours are required to install new piston rings. Additional time is needed for such services as piston-pin or bushing replacement. On most engines, the piston-and-rod assemblies are removed from the top of the engine (on a few, from the crankcase end). Thus, the first step is to remove the cylinder head (§ 17-15). Cylinders should be examined for wear. If wear has taken place, there will be a ridge at the top of the cylinder that marks the upper limit of the top-ring travel (Fig. 18-2). If this ridge is not removed, the top ring could jam under it as the piston is moved upward. This might break the rings or the piston-ring-groove lands (Fig. 18-2). Thus, the ridge, if present, should be removed.

§ 18-3. REMOVING RING RIDGE To remove ring ridges, use a special remover, as shown in Fig.

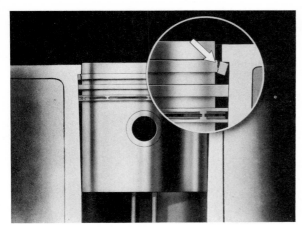

Fig. 18–2. How a ring ridge caused by cylinder wear might break the ring if the piston is withdrawn without removing the rings. *(Sealed Power Corporation)*

18–3. With the piston near the bottom of the stroke, stuff cloths into the cylinder, and install the ridge remover. Adjust the cutters to take off just enough metal to remove the ridge. Cover the other cylinders (and valves, on L-head engines) to keep cuttings from getting into them. Rotate the tool to cut the ridge away. Remove the tool, take the cloth out, and wipe the cylinder walls. Repeat for the other cylinders.

§ **18–4. REMOVING OIL PAN** The oil pan must be removed so that the connecting rods can be detached from the crankshaft. First, remove the drain plug to drain the crankcase oil. On many cars, the steering idler or other steering linkage must be removed. In such a case, note how the linkage is attached and the number and location of shims (if used). On some cars, the oil pan is more easily removed if the engine mounting bolts are removed and the engine is raised slightly. Other parts that may require removal before the oil pan can be taken off include the exhaust pipe, oil-level tube, brake-return spring, and cranking motor. Then the nuts or bolts holding the oil pan to the engine block can be removed. Steady the pan as the last two nuts or bolts are removed so that it does not drop. If the pan strikes the crankshaft so that it does not come free, turn the engine over a few degrees.

Clean the oil pan, oil screen, and oil pump thoroughly before replacing the pan. Make sure that the gasket material is scraped from the pan and block gasket surfaces. Apply new gasket cement (if specified); lay the gasket (or gaskets)

Fig. 18–3. Ridge-removing tool in place in the top of a cylinder. Cutters remove the ridge as the tool is turned in the cylinder.

in place. Be sure that the boltholes in the gasket and the pan line up. Install the pan, and tighten the bolts or nuts to the proper tension.

§ **18–5. REMOVING AND REPLACING PISTON-AND-ROD ASSEMBLIES** After the preliminaries are out of the way, as noted in previous articles, proceed as follows to remove and replace piston-and-rod assemblies.

1. Removal. With the head and pan off, crank the engine so that the piston of cylinder 1 is near bottom. Examine the rod and rod cap for identifying marks. If none can be seen, mark them with metal numbering dies (do this before removing them, and tap dies lightly to avoid distorting the rod or cap). Marks are needed to make sure that the parts go back into the same cylinders from which they were removed (each piston should also be numbered if not already marked).

Remove the rod nuts and cap. Slide the rod-and-piston assembly up into the cylinder away from the crankshaft. Use guide sleeves on the rod bolts, if specified, to keep the bolt threads from scratching the crankshaft journals (see Fig 18–4). The long handle permits easy piston and rod removal and replacement.

Turn the crankshaft as you go from rod to rod

285

Fig. 18-4. Using a special short guide and long guide to remove a connecting rod. *(Buick Motor Division of General Motors Corporation)*

so that you can reach the rod nuts. When all rods are detached and the piston-and-rod assemblies have been pushed up in the cylinders, remove the assemblies from the top of the engine.

2. Separating rods and pistons. Lay the piston-and-rod assemblies out on the bench in order as they are removed from the engine. Detach the pistons from the rods by removing the piston pins. On the free-floating type, push the pin out after removing the retainer rings (Fig. 18-5). On the type with a locking bolt, loosen the bolt and slip the pin out. On the press-fit type, use a special tool and press the pin out with an arbor press. Figures 18-6 and 18-7 show the details of one pin-removing tool and its use.

Never clamp the piston in an ordinary vise when it is necessary to hold the piston firmly; this could distort and ruin it. Instead, use a special piston vise which has curved jaws that will not distort the piston or damage its finish. Be very careful to avoid scratching, nicking, or otherwise damaging the pistons, rings, or rods. Check the rods, pistons, pins, and rings as noted in following articles.

NOTE: Make sure that oil passages in rods are clear. After cleaning rods, blow out passages with compressed air.

3. Checking piston-pin fit. On some Chevrolet engines having a press fit of the piston pin in the connecting rod, the manufacturer specifies a clearance check of the pin to the piston-pin bushings or

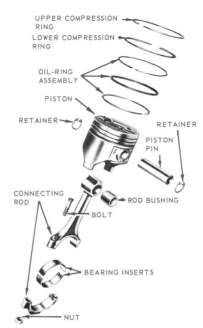

Fig. 18-5. Piston and connecting-rod assembly of type using piston-pin retaining rings. *(Ford Division of Ford Motor Company)*

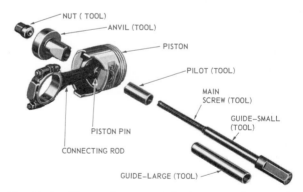

Fig. 18-6. Piston-pin-removal tool arranged properly to remove a pin. *(Chrysler-Plymouth Division of Chrysler Motors Corporation)*

bores in the piston. Bushings and pin must be clean and unscuffed. Measure the pin with a micrometer and the bushings or bores with an inside micrometer or dial bore gauge. Clearance of more than 0.001 inch requires replacement of the piston and piston-pin assembly. In this case, the piston and pin are supplied as a matched set and are not serviced separately.

On some Plymouth engines, the manufacturer

286

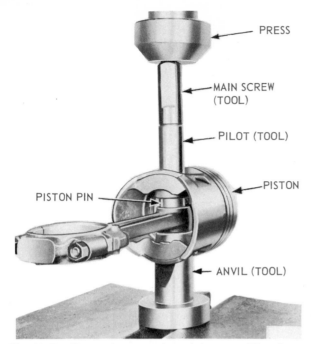

Fig. 18-7. Piston-pin-removal tool in use. (*Chrysler-Plymouth Division of Chrysler Motors Corporation*)

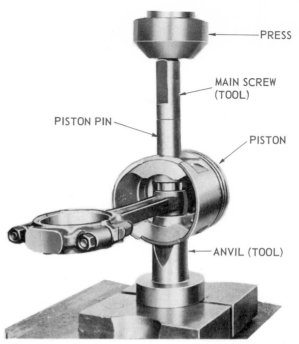

Fig. 18-9. Installing piston pin. (*Chrysler-Plymouth Division of Chrysler Motors Corporation*)

recommends a fit test after the piston pin has been pressed into position in the piston and connecting rod. The tool arrangement to install the piston pin is shown in Fig. 18-8. The actual installation procedure is shown in Fig. 18-9. The parts are aligned as shown and the nut put on the end of the main screw to hold everything in place. Then the temporary assembly is put on the press so that the pin can be pressed down into place, as shown in Fig. 18-9. Finally, the assembly is placed in a press, as shown in Fig. 18-10, and a torque wrench

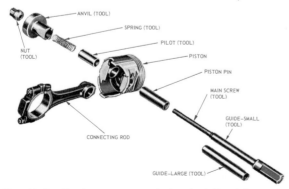

Fig. 18-8. Tool arrangement to install piston pin. (*Chrysler-Plymouth Division of Chrysler Motors Corporation*)

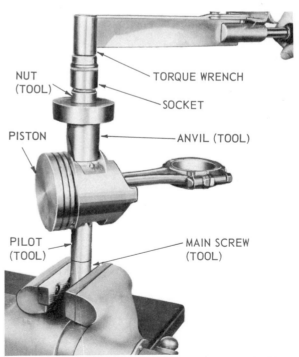

Fig. 18-10. Testing piston fit in connecting rod with a torque wrench. (*Chrysler-Plymouth Division of Chrysler Motors Corporation*)

287

is used to apply 15 lb-ft of torque to the nut on the end of the tool. If this amount of torque causes the connecting rod to move down on the piston pin, the interference or press fit is too loose and the connecting rod must be rejected. Try a new connecting rod. If the connecting rod does not move, the fit is satisfactory.

4. Reinstalling piston-and-rod assemblies. As the rods, pistons, and rings are assembled, make sure that they are rematched. Check fit of all parts as explained in following articles. Observe the proper relationship of the piston to the rod. Note, for example, that, in the assembly shown in Fig. 18-11, the notch in the piston faces to the front of the engine with the oil hole in the rod to the right side of the engine. Parts should go back into the same cylinders from which they were removed. Rings should be positioned so that the gaps are uniformly spaced around the piston (except on pistons where rings are pinned). Then the piston-ring-and-rod assembly should be dipped in light oil or castor oil to provide initial lubrication. Castor oil is considered better by many mechanics, since it has greater film strength and will not wash out as easily as mineral oil. Install pistons in cylinders, using a ring compressor (see § 18-17). Use a bolt guide sleeve and replacement tool, if specified, to keep the bolts from scratching the crankshaft journals (see Fig. 18-4). Attach the rod cap with

INDENT—ASSEMBLE TOWARD FRONT OF ENGINE

OIL HOLE—ASSEMBLE TOWARD RIGHT SIDE OF ENGINE

Fig. 18-11. Relationship of rod and piston. *(Chrysler-Plymouth Division of Chrysler Motors Corporation)*

the nuts turned down lightly. Then tap the bearing cap on its crown lightly with a brass hammer to help center it. Use a torque wrench to final-tighten nuts.

● **CAUTION:** Bearing clearances should be checked (§ 18-10).

5. Checking side clearance. On V-8 engines, some manufacturers recommend a check of side clearance between connecting rods after the rods are installed. The check is made between rods on each crankshaft journal (Fig. 18-12). Incorrect side clearance indicates bent rods (§ 18-6).

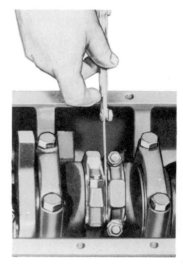

Fig. 18-12. Checking connecting-rod side clearance. *(Ford Division of Ford Motor Company)*

§ 18-6. CHECKING ROD ALIGNMENT Figure 18-13 is an exaggerated view showing the effects of a misaligned connecting rod. Heavy loading at points *A* and *B* on the bearing would cause bearing failure at these points. The heavy-pressure spots *C* and *D* on the piston will cause heavy wear and possibly scoring of the piston and cylinder wall. This is a basic inspection check recommended by engine manufacturers—that is to look for uneven wear or shiny spots on the pistons. If this condition is found, the piston, pin, and rod should all be replaced.

A rough check for rod alignment can be made by detaching the oil pan and watching the rod while the engine is cranked. If the rod moves back and forth on the piston pin, or is not centered,

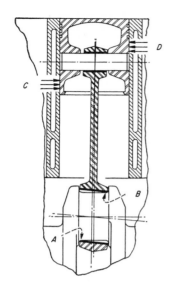

Fig. 18-13. Heavy-pressure areas caused by a bent rod. The bent condition is exaggerated. Areas of heavy pressure, (A, B, C, and D) will wear rapidly so that early failure will result. *(Federal-Mogul Service Division of Federal-Mogul-Bower Bearings, Incorporated)*

the rod is out of line. It should stay centered on the pin.

To check rod alignment out of the engine, reinstall the piston pin in the rod. Then mount the rod on the arbor of the special fixture by attaching the rod cap (Fig. 18-14). Put the V block over

FACE PLATE
V BLOCK
CLAMP SCREW
PISTON PIN
ARBOR

Fig. 18-14. Connecting-rod alignment fixture being used to check the alignment of a connecting rod. *(Chevrolet Motor Division of General Motors Corporation)*

the piston pin, and move it in against the faceplate. If the V block does not fit squarely against the faceplate, the rod is out of line. This same fixture can be used to check alignment of the rod-and-piston assembly before the rings are installed.

If the rod is out of line, check the crankpin for taper (§ 18-11). A tapered crankpin causes the rod to be subjected to bending stress.

Bent rods must be straightened or replaced. To straighten a rod, use a straightening bar inserted into the piston-pin hole. Bend the rod a little past straight and then back to straight again. This relieves stress set up by the bending process.

NOTE: Most engine manufacturers call for replacement of bent connecting rods. Their experience has shown that their rods, if bent, tend to take on a permanent set. Even if straightened, they may drift back to the permanent-set, or bent, condition.

§ 18-7. PISTON-PIN BUSHINGS IN RODS When the rod has a piston-pin bushing, check the fit of the pin. If the fit is correct, the pin will not drop through the bushing of its own weight when held vertical. It will require a light push to force it through. If the fit is too loose, the bushing should be reamed or honed for an oversize pin or else replaced. On some rods, the bushing cannot be replaced; if the bushing is so worn that it cannot be reamed or honed for an oversize pin, the complete rod must be replaced. On other rods, the worn bushings can be replaced and the new bushings reamed or honed to fit the present pins (if they are in good condition) or new standard-sized pins. Pins that are worn, pitted, or otherwise defective should be discarded. To replace a bushing, press out the old bushing in an arbor press. Burrs on the edges of the bushing bore in the rod should be removed with a hand scraper or tapered burring reamer. Then, a new bushing can be pressed in with an arbor press. A tapered mandrel should then be used to expand the edges of the bushing and thereby swage, or expand, them firmly in the rod. Make sure the oilholes in the bushing and rod align. Ream or hone the new bushing to size.

Some rods have two piston-pin bushings, separated a fraction of an inch to form an oil groove. On these, each bushing must be swaged into place with a burnishing tool (Fig. 18-15). To do this, install one bushing flush with the edge of the bore. Put the rod in the arbor press, bushing side down. Push the burnisher through. Install the second bushing, turn the rod over, and pass the burnisher

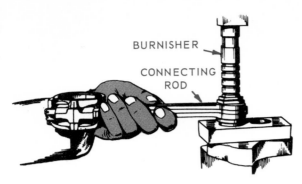

Fig. 18-15. Using a burnisher to burnish the piston-pin bushings in a connecting rod. *(Studebaker Corporation)*

through the first bushing and then through the second bushing. Ream or hone the bushings as necessary.

When reaming a set of bushings, proceed slowly on the first rod. Use an expansion reamer, and expand the reamer by easy stages, taking off a little metal each time. Try the pin fit after each reaming operation. This procedure guards against overreaming. Then, after the first rod is reamed, all others may be quickly reamed by reducing the reamer diameter about 0.0005 inch to rough-ream all the rods. Then expand the reamer to take the final cut. At this stage, check the pins with a micrometer so that any slight variation can be taken care of. Thus, if one pin is slightly larger than the others, the bushing into which it will fit can be reamed slightly larger to provide a good fit. This assures a good matching fit of pins to bushings.

To hone a set of bushings, follow the same two-step procedure. Rough-hone the bushings to within about 0.0005 inch of the proper size. Then change hone, and finish-hone to size. Check pins with a micrometer during finish-honing so that variations in pin size can be taken care of. Figure 18-16 shows a clamp to hold the connecting rod and the method of holding the rod and clamp during honing. The bushing should be moved from one end of the stone to the other and should not

Fig. 18-16. Connecting rod in a clamp, and method of holding the rod and clamp while honing, or grinding, the piston-pin bushing.

be held in one spot. However, the bushing should not be moved past the end of the stone, since this would wear the edges of the bushing bell-shaped.

NOTE: If oversize pins are used, piston bushings must be reamed or honed oversize (§ 18-13).

§ 18-8. CONNECTING-ROD BEARINGS Connecting-rod big-end bearings are of two types, direct-bonded and precision-insert (§ 6-13). Some adjustment is possible on the direct-bonded type (§ 18-10), but if this bearing is worn, the complete rod and cap must be replaced. The precision-insert type is not adjustable. However, this type of bearing can be replaced without difficulty provided the rod, crankpin, and other engine components are in good condition. Whenever a rod bearing fails, an analysis should be made so that the cause can be determined. Then the cause can be eliminated so that the failure will not be quickly repeated (see § 18-9).

§ 18-9. ANALYSIS OF BEARING FAILURES Types of bearing failure are discussed below.

1. Bearing failure due to lack of oil (A in Fig. 18-17). When insufficient oil flows to a bearing, actual metal-to-metal contact results. The bearing overheats, and the bearing metal melts or is wiped out of the bearing shell. Welds may form between the rotating journal and bearing shell. There is a chance that the engine will "throw a rod"; that is, the rod will "freeze" to the crankpin and break, and parts of the rod will go through the engine block. Oil starvation of a bearing could result from clogged oil lines, a defective oil pump or pressure regulator, or insufficient oil in the crankcase. Also, if other bearings have excessive clearance, they may pass all the oil from the pump so that some bearings are starved and thus fail.

2. Fatigue failure of bearings (B in Fig. 18-17). Repeated application of loads on a bearing will ultimately fatigue the bearing metal so that it starts to crack and flake out. Craters, or pockets, form in the bearing. As more and more of the metal is lost, the remainder is worked harder and fatigues at a faster rate. Ultimately, complete bearing failure occurs.

Fatigue failure seldom occurs under average operating conditions. However, certain special conditions will cause this type of failure. For instance, if a journal is worn out of round, the bearing will be overstressed with every crankshaft revolution.

OVERLAY WIPED OUT

A. LACK OF OIL

CRATERS OR POCKETS

B. FATIGUE FAILURE

SCRATCHES   DIRT EMBEDDED INTO BEARING MATERIAL

C. SCRATCHED BY DIRT

OVERLAY GONE FROM ENTIRE SURFACE

D. TAPERED JOURNAL

RADIUS RIDE

E. RADIUS RIDE

BRIGHT (POLISHED) SECTIONS

F. IMPROPER SEATING

Fig. 18–17. Types of engine-bearing failure. The appearance of a bearing usually indicated the cause of its failure. *(Ford Motor Company)*

Also, if the engine is idled or operated at low speed a good part of the time, the center part of the upper rod-bearing half will carry most of the load and will "fatigue out." On the other hand, if the engine is operated at maximum torque with wide-open throttle (that is, if the engine is "lugged"), then most or all of the upper bearing half will fatigue out. High-speed operation tends to cause fatigue failure of the lower bearing half.

3. Bearing scratched by dirt in the oil (C in Fig. 18–17). The property of embeddability (§ 6–14) enables a bearing to protect itself by allowing particles to embed so that they will not gouge out bearing material or scratch the rotating journal. Figure 18–18 shows, in exaggerated view, what happens when a particle embeds. The metal is

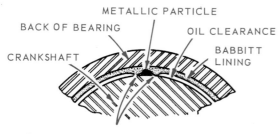

METALLIC PARTICLE

BACK OF BEARING

OIL CLEARANCE

CRANKSHAFT

BABBITT LINING

BABBITT DISPLACED BY PARTICLE AND RAISED UP AROUND IT, GREATLY REDUCING OR DESTROYING THE OIL CLEARANCE LOCALLY.

Fig. 18–18. Effect of a metallic particle embedded in bearing metal (the babbitt lining). *(Federal-Mogul Service Division of Federal-Mogul-Bower Bearings, Incorporated)*

pushed up around the particle, reducing oil clearance in the area. Usually the metal can flow outward enough to restore adequate oil clearance. However, if the dirt particles are too large, they will not embed completely and will be carried with the rotating journal, gouging out scratches in the bearing. Also, if the oil is very dirty, the bearing will become overloaded with particles. In either case, bearing failure will soon occur.

4. Bearing failure due to tapered journal (D in Fig. 18–17). If the journal is tapered, one side of the bearing will carry most or all of the load. This side will overheat and lose its bearing metal. Do not confuse this type of failure with the failure that would result from a bent connecting rod. With a tapered journal, both bearing halves will fail on the same side. With a bent rod, failure will be on opposite sides (*A* and *B* in Fig. 18–13).

5. Bearing failure from radii ride (E in Fig. 18–17). If the journal-to-crank-cheek radius is not cut away sufficiently, the edge of the bearing will ride on this radius. This would cause cramming of the bearing, possibly poor seating, rapid fatigue, and early failure. This trouble would be most likely to occur after a crankshaft-grind job during which the radii were not sufficiently relieved.

6. Bearing failure from poor seating in bore (F in Fig. 18–17). Poor seating of the bearing shell in the bore will cause local high spots where oil clearances will be too low. Figure 18–19 shows, in exaggerated view, what happens when particles of dirt are left between the bearing shell and the

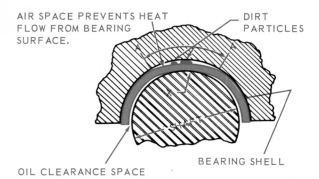

AIR SPACE PREVENTS HEAT FLOW FROM BEARING SURFACE.

DIRT PARTICLES

OIL CLEARANCE SPACE

BEARING SHELL

Fig. 18-19. Effect of dirt particles under the bearing shell due to poor installation. *(Federal-Mogul Service Division of Federal-Mogul-Bower Bearings, Incorporated)*

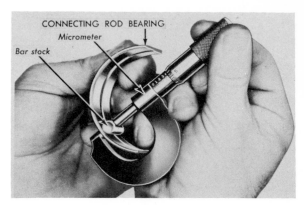

CONNECTING ROD BEARING

Micrometer

Bar stock

Fig. 18-20. Using a micrometer and finished bar stock to measure the thickness of a bearing and thereby determine the amount of wear.

counterbore. Not only does this reduce oil clearance (as at *X*) but, also, an air space exists which prevents proper cooling of the bearing. The combination can lead to quick bearing failure.

7. Bearing failure from ridging. Crankpin ridging, or "camming," may cause failure of a partial-oil-groove type of replacement bearing which has been installed without removal of the ridge. The ridge forms on the crankpin as a result of uneven wear between the part of the crankpin in contact with the partial oil groove and the part that runs on the solid bearing. The original bearing wears to conform to this ridge. However, when a new bearing is installed, the center zone may be overloaded (at the ridge) and may soon fail. A ridge so slight that it can scarcely be detected (except with a carefully used micrometer) may be sufficient to cause this sort of failure. Failures of this sort have been reported in engines having ridges of less than 0.001 inch.

§ 18-10. CHECKING CONNECTING-ROD-BEARING FIT
Precision-insert bearings are checked in one way, the direct-bonded type in another, as noted below.

● **CAUTION:** Before installing new bearings, the crankpins should always be checked for taper or out-of-roundness (§ 18-11).

1. Precision-insert bearings. Fit of these bearings can be checked in any of three ways: with Plastigage, feeler stock, or micrometer and telescope gauge. Also, the amount of bearing wear can be checked with a micrometer and a piece of round bar stock (Fig. 18-20). There is also

available a ball micrometer which has a rounded spindle end. This permits direct measurement of curved surfaces, such as on the bearing shell.

a. Plastigage. Plastigage is a plastic material that comes in strips and flattens when pressure is applied to it. A strip of the material is put into the bearing cap, the cap is installed, and the rod nuts are tightened to the specified tension. Then, the cap is removed, and the amount of flattening is measured. If the Plastigage is flattened only a little, then oil clearances are large. If it is flattened considerably, oil clearances are small. Actual clearance is measured with a special scale supplied with the Plastigage (Fig. 18-21).

The bearing cap and crankpin should be wiped clean of oil before the Plastigage is used and the crankshaft turned so that the crankpin is about

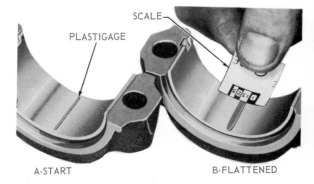

SCALE

PLASTIGAGE

A-START

B-FLATTENED

Fig. 18-21. Bearing clearance being checked with Plastigage. (Left) Plastigage in place before tightening the cap. (Right) Measuring the amount of flattening (or bearing clearance) with a scale. *(Buick Motor Division of General Motors Corporation)*

30 degrees back of BDC (bottom dead center). Do not move the crankshaft while the cap nuts are tight. This would further flatten the Plastigage and throw off the clearance measurement.

b. Feeler stock. Lubricate a strip of feeler stock, and lay it lengthwise in the center of the bearing cap. Install the cap, and tighten cap nuts lightly. Note the ease with which the rod can be moved endwise on the crankpin. If the rod moves easily, tighten the nuts a little more and recheck. Repeat the procedure until the nuts have been drawn down to the specified tightness or until the rod tightens up on the crankpin. If the rod tightens up, the clearance is less than the thickness of the feeler stock. If the rod does not tighten up, the clearance is greater than the thickness of the feeler stock. With the latter condition, lay an additional strip of feeler stock on top of the first and repeat the checking procedure. If the rod still does not tighten up, keep adding feeler stock until the actual bearing clearance is determined. Excessive clearance requires bearing replacement (§ 18–11).

c. Micrometer and telescope gauge. Check the crankpin diameter with a micrometer. Check the bearing diameter (cap in place) with a telescope gauge and micrometer (or an inside micrometer). The two diameters can then be compared to determine the difference, or bearing clearance. At the same time, the crankpin can be checked for taper or eccentric wear. Measure the diameter at several places along the crankpin (to check for taper) and also around the crankpin (to check for eccentricity, or out-of-roundness).

2. Direct-bonded connecting-rod bearings. On these, adjustment is made by installation or removal of shims under the cap. Shims are thin strips of copper or similar metal. Shims placed between the cap and rod (at the bolt bosses) hold the cap away from the rod when the nuts are tightened. This increases the bearing clearance. Clearance can be checked with a micrometer and telescope gauge, as noted above. It can also be checked by attempting to snap the rod back and forth on the crankpin with one hand. If the rod moves easily, take off the rod cap and remove one shim only from each side of the cap. Replace the cap and try to move the rod. If the rod still moves easily, take off another pair of shims. Repeat this procedure until the rod will not move. Then add one shim to each side of the cap, replace and tighten cap, and retest.

If the bearing is worn, pitted, scored, chipped, or otherwise damaged, replace the rod and cap as a unit. Rebabbitting of this type of rod should not be attempted in the field, since special equipment is required to do this job.

§ 18–11. INSTALLING PRECISION ROD BEARINGS New precision connecting-rod bearings are required if the old ones are defective (§ 18–9) or have worn so much that clearances are excessive. They are also required if the crankpins have worn out of round or tapered so much that they have to be reground. In this case, new undersize bearings are required. In addition, it is the usual practice of engine rebuilders to replace the bearings in an engine when it is torn down, regardless of whether or not the old bearings are in bad condition. Their reasoning is that it costs little more to put in new bearings when the engine is torn down for rebuilding. However, if the engine had to be torn down especially for bearing installation, the cost would be high. They believe it is cheaper insurance against failure to install new bearings during the engine-rebuilding job.

1. Checking crankpins. Crankpins should always be checked with a micrometer for taper or eccentricity. If crankpins are out of round or tapered more than 0.0015 inch, the crankshaft must be replaced or the crankpins reground (§ 19–9). Bearings working against taper or out-of-roundness of more than 0.0015 inch will not last long. And when bearings go, there is the chance that the engine will be severely damaged. Measurements should be taken in several places along the crankpin to check for taper. Diameter should be checked all the way around for out-of-roundness.

2. Taper shim bearing adjuster. If the crankpins are not excessively out of round or tapered, yet there is excessive clearance, new bearings should be installed. Sometimes, however, the new bearings will not reduce clearances to specified limits (because of crankpin wear). This calls for crankpin grinding and installation of new undersize bearings. There is, however, a compromise repair that can be made in case the value of the car does not warrant the more expensive but correct (from the engineering standpoint) crankpin-regrind and new-bearing job. This compromise involves the use of taper shim bearing adjusters (Fig. 18–22) under the bearing shells. The adjusters come in different thicknesses. The correct thickness must be selected for each bearing to provide the proper clearance at that bearing. Note that the adjuster is tapered from the center to half thickness at the ends. The adjuster shown, for example, is

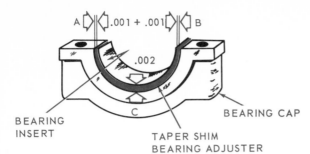

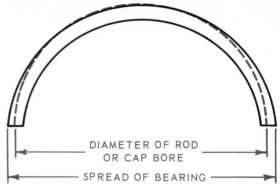

Fig. 18-23. Bearing spread.

Fig. 18-22. Taper shim bearing adjuster. The thickness of the taper shim is exaggerated. *(Perfect Circle Company)*

0.002 inch thick at the center (*C*) but only 0.001 inch thick at the ends (*A* and *B*). This provides the same correction of clearance at the ends as at the center of the bearing shell (that is, $A + B = C$).

● **CAUTION:** This is not a recommended repair procedure but is a relatively inexpensive way to get some added mileage out of an old car. It should never be used in a late-model car, since the small saving achieved is not worth the risk of subsequent bearing and engine failure.

3. Installing new bearings. When new bearings are to be installed, make sure that your hands, the workbench, your tools, and all engine parts are clean. Keep the new bearings wrapped up until you are ready to install them. Then handle them carefully, wiping each with a fresh piece of cleaning tissue just before installing it. Be very sure that the bores in the cap and rod are clean and not excessively out of round.* Then put the bearing shells in place. If they have locking tangs, make sure that the tangs enter the notches provided in the rod and cap. Note comments about bearing spread and crush, below. Check clearance after installation (§ 18-10).

● **CAUTION:** Do not attempt to correct clearance by filing the rod cap. This destroys the original relationship between cap and rod and will lead to early bearing failure.

4. Bearing spread. Bearing shells are usually manufactured with "spread," that is, with the shell

---

* Some manufacturers recommend a check of bore symmetry with the bearing shells out. The cap should be attached with nuts drawn up to specified tension. Then a telescope gauge and micrometer or a special out-of-round gauge can be used to check the bore.

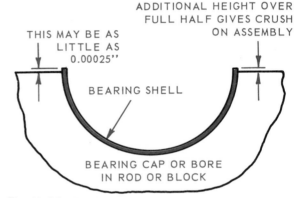

Fig. 18-24. Bearing crush.

Fig. 18-25. Ring removing and replacing tool in use. *(Aircraft Specialties, Incorporated)*

diameter somewhat greater than the diameter of the rod cap or rod bore into which the shell will fit (Fig. 18-23). When the shell is installed into the cap or rod, it will snap into place and will hold its seat during subsequent assembling operations.

5. Bearing crush. In order to make sure that the bearing shell will "snug down" into its bore in the rod cap or rod when the cap is installed, the bearings have "crush" (Fig. 18-24); that is, they are manufactured to have some additional height over a full half. This additional height must be crushed down when the cap is installed. Crushing down the additional amount forces the shells into the bores in the cap and rod, assuring firm seating and snug contact with the bores.

● **CAUTION:** Never file off the edges of the bearing shells in an attempt to remove crush. When you select the proper bearings for an engine (as recommended by the engine manufacturer), you will find that they have the correct crush. Precision-insert bearings must not be tampered with in any way in an attempt to make them "fit better." This will usually lead only to rapid bearing failure.

PISTONS AND RINGS

§ 18–12. PISTON SERVICE After the piston-and-connecting-rod assemblies have been removed from the engine and the pistons and rods separated (§§ 18–2 to 18–5), the rings should be removed from the piston (Fig. 18–25). (The rings can be removed from the piston before the piston and rod are separated.) A special ring tool is required for ring removal. The tool has two small claws that catch under the ends of the ring. Then, when pressure is applied to the tool handles, the ring is sprung enough that it can be lifted out of the ring groove and off the piston. Examine the rings as explained in § 18–15.

1. Piston cleaning. Remove carbon and varnish from piston surfaces. Do not use a caustic cleaning solution or a wire brush! These could damage the piston-skirt finish. Use solvent to remove deposits. Clean out ring grooves with a clean-out

Fig. 18–26. Groove-cleanout tool in use on piston-ring grooves. *(Ford Motor Company)*

Fig. 18–27. Using a micrometer to measure piston diameter. *(Pontiac Motor Division of General Motors Corporation)*

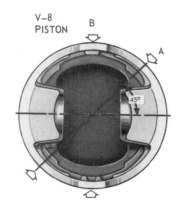

V–8 PISTON

B

A

45°

THE ELLIPTICAL SHAPE OF THE PISTON SKIRT SHOULD BE .008 TO .010 INCH FOR 273 CUBIC INCH AND .010 TO .013 INCH FOR 318 CUBIC INCH LESS AT DIAMETER (A) THAN ACROSS THE THRUST FACES AT DIAMETER (B).

.027 TO .035 IN. LESS THAN DIAMETER AT (C)

C

D

273 CUBIC INCH DIAMETER (D) SHOULD BE .0005 INCH LARGER THAN (C)

318 CUBIC INCH DIAMETERS AT (C) AND (D) SHOULD BE EQUAL ± .0005 INCH

Fig. 18–28. Piston measurements. On these Plymouth pistons, measurements should be within specifications shown. *(Chrysler-Plymouth Division of Chrysler Motors Corporation)*

tool (Fig. 18–26). Oil ring slots, or holes, must be clean; a drill of the proper size is handy for this job. Be sure that you do not remove metal when cleaning ring grooves or oil slots.

2. *Piston inspection.* Examine the pistons carefully for worn, scuffed, or scored skirts and for cracks at the ring lands, skirts, ring bosses, and heads. Defects such as excessive wear, scuffs, scores, or cracks require piston replacement. Check piston-pin bushings for wear and service then if required (§ 18–13). Also, check fit of piston rings in grooves (§ 18–16).

Check the piston with a micrometer (Fig. 18–27). Some manufacturers specify taking various measurements (Fig. 18–28). Others specify taking the measurements perpendicular to the piston-pin bore at the sizing point (Fig. 18–29) and parallel to the piston-pin bore.

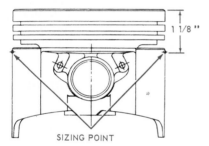

Fig. 18–29. Piston sizing point. *(Pontiac Motor Division of General Motors Corporation)*

Fig. 18–30. Taking cylinder measurement with dial indicator. Once the reading is taken, the dial should be set at zero and the reading measured with a micrometer (see next illustration). *(Pontiac Motor Division of General Motors Corporation)*

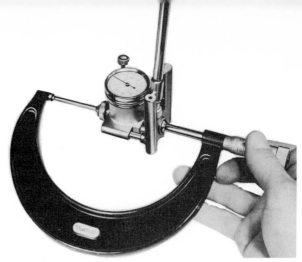

Fig. 18–31. Measuring the dial indicator reading with a micrometer. *(Pontiac Motor Division of General Motors Corporation)*

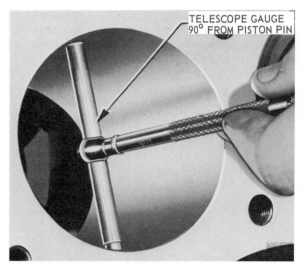

Fig. 18–32. Checking cylinder diameter with a telescope gauge. *(Buick Motor Division of General Motors Corporation)*

Compare the sizing-point reading with the measurement of the cylinder diameter taken with an inside micrometer, an outside micrometer and a dial indicator (Figs. 18–30 and 18–31), or a telescope gauge and a micrometer (Figs. 18–32 and 18–33). If the cylinder wall is excessively worn, it will require refinishing (§§ 19–15 to 19–18). Cylinder wall refinishing means that an oversize piston will be required.

NOTE: Prior to the introduction of the modern piston, the fitting process was more complicated. For instance, Ford specified the use of a piece of

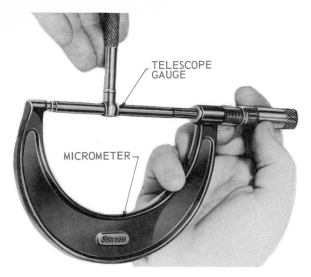

Fig. 18–33. Measuring setting of telescope gauge, which is cylinder diameter. *(Buick Motor Division of General Motors Corporation)*

feeler stock placed between the piston and cylinder, with the piston pushed down into the cylinder, upside down. The amount of pull to pull the feeler stock out was then measured. If it was too little, the fit was too loose.

3. *Piston resizing.* Resizing of modern pistons is not recommended by the automotive manufacturers. On earlier, full-skirt pistons, it was possible to resize them so as to make the skirt somewhat larger and thus reduce the clearance between the skirt and cylinder wall to normal. One resizer is shown in Fig. 18–34. It has a pair of rollers that applies pressure to the skirt as it is moved back and forth. This squeezes the metal and expands the skirt. In addition to this type of tool, there are

Fig. 18–34. Simple type of piston resizer. Pressure between the inner and the outer roller wheels squeezes the metal and expands the skirt. *(Sealed Power Corporation)*

piston-skirt expanders that can be inserted in the piston. These devices spring-load the skirt from the inside and thus increase the skirt diameter slightly.

4. *New pistons.* New pistons are supplied either finished or semifinished. The finished type, ready for installation, is available in a number of sizes. When these are used, the cylinders must be finished to fit the pistons. As a rule, engine manufacturers supply oversize pistons of the same weight as the standard pistons. Thus, it is not necessary to replace all pistons when only part of the cylinders require service. There is no problem of balance if all pistons are of the same weight, even if some are oversize. Semifinished pistons are oversize and must be finished down to size to fit the cylinders.

● **CAUTION:** Finished pistons usually have a special finish and must not be turned down or finished to a smaller size. This would remove the finish and probably cause rapid piston wear after installation.

§ 18–13. FITTING PISTON PINS IN PISTON If the piston-pin bushings are worn, they should be reamed or honed oversize (Fig. 18–35) and oversize pins installed. The pins should be replaced

Fig. 18–35. Piston-pin bushings being honed. *(Sunnen Products Company)*

297

if they are worn or pitted. The reaming and honing procedures are very similar to those used on connecting-rod piston-pin bushings (§ 18–7). When the pin is of the type that is free in the bushing, fit is correct if the pin will pass through with light thumb pressure when both piston and pin are at room temperature. When the pin is a press fit, it is forced into place under pressure. Another method is to heat the piston and then install the pin with a pilot tool. Some pistons have a locking bolt for locking the pin in the piston after it is installed.

§ 18–14. ROD AND PISTON ALIGNMENT After the rod and piston have been reassembled, but before the rings are installed on the piston, rod and piston alignment should be checked. The alignment tool shown in Fig. 18–14 is used for this check. If the V block does not line up with the face plate as the piston is moved to various positions, the connecting rod is twisted.

§ 18–15. PISTON-RING SERVICE If an engine is torn down for overhaul after considerable mileage, the chances are that the rings will require replacement. Sometimes, all that is required is to free up the rings in the ring grooves by cleaning out carbon. Special compounds that can be introduced into the intake manifold and engine oil to help free the rings without tearing down the engine have already been mentioned (§ 17–3).

In examining rings to determine whether or not they should be reused, several conditions may be found. Conditions requiring ring replacement include loss of tension, irregular light and dark areas (showing uneven wear caused by warped or worn rings), and scores or scratches.

Proper selection of new rings depends on the condition of the cylinder walls and whether or not they are to be reconditioned. Article 19–14 describes the checking of cylinder walls for wear and taper. If they are only slightly tapered or out of round (consult manufacturer's specifications for maximum allowable deviations), then standard-type rings can be installed. Where the walls have some taper, but not enough to warrant the extra expense of a rebore or hone job, special "severe," or "drastic," rings should be used. These rings have greater tension and are more flexible. This enables them to expand and contract as they move up and down in the cylinder. Thus, they follow the changing contours of the cylinder wall and provide adequate sealing (preventing blow-by) and

Fig. 18–36. Disassembled view of one type of replacement piston rings: (1) top compression ring; (2) second compression ring, which includes an expander ring; (3) upper oil-control ring; (4) lower oil-control ring. The last has a three-part construction; it consists of an upper and lower rail with an expanding spring. *(Chrysler-Plymouth Division of Chrysler Motors Corporation)*

oil control. Figure 18–36 shows a set of replacement rings for tapered cylinder walls.

The pistons of some engines have an extra piston groove cut at the lower end. When walls wear tapered, an extra oil-control ring can be fitted into this groove to improve oil control.

Automotive manufacturers generally recommend honing the cylinder walls lightly (§ 19–16) before ring installation to "break the glaze." Cylinder walls take on a hard, smooth glaze after the engine has been in use for a while. It is the practice of some engine servicemen to knock off this glaze by running a hone up and down the cylinder a few times before putting in new rings. However, at least one ring manufacturer says this does not need to be done on cast-iron cylinder walls, *provided the walls are not wavy or scuffed.* The glaze is a good antiscuff material and will not unduly retard the wear-in of new rings if the walls are reasonably concentric and in relatively good condition.

The best honing job leaves a cross-hatch pattern (Fig. 18–37) with hone marks intersecting at a 60-degree angle, as shown. This leaves the best surface for proper seating of new rings. See § 19–16 on honing procedures.

§ 18–16. FITTING PISTON RINGS Piston rings must be fitted to the cylinder and to the ring grooves in the piston. As a first step, the ring should be

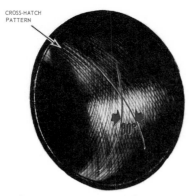

CROSS-HATCH
PATTERN

Fig. 18-37. Cross-hatch pattern left on a cylinder wall after a good honing job. *(Chrysler-Plymouth Division of Chrysler Motors Corporation)*

pushed down into the cylinder with a piston and the ring gap (space between ends of the ring) checked with a feeler gauge (Fig. 18-38). If the ring gap is too small, try a slightly smaller ring, which will have a larger gap. On earlier engines, the recommendation was to file the ends of the

ring with a fine-cut file. The file was clamped into a vise and the ring worked back and forth on the file (with the ring ends on the two sides of the file). Many manufacturers' shop manuals no longer carry instructions for filing rings.

● **CAUTION:** If the cylinder is worn tapered, the diameter at the lower limit of ring travel (in the assembled engine) will be smaller than the diameter at the top (Fig. 19-14). In this type of cylinder, *the ring must be fitted to the diameter at the lower limit of ring travel.* If fitted to the upper part of the cylinder, the ring gap will not be great enough as the ring is moved down to its lower limit of travel. This means that the ring ends will come together and the ring will be broken or the cylinder walls scuffed. In tapered cylinders, measure the ring gap with the ring at the point of minimum diameter, or at the lower limit of ring travel.

After the ring gap has been found to be correct, the outside surface of the ring should be inserted into the proper ring groove in the piston and the ring rolled around in the groove to make sure that the ring has a free fit around the entire piston circumference (Fig. 18-39). An excessively tight

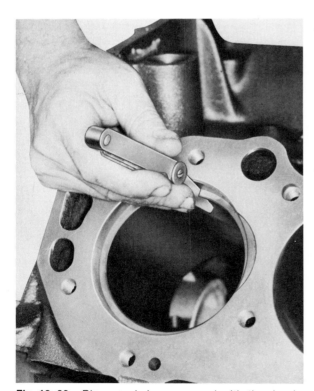

Fig. 18-38. Ring gap being measured with the ring in the cylinder. *(Chevrolet Motor Division of General Motors Corporation)*

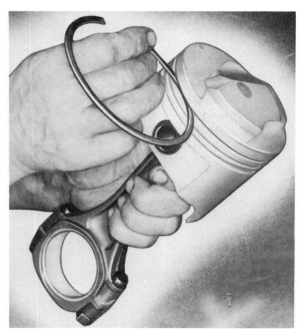

Fig. 18-39. Checking the fit of the ring in the ring groove. *(Chevrolet Motor Division of General Motors Corporation)*

Fig. 18–40. Piston-ring clearance being checked with a gauge. *(Chevrolet Motor Division of General Motors Corporation)*

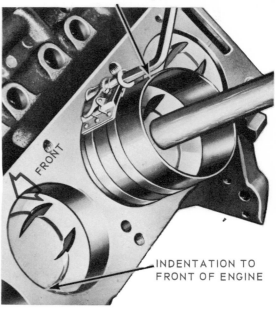

FRONT

INDENTATION TO FRONT OF ENGINE

Fig. 18–41. Using a piston-ring compressor tool to install a piston with rings. *(Chevrolet Motor Division of General Motors Corporation)*

fit probably means that the ring groove is dirty, and it should be cleaned (Fig. 18–26). After the rings are installed in the ring groove (by using the ring tool as shown in Fig. 18–25), fit should again be tested. This test is made by inserting a feeler gauge between the ring and the side of the groove (Fig. 18–40).

§ 18–17. INSTALLING PISTON IN CYLINDER To install the piston in the cylinder after the piston, rings, and rod are reassembled, it is necessary to compress the rings in their grooves so that they will enter the cylinder. A piston-ring compressor

(Fig. 18–41) can be used for this operation. The compressor clamps around the rings, compressing them into their grooves so that the piston-and-ring assembly can be pushed into the cylinder. Also, be sure to use the guide sleeve and rod replacement tool to protect the crankshaft crank journals. (See § 18–5, item 4, for replacement procedure of rod-and-piston assemblies.)

● **CAUTION:** Be sure to install pistons facing in the right direction. Many pistons have a notch or other marking that must face to the front of the engine.

Review Questions

1. Explain how to use the bearing oil-leak detector.
2. What is the first step in piston and rod removal when removal is to be made from the top of the engine?
3. What is a ring ridge, and how is it caused? What would be likely to happen if the piston were taken out from the top of the engine before the ring ridge was removed?
4. Explain how to remove and replace piston-and-rod assemblies.
5. How is connecting-rod alignment checked?
6. Explain how to check, replace, and ream or hone a set of piston-pin bushings.
7. Describe different types of bearing failure and their causes.
8. Describe checking of rod-bearing clearance on precision-insert-type bearings.
9. Describe the adjustment of direct-babbitted rod bearings.
10. Explain how to install new rod bearings.
11. What is bearing spread? What is bearing crush?
12. What is a taper shim bearing adjuster?
13. When are oversize pistons required in an engine?
14. Why is it desirable to use a piston vise for piston work?
15. How is the fit of the piston in the cylinder checked?
16. What is piston resizing? How is it done?
17. Describe the procedure of fitting piston rings.
18. Describe the procedure of installing a piston in a cylinder.
19. On what does the selection of new piston rings depend?

Study Questions

1. Refer to the shop manual on a car using precision rod big-end bearings, and write a sequence story on installing new bearings.
2. Make a list of the steps required in the removal of piston and connecting-rod assemblies from the top of the cylinder block.
3. Refer to a car-shop manual to find the procedure for selecting piston rings. Write a story on how this is done.
4. Write a sequence story telling about removing, servicing, and replacing piston-and-rod assemblies.

19

Engine Service — Crankshaft and Engine Block

This chapter concludes the discussion of engine service and describes the servicing of crankshafts, main bearings, and engine blocks and cylinders.

CRANKSHAFT AND MAIN BEARINGS

§ 19-1. CRANKSHAFT AND BEARING SERVICE

Most modern automotive engines have precision-insert-type main bearings which can be replaced without removing the crankshaft. Many bearing difficulties can be taken care of by this method of bearing replacement. However, if the bearing problem has been caused by such conditions as a warped engine block, stopped-up oil passages, a worn crankshaft journal, or a bent crankshaft, then simply replacing the bearings will not correct the condition. Such conditions as these will cause uneven bearing wear, with some bearings wearing faster (and more unevenly) than others. See § 18-9 on causes of bearing failure.

If the bearings seem to have worn fairly uniformly, then the chances are that only crankshaft-journal checks and bearing replacement will be required. Use of the bearing oil-leak detector (§ 18-1) will determine whether or not bearing wear has been uneven.

If bearing wear is uneven, then the safest procedure is to remove the crankshaft from the engine block and check both separately for alignment (§§ 19-9 and 19-11) and for clogged oil passages.

Replacing precision-insert main bearings without removing the crankshaft requires about 5 hours. Removing and replacing the crankshaft requires several additional hours.

Semifinished main bearings (§ 6-13) require finishing and fitting after installation, so that the crankshaft must be taken out. To perform the complete replacement job on semifinished main bearings requires about 19 to 22 hours.

§ 19-2. CHECKING CRANKSHAFT JOURNALS

Both the crankpins and the crankshaft main journals should be checked whenever the bearings are removed. Checking crankpins has already been discussed (§ 18-11, item 1). Journals can be checked on the engine with a special crankshaft gauge or with a special micrometer. Measurements should be taken in several places along the journal to check for taper. Also, the crankshaft should be rotated by quarter or eighth turns to check for out-of-round wear. (See § 18-9 for discussions of what a tapered, ridged, or out-of-round journal does to a bearing.) If journals are tapered or out of round by more than 0.003 inch, they should be reground (§ 19-9). As a matter of fact, some authorities consider 0.0015 inch the outside tolerable limit; they point out that *any* appreciable eccentricity or taper will shorten bearing life.

To check journals, remove the oil pan (§ 18-4) and bearing caps. It is not necessary to detach the connecting rods from the crankshaft, but the spark plugs should be removed so that the engine can be turned over easily.

1. Removing bearing caps. Remove only one bearing cap at a time if journals and bearings are being checked. Remove all caps if the crankshaft is to come out of the engine. Caps should be marked so that they can be replaced on the same journals from which they were removed. To remove a cap, loosen the nuts or bolts. Cut the lock wire (if used), or bend back the lock-washer tangs (if used). Also, disconnect the oil lines where necessary.

NOTE: Use new lock washers or lock wires on reassembly.

If the cap sticks, work it loose carefully to avoid distorting it. In some engines, a bearing-cap puller can be used; the puller bolt is screwed into the oil-coupling hole. In other engines, a screwdriver or pry bar can be used to work the cap loose. Sometimes tapping the cap lightly on one side and then on the other with a brass hammer will loosen it.

● **CAUTION:** Heavy hammering or prying will distort the cap, bend the dowel pins, or damage the dowel holes. In such a case, the bearing may not fit when the cap is replaced, and early bearing failure will occur.

2. Measuring journal with special crankshaft gauge. The special gauge (Fig. 19–1) is used as shown in Fig. 19–2. The journal and the gauge pads and plunger must be clean. Then, the plunger is retracted, the gauge held tightly against the journal (Fig. 19–2), and the plunger released so that it contacts the journal. The plunger is then locked in this position by tightening the thumbscrew. Finally, a micrometer is used to measure the distance between *D*, or the end of the plunger, and *C*, or the button on the bottom of the gauge. This measurement, multiplied by 2, is the diameter of the journal.

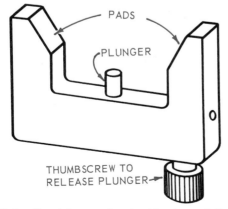

Fig. 19–1. Special gauge for checking journal diameter. (*Federal-Mogul Service Division of Federal-Mogul-Bower Bearings, Incorporated*)

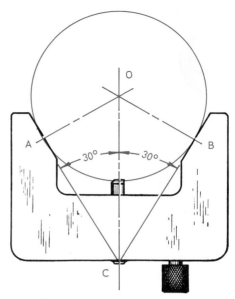

Fig. 19–2. Using a gauge to check journal diameter. (*Federal-Mogul Service Division of Federal-Mogul-Bower Bearings, Incorporated*)

3. Measuring journal with micrometer. To use the micrometer, the upper bearing half must be removed. If it is the precision-insert type, this can be done with a special "roll-out" tool, as explained in § 19–5. Then the micrometer can be used as shown in Fig. 19–3.

§ 19–3. CHECKING MAIN BEARINGS Main, or crankshaft, bearings are of two types, precision-insert and semifinished. They should be replaced if they are worn, burned, scored, pitted, rough, flaked, cracked, or otherwise damaged. (See § 18–9 on bearing failures.) It is very important to check the crankshaft journals (§ 19–2) before installing new bearings; if the journals are not in good condition, the new bearings may soon fail. Also, if bearing wear is uneven, and if part of the bearings are damaged or badly worn, then the possibility of a warped block, bent crankshaft, or clogged oil passages should be considered (see § 19–1). A compromise repair using taper shim bearing adjusters (§ 18–11) can be made where journals and bearings are in good condition but have too much clearance. Following articles describe checking of bearing fit, replacement of bearings, and servicing of crankshafts.

§ 19–4. CHECKING MAIN-BEARING FIT Bearing fit (or oil clearance) should always be checked

303

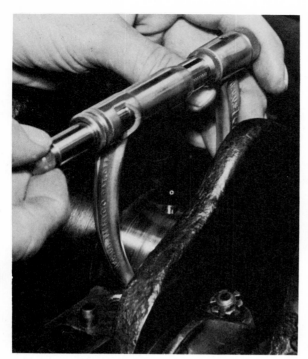

Fig. 19-3. Crankshaft-journal diameter being measured with a special micrometer.

after new bearings are installed. The fit should also be checked at other times when the condition of the bearings is being determined. Crankshaft-journal condition should also be checked at the same time.

1. Precision-insert type. Bearing clearance can be checked with feeler stock or Plastigage.

a. With feeler stock. Put a piece of feeler stock of the right size and thickness in the bearing cap after the cap has been removed (Fig. 19-4). Coat the feeler stock lightly with oil. Replace the cap, and tighten the cap nuts or bolts to the specified tension. Note the ease with which the crankshaft can be turned.

● **CAUTION:** Do not attempt to rotate the crankshaft, as this could damage the bearing. Instead, see whether it will turn about an inch in one direction or the other.

If the crankshaft is locked or drags noticeably, the bearing clearance is less than the thickness of the feeler stock. If it does not, an additional thickness of feeler stock should be placed on top of the first and the ease of crankshaft movement again checked. Clearance normally should be

Fig. 19-4. Main-bearing clearance being checked with a shim, or feeler stock. *(Dodge Division of Chrysler Motors Corporation)*

Fig. 19-5. Plastigage strip in place for bearing-clearance check. *(Chevrolet Motor Division of General Motors Corporation)*

about 0.002 inch (see the engine manufacturer's specifications for exact clearance).

b. With Plastigage. Wipe the journal and the bearing clean of oil. Put a strip of Plastigage lengthwise in the center of the journal (Fig. 19-5); replace and tighten the cap. Then remove the cap, and measure the amount the Plastigage has been flattened (Fig. 19-6). Do not turn the crankshaft with the Plastigage in place. (See § 18-10 for more detailed information on Plastigage.)

● **CAUTION:** The crankshaft must be supported so that its weight will not cause it to sag

304

Fig. 19-6. Checking flattening of Plastigage to determine bearing clearance. *(Chevrolet Motor Division of General Motors Corporation)*

and result in an incorrect measurement. One way to do this is to position a small jack under the crankshaft so that it bears against the counterweight next to the bearing being checked. Another method is to put shims in the bearing caps of the two adjacent main bearings and then tighten the cap bolts. This lifts and supports the crankshaft. Of course, if the engine is off the car and inverted, this is not necessary.

2. Semifitted (shim-adjusted) main bearings. Loosen all bearing caps just enough to permit the crankshaft to turn freely. Take off the rear main-bearing cap, and remove one shim from each side of the cap. Replace and tighten the cap bolts or nuts to the specified tension. Rotate the crankshaft to see whether it now drags. If it does not drag, remove additional shims (in pairs), and check for drag after each pair is removed. When a drag is felt, replace one shim on each side of the cap. If the crankshaft now turns freely when the cap is tightened, the clearance is correct. Loosen the cap bolts or nuts. Go to the next bearing, and adjust its clearance in the same way. Finally, when all bearings are adjusted, tighten all cap bolts or nuts to the proper tension, and recheck for crankshaft drag as it is turned. If it drags, then recheck and readjust the bearings.

3. Checking crankshaft end play. Crankshaft end play will become excessive if the end-thrust bearings are worn. This produces a noticeably sharp, irregular knock. If the wear is considerable, the knock will occur every time the clutch is released

and applied; this action causes sudden endwise movements of the crankshaft. Check end play by forcing the crankshaft endwise as far as it will go and then measuring the clearance at the end-thrust bearing with a feeler gauge (Fig. 19-7). Consult the engine manufacturer's shop manual for allowable end play.

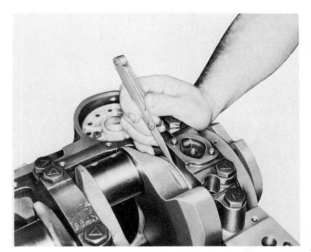

Fig. 19-7. Crankshaft end play being checked at end-thrust bearing with a feeler gauge. *(Chevrolet Motor Division of General Motors Corporation)*

§ 19-5. REPLACING PRECISION MAIN BEARINGS Before replacing bearings, crankshaft journals should be checked (§ 19-2). Also, after bearings are installed, bearing fit should be checked (§ 19-4). Precision-insert main bearings can be replaced without removing the crankshaft. However, some authorities do not advocate this. They say that you are working blind. You cannot be sure that the counterbore in the cylinder block is perfectly clean and that the shell is seating tightly. Furthermore, neither the crankshaft nor the block can be checked for alignment. As previously noted (§ 19-1), with uneven bearing wear the crankshaft should be removed for further checking.

To install a precision-insert main bearing without removing the crankshaft, use a special roll-out tool as shown in Fig. 19-8. The tool is inserted into the oilhole in the crankshaft journal, as shown. Then, the crankshaft is rotated. The tool forces the bearing shell to rotate with the crankshaft so that it is turned out of the bore. The crankshaft must be rotated in the proper direction so that

305

Fig. 19–8. Removing and installing upper main bearing. The crankshaft journal is shown partly cut away so that the tool can be seen inserted into the oil hole in the journal. *(Chrysler-Plymouth Division of Chrysler Motors Corporation)*

the lock, or tang, in the bearing is raised up out of the notch in the cylinder block.

To install a new bearing half, coat it with engine oil. Make sure that the bore, or bearing seat, in the block is clean. Do not file the edges of the shell (this would remove its crush). Use the tool as shown in Fig. 19–8 to slide the bearing shell into place. Make sure that the tang on the bearing shell seats in the notch in the block. Then place a new bearing shell in the cap. Install the cap, and tighten the cap bolts or nuts to the specified tension. Tap the crown of the cap lightly with a brass hammer while tightening it. This helps to align the bearings properly. After all bearings are in place, check bearing fit.

Some crankshaft journals have no oil hole. For example, the rear main journal of many in-line engines does not. To remove and replace the upper bearing half on these, first start the bearing half with a small pin punch and hammer. Then use a pair of pliers with taped jaws to hold the bearing half against the oil slinger and rotate the crankshaft (Fig. 19–9). This will pull the old bearing out. The new bearing is put into position in the same manner. The last fraction of an inch can be pushed into place by holding only the oil slinger with the pliers while rotating the crankshaft. Or the bearing may be tapped down with a pin punch

and hammer. Be careful, so that you do not damage the bearing.

While removing and replacing the upper bearing shell of a rear main bearing, hold the oil seal in position in the cylinder block so that it does not come out of position (see § 19–6 on oil-seal replacement).

On all but a very few engines, precision-insert bearings are installed without shims. Never use shims on these bearings unless the engine manufacturer specifies them. Similarly, bearing caps must not be filed in an attempt to improve bearing fit.

§ 19–6. REPLACING MAIN-BEARING OIL SEAL

An oil seal is required at the rear main bearing to prevent oil leakage at that point (Fig. 19–10). When main-bearing service is being performed, or whenever leakage is noted at the rear main bearing, the oil seal must be replaced.

The procedure of replacement varies with different constructions. On some engines using a split-type oil seal, the crankshaft must be removed and a special oil-seal compressor or installer used to insert the new seal in the cylinder-block bearing. The seal should then be trimmed flush with the block as shown in Fig. 19–11. The oil seal in the cap can be replaced by removing the cap, install-

Fig. 19–9. Replacing rear-main-bearing half with pliers on engine where crankshaft has no oil hole in the rear journal. *(Chevrolet Motor Division of General Motors Corporation)*

Fig. 19–10. Crankshaft rear-main-bearing oil seal: (1) oil seal, (2) left cap gasket, (3) right cap gasket, (4) oil seal. *(Chrysler-Plymouth Division of Chrysler Motors Corporation)*

ing the oil seal, and trimming it flush. On other engines (the type shown in Fig. 19–10, for example), it is not necessary to remove the crankshaft, since removal of the flywheel will permit access to the upper oil-seal retainer. The retainer

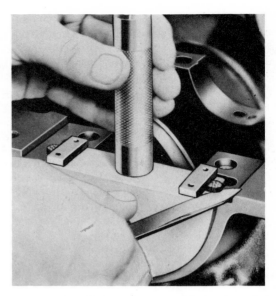

Fig. 19–11. Installation of a rear-main-bearing oil seal in a cylinder block with a special tool. *(Ford Motor Company)*

cap screws can then be removed along with the retainer for oil-seal replacement. Some engines use a one-piece rubber-type oil seal which can be pulled from around the crankshaft with a pair of pliers and a new oil seal then worked into place. It should be coated with cup grease (except on the ends, since this would prevent the ends from meeting tightly). Then, one end of the seal should be forced up into the slot on one side until it is at the top of the bearing. Next, the other end can be forced up into the slot on the opposite side so that the ends meet at the top of the bearing.

§ 19–7. REPLACING SEMIFITTED BEARINGS To replace these bearings, the crankshaft must be removed. Then, after the bearings are installed, they must be machined to size with a special boring machine. Also, the end-thrust-bearing faces must be machined, or "faced," to provide the correct amount of crankshaft end play.

§ 19–8. REMOVING THE CRANKSHAFT Such parts as the oil pan, timing-gear or timing-chain cover, crankshaft timing gear or sprocket, interfering oil lines, and oil pump must be removed before the crankshaft can be taken off. Also, on some engines, the flywheel must be detached from the crankshaft. With other parts off, the bearing caps are removed to release the crankshaft.

§ 19-9. **SERVICING CRANKSHAFT** Check the crankshaft for alignment and for journal and crankpin wear. Alignment can be checked with the setup shown in Fig. 19-12. As the crankshaft is rotated in the V blocks, the dial indicator will show any misalignment. A bent crankshaft can sometimes be straightened in a heavy press.

● **CAUTION:** Do not leave a crankshaft supported only at the ends as shown in Fig. 19-12. This could cause the crankshaft to sag and go out of alignment. Support the crankshaft on wood blocks of equal thickness placed under each journal. Or set the crankshaft on its end.

Fig. 19-12. Checking a crankshaft for alignment with V blocks and a dial indicator.

Checking of the journals and crankpins for taper or eccentricity has already been discussed (§§ 18-11 and 19-2). If journal or crankpin taper or eccentricity exceeds safe limits or if they are rough, scratched, pitted, or otherwise damaged, they must be ground undersize. Then new undersize bearings must be installed. Journals and crankpins must be ground down to fit the next undersize bearing available.

NOTE: It is possible to "metalize" journals and crankpins and then regrind them to their original sizes. This is done by first rough-turning the journals and crankpins in a lathe. Then, a high-temperature flame is used to spray liquid metal onto the prepared surfaces. This metal adheres and can be ground to form a new journal surface.

1. Finishing journals and crankpins. A special grinder or lathe is required to service journals and crankpins. The bearing surfaces must be finished to extreme smoothness. The grinding wheel may leave a certain amount of "fuzz" on the reground surfaces; this can be removed with fine crocus cloth, as follows: Cover the journals and crankpins with oil, and wrap a long strip of crocus cloth halfway around a journal. Take the

ends of the strip in your two hands and pull the strip back and forth, working uniformly all around each journal and crankpin. This removes any roughness. As a final test, wipe off the oil, and rub a copper penny across the surface. If it leaves any trace of copper on the steel, there is still roughness that should be removed.

● **CAUTION:** Be sure to relieve (grind back) the journal and crankpin radii (where they curve up to the crank cheeks). This will guard against bearing failure from radii ride (§ 18-9, item 5). Also, use care in touching up the thrust faces on the journal that takes the flanged or end-thrust main bearing. Make sure that these faces are smooth and square with the crankshaft journal.

2. Cleaning crankshaft. After grinding journals or crankpins, or at any time that the crank-

Fig. 19-13. Using a small brush to clean out oil passages in the crankshaft. (*Federal-Mogul Service Division of Federal-Mogul-Bower Bearings, Incorporated*)

shaft has been removed from the engine, the crankshaft should be thoroughly cleaned in a suitable solvent. A rifle-type brush should be used to clean out oil passages (Fig. 19–13). Remember that any trace of abrasive left in an oil passage could work out onto bearing surfaces and cause early bearing failure. Reoil the bearing surfaces immediately after they have been cleaned to keep them from rusting.

3. *Grinding crankpins on engine.* With the use of a special grinder, crankpins can be ground with the crankshaft still in the engine. To do this, the grinder is attached to a crankpin, and the crankshaft is rotated by a driving device at the rear wheel (transmissions in gear).

CYLINDER BLOCKS

§ 19–10. CYLINDER WEAR The piston and ring movement, the high temperatures and pressures of combustion, the washing action of gasoline entering the cylinder—all these tend to cause cylinder-wall wear. At the start of the power stroke, when pressures are the greatest, the compression rings are forced with the greatest pressure against the cylinder wall. Also, at the same time, the temperatures are highest, and the oil film is therefore at its least effective in protecting the cylinder walls. Thus, it is obvious that the most wear will take place at the top of the cylinder. As the piston moves down on the power stroke, the combustion pressure and temperature decrease so that less wear takes place. The cylinder thus wears irregularly, as shown in Fig. 19–14.

The cylinder also tends to wear somewhat oval-shaped. This is due to the side thrust of the piston as it moves down in the cylinder on the power stroke. The side thrust results from the swing, from vertical, of the connecting rod. Another factor is the washing action of the gasoline. At times the air-fuel mixture is not perfectly blended, and small droplets of gasoline, still unvaporized, enter the cylinder. They strike the cylinder wall (at a point opposite the intake valve) and wash away the oil film. Therefore, this area wears somewhat more rapidly.

§ 19–11. CLEANING AND INSPECTING CYLINDER BLOCK Before any service operations are performed, the cylinder block should be cleaned and inspected. There are several methods of cleaning. One method uses steam directed by a nozzle onto the block to wash away oil, sludge,

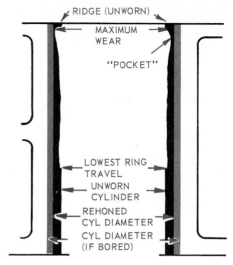

Fig. 19–14. Taper wear of engine cylinder (shown exaggerated). Maximum wear is at top, just under the ring ridge. Honing the cylinder usually requires removal of less material than boring, as indicated. Material to be removed by honing is shown solid. Material to be removed by boring is shown both solid and shaded. *(Sunnen Products Company)*

and dirt. A good solvent applied with a brush will also clean the block. Be sure all old gasket material is removed from machined surfaces. All pipe plugs that close off oil passages should be removed so that the passages can be blown out with compressed air. Long rods of the proper diameter can be pushed through the oil passages to clear out sludge that will not easily blow out. Remember that clogged oil passages will prevent normal bearing lubrication so that the bearings will wear rapidly and fail after a short time. Make sure that the passages are clean.

Threaded holes in the block should be blown out with compressed air. If the threads in the holes are not in good condition, use a tap of the correct size to clean up the threads. Then blow out the holes. Dirty or battered threads may give false torque readings that will prevent normal tightening of bolts on reassembly. This could cause engine failure from loose engine parts.

After the block is cleaned, inspect it for cracks, especially in the cylinder walls, top, water jackets, and main-bearing webs. Minute cracks not visible to the naked eye will show up if the suspected area is first coated with a mixture of kerosene and light engine oil and then wiped with zinc oxide dissolved in wood alcohol. The coating will discolor the cracks and show them up clearly.

Machined gasket surfaces should be inspected for burrs, nicks, and scratches. Minor damage can be removed with a fine oilstone. Check the head end of the block for warpage by laying a long straightedge against the sealing surfaces.

Check the main-bearing bores for alignment and out-of-roundness (§ 19–12). Bearing shells must be out, but caps must be in place for this check.

Check all expansion plugs, and replace any that show signs of leakage (§ 19–21).

§ 19–12. BEARING-BORE CHECKS

If uneven bearing wear has occurred, with some bearings wearing more than others, out-of-round bearing bores or a warped cylinder block should be considered as possible causes. Inadequate oiling could also be a factor, possibly resulting from clogged oil passages (§ 19–11).

To check bores for roundness, the crankshaft and bearing shells must be out, bearing bores must be clean, and the bearing caps must be in place, with the cap nuts or bolts tightened to the proper tension. A special dial indicator can be used to check for out-of-roundness. If bores are out-of-round, the block and caps must be machined with special boring equipment. Most of the material to correct the condition should be taken from the caps, with as little as possible being taken from the block. Oversize bearings will then be required.

To check bores for alignment, a special alignment bar must be installed in place of the crankshaft with the bearing shells out (Fig. 19–15). The bar is ground 0.001 inch smaller than the diameter of the bores. When the bearing caps (without shells) are tightened, the bar should turn by hand with the help of an extension handle on the bar. If it does not, the cylinder block is out of alignment and the bores must be machined, as explained in the previous paragraph.

§ 19–13. CYLINDER SERVICE

There are certain limits to which cylinders may wear tapered or out of round before they require refinishing. As mentioned in § 18–15, special drastic replacement rings will control compression and oil in cylinders with some taper and out-of-round wear. But when wear goes beyond a certain point, even the severest rings cannot hold compression and control oil; loss of compression, high oil consumption,

Fig. 19–15. Checking for main-bearing-bore alignment in the block with bearing caps in place. The alignment-checking bar should turn with all caps tightened to specified tension. *(Federal-Mogul Service Division of Federal-Mogul-Bower Bearings, Incorporated)*

poor performance, and heavy carbon accumulations in the cylinders will result. In such a case, the only way to get the engine back into good operating condition is to refinish the cylinders and fit new pistons (or resized pistons) and new rings to them.

Refinishing cylinders requires 12 to 20 hours (according to the type of engine). This includes fitting and installing new pistons, rings, piston pins, and connecting rods. When new bearings are fitted, about 10 additional hours is required. Grinding valves would require several more hours. These various times are mentioned because an engine that requires cylinder refinishing is usually in need of a general overhaul and these other services will also be required.

§ 19–14. CHECKING CYLINDER WALLS

Wipe walls, and examine them for scores and spotty wear (which shows up as dark, unpolished spots). Hold a light at the opposite end of the cylinder so that you can see the walls better. Scores or spots mean the walls must be refinished. Even drastic rings cannot give satisfactory performance on such walls.

Next, measure the cylinders for taper and oval wear. This can be done with an inside micrometer, with a telescope gauge and an outside micrometer, or with a special dial indicator. The dial indicator is shown in use in Fig. 18–30. It should be moved up and down in the cylinder and rotated in various positions to detect irregularities. Any irregularities will be indicated by movement of the needle. If irregularities are too great, the cylinders must be rebored or honed.

§ 19–15. REFINISHING CYLINDERS As a first step, the block should be cleaned (§ 19–11). A decision must be made on whether the cylinders are to be honed or bored. The boring machine uses a revolving cutting tool. The hone has a set of abrasive stones which are turned in the cylinder. Where cylinder wear is not too great, only honing is necessary. But if wear has gone so far that a considerable amount of metal must be removed, then honing will not do the job; a reboring job is required.

● **CAUTION:** If the crankshaft has not been removed, the main bearings and crankshaft must be protected from grit and cuttings. Quantities of clean rags should be stuffed down in the cylinder to catch the cuttings.

§ 19–16. HONING CYLINDERS If wear, taper, or eccentricity is not too great, only honing will be required. Figure 19–16 shows a cylinder hone in place, ready for the honing operation. The usual recommendation is to use honing oil or cutting fluid during the honing operation. However, dry honing of cylinders has been done; the use of a vacuum device is desirable when dry honing to remove the dust raised by the honing operation.

If a considerable amount of material must be removed, start with coarse stones. Sufficient material must be left, however, so that all rough hone marks can be removed when the final honing is done with the fine, or finishing, stones. See § 18–15 and Fig. 18–37 for information on how the cylinder wall should look after final honing. The proper honing pattern is important in obtaining good wearing-in of the new piston rings.

Final honed size should be such that the cylinder will take a standard or oversize set of rings and also a standard or oversize (or resized) piston. In other words, the cylinder must be finished to the size called for by the piston and rings to be installed.

Occasionally, during the latter stage of the honing operation, the cylinder walls should be cleaned

Fig. 19–16. Cylinder hone in place in a cylinder. In operation, the hone revolves in the cylinder, and the abrasive stones in the hone remove material from the cylinder wall. *(Hall Manufacturing Company)*

up and the piston fit checked (§ 18–12). This will guard against oversizing the cylinder, which would then require a larger oversize piston.

● **CAUTION:** Clean up the cylinders after honing (§ 19–18).

NOTE: Only those cylinders requiring service need be honed, since oversize pistons can be installed in some cylinders of an engine and standard pistons used in other cylinders (on most engines). For most engines, manufacturers supply oversize pistons that weigh the same as the standard pistons. Thus, there is no problem of balance when pistons of different sizes are used in an engine.

§ 19–17. BORING CYLINDERS If wear is too great to be taken care of by honing alone, cylinders must be bored first and then honed. The size to which the cylinders must be rebored is determined by the amount of material that needs to be removed from the walls (see § 19–10). In addition, the type of piston to be installed must be considered. With a semifinished piston, only enough material need be removed to clean up the bores. Then the pistons are finished to fit the cylinders. But when new finished pistons are to be installed, the bores will have to be finished to the proper size to take the correct oversize piston (and matching new rings).

NOTE: Refinish the cylinder with the most wear first. If you cannot clean up the cylinder when refinishing it to take the maximum-sized piston available, discard the cylinder block.

Figure 19–17 shows one type of boring bar. Figure 19–18 shows the centering fingers of the cutting head extended so that the head is centrally located in the cylinder. Figure 19–19 shows the cutting tool in place and cutting as the head revolves. This is one of several types of boring bar.

Several cautions must be observed in the use of the boring bar. First, the top of the cylinder block must be smooth and free of any nicks or burrs. These would upset the alignment of the bar and cause the cylinder to be bored at an angle to the crankshaft. Nicks and burrs should be removed with a fine-cut file. All main bearing caps should be in place with the cap bolts or nuts tightened to the specified tension. If this is not done, the bearing bores may become distorted from the cylinder-boring operation.

The boring operation should remove just enough material to clean up the cylinder wall so that all irregularities are gone. One recommended procedure is to bore the cylinder to the same diameter as the oversize piston to be installed. The final honing will remove enough additional material to give the recommended clearance (usually 0.0010 to 0.0020 inch, according to the engine model).

NOTE: Only those cylinders requiring it need to be rebored and final-honed. See the note at the end of § 19–16 about oversize and standard pistons of the same weight.

The last step in the boring operation is to use a hone with a fine stone to clean up the bore and give it a satisfactory surface for initial wear-in of the piston rings (see § 18–15 and Fig. 18–37).

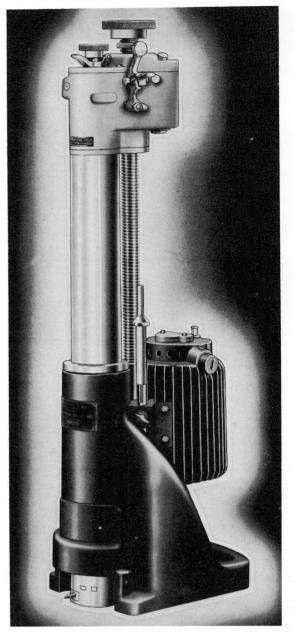

Fig. 19–17. Cylinder-boring machine. The cutting tool is carried in a rotating bar that feeds down into the cylinder as it rotates. This causes the cutting tool to remove material from the cylinder wall. *(Rottler Boring Bar Company)*

§ 19–18. CLEANING CYLINDERS Cylinders must be cleaned thoroughly after the honing or boring operation. Even slight traces of grit or dust

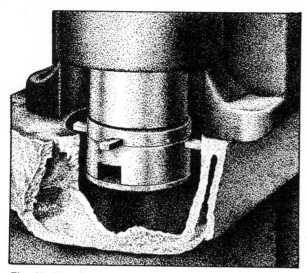

Fig. 19-18. Centering fingers extended to center the cutting head of the boring bar in the cylinder.

left on the cylinder walls may cause rapid ring and wall wear and early engine failure. As a first step, some engine manufacturers recommend wiping down the cylinder walls with very fine crocus cloth. This loosens embedded grit and also knocks off "fuzz" left by the honing stones or cutting tool. Then use a stiff brush and hot, soapy water to wash down the walls. It is absolutely essential for a good job to clean the walls of all abrasive material, since such material will

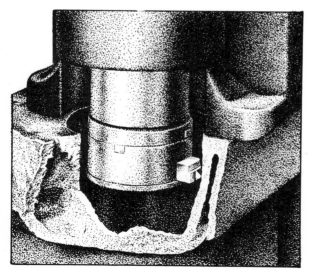

Fig. 19-19. Revolving head of a cylinder-boring machine, showing the cutting tool.

cause rapid wear of pistons, rings, and bearings if not removed.

After washing down the walls, swab them down several times with a cloth and light engine oil, wiping off the oil each time with a clean, dry cloth. At the end of the cleaning job, the cleaning cloth should come away from the walls with no trace of dirt showing on it.

Clean out all oil passages in the block, as well as stud and bolt holes, after the walls are cleaned (see § 19-11).

NOTE: Gasoline or kerosene will not remove all the grit from the cylinder walls; their use to clean up grit or dust on the cylinder walls is not recommended.

§ 19-19. REPLACING CYLINDER SLEEVES On engines equipped with removable cylinder sleeves, the sleeves usually can be removed and replaced at room temperature. A special sleeve puller is required.

Cracked blocks, scored cylinders, cylinders worn so badly that they must be bored to an excessively large oversize—all these can often be repaired by the installation of cylinder sleeves (Fig. 19-20). As a first step, the cylinder must be bored out with a boring machine to take the cylinder sleeve. Then the sleeve should be installed and bored to the proper size.

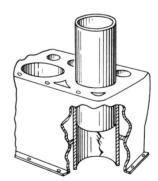

Fig. 19-20. Cracked blocks and badly scored or worn cylinder bores can sometimes be repaired by installing cylinder sleeves. *(Sealed Power Corporation)*

§ 19-20. REPAIRING CYLINDER-BLOCK CRACKS OR POROSITY If the block is in otherwise good condition, it may be worthwhile to repair cracks or sand holes (left in the block during casting). Areas which are not subjected to temperatures of more than 500°F or pressure (from coolant, oil, or cylinder) can be repaired with a metallic plastic or epoxy. Permissible repair areas for one manufacturer's engines are shown in Fig. 19–21. Other areas can sometimes profitably be repaired by welding (with copper or iron). Iron welding requires a higher temperature and this may warp the block. Unless the welding can be done inexpensively and expertly, it will usually be found better to replace the block.

The epoxy repair is started by cleaning the porous or cracked area down to bright metal with a grinder. Chamfer or undercut the crack or holes. If a hole is larger than 1/4 inch, drill, tap, and plug it. Smaller holes or cracks can be repaired with epoxy. Mix the two ingredients according to the directions on the package. Apply the mixture with a putty knife or similar tool. Fill cracks and holes and smooth the surface as much as possible. Allow the mixture to cure according to directions on the package. Then sand or grind the surface smooth and paint it.

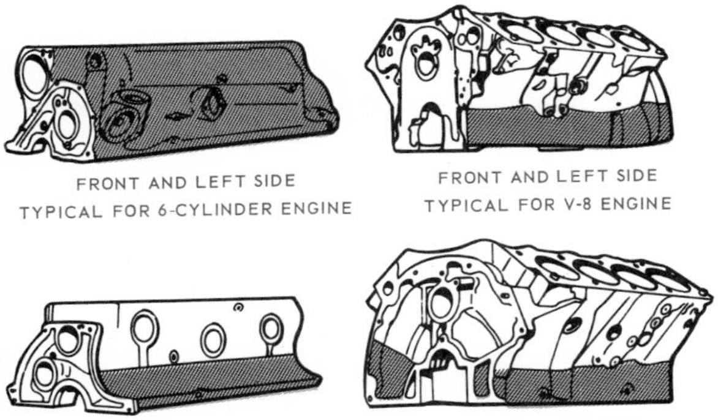

SHADED AREAS MAY BE REPAIRED WITH EPOXY

FRONT AND LEFT SIDE
TYPICAL FOR 6-CYLINDER ENGINE

FRONT AND LEFT SIDE
TYPICAL FOR V-8 ENGINE

REAR AND RIGHT SIDE

REAR AND RIGHT SIDE

Fig. 19–21. Areas of cylinder blocks that can be repaired with epoxy. *(Ford Division of Ford Motor Company)*

§ 19–21. EXPANSION CORE PLUGS If an expansion plug must be removed from the block (because of water leakage past the plug, for example), it can be drilled in the center and then pried out with a punch or small pry bar. Inspect the bore for roughness or damage that would prevent proper sealing of the new plug. If necessary, bore out the bore to take the next larger plug. When installing the new plug, coat it with the proper sealer

(water-resistant for cooling system, oil-resistant for oil galleries). Use the proper installation tool and proceed as follows, according to type of plug (Fig. 19–22).

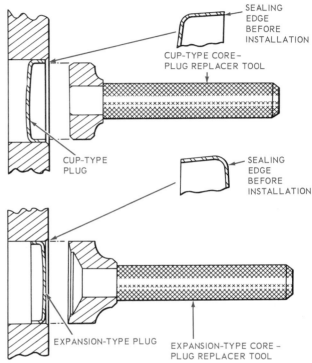

Fig. 19–22. Expansion core plugs and installation tools. *(Ford Division of Ford Motor Company)*

1. Cup type. This type is installed flanged edge outward. The proper size of tool must be used. It must not contact the flange, but all driving must be against the internal cup. The flange must be brought down below the chamfered edge of the bore.

2. Expansion type. This type is installed with the flanged edge inward, as shown. The proper tool must be used. The crowned center part must not be touched when the plug is driven in. Instead, the tool must drive against the outer part of the plug, as shown. The plug should be driven in until the top of the crown is below the chamfered edge of the bore.

Review Questions

1. Name some conditions in the cylinder block that could cause rapid and uneven main-bearing wear.
2. Explain how to check crankshaft journals and crankpins.
3. Explain how to check main-bearing fit with feeler stock. With Plastigage.
4. Explain how to check crankshaft end play.
5. Explain how to replace precision-insert main bearings.
6. Explain how to replace the main-bearing oil seal.
7. Explain how to service the crankshaft.
8. Discuss various types and causes of cylinder wear.
9. Explain how to check cylinder walls.
10. What is a cylinder-boring machine? How does it operate?
11. What is a cylinder hone? How does it operate?
12. Discuss in detail how to hone cylinder walls. How to bore a cylinder.
13. Explain how to replace worn cylinder sleeves.
14. Explain how to repair cylinder blocks.
15. Explain how to remove and replace expansion core plugs.

Study Questions

1. Write a sequence story on how to check a crankshaft.
2. Write a sequence story on how to check and replace precision-insert main bearings.
3. Write a sequence story on honing cylinder walls.
4. Write a sequence story on boring cylinder walls.

CHAPTER

20

COVER

HOSE FITTING

FILTER ELEMENT

HOUSING

Fuel-system Service

This chapter describes various types of trouble that develop in the fuel system and discusses the services required on the different fuel-system components.

§ 20–1. ANALYZING FUEL-SYSTEM TROUBLES Fuel-system troubles usually show up in engine operation, causing such troubles as poor acceleration, missing, loss of power, failure to start, backfiring, stalling, and so on. These various conditions are discussed in detail in the trouble-diagnosis chapter (Chap. 26). Fuel-pump and fuel-mileage testers can be used to check the pump action and the miles per gallon that the engine is delivering (§ 20–8). These and other checking devices will help track down trouble causes. An engine tune-up (Chap. 27) will disclose malfunctioning fuel-system components, since the carburetor and fuel pump are checked during the tune-up job. Quick checks of carburetor circuits plus servicing of the fuel-system components are discussed below.

§ 20–2. QUICK CARBURETOR CHECKS A number of quick checks can be made that will give a rough idea of whether the various carburetor circuits are functioning satisfactorily. The results of these checks should not be considered final. Accurate analysis of carburetor operation requires the use of an exhaust-gas analyzer and an intake-manifold vacuum gauge. (See the footnote in § 26–16 for the spark-plug test for an excessively rich mixture.)

1. Float-level adjustment. With the engine running at idling speed, remove the air cleaner, and note the condition of the high-speed nozzle. If the nozzle tip is wet or is discharging gasoline, the probability is that the float level is high, causing a continuous discharge of gasoline from the nozzle.

2. Low-speed and idle circuits. If the engine does not idle smoothly, the idle circuit is malfunctioning. Slowly open the throttle to give about

25 mph (miles per hour) engine speed. If the speed does not increase evenly and the engine runs roughly through this speed range, the low-speed circuit is out of order.

3. Accelerator-pump circuit. Open the throttle suddenly, and note whether the accelerator-pump circuit discharges a flow of gasoline into the air horn. The flow should continue for a few moments after throttle reaches the "open" position. On some carburetors, this can be better observed with the engine not running.

4. High-speed circuit. With the engine running at approximately 25 mph, slowly cover part of the air horn with a piece of stiff cardboard. (Caution: Do not use your hand. The vacuum could pull fingers into the air horn and damage them seriously.) The engine should speed up slightly, since this should cause a normally operating high-speed circuit to discharge more gasoline. The high-speed circuit is probably working improperly if the engine does not speed up somewhat.

§ 20–3. CAUTIONS IN FUEL-SYSTEM WORK The following cautions should be carefully observed in fuel-system work:

1. Remember that even a trace of dirt in a carburetor or fuel pump can cause fuel-system and engine trouble. Be very careful about dirt when repairing these units. Your hands, the workbench, and the tools should be clean.

2. Gasoline vapor is very explosive. Wipe up spilled gasoline at once, and put cloths outside to dry. Never bring an open flame near gasoline!

3. When air-drying parts with the air hose, handle the hose with care (see § 2–29).

§ 20–4. AIR-CLEANER SERVICE Air cleaners should be removed periodically and the filter ele-

Fig. 20-1. Carburetor air cleaner of the type using a paper element. *(Chrysler-Plymouth Division of Chrysler Motors Corporation)*

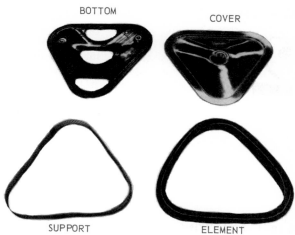

Fig. 20-2. Carburetor air cleaner of the type using a polyurethane element. *(Chevrolet Motor Division of General Motors Corporation)*

ment washed. The usual recommendation is that this should be done every time the engine oil is changed. However, if the car encounters unusually dusty conditions, then the air-cleaner element should be cleaned immediately afterward. Remember that the primary purpose of the air cleaner is to keep damaging dust from entering the engine. If the element becomes clogged with dust, it cannot do its job, and the engine will suffer.

Elements are removed by removing wing nuts, screws, and supporting clamps (if present). The method of cleaning the element varies with its type.

1. Paper element. After the cover has been removed and the element lifted off (Fig. 20-1), the element should be cleaned with compressed air. Hold the nozzle at least 2 inches away from the inside screen and blow from the center of the element outward. Examine the paper element for punctures. Discard it if it has even so much as a pinpoint puncture. Make sure that the plastic sealing rings on the upper and lower sides of the element are smooth. They must seal effectively when the element is replaced in the filter. Clean the top and bottom parts of the filter before reassembly. Install a new element every 30,000 miles, or less if the element is damaged.

2. Polyurethane element. After the element has been removed (Fig. 20-2), inspect it carefully for rips or other damage. Discard it if it is not in good condition. Wash the element in kerosene (Fig. 20-3), squeezing it gently to remove excessive kerosene.

Fig. 20-3. Washing a polyurethane air-cleaner element. *(Chevrolet Motor Division of General Motors Corporation)*

● **CAUTION:** Do not use solvents containing acetone or similar compounds, since they would ruin the element. Also, never wring out, shake, or swing the element; this would tear it. Instead, fold it over and gently squeeze it, as shown in Fig. 20-3.

Dip the cleaned element in engine oil, and squeeze out excess oil. Clean the cover and bottom parts of the cleaner. Reinstall the ele-

317

ment and its support in the cleaner bottom. Make sure that the element is not folded or creased and that it seals all the way around the bottom. Replace the cover, making sure that the element seals all the way around. Use a new gasket when installing the air cleaner on the carburetor.

3. *Oil-bath cleaner (Fig. 20-4).* After removing the filter element, clean it by sloshing it up and down in cleaning solvent. Dry it with compressed air. Dump the old oil from the cleaner body, wash it out with solvent, and dry it. Refill the body to the full mark with clean engine oil. Reinstall the filter element and cleaner body on the engine.

● **CAUTION:** Air filters which are not installed directly on the carburetor are connected to the carburetor by a flexible hose. This hose must be connected air-tight to both the filter and the carburetor. Also, the hose must have no tears or punctures that would admit unfiltered air.

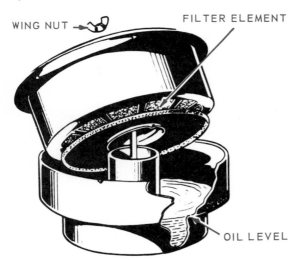

WING NUT

FILTER ELEMENT

OIL LEVEL

Fig. 20-4. Oil-bath air cleaner with the wing nut and filter element removed and the side partly cut away to show the oil level.

§ **20-5. THERMOSTATICALLY CONTROLLED AIR CLEANER** The thermostatically controlled air cleaner (§ 9-11) can be checked for proper operation with a temperature gauge or thermometer. Remove the air-cleaner cover and install the gauge as close as possible to the sensor. Allow the engine to cool to below 85°F if it is hot. Replace the air-cleaner cover without the wing nut.

Start and idle the engine. When the damper begins to open, remove the air-cleaner cover and note the temperature reading. It should be between

85 and 115°F. If it is difficult to see the damper, use a mirror.

If the damper does not open at the correct temperature, check the vacuum motor and sensor.

With the engine off, the control damper should be in the compartment or cold-air delivery mode position (see Fig. 9-20). To determine if the vacuum motor is operating, apply at least 9 inches of vacuum to the fitting on the vacuum motor. The vacuum can be from the engine or from a vacuum source in the shop. With vacuum applied, the damper should move to the hot-air delivery mode position (Fig. 9-20).

If the vacuum motor does not work satisfactorily, it should be replaced. This can be done by drilling out the spot welds and unhooking the linkage. The new motor can be installed with a retaining strap and sheet-metal screws.

If the vacuum motor does work well, the sensor should be replaced. This is done by prying up the tabs on the retaining clip. The new sensor is then installed and the tabs bent down again.

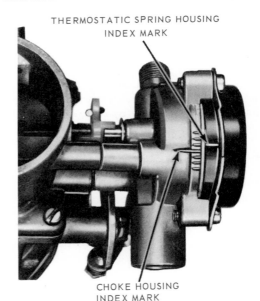

THERMOSTATIC SPRING HOUSING
INDEX MARK

CHOKE HOUSING
INDEX MARK

Fig. 20-5. Automatic choke of the type shown is adjusted by turning the cover. *(Ford Division of Ford Motor Company)*

§ **20-6. AUTOMATIC CHOKES** As a rule, automatic chokes require no service once they are adjusted for the operating conditions and engine. To adjust an automatic choke (type with adjustable cover), loosen the cover clamp screws, and turn the cover one way or the other to enrich or lean out the mixture (Fig. 20–5). Other types of choke are adjusted by bending a linkage rod.

§ 20–7. FUEL GAUGES   There is very little in the way of service that fuel gauges require. Defects in either the dash unit or the tank unit usually require replacement of the defective unit. However, on the type of gauge that makes use of vibrating thermostatic blades, dirty contact points, which may cause fluctuations of the needle, can be cleaned by pulling a strip of clean bond paper between them.

§ 20–8. FUEL-PUMP AND FILTER SERVICE   Fuel-pump pressure and capacity can be checked with special gauges. Low pump pressure will cause fuel starvation and poor engine perform-

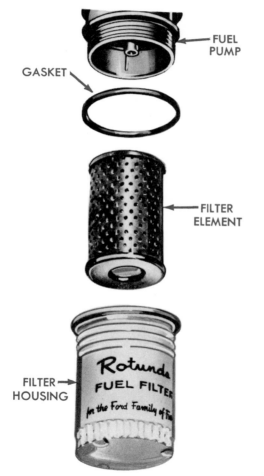

Fig. 20–6. The fuel-filter element is replaced by unscrewing the filter housing. *(Ford Division of Ford Motor Company)*

ance. High pressure will cause an overrich mixture, excessive fuel consumption, and such troubles as fouled spark plugs, rings, and valves (from excessive carbon deposits). Fuel-pump testers are connected into the fuel line from the pump and measure either the pressure that the pump can develop or the amount of fuel the pump can deliver during a timed interval. There is also a vacuum gauge for checking the vacuum pump on fuel pumps so equipped.

Fuel filters require no service except periodic checks to make sure that they are not clogged, and replacement of the filter element or cleaning of the filter, according to type. On many models, the filter is part of the fuel pump (Fig. 20–6) and can be removed so that the element can be replaced. Another type is the in-line filter (Figs. 9–4 and 9–5). In the type shown in Fig. 9–4, the filter is replaced by unclamping and detaching the fuel hose from the filter. Then, the filter can be unscrewed from the carburetor and replaced. In the type shown in Fig. 9–5, the fuel line is detached and then the nut is removed so that the old filter element can be slipped out and replaced.

§ 20–9. FUEL-PUMP TROUBLES   Fuel-system troubles that might be caused by the fuel pump are discussed below.

1. Insufficient fuel delivery. This could result from low pump pressure, which in turn could be due to any of the following:

    a. Broken, worn-out, or cracked diaphragm
    b. Improperly operating fuel-pump valves
    c. Broken or damaged rocker arm
    d. Clogged pump-filter screen or filter
    e. Leakage of air into sediment bowl because of loose bowl or worn gasket

In addition to these causes of insufficient fuel delivery due to conditions within the pump, many other conditions outside the pump could prevent delivery of normal amounts of fuel. These include such things as a clogged fuel-tank-cap vent, clogged fuel line or filter, air leaks into the fuel line, and vapor lock. Of course, in the carburetor, an incorrect float level, a clogged inlet screen, or a malfunctioning inlet needle valve would prevent delivery of adequate amounts of fuel to the carburetor.

2. Excessive pump pressure. High pump pressure will cause delivery of too much fuel to the carburetor. The excessive pressure will tend to lift the needle valve off its seat so that the fuel level in the float bowl will be too high. This results in an overrich mixture and excessive fuel consumption. Usually, high pump pressure occurs only after a fuel pump has been removed, repaired, and replaced. If a fuel pump has been operating satisfactorily, it is hardly likely that its pressure would increase enough to cause trouble. High pressure could come from installation of an excessively strong diaphragm spring or from incorrect reinstallation of the diaphragm. If the diaphragm is not flexed properly when the cover and housing are reattached, it will have too much tension and will produce too much pressure.

3. Fuel-pump leaks. The fuel pump will leak fuel from any point where screws have not been properly tightened and also where the gasket is damaged or incorrectly installed. If tightening screws does not stop the leak, then the gasket or diaphragm will require replacement. Note, also, that leaks may occur at fuel-line connections which are loose or improperly coupled.

4. Fuel-pump noises. A noisy pump is usually the result of worn or broken parts within the pump. These include a weak or broken rocker-arm spring, a worn or broken rocker-arm pin or rocker arm, or a broken diaphragm spring. In addition, a loose fuel pump or a scored rocker arm or cam on the camshaft may cause noise.

Fuel-pump noise may sound something like engine-valve tappet noise, since its frequency is the same as camshaft speed. If the noise is bad enough, it can actually be "felt" by gripping the fuel pump firmly in the hand. Also, careful listening will usually disclose that the noise is originating in the vicinity of the fuel pump. Tappet noise is usually distributed along the engine or is located more distinctly in the valve compartment of the engine.

§ 20–10. FUEL-PUMP REMOVAL As a first step in removing the fuel pump, wipe off any dirt or accumulated grease so that dirt will not get into the engine. Then take off the heat shield (where present), and disconnect the fuel lines and vacuum-pump lines (on a combination pump). Remove the attaching nuts or bolts, and lift off the pump. If it sticks, work it gently from side to side or pry lightly under its mounting. flange or attaching studs. On an engine using a push rod to operate the fuel pump, remove the rod so that it can be examined for wear or sticking.

§ 20–11. FUEL-PUMP DISASSEMBLY AND ASSEMBLY Many automotive service departments do not attempt to disassemble and repair fuel pumps, because pump manufacturers have ar-

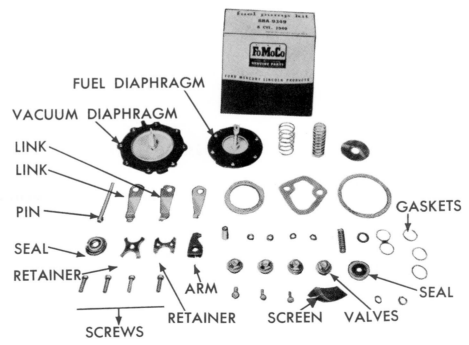

Fig. 20–7. Repair kit for a combination fuel and vacuum pump. *(Ford Division of Ford Motor Company)*

ranged a special pump-exchange program. The old pumps can be traded in on new or factory-rebuilt units. For those who prefer to repair fuel pumps, special repair kits are supplied. These repair kits contain diaphragms, valves, springs, and gaskets. Figure 20-7 shows an overhaul kit for a combination pump. Refer to the manufacturer's shop manual for overhaul procedures on specific models.

NOTE: Most late-model fuel pumps are assembled by crimping and cannot be disassembled. If defective, they must be replaced with a new assembly.

§ 20-12. FUEL-PUMP INSTALLATION Make sure that the fuel-line connections are clean and in good condition. Connect the fuel and vacuum lines to the pump before attaching the pump to the engine. Then place a new gasket on the studs of the fuel-pump mounting or over the opening in the crankcase. The mounting surface of the engine should be clean. Insert the rocker arm of the fuel pump into the opening, making sure that the arm goes on the proper side of the camshaft (or that it is centered over the push rod). If it is hard to get the holes in the fuel-pump flange to align with the holes in the crankcase, turn the engine over until the low side of the camshaft eccentric is under the fuel-pump rocker arm. Now the pump can be installed without forcing or prying it into place. Attach it with bolts or nuts. Check the pump operation as explained in § 20-8.

§ 20-13. CARBURETOR TROUBLES The trouble-diagnosis chart and trouble explanations in Chap. 26 relate many engine troubles to fuel-system and carburetor troubles. Let us list these various troubles that can be caused by the carburetor. Remember that many other conditions outside the carburetor can also cause these troubles, as noted in Chap. 26.

1. Excessive fuel consumption can result from a high float level or a leaky float, a sticking or dirty float needle valve, worn jets or nozzles, a stuck metering rod or full-power piston, idle too rich or too fast, a stuck accelerator-pump check valve, or a leaky carburetor.

2. Lack of engine power, acceleration, or high-speed performance can result from a malfunctioning accelerator pump, from the power step-up on the metering rod not clearing the jet, from dirt or gum clogging the fuel nozzle or jets, from a stuck power piston or valve, a low float level, a

dirty air filter, the choke stuck or not operating, air leaks into the manifold, the antipercolator valve stuck, the throttle valve not fully opening, or a rich mixture due to causes listed in the previous paragraph.

3. Poor idle can result from an incorrectly adjusted idle mixture or speed, a clogged idle circuit, or any of the causes listed in the previous paragraph.

4. Failure of the engine to start unless primed could be due to carburetor jets or lines clogged, a defective choke, a clogged fuel filter, or air leaks into the manifold.

5. Hard starting with the engine warm could be due to a defective choke, a closed choke valve, or improperly adjusted throttle-cracker linkage.

6. Slow engine warm-up could be due to a defectively operating choke.

7. A smoky, black exhaust is due to a very rich mixture. Carburetor conditions that could cause this are listed in item 1 above.

8. If the engine stalls as it warms up, this could be due to a defective choke or a closed choke valve.

9. If the engine stalls after a period of high-speed driving, this could be due to a malfunctioning antipercolator.

10. If the engine backfires, this could be due to an excessively rich or lean mixture.

11. If the engine runs but misses, it could be that the proper amount and ratio of air-fuel mixture are not reaching the engine, and this might be due to clogged or worn carburetor jets or to an incorrect fuel level in the float bowl.

Several of the conditions noted above can be corrected by carburetor adjustment. Other conditions require removal of the carburetor from the engine so that it can be disassembled, repaired, and reassembled. Following articles discuss carburetor adjustments and servicing procedures.

§ 20-14. CARBURETOR ADJUSTMENTS An estimated 500 different models of carburetor have been used in automotive vehicles during the past 10 years. Thus, it is obviously beyond the scope of this book to provide detailed adjustment and servicing procedures for all. However, we do discuss certain adjusting and servicing fundamentals. For servicing procedures on specific carburetor models, refer to the manufacturer's shop manuals.

1. Idle-speed and idle-mixture adjustments (Fig. 20-8). These are made together and determine the engine idling speed and mixture richness. Idling speed is adjusted by turning the adjustment screw in or out until the specified engine rpm (revolutions per minute) is attained. Then, the idle mixture is adjusted by turning the idle-mixture screw in or out. The correct setting gives the smoothest idle. On most carburetors, the proper setting is one or two turns of the screw back from the "fully seated" position. On dual or quadrijet carburetors, there are two idle-mixture screws to adjust.

2. *Throttle linkage.* The throttle linkage on the car must be adjusted so that the throttle opens wide when the foot pedal is fully depressed. In addition, the throttle must be fully closed when the foot pedal is released.

3. *Accelerator pump.* Some carburetors have an adjustable accelerator pump. A linkage rod can be shifted into various holes provided in the throttle or pump lever. Thus, a longer stroke, and richer mixture, can be obtained for winter operation and a shorter stroke for summer operation.

4. *Other adjustments.* Carburetors also require adjustments to the float or floats, metering rod or rods, antipercolator, and so on. These adjustments are covered in the applicable manufacturer's shop manual.

§ 20–15. CARBURETOR REMOVAL

To remove a carburetor, first disconnect air and vacuum lines and take off the air cleaner. Then disconnect the throttle and choke linkages. Disconnect the hot-air tube to the choke (if present). Disconnect the fuel line and the distributor vacuum-advance line from the carburetor, using two wrenches, as necessary, to avoid damage to the lines or couplings. Disconnect wires from switches and other electric controls (where present). Take off the carburetor attaching nuts or bolts, and lift off the carburetor. Try to avoid jarring the carburetor, since it may have accumulations of dirt in the float bowl, and rough treatment may stir this dirt up and cause it to get into carburetor jets or circuits.

After the carburetor is off, it should be put in a clean place where dirt or dust cannot get into the fuel inlet or other openings.

§ 20–16. CARBURETOR OVERHAUL PROCEDURES

Disassembly and reassembly procedures on carburetors vary according to their design; the manufacturer's recommendations should be carefully followed. The time required to overhaul a carburetor varies from approximately ¾ to 2

hours, according to type. Special carburetor tools are required. Gauges particularly are needed to gauge float clearance, float centering, float height, choke clearance, and so on.

Special carburetor overhaul kits are supplied for many carburetors. These kits contain all necessary parts (jets, gaskets, washers, and so forth) required to overhaul the carburetor and restore it to its original performing condition.

1. *General overhaul instructions.* Jets or nozzles should never be cleaned with drills or wires, since this would probably enlarge the openings and cause an excessively rich mixture. Instead, the openings should be cleaned out with denatured alcohol or a similar recommended solvent. This solvent will remove any gum that is clogging the opening. Similarly, all circuits or passages in the carburetor body should be washed out with solvent and then blown out with compressed air. Double-check the passages with a flashlight to be sure that they are cleaned out.

Power pistons that are scored or burred should be replaced; the piston must slide freely in the bore in the carburetor body. Worn or scored needle valves or seats must be replaced. Filter screens must be clean. Accelerator-pump plungers must fit snugly in their wells. If the leather is damaged, a new plunger must be used.

If the air horn is coated with dirt or carbon, it should be scraped lightly or sanded with sandpaper and then washed in solvent. Never use emery cloth, since particles of emery may embed and later loosen to clog jets or circuits in the carburetor.

Be sure that all residue is washed from the carburetor and that the carburetor body is clean inside and out.

New carburetor gaskets should be used when the carburetor is reassembled. The old gaskets are usually damaged when the carburetor is torn down, and there is no use taking a chance on a leak developing later that would require disassembling the carburetor again.

2. *Cautions.* Several important cautions should be observed in carburetor work.

a. Be sure your hands, the workbench, and tools are really clean.

b. Gasoline, as well as denatured alcohol or other solvent used to dissolve the gum from carburetor jets and other parts, is highly flammable. Extreme care must be used in handling these liquids—particularly some of the solvents, since they will ignite easily.

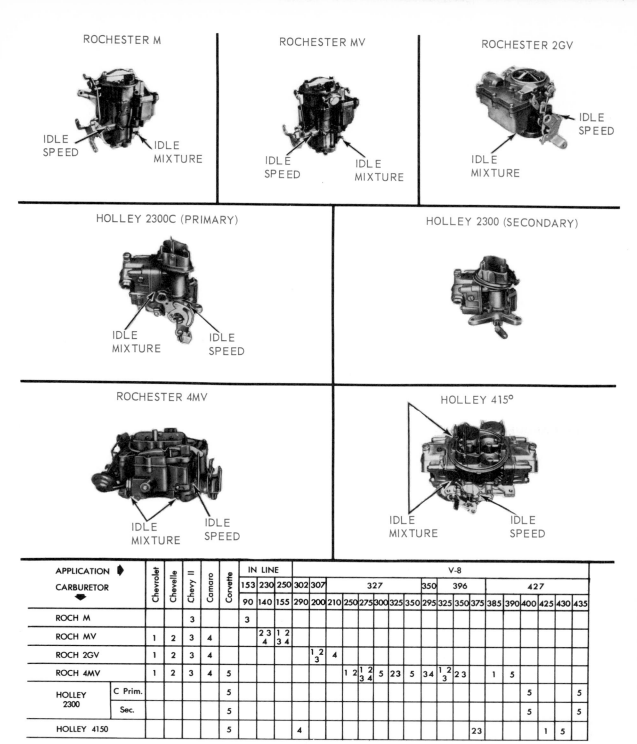

Fig. 20–8. Idle speed and idle mixture adjustments on various carburetors used in a recent model year on one make of automobile. *(Chevrolet Motor Division of General Motors Corporation)*

APPLICATION / CARBURETOR	Chevrolet	Chevelle	Chevy II	Camaro	Corvette	153 / 90	230 / 140	250 / 155	302 / 290	307 / 200	307 / 210	327 / 250	327 / 275	327 / 300	327 / 325	327 / 350	350 / 295	396 / 325	396 / 350	396 / 375	427 / 385	427 / 390	427 / 400	427 / 425	427 / 430	427 / 435
ROCH M			3			3																				
ROCH MV	1	2	3	4			2 3 / 4	1 2 / 3 4																		
ROCH 2GV	1	2	3	4						1 2 / 3	4															
ROCH 4MV	1	2	3	4	5							1 2	1 2 / 3 4	5	23	5	34	1 2 / 3	23		1	5			
HOLLEY 2300 C Prim.					5																			5		5
HOLLEY 2300 Sec.					5																			5		5
HOLLEY 4150					5				4											23				1	5	

323

c. Handle the air hose with care. Remember that high-pressure air can drive dirt particles at high speed. If one of these particles should be blown into the eye, it might damage the eye irreparably. Wear goggles to be safe when using the air hose.

d. Never clean carburetor jets or orifices with wire or drills. This would probably enlarge the openings and result in excessive fuel consumption.

e. Always use new gaskets when reassembling the carburetor.

f. The correct carburetor parts must be used in reassembly. Substitute parts that may be somewhat different should not be installed unless the carburetor manual specifically states that this may be done. Otherwise, performance and economy may be lost.

g. Carburetor adjustments should not be made until other components affecting engine operation are in good order. Adjusting the carburetor to compensate for faulty conditions elsewhere will probably result in poorer engine performance and higher fuel consumption.

h. Do not oil the automatic-choke linkage or the automatic choke.

§ 20–17. CARBURETOR INSTALLATION Examine the carburetor gasket, and make sure that it is in perfect condition. Replace it if you have any doubt as to its condition. Put the carburetor into position on the intake manifold, and attach it with nuts or bolts. Connect the fuel line and the distributor vacuum-advance line to the carburetor, using two wrenches if necessary to avoid damage to the lines or couplings. Connect wires to switches and other electric controls (where present). Make idle-speed, idle-mixture, and other adjustments. Install the air cleaner.

Study Questions

1. Explain how to check the carburetor float-level adjustment quickly.
2. Explain how to check the low-speed circuit quickly.
3. Explain how to check the accelerator-pump action quickly.
4. Explain how you can get an idea of the operating condition of the high-speed circuit.
5. What cautions should be observed in any fuel-system work?
6. Describe air-cleaner service.
7. Explain how to test and repair a thermostatically controlled air cleaner.
8. Explain how you can determine whether it is the tank unit or the dash unit that is at fault when the fuel gauge is not operating correctly.
9. Describe various fuel-pump troubles and their causes.
10. Explain how to remove and install a fuel pump.
11. Mention various engine-operating conditions that could result from faulty fuel systems.
12. Describe typical carburetor adjustments.
13. Explain how to remove and install a carburetor.
14. What are the important points to watch during carburetor overhaul?

Study Questions

1. List and describe the quick carburetor checks.
2. Write down the cautions you must observe when doing fuel-system work.
3. List and describe the various fuel-system troubles.
4. List the various engine conditions that could result from faulty fuel-system operation.
5. List various carburetor adjustments.
6. Describe in detail the various general overhaul instructions on carburetors.
7. Select a carburetor for which the servicing instructions are available, and overhaul the carburetor. Write down the important steps of overhauling a carburetor as you do them.

CHAPTER

21

Lubricating-system Service

This chapter discusses various types of trouble that may occur in the engine lubricating system and explains the services required on the lubricating-system components.

§ 21–1. TROUBLE TRACING IN LUBRICATING SYSTEM Few troubles occur in the lubricating system that are not intimately related to engine troubles. We have already discussed causes of excessive oil consumption (§ 11–6*), oil dilution, and water-sludge formation (§ 11–3) and why it is necessary to change oil periodically (§ 11–5). Figure 21–1 shows places in the engine where oil

---

* Chapter 26 (§ 26–14) has additional information on excessive oil consumption.

may be lost, causing high oil consumption. Using the bearing oil-leak detector to check for excessive bearing wear has also been described (§ 18–1). Other lubricating-system troubles that may require checking into include low oil pressure and high oil pressure.

1. Low oil pressure. Low oil pressure can result from a weak relief-valve spring, a worn oil pump, a broken or cracked oil line, obstructions in the oil lines, insufficient or excessively thin oil, or bearings that are so badly worn that they can pass more oil than the oil pump is capable of deliver-

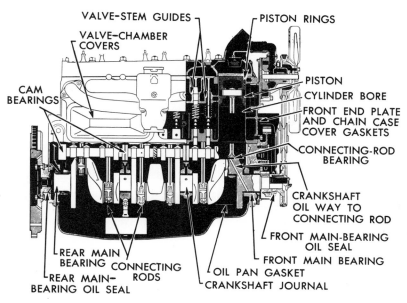

Fig. 21–1. Partial sectional view of an engine, showing points where oil may be lost. *(Federal-Mogul Service Division of Federal-Mogul-Bower Bearings, Incorporated)*

ing. A defective oil-pressure indicator may be recording low.

2. *Excessive oil pressure.* This may result from a stuck relief valve, an excessively strong valve spring, a clogged oil line, or excessively heavy oil. A defective oil-pressure indicator may read high.

§ 21-2. LUBRICATING-SYSTEM SERVICE
There are certain lubricating-system jobs that are done more or less automatically when an engine is repaired. For example, the oil pan is removed and cleaned during such engine-overhaul jobs as replacing bearings or rings (§ 18-4). When the crankshaft is removed, it is the usual procedure to clean out the oil passages in the crankshaft (§ 19-9). Also, the oil passages in the cylinder block should be cleaned out as part of the engine-block service job (§ 19-11). Following articles describe such lubricating-system service jobs as changing oil, servicing the oil-pressure relief valve and the crankcase ventilator valve, changing the oil filter, and servicing the oil pump and the oil-pressure indicator.

§ 21-3. CHECKING OIL LEVEL
Most engines use a bayonet type of oil-level gauge (the dipstick) that can be withdrawn from the crankcase to determine the oil level in the crankcase. The gauge should be withdrawn, wiped clean, reinserted, and again withdrawn so that the oil level on the gauge can be seen. The gauge is usually marked to indicate the proper oil level. The appearance of the oil should be noted to see whether it is dirty, thin, or thick. A few drops of oil can be placed between the thumb and fingers and rubbed to detect dirt or to find out whether the oil has sufficient body, that is, whether it is sticky. If the oil level is low, oil should be added to the crankcase. If the oil is thin or dirty, it should be drained and clean oil added.

§ 21-4. CHANGING OIL
Up to about 1960, standard practice called for changing the engine oil at 500-, 1,000-, or 2,000-mile intervals, according to the type of operation. With the development of improved lubricating oil* and more efficient oil and air filters, automotive manufacturers have liberalized their recommendations. With favorable operating conditions, the specified interval for oil changes on some automobiles is every 2 months or

4,000 miles, whichever occurs first. Other manufacturers put the change intervals at every 2 months or 6,000 miles. However, oil should be changed more frequently for such conditions as start-and-stop, cold-weather, low-mileage, or dusty driving, as noted below.

● **CAUTION:** Most manufacturers specify that, with the more liberal oil-change recommendations, the oil filter should be changed every time the engine oil is changed.

Oil filters installed in the system tend to reduce the frequency with which oil will require changing. But they do not eliminate the need for oil changes. Oil should be changed more frequently during cold weather, particularly when short-trip operation predominates. With short-trip operation, the engine operates cold a greater part of the time, and this increases the chances for water sludge to form. More frequent oil changes will remove this sludge before dangerous amounts can accumulate. When the car is operated on very dusty roads, the oil should be changed more frequently. Despite the air filters in the carburetor air cleaner and crankcase ventilator, dust does work its way into the engine, and this is particularly true when the car operates in dusty areas. Changing oil flushes this dust out so that it cannot harm the engine. Car manufacturers recommend that a car that has been driven through a dust storm, for example, have the oil changed immediately, regardless of how recently the last oil change was made. At the same time, the air filter should be cleaned and the oil filter (if used) changed. In addition to the changing of engine oil, the lubrication of various points in the engine accessories and chassis is periodically necessary.

§ 21-5. OIL-PAN SERVICE
Removing and cleaning the oil pan has already been discussed (§ 18-4).

§ 21-6. RELIEF VALVE
Relief valves are not usually adjustable, although springs of different tension may be installed to change the regulating pressure. This is not usually recommended, however, since a spring of the proper tension was originally installed on the engine. Any change of pressure is usually brought about by some defect that requires correction. For example, badly worn bearings may pass so much oil that the oil pump cannot deliver sufficient oil to maintain normal pressure in the lines. Installing a stronger spring

---

* See § 11-2 on properties of modern engine oils.

in the relief valve would not increase oil pressure; the relief valve is not operating under the circumstances.

§ 21-7. OIL FILTERS

Oil filters are serviced by replacing the oil-filter element or the complete filter, according to the type. Oil screens are serviced by flushing out accumulated sludge and dirt. Where a floating type of oil intake is used, the float and screen should also be cleaned.

As the oil filter becomes clogged, it passes less and less oil. Some indication of the condition of the oil filter can be had by feeling it after the engine has been operated for a short time. If the filter is hot to the touch, this indicates that oil is flowing through the filter. If it is cold, the probability is that the filter is clogged and is not passing oil. An additional check can be made by disconnecting the filter outlet with the engine running at low speed to see whether oil is flowing through the filter. However, rather than depend on some such check as this to determine filter efficiency, the best procedure is to replace the filter or filter element at periodic intervals. The usual recommendation is to replace the filter element every 5,000 miles or whenever engine oil is changed. More frequent replacement should be made if the car is operated in unusually dusty conditions.

§ 21-8. FILTER-ELEMENT REPLACEMENT

On some engines, the filter element and container are replaced as a unit. For example, on the type shown in Fig. 11-9, the old filter can be unscrewed and a new filter screwed into place by hand (Fig. 21-2). A drip pan should be placed under the old filter as it is removed to catch any oil that runs out. With the old filter off, the recess and sealing face of the filter bracket should be cleaned. Then, the sealing gasket of the new filter should be coated with oil. Finally, the new filter should be hand-tightened until the gasket comes up against the bracket face. It should then be tightened another half turn. After installation, the engine should be operated at fast idle to check for leaks. Check the oil level in the crankcase and add oil if necessary.

● **CAUTION:** Engine oil should be changed before the new filter is installed. A new filter should always start out with new oil.

On other filters, oil lines must be disconnected and reconnected when they are changed. Some filters have replaceable elements, and on these, the procedure is as follows. Remove the drain plug (if present) from the bottom of the housing. Take the cover off by loosening the center bolt or clamp. Lift out the element. If the filter housing has no drain plug, remove the old oil or sediment with a siphon gun. Wipe out the inside of the housing with a clean cloth. Be sure that no traces of lint or dirt remain. Install the new filter element. Replace the plug and cover, using a new gasket. Start the engine, and check for leaks around the cover. Note whether the oil pressure has changed (with a new element, which passes oil more easily, it may be lower). Check the level of oil in the crankcase, and add oil if necessary. Installing a new filter element usually requires the addition of a quart of oil to bring the oil level up to the proper height in the crankcase. Note also the caution above about changing oil every time the filter is changed.

After a filter element or filter is replaced, the mileage should be marked on the doorjamb sticker and the filter housing. Then, after 5,000 miles (or

Fig. 21-2. Replacing an oil filter. Some recommendations call for the use of a tool, as shown, to final-tighten filter. (*Chrysler-Plymouth Division of Chrysler Motors Corporation*)

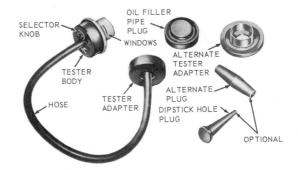

Fig. 21-3. A-c positive crankcase-ventilating-system tester. (*Ford Division of Ford Motor Company*)

COLOR	CAUSE
GREEN	System operating properly.
GREEN AND YELLOW	Regulator valve or system partially plugged. Slight kink in tester hose. Slight engine blow-by. Plugs from the kit or the engine vacuum lines are not properly sealed. Tester knob improperly set.
YELLOW	Regulator valve or system partially plugged. Tester hose kinked or blocked. Blow-by at maximum capacity of regulator valve. Plugs from the kit or the engine vacuum lines are not properly sealed. Tester knob improperly set.
YELLOW AND RED	Regulator valve or system partially or fully plugged. More engine blow-by than regulator valve can handle. Vent hose plugged or collapsed.
RED	Regulator valve or system fully plugged or stuck. Vent hose plugged or collapsed. Extreme blow-by.

Fig. 21–4. Colors displayed by the a-c tester and the conditions they indicate. *(Ford Division of Ford Motor Company)*

the specified replacement mileage) the driver and serviceman will know that it is time to replace the filter element again.

§ **21–9. OIL PUMPS** Oil pumps are relatively simple mechanisms and require little service in normal operation. If a pump is badly worn, it will not maintain oil pressure and should be removed for repair or replacement. In such a case, refer to the applicable manufacturer's shop manual for details of servicing.

§ **21–10. OIL-PRESSURE INDICATORS** Oil-pressure indicators are discussed in detail in § 11–11. These units require very little service. Defects in either the dash unit or the engine unit usually require replacement of the defective unit. On the type of unit that makes use of vibrating thermostatic blades, dirty contact points, which may cause incorrect readings, can usually be cleaned by pulling a strip of bond paper between them. Be

sure that no particles of paper are left between the points. Never use emery cloth to clean the points, since particles of emery might embed and prevent normal indicator action. If the indicator is not functioning in a normal manner, a new engine indicating unit may be temporarily substituted for the old one in order to determine whether the fault is in the engine unit or the dash unit.

§ **21–11. SERVICING CRANKCASE VENTILATOR (PCV) VALVE** A widely accepted recommendation is to replace this valve every year. If the valve becomes clogged, it will cause engine loping and rough idle. It cannot be cleaned satisfactorily—a clogged valve must be replaced. With engine loping and rough idle, install a new PCV valve, and see if the idling condition improves. If it does, leave the new valve in. If the loping or rough idle persists, check for restrictions in the lines. A test can be made to pinpoint the trouble with an a-c PCV tester (Fig. 21–3), as follows:

1. With engine at operating temperature, remove the oil-filler cap and dipstick. Plug the dipstick tube with the hole plug (Fig. 21–3).

2. With the tester body and proper tester adaptor attached to the hose, as shown, insert the adaptor into the oil-filler opening. Turn the selector knob to the correct setting for the engine under test.

3. Start the engine and let it idle. Hold the tester body upright, and note color displayed in the tester windows. Figure 21–4 shows what various colors mean and the corrections to be made.

A second type of tester is shown in Fig. 21–5. It is used as follows:

1. With the engine at normal operating temperature, remove the oil filler cap, and hold the tester over the opening in the valve cover. Make sure that there is a tight seal between the cover and the tester. An air leak here will prevent tester operation.

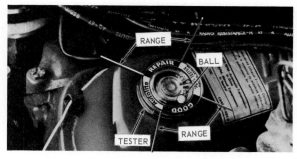

Fig. 21–5. PCV tester on valve cover in readiness for test. *(Ford Division of Ford Motor Company)*

2. Start the engine and operate it at idle. Note the position of the ball. If the ball settles in the GOOD (green) area, the system is functioning properly. If it settles in the REPAIR (red) area, check out the system components as previously noted.

*R*eview *Questions*

1. What could cause low oil pressure? High oil pressure?
2. Explain how to check the oil level in the oil pan.
3. Explain why engine oil must be changed.
4. Explain how to replace an oil-filter element.
5. Explain how to service a crankcase ventilator valve.
6. Explain how to test a PCV system and what troubles the tester might point out.

*S*tudy *Questions*

1. Write down the procedure for servicing an oil pump as explained in a manufacturer's shop manual.
2. If an engine has badly worn bearings, would you recommend using a stronger spring in the relief valve in order to maintain pressure?

22

Cooling-system Service

This chapter describes the testing, care, servicing, and repair of automotive-engine cooling-system components.

§ 22-1. COOLING-SYSTEM TESTS Over a period of time, rust and scale accumulate in the radiator and engine water jackets; the rust and scale restrict the circulation of water, and the engine tends to overheat (Fig. 22-1). In addition, the hose and connections between the radiator and the engine may deteriorate, causing leakage or inadequate passage of water. The thermostat, if stuck or distorted, may not close and open properly, thus reducing the effectiveness of the cooling system. A number of tests of the cooling system and its components can be made to determine the condition of these parts. In addition, the strength of the antifreeze solution can be tested.

● **CAUTION:** Use care when removing a pressure-type radiator cap, especially when the engine is hot. Turn the cap only to the first stop to per-

mit any pressure in the system to be released through the overflow tube. Then turn the cap further to remove it. Some manufacturers warn against taking off the cap when the engine is hot and pressure in the cooling system is high. They state that, if the cap is turned slightly and a hissing sound results, indicating pressure, the cap should immediately be retightened and *left tight until the engine has cooled and the pressure has dropped.* They say further that it should never be necessary to check the liquid level in the cooling system unless the temperature gauge shows overheating and that then the liquid level should be checked only after the engine has cooled off.

● **CAUTION:** Keep your hands away from the revolving engine fan! You can be seriously cut by the whirling blades.

1. Testing thermostat. The action of the thermostat can be observed by placing it in a pan of water and heating the pan. A thermometer should be suspended in the water so that the temperature at which the thermostat starts to open, as well as the full-open temperature, can be determined. The thermostat should not be placed on the bottom of the pan but should be suspended by a wire or placed on a screen an inch or so above the bottom (see Fig. 22-2). Thermostats are calibrated to operate at various temperatures. If a thermostat does not function according to specifications, it should be replaced.

2. Testing system for rust and scale. The appearance of the water is some indication of whether rust and scale have accumulated in the cooling system. If the water is rusty or muddy in appearance, rust is present. A fairly accurate measurement of the amount of rust and scale present can

Fig. 22-1. Accumulation of rust and scale in engine water jackets. *(Chevrolet Motor Division of General Motors Corporation)*

330

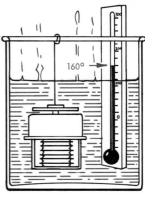

Fig. 22–2. Testing a cooling-system thermostat.

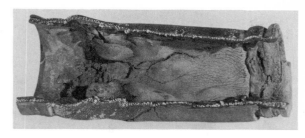

Fig. 22–3. Water hose that has become defective. *(Federal-Mogul Service Division of Federal-Mogul-Bower Bearings, Incorporated)*

be made if the capacity of the cooling system is known. All water should be drained and fresh water measured and added until the system is filled. Comparison of the amount of added water with the specified capacity of the system provides an indication of the amount of rust and scale present.

3. Testing radiator for restriction. If the radiator-hose connections are removed, the radiator drained, and a stream of water from an ordinary garden hose introduced into the top of the radiator, the water should run through the radiator and out without filling up the radiator. If the water runs out slowly, the radiator is clogged. Another test for restrictions in the radiator is to start the engine, allow it to warm up, and then turn the engine off and feel the radiator with the hand. It should be hot at the top and warm at the bottom, with an even temperature increase from bottom to top. Cold spots indicate clogged sections.

● **CAUTION:** Be sure that the engine is turned off. More than one person has injured his hand seriously by placing it in an engine fan when the engine was running.

4. Examining hose and hose connections. The appearance of the hose and connections will usually indicate their condition. If the hose is rotten and soft and collapses easily when squeezed, it should be replaced. Figure 22–3 illustrates a badly deteriorated section of hose that has been split open to show its internal appearance.

5. Testing water pump. There is no accurate way to test the action of the water pump on the car. However, some idea of its operating condition can be obtained by squeezing the upper-hose connection in the hand, with the engine warm and running. If pressure can be felt as the engine is

speeded up, this is an indication that the water pump is operating in a normal manner.

6. Testing for air suction into system. If leaks exist at any point between the radiator and the water pump, air will be drawn into the system, as shown in Fig. 22–4. Air bubbles will cause foaming and loss of the cooling water. The water could, of course, be replaced, but if antifreeze is also lost, then replacement is an expense. There is also the danger of losing antifreeze protection in this way. Air in the system speeds up corrosion and rust. To check for air suction, fill the radiator,

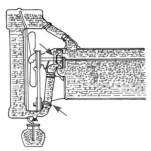

Fig. 22–4. Testing for air suction into a cooling system. Arrows indicate points at which air might enter.

attach a hose from the overflow pipe, and put the lower end of the hose into a container of water, as shown (Fig. 22–4). Start the engine, and run it until it is warmed up. If bubbles appear in the container of water, then air is being sucked into the cooling system. (It might be exhaust-gas leakage, as noted in the following paragraph.) Repair the system by tightening or replacing hoses and hose clamps. If this does not cure the trouble, then either there is exhaust-gas leakage or the water pump is leaking. Check the system as noted in the following paragraph. If no exhaust-gas leakage is found, then the trouble is probably in the pump.

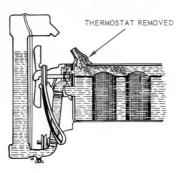

Fig. 22-5. Testing for exhaust-gas leakage into a system.

7. Testing for exhaust-gas leakage. A defective cylinder-head gasket may allow exhaust gas to leak into the cooling system. This is very damaging, since strong acids will form as the gas unites with the water in the cooling system. These acids corrode the radiator and other parts in the cooling system. A test for exhaust-gas leakage can be made by disconnecting the upper hose, removing the thermostat and the fan belt, and draining the system until the water level stands just above the top of the cylinder head (Fig. 22-5). The engine should be started and accelerated quickly several times. If the water level rises appreciably or if bubbles appear, exhaust gas is leaking into the cooling system. A new gasket should be installed and the cylinder-head bolts properly tightened.

8. Pressure-testing the system. A pressure tester (Fig. 22-6) can be used to check the system for leaks, and makes it easy to do the testing described in items 6 and 7 above. All that need be done is to fill the radiator to within $\frac{1}{2}$ inch of the filler neck, wipe the neck sealing surface, attach the tester, and apply a pressure of 15 psi. If the pressure holds steady, the system is not

leaking. If the pressure drops, further testing can be done as follows.

Look for external leaks at hose connections, engine expansion plugs, water pump, and radiator. If no external leaks are visible, remove the tester and start the engine, running it until operating temperature is reached. Reattach the tester, apply a pressure of 15 psi, and increase engine speed to about half throttle. If the needle of the pressure meter fluctuates, it indicates a combustion leak, probably through a damaged cylinder-head gasket. On a V-8 engine, you can determine which bank is at fault by grounding the spark-plug leads on one bank.

If the needle does not fluctuate, sharply accelerate the engine several times and check for abnormal discharge of water through the tail pipe. This would indicate a cracked block or head or a defective head gasket.

9. Pressure-testing the pressure cap. The same pressure tester shown in Fig. 22-6 can be used to test the radiator pressure cap. If the cap will not hold the rated pressure, it should be discarded.

10. Testing fan belt. Fan-belt adjustment should be checked as shown in Fig. 24-12. The fan belt should be checked every few thousand miles to make sure that it is still in good condition. A belt that has become worn or frayed or that has separated plies should be discarded and a new belt installed. A defective or loose belt will not only cause overheating of the engine but may also result in a run-down battery, since it cannot drive the generator fast enough to keep the battery charged.

11. Testing antifreeze-solution strength. The strength of the antifreeze solution must not be below that required to furnish adequate protection in the lowest temperatures expected. The strength of the solution is tested by use of a special antifreeze-solution hydrometer, which measures its specific gravity, or heaviness. The so-called "permanent" antifreeze compounds (ethylene glycol) are heavier than water, while alcohol-base antifreeze compounds are lighter than water. The specific-gravity reading will determine what percentage of the solution is water and what percentage is antifreeze compound. Then, by reference to a chart, the lowest temperature at which the solution will remain a liquid can be determined. Additional antifreeze compound can be added.

§ 22-2. COOLING-SYSTEM-TROUBLE DIAGNOSIS Complaints that may lead the mechanic to

Fig. 22-6. Using pressure tester to check a cooling system for leaks. *(Chrysler-Plymouth Division of Chrysler Motors Corporation)*

332

check the cooling system include slow warm-up and overheating. Slow warm-up could be caused by a thermostat that fails and remains open. This causes the water to circulate between the radiator and the engine block even when the engine is cold, making it necessary for the engine to run for a longer period of time before reaching operating temperature.

Overheating, when due to trouble in the cooling system, is most often caused by accumulations of rust and scale, defective hose or connections, malfunctioning of the water pump or thermostat, or a loose or defective fan belt. If the engine overheats without the radiator becoming normally warm and if the fan belt is tight and in good condition, the thermostat probably is not opening and will therefore require replacement. If the radiator is hot, test the water pump by pinching closed the upper hose by hand, as described in § 22–1. If the thermostat and water pump seem to be operating normally and the hose appears to be in good condition, the overheating, if actually caused by troubles in the cooling system, is probably due to accumulations of rust or scale in the cooling system. Such rust or scale should be cleaned and flushed out (§ 22–3).

The water may start to boil after the engine has been turned off; this is called *afterboil*. This could happen, for example, after a long, hard drive. The engine has so much heat in it (though it has not actually overheated) that, after the engine is turned off, the water in the cooling system boils (Fig. 22–7). It is still absorbing heat from the engine which it cannot get rid of because the cooling system is no longer working.

Boiling can also occur if the radiator has frozen up. This hinders or stops the circulation of the cooling water. Consequently, the water in the water jackets becomes so hot that it boils. Freezing of the water in the radiator, engine block, and head may crack the block or head and may open up seams in the radiator. A frozen engine is apt to be seriously damaged.

It must be remembered that there are other causes of engine overheating which have nothing to do with conditions in the cooling system. High-altitude operation, insufficient oil, overloading of the engine, hot-climate operation, improperly timed ignition, long periods of low-speed or idling operation — any of these may cause overheating of the engine (see § 26–10).

§ 22–3. CLEANING THE COOLING SYSTEM   The cooling system should be cleaned at periodic intervals to prevent the accumulation of excessive rust and scale. Accumulated rust and scale can be loosened by a good cleaning compound. There are various types of cleaning compounds; all must be used carefully in accordance with the manufacturer's instructions. A general cleaning procedure is outlined below. If considerable scale and rust have accumulated, it may be that cleaning alone will not remove them all. In this case, the radiator and engine water jackets must be flushed out with a special air-pressure flushing gun, as shown in Figs. 22–8 and 22–9. The hot-water heater can be flushed out at the same time. Some car manufacturers recommend reverse flushing, that is, flushing in which the water is forced through the radiator and water jackets in the opposite direc-

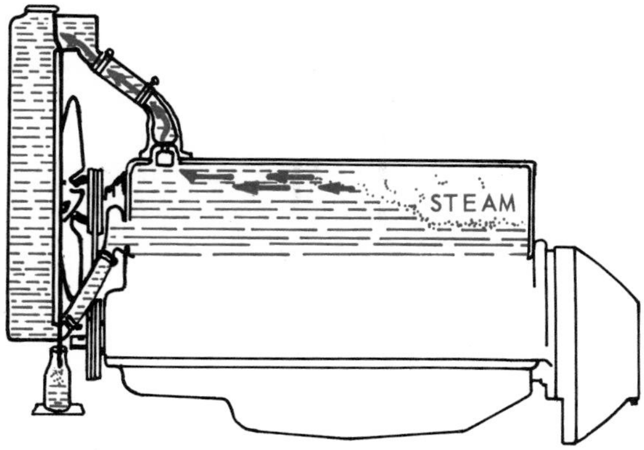

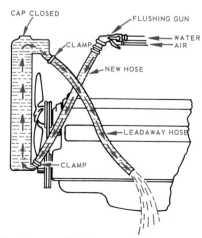

Fig. 22–7. Afterboil of water after the engine is stopped.

Fig. 22–8. Reverse-flushing a radiator.

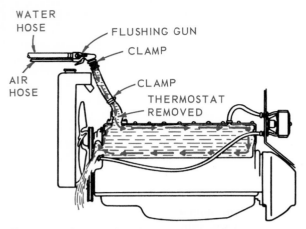

WATER HOSE
FLUSHING GUN
CLAMP
AIR HOSE
CLAMP
THERMOSTAT REMOVED

Fig. 22–9. Reverse-flushing engine water jackets.

tion to that in which the water normally circulates. This gets behind the scale and loosens it.

1. Cooling-system cleaning procedure. Completely drain the system by opening the drain cocks. Add cleaning compound, and fill the system with water. Run the engine on fast idle for at least 30 minutes after the engine reaches operating temperature. Completely drain the system again, add neutralizer (if the cleaner requires its use), fill with water, and run the engine at a fast idle for at least 5 minutes. Drain the system, refill with water, and run for at least 5 minutes after the water has reached operating temperature. Then drain and refill once again, this time with antifreeze (if it is to be used).

NOTE: During the procedure, keep the radiator covered so that the engine develops as much heat as possible. Otherwise, the engine may not get hot enough to make the thermostat open wide. This would slow water circulation and reduce the cleaning effect.

2. Cleaning radiator air passages. At the same time that the cooling system is cleaned, the radiator air passages should be cleaned out. This can be done by blowing them out, from back to front, with compressed air. This removes insects, leaves, and dirt that could clog the air passages and reduce the cooling efficiency of the radiator.

3. Flushing radiator. If cleaning alone does not remove all the accumulated rust and scale, the radiator and water jackets should be flushed. This job is done with a flushing gun that uses air pressure to force the water through. The radiator can be straight-flushed or reverse-flushed. For reverse flushing, a new hose is attached to the lower tank

of the radiator, and a leadaway hose is attached to the upper tank (Fig. 22–8). The water will, of course, drain out as this is done. Clamp the flushing gun in the hose to the lower tank, as shown, and turn on water to fill the radiator. When water runs out the leadaway hose, apply air pressure to force the water out. Apply the pressure gradually to avoid damaging the radiator. Sudden full-pressure application might rupture the radiator core. Refill the radiator, and again apply air pressure. Repeat until the water running from the leadaway hose is clean.

To straight-flush the radiator, follow the above procedure, but attach the leadaway hose to the lower tank of the radiator and the flushing-gun hose to the upper tank.

4. Flushing engine water jackets. Engine water jackets also can be straight-flushed or reverse-flushed. Some engine manufacturers warn that seals and other engine parts may be damaged if their engines are reverse-flushed. Make sure the specifications permit reverse flushing before doing the job. To reverse-flush, remove the thermostat and attach the flushing gun to the thermostat housing with a short length of hose (Fig. 22–9). The illustration does not show a leadaway hose from the water-pump inlet, but to avoid getting water all over the engine it is best to use a leadaway hose. Fill the water jackets with water, and then apply air. Repeat as for the radiator until the water runs clear from the leadaway hose.

To straight-flush the water jackets, follow the above procedure, but attach the leadaway hose to the thermostat housing and the flushing-gun hose to the pump-inlet connection.

● **CAUTION:** Do not apply too much air pressure or sudden bursts of pressure. This might damage engine seals, gaskets, or other parts.

5. Refilling system. When the cooling system has been cleaned, the thermostat replaced, and all hoses and clamps reconnected, the system should be refilled. Since the water that is put in will probably be cold, the thermostat may close and prevent quick filling. With the thermostat closed, air is trapped below the thermostat in the engine water jackets (Fig. 22–10). The thermostat usually has a small hole or two that permits this air to leak out. But it takes a little time for the air to escape. This means that you may have to fill and refill the radiator several times, waiting each time for some of the trapped air to get out.

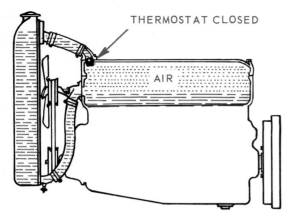

THERMOSTAT CLOSED

AIR

Fig. 22-10. Air trapped back of a closed thermostat as engine cooling system is filled.

The engine should be started and run long enough for the thermostat to heat up and open. More water can be added to make sure the system is filled.

6. *Fast-flush method.* The following procedure does not require removal of the engine thermostat and cylinder-block drain plugs, and thus the flushing procedure is quicker. With this method, the water supply is connected to the heater-supply nipple, and it flows through the engine water jacket, the water pump, and the bottom of the radiator; it exhausts mainly through the filler neck of the top radiator tank. The specific directions, keyed to Fig. 22-11, follow.

a. Set the heater temperature control (1) to high. If the car has a vacuum-operated heater valve, start the engine and run it at idle during flushing,

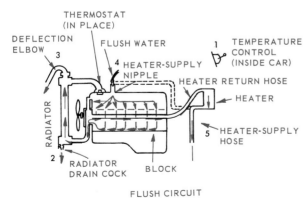

THERMOSTAT
(IN PLACE)

DEFLECTION
ELBOW   FLUSH WATER   1   TEMPERATURE
3   CONTROL
                  4 HEATER-SUPPLY   (INSIDE CAR)
                     NIPPLE
                        HEATER RETURN HOSE
RADIATOR   HEATER
                                    5 HEATER-SUPPLY
                                       HOSE
2   RADIATOR
    DRAIN COCK   BLOCK

FLUSH CIRCUIT
(COUNTER TO NORMAL CIRCULATION)

Fig. 22-11. The Union Carbide, or Prestone, fast-flush method of flushing the engine cooling system. *(Union Carbide Corporation)*

but be sure to turn it off before shutting off the water.

b. Open the radiator drain cock (2).

c. Remove the radiator cap and install a lead-away hose or a deflection elbow (3).

d. Remove the hose from the heater-supply nipple at the engine block (4), and point the hose down so that it will drain. (If the nipple is hard to get at, remove the heater-supply hose at the heater and connect the water supply to flow into this hose—not into the heater. Attach a short piece of hose at the heater and point it down [5]. *Never connect the water supply directly to the heater!* This could damage the heater.)

e. After connecting the water supply either to the heater-supply nipple (4) or to the heater-supply hose, turn on the water. A flushing gun can also be used, as noted in the flushing instructions given earlier. Avoid excessive air pressure if air is used. During the last minute squeeze the upper radiator hose to remove any trapped liquid.

f. Turn off the water, reconnect the heater-supply hose, disconnect the deflection elbow, and close the radiator drain cock after allowing enough water to drain to have room in the cooling system for adding antifreeze (or summer antirust compound). Add and adjust the antifreeze compound.

● **CAUTION:** Make sure that all hoses are fully engaged on the tubes and that the clamps are properly tightened.

§ 22-4. LOCATING AND REPAIRING RADIATOR LEAKS Leaks in the radiator are usually obvious, since telltale scale marks or water marks will form on the outside of the core below the leaks. An accurate way to locate radiator leaks is to remove the core from the car, drain out all the water, close the openings at top and bottom, and immerse the core in water. Air bubbles will escape from the core through any leaks. Small leaks can sometimes be repaired without removing the radiator from the car by use of certain liquid compounds poured into the radiator. These compounds, seeping through the leaks, harden upon coming in contact with the air, sealing off the openings. A more effective way of repairing leaks is to solder them. If there are several leaks at various places in the core, it may not be worthwhile to attempt repair, since the core is probably corroded to a point where other leaks will soon develop.

Removing a radiator core is a relatively simple job, although there is a considerable amount of work involved. The procedure varies somewhat from car to car but, in general, is as follows: First, drain the engine and radiator by opening the drain cocks in the radiator and engine block. Then detach the upper and lower radiator hoses. Remove any support bolts, horns, wiring harnesses, and so forth, that might interfere with core removal. With these parts out of the way and the radiator loose, lift it straight up and off the car.

§ 22–5. WATER-PUMP SERVICE The water pump is a relatively simple mechanism that requires little service in normal operation. Some pumps require periodic lubrication. Others, with sealed ball bearings, require no lubrication. If the pump develops noise or leaks or becomes otherwise defective, it must be removed for repair. Refer to the applicable manufacturer's shop manual for details of the servicing procedure to be followed.

Review Questions

1. Describe how to test a thermostat.
2. Explain how to test a cooling system for rust or scale.
3. Explain how to test a radiator for restrictions.
4. Explain how to test a cooling system for air being sucked into it.
5. Explain how to test a cooling system for exhaust-gas leakage.
6. Explain how to adjust a fan belt.
7. Explain how to test the strength of antifreeze solutions.
8. What could cause slow warm-up of the engine? What could cause overheating of the engine?
9. What is afterboil?
10. Explain how to clean the cooling system.

Study Questions

1. Make a list of various cooling-system tests. How is each made?
2. Write an essay describing in detail how to clean a cooling system by reverse-flushing.
3. Refer to a manufacturer's shop manual, and write a step-by-step story on all procedures involved in overhauling a defective water pump.

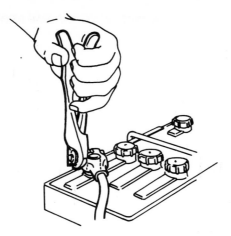

Electric-system Service — The Starting System

This and the following two chapters describe the servicing of the various components of the electric systems on the automobile, including the battery, cranking motor, regulator, generator, and ignition system. This chapter deals with the starting system, which includes the battery and the cranking motor.

The importance of good electrical service becomes apparent when we note the results of studies of car failures made by the American Automobile Association (AAA). They reported that, in one recent year, there were a total of 71,000,000 car breakdowns and that 30,000,000 of these, or 43 percent, were due to battery, cranking motor, and ignition-system failures.

STORAGE BATTERY

§ 23-1. BATTERY-TESTING METHODS Several methods of battery testing are recommended by battery manufacturers. No one automotive manufacturer recommends them all. For instance, Chevrolet recommends the instrument (or "421") test and the hydrometer (specific gravity) test. Ford recommends the cadmium-tip, a capacity or high-discharge, and the hydrometer tests. Plymouth recommends the cadmium-tip, the high-discharge, and the hydrometer tests. These are discussed below.

● **CAUTION:** Sulfuric acid is very corrosive and will destroy most things with which it comes into contact. It will cause painful and serious burns if it gets on the skin. In case of accident, the acid should be quickly flushed away with a large quantity of water, which dilutes while washing away the acid. Also, baking soda may be used to neutralize the acid. A quantity of baking soda can be kept at hand to sprinkle on anything on which the acid is spilled. Water should be used to flush off the acid and soda.

● **CAUTION:** The gases that form in the tops of the cells during battery charging are very ex-plosive. An open flame should never be brought near batteries that have been recently charged without first blowing out the gas from the tops of the cells. Use your breath, not an air hose. An air hose could splash the electrolyte or lift cell covers.

1. Light-load test. This test can be used on all batteries except those batteries having the one-piece cover (which Delco-Remy calls Energizers). With a one-piece cover, the individual cell voltages cannot be checked as required in the light-load test.

The light-load test is made by first stabilizing the battery with a momentary heavy load and then checking cell voltages with a light load applied. Make sure that the battery is in good physical condition, without a broken case or covers, and that the electrolyte is at the proper level. Use the cranking motor for 3 seconds. Turn off the engine if it starts. Then turn on the low headlight beam, and after 1 minute, read the individual cell voltages with an accurate voltmeter (Fig. 23-1).

If all cells read 1.95 volts or more and the difference between cells is no greater than 0.05 volt, the battery is in good condition.

If cells read both above and below 1.95 volts and the difference between cells is no more than

Fig. 23–1. Checking battery cell voltage with an expanded-scale voltmeter. *(Delco-Remy Division of General Motors Corporation)*

0.05 volt, the battery is in good condition but requires charging.

If all cells read below 1.95 volts, the battery is too low to test. Boost-charge (§ 23–2, item 5) and retest it.

Even if some cells read more than 1.95 volts but there is a difference between cells of more than 0.05 volt, then the battery is defective and should be discarded.

2. High-discharge or capacity test. The battery should be in good physical condition, without broken cell covers or case. Figure 23–2 shows the use of a high-discharge battery tester. The load applied can be varied by turning the knob. Actual specifications vary with different batteries. For example, the specifications for one 12-volt battery call for applying a 200-ampere load, with the battery voltage falling no lower than 9.5 volts after 15 seconds. Another calls for applying a load three times the ampere-hour rating of the battery, and then reading the voltage after 15 seconds (see Fig. 23–3). Always refer to the specifications of the battery being tested before making the test. If the voltage falls below specifications, recharge and recheck the battery. If the voltage still reads low, the battery should be discarded.

3. Hydrometer test. We have already seen that, as the battery is discharged, the electrolyte loses sulfuric acid and gains water (§ 13–4). The sulfuric acid is nearly twice as heavy as water. Thus, measuring the weight per unit volume, or the specific gravity, of the electrolyte will disclose the state of charge of the battery. The hydrometer (Fig. 23–4), a device for measuring specific gravity, contains a float that floats in the electrolyte which is drawn into the hydrometer tube from the battery. The float stem protrudes varying amounts from the electrolyte, according to the amount of sulfuric acid in the electrolyte. The stem of the float is so calibrated that the amount the stem protrudes above the electrolyte indicates the specific gravity of the electrolyte.

a. Variations of specific gravity. The specific gravity of the battery electrolyte varies as a result of several conditions: state of charge, temperature, age of battery, and self-discharge.

b. Variation with state of charge. As the state of charge of the battery changes, more or less sulfuric acid will be present in the electrolyte, causing a higher or lower specific-gravity reading when the battery is tested with a hydrometer. The following specific-gravity readings are an approximate guide to battery condition:

1.265–1.299	Fully charged battery
1.235–1.265	Three-fourths charged
1.205–1.235	One-half charged
1.170–1.205	One-fourth charged
1.140–1.170	Barely operative
1.110–1.140	Completely discharged

NOTE: Some of the late-model 12-volt batteries for passenger-car service have a somewhat lower specific gravity when charged. For instance, one type of 12-volt Delco battery is fully charged with

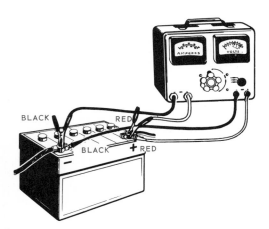

Fig. 23–2. Testing battery voltage under high discharge. *(Chrysler Motors Corporation)*

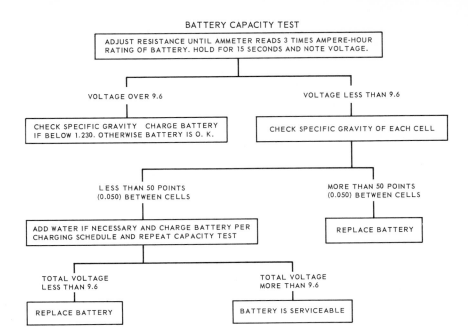

BATTERY CAPACITY TEST

ADJUST RESISTANCE UNTIL AMMETER READS 3 TIMES AMPERE-HOUR
RATING OF BATTERY. HOLD FOR 15 SECONDS AND NOTE VOLTAGE.

VOLTAGE OVER 9.6

VOLTAGE LESS THAN 9.6

CHECK SPECIFIC GRAVITY   CHARGE BATTERY
IF BELOW 1.230. OTHERWISE BATTERY IS O. K.

CHECK SPECIFIC GRAVITY OF EACH CELL

LESS THAN 50 POINTS
(0.050) BETWEEN CELLS

MORE THAN 50 POINTS
(0.050) BETWEEN CELLS

ADD WATER IF NECESSARY AND CHARGE BATTERY PER
CHARGING SCHEDULE AND REPEAT CAPACITY TEST

REPLACE BATTERY

TOTAL VOLTAGE
LESS THAN 9.6

TOTAL VOLTAGE
MORE THAN 9.6

REPLACE BATTERY

BATTERY IS SERVICEABLE

Fig. 23-3. Outline of battery capacity test recommended by Ford. *(Ford Division of Ford Motor Company)*

a specific gravity of 1.270. Other batteries, for example, those used in hot climates, have a specific gravity when fully charged of 1.225.

The decimal point is not normally referred to in a discussion of specific gravity. For example, "twelve twenty-five" means 1.225, and "eleven fifty" means 1.150. Also, the word "specific" is dropped, so that the term becomes just "gravity."

c. Variation of gravity with temperature. In addition to the effect of varying states of charge on the gravity, temperature also changes the gravity. This effect is due to the fact that as a liquid cools

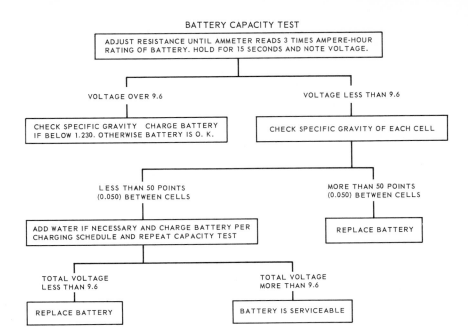

Fig. 23-4. Hydrometer being used to measure specific gravity of battery electrolyte. *(Delco-Remy Division of General Motors Corporation)*

it becomes thicker and gains gravity, and as a liquid warms it becomes thinner and loses gravity. Thus temperature must be considered when a gravity reading is taken. A correction must be made if the temperature varies from standard. This correction involves the addition or subtraction of gravity points, according to whether the electrolyte temperature is above or below the 80°F standard. The gravity of electrolyte changes about four points, or thousandths (0.004), for every 10° temperature. To make temperature correction, four points must be added for every 10° above 80°F. Four points must be subtracted for every 10° below 80°F.

EXAMPLES: 1.250 at 120°F. Add 0.016 (4 × 0.004). Corrected reading is 1.266. 1.230 at 20°F. Subtract 0.024 (6 × 0.004). Corrected reading is 1.206.

d. Loss of gravity from age. As the battery ages, the electrolyte gradually loses gravity. This is because of the loss of active material from the plates (as it sheds and drops into the bottom of the cells) and because of the loss of acid due to gassing. Over a period of 2 years, for example, battery electrolyte may drop to a top gravity, when fully charged, of not more than 1.250 from an original top gravity, when new, of possibly 1.290. Little can then be done to restore gravity since the loss is an indication of an aging battery.

e. Loss of gravity from self-discharge. If a battery is allowed to stand idle for a long period of time, it will slowly self-discharge. This condition is brought about by internal chemical reactions between the battery materials, which, although not productive of a flow of current at the time, are chemically active. The higher the battery temperature, the more rapidly self-discharge will take place. The lead sulfate that forms on the battery plates as a result of self-discharge is difficult to reconvert into active material; thus a battery that has badly self-discharged may be ruined.

f. Battery gravities for hot climates. In hot climates, where the chemical activities can take place more readily in the battery, it is often desirable to adjust the gravity reading to as low as 1.210 (28.5 percent acid) for a fully charged battery. This reduces the amount of self-discharge and prolongs the life of the battery. On discharge, the battery electrolyte may be reduced to a gravity as low as 1.075 before the battery stops delivering current. Where there is no danger of freezing, low gravities can be used.

g. Freezing point of electrolyte. The higher the gravity of the electrolyte, the lower its temperature must be before it will freeze. The battery must be kept in a sufficiently charged condition to prevent its freezing. Freezing usually ruins the battery (see Table 23–1).

4. 421 test. The 421 test is designed for use on batteries with a one-piece cover, but it can be used on other types also. The test requires a special tester which applies a specific series of timed discharge and charge cycles to the battery. The battery condition can thus be determined very accurately within a few minutes. When using this tester, follow the tester manufacturer's instructions carefully.

5. Cadmium-tip test. This test requires a special tester with cadmium tips that are inserted into the electrolyte of adjacent cells (Fig. 23–5), after filler plugs are removed. Electrolyte must be up to the proper level. If the car has been operated, or

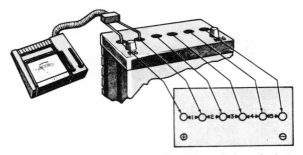

Fig. 23–5. Testing battery cells with cadmium-tip battery-cell analyzer. *(Chrysler-Plymouth Division of Chrysler Motors Corporation)*

the battery charged, within 8 hours, turn on the headlights for 1 minute. Then turn the headlights off. Start the test by putting the red probe into the cell that has the positive terminal and the black probe into the adjacent cell. Note the meter reading. Move the probes to cells 2 and 3, and so on, noting the meter readings. Compare the readings. Figure 23–6 shows various readings and the conditions they indicate.

a. If any two cells vary five scale divisions or more (top scale), the battery is at the point of failure and should be replaced.

b. If all cells vary less than five scale divisions and all read in the green section, the battery is charged and in good condition.

c. If all cells vary less than five scale divisions but if any fall in the red section, the battery is in good condition but needs charging.

d. If any reading falls in the RECHARGE AND RETEST area, the battery is too low to make a good test. Recharge and retest it.

§ 23–2. BATTERY SERVICE Battery service can be divided into four parts: testing, repair, charging, and care of batteries in stock.

1. Battery testing. Battery testing should include not only an analysis of the condition of the battery but an analysis of any abnormality found so that

Table 23–1

SPECIFIC GRAVITY AND FREEZING TEMPERATURES			
Specific gravity	Freezing temperature, degrees F	Specific gravity	Freezing temperature, degrees F
1.100	18	1.220	−31
1.160	1	1.260	−75
1.200	−17	1.300	−95

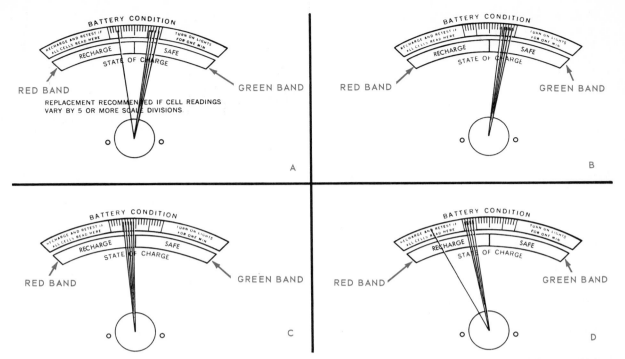

Fig. 23-6. Interpretation of meter readings for the cadmium-tip test. *(Chrysler-Plymouth Division of Chrysler Motors Corporation)*

correction can be made. This will prevent a repetition of the trouble.

a. Adding water. The first step in testing a battery is to check the electrolyte level in the battery cells. Add water, if necessary. Distilled water is preferred, but any water that is fit to drink can be used.

● **CAUTION:** Avoid overfilling the battery.

b. Overcharging. If the battery requires a considerable amount of water, the indication is that it is being overcharged; that is, too much current is being supplied to the battery. This is a damaging condition, since the active materials in the battery are overworked, causing battery life to be shortened. In addition, overcharging causes a more rapid loss of water from the battery electrolyte. Unless this water is replaced at frequent intervals, the electrolyte level is likely to fall below the tops of the plates, exposing the plates and the separators to the air. This may ruin the plates and the separators. A badly overcharged battery is fairly easy to detect, since the overcharging causes the positive-plate grids to swell and push up the positive sides of the cell covers. Thus, when a battery is found with the positive sides of

the cell covers raised above the edge of the battery case, it is probable that the battery has been badly overcharged. In addition to this action, the swelling of the grids causes them to crumble and the plates to buckle. Thus, a battery subjected to severe overcharging will soon be ruined. Where overcharging is experienced or suspected, the generator-regulator system should be checked and adjusted if necessary so that the current input to the battery is brought within reasonable limits (Chap. 24).

c. Undercharging. If the battery is discharged, it should be recharged as outlined in a following paragraph. In addition, an attempt should be made to determine the cause of the discharged battery. It could be caused by generator-regulator system malfunctioning (§§ 24-1 and 24-6); by defective connections in the charging circuit between the generator and the battery (§§ 24-1 and 24-6); by excessive load demands on the battery; by a defective battery; or by permitting the battery to stand idle for long periods so that it self-discharges excessively. In addition, an old battery may have a low specific-gravity reading because it is approaching failure.

d. Sulfation. The active materials in the plates

341

are converted into lead sulfate during discharge, as has already been noted. This lead sulfate is reconverted into active material during recharge. However, if the battery is allowed to stand for long periods in a discharged condition, the lead sulfate becomes converted into a hard, crystalline substance that is difficult to reconvert into active materials by normal charging processes. Such a battery should be charged at half the normal rate for 60 to 100 hours. Even though this long charging period may reconvert the sulfate to active material, the battery may still remain in a damaged condition, because the crystalline sulfate, as it forms, tends to break the plate grids.

e. Cracked case. A cracked case may result from excessively loose or tight hold-down clamps, from battery freezing, or from flying stones.

f. Bulged cases. Bulged cases result from tight hold-down clamps or from high temperatures.

g. Corroded terminals and cable clamps. This condition occurs naturally on batteries, and the serviceman should be prepared to remove excessive corrosion periodically from terminals and clamps. Cable clamps should be disconnected from the terminals (see *2, Removing and replacing a battery*, below) and both cleaned with cleaning tools (Fig. 23–7). After the clamps are replaced, they may be coated with petroleum jelly to retard the formation of corrosion.

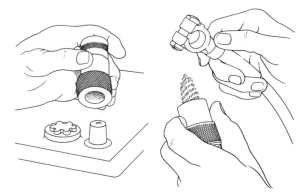

Fig. 23–7. Using special wire brushes to clean battery terminal posts and cable clamps. *(Buick Motor Division of General Motors Corporation)*

h. Corroded battery holder. Since some spraying of battery electrolyte is natural as the battery is being charged, the battery holder may become corroded from the effects of the electrolyte. Such corrosion may be cleaned off, when the battery is removed, by use of a wire brush and common baking-soda solution.

i. Dirty battery top. The top of the battery may become covered with dirt and grime mixed with electrolyte that has been sprayed from the battery. This should be cleaned off periodically by tightening the battery vent plugs, sprinkling the battery top with soda solution, waiting until the foaming stops, and then flushing off with clean water. Care should be taken that the solution does not get into the battery.

j. Discharge to metallic hold-down. If the hold-down clamps are of the uncovered metallic type, and near the insulated battery terminal, it is possible for a slow discharge to occur from the insulated terminal to the hold-down clamp. This is more apt to occur with a dirty battery top across which current can leak. The remedy is to keep the battery top clean and dry.

2. *Removing and replacing a battery.* To remove a battery from a car, first take off the grounded-battery-terminal cable clamp to prevent accidental grounding of the insulated terminal when it is disconnected. To remove a nut-and-bolt type of cable, loosen the clamp nut about 3/8 inch. Use a box wrench or special cable pliers (Fig. 23–8). Do not use ordinary pliers or an open-end wrench; either might break a cell cover when swung around. If the clamp sticks, use a clamp puller (Fig. 23–9). Do not use a screwdriver or bar to pry on the clamp; this could damage the battery cell or cover. To detach the spring-ring type of clamp, squeeze the ends of the rings apart with vise-grip or channel-lock pliers (Fig. 23–10).

After the grounded cable is disconnected, disconnect the insulated terminal cable. Clean both battery terminals and cable clamps with special

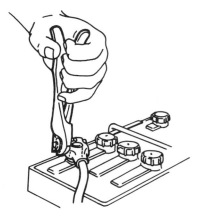

Fig. 23–8. Using battery-cable pliers to loosen the nut-and-bolt type of battery cable. *(United Delco Division, General Motors Corporation)*

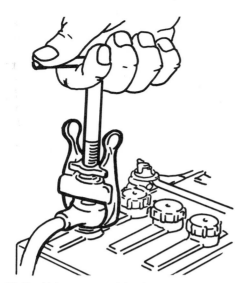

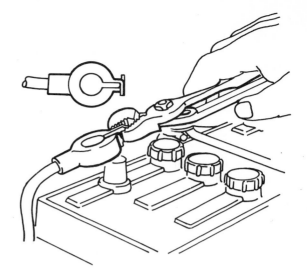

Fig. 23–9. Using a special clamp puller to pull the cable from a battery terminal. *(United Delco Division, General Motors Corporation)*

Fig. 23–10. Using pliers to loosen the spring-ring type of cable clamp from a battery terminal. *(United Delco Division, General Motors Corporation)*

tools (Fig. 23–7). Loosen the battery hold-downs, and take out the battery. When installing a battery, do not reverse the terminal connections (some automobiles have the negative terminal grounded, others the positive terminal). Reconnect the insulated terminal cable first, and then reconnect the grounded terminal cable. Apply corrosion inhibitor to clamps and terminals. Install and tighten the hold-downs. Avoid overtightening.

3. Battery repairs. If a battery is generally in good condition and not too old, such repairs as resealing cell covers or replacing a battery element may be worthwhile. Such repairs require special battery-repair equipment.

4. Battery "dopes." "Dopes" is a term applied to certain chemical compounds that are supposed to restore a battery to a charged condition when they are placed in the cells. Such chemicals should never be added to the battery. Their use may void the battery guarantee and cause battery failure.

5. Battery charging. Two methods of charging batteries are in use, the constant-current and the constant-voltage (constant-potential) methods. In the constant-current method, the current input to the battery is adjusted to the manufacturer's specifications for the battery being charged. The charging is continued until the battery is gassing freely and there is no further rise in gravity for 2 hours.

In the constant-voltage method, the voltage is held at a constant value. The battery, as it approaches a charged condition, increases in resistance to the charging current. At the same time, the current input gradually tapers off until, when the battery is fully charged, the current input has been reduced to a few amperes. This action is based on the assumption that the battery-electrolyte temperature will remain within bounds. If the battery-electrolyte temperature increases excessively, the resistance of the battery to the charging rate will remain low. Consequently the battery will be subject to damaging overcharge unless it is removed from the charging line in time.

The "quick chargers" which have recently come into use operate by charging the battery at a high rate (as much as 100 amperes) for a short time—30 to 45 minutes—so that the battery is brought up to a fair state of charge before the battery temperature increases to excessive values. If the battery is not subject to excessive temperatures, the quick-charger method of battery charging does not seem to be damaging to the battery. It should be remembered, however, that high charging rates combined with battery-electrolyte temperatures of above 125°F are very damaging to the battery. It is also true that quick chargers cannot, as a rule, bring a battery up to *full* charge in a short time. If the battery is quick-charged for a short time and then the charging operation is finished by a slow-charging method, the battery will come up to full charge.

● **CAUTION:** A battery with discolored electrolyte (from cycling) or with gravity readings more than 25 points apart should not be quick-charged. Likewise, a badly sulfated battery should not be quick-charged. Such batteries may be on the verge of failure, but they may give additional life if slow-charged. However, quick-charging them might further damage them. During quick-charging, check the color of the electrolyte and stop charging if it becomes discolored as a result of the stirring up of washed-out active material. Likewise, cell voltages should be checked every few minutes and charging stopped if cell voltages vary more than 0.2 volt.

6. *Care of batteries in stock.* Wet batteries (or batteries with electrolyte in them) are perishable. They are subject to self-discharge, which, if allowed to proceed for too long a time, will completely ruin them. To prevent this, batteries in stock should be recharged at 30-day intervals. They should not be stacked on top of each other without some means of individual support. The weight of a battery resting on the posts of another battery will cause the plate assemblies on the lower one to collapse so that short circuits will occur.

7. *Dry charged batteries.* Dry charged batteries contain fully charged positive and negative plates but no electrolyte. The batteries are sealed with rubber or plastic seals placed in the vent plugs. Since the batteries contain no moisture, practically no chemical action can take place in them. This means that they will remain in good condition for as long as 36 months, the manufacturers say, if they are properly stored.

The dry charged battery manufacturers also supply ready-mixed electrolyte in special cartons. The carton contains an acid-proof plastic bag which holds the electrolyte. To activate a battery or get it ready for service, all that is necessary is the following:

   a. Remove vent plugs and take out the plastic seals.
   b. Remove lid from electrolyte container. Unfold top of plastic bag and cut a small opening in one corner of the bag.
   c. Use a glass or acid-proof plastic funnel and fill each battery cell as shown in Fig. 23-11. *Wear goggles and observe all cautions already noted regarding sulfuric acid.* Wait a few minutes and then add more electrolyte if necessary. Some electrolyte will probably

Fig. 23-11. Adding electrolyte from a special container to a dry-charged battery. *(Delco-Remy Division of General Motors Corporation)*

be left; do not attempt to use it all. Do not overfill the battery.

   d. Before discarding the container, empty it and rinse out the bag thoroughly with water. Otherwise, someone who handles the carton might be severely burned.

CRANKING MOTOR

§ 23-3. CRANKING-MOTOR TESTING The testing of cranking motors can be divided into two parts: the tests made on the car when trouble occurs to determine whether the cranking motor or some other component is at fault, and the tests to be made on the cranking motor when it has been removed from the engine.

1. *Car testing of cranking motor.* The procedure of turning on the headlights and operating the cranking-motor switch to locate the source of trouble if the engine does not turn over is outlined in § 26-2. If the lights stay bright without cranking action when an attempt is made to operate the cranking motor, some further analysis may be made to determine whether the trouble lies in the cranking motor, switch, or control circuit. Turn the ignition switch to START, close the remote-control switch or depress the accelerator pedal, according to the type of control. The magnetic switch or the solenoid on the cranking motor will or will not work. If it does not, the indication is that current is not getting to or through the magnetic

switch or the solenoid. Some magnetic switches and solenoids can be operated by hand to see whether or not the cranking motor is capable of operation. If the cranking motor does operate as the magnetic switch or the solenoid is operated by hand, then the trouble is in the control circuit. A jumper lead can be connected around the control devices and switches so that the unit not operating can be located. Where the solenoid has a relay, the relay cover can be removed and the relay points closed by hand. If the solenoid and the cranking motor now operate, the relay is defective.

● **CAUTION:** If the cranking motor is to be checked with a jumper cable from the cranking motor to the battery, first disconnect the distributor primary lead from the ignition coil, and then turn the ignition switch to ON. Failure to do this can damage the ignition switch (on late-model cars).

If the magnetic switch, or the solenoid, operates when the attempt to start is made without operation of the cranking motor, there is an open circuit inside the cranking motor or switch. Usually, under this condition the trouble will be found in the motor. Remove the cover band (where present) and check the brushes and the commutator. A dirty or burned commutator, worn or jammed brushes, or weak brush-spring tension will prevent the brushes from making good contact with the commutator so that the cranking motor will not function. Defects or failure to locate the trouble require removal of the cranking motor for further analysis and correction.

NOTE: When failure to start is due to a dirty commutator, starting can sometimes be accomplished by rotating the armature slightly by hand to form better contact. (Do not use a screwdriver, for this might damage the commutator.) Number 00 sandpaper may then be held against the revolving commutator by means of a piece of wood with the ignition off so that the engine does not start. This will clean off the commutator. Do not operate the cranking motor more than 30 seconds. The commutator should be turned down in a lathe and the mica undercut at the first opportunity (§ 23-4).

2. *Testing detached cranking motor.* No-load and stall tests can be made on a detached cranking motor to determine whether or not it is up

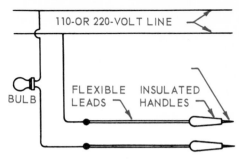

Fig. 23-12. Test points and lamp.

to specifications. These, plus the use of a set of test points and a test lamp (Fig. 23-12), should provide full information as to the unit.

a. No-load test. When the no-load test is made, the cranking motor is connected to a battery of the correct voltage, in series with a high-reading ammeter and the rpm (revolutions per minute) and current draw measured (Fig. 23-13). These should be compared with the manufacturer's specifications for the motor.

b. Stall test. This test is made by locking the drive pinion so that the armature cannot turn, and then applying a specified voltage to see what current the stalled motor will draw (Fig. 23-14).

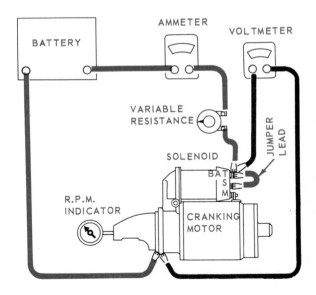

Fig. 23-13. Test setup for a no-load test. The variable resistance is used to adjust the voltage applied to the correct value. *(Delco-Remy Division of General Motors Corporation)*

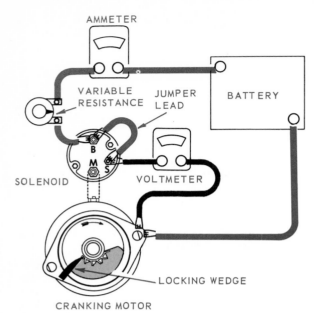

AMMETER

VARIABLE
RESISTANCE

JUMPER
LEAD

BATTERY

SOLENOID

B
M
S

VOLTMETER

LOCKING WEDGE

CRANKING MOTOR

Fig. 23-14. Stall test of a cranking motor. *(Delco-Remy Division of General Motors Corporation)*

A high-reading ammeter is required for this test as well as a high-capacity carbon-pile rheostat.

c. Interpreting no-load and stall test results. The following tabulation lists the six most common combinations of conditions found in testing cranking motors, along with further tests.

(1) Rated current draw and no-load speed indicate normal condition of the cranking motor.

(2) Low free speed and high current draw may result from:

  (a) Tight, dirty, or worn bearings; bent armature shaft; or loose field-pole screws, which allow the armature to drag on the pole shoes.

  (b) Grounded armature or fields. Raise the grounded brushes from the commutator and insulate them with cardboard. Then check with the test lamp between the insulated terminal of the cranking motor and the frame. If the test lamp lights, indicating a ground, raise the other brushes from the commutator and check fields and commutator separately to determine which is grounded. On some units, one end of the field circuit is normally grounded, and the ground screw or screws must be removed before the field can be tested for ground.

(c) Shorted armature. Check the armature further on a growler (§ 23–4).

(3) Failure to operate at all with a high current draw indicates:

  (a) Direct ground in the switch, terminal, or fields. This can be found with a test lamp by raising the grounded brushes as in (b) under item (2) above.

  (b) Frozen shaft bearings, which prevent the armature from turning.

  (c) Grounded armature windings, due, for instance, to thrown windings.

(4) Failure to operate with no current draw indicates:

  (a) Open field circuit. Inspect internal connections, and trace circuit with a test lamp, checking the brushes, armature, and fields.

  (b) Open armature coils. This condition causes badly burned commutator bars.

  (c) Broken or weak brush springs, worn brushes, high mica on the commutator, glazed or dirty commutator, or any other condition that would prevent good contact between the commutator and the brushes and thus prevent operation of the cranking motor. Most of these can be found by visual inspection.

(5) Low no-load speed with low current draw indicates:

  (a) An open field winding. Raise and insulate the ungrounded brushes from the commutator, and check the fields with a test lamp. Lamp should light as points are connected across each field.

  (b) High internal resistance due to poor connections, defective leads, dirty commutator, or any other condition listed in (c) under item (4) above.

(6) High free speed with a high current draw indicates shorted fields. Since the fields already have a low resistance, there is no practical way to test for this condition. If shorted fields are suspected, replace the fields and check for improvement in performance. But first check the other components of the cranking motor before going to this trouble.

§ 23–4. CRANKING - MOTOR SERVICE Some cranking motors require service only at the time that the engine is overhauled. Others have provision for lubrication and cover bands that can be removed to inspect the condition of the brushes and commutator. These units should be oiled and inspected every 5,000 miles.

In case of difficulty, the cranking motor should be removed from the engine and overhauled. Repair procedures are discussed in following paragraphs.

1. Damaged parts, their cause and correction. When a cranking motor is disassembled for repair or for periodic service, several types of defect may be found.

a. Thrown armature windings. Thrown armature windings are normally found only in the overrunning-clutch type of cranking motor. This condition results from excessive armature speed that has thrown the windings from the armature. Improper adjustment of the throttle-opening linkage, allowing the cranking motor to operate too ong after starting, and opening the throttle too wide all put an excessive burden on the overrunning clutch so that it tends to overheat, seize, and cause the armature to be spun at high speed. A defective overrunning clutch produces the same condition.

b. Burned commutator bars. Burned commutator bars usually indicate an open-circuited armature. The open normally will be found at one or more commutator riser bars and is most often caused by excessively long cranking periods. Such long cranking periods overheat the cranking motor so that the solder at the riser-bar connection is melted. This not only throws solder (thrown solder may be found on the cover band) but also causes the connection to loosen. Arcing then takes place each time the bar with the bad connection passes under the brushes, and the bar soon burns. If the bars are not too badly burned, the armature can be repaired by resoldering the connections at the riser bars (using rosin, not acid flux) and then turning the commutator and undercutting the mica.

c. Broken or distorted Bendix spring. A broken or distorted Bendix spring or a broken drive housing is usually caused by an attempted meshing while the engine is on a rockback or by an engine backfire during cranking. On Bendix-drive cranking motors, several seconds should elapse between attempts to start so that the drive pinion will not go into mesh with the flywheel when the engine is rocking backward. If the ignition is out of time, it may cause the engine to backfire during cranking, and this could cause a damaged drive or housing.

d. Dirty or gummy commutator. The commutator over a period of time sometimes becomes covered with a film of dirt or gum. Although this can be cleaned off with No. 00 sandpaper held against the commutator while the cranking motor is being operated (not more than 30 seconds), it is usually best to correct this condition by turning the commutator and undercutting the mica.

2. Cranking-motor disassembly, repair, and assembly. The disassembly of the cranking motor is usually simple. The solenoid or switch, where present, is removed first. Next, the cover band (where present) is removed, and the brush leads are disconnected. Or where leads are soldered, the brushes are removed from the holders. Then, after taking out the through bolts, the commutator end frame, field frame, and drive end can be separated. The Bendix drive can be removed from the armature shaft by taking out the drive-head attaching screw. The Folo-Thru drive is removed from the armature shaft by compressing the spring so that the end anchor plate clears the drive pin. The drive pin can then be pushed out of the shaft and the drive slid off the shaft. On overrunning-clutch cranking motors, the overrunning clutch can be slid off the shaft. Some models have a retainer and snap ring; these must be removed first before the overrunning clutch can be slid off. Figure 13–16 is a disassembled view of a passenger-car cranking motor.

a. Cleaning cranking-motor parts. The armature and fields should never be cleaned in any solution that dissolves or damages the insulation. They should be wiped off with a clean cloth.

b. Field-winding service. Test for a grounded field with test-lamp points on the terminal stud and frame. If the lamp lights, the field is grounded. Test for open with points at two ends of the field circuit. The lamp should light. If field windings require replacement, use a pole-shoe screwdriver and pole-shoe spreader (Fig. 23–15). The pole-shoe screwdriver prevents damage to the pole-shoe screws and assures tight reassembly of the shoes. The spreader prevents distortion of the field frame and holds the shoes firmly in place during reassembly. Rapping the frame with a plastic hammer while the screws are being tightened helps align the shoes properly. When resoldering connections, use rosin flux. Where moist conditions will be encountered, manufacturers recommend applications of special insulating varnish to field windings after reassembly to reduce the effects of moisture.

Fig. 23–15. Pole-shoe screwdriver being used on a field frame. Note that there is a pole-shoe spreader in place.

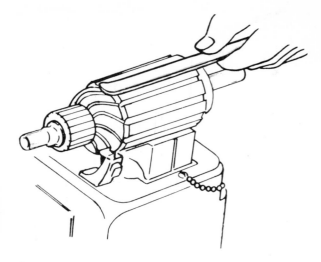

Fig. 23–16. Using a growler to test an armature for short circuits.

c. Armature service. Causes and correction of thrown armature windings and burned commutator bars have already been discussed in previous paragraphs. In addition to these conditions, inspect the armature lamination for rub marks, which would mean a worn bearing or a bent shaft that has allowed the insulation to rub on the pole shoes. A check for a bent shaft can be made by putting the armature in V blocks and rotating it while a dial indicator is placed in position to measure run-out. The run-out, or out-of-roundness, of the commutator can be checked at the same time.

The armature is tested electrically for ground by placing one test point on the lamination and the other on the commutator. If the lamp lights, the armature is grounded. It is tested for short circuits on the growler (Fig. 23–16). The armature is placed on the growler and slowly revolved

while a hacksaw blade is held above the armature core. Short circuits in the armature cause the hacksaw blade to vibrate against the core when it is held above the slot containing the shorted winding. A shorted or grounded armature should be discarded.

If the commutator is out of round, or worn, or if it has high mica, it should be turned in a lathe (Fig. 23–17). The cut should be as smooth and as light as possible. Then, the mica should be undercut $\frac{1}{32}$ inch deep. This operation may be done with a ground-down hacksaw blade (Fig. 23–18) or with a motor-driven undercutter. In either case, the undercutting should be 0.002 inch wider than the mica, to assure removal of all mica. Sand off all burrs with No. 00 sandpaper. Be sure that no burrs or copper dust remain between bars.

Where moist conditions are encountered, manufacturers recommend application of special in-

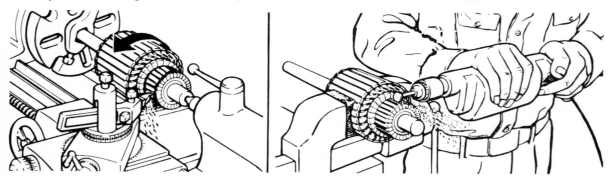

Fig. 23–17. Turning an armature commutator in a lathe and undercutting the mica with an electric drill. *(Delco-Remy Division of General Motors Corporation)*

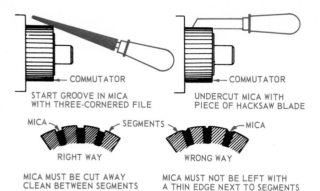

COMMUTATOR

START GROOVE IN MICA
WITH THREE-CORNERED FILE

COMMUTATOR

UNDERCUT MICA WITH
PIECE OF HACKSAW BLADE

MICA — SEGMENTS — MICA

RIGHT WAY

MICA MUST BE CUT AWAY
CLEAN BETWEEN SEGMENTS

WRONG WAY

MICA MUST NOT BE LEFT WITH
A THIN EDGE NEXT TO SEGMENTS

Fig. 23-18. Undercutting the mica on an armature commutator with a hacksaw blade. *(Delco-Remy Division of General Motors Corporation)*

sulating varnish to the armature to reduce the effects of moisture. Varnish should be kept off the shaft and commutator.

d. Brush service. Brushes that are worn to one-half of their original length should be replaced. When the brush lead is soldered, unsolder it and unclinch the lead from the connector. Where the lead terminal clip is riveted to the frame, unsolder and unclamp the lead from the clip, so that the lead of a new brush can be clamped and soldered to the clip. With new brushes in place, put the armature into position so that the brushes rest on the commutator. If the brushes do not align with the commutator bars, the brush holders

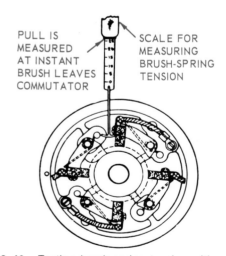

PULL IS MEASURED AT INSTANT BRUSH LEAVES COMMUTATOR

SCALE FOR MEASURING BRUSH-SPRING TENSION

Fig. 23-19. Testing brush-spring tension with a spring scale. Refer to manufacturer's specifications for actual tension of unit under check. *(Delco-Remy Division of General Motors Corporation)*

are bent, and this requires replacement of the brush holders or the end frame. The brush-spring tension should be checked with a spring scale (Fig. 23-19). Note the pull required to raise the brushes, brush arms, or holders from the contact position. Replace the springs if the tension is not correct.

e. Cranking-motor-drive lubrication. The Bendix-type and Folo-Thru drives should be cleaned by washing in kerosene. They should not be lubricated. The overrunning-clutch type of drive must never be cleaned by a high-temperature or grease-dissolving method, since this would remove the grease originally packed in the clutch. With the grease thus removed, the clutch would soon fail.

f. Testing the overrunning clutch. The overrunning-clutch pinion should turn freely and smoothly in the overrunning direction and should not slip in the cranking position with normal cranking torque imposed on it. If the pinion turns roughly in the overrunning direction, the rollers are chipped or worn and the clutch should be replaced. If the pinion slips in the cranking direction, the clutch should be replaced.

g. Cranking-motor lubrication. During reassembly of the cranking motor, all bearings should be lubricated with a few drops of light engine oil. Many cranking motors have oilless bearings that have no provision for oiling. They should be lubricated, however, before cranking-motor reassembly, with a few drops of light engine oil. On gear-reduction motors, the gear-reduction housing should be packed with graphite or high-melting-point grease before reassembly.

h. Cranking-motor assembly. The assembly procedure is the reverse of disassembly. Soldered connections should be made with rosin, not acid, flux.

i. Overrunning-clutch-pinion clearance. On the overrunning-clutch type of cranking motor, the clearance between the pinion and the thrust washer, retainer, or housing should be measured with the pinion in the cranking position after assembly is completed. It should be $5/64$ inch on Auto-Lite cranking motors, measured between the thrust washer and the pinion. On Delco-Remy units not using a retainer and snap ring on the armature shaft, the clearance between pinion and housing should be $3/16$ inch. On Delco-Remy units with the retainer and snap ring, clearance between the pinion and retainer should be 0.010 to 0.140 inch. Adjustment on some manual types is made by turning the starting-switch button in or out and on many solenoid types by turning the solenoid-plunger stud in or out. Some solenoids do not have an adjustable stud; on these, adjustment is made by loosening the four mounting screws and then moving the solenoid back or forth as necessary to obtain the proper clearance. Other solenoid types have no adjustments.

j. Folo-Thru drive. On the Folo-Thru drive, do not turn the pinion out to the extended, or cranking, position. In this position, a lockpin drops into a detent in the sleeve thread to lock the pinion in the cranking position (see Fig. 13–18). The only way the pinion can be unlocked is to mount the cranking motor on the engine and start the engine. When engine speed increases to around 400 rpm, the lockpin will be retracted by centrifugal force. The pinion will then de-mesh and move back to the retracted position.

k. Testing assembled cranking motor. The cranking motor should be submitted to no-load and torque tests, as outlined above, to make sure that it can operate according to specifications.

3. Installing cranking motor. Whenever a cranking motor is being installed or removed, the battery ground cable should be disconnected from the battery terminal in order to avoid shorting the battery by an accidental grounding of the insulated cable. When installing the cranking motor, connect the leads after the motor is bolted into place in the flywheel housing. Then check the throttle-cracker linkage on cars so equipped, and adjust as necessary in order to obtain the proper throttle opening during cranking. This is particularly important on overrunning-clutch cranking motors, since an excessive throttle opening might spin the overrunning clutch at high speed during initial engine operation, thus causing the overrunning clutch to be overloaded.

4. Checking the cranking-motor circuit. After the cranking motor has been reinstalled on the engine or whenever the circuit requires checking, the cables and connections can be tested with a low-reading voltmeter while a high-current draw is taken through the circuit. This procedure will locate any excessive resistance due to poor connections or bad cables, which would prevent the delivery of normal amounts of current to the cranking motor.

Two methods of providing the high current through the cables can be used. In one method, the cranking motor is operated. In the other, a heavy variable resistance is used. With either system, the high amperage from the battery flowing through the circuit will show up excessive resistance in the circuit, because there will be an excessive voltage drop. Too much voltage drop will reduce the voltage at the cranking motor and normal operation will not be achieved.

5. Checking with the cranking motor. A low-reading voltmeter is required for this check. Ground the ignition primary lead at the ignition distributor so that the engine will not start. Operate the cranking motor and, *very quickly,* check (1) from the insulated battery post to the solenoid battery terminal, (2) from the grounded battery post to the cranking-motor housing, and (3) from the solenoid battery terminal to the solenoid motor terminal. Do not use the cranking motor for more than 30 seconds. More than a 0.2-volt drop (0.1 volt on 6-volt circuits) on any of these indicates excessive resistance.

The remedy is to disconnect the cables and clean the cable clamps and terminal posts (see § 23–2, 2). Use new cables if the old ones seem to be in bad condition. Be sure that all connections are clean and tight. Always use cables of adequate size; undersize cables will have too much resistance and may prevent normal cranking, particularly during cold weather. If the excessive resistance is in the solenoid switch, the switch must be disassembled for cleaning or replacement of the contact disk or contacts.

NOTE: On some applications, extra-long battery cables are required because of the locations of battery and cranking motor. This may result in somewhat higher voltage drops than the recommended 0.1- or 0.2-volt. On such applications, the normal voltage drop should be established by checking several vehicles. Then when a voltage drop well above this normal value is found, excessive resistance must be located and eliminated.

Review Questions

1. In what five ways can batteries be tested?
2. Describe the light-load test.
3. Describe the high-discharge test.
4. Describe the hydrometer test of battery electrolyte.
5. Describe the 421 test.
6. Describe the cadmium-tip test.
7. Explain how the specific gravity of the electrolyte varies with the state of charge of the battery.
8. How does gravity vary with temperature?
9. What effect does age have on battery gravity?
10. What is battery self-discharge?
11. How is battery gravity adjusted for hot climates?
12. Does a discharged or a charged battery freeze more easily?
13. What cautions must be observed with regard to the gases that form in the battery during battery charge?
14. What are the four divisions of battery service?
15. Why is overcharging harmful to the battery?
16. What causes cracked battery cases? Bulged cases?
17. How are corroded battery terminals and cable clamps serviced? A corroded battery holder? A dirty battery top?
18. Explain how to remove and replace a battery.
19. Name two methods of charging batteries.
20. What is a quick charger?
21. What are battery "dopes"?
22. Name two cautions to be observed in caring for wet batteries in storage.
23. Explain how to activate a dry charged battery.
24. Describe the process of testing a cranking motor on a car.
25. Describe the process of testing a detached cranking motor.
26. What is the most common cause of thrown cranking-motor armature windings?
27. What causes burned commutator bars on a cranking-motor armature?
28. What produces broken Bendix springs?
29. What is a pole-shoe screwdriver?
30. How is it used?
31. How is an armature tested on a growler?
32. What cautions must be observed in cleaning cranking-motor parts?
33. How is an overrunning clutch tested?
34. What is the overrunning-clutch-pinion clearance?

Study Questions

1. Why does the specific gravity of the battery electrolyte change with the state of charge of the battery? With temperature?
2. List the six most common combinations of conditions found in testing cranking motors, and either explain what they mean or describe the trouble-shooting process.
3. Describe the process of repairing burned commutator bars.
4. Describe the procedure of disassembling a cranking motor.
5. What is the procedure of turning an armature commutator?
6. How is the armature-commutator mica undercut?
7. How would you apply torque on a cranking-motor overrunning-clutch pinion to check it?

24

NYLON NUT

ADJUSTING SCREW
(TURN TO ADJUST
VOLTAGE SETTING)

Electric-system Service — The Charging System

This chapter continues the discussion of electric-system service and describes the checking and servicing of the components of the charging system. These components consist of the generator and the regulator as well as the battery, already discussed in Chapter 23. Note that there are two separate testing and trouble-diagnosis procedures given in following pages, one for d-c generator-regulator systems and one for a-c alternator-regulator systems.

● **CAUTION:** Never use d-c checks on an a-c system or a-c checks on a d-c system. This could ruin the equipment.

D-C REGULATORS AND GENERATORS

§ 24–1. TESTING D-C GENERATOR-REGULATOR SYSTEMS When abnormal operation is noted in a d-c generator-regulator system of a car, it is often necessary to make preliminary checks to determine whether the regulator or the generator is causing the trouble. The first step is to check the condition of charge of the battery (§ 23–2)

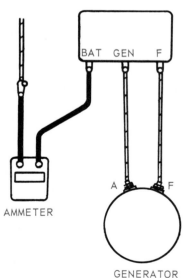

Fig. 24–1. Ammeter connections to check d-c generator output.

and the charging rate to the battery with the generator operating at medium speed with a test ammeter connected into the charging circuit as shown in Fig. 24–1.

Any one of four conditions may be found in checking the battery and the charging rate: (1) charged battery and a low charging rate, (2) charged battery and a high charging rate, (3) discharged battery and a high charging rate, and (4) a discharged battery and a low charging rate. Let us investigate further the meaning of these conditions and the defects implied when any of them is found.

1. Charged battery and a low charging rate. This is a normal condition.

2. Charged battery and a high charging rate. With the ammeter connected as shown in Fig. 24–2, operate the generator at medium speed, and disconnect the lead from the regulator F (field) terminal. This opens the generator field circuit, and if the generator is in normal condition, the output will drop off. If it does not, the generator is at fault, and it should be checked further, as outlined in § 24–3. If the output does drop off when the F-terminal lead is disconnected, the trouble is in the regulator, and it should be checked for a high voltage setting or a shorted condition.

3. Discharged battery and a high charging rate. This is a normal condition, since the regulator permits the generator output to increase when the battery is in a low state of charge.

4. Discharged battery and a low charging rate. Defective leads and bad connections in the circuit between the generator and the battery will cause

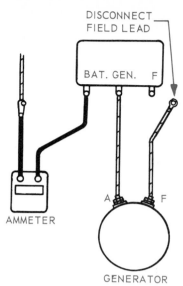

Fig. 24-2. Field lead is disconnected from the regulator F (field) terminal to locate trouble if high output is obtained with a charged battery.

the regulator to operate as though the battery were fully charged, so that the charging rate is reduced to a low value even though the battery is in a discharged condition. Thus, where a low charging rate is found with a discharged battery, the drive belt, wiring, and connections should be inspected as a first step in the analysis of the trouble. Then make the tests given below for d-c units.

● **CAUTION:** Do not try d-c tests on a-c units! This could ruin them.

On d-c generators only, bypass the generator field circuit in the regulator. This will enable you to determine whether the generator or the regulator is responsible. To bypass the generator field circuit through the regulator on the type of regulator shown in Fig. 14-15, a jumper lead should be connected between the F terminal and the ground. On the type shown in Fig. 14-16, the jumper lead should be connected between the F and GEN terminals.

● **CAUTION:** Do not ground the generator field circuit on late-model Delco-Remy double-contact regulators, since this would burn the regulator contact points.

● **CAUTION:** These tests are for d-c units only. Making such tests on a-c equipment may ruin it.

If the output does not increase after making the connection with the generator operating at medium speed, the trouble is in the generator, and it should be checked further (§ 24-3). If the output does increase, the regulator is at fault, and it should be checked for a low voltage setting or for oxidized or dirty contact points. In addition, it may be that the cutout relay is not closing because of a high setting or an open winding.

● **CAUTION:** After any regulator or generator tests (on d-c equipment only), or after installation of either unit on the car, the generator must be *polarized* to make sure that it has the correct polarity with respect to the battery. This prevents arcing and burning of the cutout-relay points that might otherwise occur. The procedure varies according to whether the generator field is externally grounded (Fig. 14-15) or internally grounded (Fig. 14-16). When the field is externally grounded, polarize the generator by momentarily connecting a jumper lead between the ammeter (or battery) and generator terminals of the regulator or the relay. When the field is internally grounded, polarize the generator by disconnecting the field lead from the F (field) terminal of the regulator and momentarily touching this lead to the regulator battery terminal. In either case, this should be done after all leads are connected and before the engine is started. The action allows a momentary flash of current to flow through the generator field so that the generator is correctly polarized.

● **CAUTION:** Never operate the generator on open circuit, that is, with the charging circuit disconnected. This would allow a damagingly high voltage to build up in the generator.

§ 24-2. REGULATORS FOR D-C SYSTEMS These regulators consist of a voltage regulator, a current regulator, and a cutout relay. Regulator electrical adjustments must be made with the regulator at operating temperature and in operating position. The electrical settings should be checked with the cover in place. Further, after each electrical adjustment, the cover must be replaced and the generator cycled (slowed until cutout relay opens and then brought back to speed).

1. Cutout relay. Connect an ammeter and a voltmeter to the regulator as shown in Fig. 24-3. Slowly increase the generator speed and note the voltage at which contact points close. Slowly decrease the generator speed and note the reverse amperage at which the points open.

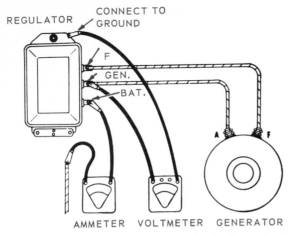

Fig. 24–3. Meter connections to check d-c cutout-relay closing voltage and opening amperage. *(Delco-Remy Division of General Motors Corporation)*

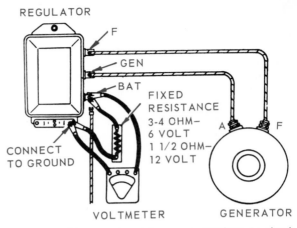

Fig. 24–4. Meter and resistance connections to check a d-c voltage regulator by the fixed-resistance method. *(Delco-Remy Division of General Motors Corporation)*

Adjust the closing voltage by changing the armature spring tension. Increasing the tension increases the closing voltage. Auto-Lite relays have a spiral spring attached to the armature; the lower spring hanger is bent to change the spring tension. Delco-Remy relays are adjusted by either bending the spring arm on which the armature spring rests or turning an adjustment screw on which the spring rests.

Recheck the closing voltage after each adjustment. If the adjustment cannot be made or if the reverse amperage is not within limits, remove the regulator and check it. Refer to a shop manual.

2. Voltage regulator. A typical meter hookup to check the voltage regulator setting is shown in Fig. 24–4. Note that a fixed resistance has been substituted for the charging circuit and battery. This will cause the voltage regulator to operate as though connected to a fully charged battery. Operate the generator at the specified speed and note the voltage reading. The regulator must be at operating temperature, and the cover must be in place.

Adjust the regulator armature by changing its spring tension. Increasing the tension increases the voltage setting. Final adjustment should be made by increasing the spring tension, not lowering it. Replace the cover and cycle the generator before rechecking the voltage setting.

On the Delco-Remy double-contact regulator, use meter connections as shown in Fig. 24–5 to check both sets of contacts. With the variable resistance out, the upper contacts will operate. With the variable resistance cut in, the lower con-

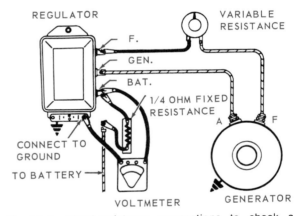

Fig. 24–5. Fixed-resistance connections to check a d-c voltage-regulator setting. Variable resistance is used to control and cycle the generator. *(Delco-Remy Division of General Motors Corporation)*

tacts will operate. Adjust the upper contacts by turning the adjustment screw in the lower spring hanger to change the spring tension. The difference between the operating voltage of the upper contacts and the lower contacts (which should be about 0.1 to 0.3 volt) can be changed by changing the armature air gap. Increasing the air gap increases the difference between the voltages.

If adjustments cannot be made correctly or if faulty operation is noted, remove the regulator for further checking. Check the right manual.

3. Current regulator. A sufficient load must be applied to prevent the voltage regulator from operating. This can be done by connecting an ammeter and heavy variable resistance as shown in Fig. 24-6. Turn on the lights and radio and apply an additional load with the variable resistance to keep the system voltage below the voltage-regulator setting. With the generator operating at the specified speed and the regulator hot, cycle the generator and note the current setting. Adjust it by changing the armature spring tension. Increasing the tension increases the current setting.

If adjustment cannot be made correctly or if faulty operation is noted, remove the regulator for further checking. Refer to the applicable automotive shop manual for specific checking instructions.

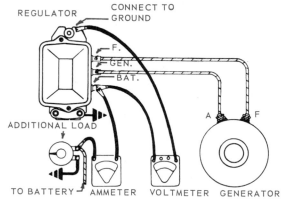

Fig. 24-6. Meter and variable resistance connections to check a d-c current regulator by the load method. *(Delco-Remy Division of General Motors Corporation)*

§ 24-3. D-C GENERATORS
If a d-c generator is found to be malfunctioning (as determined by the generator-regulator tests in § 24-1), check it further, as follows.

1. Generator produces no output. Remove the generator cover band, and check for sticking brushes, a gummed or burned commutator, or poor connections. If trouble is not readily apparent, remove the generator from the car, and test it further with a test light and points (Fig. 23-12). The procedure to be used depends on the type of generator being checked. One type (Fig. 14-15) grounds the generator field in the regulator; another type (Fig. 14-16) grounds the generator field within the generator. Tracing the field leads in the generator will permit you to determine which type the generator is. If one of the leads is connected to an insulated brush, it is of the *first* type. If one field lead is connected to a grounded brush or screw, the generator is of the *second* type.

a. First type (Fig. 14-15)

(1) Test for ground by raising the grounded generator brush from the commutator and checking with a test lamp from the generator armature terminal to the frame. If the lamp lights, the generator is grounded. Raise the other brush or brushes, and check the field circuit (field terminal to frame) and the armature (commutator to frame) separately for ground.

(2) Check for an open field by placing the test points from the armature to the field terminals of the generator. If the light does not burn, the field circuit is open.

(3) Check for a shorted field by connecting an ammeter and a battery of the specified voltage in series with the field windings. Proceed with care, since a shorted field will draw a high current that might damage the ammeter. If a shorted field is found, the regulator contact points should be checked. They are probably burned from the high field current resulting from the shorted field.

(4) Open circuits in the armature are usually readily apparent, since this condition causes burned commutator bars. Another sign of open circuits is thrown solder on the cover band. This usually develops from the overloading and overheating of the generator so that the solder at the commutator-bar connections is melted and thrown out, with a consequent development of bad connections. Where this is found, the regulator should be checked for a high setting. The bad connections cause heavy arcing to take place when the bars pass under the generator brushes, so that the bars are quickly burned. If the burning is not too serious, repair can be made by resoldering the connections at the commutator bars (using rosin, not acid, flux) and then turning the commutator and undercutting the mica (§ 23-4).

(5) The armature can be tested for short circuits on a growler (§ 23-4, item 2c).

b. Second type (Fig. 14-16)

(1) Test for a grounded armature by raising the grounded brush from the commutator and checking with a test lamp from the armature terminal to the generator frame. If the lamp lights, the armature, or the insulated brush-to-terminal circuit, is grounded.

(2) Test for grounded fields by disconnecting the field lead from the grounded brush or frame and checking from the field terminal to the frame with a test lamp. If the lamp lights, the field is grounded.

(3) Check for an open field circuit by connecting the test points between the field terminal and

the lead that was disconnected in the previous test. The lamp should light. If it does not, the circuit is open.

(4) Check for a shorted field by connecting a battery of the specified voltage and an ammeter in series with the field windings. Proceed with care, since a shorted field will draw a high current. Check the regulator points if a shorted field is found.

(5) Open circuits in the armature are, as a rule, easy to detect, since they cause burned commutator bars, and thrown solder may be found on the cover band (see item [4] above, under *First type*).

(6) Short circuits in the armature can be detected on a growler (§ 23–4, item 2c).

2. *Generator produces excessive output.* Excessive output from the type of d-c generator that normally has the field grounded in the regulator (Fig. 14–15) will result from a grounded field circuit in the generator. This can be quickly detected by raising the grounded brush and checking from the field terminal to the generator frame with a test lamp.

Excessive output from the type of generator that has the field circuit internally grounded (Fig. 14–16) may result from a shorted field or from a short between the field and the insulated brush.

3. *Generator produces unsteady or low output.* Low or unsteady output may be caused by:
   a. Loose or worn drive belt, which causes belt slippage.
   b. Sticking or worn brushes, low brush-spring tension, glazed or burned commutator, or other conditions that might prevent good contact between the brushes and the commutator.
   c. Out-of-round, dirty, rough, or worn commutator. Dirt in the commutator slots or high mica also causes low or unsteady output.

4. *Noisy generator.* There is some noise inherent in generator operation, but it may become excessive if the mounting, drive pulley, or gear is loose. Worn or dirty bearings or improperly seated brushes also may produce noise.

§ 24–4. D-C GENERATOR LUBRICATION
Many d-c generators have sealed ball bearings and do not require lubrication. Generators with hinge-cap oilers should have a few drops of medium-weight oil every engine-oil change or vehicle-lubrication period.

§ 24–5. D-C GENERATOR SERVICE
Service of d-c generators can be divided into the two types discussed below.

1. *Inspection on vehicle.* At intervals of 5,000 miles, on the average, the cover band (on units so equipped) should be removed from the generator and the brushes and commutator inspected. Look through the windows in the end frame to inspect the brushes and the commutator on units without a cover band. If the brushes are worn, they should be replaced. A dirty commutator can be cleaned by holding a strip of No. 00 sandpaper against it with a piece of soft wood while the generator is operating. Emery cloth must never be used, since particles of emery will embed and cause rapid brush wear. If the commutator is rough or out of round, has high mica, or is very dirty or gummy, it should be turned down in a lathe and the mica undercut (§ 23–4). If particles of solder are found on the inside of the cover band, it means that the generator has been overloaded and overheated so that the solder at the commutator bars has melted and been thrown out. The armature can be repaired, if the bars have not become too badly burned, by resoldering the connections with rosin flux. Then, the commutator should be turned down and the mica undercut. Be sure that all leads, nuts, screws, and terminals are tight. The generator mounting, drive-belt tension, and pulley nut should be checked. As a final step, the generator output should be tested.

2. *Generator (d-c type) disassembly, repair, and assembly.* The disassembly of the generator is usually simple. The cover band (on units so equipped) should be removed and the leads from the fields and the terminal disconnected from the brush holders. The through bolts or commutator end-frame attaching screws should be removed, followed by the field frame. The armature can then be placed in the soft jaws of a vise so that the pulley nut, pulley, and drive end frame can be removed. Figure 14–5 illustrates a disassembled view of a typical passenger-car d-c generator.

   a. *Cleaning d-c generator parts.* The armature and fields should never be cleaned in any solvent or cleaning solution that dissolves or damages the insulation. Instead, they should be wiped off with a clean cloth.

   b. *Ball bearings.* If not of the sealed type, ball bearings should be carefully cleaned by being washed in clean gasoline, kerosene, or carbon tetrachloride. Swish the bearings in the cleaner, and revolve them while submerged. After cleaning, spin the bearings in clean, light oil, and immediately relubricate them with ball-bearing grease.

c. *Field-winding service.* Test fields for open by putting test points on the two ends of the field-winding circuit. If the lamp does not light, the field circuit is open. Test fields for ground by disconnecting the lead from the brush or the ground and putting the test points on the field terminal and frame. If the lamp lights, the field circuit is grounded. Test fields for shorts by connecting them in series with an ammeter and a battery of the specified voltage. Proceed with care, because a shorted field may draw a current that is too high for the ammeter.

NOTE: If a shorted field is found, check the regulator contact points, since the high-current draw may have burned the points of the regulator that was used with the generator.

Defective field windings should be replaced by use of a pole-shoe screwdriver and a pole-shoe spreader (§ 23–4). As a rule, it is not economical to attempt to repair shorted or open field windings. In some cases, grounded field windings can be repaired with additional insulation. However, excessive bulkiness must be avoided, since the pole shoes could cut through the extra insulation and produce another ground. Make soldered connections with rosin flux. Where excessively moist operating conditions prevail, field windings can be treated with insulating varnish, after installation, as specified by generator manufacturer.

d. *Armature service.* As with cranking-motor armatures, generator armatures can be checked for run-out with V blocks and a dial indicator. Also, they can be checked for grounds with test points and for opens on a growler (§ 23–4).

EXCEPTION: A few armatures have internal connections that cause them to check shorted on the growler. On these, a special 3-volt a-c voltmeter must be used to check voltage between bars while the armature is held on the growler.

Burned commutator bars indicate open windings in the armature. Usually the openings occur at the bar, and repairs can be made (if the bars are not too badly burned) by resoldering the connections (using rosin flux) and then turning the commutator and undercutting the mica (§ 23–4). Likewise, a commutator that is out of round or worn, or one with high mica, should be repaired by turning. The mica should then be undercut.

Where moist conditions are encountered, manufacturers recommend the application of special insulating varnish to the armature. Varnish should be kept off the shaft and the commutator.

e. *Brush service.* Brushes worn to one-half of their original length should be replaced. Seat new brushes with No. 00 sandpaper or brush-seating stone. Then, with the armature in place in the commutator end frame, check the brush-spring tension as well as the brush alignment. If the brushes do not align with the commutator bars, the brush holders are bent and should be replaced. Tension is checked by measuring with a spring scale the pull required to raise brushes, brush arms, or holders from their contact position. Replace the springs if the tension is not correct.

f. *Reassembly.* Reassembly is the reverse of disassembly. Make sure that the pulley nut is drawn up to the proper tension and that the brush leads are tight. Test the generator after reassembly is complete, and if it has an adjustable third brush, adjust it to obtain the proper generator output.

g. *Polarizing d-c generator.* After any regulator or generator tests or after the removal and installation of either unit, the generator must be polarized so that it will have the proper polarity with respect to the battery (see Caution at end of § 24–1).

A-C ALTERNATOR-REGULATOR SYSTEMS

24–6. TESTING A-C ALTERNATOR-REGULATOR SYSTEMS A variety of testing equipment and procedures are recommended by the various automotive manufacturers. General Motors recommends a series of checks with jumper leads and a voltmeter. Ford has a special ARE 20–22 tester which uses lights to indicate various troubles. Chrysler's testing system is somewhat similar to General Motor's but requires a carbon-pile rheostat to load the alternator during test. There are variations from all these basic procedures, because each manufacturer supplies a variety of alternators and regulators. The following are typical.

● **CAUTION:** Do not attempt to polarize an alternator. This could seriously damage the equipment.

§ 24–7. CHRYSLER-PLYMOUTH TROUBLE DIAGNOSIS The trouble-diagnosis tabulation that follows applies especially to this manufacturer's system but also, in general, to others.

COMPLAINT	POSSIBLE CAUSE	CHECK OR CORRECTION
No output	Blown fusible wire in regulator	Correct cause and replace wire
	Drive belt loose	Readjust
	Worn or sticking brushes	Clean holders, replace brushes if necessary
	Worn slip ring	Clean or replace
	Open field	Check wiring connections, contact points, field windings
	Open stator or diodes	Check, disassemble and replace if necessary
Low output	Loose drive belt	Tighten
	Low regulator setting	Readjust
	Shorted or open diode	Check, replace as necessary
	Grounded or open stator windings	Test, replace as necessary
	High resistance in charging circuit	Check connections at battery, ground, etc.
High output and battery overcharge	High regulator setting	Adjust
	Contacts stuck	Install new regulator
	Regulator winding open	Install new regulator
	Regulator base not grounded	Connect base to good ground

§ 24–8. FORD TROUBLE DIAGNOSIS Ford recommends the use of a special ARE 20-22 charging circuit tester (Fig. 24–7), although they also outline, in their shop manuals, procedures for using an ampere-voltage tester. The ARE 20-22 tester has special harness connectors so that it can be inserted into the wiring harness at the regulator. Then, the circuit selector switch is positioned according to whether the system uses an indicator lamp or an ammeter. Next, the engine is started and operated at between 1,000 and 1,500 rpm while two tests are run by moving the

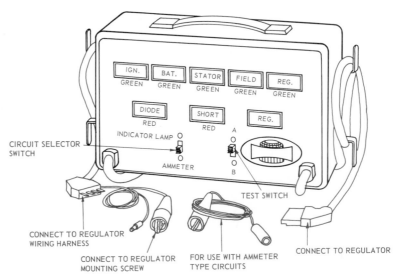

Fig. 24–7. ARE 20-22 charging circuit tester. *(Ford Division of Ford Motor Company)*

test switch to A and then to B. The pattern of lights will indicate whether or not everything is in order and, if not, what is wrong.

§ 24-9. GENERAL MOTORS TROUBLE DIAGNOSIS

This diagnosis procedure considers three troubles, faulty indicator-lamp operation, undercharged battery, and overcharged battery.

1. Faulty indicator-lamp operation. If the lamp remains on with the engine turned off, there is a shorted diode in the alternator or a short in the line. This condition will run down the battery.

If the lamp does not come on when the ignition switch is turned on, before starting the engine, there is an open in the indicator-lamp circuit, or the lamp itself is burned out.

If the lamp stays on after the engine is started, check as outlined under *2. Undercharged battery.*

2. Undercharged battery. This could be caused by a low regulator setting, loose drive belt, defective battery, poor circuit connections, open resistor (which parallels the indicator lamp), malfunctioning field relay, or a defective generator.

3. Overcharged battery. This could be caused by a high regulator setting, a defective battery, or poor circuit connections.

§ 24-10. A-C REGULATOR ADJUSTMENTS

Typical voltage adjustments for a-c regulators are described below.

1. Chrysler-Plymouth. The voltage setting is checked by making the connections with a test ammeter, voltmeter, on-off switch, and carbon-pile rheostat, as shown in Fig. 24-8.

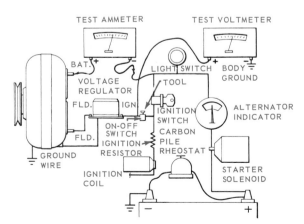

Fig. 24-8. Test connections to check a-c voltage regulator setting. *(Chrysler-Plymouth Division of Chrysler Motors Corporation)*

● **CAUTION:** Do not ground the field circuit with the ignition turned on. This will blow the fuse wire in the regulator and could ruin it.

Start the engine and operate it at 1,250 rpm. Adjust carbon pile rheostat to get a 15-ampere output. Operate for 15 minutes until system reaches operating temperature. Then readjust speed to 1,250 rpm if necessary. Readjust carbon pile to get a 15-ampere output.

Flash the voltage regulator circuit by opening and closing the on-off switch several times. Note voltage reading. Chrysler-built regulators are adjusted by bending the lower spring hanger. Essex-built regulators are adjusted by turning the adjustment screw in the regulator cover. Do not change the regulator setting more than 0.3 volt. Retest for battery-condition improvement after a week's operation with the new voltage setting and then readjust again if necessary.

2. Ford. The Ford regulator is a sealed, factory-calibrated unit, and no adjusting instructions are supplied by Ford. In case of malfunctioning, the regulator should be replaced with a new unit.

3. General Motors. The voltage regulator with the field relay used with an indicator lamp (Fig. 14-22) is checked with a voltmeter and a $1/4$-ohm 25-watt resistor. A test prod is inserted into No. 3 terminal of the regulator, and the voltmeter is connected from this test prod to ground. Then the $1/4$-ohm resistor is connected in series by disconnecting the battery ground strap from the battery and connecting the resistor between the grounded battery terminal and the ground strap.

Next, short across the resistor with a jumper cable in order to start the engine.

● **CAUTION:** Do not operate the engine with the battery disconnected!

With all accessories turned off, operate the engine at idle for 15 minutes to bring the regulator up to operating temperature. Cycle the regulator by detaching and then reattaching the harness connector at the regulator.

Bring engine speed up to 2,000 to 2,200 rpm. Note temperature at regulator and voltage setting. Compare with specifications. Adjust, if necessary, by detaching the harness connector (to avoid accidental and possibly damaging grounds), removing the cover, and reconnecting the harness connector. Then, turn the adjusting screw to change the spiral spring tension (Fig. 24-9).

NYLON NUT

ADJUSTING SCREW
(TURN TO ADJUST
VOLTAGE SETTING)

Fig. 24-9. Adjusting the upper-contact voltage setting. *(Delco-Remy Division of General Motors Corporation)*

● **CAUTION:** Make sure that the spring holder is tight against the head of the adjusting screw. To do this when backing out the screw, back it out a little more than is necessary. Then pry the spring holder up against the screw and turn the screw down to make the final adjustment.

After each adjustment, cycle the regulator by disconnecting and then reconnecting the harness connector at the regulator.

To check the lower contacts, slowly decrease engine speed until voltage decreases a few tenths of a volt, showing that the action has transferred from the upper to the lower contacts. If the differential is not correct, adjust the nylon nut (Fig. 24-9) to attain the proper differential volt-

age. If this adjustment is made, the upper-contact voltage must be rechecked and readjusted.

● **CAUTION:** When replacing the cover, first disconnect the harness connecter at the regulator. Replace it after the cover is on.

§ 24-11. A-C GENERATOR SERVICE When removing or replacing ball or roller bearings, be sure to exert pressure on the race that is tight (on the shaft or in the end frame), not on the race that is free. Service procedures for some typical units follow. See Figs. 24-10 and 24-11 for views of disassembled generators.

1. Chrysler. To disassemble the alternator, remove the brushes (insulated brush first) and then remove the through bolts and separate the stator and the slip-ring end frame from the drive end frame by prying with a screwdriver. Take off the pulley with a puller; pry off the bearing retainer (three places) from the end frame to remove the rotor and bearing from the frame.

If rectifier diodes are defective, a special tool is required to press out the old and press in the new units. Hold the diode wire close to the diode with pliers when soldering the wire to prevent heat from working back into the diode.

● **CAUTION:** The diode must not be overheated, jarred, dropped, hammered on, or otherwise treated roughly; such treatment may ruin it.

New bearings or slip rings can be installed with special puller and replacer tools.

2. Delco-Remy. There are several models of Delco-Remy a-c generators. Figure 24-10 shows

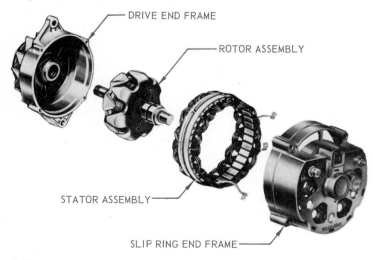

DRIVE END FRAME

ROTOR ASSEMBLY

STATOR ASSEMBLY

SLIP RING END FRAME

Fig. 24-10. Partly disassembled view of an a-c generator. *(Delco-Remy Division of General Motors Corporation)*

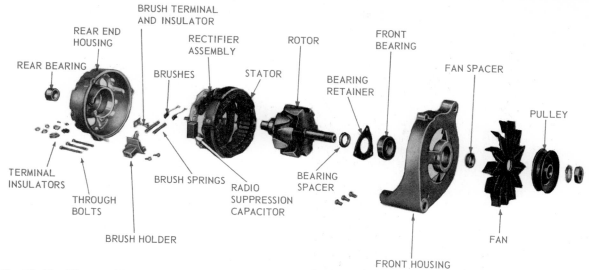

Fig. 24–11. Disassembled view of an a-c generator. *(Ford Division of Ford Motor Company)*

one type. In general, disassembly is done by removing the through bolts and separating the end frames from the stator. To avoid damaging the brushes, use through bolts to hold the brushes up when separating the end frame from the stator. Take off the pulley to separate the rotor from the end frame. Bearings are replaced with a special puller.

To service diodes, heat the end frame to 150°F to make diode removal easier. New diodes have long leads. Cut them to length, holding the lead (not the diode case) in pliers. Cover the diode threads with silicone grease and tighten in the end frame to the specified torque. Crimp the lead to flexible leads and solder with 360°F solder, using rosin flux. Avoid excessive heat on the diode.

3. Ford. Figure 24–11 is a view of a disassembled Ford a-c generator. Disassembly is done by removing the pulley (with a puller), then the nuts, washers, and insulators from the terminals, and then the screws and terminal cover. Next remove the brush-holder assembly. Pull the slip-ring end housing and stator assembly from the rotor with a puller. If bearings need replacement, pull them with a puller. If the diodes are defective, replace the complete rectifier assembly in the slip-ring end housing (diodes are not separately replaceable).

§ 24–12. BELT-TENSION ADJUSTMENT The drive belt must be properly tightened. A loose belt will slip and soon wear out, and it will not

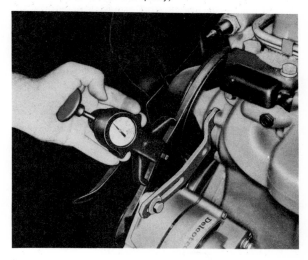

Fig. 24–12. Using a special tool to check fan-belt tension. *(Chevrolet Motor Division of General Motors Corporation)*

drive the generator fast enough to keep the battery charged. An excessively tight belt will cause rapid bearing wear. Figure 24–12 shows a belt-tension tool in place. This tool applies a measured amount of tension to the belt and checks the amount of deflection that results. If the deflection is too great, the belt tension is low and it should be increased. This is usually done by loosening the generator-mounting and adjusting-bracket bolts and moving the generator outward to increase the tension. Tighten the bolts after adjustment is complete.

Review Questions

1. What are the four conditions that may be found when the battery and the d-c generator charging rate are checked?
2. Describe the checks to be made with a charged battery and a high charging rate. (d-c system only)
3. Describe the checks to be made with a low battery and a low charging rate on a d-c system.
4. Describe the procedure for polarizing a d-c generator. Why should this be done?
5. Should a d-c generator be polarized? An a-c generator?
6. Should the generator be operated on open circuit? What might happen?
7. What units do d-c regulators contain? Explain how to check and adjust the electrical settings of each.
8. How do you check and adjust an a-c regulator?
9. What are some of the things to look for if a d-c generator produces no output?
10. What should you look for if the d-c generator produces excessive output?
11. What should you look for if the d-c generator output is unsteady or low?
12. Describe d-c generator inspection on the vehicle.
13. Describe d-c generator armature service, including checking and commutator work.
14. Explain how to disassemble and reassemble a typical d-c generator.
15. Explain how to check and adjust belt tension.
16. Describe the Chrysler-Plymouth trouble-diagnosis procedures under no-output conditions. Under low-output conditions. Under high-output conditions.
17. Describe how to use the Ford ARE 20-22 tester.
18. Describe the conditions that could cause the conditions tabulated in the General Motors trouble-diagnosis section.
19. Explain how to test and adjust a Chrysler-Plymouth a-c regulator. A Ford a-c regulator. A General Motors a-c regulator.
20. Explain how to disassemble, service, and reassemble an alternator.

Study Questions

1. See a shop manual of an automobile using a d-c regulator. Write detailed instructions for checking and adjusting the regulator.
2. Do the same for an a-c regulator.
3. Refer to a shop manual of an automobile using a d-c generator, and write detailed instructions for servicing the generator, including disassembly, testing of components, and reassembly.
4. Do the same thing again, this time for an a-c generator.
5. List the four conditions that may be found in checking the d-c generator-regulator system and the tests that should be made with each condition.
6. List the various trouble conditions and their causes on the three a-c alternator-regulator systems covered in the book.

25

Electric-system Service — The Ignition System

This chapter concludes the discussion of electric-system service and describes the checking and servicing of the components of the ignition system. These components consist of the ignition distributor, spark plugs, wiring, and ignition coil, as well as the battery (already discussed in Chapter 23).

§ 25–1. IGNITION TESTING EQUIPMENT A variety of testing equipment can be used to test the various components of the ignition system.

1. Oscilloscope. This tester (Fig. 25–1) is somewhat like a television set. It has a TV-type tube (called a cathode-ray-oscilloscope tube), on which a picture of the secondary voltage is drawn. The tester is used by connecting or clamping a

pick-up device into the ignition secondary wiring. For example, one system uses a clamp-on pick-up, as shown in Fig. 25–2. Note that the pick-up is on the high-tension lead from the coil to the center terminal on the distributor cap. Every high-voltage surge produced by the coil is sensed by the pick-up, and a signal is carried to the tester. The tester then treats the signal electronically and draws

Fig. 25–1. Electronic-diagnosis engine tester. This tester includes not only an oscilloscope (at top center), but also many other testing devices to check the condenser, distributor contact-point dwell, engine speed, combustion efficiency (exhaust-gas analyzer), and so on. These other testing devices are discussed in Chapters 26 and 27. *(Sun Electric Corporation)*

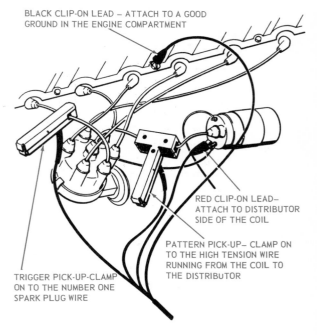

BLACK CLIP-ON LEAD – ATTACH TO A GOOD GROUND IN THE ENGINE COMPARTMENT

RED CLIP-ON LEAD– ATTACH TO DISTRIBUTOR SIDE OF THE COIL

PATTERN PICK-UP– CLAMP ON TO THE HIGH TENSION WIRE RUNNING FROM THE COIL TO THE DISTRIBUTOR

TRIGGER PICK-UP-CLAMP ON TO THE NUMBER ONE SPARK PLUG WIRE

Fig. 25–2. Clamp-on connections to pick up signals for the ignition system. *(Autoscan, Inc.)*

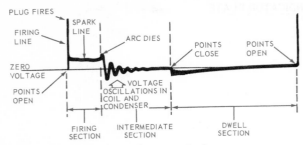

Fig. 25-3. Normal trace for one cylinder.

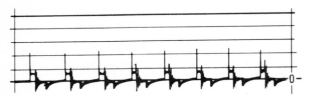

Fig. 25-4. Parade pattern for an eight-cylinder engine.

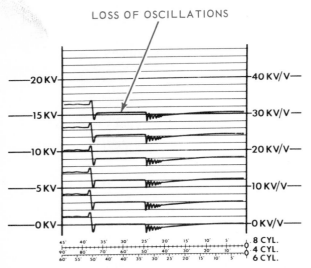

Fig. 25-5. Stacked pattern for a six-cylinder engine showing loss of oscillations after arc dies.

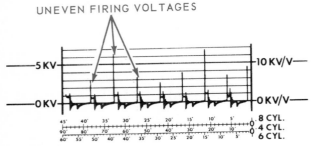

Fig. 25-6. Parade pattern showing uneven firing voltages.

a picture of the voltage on the face of the oscilloscope tube.

For example, Fig. 25-3 shows the drawing, or *trace* as it is called, resulting from the normal firing of one cylinder. Starting from the left, we see that the points open and a voltage quickly builds up in the coil secondary. Then, the plug fires and the voltage drops down to the value needed to sustain the plug arc. Soon most of the energy in the coil is used up and the arc dies. There is still some coil energy left, however, and this produces some oscillation in the system, which results in a plus-and-minus voltage. Soon this dies out and then the points close. Current flows in the coil primary and builds up a magnetic field. Then the points open and the whole cycle is repeated.

The trace in Fig. 25-3 is for one cylinder. The tester can be adjusted to pick up and display the voltage patterns for all cylinders (Fig. 25-4). Thus, the actions in all cylinders can be compared. Figure 25-4 is what is called a *parade pattern*, because the traces follow one another. The tester can also be adjusted to stack the traces (Fig. 25-5) or to superimpose all traces.

Any abnormality in the ignition system will cause a change in the trace. The manner in which the trace changes will put the finger on the trouble. For example, shorted turns in the ignition-coil secondary or a leaky condenser will kill off the voltage oscillations that normally follow the dying out of the arc (compare Figs. 25-3 and 25-5). As another example, the display might show a great variation in the voltages required to fire the different plugs (Fig. 25-6). This could result from worn spark plugs, breaks in the spark-plug wires, or a cocked distributor cap that increases the gap between the rotor and some high-tension terminals.

NOTE: The tester will also show up many abnormalities in the engine. For instance, the traces in Fig. 25-6 could result from unbalanced fuel mixtures. That is, some cylinders would be getting a much leaner mixture than others. The leaner mixtures require higher firing voltages.

2. Ignition-coil tester. Two types of ignition-coil tester are in general use, the spark-gap type and the high-frequency type. The latter type is preferred.

3. Condenser tester. A good condenser tester should be able to test the condenser for grounds or shorts and to measure the insulation resistance,

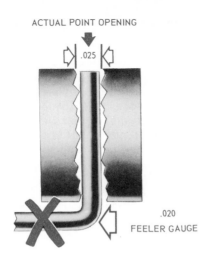

ACTUAL POINT OPENING

.025

.020
FEELER GAUGE

Fig. 25–7. A feeler gauge may not accurately measure the point opening of used and roughened points. The roughness of the points is exaggerated. *(Delco-Remy Division of General Motors Corporation)*

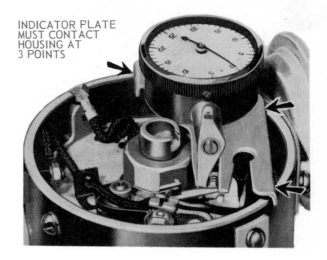

INDICATOR PLATE MUST CONTACT HOUSING AT 3 POINTS

Fig. 25–8. Two types of dial indicators used to measure contact-point openings. *(Delco-Remy Division of General Motors Corporation)*

series resistance, and capacity. These conditions all affect the performance of the ignition.

4. Distributor tester. Distributor testers are variable-speed devices that drive the distributor at various speeds so that the operation of the centrifugal advance can be checked. They also may include a cam-angle meter to measure dwell, or cam, angle (Fig. 25–9). In addition, they usually have a vacuum device to test the operation of vacuum-advance mechanisms.

5. Contact-point-opening testers. Since the opening of the distributor contact points must be correct to assure good ignition performance, their adjustment is of great importance. Three methods of testing the amount of contact-point opening are in use. One makes use of a feeler gauge placed between the points with the breaker cam turned so that the lever-arm rubbing block rests on the high point of one cam lobe. This method, although satisfactory for new points, should not be used for worn points (Fig. 25–7). Points that have been used are likely to be rough, even though they are still good for many more miles of service. To test such points, a dial indicator (Fig. 25–8) or a cam-angle meter should be used. The cam angle (contact, or dwell, angle) is the number of degrees of cam rotation from the instant the contact points close until they open again (Fig. 25–9). Increasing the cam angle decreases the contact-point opening, and vice

versa. Adjustment is made by loosening a locking screw and turning an eccentric, or by loosening a locking nut and turning the contact screw. On the unit shown in Fig. 15–3, the contacts are adjusted without removing the cap. The window can be raised to expose the adjustment screw.

6. Contact-pressure gauge. The contact-point pressure must be within specifications, since low point pressure will allow the points to bounce and burn, and high pressure will cause rapid wear of the points, cam, and rubbing block. A spring gauge can be used to measure the spring pressure. Adjustment is made by bending the breaker-lever spring.

7. Ignition timing devices. The contact points must be timed to close and open in proper relation to the piston positions in the cylinders. Several timing methods are in use. On many en-

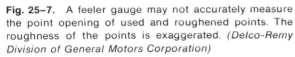

365

gines, the flywheel or dynamic balancer has a mark that aligns with a pointer on the housing when cylinder 1 is ready to fire (Fig. 25–10). At this instant, the contact points should separate so that a spark is produced. A test lamp connected across the points will indicate whether the points are opened or closed at this instant. The distributor can be loosened in its mounting and rotated so that the points will just open with the flywheel marking and pointer aligned.

The second method of timing the ignition is to use a stroboscopic light (Fig. 25–10). The light is connected to a battery as shown (some models pick up their firing energy from a 110-volt light circuit). The light flashes are triggered by the firing of plug 1. At the instant that plug 1 fires, the light flashes on. It goes off again almost at once. Thus, the repeated flashes make the flywheel or pulley seem to stand still. (This is the *stroboscopic effect.)* The timing of the ignition can therefore be observed. Correction is made by loosening and turning the distributor in its mounting. In checking timing of Fords which have the vacuum-advance mechanism connected into the carburetor venturi, the vacuum line should be disconnected.

The third method, no longer used to any extent, uses a piston-position gauge that is inserted into the cylinder through the spark-plug hole (or a special timing hole). This permits the location of top dead center in cylinder 1 so that the dis-

tributor can be timed to open its points at this instant.

8. Spark-plug cleaner. A number of spark-plug cleaning devices are in use. They operate on the sandblast principle and send a blast of gritty ceramic material against the cylinder end of the spark plug placed in the cleaner (Fig. 25–11). After cleaning, the gap should be adjusted by bending the outside electrode. The center electrode should never be bent, since this will break the porcelain shell.

§ 25–2. CAUSES OF IGNITION FAILURE Ignition failure can be classified under three main headings, as follows:

1. Loss of energy in the primary circuit. This, in turn, may be caused by several conditions.

Fig. 25–9. Cam angle. *(Delco-Remy Division of General Motors Corporation)*

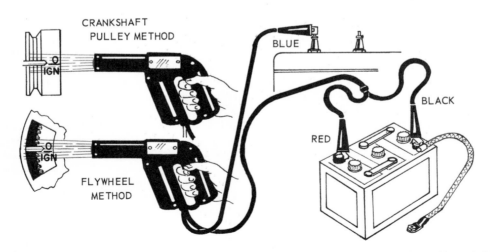

Fig. 25–10. Using stroboscopic, or ignition-timing, light to check ignition timing. Light flashes with each firing of plug number 1. Timing is correct when the pointer and the marking on the flywheel or pulley align. The unit is shown being used on a 6-volt system. Some timing lights are made for use on either a 6-volt or a 12-volt system, and there is also a 110-volt timing light.

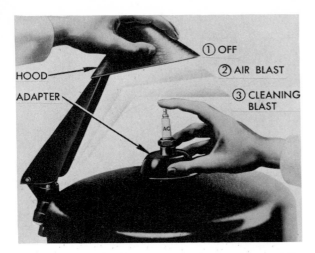

Fig. 25-11. Using a spark-plug cleaner. Moving the hood down to position 2 directs an air blast against the plug; position 3 provides the cleaning blast. *(Buick Motor Division of General Motors Corporation)*

    a. Resistance in the primary circuit due to defective leads, bad connections, burned distributor contact points or switch, or open coil primary.
    b. Points not properly set.
    c. Discharged battery or defective generator.
    d. Defective condenser (shorted, low insulation resistance, high series resistance).
    e. Grounded primary circuit in coil, wiring, or distributor.
2. Loss of energy in secondary circuit.
    a. Plugs fouled, broken, or out of adjustment.
    b. Defective high-tension wiring, which allows high-tension leaks.
    c. High-tension leakage across coil head, distributor cap, or rotor.
    d. Defective connections in high-tension circuits.
3. Out of time.
    a. Timing not set properly.
    b. Distributor bearing or shaft worn, or shaft bent.
    c. Vacuum advance defective.
    d. Centrifugal advance defective.
    e. Preignition, due to plugs of wrong heat range, fouled plugs, etc.

§ 25-3. QUICK CHECKS OF IGNITION SYSTEM

A number of quick checks can be made to determine whether or not the ignition is at fault if the engine does not operate normally.

1. Engine does not run. If the engine cranks at normal speed but does not start, the trouble could be in either the ignition or the fuel system. To check out the ignition system, disconnect the lead from one spark plug (or from the center distributor-cap terminal) and hold it about $3/16$ inch from the engine block. Crank the engine. If a good spark occurs, chances are that the ignition system is in reasonable condition (although the timing could be off). If no spark occurs, check the ignition system further.

Watch the instrument-panel ammeter (or install an ammeter in the coil primary circuit) while cranking. If there is a small, steady reading that fluctuates somewhat, the primary circuit is probably all right. The trouble is probably due to a defective coil secondary, to secondary leads, a defective condenser, or high-tension leakage across the cap, rotor, or coil head.

If the ammeter shows a fairly high and steady reading, the contact points are out of adjustment, the condenser is shorted, or the coil primary circuit is grounded.

If there is no ammeter reading, the primary circuit is open because of a loose connection, defective wiring or switch, out-of-adjustment distributor contact points, or open coil primary.

2. Engine misses. Missing is caused by such defects in the ignition system as bad or out-of-adjustment contact points; defective condenser; improper operation of centrifugal or vacuum advance; defective secondary wiring; defective coil; poor connections; high-tension leakage across coil head, rotor, or cap; or defective spark plugs. In addition, the wrong ignition coil for the engine or reversed connections to the ignition coil may cause missing.

With reversed connections, the coil polarity is reversed. This means that the electrons must jump from the relatively cool outer electrode to the center electrode. This requires a considerably higher secondary voltage and increases the possibility of engine missing, especially at high speeds. Normally, the coil is connected so as to cause the electrons to jump from the hot center electrode to the outer electrode. With the emitting electrode hot, voltage requirements are considerably lower.

To test for reversed polarity, hold an ordinary pencil tip between the high-tension wire clip and the spark-plug terminal (Fig. 25-12). The spark should flare out between the pencil tip and the spark plug, as shown. If it flares out between the

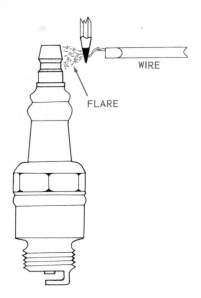

WIRE

FLARE

Fig. 25-12. Using a pencil tip to check polarity of ignition coil. If the flare is between the pencil tip and the high-tension-lead clip, and not as shown, the coil is connected backwards.

pencil tip and the wire clip, the polarity is reversed. Another test is to use a neon bulb (NE-2 or similar) between the spark-plug terminal (high-tension lead connected) and ground. With the engine running, the electrode in the neon bulb connected to the spark-plug terminal should glow. If the terminal connected to ground glows, the polarity is reversed. Reverse the coil primary leads to correct the polarity.

NOTE: For a more detailed discussion of how to diagnose a missing engine, see § 26-6.

3. Overheating and spark rap. These conditions may be caused by improper ignition timing.

§ 25-4. IGNITION SERVICE   Any check of the ignition system should start at the battery and cables and should take in the coil, distributor, condenser, low- and high-tension wiring, and spark plugs. The high-tension wiring insulation must be in good condition, since poor insulation will allow the high-voltage surges to leak to ground instead of entering the spark plugs. The distributor cap and rotor and the coil head should be examined for carbonized paths that allow high-tension leakage. The distributor contact

points should be examined, checked, and adjusted as necessary. Points that are burned or oxidized can be cleaned with a thin, fine-cut contact file or stone. Emery cloth must never be used, since particles of emery may become embedded and cause rapid burning away of the points. On the full-vacuum-control distributor (§ 15-6, item 4), the spark advance should be checked and adjusted, as necessary. The distributor should be lubricated periodically.

1. Summary of ignition troubles. Various troubles that may occur in the components of the ignition system are discussed below.

a. Burned or oxidized contact points. It is normal for ignition-distributor contact points gradually to burn away over a long period of time. Rapid burning or oxidizing of the points may be due to several conditions.

(1) Excessive resistance in the condenser circuit caused by high series resistance in the condenser or by a loose mounting or connection.

(2) High voltage produced by a high voltage-regulator setting.

(3) Contact angle too large (point opening too small). The points, closed too much of the total operating time, burn away rapidly.

(4) Weak spring tension that causes the contact points to bounce and arc.

(5) Oil or crankcase vapors entering the distributor housing are deposited on the point surfaces, causing them to burn rapidly. A glance at the breaker plate usually discloses this condition, since it causes a black smudge on the breaker plate under the points. Clogged engine breather pipes and worn distributor bearings can produce this trouble.

b. Sooty, burned, or cracked spark-plug insulator. Spark plugs may fail from a variety of reasons. Spark-plug manufacturers usually recommend replacement of spark plugs at 10,000-mile intervals in order to forestall failure and maintain the engine at good operating efficiency. One cause of spark-plug trouble is the installation of plugs of the wrong heat range. Heat range is a means of designating how hot a plug will run in operation (Fig. 25-13). The temperature that a plug will attain depends on the distance the heat must travel from the center electrode to reach the outer shell of the plug and enter the cylinder head. If the path of heat travel is long, the plug will run hotter than if the path is short. When a plug runs too cold, there will be a sooty carbon deposit on the insulator around

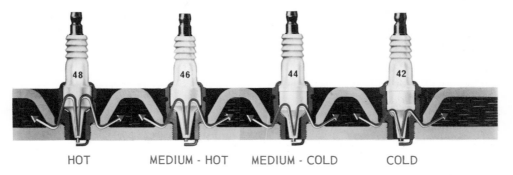

| 48 | 46 | 44 | 42 |

HOT   MEDIUM - HOT   MEDIUM - COLD   COLD

Fig. 25-13. Heat range of spark plugs. The longer the heat path (indicated by arrows), the hotter the plug runs. *(AC Spark Plug Division of General Motors Corporation)*

the center electrode. A hotter-running plug will burn this carbon away or prevent its formation. Carbon deposit may also be caused by excessive choking or by excessive oil getting into the cylinder.

If the plug runs too hot, the insulator may take on a white or grayish cast and may appear blistered. A plug that runs hot will wear more rapidly, since the higher temperatures cause the electrodes to burn away more quickly.

Cracked insulators are usually caused by careless installation of the plug or by careless adjustment of the plug gap.

2. Distributor disassembly and reassembly. Disassembly procedures vary with different constructions. A typical procedure starts with removal of the cap, rotor, terminal parts, and breaker plate. Then the coupling or gear is taken off after the head of the pin has been filed off and the pin driven out. This permits removal of the shaft from the housing.

Reassembly is the reverse of disassembly. Replace the bearing in its housing if it is worn and allows excessive side play or wobble of the shaft. The old bearing can be pressed out and the new one pressed in with an arbor press. Some bearings will require reaming to size after installation. When installing the coupling or the gear, add or remove shims (between the coupling or gear and the housing) before the pin end is peened over, in order to get the correct shaft end play.

3. Distributor lubrication. Hinge-cap oilers should have 8 to 10 drops of light engine oil every engine oil change. Grease cups should be turned down one turn every engine oil change and filled with No. 2½ grease, as required. High-pressure grease fittings should be supplied with grease every engine oil change. Sealed grease chambers should be repacked every 25,000 miles, and sealed oil reservoirs should be refilled with 20W oil every 20,000 miles. The cam should be lubricated with cam grease every engine oil change. At the same time, the breaker-lever pivot and the felt wick under the rotor should have a drop or two of oil.

Review Questions

1. Name several pieces of testing equipment for testing the components of the ignition system.
2. Explain how to use an oscilloscope tester.
3. What is a trace?
4. What is the cam angle?
5. What is meant by ignition timing? Explain the ways this ignition timing is checked.
6. How do you check the ignition system if the engine is cranked normally but will not run?
7. What conditions in the ignition system will cause the engine to miss?
8. Name a few causes of burned or oxidized distributor contact points.

Study Questions

1. Refer to the operating manual for one type of ignition-coil tester, and write a description of how to use it.
2. Do the same for a condenser tester.
3. Do the same for a distributor tester.
4. Study the manual for an oscilloscope type of ignition tester, and write an explanation of what causes various abnormal traces.
5. Explain how to measure distributor contact-point opening. How to measure cam angle.
6. Explain how to adjust ignition timing.
7. Make a list of the causes of burned or oxidized distributor contact points.
8. Explain what is meant by heat range in spark plugs.
9. Make a list of causes of ignition failure due to loss of energy in the primary.
10. Do the same for causes of loss of energy in the secondary.
11. Refer to a shop manual, and write a description of how to disassemble and reassemble an ignition distributor.

CHAPTER

26

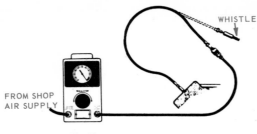

FROM SHOP
AIR SUPPLY

WHISTLE

Engine Trouble
Diagnosis

This chapter discusses various engine troubles and explains what may cause these troubles. Further, it indicates how those troubles may be cured. In other words, the chapter covers engine trouble diagnosis. Preceding chapters describe servicing and repair procedures to be used after a trouble has been tracked down to its cause.

§ 26–1. TROUBLE-DIAGNOSIS CHART The chart that follows lists various engine complaints, their possible causes, and checks or corrections to be made. Use of the information in this chart will often greatly shorten the time required to correct a trouble. For by following a logical procedure, the cause of trouble usually can be located quickly.

On the other hand, haphazard guesswork wastes both your time and your effort.

NOTE: The troubles and possible causes are not listed in the chart in the order of frequency of occurrence. That is, item 1 (or item a under "Possible Cause") does not necessarily occur more frequently than item 2 (or item b).

ENGINE TROUBLE-DIAGNOSIS CHART

See §§ 26–2 to 26–15 for detailed explanations of trouble causes and corrections listed below.

COMPLAINT	POSSIBLE CAUSE	CHECK OR CORRECTION
1. Engine will not turn over (§ 26–2)	a. Run-down battery	Recharge or replace
	b. Starting circuit open — *bad solenoid switch or bad starter*	Locate and eliminate open
	c. Bendix drive jammed	Free drive
	d. Cranking motor jammed — *unlikely*	Remove for teardown and correction
	e. Engine jammed	Check engine to find trouble
	f. Also causes listed under item 3, "Engine turns over at normal speed but does not start," below. Driver may have run battery down trying to start	
2. Engine turns over slowly but does not start (§ 26–3)	a. Run-down battery	Recharge or replace
	b. Defective cranking motor	Replace or repair
	c. Bad connections in starting circuit *ck. for loose connect.*	Clean and tighten
	d. Undersized battery cables — *should be for 12 volts*	Replace
	e. Also causes listed under item 3, "Engine turns over at normal speed but does not start," below. Driver may have run battery down trying to start	

3. Engine turns over at normal speed but does not start (§ 26–4)	a. Ignition system defective	Try spark test; check timing, ignition system
	b. Fuel system defective or overchoking	Prime engine; check fuel pump, line, choke, carburetor
	c. Air leaks in intake manifold or carburetor	Tighten mounting; replace gasket as needed
	d. Engine defective	Check compression or leakage (see § 26–5), valve action, timing, etc.
4. Engine runs but misses — one cylinder (§ 26–6) *vibrates*	a. Defective spark plug	Clean or replace
	b. Distributor cap or lead defective	Replace
	c. Stuck valve	Free valve; service stem and guide
	d. Defective rings or piston	Replace; service piston and cylinder wall as needed
	e. Defective head gasket	Replace
5. Engine runs but misses — different cylinders (§ 26–6)	a. Defective ignition	Check timing and ignition
	b. Defective fuel system	Check fuel pump, carburetor
	c. Loss of compression	Check compression or leakage (see § 26–5)
	d. Defective valve action	Check valve action with compression, leakage, or vacuum test (see §§ 26–5 and 26–7)
	e. Defective rings	Check compression or leakage and vacuum; replace rings, service pistons and cylinder walls as needed
	f. Overheated engine	Check cooling system
	g. Manifold heat-control valve sticking	Free valve
	h. Clogged exhaust	Check tail pipe and muffler; eliminate clogging
6. Engine lacks power, acceleration, or high-speed performance, hot or cold (§ 26–8)	a. Ignition defective	Check timing, distributor, wiring, condenser, coil, and plugs
	b. Fuel system defective	Check carburetor, air cleaner, and fuel pump
	c. Throttle valve not opening fully	Adjust linkage
	d. Clogged exhaust	Check tail pipe and muffler; eliminate clogging
	e. Loss of compression	Check compression or leakage (see § 26–5)
	f. Excessive carbon in engine	Remove carbon
	g. Defective valve action	Check with compression, leakage, or vacuum tester (see §§ 26–5 and 26–7)
	h. Excessive rolling resistance from low tires, dragging brakes, wheel misalignment, etc.	Correct the defect causing rolling resistance
	i. Heavy oil	Use lighter oil
	j. Wrong or bad fuel	Use good fuel of correct octane

7. Engine lacks power, acceleration, or high-speed performance, hot only (§ 26–8)	a. Engine overheats	Check cooling system (see item 9 below)
	b. Defective choke	Repair or replace
	c. Sticking manifold heat-control valve	Free valve
	d. Vapor lock	Use different fuel, or shield fuel line
8. Engine lacks power, acceleration, or high-speed performance, cold only (§ 26–8)	a. Automatic choke stuck	Repair or replace
	b. Manifold heat-control valve stuck	Free valve
	c. Cooling-system thermostat stuck	Repair or replace
	d. Stuck engine valves	Free valves; service valve stems and guides as needed
9. Engine overheats (§ 26–10) Cooling system	a. Lack of water	Add water
	b. Ignition timing late	Adjust timing
	c. Loose or broken fan belt	Tighten or replace
	d. Defective thermostat	Replace
	e. Clogged water jackets	Clean out
	f. Defective radiator hose	Replace
	g. Defective water pump	Repair or replace
	h. Insufficient engine oil	Add oil
	i. High-altitude, hot-climate operation	Drive more slowly; keep radiator filled
	j. Valve timing late	Retime
10. Rough idle (§ 26–11)	a. Carburetor idle adjustment incorrect	Readjust idle mixture and speed
	b. Malfunctioning crankcase ventilator valve*	Replace
	c. Other causes, which are listed under "Engine lacks power, etc." (items 6, 7, and 8 above)	
11. Engine stalls cold or as it warms up (§ 26–12)	a. Choke valve stuck closed	Open choke valve; free or repair automatic choke
	b. Fuel not getting to or through carburetor lean	Check fuel pump, lines, filter, float, and idle circuits.
	c. Manifold heat-control valve stuck	Free valve
	d. Engine overheats	See item 9, "Engine overheats," above
	e. Engine idling speed set too low	Increase idling speed to specified value
	f. Malfunctioning crankcase ventilator valve*	Replace
	g) bad heat riser	
12. Engine stalls after idling or slow-speed driving (§ 26–12)	a. Defective fuel pump	Repair or replace fuel pump
	b. Overheating	See item 9, "Engine overheats," above
	c. High carburetor float level	Adjust
	d. Idling adjustment incorrect	Adjust
	e. Malfunctioning crankcase ventilator valve*	Replace

* On closed-crankcase ventilating system

13. Engine stalls after high-speed driving (§ 26-12)	a. Vapor lock	Use different fuel, or shield fuel line
	b. Carburetor venting or idle compensator valve defective	Check and repair
	c. Engine overheats	See item 9, above
	d. Malfunctioning crankcase ventilator valve*	Replace
14. Engine backfires (§ 26-13)	a. Ignition timing off	Adjust timing
	b. Spark plugs of wrong heat range	Install correct plugs
	c. Excessively rich or lean mixture	Repair or readjust fuel pump or carburetor
	d. Overheating of engine	See item 9, "Engine overheats," above
	e. Carbon in engine	Clean out
	f. Valves hot or sticking	Adjust; free; clean; replace if bad
	g. Cracked distributor cap	Replace cap
15. Smoky exhaust 1) Blue smoke	Excessive oil consumption	See item 16 and § 26-14
2) Black smoke	Excessively rich mixture	See item 18 and § 26-16
16. Excessive oil consumption (§ 26-14)	a. External leaks	Correct seals; replace gaskets
	b. Burning oil in combustion chamber	Check valve-stem clearance, piston rings, cylinder walls, rod bearings, vacuum-pump diaphragm
	c. High-speed driving	Drive more slowly
17. Low oil pressure (§ 26-15)	a. Worn engine bearings	Replace
	b. Engine overheating	See item 9, above
	c. Oil dilution or foaming	Replace oil
	d. Lubricating-system defects	Check oil lines, oil pump, relief valve
18. Excessive fuel consumption (§ 26-16)	a. "Nervous" or "jackrabbit" driver	Drive more reasonably
	b. High speed	Drive more slowly
	c. Short-run operation	Make longer runs
	d. Excessive fuel-pump pressure or pump leakage	Reduce pressure; repair pump
	e. Choke partly closed after warm-up	Open; repair or replace automatic choke
	f. Clogged air cleaner	Clean
	g. High carburetor float level	Adjust
	h. Stuck or dirty float needle valve	Free and clean
	i. Worn carburetor jets	Replace
	j. Stuck metering rod or full-power piston	Free
	k. Idle too rich or too fast	Adjust
	l. Stuck accelerator-pump check valve	Free
	m. Carburetor leaks	Replace gaskets, tighten screws, etc.
	n. Faulty ignition	Check coil, condenser, timing, plugs, contact points, wiring

Handwritten annotations: "crossed wire / bad points" (near item 14); "white" (under Blue smoke); "water" (under Excessive oil consumption)

* On closed-crankcase ventilating system

o. Loss of engine compression		Check compression or leakage (see § 26–5)
p. Defective valve action		Check with compression, leakage, or vacuum tester (see §§ 26–5 and 26–7)
q. Excessive rolling resistance from low tires, dragging brakes, wheel misalignment, etc.		Correct the defects causing rolling resistance
r. Clutch slippage		Adjust or repair
19. Engine is noisy (see § 26–17)		
1) Regular clicking	Valve and tappet	Readjust valve clearance
2) Ping or chatter on load or acceleration	Spark knock due to low-octane fuel, carbon, advanced ignition timing, or causes listed under item 14, "Engine backfires," above	Use higher-octane fuel; remove carbon; adjust ignition timing
3) Light knock or pound with engine floating	Worn connecting-rod bearing or crankpin, misaligned rod, lack of oil	Replace or adjust bearings; service crankpins, replace rod; correct lack of oil
4) Light, metallic double knock, usually most audible during idle	Worn or loose piston pin or bushing or lack of oil	Service pin and bushing; correct lack of oil
5) Chattering or rattling during acceleration	Worn rings, cylinder walls, low ring tension, broken rings	Service walls; replace rings
6) Hollow, muffled bell-like sound, engine cold	Piston slap due to worn pistons, walls, collapsed piston skirts, excessive clearance, lack of oil, misaligned connecting rods	Replace or resize pistons; service walls; replace rods; correct lack of oil
7) Dull, heavy, metallic knock under load or acceleration, especially when cold	Regular noise: worn main bearings; irregular: worn end-thrust bearings	Replace or service bearings and crankshaft
8) Miscellaneous noises	Rattles, etc., from loosely mounted accessories; generator, horn, oil pan, etc.	Tighten mounting

§ 26–2. ENGINE WILL NOT TURN OVER If the engine will not turn over when starting is attempted, turn on the headlights or dome light and try to start. The lights will (1) stay bright, (2) dim considerably, (3) dim slightly, (4) go out, (5) not burn at all.

1. If the lights stay bright, there is an open circuit in the cranking motor, switch, or main or control circuit. Check as outlined in § 23–3.

2. If the lights dim considerably, the battery may be run down, or there is mechanical trouble in the cranking motor or engine. If the battery checks O.K. with a hydrometer, remove the cranking-motor cover band where present and try to turn the armature by hand (do not use a screwdriver, since this could damage the armature). If the armature is jammed, remove the cranking motor for further analysis. On the Bendix-type cranking motor (which does not use a shift lever), the drive pinion may be jammed. If the armature turns readily, the trouble is probably in the engine.

3. If the lights dim only slightly, listen for crank-

ing-motor action (sound of an electric motor running). If it runs, the pinion is not engaging the engine flywheel (this trouble could happen only on Bendix-type units and would be due to a stuck pinion). If the armature does not rotate, the pinion may be engaging the flywheel, but excessive resistance or an open circuit in the cranking motor is preventing normal action.

4. If the lights go out as cranking is attempted, the chances are that there is a bad connection in the main circuit, probably at a battery terminal.

5. If the lights burn dimly or not at all when they are turned on, even before cranking is attempted, the battery is probably run down.

§ 26-3. ENGINE TURNS OVER SLOWLY BUT DOES NOT START
Causes of this condition could be a run-down battery, a defective cranking motor, undersized battery cables, or mechanical trouble in the engine. Check the battery, cranking motor, and circuit as outlined in Chap. 23. If they are normal, the trouble probably is in the engine (defective bearings, rings, and so on, that could produce high friction). Remember that, in cold weather, cranking speed is reduced by thickening of the engine oil and reduction of battery efficiency.

NOTE: If the battery is run down, it could be that the driver has discharged the battery in a vain attempt to start. The cause of starting failure could be as noted in the following paragraphs.

§ 26-4. ENGINE TURNS OVER AT NORMAL CRANKING SPEED BUT DOES NOT START
This means that the battery and cranking motor are in normal condition. The cause of trouble is probably in the ignition or fuel system. The difficulty could be due to overchoking.* Try cranking with the throttle wide open. If the engine does not start, disconnect the lead from one spark plug (or from the center distributor-cap terminal), and hold it about $3/16$ inch from the engine block. Crank the engine to see if a good spark occurs. If no spark occurs, check the ignition system. If a spark does occur, the ignition system is probably O.K. (the timing could be off, however).

---

* The above analysis applies to a cold engine. Failure to start with a hot engine may be due to a defective choke that fails to open properly as the engine warms up. This would cause flooding of the engine (delivery of too much gasoline). Open the throttle wide while cranking (this dechokes the engine), or open the choke valve by hand while cranking.

If the ignition system seems to be operating normally, the fuel system should be analyzed. First, prime the engine by operating the carburetor accelerator pump several times. Or remove the air cleaner, and squirt a small amount of gasoline into the carburetor air horn.

● **CAUTION:** Gasoline is highly explosive. Keep back out of the way while priming the engine; the engine might backfire through the carburetor.

If the engine now starts and runs for a few seconds, the fuel system is probably faulty; it is not delivering fuel to the engine. Disconnect the fuel inlet to the carburetor temporarily, hold a container under the fuel line to catch fuel, and crank the engine to see whether fuel is delivered. If it is not, the fuel pump is defective or the fuel line is clogged. If fuel is delivered, the carburetor is probably at fault (jets or circuits clogged), the automatic choke is not working correctly, or possibly there are air leaks into the intake manifold or carburetor.

If the fuel and ignition systems seem to be OK on the preliminary checks, check the mechanical condition of the engine by the compression and leakage tests (§ 26-5).

§ 26-5. CYLINDER COMPRESSION AND LEAKAGE TESTERS
The purpose of these testers is to determine whether or not the cylinder can hold compression, or whether there is excessive leakage past the rings, valves, or head gasket. The compression tester (Fig. 26-1) has been one of the basic engine-testing instruments for many years. Recently, the cylinder-leakage tester has come into use; some operators believe that it can more accurately pinpoint defects in the cylinder.

As a first step in using either tester, loosen the spark plugs one turn, start the engine and run it at 1,000 rpm for a few moments. This blows out the carbon from around the plugs. If this carbon is not blown out, particles might fall into the engine and lodge under the valves to cause a faulty compression or leakage reading.

1. Compression tester. This instrument measures cylinder pressure, in psi (pounds per square inch), as the piston moves up to TDC (top dead center). This pressure is an indication of engine condition. If the pressure is low, then the cylinder cannot hold compression (possibly owing to worn rings, piston or cylinder walls, or to poor valve seating, and so on).

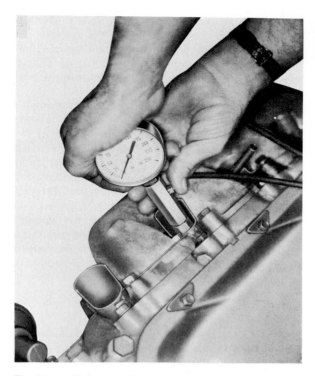

Fig. 26–1. Using a cylinder compression tester. *(Chevrolet Motor Division of General Motors Corporation)*

To use the compression tester, remove all spark plugs, hold the tester fitting tightly in the spark-plug hole of a cylinder, and crank the engine with the cranking motor. Engine should be at operating temperature and battery should be in charged condition. Be sure to hold the throttle valve wide open so that the fuel system does not deliver fuel to the engine during the test. Note the maximum compression pressure as indicated by the needle on the compression-tester dial. An excessively high compression pressure indicates carbon deposits on the piston or cylinder head.

● **CAUTION:** If engine is cranked with a jumper lead at the cranking motor, first disconnect the distributor primary lead from the ignition coil and turn the ignition switch to ON. Failure to do this can damage the ignition switch.

If compression pressure is too low, then there is leakage past the valves, piston rings, or cylinder-head gasket. This means that, in order to correct the trouble, the head must come off and the various engine parts must be inspected. But before this is done, you can make one further

check to pinpoint the trouble more accurately. Pour a small quantity of heavy oil into the cylinder through the spark-plug hole, and then retest the compression pressure. If the compression pressure increases to a more normal figure, this means that the loss of compression is due to leakage past the piston rings. This can result from worn or scored piston rings, pistons, or cylinder walls, or from piston rings being weak, broken, or stuck in their grooves. If adding oil does not help the compression pressure, the chances are that the leakage is past the valves. This could be due to weak or broken valve springs; improper valve adjustments; carboned or sticking valve stems; burned, warped, worn, or pitted valves; or worn, burned, or pitted valve seats. If the compression leakage is not past rings or valves, then the cylinder-head gasket is not holding the compression, owing to its being burned or to improper tightening of the cylinder-head attaching bolts or nuts.

Low compression in two adjacent cylinders indicates that there is a blown gasket between the cylinders that allows leakage between them.

If the compression pressure stays low for the first few piston strokes and then increases to a more normal figure, it indicates a sticking valve.

2. Cylinder leakage tester. This instrument applies air pressure to the cylinder with the piston at TDC on the compression stroke (Fig. 26–2). If excessive leakage is indicated on the instrument, the cause of the leakage can be pinpointed by listening at the carburetor, tail pipe, or crankcase filler pipe.

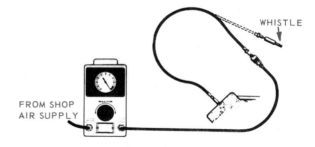

Fig. 26–2. Using a cylinder leakage tester. The whistle is used to locate TDC in number 1 cylinder. *(Sun Electric Corporation)*

As a first step in using the cylinder leakage tester, TDC must be determined on number one cylinder. Remove all spark plugs, the air cleaner, the crankcase filler cap, and the radiator cap. Set the throttle valve to wide open position. Fill the radiator to the proper level.

Connect the adaptor, with the whistle, to the spark-plug hole of the number one cylinder. Turn the engine over until the whistle sounds. This means that the number one piston is moving up on the compression stroke. Continue to rotate the engine until the TDC timing mark on the engine aligns. The piston is now at TDC. Before checking for cylinder leakage, make provisions for locating TDC in other cylinders as follows: Remove the distributor cap and ground the coil secondary lead. Install a special adaptor on the distributor shaft or rotor and make a chalk mark on an adjacent engine surface opposite the TDC mark on the adaptor plate. Connect the indicator light between the distributor primary terminal and the ground. You are now ready to make the test.

Connect a hose from the tester to the adaptor hose in place of the whistle, and turn on the tester. Air pressure (from the shop source) is now being applied to the number one cylinder (Fig. 26-2). Note the gauge reading, which shows the percentage of air leakage. If it is above 20 percent (this figure is actually high on many late-model high-compression engines), check further by listening at the carburetor, tail pipe, and crankcase filler pipe. Air escaping through the carburetor means an intake-valve leak. Air escaping through the tail pipe means a leaking exhaust valve. Air escaping through the crankcase filler pipe means leakage past the piston rings. If air is bubbling up into the radiator upper tank, the head gasket is leaking.

Test each cylinder in turn, according to the firing order, locating TDC in each cylinder by using the proper TDC marking on the adaptor plate previously mounted on the distributor. The proper TDC marking on the adaptor plate will align with the chalk mark previously made on the engine surface, and the indicator light will come on as the piston reaches TDC in each cylinder.

§ 26-6. ENGINE RUNS BUT MISSES
A missing engine is a rough engine; failure of cylinders to fire throws the engine out of balance so that roughness and loss of power are evident. It is sometimes hard to track down a miss, since it might occur at some speeds or throttle openings and not others. Also, a miss may skip around.

1. One method of tracking down a miss is to short out each cylinder spark plug in turn with a screwdriver. The screwdriver should have an insulated handle so that you do not get shocked. Put the screwdriver shank between the spark-plug terminal and the engine block. This prevents a spark from occurring, so that the cylinder will miss. If the engine rhythm or speed changes, then that cylinder was delivering power. If no change occurs, the cylinder was missing before the plug was shorted out.

2. A more accurate method of tracking down a missing cylinder is to check cylinder balance. This is done by running the engine on only two cylinders at a time. (On four-cylinder engines, run the engine on one cylinder at a time.) Two cylinders are used because running the engine on only one cylinder at a time is not conclusive. The procedure is as follows:

a. Connect the tachometer and the vacuum gauge (Fig. 26-3), start the engine, and run it until it reaches operating temperature. Then operate it at 1,000 rpm if it is a six-cylinder engine or 1,500 rpm if it is an eight-cylinder engine.

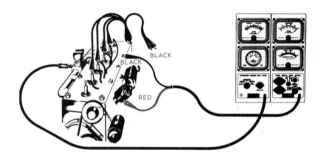

Fig. 26-3. Tachometer and vacuum-gauge connections to make a cylinder balance test. Multiple-lead plug-grounding lead assembly can be used to ground plugs as shown, or plug leads can be disconnected. Connections shown are for a negative-grounded system. Red and black leads should be reversed for a positive-grounded system. *(Sun Electric Corporation)*

b. Ground out (or disconnect spark-plug leads from) all but two cylinders so that the engine will run on two cylinders only. Determine which cylinders to use by taking the engine firing order and putting the first half over the second, as:

$$1\text{-}2\text{-}7\text{-}8\text{-}4\text{-}5\text{-}6\text{-}3 \text{ would be } \frac{1\text{-}2\text{-}7\text{-}8}{4\text{-}5\text{-}6\text{-}3}$$

Then select the cylinder whose numbers are directly above and below each other, as 1 and 4. After running on 1 and 4, run the engine on 2 and 5, then 7 and 6, then 8 and 3.

c. Note the engine rpm and intake-manifold vacuum for each pair of cylinders. If one pair shows definitely lower readings, one of the two cylinders is weak or missing. Short out half the cylinders (front or rear half in an in-line engine, one bank in a V-8). The half, or bank, giving the lower reading will contain the weak cylinder.

3. Check a missing cylinder further by removing the spark-plug lead and holding it close to the engine block while the engine is running. If no spark occurs, there is probably a high-tension leak due to a bad lead or a cracked or burned distributor cap. If a good spark occurs, install a new spark plug in the cylinder, reconnect the lead, and see whether the cylinder still misses. If it does, the cause of the trouble is probably defective engine parts, such as valves or rings.

4. If the miss is hard to locate, perform a general tune-up (Chap. 27). This will disclose and may eliminate various causes of missing, including defects in ignition system, defects in fuel system, loss of engine compression, sticky or damaged engine valves, overheated engine, manifold heat control sticking, a clogged exhaust, and so on.

§ 26–7. ENGINE VACUUM GAUGE This is an important engine tester for tracking down troubles in an engine that runs but does not perform satisfactorily. It measures intake-manifold vacuum. The intake-manifold vacuum varies with different operating conditions, and also with different engine defects. The manner in which the vacuum varies from normal indicates the type of engine trouble. Figure 26-4 shows a vacuum gauge and a tachometer connected for a test. The tachometer

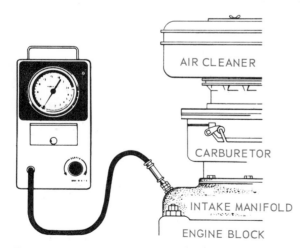

Fig. 26-4. A vacuum gauge connected to an intake manifold for a manifold vacuum test. *(Sun Electric Corporation)*

is a speed-measuring device. It is connected to the ignition primary circuit and measures the number of times per minute that the primary circuit is interrupted (by opening and closing of the distributor contact points). It then translates this information into engine rpm (revolutions per minute).

The vacuum gauge is connected to the intake manifold at the point where the windshield wiper (or vacuum pump) is normally connected. On engines with electric windshield wipers, the gauge is connected to the power-brake fitting or to the manifold itself after a pipe plug is removed. Then, the engine is operated at idle speed (after it has been warmed up) and the vacuum-gauge reading noted. Meanings of various readings are as follows.

1. A steady and fairly high reading (17 to 22 inches, depending on altitude and engine) indicates normal performance. The reading will be lower at higher altitudes because of the lowered atmospheric pressure. For every 1,000 feet above sea level, it will be reduced about 1 inch.

NOTE: Late-model engines with high-lift cams and more valve overlap are apt to have a lower and more erratic intake-manifold vacuum.

2. A low, steady reading indicates late ignition or valve timing, or possibly leakage around pistons owing to stuck piston rings or to worn or scored rings, pistons, or cylinder walls. Any of these reduces power output. With reduced power, the engine does not "pull" as much vacuum.

3. A very low reading indicates a leaky intake manifold or carburetor gasket, or leaks around the throttle-valve shaft. Air leaks into the manifold cause loss of vacuum and low engine output.

4. Oscillations of the needle, increasing with engine speed, indicate weak valve springs.

5. A gradual falling back of the needle toward zero, with the engine idling, indicates a clogged exhaust line.

6. Regular dropping back of the needle indicates a valve sticking open or a plug not firing.

7. Irregular dropping back of the needle indicates valves stick irregularly.

8. Floating motion or slow oscillation of the needle indicates an excessively rich air-fuel mixture. (See item 18, "Excessive fuel consumption," in the Engine Trouble-diagnosis Chart, § 26–1; and see § 26–16 for trouble in the fuel system that could cause an excessively rich mixture.)

9. A test for loss of compression due to leakage

around pistons (as a result of stuck piston rings or of worn or scored rings, pistons, or cylinder walls) can be made as follows: Race the engine momentarily, and then quickly close the throttle. If the needle swings around momentarily to 23 to 25 inches as the throttle is closed, the compression is probably satisfactory. If the needle fails to swing this far, there is loss of compression.

§ 26-8. ENGINE LACKS POWER This is a rather general complaint that is often difficult to analyze. The best procedure is to perform a tune-up (Chap. 27), since this will disclose various engine conditions that could cause loss of power. Some idea of the cause can be gained by determining whether the engine lacks power only when cold, only when hot, or when either hot or cold.

NOTE: The chassis dynamometer accurately measures engine horsepower (§ 4-12) and is very useful in analyzing this type of complaint.

1. If the engine lacks power and acceleration either hot or cold, the fuel system may not be enriching the mixture as the throttle is opened. This could be due to a faulty accelerator pump or a defective high-speed or full-power circuit in the carburetor. Also, the fuel system could be supplying an excessively lean or rich mixture (fuel pump defective, lines clogged, filter clogged, carburetor jets or lines worn, air leaks at the carburetor or manifold joints, malfunctioning crankcase ventilator valve, and so on). Carburetor and fuel-system action can be checked with an exhaust-gas analyzer (§ 26-9).

Another condition that could cause lack of power, with engine hot or cold, could be improper linkage adjustment that prevents full throttle opening. Also, the ignition system may be causing trouble, owing to incorrect timing, a ''weak'' coil, reversed polarity (see § 25-3), wrong spark-plug heat range, and so on. The wrong fuel or oil for the engine could reduce performance. In the engine, numerous conditions could cause loss of power, including engine deposits (carbon), lack of compression (faulty valves, rings, worn cylinder walls, pistons, and so on), and defective bearings. A clogged exhaust (bent tail pipe or clogged muffler) could create back pressure that would cause poor engine performance. Also, any sort of excessive rolling resistance would absorb engine power and hold down engine acceleration and speed. This would include dragging brakes, underinflated tires, misaligned wheels, and ex-

cessive friction in the transmission or power train.

2. If the engine lacks power only when hot, the engine may be overheating (§ 26-10), the automatic choke may not be opening normally as the engine warms up, the manifold heat-control valve may be stuck, or there may be a vapor lock in the fuel pump or line (§ 10-2).

3. If the engine lacks power when cold or reaches operating temperature too slowly, the automatic choke may be leaning out the mixture too soon (before the engine warms up), the manifold heat-control valve may not be closed (so that insufficient heat reaches the intake manifold), or the cooling-system thermostat may be stuck open. In this case, water circulation goes on between the engine and radiator even with the engine cold, and so warm-up is delayed. Ocasionally engine valves may stick when the engine is cold, but as the engine warms up, the valves become free and work normally.

§ 26-9. EXHAUST-GAS ANALYZER The exhaust-gas analyzer, or combustion tester, checks the exhaust gas to determine what percentage of the gasoline has not been burned. When mixture ratios are not correct, or when there is a fouled plug or sticky valves (among other things), not all the gasoline burns. Combustion efficiency is low, and gasoline is being wasted. The exhaust-gas analyzer draws a small part of the exhaust gas from the tail pipe and runs it through an analyzing device which then reports, by an indicating needle on a dial, the fuel ratio (mixture richness) or combustion efficiency (see Fig. 26-5). When

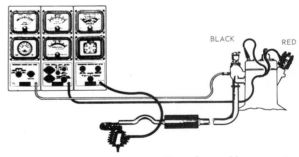

Fig. 26-5. Instrument connections for making a combustion-efficiency (or exhaust-gas) analysis on a negative-grounded system. Red and black leads must be reversed on a positive-grounded system. Note that the pickup gun is installed in the tail pipe and is connected by a hose to the analyzer. A small pump, or booster, draws exhaust gas through the hose to the analyzer. (Sun Electric Corporation)

not influenced by abnormal engine factors, the combustion efficiency and fuel ratio can be said to be directly related. The richer the ratio, the lower the efficiency (that is, a smaller percentage of the gasoline burns).

Where the engine is equipped with an air-injection system (see Fig. 9–70), the additional air injected into the exhaust manifold introduces extra oxygen and burns much of the unburned hydrocarbons in the exhaust gases. This will give a false picture of the fuel-system condition. To eliminate this, the air-injection system can be temporarily inactivated by disconnecting the air-supply hose to the air manifold (or manifolds). Then plug the manifold connection to prevent exhaust gas escaping.

§ 26–10. ENGINE OVERHEATS The first thought that comes to mind when an engine overheats is that the cooling system is not functioning properly. Such faults in the cooling system as lack of water, a loose or broken fan belt, a defective water pump, clogged water jackets, a defective radiator hose, or a defective thermostat could cause engine overheating. However, late ignition or valve timing, lack of engine oil, or high-altitude or hot-climate operation may cause overheating. Also, freezing of the cooling water could cause lack of water circulation so that local hot spots and boiling would take place.

§ 26–11. ROUGH IDLE If the engine idles roughly but runs normally above idle, chances are the idle speed and mixture are incorrectly adjusted. A rough idle could be due to other causes.

§ 26–12. ENGINE STALLS If the engine starts and then stalls, note whether the stalling takes place before or after the engine warms up, after idling or slow-speed driving, or after high-speed or full-load driving. Special note should be made of the crankcase ventilator valve (closed-crankcase ventilating systems). If this valve becomes clogged or sticks, it will cause poor idling and stalling.

1. Engine stalls before it warms up. This could be due to an improperly set fast or slow idle or to improper adjustment of the idle-fuel-mixture needle in the carburetor. Also, it could be due to a low carburetor float setting or to insufficient fuel entering the carburetor. This condition could result from a faulty float-needle valve, dirt or water in the fuel lines or filter, a defective fuel pump, or a plugged fuel-tank vent. Also, the carburetor could be icing (§ 9–35). In some instances, certain ignition troubles could cause stalling after starting, but as a rule if the ignition troubles are bad enough to cause stalling, they would also prevent starting. Consider burned contact points or defective spark plugs, however, which might permit starting but could fail to keep the engine going. One other condition might be an open primary resistance wire. When the engine is cranked, this wire is bypassed (see end of § 15–5). Then, when the engine starts and cranking stops, this wire is inserted into the ignition primary circuit. If this wire were open, the engine would then stall.

2. Engine stalls as it warms up. This could result if the choke valve is stuck closed; the mixture becomes too rich for a hot engine, and the engine stalls. If the manifold heat-control valve sticks, the air-fuel mixture might become overheated and too lean, causing the engine to stall. If the hot-idle speed is too low, the engine may stall as it warms up because the idling speed drops too low. Also, stalling may be caused by overheating of the engine, which could cause vapor lock.

3. Engine stalls after idling or slow-speed driving. This could occur if the fuel pump has a cracked diaphragm, weak spring, or defective valve. The pump fails to deliver enough fuel for idling or slow-speed operation (although it could deliver enough for high-speed operation). If the carburetor float level is set too high or the idle adjustment is too rich, the engine may "load up" and stall. A lean idle adjustment may also cause stalling. The engine may overheat during sustained idling or slow-speed driving; with this condition, the air movement through the radiator may not be sufficient to keep the engine cool. Overheating, in turn, could cause vapor lock and engine stalling. (See § 26–10 for causes of overheating.)

4. Engine stalls after high-speed driving. This could occur if enough heat accumulates to cause a vapor lock (§ 10–2). The remedy here would be to shield the fuel line and fuel pump or use a less volatile fuel. Failure of the venting or idle-compensator valve in the carburetor may also cause stalling after high-speed operation. And, of course, excessive overheating of the engine is also a primary cause of stalling (§ 26–10).

§ 26–13. ENGINE BACKFIRES This could be due to late ignition timing, ignition cross-firing (caused by the spark jumping across the distributor cap or through the cable insulation), spark plugs of the wrong heat range (which overheat and cause preignition), excessively rich or lean mixtures (caused by fuel-pump or carburetor troubles), overheating of the engine (§ 26–10), carbon in the engine, hot valves, or intake valves that stick or seat poorly. Carbon in the engine, if excessive, may retain enough heat to cause the air-fuel mixture to preignite as it enters the cylinder so that backfiring occurs. Carbon also increases the compression ratio and thus the tendency for knocking and preignition. Hot plugs may cause preignition; cooler plugs should be installed. If intake valves hang open, combustion may be carried back into the carburetor. Valves which have been ground excessively so that they have sharp edges, those which seat poorly, or those which are carboned so that they overheat often produce backfiring.

§ 26–14. EXCESSIVE OIL CONSUMPTION Oil is lost from the engine in three ways: by burning in the combustion chamber, by leakage in liquid form, and by passing out of the crankcase through the crankcase ventilating system in the form of mist or vapor.

External leakage can often be detected by inspecting the seals around the oil pan, valve cover plate, timing-gear housing, or at oil-line and filter connections.

Burning of oil in the combustion chamber gives the exhaust gas a bluish tinge. Oil can enter the combustion chamber in three ways: through a cracked vacuum-pump diaphragm, through clearance between intake-valve stems and valve guides, and past piston rings. The vacuum pump can be quickly checked by operating the windshield wipers and then quickly accelerating the engine. If the wipers stop, this means that the vacuum-pump diaphragm is cracked. Oil can pass through this crack into the combustion chamber. This check applies only to cars equipped with a combination fuel and vacuum pump.

If intake-valve-stem clearance is excessive, oil will be "pulled" through this clearance and into the combustion chamber on each intake stroke. The appearance of the intake-valve stem often indicates that this is occurring; some of the oil remains on the underside of the valve and stem to form carbon. The remedy is to install valve seals or a new valve guide and possibly a new valve.

Probably the most common cause of excessive oil consumption is passage of oil into the combustion chamber between the piston rings and the cylinder walls. This is often called "oil pumping" and is due to worn, tapered, or out-of-round cylinder walls or to worn or carboned rings. In addition, when engine bearings are worn, excessive oil will be thrown on the cylinder walls. The rings will not be able to control all of it, and too much will work up into the combustion chamber.

High speed must also be considered in any analysis of excessive oil consumption. High speed means high temperatures and thus thin oil. More oil, and thinner oil, is thrown on the cylinder walls at high speed. The piston rings, moving at high speed, cannot function so effectively, and more oil works up into the combustion chamber. In addition, the churning effect of the oil in the crankcase creates more oil vapor and mist at high speed. More oil is thus lost through the crankcase ventilating system. Tests have shown that an engine will use several times as much oil at 60 mph (miles per hour) as at 30 mph.

§ 26–15. LOW OIL PRESSURE Low oil pressure is often a warning of worn engine bearings. The bearings can pass so much oil that the oil pump cannot maintain oil pressure. Further, the end bearings will probably be oil-starved and may fail. Other causes of low oil pressure are a weak relief-valve spring, a worn oil pump, a broken or cracked oil line, or a clogged oil line. Oil dilution, or foaming, sludge, insufficient oil, or oil made too thin by engine overheating will cause low oil pressure.

§ 26–16. EXCESSIVE FUEL CONSUMPTION This condition can be caused by almost anything in the car, from the driver to underinflated tires or a defective choke. A fuel-mileage tester can be used to accurately check fuel consumption (Fig. 26–6). The compression or leakage tester (§ 26–5) and the vacuum gauge (§ 26–7) will help determine whether the trouble is in the engine, fuel system, ignition system, or elsewhere.*

---

* A rough test of mixture richness that does not require any testing instruments is to install a set of new or cleaned spark plugs of the correct heat range for the engine and to operate the car for 15 or 20 minutes, then stop the car, and remove and examine the plugs. If they are coated with a black carbon deposit, the indication is that the mixture is too rich. (See points *a* to *g* under item 4 below.) Black exhaust smoke is another indication of an excessively rich mixture: The mixture is too rich to burn fully, and so the exhaust gas contains "soot," or unburned fuel.

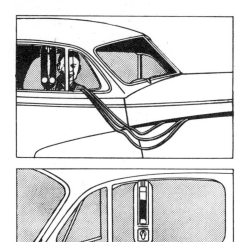

Fig. 26–6. A fuel-mileage tester as it looks from outside and inside a car when mounted in place ready for a test. The tester measures the exact amount of fuel being used during a trial run. *(Kent-Moore, Inc.)*

If the trouble seems to be in the fuel system, consider the following:

1. A "nervous" driver, who pumps the accelerator when idling and insists on being the first to get away when the stoplight changes, will use excessive amounts of fuel.

2. Operation with the choke partly closed after warm-up will use excessive amounts of fuel.

3. Short-run operation means the engine will be operating on warm-up most of the time. This means fuel consumption will be high.

These three conditions are due to the type of operation; changing operating conditions is the only cure. If the excessive fuel consumption is not due to any of these, then check the fuel pump for excessive pressure. High fuel-pump pressure will cause a high float-bowl level and a rich mixture. Special gauges check pump pressure (§ 20–8).

4. If excessive fuel consumption is not due to high fuel-pump pressure or to operating conditions, the trouble is likely to be in the carburetor and could be any of the following:

  a. If the car is equipped with an automatic choke, the choke may not be opening rapidly enough during warm-up or may not fully open. This can be checked by remov-

ing the air cleaner and observing the choke operation during warm-up.

  b. A clogged air cleaner that does not admit sufficient air will act somewhat like a partly closed choke valve. The cleaner element should be cleaned or replaced.

  c. If the float level is high in the float bowl, it will cause flooding and delivery of excessive fuel to the carburetor air horn. The needle valve may be stuck open or may not be seating fully. The float level should be checked and adjusted.

  d. If the idle is set too rich or the idle speed too high, excessive fuel consumption will result. These should be checked and adjusted as necessary.

  e. Where the accelerator-pump circuit has a check valve, failure of the check valve to close properly may allow fuel to feed through into the carburetor air horn. The carburetor will require disassembly.

  f. If the metering rod is stuck in the high-speed full-throttle position or the economizer valve holds open, it will permit the high-speed full-power circuit to function, supplying an excessively rich mixture. The carburetor will require disassembly for repair.

  g. Worn jets, permitting the discharge of too much fuel, require replacement during carburetor rebuilding.

5. Faulty ignition can also cause excessive fuel consumption; the ignition system could cause engine miss and thus failure of the engine to utilize all the fuel. This sort of trouble would also be associated with loss of power, acceleration, or high-speed performance (§ 26–8). Conditions in the ignition system that might contribute to the trouble include a "weak" coil or condenser, incorrect timing, faulty advance-mechanism action, dirty or worn plugs or contact points, or defective wiring.

6. Inferior engine action can produce excessive fuel consumption; for example, loss of engine compression from worn or stuck rings, worn or stuck valves, or a loose or burned cylinder-head gasket. Power is lost under these conditions and more fuel must be burned to achieve the same speed. (Refer to § 26–5 for compression and leakage checking procedures.)

7. Excessive fuel consumption can also result from conditions that make it hard for the engine to move the car along the road. Such factors as

low tires, dragging brakes, and misalignment of wheels increase the rolling resistance of the car. The engine must use up more fuel to overcome this excessive rolling resistance.

§ 26–17. ENGINE NOISES Various types of engine noises may be found, some of which have little significance. Other noises may indicate serious engine trouble that will require prompt attention to prevent major damage to the engine. Characteristics of various noises and their causes are described below, along with tests that may be necessary to confirm a diagnosis.

A listening rod will be of help in locating the source of a noise. The rod acts somewhat like the stethoscope that a doctor uses to listen to a patient's heartbeat or breathing. When one end is placed at the ear and the other end at some particular part of the engine, noises from that part of the engine will be carried along the rod to the ear. A long screwdriver or one of the engine stethoscopes now available can be used. When using the listening rod to locate the source of a noise, put the engine end at various places on the engine until the noise is the loudest. You can also use a piece of garden hose (about 4 feet long) to localize engine noises. Hold one end of the hose to your ear, and move the other end of the hose around the engine until the noise is the loudest. By determining the approximate source of the noise, you can, for example, locate a broken and noisy ring in a particular cylinder or a main-bearing knock.

● **CAUTION:** Keep away from the moving fan belt and fan when using the listening rod.

1. Valve and tappet noise. This is a regular clicking noise that increases in intensity as engine speed increases. The cause is usually excessive valve clearance. A feeler gauge inserted between the valve stem and lifter or rocker arm will reduce the clearance. If the noise also is reduced, then the cause is excessive clearance; the clearance should be readjusted. If inserting the feeler gauge does not reduce noise, the noise is resulting from such conditions in the valve mechanism as weak springs, worn lifter faces, lifters loose in block, rough adjustment-screw face, or rough cams; or else the noise is not from the valves at all. (See other conditions listed below.)

2. Spark knock. Spark knock or rap is a pinging or chattering sound most noticeable during acceleration or when the car is climbing a hill. Some spark knock is normal, but when it becomes excessive, it is due to conditions, such as use of fuel of too low an octane rating for the particular engine, carbon deposits in the engine which increase compression ratio, advanced ignition timing, or the conditions described in § 26–13.

3. Connecting-rod noises. Connecting-rod noises usually have a light knocking or pounding character. The sound is most noticeable when the engine is "floating" (not accelerating or decelerating). The sound becomes more noticeable as the accelerator is eased off with the car running at medium speed. To locate connecting-rod noise, short out spark plugs one at a time. The noise will be considerably reduced when the cylinder that is responsible is not delivering power. A worn bearing or crankpin, a misaligned connecting rod, inadequate oil, or excessive bearing clearances cause connecting-rod noise.

4. Piston-pin noise. Piston-pin noise is somewhat similar to valve and tappet noise, but it has a characteristic metallic double knock. In addition, it is usually most audible during idle with the spark advanced. However, on some engines, the noise becomes most audible at car speeds of around 30 mph. A check can be made by running the engine at idle with the spark advanced and then shorting out spark plugs. Piston-pin noise will be reduced somewhat when a plug in a noisy cylinder is shorted out. Causes of this noise are a worn or loose piston pin, a worn bushing, or a lack of oil.

5. Piston-ring noise. Piston-ring noise is also somewhat similar to valve and tappet noise, since it is characterized by a clicking, snapping, or rattling noise. This noise, however, is most evident on acceleration. Low ring tension, broken rings, worn rings, or worn cylinder walls produce this noise. Since the noise can sometimes be confused with other engine noises, a test can be made as follows: Remove the spark plugs, and add an ounce or two of heavy engine oil in each cylinder. Crank the engine for several revolutions to work the oil down past the rings. Then replace the plugs, and start the engine. If the noise has been reduced, it is probable that the rings are at fault.

6. Piston slap. Piston slap is characterized by a muffled, hollow, bell-like sound and is due to the rocking back and forth of the piston in the cylinder. If it occurs only when the engine is cold, it should not be considered serious. When it occurs under all operating conditions, further investigation is in order. It is caused by inadequate oil, worn cylinder walls, worn pistons, collapsed piston skirts, excessive piston clearances, or misaligned connecting rods.

7. Crankshaft knock. This noise is a heavy and dull metallic knock most noticeable when the engine is under a heavy load or accelerating, particularly when cold. When the noise is regular, it probably results from worn main bearings. When the noise is irregular and sharp, it is probably due to worn end-thrust bearing. This latter condition, when unusually bad, will cause the noise to be produced each time the clutch is released and engaged.

8. Miscellaneous noises. Other noises result from loosely mounted accessory parts, such as generator, cranking motor, horn, water pump, manifolds, flywheel, crankshaft pulley, oil pan, and so forth. In addition, other automotive components, such as the clutch, transmission, and differential, may develop various noises.

Review Questions

1. What could be the possible causes if the engine will not turn over? How do you use the lights to check for the cause?
2. What could be the cause if the engine turns over slowly but does not start?
3. What could be the cause if the engine turns over at normal cranking speed but does not start? How do you check the ignition system with this condition? The fuel system?
4. What could cause the engine to miss?
5. What could cause the engine to lack power, acceleration, or high-speed performance?
6. What could cause the engine to overheat?
7. What could cause the engine to stall as it warms up? What could cause stalls after prolonged idling?
8. What could cause the engine to backfire?
9. What could cause excessive oil consumption?
10. What could cause excessive fuel consumption?
11. Describe various engine noises, and explain what could cause them.
12. What would cause the engine to stall after high-speed driving?
13. Explain how to use the cylinder compression tester. The leakage tester. Explain what various results mean.
14. Explain how to use a vacuum gauge to test an engine and what the various test results mean.
15. Explain how to use an exhaust-gas analyzer.

Study Questions

1. Make lists of various engine troubles, their causes, and their corrections. Study these lists to learn them thoroughly.
2. Write down the procedure for using the lights to find the cause if the engine fails to turn over.
3. Write down the procedure for checking the ignition system by the spark test.
4. Write down the procedure for priming the engine to check the fuel system.
5. Write down the procedure for using a screwdriver to track down a miss.

CHAPTER
27

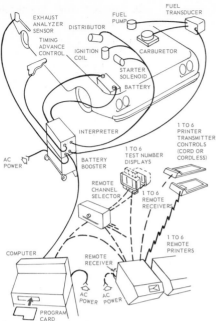

This chapter describes the procedure known as engine tune-up, a procedure which includes testing the various components and accessory systems involved in engine operation. Tune-up goes farther than mere testing, however. It also includes readjusting or replacing parts as required to restore new engine performance. In some cases, during a tune-up, serious troubles may be uncovered that will require major repair work. Previous chapters have described the various service jobs required on the various accessory systems associated with the engine as well as the engine itself. In addition, various testing procedures have been described. None of these procedures will be repeated in the pages that follow. When reference is made to a specific test, turn back to the chapter where it is described if you have forgotten how to make the test.

Engine Tune-up

§ 27-1. NEED FOR TUNE-UP The modern high-compression engine is more sensitive to variations from specifications than the earlier slow-speed, lower-output engines. To maintain an engine at peak performance and economy, it must be kept in good condition, with all components "up to spec." Often, during a tune-up, several conditions will be found which must be corrected to restore the engine to "like new" condition.

There are two general kinds of checks, the visual and mechanical, and those made with instruments. Some of the modern diagnostic instruments used in engine checking are quite elaborate and will quickly check the entire engine system. The latter part of the chapter describes one of these.

§ 27-2. TUNE-UP PROCEDURES Following is a typical tune-up procedure, including visual and mechanical checks and also checks with instruments. Some of the checks listed below are not related to the engine but should be performed in the interest of safety.

1. Loosen spark plugs, start engine to blow

out dirt and carbon, shut off engine, and remove plugs.

2. Test engine compression.

● **CAUTION:** If engine is cranked with a jumper cable at the cranking motor, first disconnect the distributor primary lead from the ignition coil and then turn ignition switch to ON. Failure to do this can damage the ignition switch (on late-model cars).

3. If compression is not up to specifications, perform engine services that will eliminate the trouble. If compression is all right, reinstall the spark plugs.

NOTE: Before reinstalling the plugs, clean, check, and adjust them.

4. Remove distributor cap, clean it, and visually check it for carbon tracks, burns, chips, or corroded terminals. Discard it if it is not in good condition.

5. Clean and inspect rotor, and discard it if it is not in good condition.

6. Inspect the high-tension leads, and if they have cracked or frayed insulation or wires, or are otherwise damaged, discard them.

7. Check distributor centrifugal advance by turning the distributor rotor in the advancing position as far as it will go. Release it. If the rotor does not readily return to its original position, the centrifugal advance is faulty and the distributor must be disassembled for repair.

8. Test the vacuum advance by turning the movable breaker plate and noting whether or not the vacuum-advance spring returns it to its original position. If it does not, the mechanism is defective and will probably require replacement.

9. Check distributor contact points and clean or replace them as necessary. Readjust point opening.

10. Reinstall distributor cap and replace wiring.

11. Check battery state of charge, adding water if necessary, and check battery top for cleanliness. Clean if necessary. Check condition of battery hold-down clamps, tightening them if necessary.

● CAUTION: Do not tighten the clamps excessively, as this could warp or break the battery case.

12. Check battery cables for damage, corrosion, and loose connections, and make necessary corrections.

13. If the battery has been overcharged or undercharged, check the alternator and regulator. This can be done later in the procedure, after the engine has been started and is running.

14. Check drive belts and tighten or replace them as required.

15. Check the condition of the manifold heat-control valve, making sure that it is free to operate. If it is sticking, free it up with an appropriate solvent.

16. Make sure the intake manifold bolts are tightened to the proper specifications. Even a slight leak will reduce engine performance.

17. Check fuel lines for tight connections and for kinks, beads, or leaks. Make necessary corrections. Clean or replace filter.

18. Inspect the cooling system for signs of leaks, weak or collapsed hoses, correct coolant level, and antifreeze protection. Make pressure check of cooling system and of pressure cap.

19. Check and adjust the accelerator linkage if necessary.

20. Service the crankcase ventilation system as necessary. Check ventilation valve and replace it if necessary.

21. Check intake-manifold air-injection system.

22. Remove carburetor air cleaner, and check choke valve to make sure choke is working normally. Clean or replace air-cleaner filter element as necessary. Check thermostatically controlled air-cleaner action after air cleaner is replaced.

23. Connect vacuum gauge, contact-point dwell meter, tachometer, and timing light, and start engine.

NOTE: Alternatively, an ignition-system oscilloscope tester can be used if available, as explained in Chap. 25.

24. Check and adjust contact-point dwell and ignition timing.

25. Adjust idle speed and mixture to specifications.

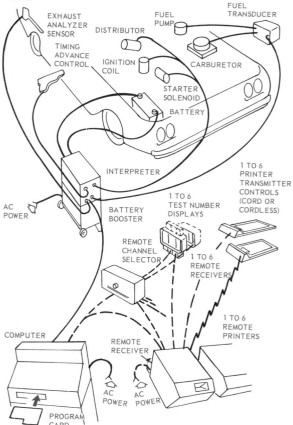

Fig. 27-1. Automotive systems test analyzer connected in readiness to make a complete analysis of the engine and accessory systems. (Universal Testproducts, Incorporated)

26. Other tests that can be made include cylinder-balance test (to find a weak cylinder), cranking-motor operation, conditions of ignition coil and condenser, tightness of mounting bolts, oil level in engine, air pressure in tires, condition of tires, and efficiency of the brakes.

27. Always check the doorjamb sticker to see if lubrication services are required.

28. Make sure that the lights and horn are working, and, if possible, check headlight alignment.

29. Test steering system for looseness and ease of action.

30. Check suspension system and shock absorbers for looseness, excessive play, and wear.

31. Check front wheels and ball joints for excessive wear or loose bearings.

§ 27–3. ENGINE ANALYZERS Figures 25–1 and 25–2 illustrate analyzers using oscilloscopes and other testing devices to make rapid and complete checks of the operating condition of the engine and accessories. Once you have learned how to use these analyzers, you will be able to make a complete analysis in a very short time.

In addition to these analyzers, there are still more complex testers that utilize punched cards to operate the testing devices in an automatic manner. For example, Fig. 27–1 shows a system which uses a computer and an interpreter. The various connections to be made are shown in the illustration. Also shown are a remote channel selector which can be used to select display devices or a printer to either display the test results on a screen or to print them out.

The operation of the tester is simple after the connections are made. You simply select the proper computer-program card (see Fig. 27–2) and insert it into the computer. The punched card has the specifications for the particular model car under test. The tester is then started and the tests listed (Fig. 27–2) are performed. As already noted, test results can be printed out on a form which can be shown to the customer.

A further refinement possible in this type of tester is for the computer to list parts to be replaced, hours of work required, and the cost of labor and parts. There is also the possibility that the computer could be programmed to schedule the work to suit the availability of manpower and space in the service shop.

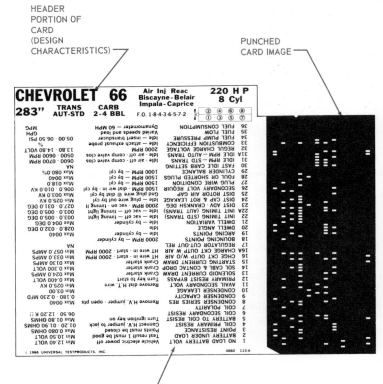

Fig. 27–2. Computer program card. *(Universal Testproducts, Incorporated)*

Review Questions

1. Why is the tune-up procedure more important for modern engines?
2. Explain what, in general, engine tune-up means.
3. Why must you blow the dirt and carbon out from around the spark plugs before removing them?
4. How is the compression test made?
5. Explain how to check the ignition distributor.
6. Explain how to check the battery.
7. Explain how to check the cooling system.
8. How do you check the crankcase ventilation system?
9. Explain how to make a cylinder-balance test.

Study Questions

1. Prepare a step-by-step list of how to tune-up an engine.
2. In the shop, follow the procedure you have listed on a car assigned to you by the instructor. Note down at each step the conditions found and the procedures followed, if required, to correct variation from specifications.

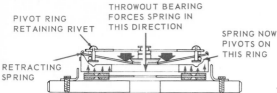

PIVOT RING
RETAINING RIVET

THROWOUT BEARING
FORCES SPRING IN
THIS DIRECTION

SPRING NOW
PIVOTS ON
THIS RING

RETRACTING
SPRING

Clutches

This chapter discusses the purpose, construction, and operation of automotive clutches. The clutch is located in the power train (§ 28–1) between the engine and the transmission.

---

§ 28–1. PURPOSE OF CLUTCH The clutch shown in Figs. 28–1 and 28–2 is of the type used with standard transmissions (not automatic). Its purpose is to permit the driver to couple or uncouple the engine and transmission. When the clutch is in the coupling (or normal running) position, power flows through it from the engine to the transmission. If the transmission is in gear (see Chap. 30), then power flows on through to the car wheels so that the car moves. Essentially, then, the clutch has the job of permitting the driver to uncouple the engine temporarily so that the gears can be shifted from one to another

foward gear position (or into reverse or neutral). It is necessary to interrupt the flow of power (by uncoupling) before gears are shifted. Otherwise, gear shifting would be extremely difficult if not impossible.

The clutch (Figs. 28–1 and 28–2) contains a friction disk (or driven plate) about a foot in diameter. It also contains a spring arrangement and a pressure plate for pressing this disk tightly against the smooth rear face of the flywheel. The friction disk is splined to the clutch shaft. The splines consist of two sets of teeth, an internal set on the hub of the friction disk and a match-

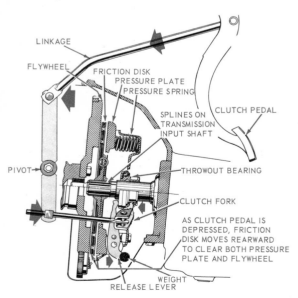

Fig. 28–1. Sectional view of a clutch, with the linkage to the clutch pedal shown schematically. *(Buick Motor Division of General Motors Corporation)*

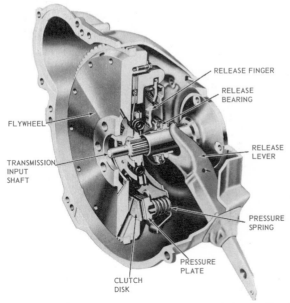

Fig. 28–2. Partial cutaway view of a typical clutch. *(Ford Division of Ford Motor Company)*

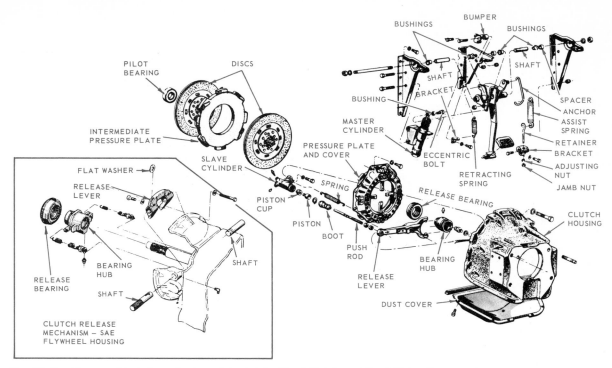

Fig. 28-3. Disassembled view of a two-disk clutch. *(Ford Division of Ford Motor Company)*

ing external set on the clutch shaft. They permit the friction disk to slide back and forth along the shaft but force the disk and the shaft to rotate together. External splines can be seen on the shaft in Fig. 28-1.

The flywheel, which is attached to the end of the engine crankshaft, rotates when the engine is running. When the clutch is engaged (that is, in the coupling position), the friction disk is held tightly against the flywheel (by the clutch springs) so that it must rotate with the flywheel. This rotary motion is carried through the friction disk and clutch shaft to the transmission.

To disengage (or uncouple) the clutch, the clutch pedal is pushed down by the foot. This causes the clutch fork to pivot so that the clutch throwout bearing is forced inward. As the throwout bearing moves inward, it operates release levers. The release levers take up the spring pressure and lift the pressure plate away from the friction disk. The friction disk is no longer pressed against the flywheel face, and the engine can run independently of the power train. Releasing the clutch pedal permits the clutch fork to release the throwout bearing so that the springs once

again cause the pressure plate to force the friction disk against the flywheel face. The two again revolve together.

§ 28-2. TYPES OF CLUTCH　All automotive clutches used with standard transmissions are very similar in construction and operation. There are some differences in the details of the linkages as well as in the pressure-plate assemblies. In addition, some clutches for heavy-duty applications have two friction disks and an intermediate pressure plate (Fig. 28-3). Also, some clutches are operated by hydraulic means (§ 28-7).

Figure 28-4 is a view of a disassembled clutch and linkage. Three types of clutch are described below: the coil-pressure-spring type, diaphragm-spring type, and semicentrifugal type.

§ 28-3. COIL-PRESSURE-SPRING CLUTCH　The clutches of this type contain three to nine coil springs. The purpose of the coil springs is to spring-load the friction disk between the pressure plate and the engine flywheel in the coupling (or clutch-engaged) position. In this position, the friction between the flywheel and the fric-

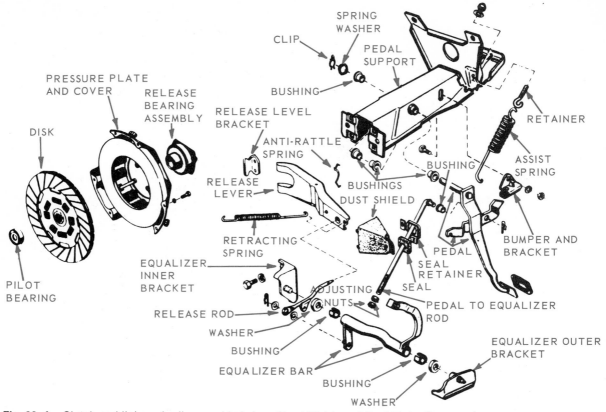

Fig. 28-4. Clutch and linkage in disassembled view. *(Ford Division of Ford Motor Company)*

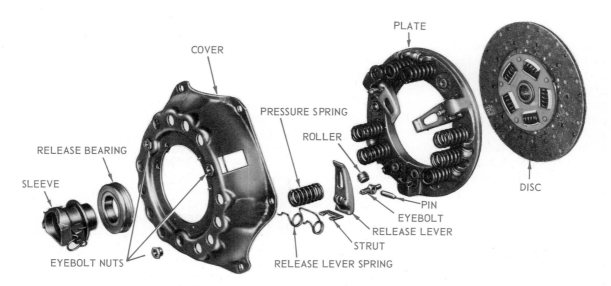

Fig. 28-5. Exploded view of a clutch. The flywheel is not shown. *(Chrysler-Plymouth Division of Chrysler Motors Corporation)*

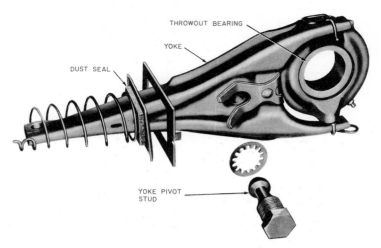

Fig. 28–6. Clutch-fork assembly with its throwout bearing. *(Oldsmobile Division of General Motors Corporation)*

tion disk, and between the pressure plate and the friction disk, causes the friction disk to rotate with the flywheel and pressure plate. The hub of the friction disk is splined to the clutch shaft. The shaft must thus rotate with the friction disk.

Figure 28–5 is a view of a disassembled clutch using nine coil-pressure springs. You can see how one of these springs is positioned in the assembly by referring to Fig. 28–1. Note that the housing cover is bolted to the flywheel. The cover, pressure plate, springs, and other clutch parts rotate with the flywheel. In the coupling position, as shown, the spring is forcing the pressure plate to clamp the friction disk between the plate and the flywheel.

To uncouple the transmission from the engine, the clutch pressure plate must be moved away from the friction disk. When this happens, the pressure on the friction disk is relieved, and it no longer has to revolve with the flywheel and pressure plate.

The driver pushes down on the clutch pedal to produce this effect. As he does so, the linkage from the pedal to the clutch causes movement of a clutch fork, or yoke. The linkage to the clutch fork is shown schematically in Fig. 28–1. The fork is pivoted so that, as the outer end is pushed back by the linkage, the inner end moves forward, toward the clutch. This action causes a throwout bearing to move inward. Figure 28–6 shows a clutch-fork assembly with its throwout bearing. As the bearing is forced inward, it moves against the inner ends of three release levers which are evenly spaced around the clutch. You

can see one of the release levers in the clutch shown in Fig. 28–1. As the throwout bearing moves in against the release levers, it causes the release levers to pivot on their supporting pins. This, in turn, causes the outer ends of the release levers to move away from the friction disk. This movement forces the pressure plate away from the friction disk so that the clutch is uncoupled. Figure 28–7 shows the engaged and released positions of the clutch. Note that the outer end of the release lever exerts its actuating force on the pressure plate through a strut.

Figure 28–8 is a view of a disassembled three-spring clutch. This clutch operates in the same way as the nine-spring clutch described in the previous paragraphs.

§ 28–4. FRICTION DISK The friction disk (Fig. 28–9) consists of a hub and plate assembly to which is attached a series of facings. The disk usually includes a cushioning device as well as a dampening device. The cushioning device provides a cushioning effect as the clutch is engaged so that smoother engagement results. In Fig. 28–9, the cushioning device consists of waved cushion springs to which the friction facings are attached. The waves compress slightly as the clutch engages to provide the cushioning effect. The dampening device uses a series of heavy coil springs placed between the drive washers and riveted to the cushion springs and the hub flange. The disk hub is thus driven through the springs, and they absorb a certain amount of torsional vibration. Stop pins limit the relative motion between

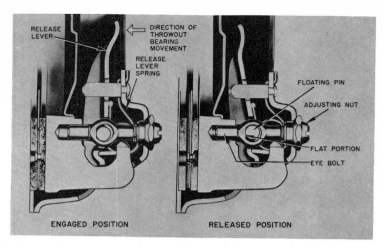

Fig. 28–7. The two limiting positions of the pressure plate and the release lever. *(Oldsmobile Division of General Motors Corporation)*

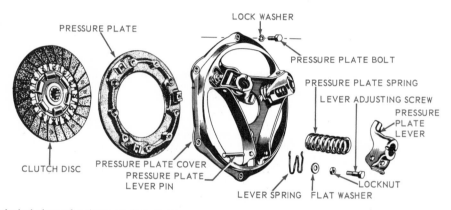

Fig. 28–8. Exploded view of a three-spring clutch.

the hub flange and the drive washers. A molded friction ring, compressed between the hub flange and the drive washers, provides frictional dampening that prevents oscillation between the hub flange and the drive washers.

§ 28–5. DIAPHRAGM-SPRING CLUTCH
One type of clutch (Fig. 28–10) has a diaphragm spring that not only provides the spring pressure required to hold the friction disk against the flywheel but also acts as the release lever that takes up the spring pressure when the clutch is disengaged.

The tapering-finger-type unit has a one-piece diaphragm that is a solid ring on the outer diameter, with a series of tapering fingers pointing inward toward the clutch. The action of the clutch

diaphragm is somewhat like the flexing action that takes place when the bottom of an oilcan is depressed. When the throwout bearing moves in against the ends of the fingers, the entire diaphragm is forced against a pivot ring. When this happens, the diaphragm dishes inward. In this way the pressure plate is raised from the friction desk.

Figures 28–11 and 28–12 illustrate the two positions of the diaphragm spring and clutch parts. In the engaged position (Fig. 28–11), the diaphragm spring is slightly dished, with the tapering fingers pointing slightly away from the flywheel. This places spring pressure against the pressure plate around the entire circumference of the diaphragm spring. The diaphragm spring is naturally formed to exert this initial pressure.

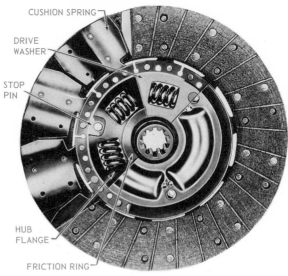

Fig. 28–9. Typical friction disk, or driven plate. *(Buick Motor Division of General Motors Corporation)*

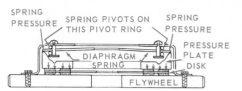

Fig. 28–11. Diaphragm-spring clutch in engaged position. *(Chevrolet Motor Division of General Motors Corporation)*

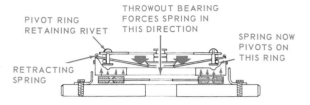

Fig. 28–12. Diaphragm-spring clutch in disengaged position. *(Chevrolet Motor Division of General Motors Corporation)*

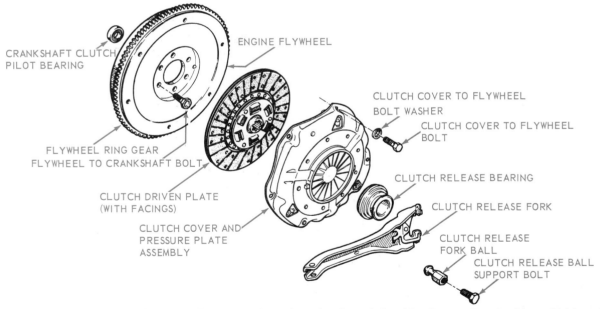

Fig. 28–10. Diaphragm-spring clutch in disassembled view, showing relationship of parts. *(Pontiac Motor Division of General Motors Corporation)*

When the throwout bearing is moved inward against the spring fingers (as the clutch pedal is depressed), the spring is forced to pivot round the inner pivot ring, dishing in the opposite direction. The outer circumference of the spring now lifts the pressure plate away, through a series of retracting springs placed around the outer circumference of the pressure plate (Fig. 28–12).

§ 28–6. SEMICENTRIFUGAL CLUTCH The semi-centrifugal-clutch release levers have weights placed at their outer ends (Fig. 28–1). The weights are so related to the release levers that as speed increases, centrifugal force on the weights causes the release levers to exert added pressure on the pressure plate. When the clutch is not rotating and is engaged, the only pressure on the pres-

395

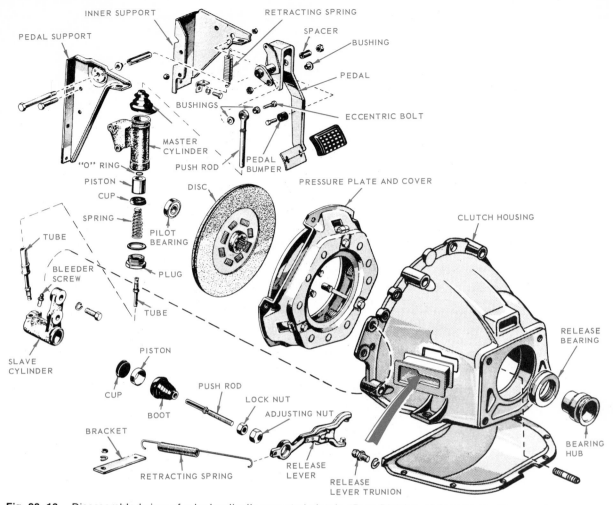

INNER SUPPORT
PEDAL SUPPORT
RETRACTING SPRING
SPACER
BUSHING
PEDAL
BUSHINGS
ECCENTRIC BOLT
MASTER CYLINDER
PEDAL BUMPER
PUSH ROD
"O" RING
PISTON
CUP
SPRING
TUBE
BLEEDER SCREW
SLAVE CYLINDER
DISC
PILOT BEARING
PLUG
TUBE
PRESSURE PLATE AND COVER
CLUTCH HOUSING
PISTON
CUP
BOOT
PUSH ROD
LOCK NUT
ADJUSTING NUT
BRACKET
RETRACTING SPRING
RELEASE LEVER
RELEASE LEVER TRUNION
RELEASE BEARING
BEARING HUB

Fig. 28–13. Disassembled view of a hydraulically operated clutch. *(Ford Division of Ford Motor Company)*

sure plate is produced by the springs. However, as soon as the clutch begins to revolve, centrifugal action on the release-lever weights causes the release levers to increase the pressure on the pressure plate. The higher the speed, the greater the pressure.

§ 28–7. HYDRAULIC CLUTCH This clutch is for use on vehicles where the clutch is remotely located so that it would be difficult to run linkages from the foot pedal to the clutch. Also it is used on medium-duty applications where heavy pressure-plate springs are required. When a clutch is designed to transmit high torques, the springs must be heavy in order to provide sufficient pressure on the friction disk. With insufficient spring

pressure, the pressure plate and flywheel would slip on the friction disk, quickly ruining it.

The heavy spring pressure, however, increases the pressure that must be applied to the clutch release lever or fork. This, in turn, increases the pressure that the driver must apply to the clutch pedal. To reduce the clutch-pedal pressure, a hydraulic system is used on the hydraulic clutch. Figure 28–13 shows one of these clutches in disassembled view. The clutch pedal does not work directly to the release lever through linkages. Instead, when the driver pushes down on the clutch pedal, a push rod is forced down into a master cylinder. This action moves a piston and cup in the master cylinder which forces hydraulic fluid out of the master cylinder, through a tube, and into a slave cylinder. (This action is much like that which takes place in a hydraulic brake system, as explained in Chap. 40.)

As the fluid is forced into the slave cylinder, it moves a piston and push rod. This movement causes the clutch release fork to move, thereby operating the pressure-plate release levers. The hydraulic system can be designed to multiply the driver's efforts so that a fairly light foot-pedal pressure produces a stronger push on the clutch release fork. There is the additional advantage that no mechanical linkage between the two is required. Thus, there is no problem of arranging long linkages if the engine is remotely located from the driver's compartment, as, for instance, at the rear of the vehicle.

*R*eview *Questions*

1. What is the purpose of the clutch?
2. Is the clutch placed between the transmission and the engine, or is the transmission between the clutch and the engine?
3. On what factors does the type of clutch used depend?
4. What is the purpose of the pressure plate in the clutch?
5. What is the purpose of the friction disk in the clutch?
6. In what way is the friction disk connected to the clutch shaft?
7. What is the purpose of the clutch release levers?
8. What causes the clutch throwout bearing to move along the clutch shaft?
9. Describe the cushioning device used on some friction disks. The dampening device.
10. Describe the operation of the diaphragm spring in the clutch using this type of spring.
11. How does the semicentrifugal clutch differ from other clutches?
12. What holds the pressure plate, friction disk, and flywheel facing together when the clutch is engaged?
13. What is a hydraulic clutch? How does it work?

*S*tudy *Questions*

1. Make a sketch of a clutch, and name the essential parts.
2. Write a sequence story of the actions that occur when the clutch pedal is depressed.
3. What do you suppose would be damaged in the clutch if a driver habitually "rode the clutch," or kept his foot continuously on the clutch pedal?

CHAPTER
29

SPRING
PRESSURE
SPRING PIVOTS ON
THIS PIVOT RING
SPRING
PRESSURE
PRESSURE
PLATE
DISK
DIAPHRAGM
SPRING
FLYWHEEL

Clutch Service

This chapter describes the trouble diagnosis, removal, overhaul, adjustment, reassembly, and installation of various types of clutches used on passenger cars.

§ 29-1. CLUTCH TROUBLE DIAGNOSIS Several types of clutch trouble may be experienced. Usually, the trouble itself is fairly obvious and falls into one of the following categories: slipping, chattering or grabbing when engaging, spinning or dragging when disengaged, clutch noises, clutch-pedal pulsation, and rapid friction-disk-facing wear. Following articles discuss these troubles and explain how to find their causes.

§ 29-2. CLUTCH SLIPS WHILE ENGAGED Slipping of the clutch while it is engaged is extremely hard on the clutch facings. The facings wear and burn badly, so that a slipping clutch may soon become completely inoperative.

Clutch slippage is particularly noticeable during acceleration, especially from a standing start or in low gear. A rough test for clutch slippage can be made by starting the engine, setting the hand brake, shifting into high gear, and then slowly releasing the clutch pedal while accelerating the engine slowly. If the clutch is in good condition, it should hold so that the engine stalls immediately after clutch engagement is completed.

Several conditions can cause clutch slippage. The clutch linkage may not be properly adjusted. With an incorrect adjustment that reduces pedal lash too much, the throwout bearing will still press against the release levers even with a fully released clutch pedal. This takes up part of the spring pressure; the pressure plate will not exert sufficient pressure to hold the friction disk tightly enough against the flywheel. As a result, there is slippage between the surfaces. The correction here is to readjust the linkage (§ 29-9).

If the clutch-release linkage binds, it may not return to the fully engaged position when the clutch pedal is released. This, of course, causes clutch slippage. Binding can be eliminated by lubricating all points of friction in the linkage and realigning and readjusting the linkage if necessary (§ 29-9). If readjusting, lubricating, and freeing the linkage do not eliminate the slippage, then the trouble is probably inside the clutch itself, and this requires removal of the clutch from the car so that it can be disassembled for service. Conditions in the clutch itself that could cause slippage include the following:

Weak or broken pressure springs (or diaphragm spring) will not exert sufficient pressure; new springs should be installed. Worn friction-disk facings or grease or oil on the disk facings will permit slippage; the facings or the complete disk should be replaced if this is the case (§ 29-12).

Incorrectly adjusted release levers (adjustable type) may act in the same manner as an incorrectly adjusted clutch linkage or a binding clutch-release linkage. That is, they may prevent full spring pressure on the pressure plate, with a resulting clutch slippage. Release levers must be adjusted, as explained in the shop manual.

§ 29-3. CLUTCH CHATTERS OR GRABS WHEN ENGAGING As a rule, this trouble is inside the clutch itself, and the clutch will have to be taken off the car for servicing. Before this is done, however, the clutch linkage should be carefully checked to make sure it is not binding; if it binds, it may release suddenly to throw the clutch into quick engagement, with a resulting heavy jerk.

In the clutch, the trouble could be due to oil

or grease on the disk facings or to glazed or loose facings. Also, binding of the friction-disk hub on the clutch shaft could prevent smooth engagement of the clutch; this condition requires cleaning up of the splines in the hub and on the shaft and lubrication of the splines. Broken parts in the clutch, such as broken disk facings, broken cushion or coil springs in the friction disk, or a broken pressure plate, could cause poor clutching action and grabbing.

§ 29-4. CLUTCH SPINS OR DRAGS WHEN DISENGAGED

The clutch friction disk spins briefly after disengagement when the transmission is in neutral. It takes a moment for the friction disk to come to rest. This normal spinning should not be confused with a dragging clutch. When the clutch drags, the friction disk is not being fully released from the flywheel or pressure plate as the clutch pedal is depressed; the friction disk continues to rotate with or to rub against the flywheel or pressure plate.

The first thing to check with this condition is the pedal-linkage adjustment. If there is excessive pedal lash, or "free" travel, even full movement of the pedal to the floorboard will not force the throwout bearing in against the release levers (or diaphragm spring) far enough to release the clutch fully. If adjustment of the linkage to reduce pedal lash does not correct the trouble (see § 29-9), the trouble is in the clutch, and the clutch must be removed for disassembly and service.

In the clutch, the trouble could be due to a warped friction disk or pressure plate or a loose friction-disk facing. On the type of clutch with adjustable release levers, improper adjustment would prevent full disengagement, so that the clutch would drag. The friction-disk hub may bind on the clutch shaft so that it does not move back and forth freely. The result is that the friction disk rubs against the flywheel when the clutch is released. Binding may be relieved by cleaning up the splines on the shaft and in the hub and lubricating the splines.

§ 29-5. CLUTCH NOISES

Clutch noises are usually most noticeable when the engine is idling. To diagnose clutch noise, first note whether it is heard when the clutch is engaged or when the clutch is disengaged.

Noises that come from the clutch when the clutch is engaged could be due to a friction-disk hub that is loose on the clutch shaft. This would require replacement of the disk or clutch shaft, or perhaps both if both are excessively worn. Friction-disk dampener springs that are broken or weak will cause noise, and this requires replacement of the complete disk. Misalignment of the engine and transmission will cause a backward-and-forward movement of the friction disk on the clutch shaft; alignment must be corrected.

Noises that come from the clutch when it is disengaged could be due to a clutch throwout bearing that is worn, is binding, or has lost its lubricant. Such a bearing squeals when the clutch pedal is depressed and the bearing comes into operation. The bearing should be relubricated or replaced. If the release levers are not properly adjusted, they will rub against the friction-disk hub when the clutch pedal is depressed. The release levers should be readjusted. If the pilot bearing in the crankshaft is worn or lacks lubricant, it will produce a high-pitched whine when the transmission is in gear, the clutch is disengaged, and the car is stationary. Under these conditions, the clutch shaft, which is piloted in the bearing in the crankshaft, is stationary, but the crankshaft and bearing are turning. The bearing should be lubricated or replaced.

In the diaphragm-spring clutch, worn or weak retracting springs will cause a rattling noise when the clutch is disengaged and the engine is idling. Eliminate by replacing the springs without removing the clutch from the engine.

§ 29-6. CLUTCH-PEDAL PULSATION

Clutch-pedal pulsation, sometimes called a *nervous pedal,* is noticeable when a slight pressure is applied to the clutch pedal with the engine running. The pulsations can be felt by the foot as a series of slight pedal movements. As the pedal pressure is increased, the pulsations cease. This condition is often an indication of trouble that must be corrected before serious damage to the clutch results. One possible cause of the condition is misalignment of the engine and transmission. If the two are not in line, the friction disk or other clutch parts will move back and forth with every revolution. The result is rapid wear of clutch parts. Correction is to detach the transmission, remove the clutch, and then check the housing alignment with the engine and crankshaft. At the same time, the flywheel can be checked for wobble, since a bent crankshaft flange, or a flywheel that is not seated on the crankshaft flange, will also produce clutch-pedal pulsations. A flywheel that is not seated on the crankshaft flange should be removed and remounted to make sure that it does seat evenly. If the flange is bent, a new flange is required.

If the clutch housing is distorted or shifted so that alignment between the engine and transmission has been lost, it is sometimes possible to restore alignment by installing shims between the housing and engine block and between the housing and transmission case. Otherwise, a new clutch housing will be required.

Other causes of clutch-pedal pulsations include uneven release-lever adjustments (so that release levers do not meet the throwout bearing and pressure plate together) and a warped friction disk or pressure plate. Release levers (adjustable type) should be readjusted. A warped friction disk must usually be replaced. If the pressure plate is out of line because of a distorted clutch cover, then the cover sometimes can be straightened to restore alignment.

§ 29-7. RAPID FRICTION-DISK-FACING WEAR
Rapid wear of the friction-disk facings will be caused by any condition that permits slippage between the facings and the flywheel or pressure plate. Thus, if the driver has the habit of "riding" the clutch (that is, if he keeps his foot resting on the clutch) part of the pressure-plate spring pressure will be taken up so that slipping may take place. Likewise, frequent use of the clutch or excessively slow releasing of the clutch after declutching will increase clutch-facing wear. The remedy here is for the driver to use the clutch properly and only when necessary.

Several conditions in the clutch itself can cause this trouble. For example, weak or broken pressure springs will cause slippage and facing wear. In this case, the springs must be replaced. If the pressure plate or friction disk is warped or out of line, it must be replaced or realignment must be reestablished. In addition to these conditions in the clutch, improper pedal-linkage adjustment or binding of the linkage may prevent full spring pressure from being applied to the friction disk. With less than full spring pressure, slippage and wear are apt to take place. The linkage must be readjusted and lubricated at all points of friction.

§ 29-8. CLUTCH PEDAL STIFF
A stiff clutch pedal, or a pedal that is hard to depress, is likely to result from lack of lubricant in the clutch linkage, from binding of the clutch-pedal shaft in the floorboard seal, or from misaligned linkage parts that are binding. In addition, the overcenter spring (on cars so equipped) may be out of adjustment. Also, if the clutch pedal has been bent so that it rubs on the floorboard, it may not operate easily. The remedy in each of these cases is obvious: Parts must be realigned, lubricated, or readjusted as necessary.

§ 29-9. CLUTCH-PEDAL ADJUSTMENT
Clutch-pedal-linkage adjustment may be required from time to time to compensate for friction-disk-facing wear. Also, the linkage requires periodic lubrication. The adjustment must provide the proper amount of free clutch pedal travel (also called pedal *lash*). The free travel is the pedal movement before the throwout bearing comes up against the clutch release levers. After this occurs, there is a definite increase in the amount of pressure required to actuate the release levers and disengage the clutch. If the pedal lash is too great, the clutch may not release fully, and this could cause clutch spinning during disengagement (§ 29-4). If the pedal lash is too small, the clutch may not be able to engage fully (§ 29-2), and this could cause rapid friction-disk-facing wear. Methods of making the adjustment vary in different cars. Refer to the manufacturer's shop manual for details and specifications.

§ 29-10. CLUTCH REMOVAL AND REPLACEMENT
Variations in construction and design require that different removal and replacement procedures be used on different cars. First, the transmission must be removed (§ 32-3). Then, the clutch-housing pan or flywheel lower cover must be removed and the clutch linkage detached. Finally, the clutch can be detached from the flywheel and removed. Refer to the shop manual.

§ 29-11. CLUTCH OVERHAUL
No general instructions that would apply to all types of clutches can be given. Whenever a clutch is to be disassembled, serviced, reassembled, and adjusted, refer to the shop manual describing these procedures.

§ 29-12. INSPECTING AND SERVICING CLUTCH PARTS
The various clutch parts can be checked as follows when they are removed from the clutch:

1. Clutch pressure springs. If the pressure springs have overheated, the paint will burn off or the springs will turn blue. Overheated springs should be replaced, since they may have lost tension and will not operate satisfactorily. Spring pressure can be tested with a spring-tension tester.

2. Pressure plate. A warped or badly scored pressure plate should be replaced. Slight scores or scratches can be cleaned off with fine emery cloth. All traces of emery should be removed.

3. Friction disk. The friction disk should be carefully inspected to make sure that it is in good condition. Several points should be considered.

● **CAUTION:** Do not get any trace of oil or grease on the friction-disk facings. Even small traces may cause clutch grabbing or slipping.

a. Facings. If the facings are worn down nearly to the heads of the rivets, then the facings or friction disk should be replaced. Many manufacturers recommend replacement of the complete disk; some supply facing-replacement data along with strong cautions to be extremely careful if installation of new facings on the disk is attempted.

b. Cushion springs. If the cushion springs under the facings appear to be cracked or weak, the friction disk should be replaced.

c. Torsional springs. Torsional springs that are loose and seem to have lost tension require replacement of the complete friction disk.

d. Hub splines. The fit of the hub to the clutch shaft should be tested. It should slide on without difficulty and should not have any noticeable rotary play. Excessive play means worn splines, and either the shaft or the disk should be replaced (or both).

4. Throwout bearing. The throwout, or release, bearing should never be cleaned in any cleaning solvent or degreasing compound, since this would remove the lubricant that is placed in the bearing on original assembly and thereby ruin the bearing. If the bearing runs roughly or seems loose or noisy, it should be replaced.

5. Housing alignment. Normally, there need be no concern about the clutch-housing alignment, since it was correct on original assembly and alignment should not be lost even if the transmission has been removed and replaced. However, if clutch-pedal pulsations are noticed or if gear shifting is hard and gears jump out of mesh, then alignment should be checked. This requires a special alignment arbor and dial indicator.

6. Pilot bearing in crankshaft. The pilot bearing in the crankshaft is usually either a bushing or a ball bearing. The old bushing can be removed and a new one installed with a special tool. A small amount of short-fiber grease should then be placed in the bushing. Do not put any kind of grease on the end of the clutch shaft.

R*eview Questions*

1. Name several causes of clutch slippage.
2. What could cause the clutch to grab or chatter while being engaged?
3. What could cause the clutch to spin or drag while disengaged?
4. Into what two groupings can clutch noises be divided?
5. When clutch noise is heard with the clutch engaged, what could be the possible causes of the noise?
6. If the clutch noise is heard with the clutch disengaged, what could be the possible causes?
7. What causes a "nervous" clutch pedal?
8. What could cause abnormally rapid friction-disk wear?
9. Give some general instructions for making the clutch-pedal adjustment.
10. Give some general instructions on inspecting and servicing clutch parts.

S*tudy Questions*

1. Make a list of clutch troubles and their causes.
2. Refer to a car shop manual, and make a list of the steps in removing a clutch from a car.
3. Write a sequence story of the disassembly procedure on a coil-pressure-spring type of clutch. On a diaphragm-spring type.
4. Write a story on the procedure for adjusting the release levers on one type of clutch.

ENGINE DELIVERING 100 LB-FT
TORQUE. GEAR RATIO THROUGH
POWER TRAIN IS 12:1

1200 POUNDS

1200 POUNDS

TIRE RADIUS
1 FOOT

Transmissions

This chapter discusses the purpose, construction, and operation of standard, manually shifted transmissions. The following chapters describe overdrives and the various types of automatic transmissions in use on late-model automobiles.

§ 30–1. PURPOSE OF TRANSMISSIONS The transmission, or gear changer, provides a means of varying the gear ratio between the engine and rear wheels. Thus, the engine crankshaft may be made to turn approximately four, eight, or twelve times for each wheel revolution. In addition, a reverse gear is provided that permits backing the car.

In automatic transmissions, the varying ratios between the engine crankshaft and the wheels are achieved by automatic means. That is, the driver does not need to shift gears because the automatic controls in the automatic transmission supply the proper ratio to suit the driving conditions. Such transmissions make use of a fluid coupling or a torque converter, as well as mechanical, hydraulic, or electrical controls. All these are discussed in detail in later chapters.

§ 30–2. GEARS AND TORQUE Before we consider the transmission further, we might take a closer look at gear action. The relative speed of rotation between two meshing gears (the gear ratio) is determined by the number of teeth in the gears. For instance, when two meshing gears have the same number of teeth, they will both turn at the same speed (Fig. 30–1). However, when one gear has more teeth than the other, the smaller gear will turn more rapidly than the larger one. Thus, a gear with 12 teeth will turn two times as fast as a gear with 24 teeth (Fig. 30–2). The gear ratio between the two gears is 2:1. If the 12-tooth gear were meshed with a 36-tooth gear, the 12-tooth gear would turn three times for every revolution of the larger gear. The gear ratio between these gears would be 3:1.

1. Torque. Not only does the gear ratio change with the relative number of teeth in the meshing gears, but the *torque* also changes. Torque is twisting, or turning effort. Torque is measured in pound-feet (lb-ft).

Any shaft or gear that is being turned has torque applied to it. The engine pistons and connecting rods push on the cranks on the crankshaft, thereby applying torque to the crankshaft and causing it to turn. The crankshaft applies torque to the gears in the transmission so that the gears turn. This turning effort, or torque, is carried through the power train to the rear wheels so that they turn.

2. Torque in gears. Torque on shafts or gears is measured as a straight-line force at a distance

Fig. 30–1. Two meshing gears with the same number of teeth.

Fig. 30–2. Two meshing gears of different sizes. The smaller gear will turn more rapidly than the larger one.

from the center of the shaft or gear. For instance, suppose that we want to measure the torque in the gears shown in Fig. 30-2. If we could hook a spring scale to the gear teeth and get a measurement of the pull, we could determine the torque. (Actually, a spring scale could not be used, although there are devices to measure the torque of rotating parts.) Suppose, for example, we find that the tooth of the driving gear is pushing against the tooth of the driven gear with a 25-pound force (Fig. 30-3). This force, at a distance of 1 foot (the radius, or distance from the center of the driving gear), means a torque of 25 lb-ft. That is, the smaller, driving gear is delivering a torque of 25 lb-ft.

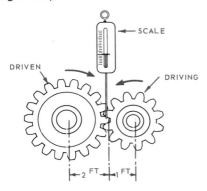

Fig. 30-3. The torque on a gear is the force on the gear teeth times the distance from the center of the shaft to the point on the tooth where the force is applied.

The 25-pound push from the gear teeth of the smaller gear is applied to the gear teeth of the larger gear. But it is applied at a distance of 2 feet from the center. Therefore, the torque on the larger gear is 50 lb-ft (25 × 2). The same force is acting on the teeth of the larger gear, but it is acting at twice the distance from the shaft center.

3. Torque and gear ratio. Now, the important point of all this is that, if the smaller gear is driving the larger gear, the gear ratio will be 2:1. But the torque ratio will be 1:2. The larger gear will turn only half as fast as the smaller gear. But the larger gear will have *twice the torque* of the smaller gear. In gear systems, *speed reduction means torque increase.* For example, in the previous article we mentioned that, when the transmission is in low gear, there is a speed reduction (or gear reduction) of 12:1 from engine to wheels. That is, the crankshaft turns 12 times to turn the rear wheels once. This means that the torque in-

creases 12 times (ignoring losses due to friction). In other words, if the engine produced a torque of 100 lb-ft, then 1,200 lb-ft torque would be applied to the rear wheels.

To see how this torque produces the forward thrust or push on the car, refer to Fig. 30-4. In the example shown, the torque being delivered by the engine is assumed to be 100 lb-ft. We assume also that the gear reduction from the engine to rear wheels is 12:1, with a torque increase of 1:12. Wheel radius is assumed to be 1 foot (for ease of figuring). With the torque acting on the ground at a distance of 1 foot (the radius of the wheel), the push of the tire on the ground is 1,200 pounds. Consequently, the push on the wheel axle, and thus the car, is 1,200 pounds.

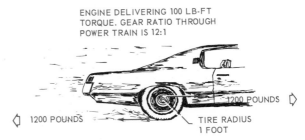

Fig. 30-4. How torque at the rear wheels is translated into forward push. The tire is turned with a torque of 1,200 lb-ft. Since, in the example shown, the tire radius is 1 ft, the push of the tire on the ground will be 1,200 lb. That is, a 1,200-lb force pushes the vehicle forward.

NOTE: Actually, the torque is split between the two rear wheels. Thus, the torque on each rear wheel is 600 lb-ft, and each tire thus pushes on the ground with a force of 600 pounds. Both tires together push with a force of 1,200 pounds, giving the car a forward thrust of 1,200 pounds.

4. Other gears. The gears discussed above are spur gears. The teeth are parallel to, and align with, the center line of the gear. Many types of gears are used in the automobile. They differ mainly from the spur gear in the shape and alignment of the gear teeth. Thus, helical gears are like spur gears except that the teeth have, in effect, been twisted at an angle to the gear center line. Bevel gears are shaped like cones with the tops cut off; the teeth point inward toward the apex of the cone. Bevel gears are used to transmit motion through angles. Some gears have their teeth pointing inward; these are internal gears. Several typical gears are shown in Fig. 30-5.

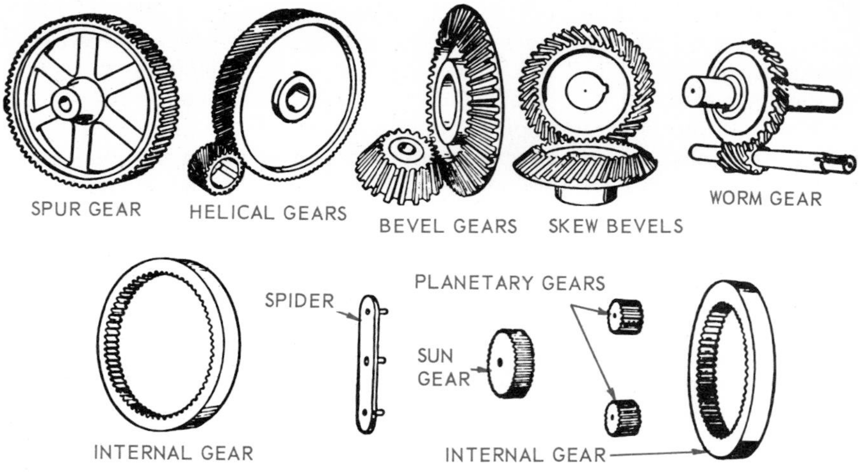

Fig. 30-5. Various types of gears. The disassembled view of the planetary-gear system (right) shows the relationship of the spider, sun, two planetary, and internal gears. Planetary gears are used in overdrives and automatic transmissions. The spider is also called a planet-pinion cage.

SPUR GEAR   HELICAL GEARS   BEVEL GEARS   SKEW BEVELS   WORM GEAR

INTERNAL GEAR   SPIDER   PLANETARY GEARS   SUN GEAR   INTERNAL GEAR

§ 30-3. OPERATION OF TRANSMISSION

We shall use a simplified version of a standard three-speed transmission to discuss transmission operation (Fig. 30-6). In the drawing, it is represented by three shafts and eight gears of various sizes. Only the moving parts are shown. The transmission housing and bearings are not shown.

Four of the gears are rigidly connected to the countershaft (Fig. 30-6). These are the driven gear, second-speed gear, first-speed gear, and reverse gear. When the clutch is engaged and the engine is running, the clutch-shaft gear drives the countershaft driven gear. This turns the countershaft and the other gears on the countershaft. The countershaft rotates in a direction opposite, or counter, to the rotation of the clutch-shaft gear. With the gears in neutral, as shown in Fig. 30-6, and the car stationary, the transmission main shaft is not turning.

The transmission main shaft is mechanically connected by shafts and gears in the final drive to the car wheels. The two gears on the transmission main shaft may be shifted back and forth along the splines on the shaft by operation of the gearshift lever in the driving compartment. The splines are matching internal and external teeth that permit endwise (axial) movement of the gears but cause the gears and shaft to rotate together. Note in the illustrations that a floor-type shift lever is shown. This type of lever is shown since it illustrates more clearly the lever action in shifting gears. The transmission action is the same, regardless of whether a floor-type shift lever or a steering-column shift lever is used.

1. First-speed gear. When the gearshift lever is operated to place the gears in *first* (Fig. 30-7), the large gear on the transmission main shaft is moved along the shaft until it meshes with the small gear on the countershaft. The clutch is disengaged for this operation, so that the clutch shaft and the countershaft stop rotating. When the clutch is again engaged, the transmission main shaft rotates as the driving gear on the clutch shaft drives it through the countershaft. Since the countershaft is turning more slowly than the clutch shaft and since the small countershaft gear is engaged with the large transmission main-shaft gear, a gear reduction of approximately 3:1 is achieved. That is, the clutch shaft turns three times for each revolution of the transmission main shaft. Further gear reduction in the differential at the rear wheels produces a still higher gear ratio (approximately 12:1) between the engine crankshaft and the wheels.

2. Second-speed gear. When the clutch is operated and the gearshift lever moved to *second* (Fig. 30-8), the large gear on the transmission main shaft de-meshes from the small first-speed countershaft gear. The smaller transmission main-shaft gear is slid into mesh with the large second-speed countershaft gear. This provides a somewhat reduced gear ratio, so that the engine crankshaft turns only about twice to the transmission main shaft's once. The differential gear reduction increases this gear ratio to approximately 8:1.

3. Third-speed gear. When the gears are shifted into *third* (Fig. 30-9), the two gears on the transmission main shaft are de-meshed from the countershaft gears and the second-and-third-

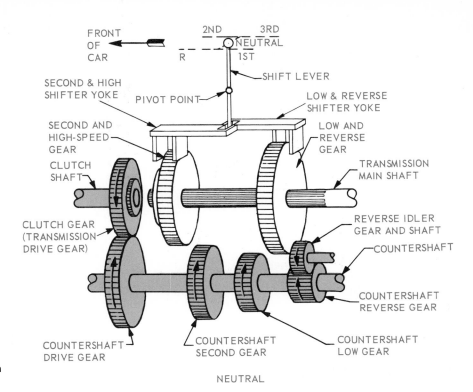

FRONT OF CAR

2ND   3RD
R   NEUTRAL   1ST

SHIFT LEVER

SECOND & HIGH SHIFTER YOKE

PIVOT POINT

LOW & REVERSE SHIFTER YOKE

SECOND AND HIGH-SPEED GEAR

LOW AND REVERSE GEAR

CLUTCH SHAFT

TRANSMISSION MAIN SHAFT

CLUTCH GEAR (TRANSMISSION-DRIVE GEAR)

REVERSE IDLER GEAR AND SHAFT

COUNTERSHAFT

COUNTERSHAFT REVERSE GEAR

COUNTERSHAFT DRIVE GEAR

COUNTERSHAFT SECOND GEAR

COUNTERSHAFT LOW GEAR

NEUTRAL

Fig. 30-6. Transmission with gears in neutral.

speed gear is forced axially against the clutch-shaft gear. External teeth on the clutch-shaft gear mesh with internal teeth in the second-and-third-speed gear so that the transmission main shaft turns with the clutch shaft, and a ratio of 1:1 is obtained. The differential reduction produces a gear ratio of about 4:1 between the engine crankshaft and the wheels.

4. Reverse gear. When the gears are placed in *reverse* (Fig. 30-10), the larger of the transmission main-shaft gears is meshed with the reverse idler gear. This reverse idler gear is always in mesh with the small reverse gear on the end of the countershaft. Interposing the idler gear between the countershaft reverse gear and the transmission main-shaft gear causes the transmission shaft to be rotated in the opposite direction, or in the same direction as the countershaft. This reverses the rotation of the wheels, so that the car backs.

While the description above outlines the basic principles of all transmissions, somewhat more complex transmissions are used on modern cars. These include helical gears and synchromesh devices that synchronize the rotation of gears that are about to be meshed. This eliminates

clashing of the gears and makes gear shifting easier.

§ 30-4. GEARSHIFTING Gearshift levers on manual transmissions are located either on the steering column or on the floorboard. With either location, the operation of the gearshift lever does two things. First, it selects the gear assembly to be moved. Second, it moves it either forward or backward into the desired gear position.

Figure 30-11 shows the shifting patterns for a column and a floorboard shift lever. Let us look at the column shift first. To shift into first or reverse, the driver depresses the clutch pedal to momentarily disconnect the engine from the transmission. Then, he lifts the shift lever and moves it forward for reverse or back for low, or first, gear. When the lever is lifted, it pivots on its mounting pin, and this forces a rod on its inner end to be pushed down the steering column. This downward movement pushes a crossover blade at the bottom of the steering column downward. A slot in the blade engages a pin on the first-and-reverse shift lever (Fig. 30-12). Now, when the shift lever is moved, say into first, the first-and-reverse lever is rotated.

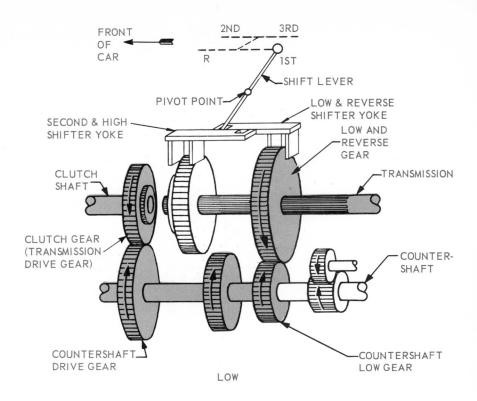

FRONT OF CAR

2ND   3RD

R   1ST

SHIFT LEVER

PIVOT POINT

SECOND & HIGH SHIFTER YOKE

LOW & REVERSE SHIFTER YOKE

LOW AND REVERSE GEAR

CLUTCH SHAFT

TRANSMISSION

CLUTCH GEAR (TRANSMISSION DRIVE GEAR)

COUNTER-SHAFT

COUNTERSHAFT DRIVE GEAR

COUNTERSHAFT LOW GEAR

LOW

Fig. 30–7. Transmission with gears in first.

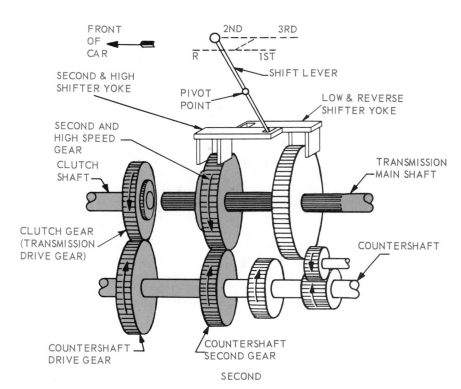

FRONT OF CAR

2ND   3RD

R   1ST

SHIFT LEVER

SECOND & HIGH SHIFTER YOKE

PIVOT POINT

LOW & REVERSE SHIFTER YOKE

SECOND AND HIGH SPEED GEAR

CLUTCH SHAFT

TRANSMISSION MAIN SHAFT

CLUTCH GEAR (TRANSMISSION DRIVE GEAR)

COUNTERSHAFT

COUNTERSHAFT DRIVE GEAR

COUNTERSHAFT SECOND GEAR

SECOND

Fig. 30–8. Transmission with gears in second.

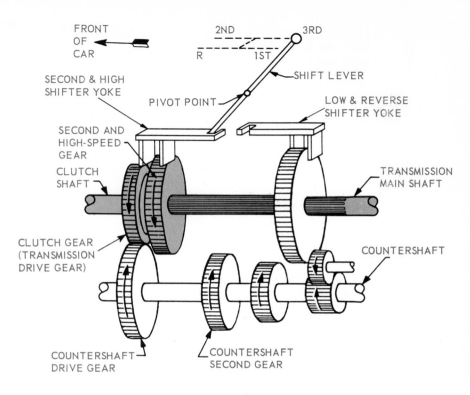

Fig. 30–9.   Transmission with gears in third.

HIGH

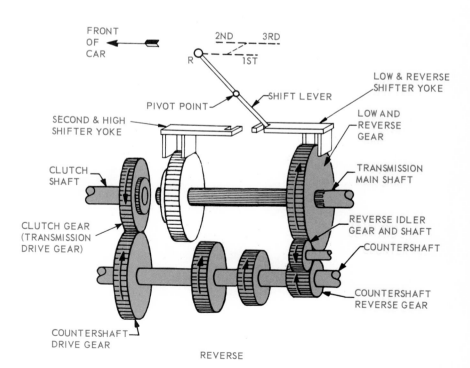

Fig. 30–10.   Transmission with gears in reverse.

REVERSE

This movement is carried by linkage to the transmission (Fig. 30-13). At the transmission, the movement causes the transmission first-and-reverse lever to move. This lever is on a shaft that extends through the transmission side cover and is connected inside the transmission to another lever (Fig. 30-14). On the end of this lever a shift fork is mounted. The arrangement does this: When the shaft is rotated by the movement of the first-and-reverse lever, it causes the shift fork to move forward or backward in the transmission.

Now, to see what effect this forward or backward movement has, refer to Fig. 30-15. When the shift is made to first, the shift fork is moved forward (to the left in Fig. 30-15). This moves the first-and-reverse synchronizer assembly to the left. When this happens, internal splines (or teeth) in the synchronizer drum engage with external splines on the first gear. Now, when the driver releases the clutch pedal, both must rotate together and the power flow is through the gears, as shown in Fig. 30-15B.

When the shift is made to reverse, the synchronizer assembly moves backward (to the right in Fig. 30-15), so that the drum splines engage the reverse-gear splines, thus putting the transmission into reverse.

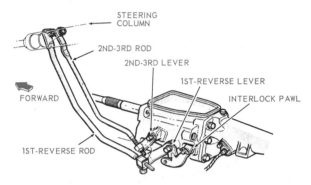

Fig. 30-13. Gearshift linkage between shift levers at the bottom of the steering column and the transmission levers on the side of the transmission. (*Chrysler-Plymouth Division of Chrysler Motors Corporation*)

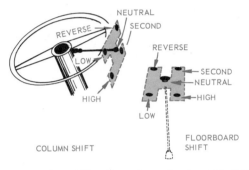

Fig. 30-11. Gearshift patterns for a steering-column and a floorboard shift lever.

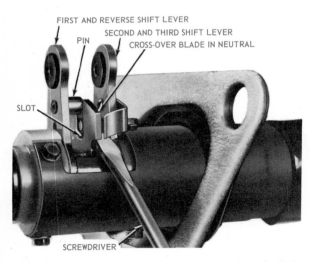

Fig. 30-12. Shift levers and cross-over blade at the bottom of the steering column. The screwdriver is shown holding the cross-over blade in neutral for an adjustment check. (*Chrysler-Plymouth Division of Chrysler Motors Corporation*)

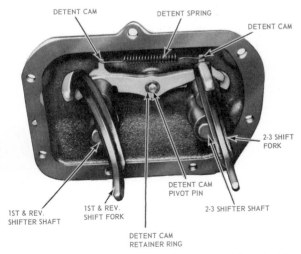

Fig. 30-14. Transmission side cover, viewed from inside the transmission. The shift forks are mounted on the ends of levers attached to shafts. The shafts can rotate in the side cover. The detent cams and springs prevent more than one of the shift forks from moving at any one time. (*Chevrolet Motor Division of General Motors Corporation*)

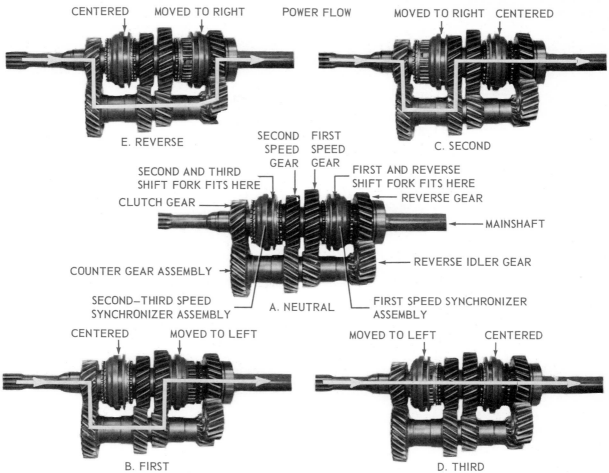

Fig. 30-15. Synchronizer-drum positions and power flow through gears in the different gear positions. Power flow in different gear positions is shown by arrows. *(Buick Motor Division of General Motors Corporation)*

Note the synchronizer-drum positions in second and third. The gear ratios attained in the various gear positions are the result of the different sizes of gear on the mainshaft and the countershaft.

Figure 30-16 shows a floorboard shift lever and linkages to the transmission. This arrangement operates in the same manner as the column-mounted shift lever.

§ 30-5. SYNCHRONIZERS To avoid the clashing of gears during shifting and to simplify the shifting action for the driver, synchronizing devices are used in transmissions. These devices assure that gears which are about to mesh will be rotating at the same speed and thus will engage smoothly. One type uses synchronizing cones on the gears and on

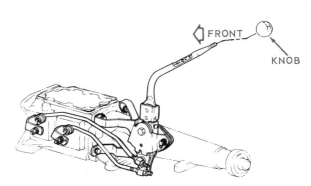

Fig. 30-16. Gearshift linkage arrangement of transmission with floorboard shift lever. *(Pontiac Motor Division of General Motors Corporation)*

409

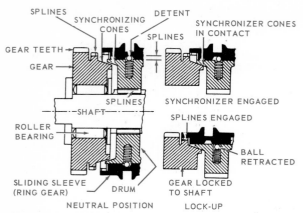

Fig. 30–17. Operation of transmission synchronizing device using cones.

the synchronizing drums (Fig. 30–17). In the neutral position, the sliding sleeve is held in place by spring-loaded balls resting in detents in the sliding sleeve (or ring gear). When a shift starts, the drum and ring gear, as an assembly, are moved toward the selected gear. The first contact is between the synchronizing cones on the selected

gear and the drum. This contact brings the two into synchronization. Both rotate at the same speed. Further movement of the shift fork forces the sliding sleeve on toward the selected gear. The internal splines on the sliding sleeve match the external splines on the selected gear. Now, the gears are locked up, or engaged, and the shift is completed. Note that the sliding sleeve moves off center from the drum for engagement and that this pushes the ball down against the spring.

The pin-type synchronizer (Fig. 30–18) is another type of snychronizer. It has a pair of stop rings, each having three pins which pin them to the clutch-gear sleeve. The clutch gear is splined to the main shaft; external teeth on the clutch gear mesh with internal teeth in the clutch-gear sleeve. Thus, the clutch gear, clutch-gear sleeve, and two stop rings are always rotating with the main shaft. When the shift is made into second, for example, the main shaft and associated parts may be rotating at a different speed from the second-speed gear. However, as the clutch-gear sleeve is moved toward the second-speed gear, the rear inner stop ring moves against the face

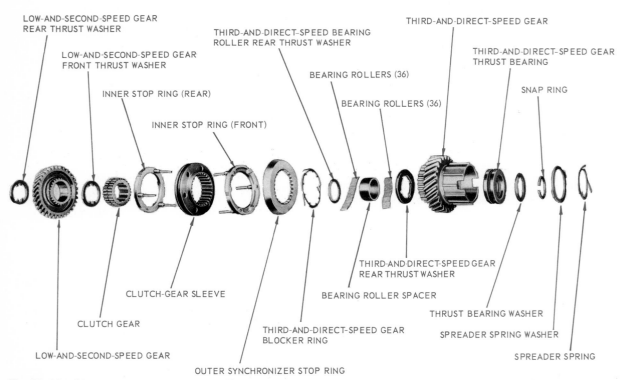

Fig. 30–18. Disassembled view of a pin-type synchronizing device used to assure gear synchronization in shifting. *(Chrysler-Plymouth Division of Chrysler Motors Corporation)*

410

of the second-speed gear, bringing it into synchronous rotation with the clutch-gear sleeve. This permits alignment of the external teeth on the clutch gear and the teeth on the small diameter of the second-speed gear. Now, the clutch-gear sleeve can slip over the teeth of the second-speed gear to couple the second-speed gear and the clutch gear. Then, when the clutch is engaged and the engine again delivers power through it, the second-speed gear drives the main shaft through the clutch gear and the clutch-gear sleeve.

The action in shifting to third is very similar. The third-and-direct-speed gear is supported on roller bearings.

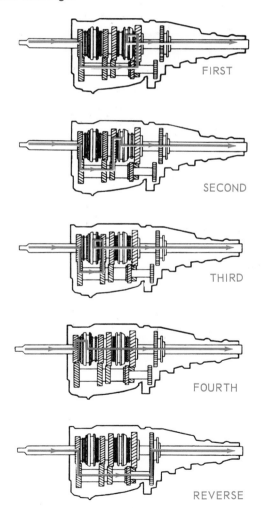

Fig. 30–19. Power flow through a four-speed transmission in the different gear positions. *(Buick Motor Division of General Motors Corporation)*

§ 30–6. OTHER MANUAL TRANSMISSIONS A number of cars are using four-speed transmissions. The four-speed transmission shown in Fig. 30–19 is a constant-mesh type, with two synchronizing clutch assemblies and with all four of the forward gears in mesh with their counterparts on the countergear assembly. Figure 30–19 shows the gear positions in the four forward and one reverse shift positions.

A variety of other designs have been used in automobiles, trucks, buses, and other heavy-duty equipment. Some of them have as many as ten forward and two reverse speeds; these are combination units with a five-forward-speed and one-reverse-speed transmission and a two-speed auxiliary.

A number of vehicles have the engine mounted in the rear (Fig. 30–20), and this requires a somewhat different transmission arrangement. The transmission and differential (Chap. 36) are assembled, as a unit, at the rear-axle location.

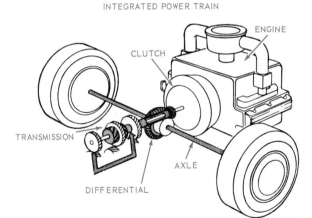

Fig. 30–20. Schematic view of the Corvair power train, showing locations of the engine, clutch, and transmission. *(Chevrolet Motor Division of General Motors Corporation)*

Figure 30–21 is a sectional view of the transmission. It is a conventional three-speed transmission similar to others previously described except for some minor modifications necessary to adapt it to the rear mount. The Corvair also is supplied with a four-speed transmission of the constant-mesh type; it is similar to other four-speed transmissions already described.

The transmission shown in Fig. 30–22 is for use on a front-drive vehicle. The engine is mounted crosswise so that the transmission is also cross-

411

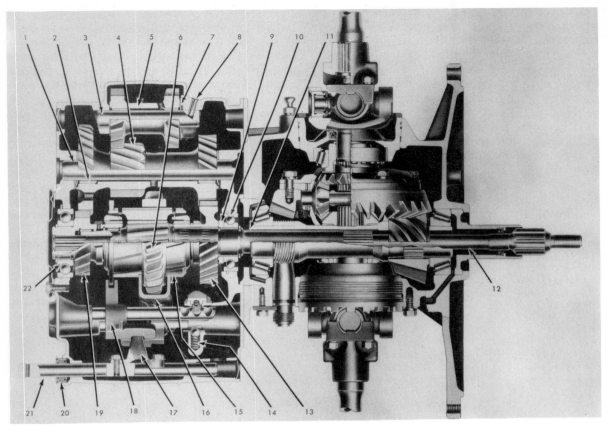

Fig. 30–21. Transmission for a rear-engine car. This assembly is called a transaxle by the manufacturer.

1. Countergear shaft
2. Countergear needle bearings
3. Reverse idler-gear shaft
4. Countergear
5. Reverse idler gear
6. First-and-reverse sliding gear
7. Radial needle bearing (Torrington)
8. Reverse idler-shaft retaining pin
9. Thrust washer
10. Main-shaft bearing
11. Main shaft
12. Clutch shaft
13. Second gear
14. First-and-reverse detent spring and ball
15. Second-and-third clutch
16. First-and-reverse shifter fork
17. Manual-shift shaft finger
18. Second-and-third shifter fork
19. Clutch gear
20. Manual-shift shaft seal
21. Manual-shift shaft
22. Clutch gear bearing

(Chevrolet Motor Division of General Motors Corporation)

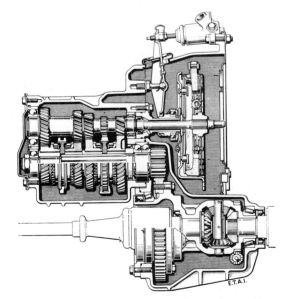

Fig. 30–22. Cutaway view of a four-forward-speed transmission for a cross-mounted engine used on a front-drive car. *(Simca)*

412

Fig. 30–23. Top view of a transmission and differential for a rear-engine car. *(Volkswagen)*

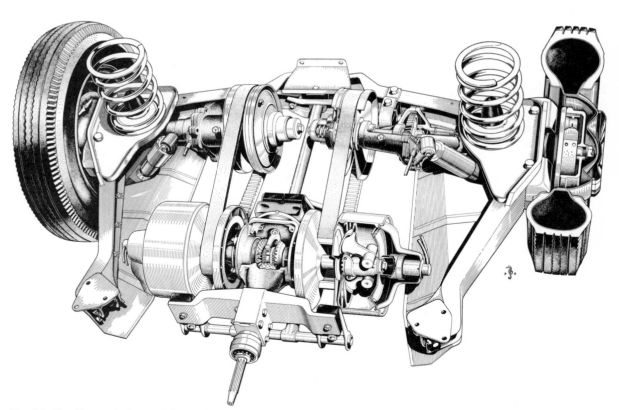

Fig. 30–24. Transmission and final-drive arrangement using variable speed pulleys. *(DAF of Holland)*

wise in the vehicle. Note that the clutch (at top) is of the hydraulically operated type. The transmission is a four-forward-speed unit.

Figure 30–23 is a sectional view of a transmission and differential for a car using a four-cylinder, rear-mounted, air-cooled engine.

Figure 30–24 shows the transmission and final drive for a small car using a two-cylinder engine (shown in Fig. 5–3). This transmission uses two sets of variable-speed pulleys and belts. The speed ratio is varied, in this arrangement, by changing the effective diameters of the pulleys. For example, when first starting, the driving pulleys (toward front of car) are small and the driven pulleys are large. The driven pulleys drive the rear wheels through reduction gears. With the driving pulleys small and the driven pulleys large, there is a large speed reduction (same as gear reduction) and a consequent torque increase. However, as the car gets into motion, centrifugal force acting on the pivoted weights next to the driving pulleys begins to force the sides of the pulleys inward, thus increasing the effective diameters of the driving pulleys. The driven pulleys become smaller at the same time, because the inner sides of these pulleys are forced outward against spring pressures. The result is that the drive ratio (or gear reduction) is reduced. Also controlling the action is engine intake-manifold vacuum acting on diaphragms in the drums next to the driving pulleys. With a high vacuum, indicating a full-open throttle, the outer sides of the driving pulleys are pulled out, reducing their effective diameters and increasing the drive ratio.

Review Questions

1. What is the purpose of the transmission?
2. What are the three forward-speed gear ratios usually provided?
3. What characteristics of the gasoline engine make the transmission necessary?
4. Explain the actions that take place in the transmission as shift is made into first. Into second. Into third. Into reverse.
5. In a gear system, does speed reduction mean torque reduction or torque increase?
6. What is the purpose of synchromesh devices?
7. Explain how the synchromesh functions as the shift is made from first to second. From second to third.
8. Why is there no synchromesh on many transmissions for shifting into first or reverse?
9. Why is the constant-mesh transmission given that name?
10. What are the two separate motions of the gearshift lever that are required to shift gears? What does the first motion do? The second motion?

Study Questions

1. Make five sketches showing only the transmission gears that are in mesh in the four gearshift positions and in neutral.
2. Make a list of the actions that take place in a transmission as the gears are shifted from neutral to first to second to third.
3. Write a sequence story of the actions that take place as the synchromesh device is brought into operation. If the actual unit can be obtained, it will be a big help toward a better understanding of the operation of this device.

CHAPTER
31

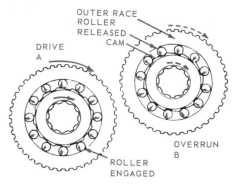

DRIVE
A

OUTER RACE
ROLLER
RELEASED
CAM

OVERRUN
B

ROLLER
ENGAGED

This chapter discusses the purpose and function of the overdrive and describes the manner in which it operates. The description of the planetary-gear system in the pages that follow is especially important, since planetary-gear systems are used in many automatic transmissions. In order to understand the automatic transmissions, you must understand planetary-gear systems. Thus, be sure to spend enough time studying planetary gears so that you understand how they operate.

Overdrives

§ 31-1. PURPOSE OF OVERDRIVE   The overdrive is a mechanism interposed between the transmission and propeller shaft (Fig. 31-1) to permit the propeller shaft to turn faster than, or overdrive, the transmission main shaft. This action, produced when the overdrive is in operation, drops engine speed about 30 percent without a change of vehicle speed. Although the vehicle has less "pep" in overdrive, there is less engine and accessory wear during overdrive operation. Also, the driver can come out of overdrive any time he wishes, as, for instance, when he accelerates to pass another car.

The overdrive includes two essential devices, a freewheeling mechanism and a planetary-gear set. These are explained in following articles.

§ 31-2. FREEWHEELING   MECHANISM   This mechanism is much like the overrunning clutch used in cranking motors (§ 13-14). It is a one-way drive mechanism. For example, in Fig. 31-2, shaft A can drive shaft B. But shaft B cannot drive

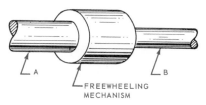

A

B

FREEWHEELING
MECHANISM

Fig. 31-2.   The freewheeling mechanism provides solid drive when shaft A is turning shaft B. But if shaft A slows or stops, shaft B can still "freewheel," or turn faster than (overrun) shaft A.

PROPELLER
SHAFT

OVERDRIVE

MOUNTING INSULATOR

TRANSMISSION

Fig. 31-1.   The overdrive is located between the transmission and the propeller shaft.

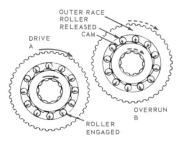

OUTER RACE
ROLLER
RELEASED
CAM

DRIVE
A

OVERRUN
B

ROLLER
ENGAGED

Fig. 31-3.   Action in overrunning clutch during driving (A), during overrunning (B). *(American Motors Corporation)*

shaft A. Figure 31–3 shows the construction. When shaft A is driving shaft B, a series of rollers roll up on ramps and lock shaft B. But if shaft B turns faster than shaft A, the rollers are rolled down off the ramps and thus unlock the two shafts.

§ 31-3. PLANETARY-GEAR SYSTEM

The planetary-gear system, as used in the overdrive and in automatic transmissions, consists of an outer ring gear (sometimes called the *internal gear* because its teeth are inside), three planet pinions held on pinion shafts in a cage or carrier, and a sun gear (Fig. 31–4). The planetary-gear system gets its name from the fact that the pinions revolve around the sun gear and rotate at the same time, just as the planets in our solar system rotate and revolve around the sun.

Before we discuss the manner in which the planetary-gear system is used in the overdrive, let us see how the system functions when we hold one of the three members (ring gear, planet-pinion cage or carrier, or sun gear) stationary and turn another member. The chart (Fig. 31–5) shows what will happen with different combinations, and following paragraphs explain these various combinations.

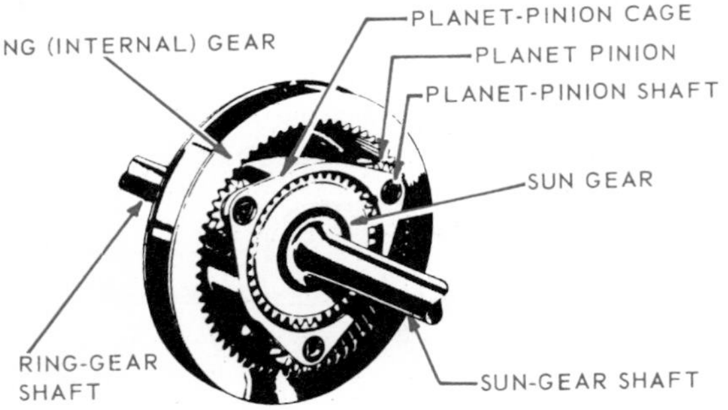

1. Speed increase. If we turn the planet-pinion cage and hold the sun gear stationary, the planet-pinion shafts will be carried around with the cage. As this happens, the planet pinions must rotate on their shafts since the pinions are meshed with the sun gear. In a sense, they "walk around" the stationary sun gear, rotating on their shafts as they, and the cage, revolve around the sun gear. And since the planet pinions are meshed with the ring gear, they also cause the ring gear to rotate. Actually, the ring gear, in this case, will rotate faster than the planet-pinion cage.

Figure 31–6 illustrates how the stationary sun gear causes the ring gear to turn faster than the planet-pinion cage. At any given instant, the pinion tooth meshed with the sun gear is stationary, since the sun gear itself is stationary. The pinion, therefore, can be said to be pivoting around this stationary tooth. If the pinion shaft is moving 1 foot per second, as shown in the illustration, then the outside tooth must be moving faster than 1 foot per second. That is, the

Fig. 31-4. Parts in a planetary-gear system. (*American Motors Corporation*)

CONDITIONS	1	2	3	4	5	6
RING GEAR	D	T	H	H	T	D
CAGE	T	D	D	T	H	H
SUN GEAR	H	H	T	D	D	T
SPEED	I	L	L	I	IR	LR

D—DRIVEN   L—REDUCTION OF SPEED
H—HOLD   R—REVERSE
I —INCREASING OF SPEED   T—TURN OR DRIVE

Fig. 31-5. Chart showing the various conditions that are possible in the planetary-gear system if one member is held and another is turned.

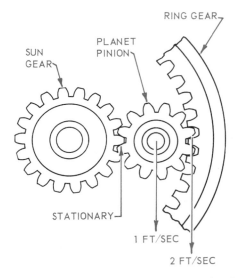

Fig. 31-6. If the sun gear is stationary and the planet-pinion cage is turned, the ring gear will turn faster than the cage. The planet pinion pivots about the stationary teeth. If the center of the pinion shaft is moving at 1 foot per second, the tooth opposite the stationary tooth must move at 2 feet per second (it is twice as far away from the stationary tooth as the center of the shaft).

outside tooth and also the ring gear with which it is meshed move faster than the shaft. Thus the ring gear rotates faster than the planet-pinion cage.

The ratio between the planet-pinion cage and the ring gear can be altered by changing the sizes of the different gears. In the example shown in Fig. 31–7, the ring gear makes one complete revolution while the planet-pinion cage turns only 0.7 revolution. In other words, the ring gear is running faster than the cage, and the gear ratio between the two is 1:0.7. The system functions as a speed-increasing mechanism since the driven member (ring gear) turns faster than the driving member (planet-pinion cage).

2. Speed reduction. If we turn the *ring gear* while holding the sun gear stationary (Fig. 31–5), the planet-pinion cage will turn more slowly than the ring gear. In this case, the system functions as a speed-reducing mechanism since the driven member (planet-pinion cage) turns more slowly than the driving member (ring gear).

3. Speed reduction. Let us try still another combination and see what happens if we hold the ring gear stationary and turn the sun gear. We shall find that the planet pinions will turn on their shafts. They must also "walk around" the ring gear since they are in mesh with it. As they do this, the planet-pinion cage is carried around. The cage therefore rotates, but at a speed less

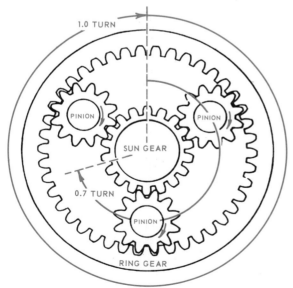

Fig. 31–7. The relative sizes of the gears, as shown, cause the ring gear to turn once while the planet-pinion cage is turned 0.7 times with the sun gear held stationary.

than the sun-gear speed. In this case, the system functions as a speed-reducing mechanism. The driven member (planet-pinion cage) turns more slowly than the driving member (sun gear).

4. Speed increase. Another combination would be to hold the ring gear and turn the planet-pinion cage. In this case, the sun gear would be forced to rotate faster than the cage, and the system would function as a speed-increasing mechanism. The driven member (sun gear) turns faster than the driving member (planet-pinion cage).

5. Reverse. Still another combination would be to hold the planet-carrier cage stationary and turn the ring gear. In this case, the planet pinions act as idlers, similar to the reverse-idler gear in a standard transmission, and thereby cause the sun gear to turn in the reverse direction to ring-gear rotation. Thus, the system functions as a reverse-rotation system, with the sun gear turning faster than the ring gear.

6. Reverse. There is still one more combination. If the cage is held and the sun gear is turned, then the ring gear will turn in a reverse direction, but slower than the sun gear.

7. Direct drive. If any two of the three members (sun gear, cage, ring gear) are locked together, then the entire planetary-gear system is locked out and the input shaft and output shaft must turn at the same speeds. That is, there is no change of speed through the system, and the drive ratio is 1:1. On the other hand, if no member is held stationary and no two members are locked together, then the system will not transmit power at all. The input shaft may turn, but the output shaft does not.

8. Planetary-gear system applied to overdrive. In the overdrive, the ring gear is attached to the output shaft while the three planet pinions are assembled into a cage that is splined to the transmission main shaft. The sun gear has an arrangement whereby it may be permitted to turn, or it may be locked in a stationary position. When it is locked, the ring gear (and thus the output shaft) is forced to turn faster than the transmission main shaft. In other words, the output shaft *overdrives* the transmission main shaft. Disassembled and cutaway views show the planetary-gear members in various positions (Figs. 31–8 to 31–11).

§ **31–4. OVERDRIVE OPERATION**   Figure 31–8 shows the component parts of one type of over-drive in exploded view, with all major parts dis-

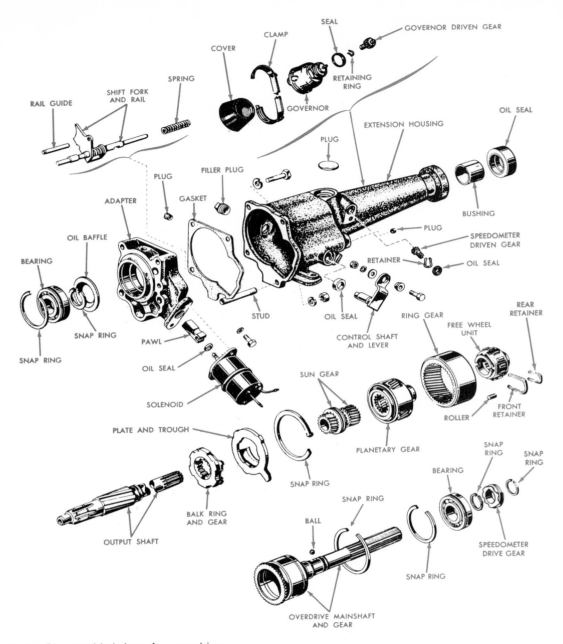

Fig. 31-8. Disassembled view of an overdrive.

assembled but lined up in their approximate relationship in the actual assembly. Figure 31-9 shows the operating components in partial cutaway view. The situation shown is with the overdrive in direct drive. That is, the transmission main shaft and the output shaft are turning at the same speed. The freewheeling mechanism is locked up.

1. Going into overdrive. In Fig. 31-9, although the overdrive is in direct drive, it is ready to go into overdrive just as soon as the car speed is great enough and the driver momentarily releases the accelerator. Note that, in the figure, the pawl (18) is out of the way of the sun-gear control plate (2). It is held in this position by the blocker ring (19), as shown at *A* in Fig. 31-10. The blocker

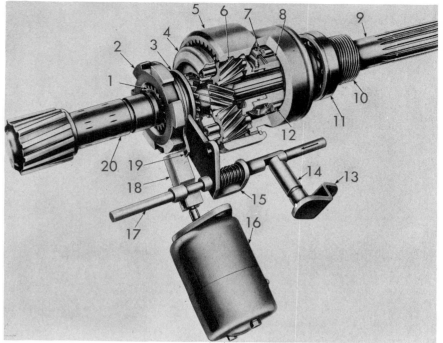

1. Sun gear
2. Sun-gear control plate
3. Sun-gear shift collar
4. Pinion-cage assembly
5. Output-shaft ring gear
6. Pinion
7. Clutch-cam-roller retainer
8. Cam
9. Output shaft
10. Speedometer drive gear
11. Output-shaft bearing
12. Clutch cam roller
13. Control lever
14. Control shaft and lever
15. Shifter fork
16. Solenoid assembly
17. Control rod
18. Sun-gear pawl
19. Blocker ring
20. Transmission main shaft

Fig. 31–9. Overdrive operating components, partly cut away. *(Chevrolet Motor Division of General Motors Corporation)*

ring is loosely assembled onto the sun-gear control plate so that it can turn a few degrees one way or the other.

When the car reaches overdrive cut-in speed (roughly between 18 and 21 mph), a governor driven from the overdrive output shaft closes electrical contacts. This connects the solenoid to the battery and the solenoid is therefore energized. This spring-loads the solenoid pawl so that it attempts to move upward and into a notch in the sun-gear control plate. However, the pawl is held away by the blocker ring, as shown in Fig. 31–10A.

When the driver momentarily releases the accelerator pedal, the engine speed drops. As it drops, the freewheeling mechanism goes into action to permit the output shaft to overrun the transmission main shaft. When this happens, the sun gear slows and then reverses directions. It does this because the ring gear (which rotates with the output shaft) begins to drive it through the planet pinions.

At the moment that the sun gear reverses directions, it moves the blocker ring around a few degrees to the position shown at *B* in Fig. 31–10. When this happens, the pawl can move inward

and into the next notch on the sun-gear control plate that comes around. This locks the control plate in a stationary position.

Since the control plate is splined to the sun gear, this action also locks the sun gear in a stationary position. Now, when the driver again steps on the accelerator and engine speed increases, the car goes into overdrive. With the sun gear locked, the power flow is that shown in Fig. 31–11. The transmission main shaft drives through the planet-

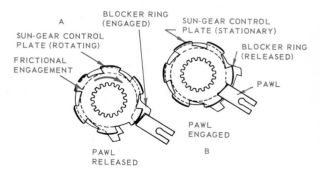

Fig. 31–10. Positions of the sun-gear control plate, blocker ring, and pawl with the pawl released (A) and with the pawl engaged (B). With the pawl engaged, the sun gear is held stationary.

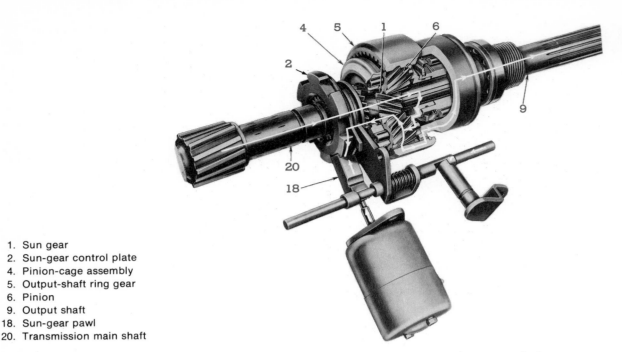

1. Sun gear
2. Sun-gear control plate
4. Pinion-cage assembly
5. Output-shaft ring gear
6. Pinion
9. Output shaft
18. Sun-gear pawl
20. Transmission main shaft

Fig. 31-11. Overdrive mechanism in overdrive. *(Chevrolet Motor Division of General Motors Corporation)*

pinion cage (splined to the transmission main shaft) and causes the pinions to rotate around the sun gear, as shown in Fig. 31-6. The ring gear is attached to the output shaft through the outer race of the freewheeling mechanism. Thus the ring gear and output shaft overdrive (turn faster than) the transmission main shaft. Note that under this condition the freewheeling mechanism is freewheeling. That is, the outer race is overrunning the clutch cam and thus the transmission main shaft.

2. Coming out of overdrive. To come out of overdrive, the driver merely pushes the accelerator all the way down. This would be the action the driver would take when he wants an extra burst of power, as, for example, to pass another car. Pushing the accelerator all the way down causes the accelerator pedal to operate a kick-down switch. Operation of this switch produces two actions. First, it opens the solenoid circuit so that the solenoid attempts to withdraw the pawl from the sun-gear control plate. However, there is considerable pressure on the pawl since it is holding the sun gear stationary and the planet pinions are thrusting hard against the sun gear as they drive the ring gear.

The second action of the kick-down switch momentarily relieves this drive, however, since

the kick-down switch also grounds out the ignition circuit and thereby prevents the engine from delivering power. Since the engine will slow down if it is not delivering power, the driving thrust of the planet pinions on the sun gear is almost instantly relieved. This frees the sun gear and sun-gear control plate, and the drive pawl is pulled back by the spring in the solenoid. As the drive-pawl plunger in the solenoid bottoms, it opens the ground-out contacts and the engine once again begins to deliver power. Now, with the sun gear unlocked, drive is again direct as shown in Fig. 31-9.

The ignition system is disconnected for such a short time that the interruption of the flow of power is not noticeable. The entire sequence of events that takes place when the kick-down switch is closed may be completed in less than a second; the car goes from overdrive into direct drive very quickly.

When the driver again wants to go into overdrive, he has merely to lift his foot momentarily from the accelerator pedal, as already explained.

3. Locking out the overdrive. If the driver wants to lock out the overdrive, he pulls out a control knob on the car dash. This forces the control rod (17 in Fig. 31-9) to the right. As the control rod moves in this direction, it forces the sun-gear

420

control plate and sun gear to move toward the planet-pinion cage. The sun-gear teeth enter into mesh with internal teeth in the planet-pinion cage so that the two lock up. Under this condition, the sun gear and pinion cage must turn together, and thus the entire assembly turns as a unit so that there can be no overrunning effect. The movement of the control rod also locks out the sun-gear pawl, as shown.

§ 31-5. OVERDRIVE ELECTRIC CONTROLS

Various types of electric controls for overdrives have been used, but, essentially, all have the same purpose. They must energize the solenoid as the car reaches cut-in speed. They must also disconnect the ignition circuit momentarily and at the same time open the solenoid circuit when the kick-down switch is closed as the driver wants to come out of overdrive.

Figure 31-12 shows a wiring circuit of the electric control system used with the overdrive described on previous pages. Some systems also have an overdrive lockout switch which is connected into the circuit between the governor switch and the solenoid. When the overdrive is locked out, this switch is open so that the electric control circuit is inoperative.

When the driver wants to go into overdrive, he pushes in the control knob on the dash. This places the system in the condition shown in Fig. 31-9. When the car reaches cut-in speed, the governor closes its contacts to connect the overdrive relay winding to the battery. The overdrive relay, in turn, closes its contacts to connect the solenoid to the battery. Now, the overdrive is ready to go into action. When the driver momentarily releases the accelerator pedal, the solenoid can send the pawl into a notch in the sun-gear control plate. This puts the transmission into overdrive.

To come out of overdrive, the driver pushes all the way down on the accelerator pedal, thus causing the upper contacts of the kick-down switch to open and the lower contacts to close.

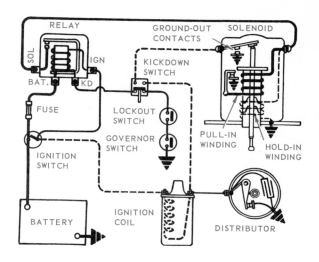

Fig. 31-12. Electric circuit of the overdrive control. Kick-down switch is shown upside down in the illustration. Actually, the contacts connected by dashed lines are the lower, or ground-out contacts. *(Chevrolet Motor Division of General Motors Corporation)*

Opening the upper contacts opens the overdrive-relay circuit. The overdrive relay therefore opens its contacts to open the solenoid circuit. Also, closing the lower contacts in the kick-down switch directly grounds the ignition coil and thereby prevents any ignition. With this interruption of ignition-system action, the engine stops delivering power and begins to slow down. As it does this, the thrust on the solenoid pawl is relieved, and the spring pressure pulls the pawl out of the notch in the sun-gear control plate. When the solenoid pawl snaps into the "out" position, the ground-out contacts in the solenoid are opened to "unground" the ignition coil and thereby permit the ignition system to function again. The engine again begins to deliver power. This series of actions takes place so quickly that no appreciable lag in power delivery is noticeable.

Review Questions

1. What is the purpose of the overdrive?
2. When the overdrive is in operation, does the propeller shaft turn faster or slower than the engine crankshaft?
3. How does the driver shift into overdrive? How can he come out of overdrive once again?
4. Describe a freewheeling mechanism used in an overdrive.
5. Describe the actions in the overdrive as the driver lifts his foot from the accelerator momentarily in order to go into overdrive. Describe the actions as the driver pushes the accelerator past wide-open throttle in order to come out of overdrive.
6. Describe the actions that take place in the electric control circuit as the driver closes the throttle switch.

Study Questions

1. Refer to the chart showing different possible combinations in the planetary-gear system, and write down descriptions of the actions taking place during each combination.
2. Write a sequence story of the actions that take place as the overdrive comes into operation. The actions that take place when the car is brought out of overdrive.
3. Write an essay explaining how the overdrive electric control system operates.

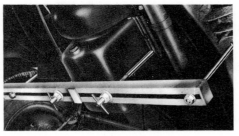

Standard-transmission and Overdrive Service

This chapter discusses trouble diagnosis, removal, overhaul, and reassembly of standard transmissions and overdrives. Following chapters describe different semiautomatic and automatic transmissions in use on passenger cars.

§ 32-1. TRANSMISSION AND OVERDRIVE TROUBLES As a first step in any transmission or overdrive service, diagnosis of the trouble should be made in an attempt to pinpoint the trouble in the malfunctioning unit. Sometimes it is not possible to determine the exact location of a trouble, and the unit must be removed from the car so that it can be torn down and examined. At other times, diagnosis will lead to the point of trouble so that it can be eliminated without major disassembly.

The chart that follows lists the various complaints that might be blamed on the transmission or overdrive, together with their possible causes, the checks to be made, and corrections needed.

§ 32-2. TRANSMISSION AND OVERDRIVE TROUBLE-DIAGNOSIS CHART This chart is divided into two parts, "Transmission Troubles" and "Overdrive Troubles." Most transmission troubles can be grouped under a few headings such as "Hard shifting," "Transmission slips out of gear," "Transmission noisy . . .," and so on, as listed in the chart.

NOTE: The complaints and possible causes are not listed in the chart in the order of frequency of occurrence. That is, item 1 (or item *a* under "Possible Cause") does not necessarily occur more frequently than item 2 (or item *b*).

TRANSMISSION TROUBLES

COMPLAINT	POSSIBLE CAUSE	CHECK OR CORRECTION
1. Hard shifting into gear	a. Clutch not releasing	Adjust (see § 29-9)
	b. Gearshift linkage out of adjustment	Adjust
	c. Improper lubrication of linkage	Lubricate
	d. Shifter fork bent	Replace or straighten
	e. Sliding gear tight on shaft splines	Clean splines or replace shaft or gear
	f. Sliding-gear teeth battered	Replace
	g. Synchronizing unit damaged	Replace defective parts
2. Transmission sticks in gear	a. Clutch not releasing	Adjust (see § 29-9)
	b. Gearshift linkage out of adjustment	Adjust
	c. Improper lubrication of linkage	Lubricate
	d. Detent balls (lockout) stuck	Free
	e. Gears tight on shaft splines	Clean splines or replace shaft or gears

3. Transmission slips out of first or reverse	a. Gearshift linkage out of adjustment	Adjust
	b. Gear loose on main shaft	Replace shaft or gear
	c. Gear teeth worn	Replace gear
	d. Excessive end play of gears	Replace worn or loose parts
	e. Insufficient shift-lever spring (lockout) tension	Install new spring
	f. Bearings worn	Replace
4. Transmission slips out of second	a. Gearshift linkage out of adjustment	Adjust
	b. Gear or drum loose on main shaft	Replace worn parts
	c. Excessive main-shaft end play	Replace worn or defective parts
	d. Gear teeth worn	Replace gears
	e. Insufficient shift-lever spring (lockout) tension	Install new spring
5. Transmission slips out of high	a. Gearshift linkage out of adjustment	Adjust
	b. Misalignment between engine and transmission	Realign
	c. Excessive main-shaft end play	Replace worn or defective parts
	d. Gear teeth worn	Replace gears
	e. Insufficient shift-lever spring (lockout) tension	Replace spring
	f. Bearings worn	Replace
	g. Synchronizing unit worn or defective	Replace worn parts
6. No power through transmission	a. Clutch slipping	Adjust (see § 29–9)
	b. Gear teeth stripped	Replace gear
	c. Shifter fork or other linkage part broken	Replace
	d. Gear or shaft broken	Replace
	e. Drive key sheared	Replace
7. Transmission noisy in neutral	a. Transmission misaligned with engine	Realign
	b. Bearings worn or dry	Replace, lubricate
	c. Gears worn	Replace
	d. Countershaft worn or bent	Replace
	e. Excessive end play of countershaft	Replace worn parts
8. Transmission noisy in gear	a. Clutch friction disk defective	Replace
	b. Engine torsional-vibration dampener defective	Replace or adjust
	c. Main rear bearing of transmission worn or dry	Replace or lubricate
	d. Gears loose on main shaft	Replace worn parts
	e. Gear teeth worn	Replace gears
	f. Speedometer gears worn	Replace
	g. Conditions noted in item 7. Transmission noisy in neutral. Refer to item 7 above for other causes	
9. Gears clash in shifting	a. Clutch not releasing	Adjust
	b. Synchronizer defective	Replace defective parts
	c. Gears sticky on main shaft	Free. Replace defective parts

10. Oil leaks	a. Foaming due to improper lubricant	Use recommended lubricant
	b. Lubricant level too high	Use proper amount, no more
	c. Gaskets broken or missing	Install new gaskets
	d. Oil seals damaged or missing	Install new oil seals
	e. Oil slingers damaged, improperly installed, or missing	Install oil slingers properly
	f. Drain plug loose	Tighten
	g. Transmission bearing retainer bolts loose	Tighten
	h. Transmission case cracked	Use new case

OVERDRIVE TROUBLES

The overdrive may have any of the troubles listed below. Be careful, in analyzing trouble on a car equipped with overdrive, not to blame the overdrive for troubles in the transmission, or vice versa. For example, a certain overdrive trouble may prevent shifting the transmission into reverse. It would be easy to blame this on the transmission, whereas the fault would actually lie in the overdrive.

COMPLAINT	POSSIBLE CAUSE	CHECK OR CORRECTION
11. Will not go into overdrive	a. Wiring defective	Tighten connections, install new wiring
	b. Governor defective	Install new governor
	c. Kick-down switch defective	Install new switch
	d. Relay defective	Install new relay
	e. Solenoid defective	Install new solenoid
	f. Linkage to control knob on dash out of adjustment	Adjust
	g. Defect in overdrive including gear jammed or broken, overrunning clutch defective, excessive shaft end play	Disassemble overdrive to eliminate defective part, tighten flange nut
12. Will not come out of overdrive	a. Wiring defective	Tighten connections, install new wiring
	b. Kick-down switch defective	Install new switch
	c. Solenoid defective	Install new solenoid
	d. Pawl jammed	Free pawl
	e. Sun gear jammed	Disassemble overdrive to eliminate jam, and replace defective parts
13. Cannot shift into reverse, and overdrive dash knob jammed in OD position ("overdrive")	a. Pawl jammed in sun-gear control plate	Replace solenoid
	b. Solenoid defective	Replace solenoid
	c. Relay defective	Replace relay
	d. Governor grounded	Replace governor
	e. Reverse lockout switch grounded	Replace switch
	f. Kick-down switch defective	Replace switch
	g. Wiring defective	Tighten connections, replace wiring
	h. Sun gear jammed	Disassemble overdrive to eliminate jam
	i. Linkage to dash knob out of adjustment	Adjust

14. No power through overdrive	a. Overrunning clutch slipping	Replace defective parts in overdrive
	b. Planetary parts broken	Replace defective parts
15. Noises in overdrive	a. Gears worn, chipped, broken	Replace defective gears
	b. Main-shaft bearing worn or scored	Replace
	c. Overrunning-clutch parts worn or scored	Replace
16. Oil leaks	a. Defective or broken gaskets or oil seals	Replace
	b. Loose mounting	Tighten mounting bolts
	c. Excessive lubricant	Put in only specified amount, no more

§ 32-3. TRANSMISSION REMOVAL AND INSTALLATION

Because of the variations in construction of transmissions on different automobiles, different procedures must be followed in the removal, disassembly, repair, assembly, and installation of their transmissions. These operations require about 5 to 7 hours, the difference in time being due to variations in the procedures. Basically, the procedures are similar. However, refer to the manufacturer's shop manual before attempting such work. In general, the following steps are required:

1. Drain lubricant. Some manufacturers recommend flushing the transmission before removal. This is done by filling the transmission with gasoline or kerosene, after the lubricant is drained, and then operating the engine with the transmission in neutral for 15 seconds. Then the cleaner should be drained.

2. Disconnect the rear axle or the front end of the propeller shaft or the universal joint, according to type. Where needle bearings are used, tape the bearing retainers to the shaft to avoid losing needles.

3. Disconnect shifting linkages from transmission, hand-brake linkage or spring, and speedometer cable.

4. Install engine support, where specified (see Fig. 32-1).

5. Remove attaching bolts or stud nuts. Where recommended, two pilot, or guide, pins should be used. These pins are substituted for transmission bolts and prevent damage to the clutch friction disk as the transmission is moved back. The transmission is then moved toward the rear until the main gear shaft clears the clutch disk. It can then be lowered to the floor.

6. In general, installation is the reverse of removal. Be sure the matching faces of the trans-

Fig. 32-1. Installing engine support prior to removal of transmission.

mission and the flywheel housing are clean. Place a small amount of lubricant on the splines of the main gear shaft. Carefully support the transmission (using guide pins if specified), and move it forward into position. Turn the shaft, if necessary, to secure alignment of the shaft and the clutch-disk hub splines. Put bolts in place, and tighten them to the correct tension.

● **CAUTION:** If the transmission does not fit snugly against the flywheel housing, do not force it. Roughness or dirt, or possibly a loose snap ring or other parts, may be blocking the transmission. If the bolts are tightened under such circumstances, the transmission case may be broken.

§ 32-4. TRANSMISSION AND OVERDRIVE OVERHAUL

The overhaul procedures differ for each model of transmission and overdrive. Thus, before disassembling, servicing, and reassembling a transmission or overdrive, always refer to the shop manual that covers the specific model being repaired. Follow the instructions step by step.

§ 32-5. GEARSHIFT - LINKAGE ADJUSTMENTS

The linkage between the gearshift lever and the shifter levers on the transmission must be properly adjusted; this permits proper selection of gears and completion of gear shifts. Typically, the adjustment is made in two steps. First, an adjustment is made which positions the gear shift lever so far as up-and-down movement is concerned. This determines the distance between the lever and the steering wheel. Second, the radial position of the lever must be established with reference to the steering wheel. Since these adjustments are different on different cars, refer to the applicable shop manual before attempting to make any adjustment on a car.

Review Questions

1. What could cause hard shifting into gear?
2. What could cause the transmission to stick in gear?
3. What might cause the transmission to slip out of first or reverse?
4. What could cause the transmission to slip out of second?
5. What could cause the transmission to slip out of third?
6. What would prevent delivery of power through the transmission?
7. Describe the various conditions that could cause the transmission to operate noisily.
8. What would cause the gears to clash while shifts were made?
9. What could cause oil to be lost from the transmission?
10. What could prevent an overdrive from going into overdrive?
11. What would prevent the overdrive from coming out of overdrive?
12. What in the overdrive might prevent shifting into reverse?
13. What would prevent power transmission through the overdrive?
14. Explain what might cause noise in the overdrive.
15. Describe in a general way the procedure for removing and installing a complete transmission.

Study Questions

1. Make a list of all types of transmission troubles, together with their possible causes and corrections.
2. Write a detailed transmission removal, overhaul, reinstallation, and adjustment story, basing it on a manufacturer's shop manual.

CHAPTER

33

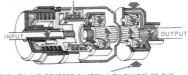

THE FORWARD CLUTCH IS APPLIED. THE FRONT PLANETARY UNIT RING GEAR IS LOCKED TO THE INPUT SHAFT.

INPUT   OUTPUT

THE LOW AND REVERSE CLUTCH (LOW RANGE) OR THE ONE-WAY CLUTCH(DI RANGE) IS HOLDING THE REVERSE UNIT PLANET CARRIER STATIONARY.

FIRST GEAR

Automatic Transmissions

This chapter describes the construction and operation of modern automatic transmissions used on automotive vehicles. Although they vary in details, all operate in a similar manner. They have a torque converter and planetary-gear sets which are controlled by brakes and clutches to provide two or three forward gear ratios.

§ **33–1. TORQUE CONVERTER** The torque converter is a type of fluid coupling that uses a fluid to transmit turning effort from one shaft to another. Two fans can demonstrate a simple fluid coupling (Fig. 33–1). When one fan is turned on and faced toward the other, the stream of air causes the second fan to turn, even though it is not plugged in. To improve the efficiency of the fluid coupling, the two members must be closely coupled.

A simple version of an actual fluid coupling is shown in Fig. 33–2. The assembly is like a hollow doughnut, sliced in two, with a series of vanes set inside each. A sectional view would look like Fig. 33–3. One member is attached to the crankshaft, the other to the transmission shaft. The two members are enclosed by an outer shell and filled with transmission fluid, an oillike substance.

When the crankshaft turns, the driving member carries oil around with it and throws it, by centrifugal force, into the driven member. The oil hits the faces of the vanes in the driven member, thus causing the driven member to turn.

Fig. 33–2. Simplified version of two members of a fluid coupling. *(Chevrolet Motor Division of General Motors Corporation)*

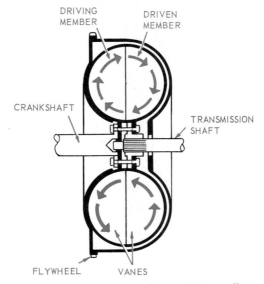

DRIVING MEMBER   DRIVEN MEMBER

CRANKSHAFT

TRANSMISSION SHAFT

FLYWHEEL   VANES

Fig. 33–3. Cross-sectional view of a fluid coupling.

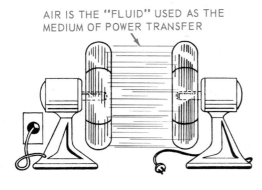

AIR IS THE "FLUID" USED AS THE MEDIUM OF POWER TRANSFER

1   2

Fig. 33–1. Rotation of fan 1 causes fan 2 to rotate. This is a simple fluid coupling with air serving as the fluid.

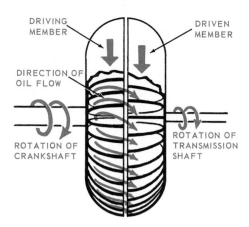

Fig. 33-4. Fluid coupling in action. Oil is thrown from the driving into the driven member. The outer casings have been cut away so that the vanes can be seen.

In the actual torque converter, the vanes are curved and not flat, as shown in Figs. 33-2 to 33-4. This curvature reduces "bounce-back" of the fluid. With flat vanes, the fluid, as it hit the vanes of the driven member, would tend to bounce back into the driving member. This would, in effect, kill off some of the driving torque and power would be lost.

But, with curved vanes (Fig. 33-5), the fluid is unable to bounce back because of the curvature of the vanes in the driven member. In the illustration, the split guide ring is a smaller doughnut-shaped ring which tends to keep the fluid in the outer part of the driving and driven members where it can do the most good.

NOTE: In actual torque converters, the driving member is called the *pump,* or impeller. The driven member is called the *turbine.* We will use "pump" and "turbine" in our discussions.

§ 33-2. THE THIRD MEMBER The coupling shown in Fig. 33-5 would not work efficiently, however. The reason is that as the fluid leaves the inner part of the turbine, it would be thrown into the pump in a hindering direction (Fig. 33-6). That is, it would oppose the rotation of the pump. To eliminate this, a third member, called a *stator,* is added (Fig. 33-7). It has curved vanes which change the direction of the fluid coming out of the turbine into a helping direction.

Figure 33-8 shows you, in a simplified manner, just how the third member changes the direction

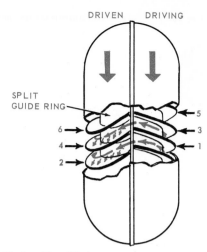

Fig. 33-5. Simplified cutaway view of two members of a torque converter, showing, with heavy arrows, how oil circulates between the driving and the driven member vanes. In operation, the oil is forced by vane 1 downward toward vane 2, as shown by small arrows. Oil then passes around behind the split guide ring and into the driving member again, or between vanes 1 and 3. Then, it is thrown against vane 4 and continues this circulatory pattern, passing continuously from one member to the other.

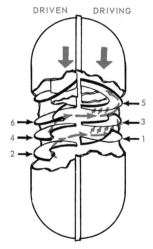

Fig. 33-6. This figure is designed to show what would happen if the vanes in Fig. 33-5 were continuous. Actually, the inner ends of the vanes are not as shown here but are as pictured in following figures. In this illustration, the split guide ring and the outer ends of the vanes have been cut away. If the vanes were as shown here, the oil leaving the trailing edges of the driven member would be thrown upward against the forward faces of the driving-member vanes, thus opposing the driving force. This effect, shown by the small arrows, would cause wasted effort and loss of torque.

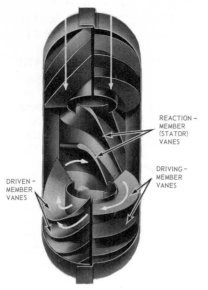

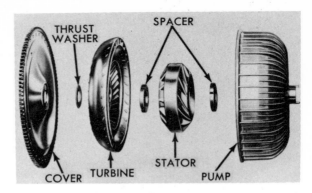

Fig. 33-7. Cutaway view of a torque converter with three members. The third member, the stator, serves as a reaction member. It changes the direction of oil flow, as shown by the curved arrows, under certain operating conditions. Compare this illustration with Figs. 33-5 and 33-6. (Chevrolet Motor Division of General Motors Corporation)

of the fluid. To the left (at A), a jet of fluid striking the curved bucket would have little effect. It would exert some push, but not much. It would leave the bucket with about the same energy as it entered. However, if a curved vane were placed as shown at B, then the fluid would be redirected into the bucket. Actually, the fluid could complete the circuit many times, adding a push to the bucket each time. To say it another way, the third member (the curved vane) increases the torque applied to the wheel on which the bucket is attached.

In a like manner, the stator, placed between the turbine and the pump (Figs. 33-7 and 33-9), changes the direction of the fluid so that it enters the pump in a helping direction. The fluid therefore exerts a harder push as it leaves the pump and enters the turbine. The effect is called *torque multiplication*. In many torque converters, the torque can be more than doubled. You can compare this with two gears of different sizes (Fig. 30-2). If the smaller gear drives the larger gear, the larger gear will turn more slowly but will have a greater torque.

In the same way, when the pump turns faster than the turbine, the turbine, while turning slower, will have a greater torque.

§ 33-3. **STATOR ACTION** The stator, we have seen, causes the torque converter to multiply torque, *when the pump is turning faster than the turbine.* This speed difference and increase in torque is equivalent to what the manual trans-

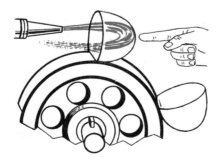

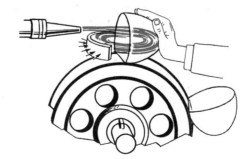

Fig. 33-8. Effect of a jet of oil on a bucket attached to a wheel. If the oil enters and leaves as at A, the push imparted to the bucket and wheel is small. But, if the oil jet is redirected into the bucket by a curved vane as at B, the push is increased. (Chrysler Motors Corporation)

mission does when in low gear. It allows the engine to turn fast while the car wheels are turning slowly so that high torque can be applied and the car can accelerate.

However, as the car comes up to speed, the turbine begins to "catch up" with the pump. When this happens, the fluid leaving the trailing edges of the turbine vanes is moving at about the same speed as the pump. Therefore, it could pass directly into the pump in a helping direction without being given an assist by the stator. In fact, under these conditions, the stator vanes get in the way.

To get the stator vanes out of the way as the turbine catches up with the pump, the stator is mounted on a freewheeling mechanism (similar to the one in the overdrive shown in Fig. 31–3). As long as the fluid from the turbine strikes the faces of the stator vanes, the stator is stationary. It is locked by the freewheeling mechanism, or clutch. But when the fluid starts to strike the back of the stator vanes, the stator starts to freewheel. It starts to rotate so that the stator vanes, in effect, get out of the way.

Actually, the turbine can never quite catch up with the pump. The pump must always be turning a little faster than the turbine in order for the fluid to have an effect on the turbine blades. A typical ratio is 9:10. That is, the pump turns 10 times while the turbine turns 9 times. This would be the ratio during cruising at a steady speed. During acceleration, the ratio increases. This produces a torque multiplication for good acceleration.

TRANSMISSION WITH TORQUE CONVERTERS

§ 33–4. VOLKSWAGEN AUTOMATIC STICK-SHIFT TRANSMISSION This transmission uses a torque converter in conjunction with a three-speed transmission and a vacuum-operated clutch (Fig. 33–10). The three forward driving ranges are "L" for steep inclines, "1" for starting off and city driving, and "2" for cruising. There is also a reverse gear, of course

The transmission, or gear box, is very similar in general construction to the three-speed units described in Chap. 30. The driver may change from one forward gear to another by simply moving the shift lever. This action closes electrical contacts in the lever base which connects a solenoid to the battery. This solenoid, as it operates, opens a vacuum valve which connects a vacuum diaphragm to the engine intake manifold. The vacuum diaphragm is moved by atmospheric pressure as pressure is lost on the other side of the diaphragm because of the vacuum. The diaphragm movement actuates a clutch lever which, in turn, releases the clutch. As this happens, the gearshift lever is released, the solenoid circuit is broken, and the vacuum valve closes. Now, the clutch is reengaged.

§ 33–5. AUTOMATIC TRANSMISSION SHIFT CONTROLS In automatic transmissions shifting from one forward speed to another is automatic and is accomplished by clutches and brakes within the transmission. These devices release or lock

Fig. 33–10. Volkswagen automatic stick-shift transmission. *(Volkswagen)*

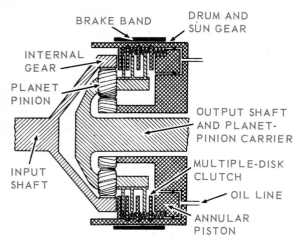

Fig. 33–11. Schematic sectional view showing the two controlling mechanisms used in the front planetary set in the Hydra-Matic. One controlling mechanism consists of a brake drum and brake band; the other is a multiple-disk clutch.

up various components of the planetary-gear system within the transmission to produce the two speeds. You will recall that, in § 31-3, we explained how a planetary-gear system works. Now let us see how the controls operate.

Figure 33–11 is a simplified cross section of a planetary-gear system with a multiple-disk clutch and a brake band for planetary-gear control. Figures 33–12 and 33–13 show clutch parts and a brake band from automatic transmissions.

If the brake band is tightened, it will hold the brake drum and sun gear stationary. This means that there will be a gear reduction through the planetary gears. On the other hand, if the brake band is released and the clutch is applied, the planet-pinion carrier and the sun gear are locked

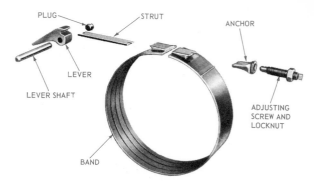

Fig. 33–13. Transmission brake band. *(Chrysler-Plymouth Division of Chrysler Motors Corporation)*

together so that the entire gear system turns as a unit for direct drive. The brake band is normally applied by a heavy spring (plus oil pressure in the actual transmission). This spring is located in the servo, a cylinder in which the spring and a piston are assembled. The clutch is applied by oil pressure against an annular, or circular, piston (Fig. 33–11). You will note that the clutch disks are alternately splined to the drum and sun gear and the planet-pinion carrier (see also Fig. 33–12). When oil pressure back of the annular piston forces the clutch disks together, the lockup of the sun gear and planet-pinion carrier is completed.

The shifting from one gear to the other must be controlled so as to take place only under certain operating conditions. Figure 33–14 illustrates, in simplified schematic view, the shift control system. There are two controlling factors: car speed and throttle opening (or intake-manifold vacuum). These two factors produce two varying oil pressures that work against opposite ends of the shift valve. One pressure is from the governor and is based on car speed. The other is from the

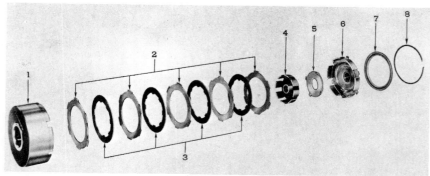

Fig. 33–12. Clutch parts: 1. Clutch-drum assembly. 2. Clutch driven plate. 3. Clutch drive plate. 4. Clutch hub. 5. Clutch-hub thrust washer. 6. Low-sun-gear-and-clutch-flange assembly. 7. Clutch-flange retainer. 8. Retainer snap ring. *(Chevrolet Motor Division of General Motors Corporation)*

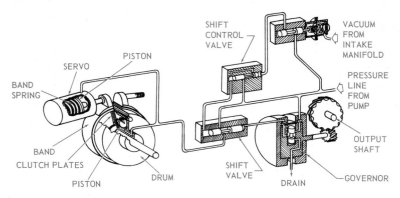

Fig. 33-14. Schematic diagram showing the hydraulic control system for the brake-band servo and the clutch. In the system shown, the band is normally on and the clutch off; this produces gear reduction. But when the shift valve is moved, pressure from the oil pump is admitted to the front of the brake-band piston and to the clutch piston. This causes the brake to release and the clutch to apply. Now, with the clutch locking two planetary members together, the planetary system goes into direct drive.

modulator valve and is based on engine intake-manifold vacuum.

1. Governor pressure. The governor has a rotor, or housing, driven from the output shaft of the transmission. Inside the housing there is a governor valve. The governor valve has two opposing forces acting on it, centrifugal force from rotation, and pump oil pressure. With low car and governor speed, the valve is positioned near the center of the housing and passes only a small oil pressure. As car speed increases, the governor housing rotates more rapidly and this increases the centrifugal force on the valve, causing it to move outward. This passes more oil pressure to the end of the shift valve.

2. Shift-control-valve pressure. The shift control valve is controlled by the modulator valve. The modulator valve has a bellows that is operated by engine intake-manifold vacuum. When the intake-manifold vacuum is low, as it would be during part or wide-open throttle, the bellows is at its full length and has moved the modulator valve to the left (in Fig. 33–14). In this position, oil pressure is passed through the valve to one end of the shift control valve. This pushes the shift control valve to the left, thus admitting pump pressure to the left end of the shift valve. This holds the shift valve to the right, blocking oil pressure to the servo and clutch piston. The gears remain in low.

3. Upshifting. When the driver has attained cruising speed and eases off on the throttle, intake manifold goes up. When this happens, the bellows collapses, pulling the modulator valve to the right. This cuts off oil pressure to the shift control

valve so that it moves to the right, blocking oil pressure to the left end of the shift valve. Meanwhile, governor pressure has increased. The combination of low pressure on one end and high pressure on the other end of the shift valve causes the shift valve to move to the left, thus admitting oil pressure to the clutch piston and the servo. The servo therefore releases the brake band and the clutch piston engages the clutch. With the brake band released and the clutch engaged, the planetary-gear system upshifts to direct drive.

4. Other valves. The above is a very simplified description of how the upshifting is accomplished. The actual valves are more complicated, having springs for initial loading of the valves. There are other valves beside the ones mentioned to ease the shifts, regulate pressures, time downshifts, and so on. There is also the manual-shift valve.

5. Manual-shift valve. This valve is controlled by the driver by movement of a shift lever on the steering column. As the manual valve is moved, it opens or closes various lines that direct oil pressure to the valves in the transmission. For instance, when the valve is moved to D, or drive, oil pressure is directed to the transmission valves so that they are ready to shift into D whenever the speed and throttle conditions are right. This has already been discussed in previous paragraphs. If the manual-shift valve is placed in L, or low, the oil pressure is directed to the valves so that the modulator valve is blocked from producing an upshift.

6. Transmission fluid. We have been saying "oil" through our discussion of how the transmission works. Transmission fluid could be considered a form of oil, but it is a very special sort of oil, with several additives such as viscosity-index improvers, oxidation and corrosion inhibitors, extreme-pressure and antifoam agents, detergents, dispersants, friction modifiers, pourpoint depressants, seal-swell agents, and fluidity modifiers. A number of these are discussed in the section on engine oils (§ 11–2).

● **CAUTION:** It is extremely important to use the proper transmission fluid recommended by the automobile manufacturer. Use of a transmission fluid that is not on the recommended list can cause serious transmission trouble.

§ 33–6. GENERAL MOTORS TYPE 300 AUTOMATIC TRANSMISSION This is a two-speed automatic transmission with torque converter which, with various modifications and different names, has been used in many General Motors automobiles (Buick Super Turbine 300, Chevrolet Aluminum Powerglide, Oldsmobile Jetaway,

Pontiac). A cutaway view of this transmission is shown in Fig. 33–15. Figures 33–16 to 33–20 show conditions in the transmission in low, drive, and reverse.

Note first that the planetary-gear system is more complicated than the one we previously described. It has extra gears. Refer to Figs. 33–15 and 33–16 as you read the following explanation of the gears.

The clutch hub is splined to the input shaft so that the two must turn together. The clutch drum is splined to the low sun gear so that they must turn together. The low sun gear and clutch drum, if released, can turn freely on the input shaft. The input sun gear is splined to the input shaft so that it must turn with the input shaft. The input sun gear is meshed with the three planet long gears which are carried by a flange on the output shaft. The planet long gears are meshed with the planet short gears (also carried by the flange on the output shaft). The planet short gears are, in turn, meshed with the low sun gear. Note that both the planet short and planet long pinions are carried in the same cage or carrier.

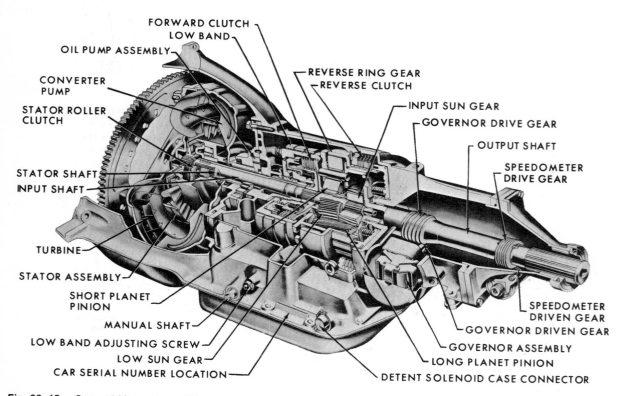

Fig. 33–15. General Motors type 300 automatic transmission. *(General Motors Corporation)*

434

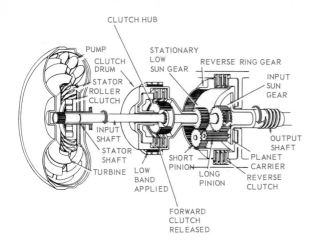

Fig. 33-16. Power flow in L (low) range. The forward clutch is released and the low band is applied so that the low sun gear is held stationary. *(Pontiac Motor Division of General Motors Corporation)*

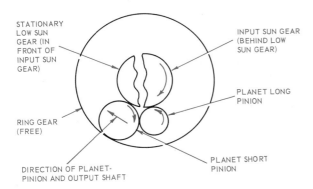

Fig. 33-17. End view of gears in transmission planetary-gear system with the system in low gear. The two sun gears are shown partly cut away so that the locations of the two can be seen. The input sun gear is behind the low sun gear.

It is important for you to understand how these gears are meshed and their relationship to each other. If you are not clear on this, reread the previous paragraph and study the illustrations again.

1. Transmission in low. Now look at Figs. 33-16 and 33-17 once more. This shows the situation when the transmission is in low. The forward clutch is released and the brake band is applied. Thus, the clutch drum and low sun gear are held stationary. The power flow is from the input sun gear, through the planet long pinions, and the planet short pinions. Since the planet short pinions are

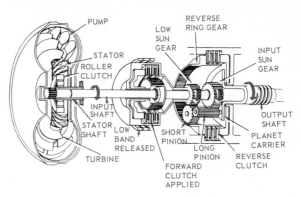

Fig. 33-18. Power flow in D (drive) range. The low band is released and the forward clutch is applied, locking the low sun gear to the input shaft. *(Pontiac Motor Division of General Motors Corporation)*

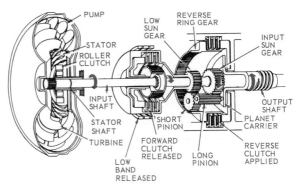

Fig. 33-19. Power flow in R (reverse). The forward clutch and low band are released and the reverse clutch is applied to hold the reverse ring gear stationary. *(Pontiac Motor Division of General Motors Corporation)*

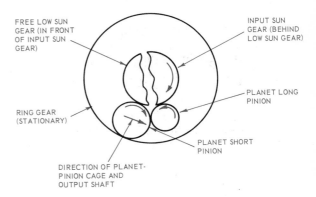

Fig. 33-20. End view of gears in transmission planetary-gear system with the system in reverse gear.

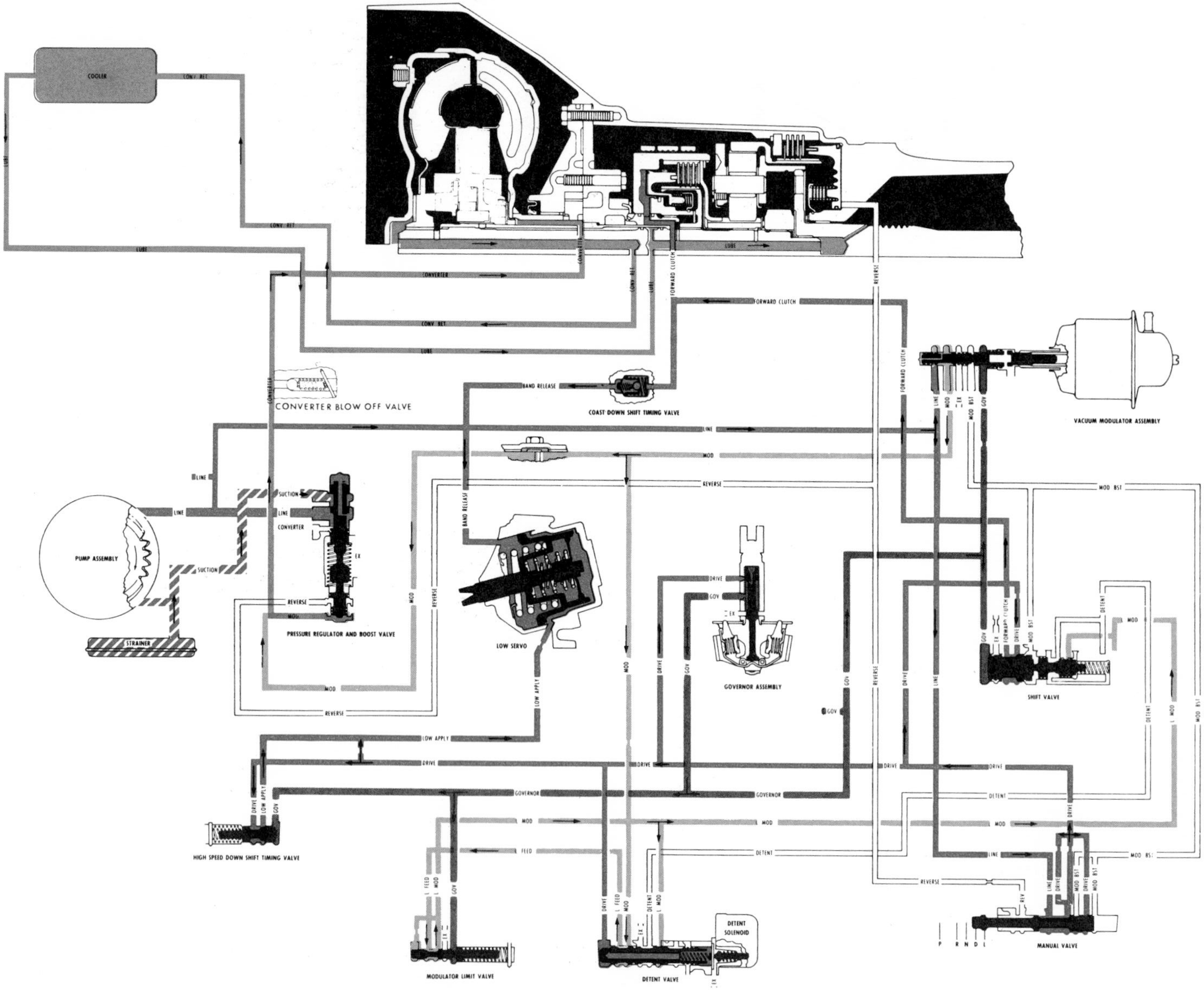

Fig. 33-21. Hydraulic control circuits of an automatic transmission with transmission upshifted. (*Oldsmobile Division of General Motors Corporation*)

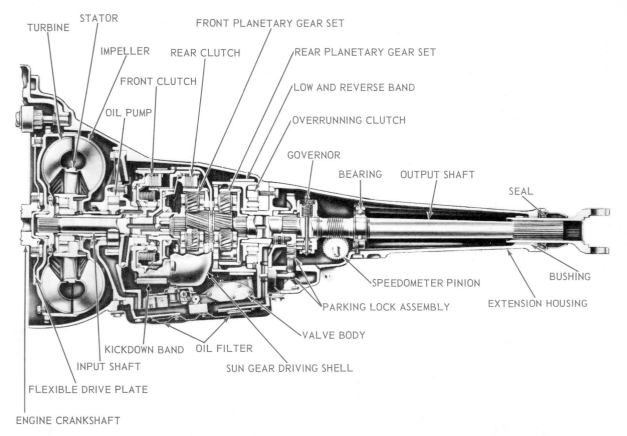

Fig. 33-22. Sectional view of Torque-Flite transmission. *(Chrysler-Plymouth Division of Chrysler Motors Corporation)*

meshed with the stationary low sun gear, these pinions must circle around the low sun gear as they rotate. Thus, they carry the planet-pinion cage around in the direction shown. Note, in Fig. 33-17, the directions in which the various gears rotate. Gear reduction is achieved through the combination of short and long pinions and the fact that the planet-pinion cage, or carrier, is being driven through the planet-pinion shafts.

2. Transmission in drive. The forward clutch is applied and the low band released in drive (Fig. 33-18). With this situation, the low sun gear is locked to the input shaft so that the entire planetary-gear system must turn as a unit. There is no gear reduction in the transmission.

3. Transmission in reverse. The low band and forward clutch are released and the reverse clutch is applied (Figs. 33-19 and 13-20). With this condition, the reverse ring gear is held stationary by

the clutch.* Now, the planet short pinion, as it rotates, is forced to circle around inside the stationary ring gear. This turns the planet-pinion cage and the output shaft in the reverse direction so that the vehicle is backed. Gear reduction is achieved in this gear position.

4. Hydraulic control circuit. Figure 33-21 shows the hydraulic control circuit of an automatic transmission similar to the one just discussed, with the transmission shifted into drive. The manual shift-control valve is positioned by the driver as he moves the shift lever on the steering column.

---

* On earlier models, a brake band and drum were used instead of the clutch. The clutch was found to have greater holding power and was therefore substituted for the brake on later models used with higher output engines.

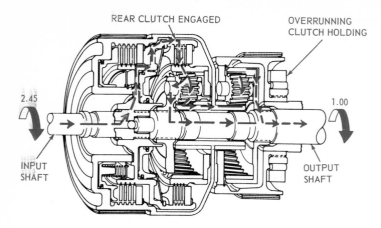

Fig. 33-23. Power flow in D (drive) position when first breaking away from a standing start. *(Chrysler-Plymouth Division of Chrysler Motors Corporation)*

Fig. 33-24. Power flow in D (drive) after up-shift from low to second, or after kickdown from D to second. *(Chrysler-Plymouth Division of Chrysler Motors Corporation)*

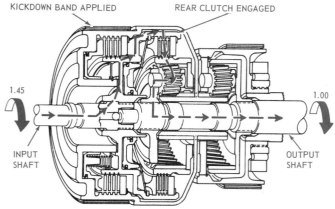

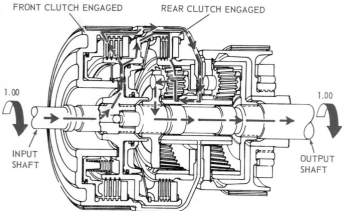

Fig. 33-25. Power flow in D (drive) after up-shift to direct drive. *(Chrysler-Plymouth Division of Chrysler Motors Corporation)*

When the shift-control lever is in the drive position, the transmission starts out in low and then shifts up into drive, as already explained (§ 33-5).

§ 33-7. CHRYSLER TORQUE-FLITE TRANSMISSION
This transmission has two clutches and two brake bands to provide three forward speeds. A sectional view of the transmission is shown in Fig. 33-22, and the various gear positions are shown in Figs. 33-23 to 33-28. In D, or drive, the transmission starts out in low and up-shifts through second to high, or D, automatically as conditions require. There is also a kick-down condition where depressing the accelerator, as for instance when passing, will cause the transmission to drop back from D into second gear.

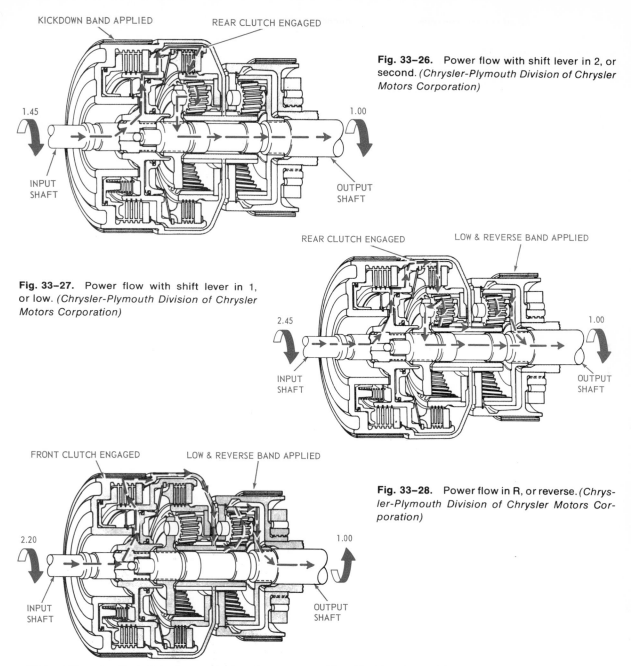

KICKDOWN BAND APPLIED   REAR CLUTCH ENGAGED

Fig. 33-26. Power flow with shift lever in 2, or second. *(Chrysler-Plymouth Division of Chrysler Motors Corporation)*

1.45

1.00

INPUT SHAFT

OUTPUT SHAFT

Fig. 33-27. Power flow with shift lever in 1, or low. *(Chrysler-Plymouth Division of Chrysler Motors Corporation)*

REAR CLUTCH ENGAGED   LOW & REVERSE BAND APPLIED

2.45

1.00

INPUT SHAFT

OUTPUT SHAFT

FRONT CLUTCH ENGAGED   LOW & REVERSE BAND APPLIED

Fig. 33-28. Power flow in R, or reverse. *(Chrysler-Plymouth Division of Chrysler Motors Corporation)*

2.20

1.00

INPUT SHAFT

OUTPUT SHAFT

You will note that this transmission has two semiseparate planetary-gear systems. There are two ring gears, two planet-pinion carriers, but only one sun gear. This is called a compound planetary-gear system. If you study the various illustrations, you will see how operation of the clutches and brake bands will produce the various gear positions. It may help you to look at

Fig. 33-29, also, which shows the planetary-gear train in exploded view.

§ 33-8. FORD C6 AUTOMATIC TRANSMISSION This transmission has three clutches and one brake band to provide three forward speeds. A cutaway view of the transmission is shown in Fig. 33-30. Figure 33-31 shows a sectional view of the

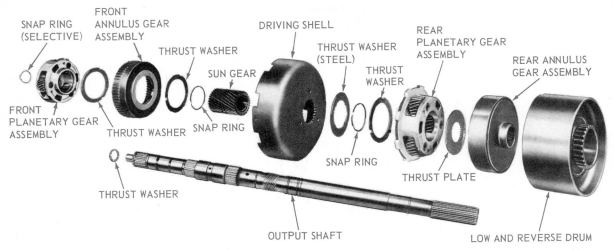

Fig. 33–29. Exploded view of the Torque-Flite planetary-gear train. *(Chrysler-Plymouth Division of Chrysler Motors Corporation)*

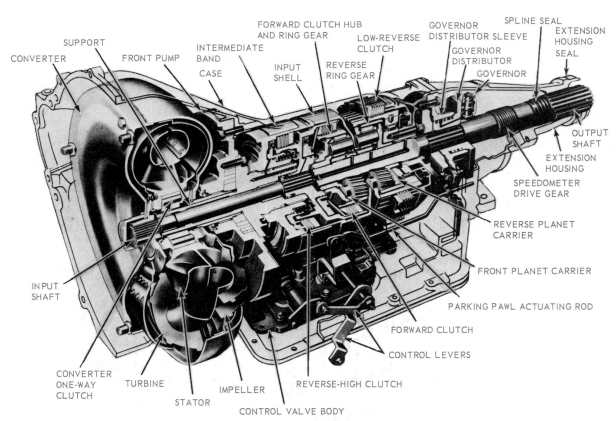

Fig. 33–30. Cutaway view of the Ford C6 automatic transmission. *(Ford Division of Ford Motor Company)*

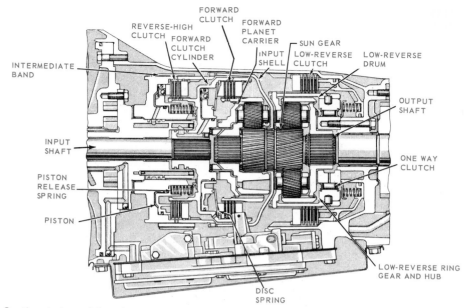

Fig. 33–31. Sectional view of the planetary-gear train in the Ford C6 automatic transmission. *(Ford Division of Ford Motor Company)*

THE FORWARD CLUTCH IS APPLIED. THE FRONT PLANETARY UNIT RING GEAR IS LOCKED TO THE INPUT SHAFT.

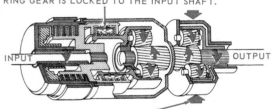

THE LOW AND REVERSE CLUTCH (LOW RANGE) OR THE ONE-WAY CLUTCH(DI RANGE) IS HOLDING THE REVERSE UNIT PLANET CARRIER STATIONARY.

FIRST GEAR

Fig. 33–32. Transmission in first gear. *(Ford Division of Ford Motor Company)*

THE INTERMEDIATE BAND IS APPLIED. THE REVERSE AND HIGH CLUTCH DRUM, THE INPUT SHELL AND THE SUN GEAR ARE HELD STATIONARY.

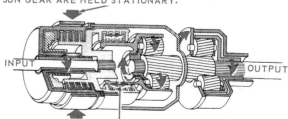

THE FORWARD CLUTCH IS APPLIED. THE FRONT PLANETARY UNIT RING GEAR IS LOCKED TO THE INPUT SHAFT.

SECOND GEAR

Fig. 33–33. Transmission in second gear. *(Ford Division of Ford Motor Company)*

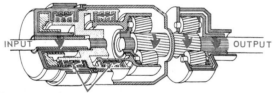

BOTH THE FORWARD AND THE REVERSE AND HIGH CLUTCH ARE APPLIED. ALL PLANETARY GEAR MEMBERS ARE LOCKED TO EACH OTHER AND ARE LOCKED TO THE OUTPUT SHAFT.

HIGH GEAR

Fig. 33–34. Transmission in high gear. *(Ford Division of Ford Motor Company)*

THE REVERSE AND HIGH CLUTCH IS APPLIED. THE INPUT SHAFT IS LOCKED TO THE REVERSE AND HIGH CLUTCH DRUM, THE INPUT SHELL AND THE SUN GEAR.

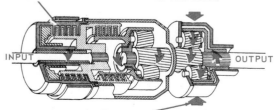

THE LOW AND REVERSE CLUTCH IS APPLIED. THE REVERSE UNIT PLANET CARRIER IS HELD STATIONARY.

REVERSE

Fig. 33–35. Transmission in reverse. *(Ford Division of Ford Motor Company)*

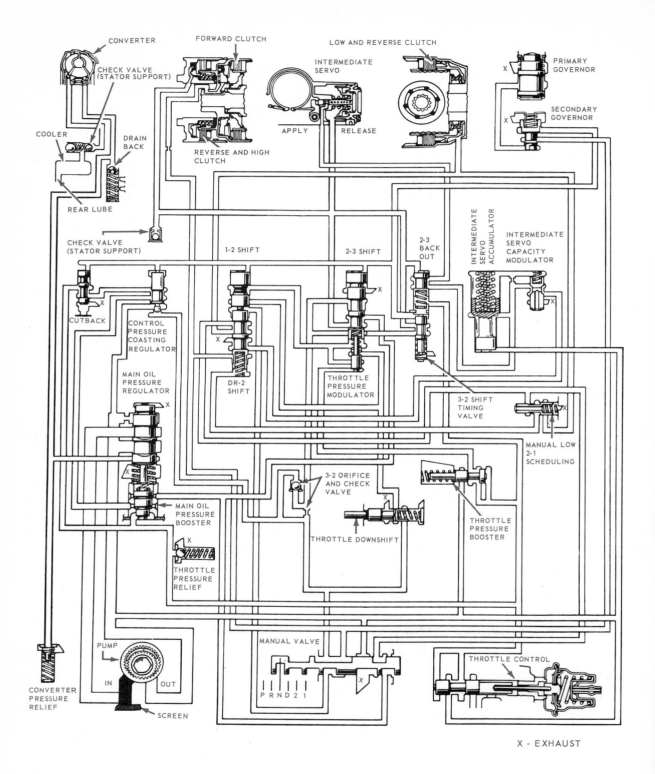

Fig. 33-36. Complete hydraulic system of the Ford C6 automatic transmission. *(Ford Division of Ford Motor Company)*

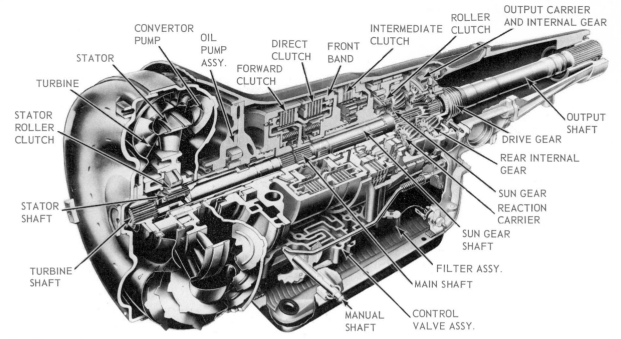

Fig. 33-37. Cutaway view of the General Motors type 400 automatic transmission. *(Cadillac Motor Car Division of General Motors Corporation)*

gear train. Figures 33–32 to 33–35 show the various gear positions. In D, or drive, the transmission starts in low and upshifts through second to D. The transmission has two semiseparate planetary-gear systems (similar to Torque-Flite). Study the illustrations to learn how the various gear positions function as the clutches and band are applied or released.

Figure 33–36 shows the hydraulic control system for the transmission. As you can see, this is much more complicated than our simplified control system shown in Fig. 33–14. The numerous valves serve to smooth shifts, compensate for variations in engine torque and throttle opening (and thus prevent hard shifts), regulate fluid pressure, produce the shifts from low to second to high, control rate of brake-band application, and so on.

§ 33–9. GENERAL MOTORS TYPE 400 AUTOMATIC TRANSMISSION This is a three-speed automatic transmission with torque converter which, with various modifications and different names, has been used in many General Motors automobiles (Buick Super Turbine 400, Cadillac, Chevrolet, Oldsmobile, Pontiac Turbo Hydra-Matic, etc.). A cutaway view of this transmission is shown in Fig. 33–37. Figures 33–38 to 33–41

show conditions in the transmission in low, second, D or drive, and R or reverse.

Note that this transmission has a compound planetary-gear system, three clutches, and two brake bands. A study of the illustrations will show you how the various gear positions are attained.

§ 33–10. AUTOMATIC TRANSMISSION FOR FRONT DRIVE The transmission shown in Fig. 33–42 is for the front-drive Cadillac automobile. It is essentially a Turbo Hydra-Matic automatic transmission which has been cut in two just back of the torque converter so that the planetary-gear system and controls can be placed along side the torque converter. The transmission operates in the same manner as the one described in § 33–9.

§ 33–11. AUTOMATIC TRANSMISSION FOR REAR ENGINE The transmission shown in Fig. 33–43 is used on the Chevrolet rear-engine Corvair. It is very similar in construction and operation to other Powerglide models except that the torque converter and planetary-gear system have been separated and the differential placed between them. Chapter 36 describes differentials.

443

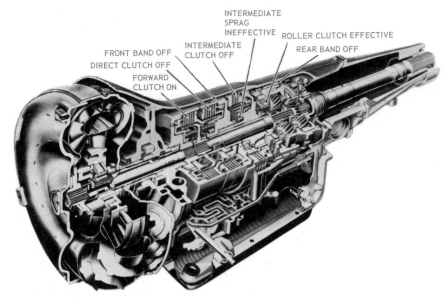

Fig. 33–38. Transmission in first gear with manual shift lever in D. The forward clutch is applied so that the rear internal gear is turned in a clockwise direction. This causes the rear pinions to turn clockwise to drive the sun gear counterclockwise. The sun gear therefore drives the front pinions clockwise, thus turning the front internal gear, output carrier, and output shaft clockwise with a reduction of approximately 2.5/1. The reaction of the front pinions against the front internal gear is taken by the reaction carrier and one-way roller clutch assembly. *(Buick Motor Division of General Motors Corporation)*

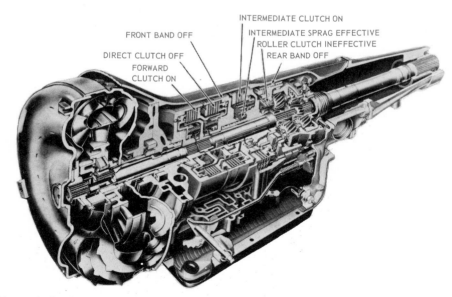

Fig. 33–39. Transmission in second gear with manual shift lever in D after having upshifted from first. The intermediate clutch is applied to allow the intermediate sprag to hold the sun gear against counterclockwise rotation. Torque is now applied from the input shaft through the forward clutch and mainshaft to the rear internal gear in a clockwise direction. Clockwise rotation of the rear internal gear turns the rear pinions clockwise against the stationary sun gear. This causes the output carrier and output shaft to turn clockwise with a reduction of approximately 1.5/1. *(Buick Motor Division of General Motors Corporation)*

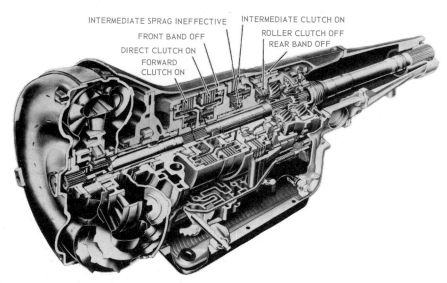

Fig. 33-40. Transmission in direct drive. Torque from the input shaft is transmitted through the forward clutch to the mainshaft and rear internal gear. With the direct clutch applied, equal power is also transmitted to the sun-gear shaft and the sun gear. Since both the sun gear and internal gears are now turning at the same speed, the planetary-gear system is locked and turns as one unit in direct drive, or with a ratio of 1/1. (*Buick Motor Division of General Motors Corporation*)

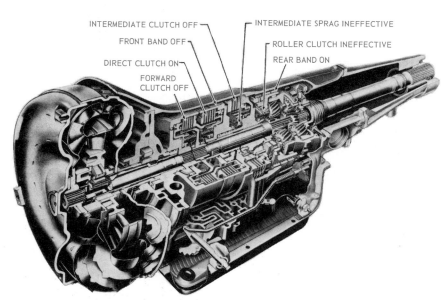

Fig. 33-41. Transmission in reverse. The direct clutch is applied to direct the turbine torque to the sun-gear shaft and sun gear. The rear band is applied, holding the reaction carrier. Clockwise torque to the sun gear causes the front pinions and front internal gear to turn counterclockwise with a gear-ratio reduction of approximately 2/1. The output shaft rotates in the reverse direction to back the car. (*Buick Motor Division of General Motors Corporation*)

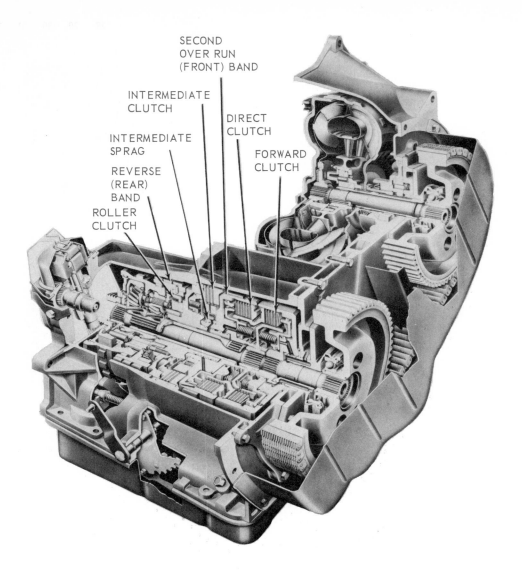

SECOND OVER RUN (FRONT) BAND

INTERMEDIATE CLUTCH

INTERMEDIATE SPRAG

REVERSE (REAR) BAND

ROLLER CLUTCH

DIRECT CLUTCH

FORWARD CLUTCH

SELECTOR POSITION	PUMP PRESSURE	FORWARD CLUTCH	DIRECT CLUTCH	2ND OVERRUN BAND	INT. CLUTCH	INT. SPRAG	ROLLER CLUTCH	REV. BAND
PARK—NEUT.	60-150	OFF	OFF	OFF	OFF	OFF	OFF	OFF
DRIVE 1	60-150	ON	OFF	OFF	OFF	OFF	ON	OFF
LEFT 2	60-150	ON	OFF	OFF	ON	ON	OFF	OFF
3	60-150	ON	ON	OFF	ON	OFF	OFF	OFF
DRIVE 1	150	ON	OFF	OFF	OFF	OFF	ON	OFF
RIGHT 2	150	ON	OFF	ON	ON	ON	OFF	OFF
LO 1	150	ON	OFF	OFF	OFF	OFF	ON	ON
2	150	ON	OFF	ON	ON	ON	OFF	OFF
REV.	95-230	OFF	ON	OFF	OFF	OFF	OFF	ON

Fig. 33–42. Turbo Hydra-Matic automatic transmission for a front-drive automobile, partly cut away so that internal construction can be seen. The table shows the internal conditions for different selector positions. *(Cadillac Motor Car Division of General Motors Corporation)*

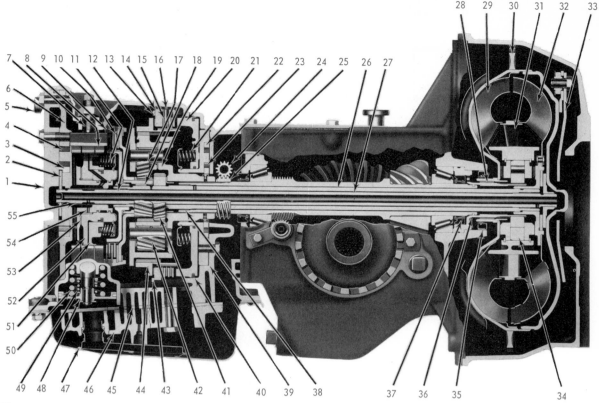

Fig. 33–43. Powerglide used with rear-engine Corvair.

1. Front pump cover
2. Front pump shaft drive hub
3. Front pump drive gear
4. Front pump driven gear
5. Transmission vent
6. Front pump body
7. Low-band adjusting screw and lock nut
8. Low band
9. Clutch drum reaction plate (3 used)
10. Clutch drum faced plate (2 used)
11. Clutch piston return spring (15 used)
12. Turbine shaft
13. Reverse clutch retaining ring clip
14. Reverse clutch front reaction plate (thick)
15. Reverse clutch faced plate (3 used)
16. Reverse clutch reaction plate (3 used)
17. Short pinion
18. Low sun-gear bushing
19. Planet carrier hub (transmission output)
20. Reverse piston
21. Reverse piston return spring (17 used)
22. Rear pump driven gear
23. Rear pump drive gear
24. Governor driven gear
25. Governor drive gear
26. Turbine shaft
27. Front pump shaft
28. Converter hub bushing
29. Converter pump
30. Starter gear
31. Stator
32. Turbine
33. Engine flex plate
34. Stator cam race
35. Converter hub seal
36. Stator shaft
37. Pinion shaft rear oil seal
38. Pinion shaft bushing
39. Rear pump wear plate
40. Reverse piston outer seal
41. Planet carrier input sun gear
42. Long pinion gear
43. Reverse clutch plate retaining ring
44. Ring gear
45. Valve body ditch plate
46. Valve body
47. Oil pick-up pipe
48. Low servo piston
49. Low servo piston cushion spring
50. Low servo piston return spring
51. Clutch drum piston
52. Clutch drum hub
53. Clutch drum selective thrust washer
54. Clutch drum bushing
55. Front pump body bushing

(Chevrolet Motor Division of General Motors Corporation)

Review Questions

1. Name some differences between a fluid coupling and a torque converter.
2. Describe the bounce-back effect resulting when there are only two members in the coupling.
3. Explain how adding a third member to the torque converter permits the torque converter to multiply torque when there is speed reduction.
4. Describe the stator action.
5. Describe the Volkswagen stick-shift transmission.
6. Describe the basic automatic-transmission shift controls.
7. Describe the construction and operation of the GM type 300 transmission. The Ford C6 transmission. The GM type 400 transmission.

Study Questions

1. Write an essay describing the construction and operation of a torque converter. Show how torque is multiplied.
2. Write an essay describing the construction and operation of one of the automatic transmissions which has automatic shifts.

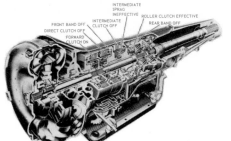

CHAPTER
34

Automatic-transmission Service

This chapter discusses general trouble diagnosis and servicing procedures on automatic transmissions. The instructions that follow apply, in general, to all automatic transmissions. However, the manufacturer's shop manual applying to the specific model of transmission being serviced should be carefully followed when any work is done on an automatic transmission.

§ 34–1. AUTOMATIC-TRANSMISSION TROUBLE DIAGNOSIS Manufacturers supply diagnosis guides such as the one shown in Fig. 34–1. As you will see when you study the guide sheet, it lists various troubles and is cross-referenced by letters to probable trouble sources. For example, suppose the trouble is no drive in D, 2, and 1. With the transmission in the vehicle, check items C, W, E, and R. These items are, as shown at the bottom of the guide sheet, C, manual linkage, W, control pressure check, E, valve body, and R, air pressure check. If the transmission is out of the vehicle, check a and c. Look to the bottom of the sheet to see what a and c are; a is the forward clutch, and c is leakage in the hydraulic system.

In regular transmission work, you would follow the procedures outlined in the manufacturer's shop manual to track down the cause of trouble. Then, continuing to follow the instructions, you would test, disassemble, repair, and adjust as indicated.

§ 34–2. AUTOMATIC-TRANSMISSION SERVICE For specific servicing procedures on automatic transmissions, always refer to the applicable shop manual that covers the model being worked on. Further, use the special service tools that the shop manual calls for. General points of transmission testing and servicing, and precautions to observe are noted below.

1. Road tests. If you road-test a car to check the transmission operation, be sure to observe all traffic laws. If a chassis dynamometer is available, it can be used, and it will not be necessary to take the car out on the road to check shift

points and other operating characteristics of the transmission.

2. Towing or pushing a car to start it. It is often the practice to push or tow a car with a run-down battery to start the engine. If this is done, the special instructions supplied by the manufacturer should be observed. For instance, one manufacturer specifies that the car should be pushed, with the selector lever in neutral, until a speed of about 16 mph (miles per hour) is reached. Then a shift should be made into low. After the engine starts, the selector lever should be returned to neutral until the engine warms up. It is better to push, rather than tow, a car to start it. If the car is towed, the engine might start and cause the car to ram the car ahead of it before it could be brought under control.

3. Towing a disabled car. If a car with an automatic transmission is disabled, it can usually be towed short distances without danger. However, towing speed should be low. The selector lever should be in neutral. On some cars, the recommendation is to use a rear-end pickup truck or else to remove or disconnect the propeller shaft if the car is to be towed any distance. When the car is towed, the transmission may not be furnished normal lubrication. Thus it could be ruined in fairly short distances, particularly if the car were towed at fairly high speeds.

4. Engine performance. Before the automatic transmission is checked, the engine should be tested to make sure that it is in good condition. A sluggish engine will not give the transmission a chance to perform normally. Shifting may be delayed. Further, the engine may not have enough

449

Trouble Symptom	Transmission In Vehicle	Transmission Out of Vehicle
No Drive in D, 2 and 1	CWER	ac
Rough Initial Engagement in D or 2	KBWE	a
1-2 or 2-3 Shift Points Incorrect or Erratic	ABLCDWER	
Rough 1-2 Upshifts	BJGWE	
Rough 2-3 Shifts	BJWGER	br
Dragged Out 1-2 Shift	ABJWGER	c
Engine Overspeeds on 2-3 Shift	CABJWEG	br
No 1-2 or 2-3 Shift	CLBDWEGJ	bc
No 3-1 Shift in D	DE	
No Forced Downshifts	LWE	
Runaway Engine on Forced 3-2 Downshift	WJGEB	c
Rough 3-2 or 3-1 Shift at Closed Throttle	KBJWE	
Shifts 1-3 in D	GJEDR	
No Engine Braking in First Gear—Manual Lo Range	CHEDR	c
Creeps Excessively	K	
Slips or Chatters in First Gear, D	ABWE	aci
Slips or Chatters in Second Gear	ABJGWER	ac
Slips or Chatters in R	ABCHWER	bcr
No Drive in D Only	CWE	i
No Drive in 2 Only	ACWJER	c
No Drive in 1 Only	AWER	c
No Drive in R Only	ACHWER	bcr
No Drive in Any Selector Lever Position	ACWER	cd
Lockup in D Only	E	gc
Lockup in 2 Only	HE	bgci
Lockup in 1 Only	E	gc
Lockup in R Only	E	agc
Parking Lock Binds or Does Not Hold	C	g
Transmission Overheats	OEBW	ns
Maximum Speed Too Low, Poor Acceleration	YZ	n
Transmission Noisy in N and P	AE	d
Transmission Noisy in First, Second, Third or Reverse Gear	AE	hadi
Fluid Leak	AMNOPQSUXBJ	imp
Car Moves Forward in N	C	a

PROBABLE TROUBLE SOURCES

A	Fluid Level	W	Perform Control Pressure Check
B	Vacuum Diaphragm Unit or Tubes Restricted—Leaking—Adjustment	X	Speedometer Driven Gear Adapter Seal
C	Manual Linkage	Y	Engine Performance
D	Governor	Z	Car Brakes
E	Valve Body	a	Forward Clutch
G	Intermediate Band	b	Reverse-High Clutch
H	Low-Reverse Clutch	c	Leakage in Hydraulic System
J	Intermediate Servo	d	Front Pump
K	Engine Idle Speed	g	Parking Linkage
L	Downshift Linkage—Including Inner Lever Position	h	Planetary Assembly
M	Converter Drain Plugs	i	Planetary One-Way Clutch
N	Oil Pan Gasket, Filler Tube or Seal	j	Engine Rear Oil Seal
O	Oil Cooler and Connections	m	Front Pump Oil Seal
P	Manual or Downshift Lever Shaft Seal	n	Converter One-Way Clutch
Q	1/8 Inch Pipe Plugs in Case	p	Front Pump to Case Gasket or Seal
R	Perform Air Pressure Check	r	Reverse-High Clutch Piston Air Bleed Valve
S	Extension Housing to Case Gasket	s	Converter Pressure Check Valves
U	Extension Housing Rear Oil Seal		

Fig. 34-1. Trouble-diagnosis guide for Ford C6 automatic transmission. *(Ford Division of Ford Motor Company)*

power to pull the car and accelerate normally. This may lead to wrong guesses about the transmission.

5. Throttle and control linkages. For the transmission to function properly, the linkages between the selector lever and transmission must be correctly adjusted. Incorrect selector-lever-linkage adjustment could keep the transmission from functioning in the selected operating range.

6. Oil level and cleanliness. The oil level must be correct in the transmission and the fluid coupling or torque converter. If the fluid level is low, transmission parts may not be adequately lubricated and may thus fail. Further, inadequate oil may cause the fluid coupling or torque converter to function below par and not transmit the power fed into it. Servos may not work properly if they are oil-starved. Thus, the oil level must be maintained properly. Naturally, the oil must be clean and of the proper type. Any trace of dirt in the oil is likely to cause a valve to hang up, and this could throw the operation of the transmission completely off. Also, if the wrong type of oil is used, it may foam or prove otherwise unsuitable. In such a case, transmission malfunctioning and damage could be expected.

● **CAUTION:** It is of the greatest importance to use the proper transmission fluid when refilling or adding fluid to an automatic transmission. Using the wrong fluid is apt to lead to quick failure of the transmission. Always follow the manufacturer's recommendations.

7. Oil-pressure checks. One of the checks commonly made on automatic transmissions measures the oil pressures in various parts of the hydraulic circuit. These measurements will disclose whether or not oil pressures are getting through to the valves and servos as they should. If they are not, then there is some fault in the hydraulic system. If they are, and yet valve or servo action is not correct, then the cause of trouble is pin-pointed at the valve or servo.

8. Stall test. Another test to be made on many automatic transmissions is to apply the car brakes so that the car cannot move, put the selector lever in a "drive" position, and open the throttle wide. If engine speed increases excessively, this is a sign that brake bands are slipping in the transmission. If the engine does not come up to speed, the chances are the engine is not in good condition and should be tuned up.

9. Brake-band adjustments. Brake bands are adjusted in different ways on the various automatic transmissions. When correct, they will not slip on the stall test but will release fully under the proper operating conditions.

10. Automatic-transmission overhaul. Always follow the instructions given in the applicable manufacturer's shop manual when overhauling, adjusting, or otherwise servicing an automatic transmission. These mechanisms, although very sturdy, must be serviced correctly to provide normal operation. Of special importance in the disassembly-reassembly procedure is cleanliness. It must be remembered that many parts in the automatic transmission are fitted with extremely close tolerances. Thus, even tiny particles of dirt or grit can cause serious malfunctioning and damage. For example, a particle of dirt in the valve body could cause valves to hang up so that the transmission would not shift normally.

Review Questions

1. Explain the purpose of the diagnosis guides that manufacturers supply for their automatic transmissions.

2. Discuss the various precautions to observe when engaged in automatic-transmission service.

Study Question

1. Select an automatic transmission, and write an overhaul story on it. You should base your story on both the shop manual and your actual shopwork, if that is possible. Be sure that you cover details of adjustments.

CHAPTER
35

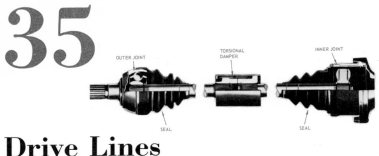

OUTER JOINT | TORSIONAL DAMPER | INNER JOINT

SEAL | SEAL

Drive Lines

This chapter describes the purpose, construction, operation, and servicing of drive lines. Drive lines, in automobiles, are the driving connection between the transmission and the driving mechanism at the rear wheels (the differential). The purpose of the drive line is to carry the driving power from the transmission to the rear wheels. It consists of the propeller shaft, a universal joint (or joints), and a slip joint.

---

§ 35-1. FUNCTION OF PROPELLER SHAFT The propeller shaft is a driving shaft that connects the transmission main, or output, shaft to the differential at the rear axles. Rotary motion of the transmission main, or output, shaft carries through the propeller shaft to the differential, causing the rear wheels to rotate. The propeller-shaft design must take two facts into consideration. First, the engine and transmission are more or less rigidly attached to the car frame. Second, the rear-axle housing (with wheels and differential) is attached to the frame by springs. As the rear wheels encounter irregularities in the road, the springs compress or expand. This changes the angle of drive between

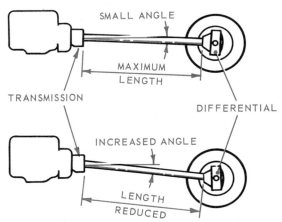

SMALL ANGLE

MAXIMUM LENGTH

TRANSMISSION

DIFFERENTIAL

INCREASED ANGLE

LENGTH REDUCED

Fig. 35-1. As the rear axle housing, with differential and wheels, moves up and down, the angle between the transmission output shaft changes and the length of the propeller shaft also changes. The reason the propeller shaft shortens as the angle increases is that the rear axle and differential move in a shorter arc than the propeller shaft. The centerpoint of the axle-housing arc is the rear-spring or control-arm attachment to the frame.

the propeller shaft may take care of these two changes the distance between the transmission and the differential (see Fig. 35-1). In order that the propeller shaft may take care of these two changes, it must incorporate two separate types of device. There must be one or more universal joints to permit variations in the angle of drive. There must also be a slip joint that permits the effective length of the propeller shaft to change.

The propeller shaft may be solid or hollow, protected by an outer tube or exposed. Some applications include bearings at or near the propeller-shaft center to support the shaft. Figures 35-2 to 35-4 illustrate various types of propeller shaft. On some applications, the propeller shaft is in two sections (see Figs. 35-3 and 35-4), supported by a center bearing and coupled together by universal joints. The two-section shaft shown in Fig. 35-3 has a center support, as shown in Fig. 35-4.

§ 35-2. UNIVERSAL JOINTS A simple universal joint is illustrated in Fig. 35-5. It is essentially a double-hinged joint consisting of two Y-shaped yokes, one on the driving shaft and the other on the driven shaft, and a cross-shaped member called the *spider*. The four arms of the spider, known as *trunnions*, are assembled into bearings in the ends of the two shaft yokes. The driving shaft causes the spider to rotate, and the other two trunnions of the spider cause the driven shaft to rotate. When the two shafts are at an angle to each other, the bearings in the yokes permit the yokes to swing around on the trunnions with each revolution. A variety of universal joints have been used on automobiles, but the types now in most common use are the spider and two-yoke, the constant-velocity, and the ball-and-trunnion joints.

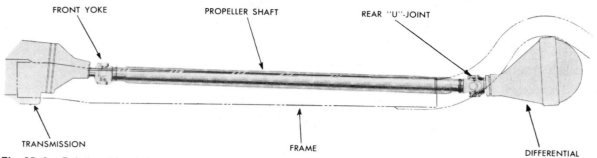

Fig. 35-2. Relationship of the propeller shaft to the transmission, frame, and differential. This is a one-piece propeller shaft supported at the front and rear by universal joints. (*Pontiac Motor Division of General Motors Corporation*)

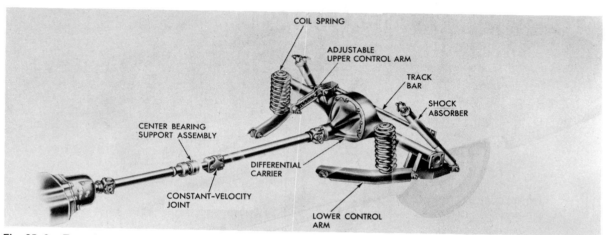

Fig. 35-3. Two-piece propeller shaft using three universal joints. The front shaft section is supported at its rear by a bearing. The universal joint immediately back of this bearing is a constant-velocity unit. (*Buick Motor Division of General Motors Corporation*)

The spider and two-yoke design is essentially the same as the simple universal joint discussed above except that the bearings are often of the needle type (upper left in Fig. 35-4). As will be noted, there are four needle bearings (one is shown disassembled in Fig. 35-4), one for each trunnion of the spider. The bearings are held in place by rings that drop into undercuts in the yoke-bearing holes.

The ball-and-trunnion type of universal joint combines both the universal and the slip joint in one assembly. A universal joint of this design is shown in Fig. 35-6 in exploded view. The shaft has a pin pressed through it, and around both ends of the pin are placed balls drilled out to accommodate needle bearings. The other member of the universal joint consists of a steel casing, or body, that has two longitudinal channels into which the balls fit. The body is bolted to a flange on the mat-

ing shaft. The rotary motion is carried through the pin and balls. The balls can move back and forth in the channels of the body to compensate for varying angles of drive. At the same time, they act as a slip joint by slipping into or out of the channels.

Constant-velocity universal joints are shown on propeller shafts in Figs. 35-3 and 35-4 and in sectional view in Fig. 35-7. This joint consists of two individual universal joints linked by a ball and socket. The ball and socket splits the angle of the two propeller shafts between the two universal joints. Because the two joints are operating at the same angle, the normal fluctuations that could result from the use of a single universal joint are cancelled out. That is, the acceleration resulting at any instant from the action of one universal joint is nullified by the deceleration of the other and vice versa.

453

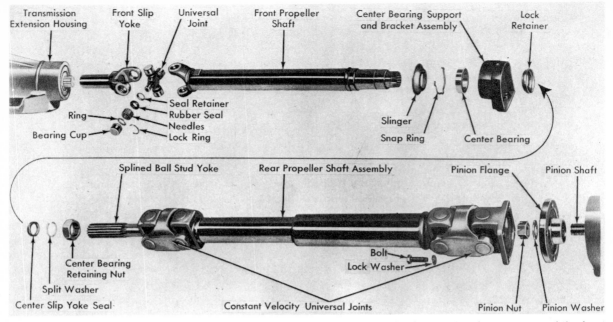

Transmission Extension Housing — Front Slip Yoke — Universal Joint — Front Propeller Shaft — Center Bearing Support and Bracket Assembly — Lock Retainer

Ring — Seal Retainer — Rubber Seal — Needles — Bearing Cup — Lock Ring — Slinger — Snap Ring — Center Bearing

Splined Ball Stud Yoke — Rear Propeller Shaft Assembly — Pinion Flange — Pinion Shaft

Center Bearing Retaining Nut — Split Washer — Center Slip Yoke Seal — Constant Velocity Universal Joints — Bolt — Lock Washer — Pinion Nut — Pinion Washer

Fig. 35–4. Disassembled view of a two-piece propeller shaft, showing details of center bearing support and the front universal joint. The center and rear universal joint are constant-velocity units. (*General Motors Corporation*)

Fig. 35–5. A simple universal joint.

§ 35-3. SLIP JOINT A slip joint is illustrated in Fig. 35-4. As previously explained, the slip joint consists of outside splines on one shaft and matching internal splines on the mating hollow shaft. The splines cause the two shafts to rotate together but permit the two to move endwise with each other. This accommodates any effective change of length of the propeller shaft as the rear axles move toward or away from the car frame. A slip joint can be seen in Fig. 35-7.

§ 35-4. TYPE OF DRIVE The rotation of the propeller shaft transmits torque through the differential to the rear wheels, causing them to rotate and move the car. The wheels rotate because torque is applied to them. This torque not only rotates the wheels in one direction, but it also attempts to rotate the differential housing in the opposite direction. To understand why this occurs it is necessary to review briefly the construction

of the differential (Fig. 36-2). The ring gear is connected through other gears to the rear-wheel axles; the torque applied through the drive pinion forces the ring gear and wheels to rotate. It is the side thrust of the drive-pinion teeth against the ring-gear teeth that makes the ring gear rotate. This side thrust also causes the drive-pinion shaft to push against the shaft bearing. The thrust against the shaft bearing is in a direction opposite to the thrust of the pinion teeth against the ring-gear teeth. Since the drive-pinion bearings are held in the differential housing, the housing tries to rotate in a direction opposite to the ring-gear and wheel rotation. This action is termed "rear-end torque," and, to prevent excessive movement of the differential housing from this action, several methods of bracing the housing are used. The two most common types are the torque-tube drive and the Hotchkiss drive (Fig. 35-8).

In the torque-tube drive, the propeller shaft is encased in a hollow tube. The tube is rigidly bolted to the differential housing at one end and is fastened at the other end to the transmission case through a somewhat flexible joint. On many cars, a pair of truss rods are attached between the rear-axle housings and the transmission end of the torque tube. The torque tube and the truss rods brace the differential housing to prevent excessive differential-housing movement. In other words, these members absorb the rear-end torque.

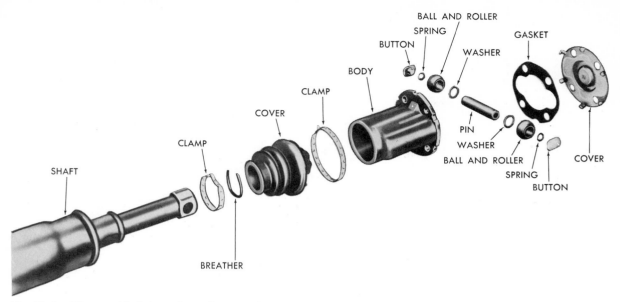

Fig. 35–6. Disassembled view of a ball-and-trunnion universal joint. (*Chrysler-Plymouth Division of Chrysler Motors Corporation*)

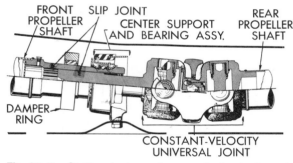

Fig. 35–7. Sectional view of a constant-velocity universal joint. (*Buick Motor Division of General Motors Corporation*)

In the Hotchkiss drive, the rear-end torque is absorbed by the rear springs. The rear springs are attached to brackets bolted to the rear-axle housing so that the springs themselves act as the torque-absorbing members. Thus, when the car is moving forward, the rear-end torque causes the front halves of the springs to be compressed as the rear halves of the springs are expanded. Two universal joints are required on the propeller shaft in the Hotchkiss drive, one at each end of the shaft (see Fig. 35–2). The reason for this is obvious: The differential housing does rotate as a result of rear-end torque within the limits imposed by car springs. Most cars today use the Hotchkiss drive.

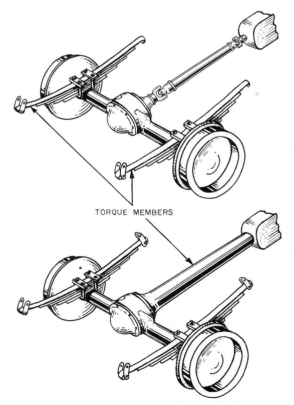

Fig. 35–8. Hotchkiss drive (top) compared with a torque-tube drive (bottom).

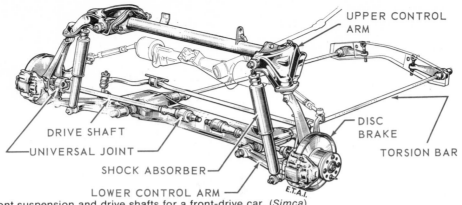

Fig. 35-9. Front suspension and drive shafts for a front-drive car. (*Simca*)

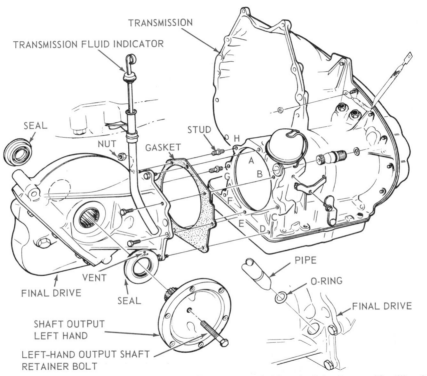

Fig. 35-10 Final drive attachment for a front-drive car. The left-hand drive shaft is shown. (*Cadillac Motor Car Division of General Motors Corporation*)

§ 35-5. FRONT-END DRIVE Some vehicles have front drives. That is, the transmission is connected through driving axles to the front wheels. Figure 30-22 shows a manual transmission and differential for such an arrangement. Figure 35-9 shows the front suspension system and drive shafts for this same vehicle. Each drive shaft has two universal joints to permit the front wheels to move up and down and also pivot from one side to the other for steering.

Some models of Cadillac and Oldsmobile also are front-drive vehicles. Figure 33-42 shows the Turbo Hydra-Matic transmission used on these cars. Figure 35-10 shows the transmission and final drive, or differential, with the left-hand output shaft. The right-hand output shaft is shown in Fig. 35-11. The left-hand output shaft is shorter than the right-hand output shaft because the differential is offset to the left. The output shafts maintain their alignment with the differential. They are

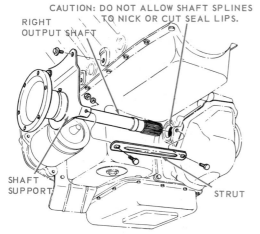

CAUTION: DO NOT ALLOW SHAFT SPLINES TO NICK OR CUT SEAL LIPS.

RIGHT OUTPUT SHAFT

SHAFT SUPPORT

STRUT

Fig. 35–11. Location of right-hand output shaft in relation to the final drive. *(Cadillac Motor Car Division of General Motors Corporation)*

connected by drive shafts to the two front wheels in a manner much like the Simca shown in Fig. 35–9. Each drive shaft has two universal joints to permit vertical movement of the wheels and pivoting for steering. See Figs. 35–12 and 35–13.

Figure 35–14 shows another front-drive arrangement for a small car.

§ 35–6. REAR DRIVE WITH REAR-MOUNTED ENGINE Some cars have the engine mounted at the rear and use short output shafts to carry the engine power to the rear wheels. Figure 35–15 shows one such vehicle. The two output shafts each have two universal joints. The rear wheels are independently suspended.

§ 35–7. REAR-MOUNTED ENGINE WITH FOUR-WHEEL DRIVE Some vehicles have the engine mounted at the rear with all four wheels being

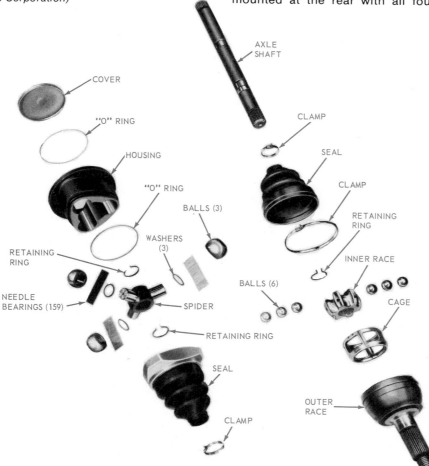

AXLE SHAFT

COVER

"O" RING

HOUSING

"O" RING

BALLS (3)

WASHERS (3)

RETAINING RING

NEEDLE BEARINGS (159)

SPIDER

RETAINING RING

SEAL

CLAMP

CLAMP

SEAL

CLAMP

RETAINING RING

INNER RACE

BALLS (6)

CAGE

OUTER RACE

Fig. 35–12. Left-hand drive axle assembly for front-drive car. *(Oldsmobile Division of General Motors Corporation)*

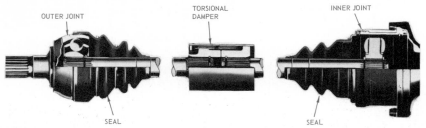

Fig. 35–13. Right-hand drive axle assembly for front-drive car. *(Oldsmobile Division of General Motors Corporation)*

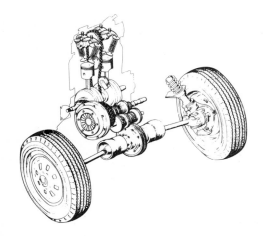

Fig. 35–14. Front-drive arrangement for a small car using a two-cylinder engine. *(Honda)*

driven (Fig. 35–16). This requires an arrangement at the rear wheels much like that for the Corvair shown in Fig. 35–15. In addition, a propeller shaft is required to carry the power to the front differential. From there, it is carried to the two front wheels by output shafts, each having universal joints. Figure 1–20 shows a four-wheel-drive vehicle from the bottom.

§ 35–8. UNIVERSAL-JOINT SERVICE Little maintenance of universal joints is required aside from periodic lubrication. When disassembly is required, it may take 1 hour, when only one universal joint is to be overhauled, to approximately 4 hours, when the propeller shaft is removed and replaced. On many cars, the propeller-shaft and universal-joint parts are carefully balanced during original

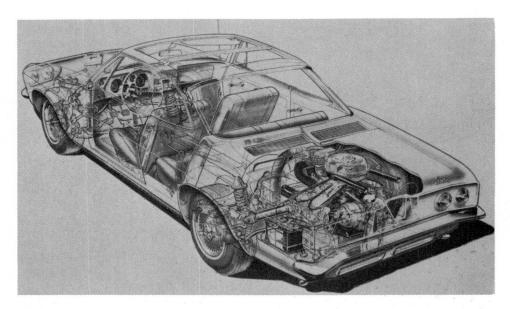

Fig. 35–15. Phantom view of Corvair showing rear-engine mounting and drive arrangement. *(Chevrolet Motor Division of General Motors Corporation)*

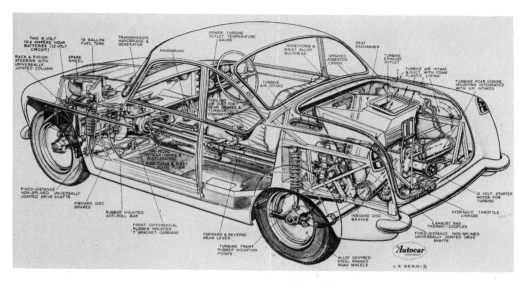

Fig. 35–16. Automobile with engine at rear and using four-wheel drive. *(Autocar)*

assembly. To assure reassembly in the correct relationship, so that the balance will be maintained, the parts are marked. If the marks cannot be found before disassembly, new marks should be made so that the parts can be reasembled correctly. Refer to the applicable car shop manual for service procedures on specific models.

Review Questions

1. What is the function of the propeller shaft?
2. What two actions take place as the rear springs compress and expand, insofar as the propeller shaft is concerned? What two devices are used to take care of these actions?
3. Describe the action of a two-yoke and cross universal joint.
4. Describe the action of a ball-and-trunnion type of universal joint.
5. Describe the action of a constant-velocity universal joint.
6. What is the purpose of the universal joint?
7. What is the purpose of a slip joint?
8. What is rear-end torque? Describe in detail what causes rear-end torque.
9. What absorbs the rear-end torque in the torque-tube drive?
10. What absorbs the rear-end torque in the Hotchkiss drive?
11. How many universal joints are required on the Hotchkiss drive? Why that number?
12. Describe a front drive.
13. Describe a rear drive used with a rear-mounted engine.

Study Questions

1. Make a sketch of a universal joint, and write an explanation of its operation.
2. Make a sketch of a slip joint, and write an explanation of its operation.
3. Write a brief article explaining why rear-end torque occurs.
4. Make sketches of a torque tube and a Hotchkiss drive, indicating the members that absorb rear-end torque.
5. Write a service story on one propeller shaft, including the universal joints. Base your story on a shop manual or actual shopwork.

CHAPTER

36

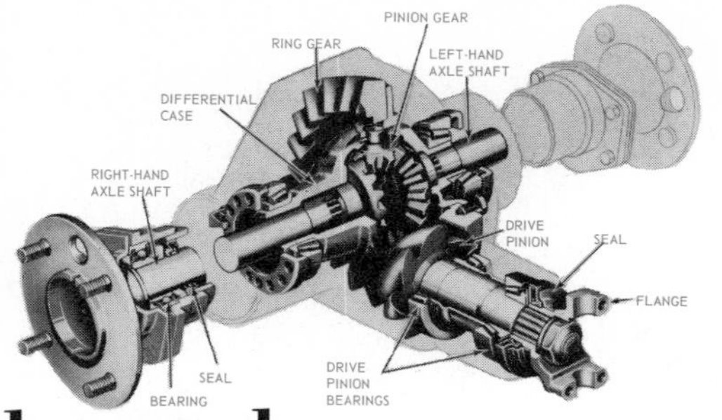

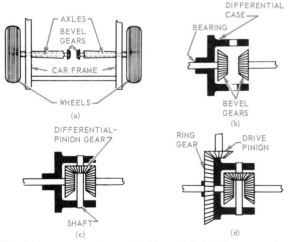

Rear Axles and Differentials

This chapter discusses the purpose, construction, operation, and servicing of differentials and rear axles. The differential is part of the rear-axle-housing assembly, which includes the differential, rear axles, wheels, and bearings.

---

§ 36–1. FUNCTION OF DIFFERENTIAL If the car were to be driven in a straight line without having to make turns, then no differential would be necessary. However, when the car rounds a turn, the outer wheel must travel farther than the inner wheel. If a right-angle turn is made with the inner wheel turning on a 20-foot radius, this wheel travels about 31 feet (Fig. 36–1). The outer wheel, being nearly 5 feet from the inner wheel, turns on a 24⅔-foot radius (in the car shown), and it travels nearly 39 feet.

If the propeller shaft were geared rigidly to both rear wheels so that they would both have to rotate together, then each wheel would have to skid an average of 4 feet in making the turn discussed

above. On this basis, tires would not last long. In addition, the skidding would make the car hard to control on turns. The differential eliminates these troubles because it allows the wheels to rotate different amounts when turns are made.

To study the construction and action of the differential, let us build up, in effect, a simple differential (Fig. 36–2). The two rear wheels are attached, through the axles, to two small bevel side gears

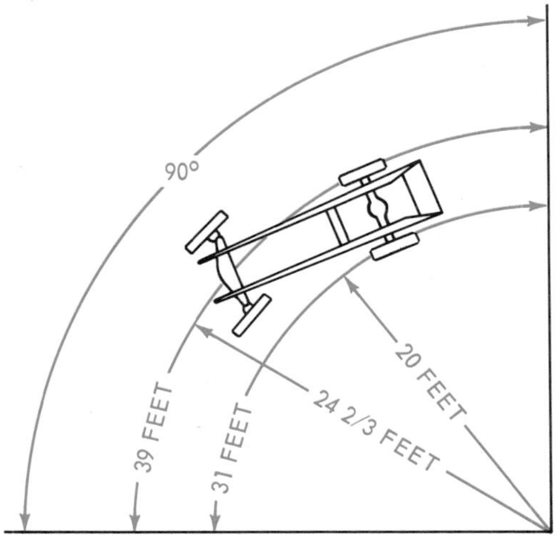

Fig. 36–2. Rear axles and differential. (a) The rear axles are attached to the wheels and have bevel side gears on their inner ends. (b) The differential case is assembled on the left axle but can rotate on a bearing independently of the axle. (c) The differential case supports the differential-pinion gear on a shaft, and this gear meshes with the two bevel gears. (d) The ring gear is attached to the differential case so that the case rotates with the ring gear when the latter is driven by the drive pinion.

Fig. 36–1. Difference of wheel travel as car makes a 90-degree turn with the inner rear wheel on a 20-foot radius.

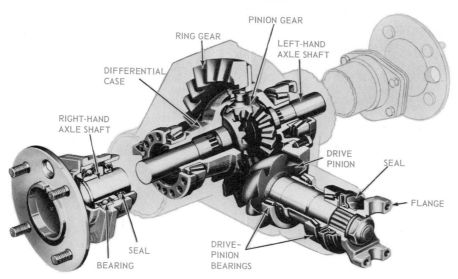

Fig. 36–3. Cutaway view of a differential and rear axle. *(Ford Division of Ford Motor Company)*

(Fig. 36–2*a*). There is a differential case assembled around the left axle (Fig. 36–2*b*). The case has a bearing that permits it to turn independently of the left axle. Inside the case is a shaft that supports a third bevel gear (Fig. 36–2*c*). This third bevel gear, called the *differential-pinion* gear, is meshed with the two axle bevel side gears. Thus, when the differential case is rotated, both axle bevel gears rotate and thus both wheels turn. However, let us suppose that one wheel is held stationary. Then, when the differential case is rotated, the differential-pinion gear will also rotate as it "runs around" on the stationary axle bevel gear. As it rotates in this manner, it carries rotary motion to the other axle bevel gear, causing it, and the wheel, to rotate.

It can be seen that, when one rear wheel turns more rapidly than the other, the differential-pinion gear spins on its shaft, transmitting more rotary motion to one rear wheel than to the other. When both turn at the same speed, the differential-pinion gear does not rotate on its shaft.

The differential case is rotated by means of a ring gear attached to it. This ring gear is meshed with a drive pinion on the end of the propeller shaft (Fig. 36–2*d*). When the car is on a straight road, the ring gear, differential case, differential-pinion gear, and two axle bevel gears all turn as a unit without any relative motion. However, when the car begins to round a curve, the differential-pinion gear rotates on its shaft to permit the outer

rear wheel to turn more rapidly than the inner rear wheel.

1. Standard differential. The actual differential is more complicated than that in Fig. 36–2. An actual differential, partially cut away, is illustrated in Fig. 36–3 and, in disassembled view, in Fig. 36–4. The driving power enters the differential through the drive pinion on the end of the propeller shaft. The drive pinion is meshed with a large ring gear so that the ring gear revolves with the pinion. Attached to the ring gear (through the differential case) is a differential-pinion shaft on which are assembled two differential-pinion gears. Each rear car wheel has a separate axle, and there are two side gears splined to the inner ends of the two wheel axles. The two differential-pinion gears mesh with these two side gears. When the car is on a straight road, the two differential-pinion gears do not rotate on the pinion shaft, but they do exert pressure on the two side gears so that the side gears turn at the same speed as the ring gear, causing both rear wheels to turn at the same speed, also. When the car rounds a curve, the outer wheel must turn faster than the inner wheel. To permit this, the two pinion gears rotate on their pinion shaft, transmitting more turning movement to the outer side gear than to the inner side gear. Thus, the side gear on the outer-wheel axle turns more rapidly than the side gear on the inner-wheel axle. This permits the outer wheel to turn more rapidly while the car is rounding the curve.

461

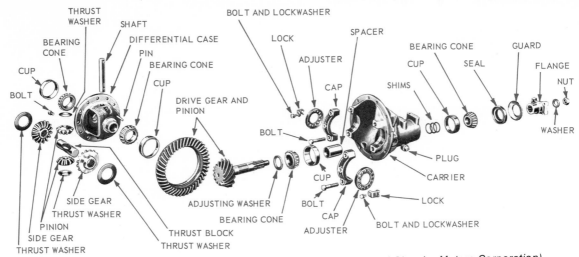

Fig. 36-4. Disassembled view of a differential. *(Chrysler-Plymouth Division of Chrysler Motors Corporation)*

2. Nonslip differential. The conventional differential delivers the same amount of torque to each rear wheel. If one wheel slips on ice, then the other wheel cannot deliver torque. To prevent this, many cars are now equipped with a nonslip differential (Figs. 36-5 and 36-6). This differential is very similar in construction to conventional types except that it has two sets of clutch plates, and, in addition, the ends of the pinion shafts lie rather loosely in notches in the two halves of the differential case. During normal straight-road driving, power flow is as shown in Fig. 36-7. The turning effort passes from the drive pinion through the axle drive gear and the differential case to the pinion shafts, and through the differential pinions

and differential side pinions to the axle shaft. Note that the turning differential case carries the pinion shafts around with it. Since there is considerable side thrust, the pinion shafts tend to slide up the sides of the notches in the two halves of the differential case (these notches can be seen in Fig. 36-5). As they slide up, they are forced outward, and this force is transmitted to the clutch plates. The clutch plates thus lock the axle shafts to the differential case. Then, if one wheel encounters a patch of ice or mud that causes it to lose traction temporarily, it will not spin, since it cannot turn faster than the other wheel.

When rounding a curve (Fig. 36-8), the differential acts in the conventional manner to permit

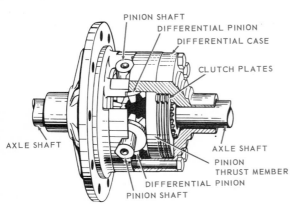

Fig. 36-5. Cutaway view of a nonslip differential. *(Dodge Division of Chrysler Motors Corporation)*

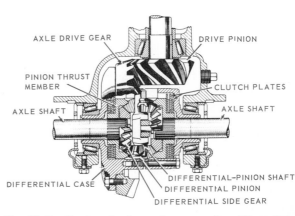

Fig. 36-6. Sectional view of a nonslip differential. *(Dodge Division of Chrysler Motors Corporation)*

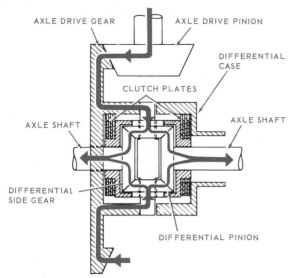

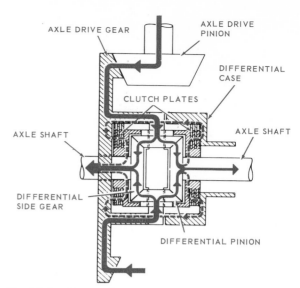

Fig. 36-7. Power flow through a nonslip differential on a straightaway. *(Dodge Division of Chrysler Motors Corporation)*

Fig. 36-8. Power flow through a nonslip differential when rounding a turn. *(Dodge Division of Chrysler Motors Corporation)*

the outer wheel to rotate a little faster than the inner wheel. This action is permitted by slipping of the clutches.

§ 36-2. DIFFERENTIAL GEARING Since the ring gear has many more teeth than the drive pinion,

a considerable gear reduction is effected in the differential. The gear ratios vary somewhat on different cars, depending on car and engine design. Ratios of 3.36:1 upward to about 5:1 are used on passenger cars. This means that the ring gear has 3.36 to 5 times as many teeth as the drive

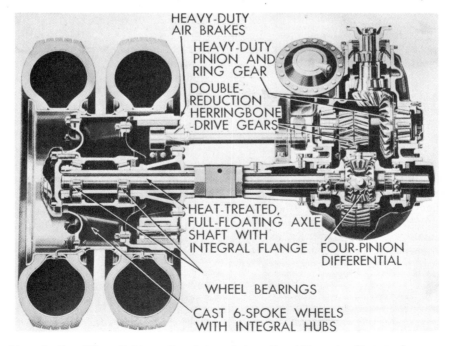

Fig. 36-9. Double-reduction differential in sectional view. *(International Harvester Company)*

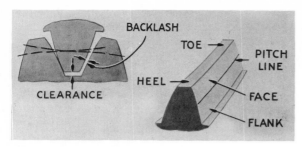

Fig. 36–10. Gear-tooth nomenclature. *(Chrysler-Plymouth Division of Chrysler Motors Corporation)*

pinion, so that the drive pinion has to rotate 3.36 to 5 times (according to gear ratio) in order to cause the ring gear to rotate once. For heavy-duty applications, such as large trucks, ratios of about 9:1 may be used. Such high ratios are secured by use of double-reduction gearing (Fig. 36–9).

The gear ratio in the differential is usually referred to as the *axle ratio*, although it would be more accurate to call it the differential ratio.

Figure 36–10 illustrates gear-tooth nomenclature. The mating teeth to the left illustrate clearance and backlash, while the tooth to the right has the various tooth parts named. Clearance is the distance between the top of the tooth of one gear and the valley between adjacent teeth of the mating gear. Backlash is the distance between adjacent meshing teeth in the driving and driven gears; it is the distance one gear can rotate backward, or backlash, before it will cause the other gear to move. The toe is the smaller section of the gear tooth; the heel is the larger section.

§ 36–3. DOUBLE-REDUCTION DIFFERENTIALS

In order to secure additional gear reduction through the differential and thus provide a higher gear ratio between the engine and the rear wheels, some heavy-duty applications use double-reduction differentials (Fig. 36–9). In this type of differential, the drive pinion meshes with a ring gear assembled to a straight shaft on which there is a reduction-drive gear set. The reduction-drive gear set drives a driven gear set that has a greater number of gear teeth. Gear reduction is thus obtained between the drive pinion and the ring gear and also between the two-reduction gear sets.

§ 36–4. TYPES OF REAR AXLE

There are two basic types of axle: dead axles and live axles. The dead axle does not rotate; the wheel rotates on it. A common example is the axle on a horse-drawn wagon. Live axles are attached to the wheel so that both the wheel and the axle rotate together. Live axles are classified according to the manner in which they are supported: semifloating, three-quarter-floating, and full-floating.

A special type of rear axle using two universal joints is illustrated in Fig. 37–10. Each rear wheel is independently suspended by a control arm.

§ 36–5. DIAGNOSING DIFFERENTIAL TROUBLES

Most often, it is noise that draws attention to trouble existing in the rear axles or differential. It is not always easy, however, to diagnose the trouble by determining the source of noise and the operating conditions under which noise is produced. Such conditions as defective universal joints, rear-wheel bearing or muffler or tire noises may be improperly diagnosed as differential or rear-axle trouble. Some clue as to the cause of trouble may be gained, however, by noting whether the noise is a hum, growl, or knock; whether it is produced when the car is operating on a straight road or on turns only; and whether the noise is most noticeable when the engine is driving the car or when the car is coasting.

A humming noise in the differential is often caused by improper drive-pinion or ring-gear adjustment which prevents normal tooth contact between the gears. This produces rapid gear-tooth wear, so that the noise will gradually take on a growling characteristic. Correction should be made before the trouble progresses to this extent, since abnormal tooth wear will require pinion and gear replacement.

If the noise is most evident when the car is being accelerated, the probability is that there is heavy heel contact on the gear teeth; the ring gear must be moved near the drive pinion. If the noise is most evident when the car is coasting with the car in gear and the throttle closed, it is probable that there is heavy toe contact on the gear teeth; the ring gear must be moved away from the drive pinion.

NOTE: Tire noise may sometimes be mistaken for differential noise. Since tire noise varies considerably according to the type of pavement, while differential noise does not, the car should be driven over various types of pavement to determine whether the noise is resulting from tires or from the differential.

If the noise is present only when the car is rounding a curve, the trouble is due to some condition in the differential-case assembly. Differential-pinion gears tight on the pinion shaft, differential side gears tight in the differential case, damaged gears or thrust washers, or excessive backlash between gears could produce noise when the car turns. A knocking noise will result if bearings or gears are damaged or badly worn.

The *axle ratio* of a car can be determined easily when the propeller shaft is exposed (Hotchkiss drive) by marking one rear tire and the propeller shaft with chalk and then pushing the car forward, counting at the same time the revolutions the propeller shaft makes for one wheel revolution. The car transmission should be in neutral. If the propeller shaft makes 4.4 revolutions while the wheel revolves once the axle ratio is 4.4 : 1.

Backlash in the differential and power train can be checked by placing the transmission in high gear, raising one rear wheel off the floor, and noting the amount of free rotary motion the raised wheel has.

§ 36–6. DIFFERENTIAL REPAIR Repair and overhaul procedures on rear axles and differentials vary somewhat from one car to another. Always consult the applicable car shop manual before attempting to service any of these mechanisms.

Review Questions

1. What is the purpose of the differential?
2. Name in order the various parts in the differential through which power is carried from the drive pinion to the axle shafts.
3. When the car is being operated on a straight road, do the differential-pinion gears rotate on their shafts?
4. What occurs to the differential-pinion gears when the car rounds a curve?
5. About what gear reduction is obtained in the differential on passenger cars? Does it vary from car to car?
6. What is the purpose of the nonslip differential?
7. Describe the operation of a nonslip differential.
8. In gears, what is clearance? Backlash? Face? Flank?
9. What are double-reduction differentials?
10. What are the two basic types of axle? In what way do they differ?
11. What are the three general types of live axle?
12. What is it that most often draws attention to trouble existing in the differential?
13. What does a humming noise in the differential often indicate?
14. When differential noise is most evident during car acceleration, what is the probable trouble?
15. If the noise is most evident when the car is coasting in gear, what is the probable trouble?
16. If the noise is present only when the car rounds a turn, what is the probable location of the trouble?
17. On a Hotchkiss-drive car, how can the axle ratio be determined? What is the meaning of the term "axle ratio"?
18. How is backlash in the power train checked?

Study Questions

1. List the parts in a differential in the order in which they transmit power from the propeller shaft.
2. Describe standard differential operation.
3. Describe the operation of a nonslip differential.

CHAPTER
37

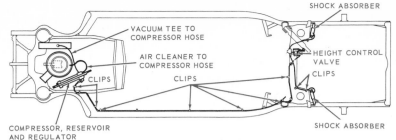

VACUUM TEE TO COMPRESSOR HOSE

AIR CLEANER TO COMPRESSOR HOSE

CLIPS

CLIPS

COMPRESSOR, RESERVOIR AND REGULATOR

SHOCK ABSORBER

HEIGHT CONTROL VALVE

CLIPS

SHOCK ABSORBER

Automotive Springs and Suspension

This chapter describes the various springs and suspension systems used in automotive vehicles, including shock-absorber construction and operation.

---

§ 37–1. FUNCTION OF SPRINGS The car frame supports the weight of the engine, power-train components, body, and passengers. The frame, in turn, is supported by the springs. The springs are placed between the frame and the wheel axles. Illustrations on the following pages show different types of springs used at the front and rear wheels. Regardless of the type of spring, all work in a similar manner. The weight of the frame, body, and so on, applies an initial compression to the springs. The springs will further compress or expand as the car wheels encounter irregularities in the road. Thus, the wheels can move up and down somewhat independently of the frame. This allows the springs to absorb a good part of the up-and-down motion of the car wheels. The motion therefore is not transmitted to the car frame and from it to the passengers.

§ 37–2. TYPES OF SPRINGS The automobile uses three basic types of spring: coil, leaf, and torsion bar. Also, air suspension was at one time offered by automotive manufacturers as optional equipment. Most cars use either coil springs or torsion-bar springs at the two front wheels (Figs. 35–9 and 37–1). Some cars use coil springs at the rear wheels (Fig. 35–3). Other cars use leaf springs at the rear wheels. A few cars (and many heavy-duty vehicles) also use leaf springs at the front wheels.

1. Coil springs. The coil spring is made of a length of special spring steel (usually round in cross section) which is wound in the shape of a coil. The spring is formed at high temperature (the steel is white hot), and it is then cooled and properly heat-treated so as to give it the proper characteristics of elasticity and "spring-

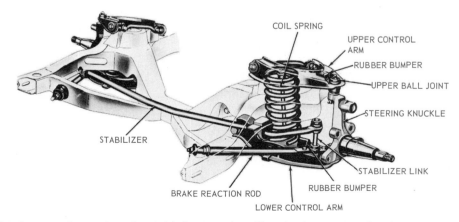

COIL SPRING

UPPER CONTROL ARM

RUBBER BUMPER

UPPER BALL JOINT

STEERING KNUCKLE

STABILIZER LINK

RUBBER BUMPER

LOWER CONTROL ARM

BRAKE REACTION ROD

STABILIZER

Fig. 37–1. Front-suspension system shown in phantom view. The wheels mount on bearings on the tapered spindles of the steering knuckles. *(Buick Motor Division of General Motors Corporation)*

466

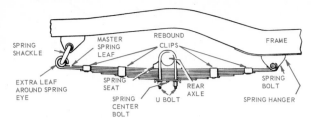

Fig. 37-2. A typical leaf spring, showing attachments to the frame and also the method of attachment to the axle.

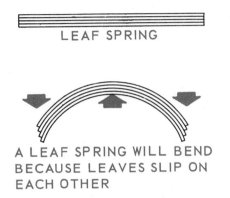

LEAF SPRING

A LEAF SPRING WILL BEND BECAUSE LEAVES SLIP ON EACH OTHER

Fig. 37-3. If a leaf spring made of equal-length leaves is bent, the amount of slippage between leaves will be as shown.

iness." Spring characteristics are discussed below.

2. Leaf springs. There are two types of leaf spring, the multileaf and the single leaf. The latter has been designated as a tapered-plate spring by the manufacturer.

The multileaf spring is made up of a series of flat steel plates of graduated length placed one on top of another, as shown in Fig. 37-2. The plates, or leaves, are held together at the center by a center bolt which passes through holes in the leaves. Clips placed at intervals along the spring keep the leaves in alignment. Instead of clips, as shown in Fig. 37-2, some leaf springs are sheathed in a metal cover. The longest, or master, leaf is rolled at both ends to form spring eyes through which bolts are placed to attach the spring ends. On some springs, the ends of the second leaf are also rolled part way around the two spring eyes to reinforce the master leaf.

In operation, the leaves not only bend but also slip against each other. The reason for this is shown in Fig. 37-3. As the spring is bent, the individual leaves remain the same length, and this means that slippage must occur, as shown.

In the actual leaf spring, the leaves are of graduated length. To permit them to slip, various

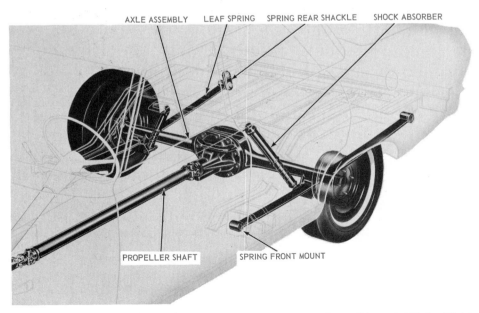

Fig. 37-4. Rear-suspension system using tapered-plate, or single-leaf, springs. *(Chevrolet Motor Division of General Motors Corporation)*

means of applying lubricant between the leaves are used. In addition, some leaf springs have special inserts of various materials, placed between the leaves, to permit easier slipping. The clips shown on the spring in Fig 37-2 are called *rebound* clips because they prevent excessive

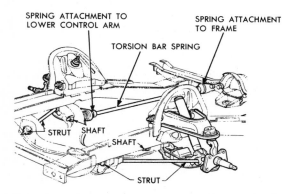

Fig. 37-5. Front-suspension system using torsion-bar springs. *(Chrysler-Plymouth Division of Chrysler Motors Corporation)*

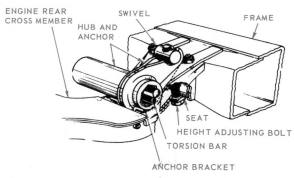

Fig. 37-6. Method of attaching the rear of a torsion bar to the frame. The hub and anchor, swivel, and adjusting bolt are for adjusting the height of the car. *(Chrysler-Plymouth Division of Chrysler Motors Corporation)*

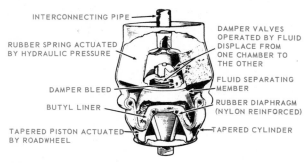

Fig. 37-7. Partial cutaway view of a Hydrolastic spring. *(British Motor Corporation)*

leaf separation during rebound, or after the wheel has passed over an obstruction in the road. In addition, springs may be covered with a metal sheath, as shown in Fig. 37-8, to retain lubricant and prevent the entrance of moisture and dirt.

3. Single-leaf springs. This spring, also called a *tapered-plate spring,* is made of a single steel plate which is heavier at the center and tapered to the two ends. Figure 37-4 shows a rear suspension system using two single-leaf springs. The method of mounting and operating is generally the same as with the multileaf spring.

4. Torsion-bar suspension. Figures 35-9 and 37-5 show torsion-bar front-suspension systems using two torsion bars. The rear end of each torsion bar is attached to a frame cross member through a car-leveling device. This car-leveling device can be adjusted to level up the car in case any sag occurs in the suspension after long mileage. The rear ends of the torsion bars are kept from turning by this attachment. The front ends of the torsion bars are attached to the lower control arms at the pivot points of the arms. Thus, as the lower control arms move up and down in response to up-and-down front-wheel movement, the torsion bars twist. The car weight places an initial twist on the bars, just as it places an initial compression on the coil springs of cars with coil-spring suspension. The twisting of the torsion bars provides the springing effect. Figure 37-6 shows the car-leveling device at one rear end of one torsion bar. Turning the height-adjustment bolt causes the hub and anchor assembly to turn. This rotates the rear end of the torsion bar so that the front end of the car is raised or lowered.

5. Air suspension. In air suspension, the four conventional springs are replaced by four air bags, or air-spring assemblies. Essentially, the air-spring assembly is a flexible bag enclosed in a metal dome or girdle. The bag is filled with compressed air which supports the weight of the car. When a wheel encounters a bump in the road, the air is further compressed and absorbs the shock. An air compressor, driven by the engine, maintains pressure in the air bags.

6. Hydrolastic suspension. This suspension uses rubber springs actuated by hydraulic pressure. There is a spring unit (Fig. 37-7) at each wheel. Front and rear units on each side are connected by a pipe so that the liquid (water) can flow between the units. When a wheel encounters a bump, the tapered piston is pushed upward. This forces the fluid which is beneath and in the center of the rubber spring to actuate the spring. At the same time, water is forced up through the interconnecting pipe to the other unit on the same side of the car. This causes the other wheel to be lifted also, thus distributing the shock of the bump between the front and rear wheels.

§ 37–3. SPRUNG AND UNSPRUNG WEIGHT

In the automobile, the terms "sprung weight" and "unsprung weight" refer to the part of the car that is supported on springs and the part that is not. The frame and the parts attached to the frame are sprung; that is, their weight is supported on the car springs. However, the wheels and wheel axles (and rear-axle housing and differential) are not supported on springs; they represent unsprung weight. Generally speaking, unsprung weight should be kept as low as possible. The reason for this is that as unsprung weight increases, so does the roughness of the ride. For example, consider a single wheel. If it is light, it can move up and down as road irregularities are encountered without causing much reaction to the car frame. But if the weight of the wheel is increased, then its movement will become more noticeable to the car occupants. To take a ridiculous example, suppose the unsprung weight at the wheel is equal to the sprung weight above the wheel. In such a case, the sprung weight would tend to move about as much as the unsprung weight. The unsprung weight, which must move up and down as road irregularities are encountered, would tend to cause a like motion of the sprung weight. This is the reason for keeping the unsprung weight as low as possible so that it represents only a small portion of the total weight of the car.

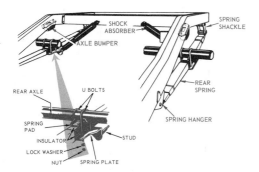

Fig. 37–8. Rear leaf springs, showing details of attaching spring to the axle housing.

§ 37–4. CHARACTERISTICS OF SPRINGS

The ideal spring for automotive suspension would be one which would absorb road shock rapidly and then return to its normal position slowly. Such an ideal is not possible, however. An extremely flexible, or soft, spring would allow too much movement, and a stiff, or hard, spring would give too rough a ride. However, satisfactory riding qualities are attained by using a fairly soft spring with a shock absorber (§ 37–11).

Softness or hardness of a spring is referred to as its *rate*. The rate of a spring is the weight required to deflect it 1 inch. The rate of automotive springs is about constant through their operating range, or deflection, in the car. This is stated by Hooke's law, as applied to coil springs: The spring will compress in direct proportion to the weight applied. Thus, if 600 pounds will compress the spring 3 inches, 1,200 pounds will compress the spring twice as far, or 6 inches.

§ 37–5. LEAF-SPRING INSTALLATION

The leaf spring most commonly used in automotive vehicles is a semielliptical spring. It is in the shape of half an ellipse, and that is the reason for its name. Figure 37–2 and 37–8 show springs of this type. The method of attachment in these figures is a common one for leaf springs. The center of the spring is attached to the axle housing with two U bolts so that the spring is, in effect, hanging from the axle housing. A spring plate or straps are used at the bottom of the spring, and a spring pad is used between the axle and the spring. There may also be an insulating strip of rubber or similar material to reduce noise transference between the axle and spring.

1. Spring hanger. One end of the spring is attached to a hanger on the frame by means of a bolt and bushing in the spring eye. The spring, as it bends, causes the spring eye to turn back and forth with respect to the spring hanger. The attaching bolt and bushing must permit this rotation. Some applications have a hollow spring bolt with a lubricating fitting. This permits lubrication of the bushing. Other designs do not require lubrication. Many designs have a bushing made up of an inner and an outer metal shell. Between these two shells is a molded rubber bushing. The weight is carried through the rubber bushing. The rubber acts to dampen vibration and noise and thus prevents them from entering the car frame.

2. Spring shackle. As the spring bends, the distance between the two spring eyes changes. If

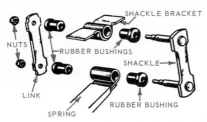

Fig. 37-9. Details of a rubber-bushed spring shackle.

both ends of the spring were fastened rigidly to the frame, then the spring would not be able to bend. To permit bending, the spring is fastened at one end to the frame through a link called a *shackle.* The shackle is a swinging support attached at one end to the spring eye and at the other end to a supporting bracket on the car frame. Spring shackles can be seen in Figs. 37-2 and 37-8. A spring shackle is shown in disassembled view in Fig. 37-9. The two links provide the swinging support that the spring requires, and the bolts attach the links to the shackle bracket on the frame and to the spring eye. The rubber bushings insulate the spring from the frame to prevent transference of noise and vibration between the two.

Shackles with lubrication fittings require periodic lubrication. However, the rubber-bushed

shackle must not be lubricated. Oil or grease on the rubber bushings will cause them to soften and deteriorate.

3. Transverse mounting. This mounting (Fig. 37-10) uses a single multileaf spring at the rear of the car, each rear wheel being independently suspended by one end of the spring. Each rear wheel is driven by a shaft with two universal joints.

§ 37-6. HOTCHKISS AND TORQUE-TUBE DRIVES
Before we discuss rear-suspension systems further, we should note that the rear springs may have an additional job to do besides supporting the car load. This additional job is to absorb *rear-end torque* (see § 35-4). Whenever the rear wheel is being driven, through the power train, by the engine, it rotates as shown in Fig. 37-11 (for forward car motion). At the same time, the wheel-axle housing tries to rotate in the opposite direction, as shown (Fig. 37-11). The twisting motion thus applied to the axle housing is called *rear-end torque.* Two different rear-end designs are used to combat this twisting motion of the axle housing. They are the Hotchkiss drive and the torque-tube drive (Fig. 35-8).

§ 37-7. REAR SUSPENSION
We have illustrated and discussed rear-suspension systems in some

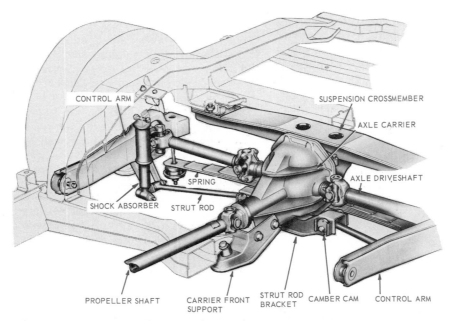

Fig. 37-10. Rear-suspension and drive-line components used in the Corvette, showing the transverse leaf spring and the axle driveshafts with their two universal joints each. *(Chevrolet Motor Division of General Motors Corporation)*

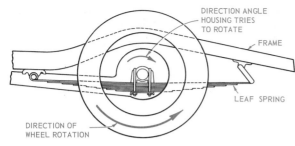

Fig. 37–11. Axle housing tries to rotate in a direction opposite to that of wheel rotation.

detail. Figures 37–4, 37–8, and 37–11 show rear-suspension systems using leaf springs. Methods of attaching the springs through hangers and shackles have also been shown and described (§ 37–5). No additional bracing is needed with leaf springs mounted as shown in Fig. 37–11, since the springs absorb rear-end torque and side thrust

(as when rounding a corner). However, the leaf spring mounted transversally (Fig. 37–10) does require additional bracing; control arms and strut rods are therefore used.

With coil springs, the rear-suspension system requires some method of holding the axle housing in place. Figure 35–3 shows a coil-spring rear suspension in phantom view, and Fig. 37–12 is a disassembled view of a rear suspension of somewhat different construction. The coil springs are assembled between spring seats in the car frame and pads on the axle housing. Note that two control arms, or links, are used. They are attached between the rear-axle housing and the car frame and permit upward or downward movement of the axle housing with respect to the car frame. They prevent side movement or forward and backward movement. In the installation shown in Fig. 35–3, a track bar is used to prevent side movement.

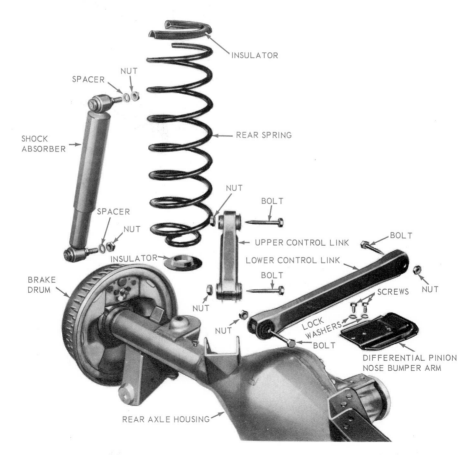

Fig. 37–12. Rear-suspension system using coil springs in disassembled view. *(Cadillac Motor Car Division of General Motors Corporation)*

471

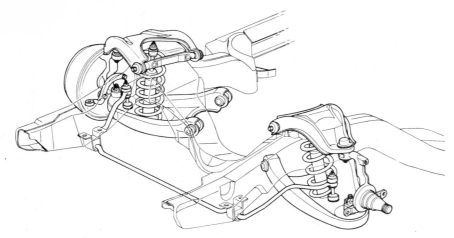

Fig. 37–13. Coil-spring front-suspension system of type with two frame attachment points for lower control arm. *(Chevrolet Motor Division of General Motors Corporation)*

§ 37–8. FRONT SUSPENSION The suspension of the front wheels is more complicated than the suspension of the rear wheels. Not only must the front wheels move up and down with respect to the car frame (for spring action), but also they must be able to swing at various angles to the car frame for steering. In the pages that follow, we discuss the various types of suspension systems used on modern cars. Chapter 38 covers steering systems.

In order to permit the front wheels to swing to one side or the other for steering, each wheel is supported on a spindle which is part of a steering knuckle. The steering knuckle is then supported through ball joints, by upper and lower control arms which are attached to the car frame.

§ 37–9. INDEPENDENT FRONT SUSPENSION Practically all passenger cars now use the independent type of front suspension system in which each front wheel is independently supported by a coil, torsion-bar, or leaf spring. The coil-spring arrangement is the most common. There are three types of coil-spring front suspension. In one, the coil spring is located between the upper and lower control arms (Fig. 37–1), and the lower control arm has one point of attachment to the car frame. In the second type, the coil spring is located between the upper and lower control arms (Fig. 37–13), and the lower control arm has two points of attachment to the car frame. In the third type, the coil spring is between the upper control arm and spring tower or housing that is part of the front-end sheet-metal work (Fig. 37–14).

In the type with a single point of attachment for the lower control arm (Fig. 37–1), a strut, or brake reaction rod, is used to prevent forward or backward movement of the lower control arm. This strut, or rod, can also be seen in Fig. 37–14. It is attached between the outer end of the lower control arm and the car frame.

The geometry of a front-end suspension is shown in Fig. 37–15. The lower arm is considerably

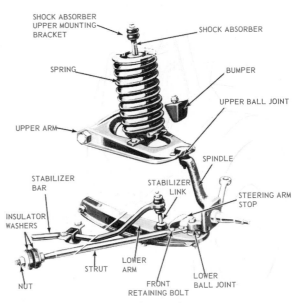

Fig. 37–14. Front-suspension system of type with coil springs mounted above the upper control arms. *(Ford Division of Ford Motor Company)*

longer than the upper arm. The points of attachment are arranged to allow the steering-knuckle support to move up and down almost vertically as the wheel meets irregularities in the road. At the same time, the steering knuckle and wheel can pivot on the ball joints to steer the car (see Chap. 38).

Note that the steering knuckle is maintained in nearly vertical alignment as it moves up and down. This keeps the wheel in almost vertical alignment, which is desirable from the standpoint of steering control and tire wear. This maintenance of alignment is achieved by the relationship between the frame and the suspending members.

In 1969 Buick came out with an altered front-suspension design that put the instant center *outside* the car, instead of inside (see Fig. 37–16). The instant center is the point of intersection of lines drawn through the control arm attachment points for any one position of the wheel. Note that, in the 1968 design, the wheel tilted inward as it moved upward. That is, it took on a negative camber (see § 38–3). On the 1969 design, with the instant center outside the car, the wheel tilts outward as it moves upward. That is, it takes on a positive camber. Now, refer to Fig. 37–17 to see how this affects car stability. When a front wheel encounters a bump, as shown, the 1969 design causes the wheel to tilt outward as it moves up. The effect of this is to impart an outward thrust

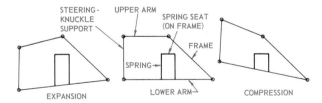

Fig. 37–15. Geometry of a front-suspension system. As the steering-knuckle support and wheel move up and down, the upper and lower arms pivot on the frame, causing the spring to expand or compress.

Fig. 37–16. Comparison of 1968 and 1969 front-suspension systems. In the 1969 design, the inner attachment points of the control arms have been moved apart so that the instant center is outside the car. *(Buick Motor Division of General Motors Corporation)*

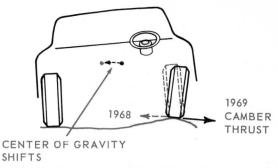

Fig. 37–17. Showing how the 1969 design causes the center of gravity to shift as the wheel moves up. *(Buick Motor Division of General Motors Corporation)*

at the road which reduces the side effect of the bump (which tends to push the car to the left in Fig. 37–17). The stability factor is even more pronounced as the car rounds a curve. Centrifugal force throws more of the weight on the outer wheel so that this wheel moves up. As it does so, it tilts outward, as shown in Fig. 37–17, and the tire opposes the centrifugal force that is trying to push the car sideways. In addition, because the bottom of the tire shifts inward as it moves up, the center of gravity of the car shifts also. It shifts into the curve to help counteract the centrifugal force pushing the car outward.

Rubber bumpers are placed on the frame and lower suspension arm to prevent metal-to-metal contact between frame and arms as limits of spring compression or expansion are reached.

A stabilizer bar, or sway eliminator, is used on many cars to interconnect between the two lower suspension arms (Figs. 37–1 and 37–14). The shaft prevents too great a difference in spring action, thus providing better steering ability and control of body roll. Body roll is the leaning out of the car body caused by centrifugal force as the car rounds a turn. This tends to compress the outer spring and expand the inner spring. When this happens, the stabilizer shaft is twisted. The resistance of the shaft to the twisting effect com-

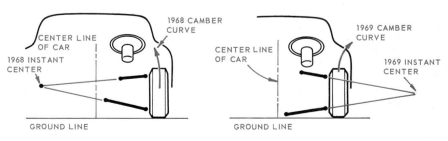

bats the tendency toward differences in spring length. This, in turn, tends to prevent excessive body roll.

§ 37–10. OTHER TYPES OF FRONT SUSPENSION

There are other types of front suspension besides the coil-spring type. We have already mentioned the torsion-bar type (Figs. 35–9 and 37–5). The twin I-beam construction is another type, used on some models of Ford trucks (Fig. 37–18). Each front wheel is supported at the end by a separate I beam. The opposite ends of the I beams are attached to the frame by pivots. The wheel ends of the two I beams are attached to the frame by radius arms which prevent backward or forward movement of the wheels. The design provides adequate suspension flexibility with the added strength of the I-beam construction.

For larger trucks, the single I-beam design is usual (Fig. 37–19). The I beam has a hole in each end through which a kingpin is assembled to hold the steering knuckle in place. Each end of the I beam is supported by a leaf spring.

§ 37–11. PURPOSE OF SHOCK ABSORBERS

Springs alone are not satisfactory for a car suspension system. As has already been mentioned (in § 37–4), the spring must be a compromise between flexibility and stiffness. It must be flexible so that it can absorb road shocks. But if it is too flexible, it will flex and rebound excessively and repeatedly, giving a rough ride. A stiff spring will not flex and rebound so much after a bump has been passed. But on the other hand it will give a hard ride because it will transmit too much of the road shock to the car. By using a relatively flexible, or soft, spring and a shock absorber, a satisfactorily smooth ride will be achieved.

You can demonstrate to yourself why a spring alone would be unsatisfactory for a vehicle suspension. Hang a weight on a coil spring as shown in Fig. 37–20. Then lift the weight and let it drop. It will expand the spring as it drops. Then, it will rebound, or move up. The spring, as it expands and contracts, will keep the weight moving up and down (oscillating) for some time.

On the car, a very similar action will take place with a flexible spring. The spring is under an initial compression because of the car weight. Then, as a wheel passes over a bump, the spring is further compressed. After the bump is passed, the spring attempts to return to its original position. But it overrides this position and expands too much. This

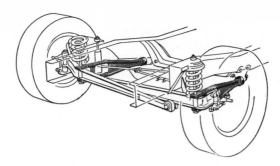

Fig. 37–18. Twin I-beam front suspension using coil springs. *(Ford Division of Ford Motor Company)*

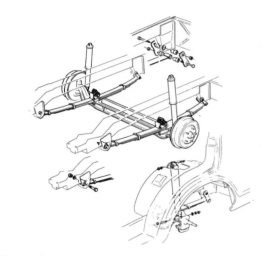

Fig. 37–19. Front-suspension system for a truck using an I-beam front axle and two leaf springs. *(Chevrolet Motor Division of General Motors Corporation)*

Fig. 37–20. If a weight hanging from a coil spring is set into up-and-down motion, it will oscillate for some time, the distance it moves up and down gradually shortening as indicated by the curve. Finally, the motion will die out.

action causes the car frame to be thrown upward. Now, having overexpanded, the spring compresses. Again it overrides and compresses too much. As this happens, the wheel may be raised clear of the road, and the frame may drop. Now, the spring expands again, and so the oscillations continue, gradually dying out. But every time the wheel encounters a bump or hole in the road, the same series of oscillations will take place.

Such spring action on a vehicle produces a rough and unsatisfactory ride. On a bumpy road, and especially on a curve, the oscillations might become serious enough to cause the driver to lose control of the car. Therefore, it is necessary to use some device to dampen out the spring oscillations quickly once the wheel has passed the hole or bump in the road. The shock absorber is the device universally used today. There have been many types of shock absorber, operating on friction, on compressed air, and hydraulically. The hydraulic shock absorber is the only type in common use at present. It contains a fluid that is forced through restricting orifices as the shock absorber is operated by spring flexure. The resistance to the movement of the fluid through the restricting orifices imposes a drag on spring movement, thus quickly dampening out spring oscillations.

§ 37–12. SHOCK-ABSORBER OPERATION

The direct-acting, or telescope, shock absorber is the most widely used shock absorber and is found on both front- and rear-suspension systems. Several of the illustrations in this chapter show methods of mounting the shock absorber at front and rear wheels.

Regardless of the method of mounting, the shock absorber is attached in such a way that as the wheel moves up and down, the shock absorber shortens and lengthens (telescopes and extends). Since the shock absorber imposes a restraint on this movement, excessive wheel and spring movements as well as spring oscillation are prevented.

A direct-acting shock absorber is shown in cutaway view in Fig. 37–21. Figure 37–22 shows the operation of the shock absorber during compression and extension (rebound). With either action, the fluid in the shock absorber moves one way or the other through small passages in the piston. This imposes a restraint on the spring and wheel action as noted in the previous section.

§ 37–13. SHOCK-ABSORBER TYPES

Several other types of shock absorber have been used, including the parallel-cylinder, opposed-cylinder,

and vane types. In the two-cylinder type, there was one cylinder for compression and another for rebound. The vane type used vanes that rotated in a cylindrical chamber filled with fluid. The direct-acting shock absorber is almost universally used today.

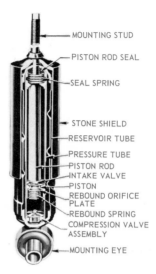

Fig. 37–21. Cutaway view of a direct-acting shock absorber. *(Buick Motor Division of General Motors Corporation)*

Labels: MOUNTING STUD, PISTON ROD SEAL, SEAL SPRING, STONE SHIELD, RESERVOIR TUBE, PRESSURE TUBE, PISTON ROD, INTAKE VALVE, PISTON, REBOUND ORIFICE PLATE, REBOUND SPRING, COMPRESSION VALVE ASSEMBLY, MOUNTING EYE

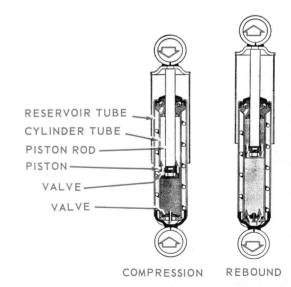

RESERVOIR TUBE, CYLINDER TUBE, PISTON ROD, PISTON, VALVE, VALVE

COMPRESSION REBOUND

Fig. 37–22. Operation of a direct-acting shock absorber during compression (left) and extension, or rebound (right). Fluid movement is shown by arrows. *(Chrysler-Plymouth Division of Chrysler Motors Corporation)*

475

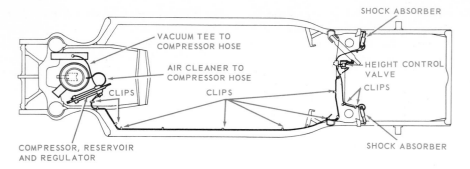

Fig. 37–23. Schematic view of automatic level control. *(Cadillac Motor Car Division of General Motors Corporation)*

§ 37–14. AUTOMATIC LEVEL CONTROL This system compensates for variations in load in the rear of the car. To explain why this is desirable, consider the following. When a heavy load is added to the trunk or rear seat, the springs will give and allow the rear end to settle. This changes the handling characteristics of the car and also causes the headlights to point upward. The automatic level control prevents all this by automatically raising the rear back to level when a load is added, and automatically lowering the rear back to level when

the load is removed. The system consists of a compressor (with reservoir and regulator), a height-control valve, two special shock absorbers, and air-pressure lines connecting the components (Fig. 37–23).

The compressor is operated by engine intake-manifold vacuum. The vacuum actuates a pump which builds up air pressure in the compressor reservoir. When a load is added to the rear of the car, this air pressure is passed through the height-control valve to the two rear shock absorbers. Each shock absorber contains an air chamber (Fig. 37–24). The air pressure, entering this chamber, will raise the upper shell of the shock absorber to bring the rear of the car back up to level again.

The height-control valve (Fig. 37–25) has a linkage to the rear suspension. When this linkage is

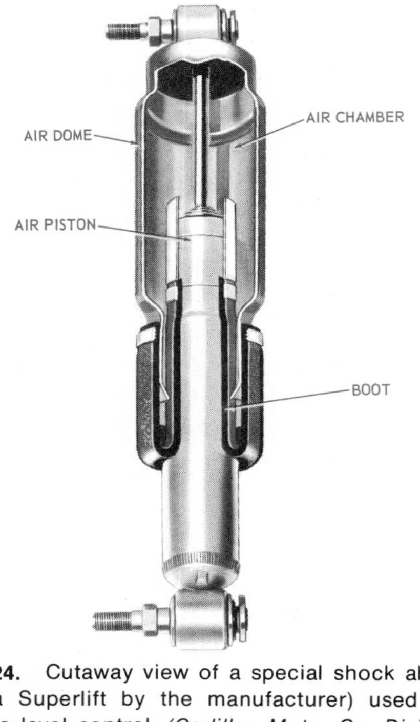

Fig. 37–24. Cutaway view of a special shock absorber (called a Superlift by the manufacturer) used in the automatic level control. *(Cadillac Motor Car Division of General Motors Corporation)*

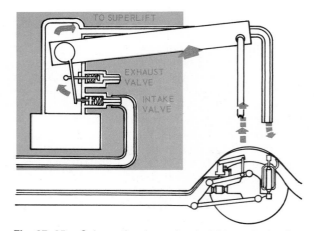

Fig. 37–25. Schematic view of a height control valve and the actions taking place when a load is added to the car. The components are not in proportion. *(Buick Motor Division of General Motors Corporation)*

476

raised by the addition of a load, it opens the intake valve, thus allowing compressed air to flow to the shock absorbers. When the load is removed, and the rear of the car is thus raised, the linkage operates the exhaust valve, allowing air to exit from the shock absorber until the correct level is achieved. The height-control valve has a time-delay mechanism that allows the valve to respond only after several seconds. This eliminates fast valve action which would tend to cause the system to function every time a wheel encountered a bump in the road. That is, the system functions on load changes only, and not on road shocks.

*R*eview Questions

1. What is the purpose of the car springs?
2. Describe a coil spring.
3. Describe the construction of a leaf spring.
4. Describe a torsion-bar suspension system.
5. What is a tapered-plate spring?
6. Describe one method of attaching a leaf spring to a car.
7. What is the purpose of the spring shackle? Describe a spring shackle.
8. What is meant by sprung and unsprung weight?
9. What absorbs rear-end torque in the Hotchkiss drive? In the torque-tube drive?
10. What is the purpose of the stabilizer shaft? Describe how this shaft functions.
11. In a rear suspension using coil springs, between what two members is the coil spring retained?
12. What is the purpose of the two rear-axle control arms in a coil-spring rear suspension?
13. Between what two members is the coil spring retained on most front-suspension systems?
14. Describe the ball-joint front-suspension system.
15. Why are shock absorbers desirable?
16. Describe the action of a spring on a car without shock absorbers as a wheel encounters a bump in the road. Why is this action troublesome?
17. On what hydraulic principle is most modern shock-absorber action based?
18. What is another name for the direct-acting shock absorber? Describe briefly the actions that take place in this shock absorber when it is telescoped because of spring compression. Describe briefly the actions that take place when it is extended because of spring expansion.
19. Describe how the automatic level control works.

*S*tudy Questions

1. What is Hooke's law, as applied to coil springs?
2. Make a sketch of a rear-suspension system using a leaf spring, and show the actions that take place when the wheel encounters a hole. When it encounters a bump.
3. Make a sketch of a front-suspension system using coil springs, and show the actions that take place when the wheel encounters a hole. When it encounters a bump.
4. Write a story explaining what takes place when a direct-acting shock absorber goes into operation.

CHAPTER
38

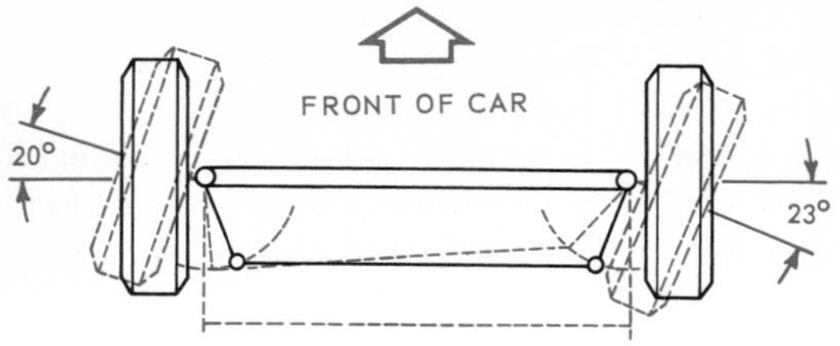

FRONT OF CAR

20°

23°

Steering Systems

This chapter covers the various types of steering systems used in automotive vehicles. The requirements of a steering system as well as types of steering gears and linkages are described. The discussion of steering gears takes up most of the chapter, since there are many varieties of steering gears, both manually and hydraulically operated. The latter type is known as power steering.

§ 38–1. FUNCTION OF THE STEERING SYSTEM A simplified drawing of a steering system is shown in Fig. 38–1A. We have already described the various methods of supporting the front-wheel spindle (Chap. 37) so that the wheels can be swung to the left or right for steering. This movement is produced by gearing and linkage between the steering wheel in front of the driver and the steering knuckle (or wheel). The complete arrangement is called the *steering system.* Actually, the steering system is composed of two elements, a steering gear at the lower end of the steering column and linkage between the gear and the wheel steering knuckles. Before we discuss linkages and steering gears in detail, let us take a look at the steering system from the standpoint of geometry, or the angles involved.

§ 38–2. FRONT - END GEOMETRY The term "front-end geometry" refers to the angular relationship between front wheels, front-wheel attaching parts, and car frame. The angle of the steering axis away from the vertical, the pointing in, or toe-in, of the front wheels, the tilt

of the front wheels from vertical—all these are involved in front-end geometry. Every one of them influences the steering ease, steering stability, and riding qualities of the car and has a direct effect on tire wear. The various factors that enter into front-end geometry are classified under the following terms: camber, steering-axis inclination (or kingpin inclination), caster, toe-in, and toe-out on turns. These are discussed in detail below.

§ 38–3. CAMBER Camber is the tilting of the front wheels from the vertical (Fig. 38–1B). When the tilt is outward, so that the wheels are farther apart at the top than at the bottom, the camber is positive. Positive camber is shown in Fig. 38–1. When the tilt is inward, so that the wheels are closer together at the top than at the bottom, the camber is negative. The amount of tilt is measured in degrees from the vertical, and this measurement is called the *camber angle.* The purpose

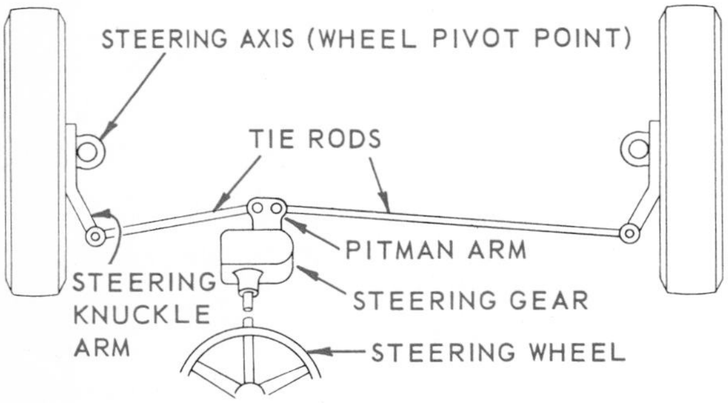

STEERING AXIS (WHEEL PIVOT POINT)

TIE RODS

PITMAN ARM

STEERING GEAR

STEERING WHEEL

STEERING KNUCKLE ARM

Fig. 38–1A Simplified drawing of a steering system.

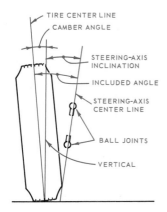

TIRE CENTER LINE

CAMBER ANGLE

STEERING-AXIS INCLINATION

INCLUDED ANGLE

STEERING-AXIS CENTER LINE

BALL JOINTS

VERTICAL

Fig. 38–1B. Camber angle and steering-axis inclination. Positive camber is shown.

of camber is to give the wheels a slight outward tilt to start with. Then, when the vehicle is loaded and rolling along on the road, the load will just about bring the wheels to a vertical position. If you started with no camber angle (wheels vertical), then loading the car might give them a negative camber. Any amount of camber (positive or negative) tends to cause uneven or more rapid tire wear, since the tilt puts more of the load on one side of the tread than on the other.

§ 38-4. STEERING-AXIS (OR KINGPIN) INCLINATION

At one time, all steering systems had a kingpin which attached the steering knuckle to a support. Later, ball-joint supports were adopted (Fig. 38-2). In this design, the steering knuckle and the steering-knuckle support were combined into a single part, called the *steering knuckle.* The steering knuckle is supported at top and bottom by the control arms and is attached to the arms by ball joints.

The inclination from the vertical of the kingpin, or the center lines of the ball joints, is a very important factor in steering action. This inclination, called *kingpin* or *steering-axis inclination,* is the inward tilt of the kingpin or ball-joint center line from the vertical (Figs. 38-1B and 38-2). This inward tilt is desirable for several reasons. In the first place, it helps provide steering stability by tending to return the wheels to the straight-ahead position after any turn. It also reduces steering effort, particularly when the car is stationary. In addition, it reduces tire wear.

The inward tilt, or inclination, of the steering axis tends to keep the wheels straight ahead. It helps recovery, or the return of the wheels to the straight-ahead position after a turn has been made. You can make a table-top demonstration of why this is so with a pencil, a rubber band, a cardboard disk, and a piece of cardboard (Fig. 38-3). Put them together as shown in Fig. 38-3. The cardboard disk represents the wheel, the pencil the kingpin, and the cardboard brace at the top holds the two apart at the top so as to get steering-axis inclination. Needless to say, the angle is greatly exaggerated in the figure. Now, hold the pencil at an angle to the table top so that the wheel is vertical, as shown in Fig. 38-3. Then rotate the pencil, but do not change its angle with the table top. Notice that, as you turn the pencil, the wheel is carried around and down toward the table top (Fig. 38-4). If the wheel could not move down, what would happen? As you turned the pencil, then the pencil would have to be moved up (always maintaining the same angle with the table top).

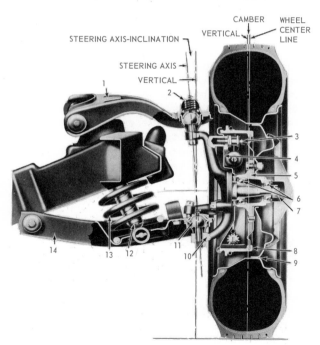

Fig. 38-2. Spherical, or ball-joint, front-suspension system.

1. Upper control arm
2. Upper spherical joint
3. Brake anchor pin
4. Brake backing plate
5. Front-wheel hub
6. Front-wheel bearings
7. Front-wheel spindle (part of knuckle)
8. Brake drum
9. Wheel
10. Steering knuckle
11. Lower spherical joint
12. Shock absorber
13. Front spring
14. Lower control arm

(Chevrolet Motor Division of General Motors Corporation)

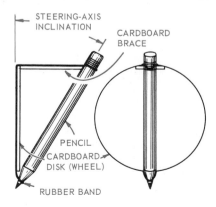

Fig. 38-3. A cardboard disk to serve as the wheel, a rubber band, a pencil, and a cardboard brace will demonstrate the effect of steering-axis inclination.

This last movement is what actually takes place in the automobile. The wheel is in contact with the ground. It cannot move down. Therefore, as it is swung away from straight ahead, the ball joints and supporting parts are moved upward. This means that the car body is actually lifted. In other words, steering-axis inclination causes the car to be raised every time the front wheels are swung away from straight ahead. Then, the weight of the car tends to bring the wheels back to straight ahead after the turn is completed and the steering wheel is released.

§ 38-5. INCLUDED ANGLE   The included, or combined, angle is the camber angle plus the steering-axis angle (Fig. 38-1B). The included

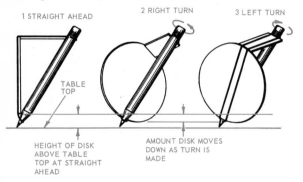

Fig. 38-4. The cardboard disk represents the left front wheel as viewed from the driver's seat: (1) the "straight-ahead" position, (2) a right turn, (3) a left turn.

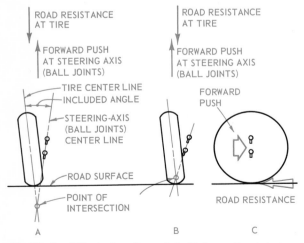

Fig. 38-5. Effect when the point of intersection is below the road surface (A), and above the road surface (B). The left front wheel as viewed from the driver's seat is shown in A and B. C is a side view of the wheel to show two forces acting on the wheel and ball joints.

angle is important because it determines the point of intersection of the wheel and the steering-axis center lines (Fig. 38-5). This, in turn, determines whether the wheel will tend to toe out or toe in. "Toe-out" is a term used to describe the tendency of the wheel to point outward. A soldier standing at attention has his feet "toed out." "Toe-in" is just the opposite; a pigeon-toed person turns the toes of his feet inward. Likewise, a wheel that toes in tries to point inward as it rolls. Figure 38-10 shows what toe-in is on a vehicle. The tire on a wheel that is toed in or toed out will wear more rapidly. The tire has to go in the direction in which the car is moving. But since it is not pointed in that direction (it is toed out or toed in), it is dragged sideways as it rolls forward. The more toe-out or toe-in, the more it is dragged sideways and the faster the tire wears.

When the point of intersection (Fig. 38-5) is below the road surface, then the wheel will tend to toe out. This is because the forward push (which is through the steering axis or center lines of the ball joints) is inside the tire center line at the road surface. In the right-hand picture in Fig. 38-5, the two opposing forces working on the wheel are shown. One is the forward push through the ball joints; the other is the road resistance to the tire. If these two forces are exactly in line, then the wheel will have no tendency to toe out or toe in. The two forces will be in line with each other only when the point of intersection is at the road surface. When it is below the road level, as shown at A in Fig. 38-5, then the wheel attempts to swing outward, or toe out. When the point of intersection is above the road level, as shown at B in Fig. 38-5, then the wheel attempts to swing inward, or toe in.

§ 38-6. CASTER   In addition to being tilted inward toward the center of the car, the steering axis may also be tilted forward or backward from the vertical (Fig. 38-6). Backward tilt from the vertical is called *positive caster.* Positive caster aids directional stability, since the center line of the ball joints passes through the road surface ahead of the center line of the wheel. Thus, the push on the ball joints is ahead of the road resistance to the tire. The tire is trailing behind, just as the caster on a table leg "trails behind" when the table is pushed (Fig. 38-7).

Caster has another effect that is important. When both front wheels have positive caster, the car tends to roll out or lean out on turns. But if the front wheels have negative caster, then the car tends to bank, or lean in, on turns. Let us use a pencil, rubber band, and cardboard disk to demonstrate why this is so (Fig. 38–8). Fasten the cardboard disk and the pencil together as shown. The disk represents the left front wheel. Note that we do not include any steering-axis inclination here; we want to show only the effect of positive caster. Hold the disk vertical with the pencil at an angle so that both the pencil point and the edge of the disk rest on the table top. Now, rotate the pencil as shown. Note that the disk is lifted from the table top. Actually, in the car, the wheel (disk) would not be lifted. Instead, the ball joints (pencil) would move down. In other words, on a right turn, the left side of the car would drop.

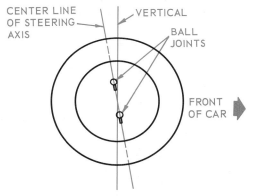

Fig. 38–6. Left front wheel (as viewed from the driver's seat), shown from inside so that the backward tilt of the steering axis from vertical can be seen. This backward tilt is called positive caster.

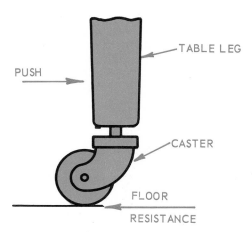

Fig. 38–7. The wheel of the caster trails behind and follows in the direction of the push when the table leg is moved.

Now, let us see what happens at the right front wheel (Fig. 38–9). As the right turn is made, the wheel pivots on the road surface, causing the ball joints (pencil) to be lifted. The right side of the car is lifted.

When the left side of the car is lowered and the right side of the car is lifted as a right turn is made (as described above), then the car rolls, or leans

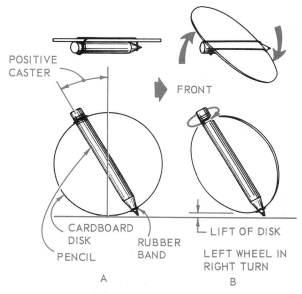

Fig. 38–8. Using a cardboard disk, a pencil, and a rubber band to show the effects of positive caster in a right turn. The disk represents the left front wheel.

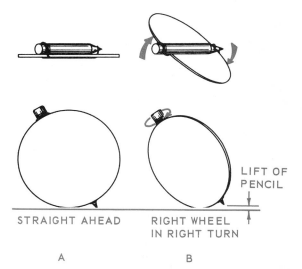

Fig. 38–9. The effect of positive caster on the right front wheel during a right turn.

out, on the turn. This is just the opposite of what would be the most desirable, since it adds to the effect of centrifugal force on the turn. By using negative caster (tilting the steering axis forward), the car can be made to lean in on a turn (and thus decrease the effect of centrifugal force). For instance, with negative caster the left side of the car would lift during a right turn, and the right side of the car would drop. This would combat the roll-out effect of centrifugal force.

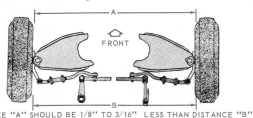

DISTANCE "A" SHOULD BE 1/8" TO 3/16" LESS THAN DISTANCE "B"

Fig. 38–10. Front-wheel toe-in. The wheels are viewed from above and the front of the car is at the top of the illustration. Specifications shown are for one particular model of car. *(Oldsmobile Division of General Motors Corporation)*

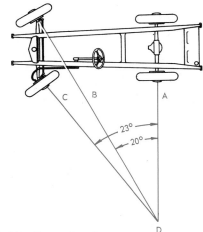

Fig. 38–11. Toe-out on turns.

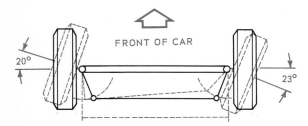

Fig. 38–12. Manner in which toe-out on turns is obtained. *(Chevrolet Motor Division of General Motors Corporation)*

There is another important effect that caster has. Positive caster tries to make the front wheels toe in. With positive caster, the car is lowered as the wheel pivots inward. Thus, the weight of the car is always trying to make the wheel toe in. With negative caster, the wheels would try to toe out.

Note that positive caster increases the effort required to steer. Positive caster tries to keep the wheels straight ahead. To make a turn, this tendency must be overcome. Note, too, that steering-axis inclination also tries to keep the wheels straight ahead. Thus, to make a turn, the effects of both caster (when positive) and steering-axis inclination must be overcome. Late-model vehicles, and particularly heavy-duty trucks, tend toward a negative caster. This makes steering easier, and there is still sufficient tendency toward recovery, or the return of the wheels to straight ahead (provided by steering-axis inclination).

§ **38–7. TOE-IN** As we have already mentioned, toe-in is the turning in of the front wheels; they attempt to roll inward instead of straight ahead. On a car with toe-in (Fig. 38–10), the distance between the front wheels is less at the front (A) than at the rear (B). The actual amount of toe-in is normally only a fraction of an inch. The purpose of toe-in is to ensure parallel rolling of the front wheels, to stabilize steering, and to prevent sideslipping and excessive wear of tires. The toe-in on the front wheels of a car serves to offset the small deflections in the wheel-support system which come about when the car is moving forward. These deflections are due to the rolling resistance of the tires on the road. In other words, even though the wheels are set to toe in slightly when the car is standing still, they tend to roll parallel on the road when the car is moving forward.

§ **38–8. TOE-OUT DURING TURNS** Toe-out during turns, also called *steering geometry*, refers to the difference in angles between the two front wheels and the car frame during turns. Since the inner wheel is rotating on or following a smaller radius than the outer wheel when the car is rounding a curve, its axle must be at a sharper angle with the car frame; that is, it must toe out more. This condition is shown in Fig. 38–11. When the front wheels are steered to make the turn illustrated, the inner wheel turns to an angle of 23 degrees with the car frame. But the outer wheel turns only 20 degrees with the car frame. This permits the inner wheel to follow a shorter radius than the outer wheel, and the circles on which the two front wheels turn are concentric; that is, their centers are at the same place, D. Toe-out is secured by providing the proper relationship between the steering-knuckle arms, tie rods, and pitman arm. This relationship is such that the inner wheel on a curve always toes out more than the outer wheel. Figure 38–12 illustrates the manner of securing this condition. When the tie rod is moved to the left during a right turn, it pushes at almost a right angle against the left steering-knuckle arm. The right end of the tie rod, however, not only moves to the left, but it also swings forward, as shown by the dotted line, so that the right wheel is turned an additional amount. When a left turn is made, the left wheel is turned an additional amount over that which the right wheel turns. Figure 38–12 shows a parallelogram type of linkage (see § 38–9). Other types of linkage give a similar effect and provide a like toe-out on turns.

Fig. 38–13. Steering linkage identification. *(Pontiac Motor Division of General Motors Corporation)*

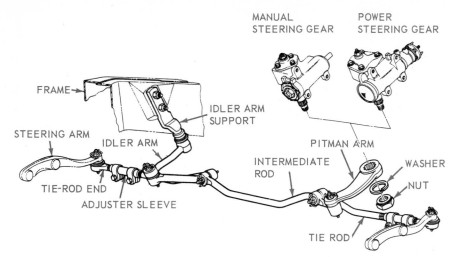

FRAME

IDLER ARM
SUPPORT

STEERING ARM

IDLER ARM

PITMAN ARM

INTERMEDIATE
ROD

WASHER

NUT

TIE-ROD END

ADJUSTER SLEEVE

TIE ROD

Fig. 38–14. Steering linkage details. *(Pontiac Motor Division of General Motors Corporation)*

§ 38–9. STEERING LINKAGES

Many types of steering linkage have been made to connect between the steering knuckles of the front wheels and the pitman arm of the steering gear. You will recall that the pitman arm swings from one side to the other (or forward and backward on some cars) as the steering wheel is turned. This movement must be carried to the steering arms at the wheels by some form of linkage. All have some means of adjusting the lengths of the tie rods or links so that proper alignment can be established between the front wheels. This alignment gives the front wheels a slight toe-in when the car is at rest. Then, when the car begins to move forward, this

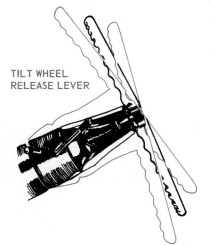

TILT WHEEL
RELEASE LEVER

Fig. 38–15. Tilt steering wheel. Lifting the release lever permits the steering wheel to be tilted to various positions, as shown. *(Buick Motor Division of General Motors Corporation)*

toe-in practically disappears as all looseness, or "sloppage," in the steering system is taken up.

Figure 38–13 shows one form of parallelogram linkage with the connecting-rod assembly connected at one end to the pitman arm and at the other end to the steering idler arm. The steering-arms are connected to the connecting-rod assembly by two secondary connecting-rod, or tie-rod, assemblies. Figure 38–14 shows the linkage details of a similar system.

§ 38–10. TILT STEERING WHEEL AND COLUMN

A number of automobiles have steering wheels that tilt up or down and also can be moved out of or into the steering column (Figs. 38–15 and 38–16). This makes it easier for the driver to get into or out of the car. Also, the driver can vary the position of the wheel to suit his build. He can also change the position during a long drive to vary his driving posture.

Some Ford automobiles have, as optional equipment, a steering column that can be moved inward toward the center of the car to make it easier for the driver to get in and out of the car. The pivot point on this arrangement is just above the steering gear, at the lower end of the steering column. At that point there is a flex joint that connects between the upper steering shaft and the worm shaft in the steering gear. This permits the steering shaft and steering column to be pivoted toward the center of the car. There is a locking mechanism connected to the transmission selector lever. The steering column is locked in the drive position and in all selector lever positions except park. To unlock the steering column, the selector lever must

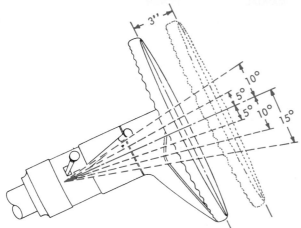

Fig. 38–16. Tilting and telescoping steering wheel. *(Cadillac Motor Car Division of General Motors Corporation)*

be moved to park. Also, if the steering column is moved out of the driving position, the selector lever is locked in the park position. This interlocking is a safety feature which prevents the steering column from being accidentally moved while the car is in operation.

§ 38–11. COLLAPSIBLE STEERING COLUMN

The collapsible steering column (Figs. 38–17 and 38–18), used on modern cars as a protective device, will collapse on impact. Thus, if the car should become involved in a front-end collision that throws the driver forward, the steering column will absorb the energy of his forward movement and greatly reduce the possibility of his being injured. The steering shaft is made in two parts which are fitted together so that they can telescope as the steering column collapses.

The steering column shown in Fig. 38–17 is called the *Japanese lantern* design because, on impact, it folds up like a Japanese lantern. The type shown in Fig. 38–18 is of the tube-and-ball design and is more recent than the other. In the tube-and-ball design, two tubes are placed one inside the other with tight fitting ball bearings between. On impact, the tubes are forced together as shown, and the balls must plow furrows in the tubes to permit the relative motion. This design is said to give a more uniform collapse rate than the earlier design.

§ 38–12. STEERING LOCK

In 1969, General Motors came out with a combination ignition

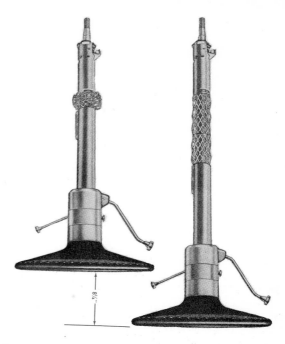

Fig. 38–17. Energy absorbing, or collapsible, steering column of the "Japanese lantern" design. The column can collapse, as shown in the lower view, during impact. *(Cadillac Motor Car Division of General Motors Corporation)*

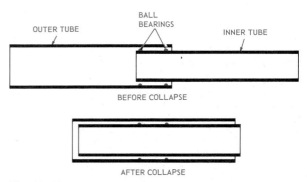

Fig. 38–18. Energy absorbing, or collapsible, steering column of the tube and ball design. *(General Motors Corporation)*

switch and steering-wheel lock (Fig. 38–19). The ignition switch is mounted on the steering column, as shown, and it has a gear attached to the cylinder in the lock. When the ignition key is inserted and the ignition switch is turned to ON, the gear rotates and pulls the rack and plunger out of the notch in the disk. The disk is mounted on the steering shaft. This frees the steering shaft and wheel so that the car can be steered. When the

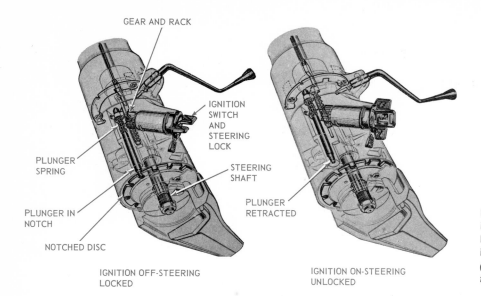

GEAR AND RACK

IGNITION SWITCH AND STEERING LOCK

PLUNGER SPRING

STEERING SHAFT

PLUNGER IN NOTCH

PLUNGER RETRACTED

NOTCHED DISC

IGNITION OFF-STEERING LOCKED

IGNITION ON-STEERING UNLOCKED

Fig. 38-19. Combination ignition switch and steering lock in phantom view, showing two positions of the lock. *(General Motors Corporation)*

ignition switch is turned off, the gear's rotation moves the rack and plunger toward the locked position. If the plunger is lined up with a notch in the disk, it will enter the notch and lock the steering wheel. But, if the wheel and disk are in a position where the plunger cannot enter a notch in the disk, the plunger will be spring-loaded against the side of the disk. Now, a slight turn of the wheel will turn the disk enough for the plunger to enter a notch and lock the steering wheel.

§ 38-13. STEERING GEARS The steering gear is a device for converting the rotary motion of the steering wheel into straight-line motion (of linkage). Essentially, the steering gear consists of two parts, a worm on the end of the steering shaft and a pitman-arm shaft on which there is a gear sector, toothed roller, or stud. The gear sector, toothed roller, or stud meshes with the worm. In Fig. 38-20, the steering gear uses a toothed roller. The roller and worm teeth mesh. When the worm is rotated (by rotation of the steering wheel), the roller teeth must follow along, and this action causes the pitman-arm shaft to rotate. The other end of the pitman-arm shaft carries the pitman arm; rotation of the pitman-arm shaft causes the arm to swing in one direction or the other. This motion is then carried through the linkage to the steering knuckles at the wheels.

NOTE: The pitman-arm shaft is also called the *cross shaft, pitman shaft, roller shaft, steering-arm shaft,* and *sector shaft.*

A somewhat different type of steering gear is shown in Fig. 38-21. In this unit, friction is kept exceptionally low by interposing balls between the major moving parts, or between the worm teeth and grooves cut in the inner face of a ball nut. The rotation of the worm gear causes the balls to roll in the worm teeth. The balls also roll in grooves cut in the inner face of the nut. Thus, as

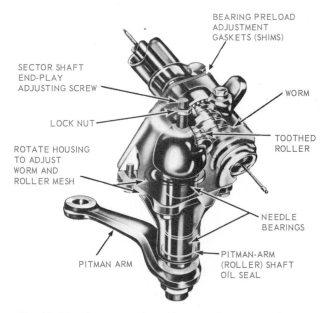

BEARING PRELOAD ADJUSTMENT GASKETS (SHIMS)

SECTOR SHAFT END-PLAY ADJUSTING SCREW

WORM

LOCK NUT

TOOTHED ROLLER

ROTATE HOUSING TO ADJUST WORM AND ROLLER MESH

NEEDLE BEARINGS

PITMAN ARM

PITMAN-ARM (ROLLER) SHAFT OIL SEAL

Fig. 38-20. Phantom view of a steering gear using a toothed roller attached to the pitman-arm shaft. Worm and roller teeth mesh. *(Ford Motor Company)*

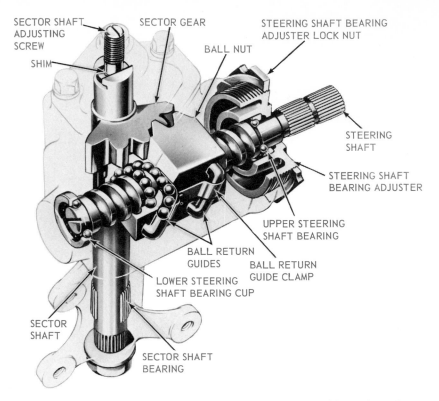

SECTOR SHAFT ADJUSTING SCREW

SECTOR GEAR

STEERING SHAFT BEARING ADJUSTER LOCK NUT

SHIM

BALL NUT

STEERING SHAFT

STEERING SHAFT BEARING ADJUSTER

UPPER STEERING SHAFT BEARING

BALL RETURN GUIDES

BALL RETURN GUIDE CLAMP

LOWER STEERING SHAFT BEARING CUP

SECTOR SHAFT

SECTOR SHAFT BEARING

Fig. 38–21. Phantom view of a recirculating-ball steering gear. *(Ford Division of Ford Motor Company)*

the worm rotates, the balls cause the nut to move up or down along the worm. This up-or-down motion is carried to the gear sector by teeth on the side of the ball nut. This then forces the gear sector to move along with the ball nut so that the pitman-arm shaft rotates.

The balls are called *recirculating balls* because they can continuously recirculate from one to the other end of the ball nut through a pair of ball return guides. For example, suppose that the driver makes a right turn. The worm gear is rotated in a clockwise direction (viewed from the driver's seat), and this causes the ball nut to move upward. The balls roll between the worm and ball nut, and as they reach the upper end of the nut, they enter the return guide and then roll back to a lower point, where they reenter the groove between the worm and ball nut.

§ 38–14. **POWER STEERING** The principle of power steering is very simple. A booster arrangement is provided which is set into operation when the steering-wheel shaft is turned. The booster then takes over and does most of the work of steering. Power steering has used compressed

air, electrical mechanisms, and hydraulic pressure. Hydraulic pressure is used on the vast majority of power-steering mechanisms today.

In the hydraulic power-steering system, a continuously operating pump provides hydraulic pressure when needed. As the steering wheel is turned, valves are operated that admit this hydraulic pressure to a cylinder. Then the pressure causes a piston to move, and the piston does most

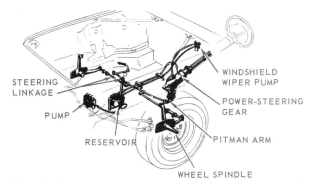

STEERING LINKAGE

PUMP

RESERVOIR

WINDSHIELD WIPER PUMP

POWER-STEERING GEAR

PITMAN ARM

WHEEL SPINDLE

Fig. 38–22. Integral type of power-steering system. *(Lincoln-Mercury Division of Ford Motor Company)*

487

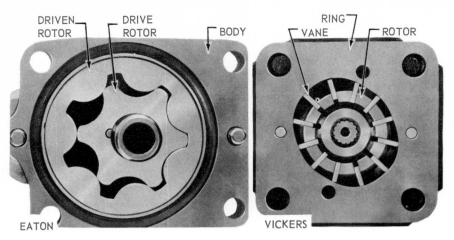

Fig. 38-23. End views, with their covers removed, of two types of pump used with power steering: (left) Eaton pump and (right) Vickers pump. *(Buick Motor Division of General Motors Corporation)*

of the steering work. Specific power-steering systems are described in the articles that follow. There are actually two general types of power-steering systems. In one, the integral type, the power operating assembly is part of the steering gear. In the other, the linkage type, the power operating assembly is part of the linkage. Figure 38-22 shows, in phantom view, a power-steering system of the integral type.

§ 38-15. GENERAL MOTORS POWER STEERING
Two models used in recent years are the in-line and

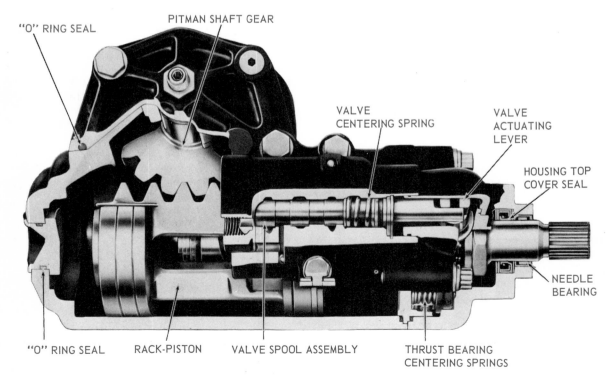

Fig. 38-24. Cutaway view of a Saginaw in-line power-steering unit. *(Buick Motor Division of General Motors Corporation)*

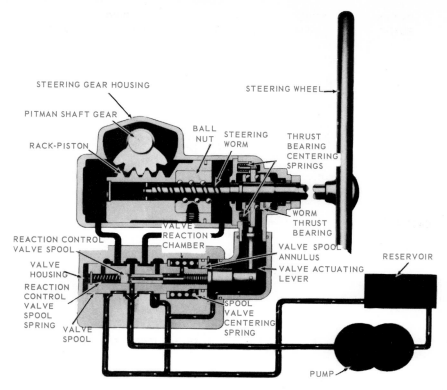

Fig. 38–25. Circulation of oil through a power-steering unit in the straight-ahead position. *(Buick Motor Division of General Motors Corporation)*

the rotary-valve (or torsion-bar) system. Although much alike in action, they are somewhat different in construction. Both are integral units and are mounted on the lower end of the steering shaft (Fig. 38–22). The steering unit consists of a recirculating-ball-and-nut steering gear (such as is illustrated in Fig. 38–21), to which has been added a hydraulic booster actuated by the pressure from an oil pump.

1. Oil pump. Figure 38–23 shows two types of pump used with power-steering systems. In the Eaton pump, an inner drive rotor causes the driven rotor to rotate with it. As they rotate, the pockets between the rotors increase and then decrease in size. During increase, oil flows into the pockets through an inlet port from the pump reservoir. Then, during decrease, this oil is forced out of the pump through an exit port. In the Vickers pump, there is a slotted driving rotor in which 12 vanes are assembled. These vanes slide outward to contact the inner face of the pump body. The inner face is so shaped (oval) as to provide two pumping chambers. As the rotor rotates, the vanes slide out and in to increase and then decrease the

pockets between the vanes. During increase, oil enters the pockets from the pump reservoir. During decrease, the oil is forced from the pockets through exit ports. Both pumps have an overload relief valve set to open when the pressure goes above about 750 psi (pounds per square inch).

2. In-line power steering. This unit consists of a recirculating-ball steering gear to which has been added a control valve and an actuating piston. Figure 38–24 is a cutaway view of the unit. The piston has a rack on it, as shown in Fig. 38–24. The rack meshes with the sector on the pitman shaft. When the steering wheel is turned, the worm at the lower end of the steering shaft turns. This action causes the ball nut and the piston to move endwise. The sector therefore turns the pitman shaft for steering. Figure 38–25 shows the oil circulation through the unit in the straight-ahead position.

The assisting action of the unit comes into effect whenever more than about 3 pounds is required to turn the wheel. When this occurs, because of the resistance of the wheels to turning, the worm shifts endwise slightly to cause the valve

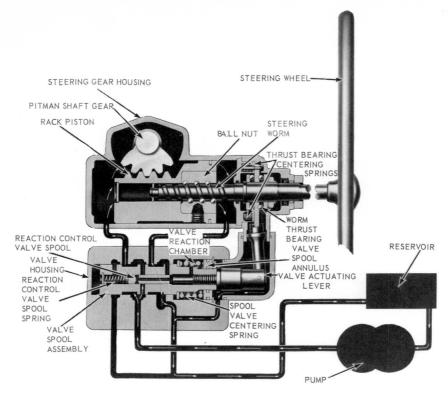

STEERING GEAR HOUSING

PITMAN SHAFT GEAR

RACK PISTON

STEERING WHEEL

BALL NUT

STEERING WORM

THRUST BEARING CENTERING SPRINGS

REACTION CONTROL VALVE SPOOL

VALVE HOUSING

REACTION CONTROL VALVE SPOOL SPRING

VALVE SPOOL ASSEMBLY

VALVE REACTION CHAMBER

WORM THRUST BEARING

VALVE SPOOL ANNULUS

VALVE ACTUATING LEVER

SPOOL VALVE CENTERING SPRING

RESERVOIR

PUMP

Fig. 38–26. Circulation of oil when the car is making a right turn. *(Buick Motor Division of General Motors Corporation)*

to operate. This admits oil at high pressure from the pump to one side or the other of the piston, and the piston is moved to assist in the turning effort.

For instance, on a right turn (Fig. 38–26), the worm moves downward (to the left) a small amount. This movement carries the thrust bearing downward, also. As the thrust bearing moves downward (to the left in Fig. 38–26), it causes the actuating lever to tilt, as shown. This brings the spool valve to the right. Now oil at high pressure is admitted to the left side of the piston. The piston is moved to the right. The higher the turning resistance, the more the valve spool is moved and the higher the oil pressure on the piston. Thus, a proportional effect is at work. Most of the turning effort is handled by the oil pressure on the piston.

When a left turn is made, the valve spool is moved to the left and oil under pressure is admitted to the right side of the piston.

3. Rotary-valve (torsion-bar) power steering. This unit (Figs. 38–27 to 38–30) uses a small

torsion bar that twists as the steering wheel is turned and a rotary valve. In the straight-ahead position, the rotary valve is centered on the valve spool so that oil is permitted to flow past both sides of lands on the spool. The oil can thus readily flow to the oil return, and no oil pressure builds up. When a turn is made, the turning effort is applied through the torsion bar; it twists slightly and causes the valve spool to move slightly with respect to the rotary valve. Now oil is forced to flow to one end of the piston; oil pressure therefore assists the turn (Fig. 38–30). The more resistance to turning the driver encounters, the more the valve spool is displaced and the higher the oil pressure that is applied to the piston. Thus, although most of the steering effort is handled by oil pressure, a proportional amount is "sensed" by the driver so that he is always aware of variations in steering effort.

§ 38-16. CHRYSLER POWER STEERING This unit is similar in many ways to the in-line power-

490

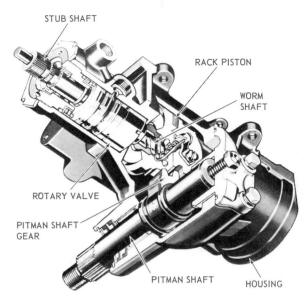

STUB SHAFT

RACK PISTON

WORM SHAFT

ROTARY VALVE

PITMAN SHAFT GEAR

PITMAN SHAFT

HOUSING

Fig. 38-27. Rotary-valve power-steering gear, cutaway view. *(Cadillac Motor Car Division of General Motors Corporation)*

steering unit. Figure 38–31 is a cutaway view of the unit. Note that it has a pivot lever which forms a linkage between the thrust bearing and the spool valve.

The operation of the unit is similar to others already described. When the steering wheel is turned, a slight endwise movement of the worm shaft occurs. This is due to end thrust through the worm. The endwise movement moves the thrust bearing, causing the pivot lever to pivot.

Figure 38–32 shows the position of the pivot lever and spool valve when the car is moving straight forward. Figure 38–33 shows their positions when a left turn is made. Here, the worm shaft has been thrust upward (to the right in Fig. 38–31) so that the upper end of the pivot lever moves downward (to the left in Fig. 38–33). This moves the spool valve as shown so that high-pressure oil is directed to the lower side of the power piston (to the left in Fig. 38–31) while the return line from the upper side of the power piston is opened. The oil pressure therefore assists the turn.

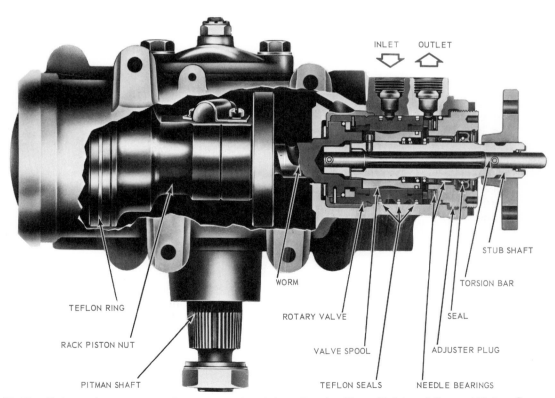

INLET   OUTLET

STUB SHAFT

TORSION BAR

SEAL

ADJUSTER PLUG

NEEDLE BEARINGS

TEFLON SEALS

VALVE SPOOL

ROTARY VALVE

WORM

TEFLON RING

RACK PISTON NUT

PITMAN SHAFT

Fig. 38-28. Rotary-valve power-steering gear, sectional view. *(Pontiac Motor Division of General Motors Corporation)*

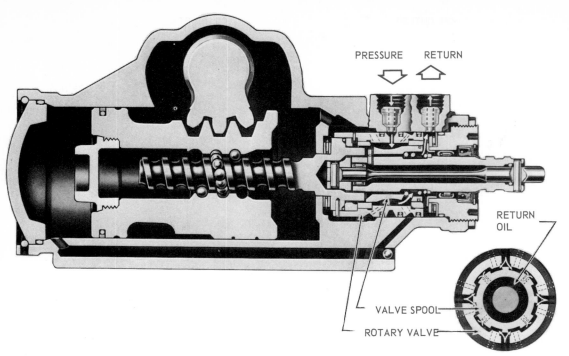

PRESSURE RETURN

RETURN
OIL

VALVE SPOOL
ROTARY VALVE

NEUTRAL POSITION

Fig. 38-29. Rotary-valve power-steering unit in the straight-ahead position. *(Pontiac Motor Division of General Motors Corporation)*

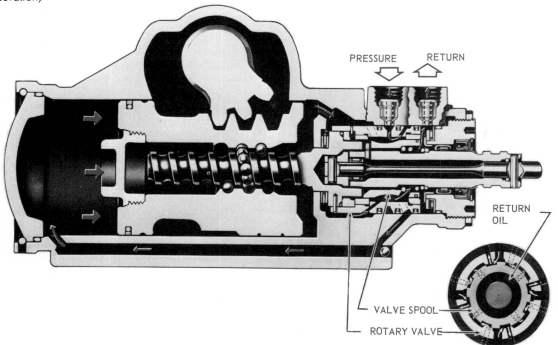

PRESSURE RETURN

RETURN
OIL

VALVE SPOOL
ROTARY VALVE

RIGHT-TURN POSITION

Fig. 38-30. Rotary-valve power-steering unit during a right turn. *(Pontiac Motor Division of General Motors Corporation)*

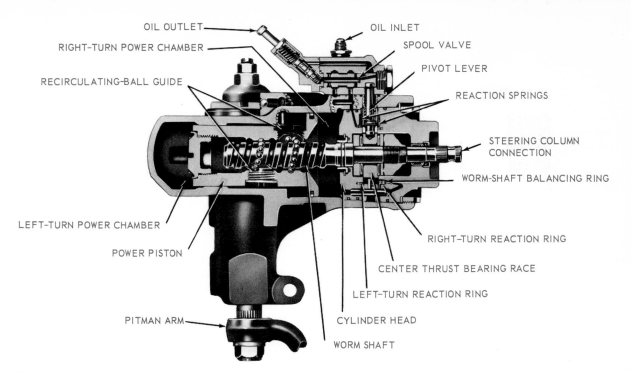

Fig. 38–31. Cutaway view of a constant-control power-steering unit. *(Chrysler-Plymouth Division of Chrysler Motors Corporation)*

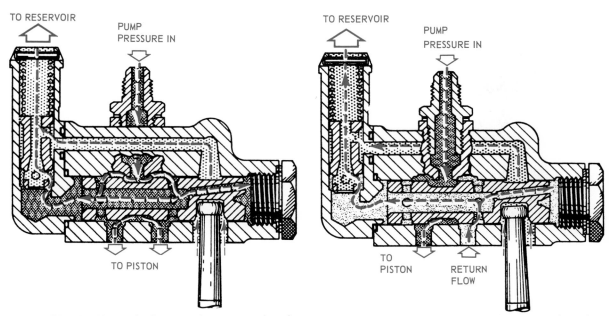

Fig. 38–32. Position of the steering-gear valve in straight-ahead driving. *(Chrysler-Plymouth Division of Chrysler Motors Corporation)*

Fig. 38–33. Position of the steering-gear valve when the car makes a left turn. *(Chrysler-Plymouth Division of Chrysler Motors Corporation)*

§ 38-17. LINKAGE-TYPE POWER STEERING In the linkage-type power-steering system, the power cylinder is not part of the steering gear. Instead, the power cylinder (or booster cylinder, as it is also called) is connected into the steering linkage. In addition, the valve assembly is included in the steering linkage, either as a separate assembly or integrally with the power cylinder. Figure 38-34 shows one linkage-type power-steering system in which the booster cylinder and valve assembly are separate units. In operation, the steering gear works in exactly the same way as the mechanical types described in § 38-13. However, the swinging end of the pitman arm is not directly connected to the steering linkage. Instead, it is connected to a valve assembly. As the end of the pitman arm swings when a turn is made, it actuates the valve assembly. Then, the valve assembly directs hydraulic oil pressure from the oil pump to the booster cylinder. Inside the booster cylinder, pressure is applied to one or the other side of a piston. Movement then takes place (actually, in this unit, the cylinder moves instead of the piston), and this movement is transferred to the connecting rod in the steering linkage. Thus, most of the effort required to move the connecting rod and steer the car is furnished by the booster cylinder.

1. Valve-assembly operation. In many ways, the valve assembly is very similar to that used in the in-line power-steering unit. The operating part consists of a valve spool assembled into a valve body as shown in Fig. 38-35. The ball on the end of the pitman arm fits a socket in the stem of the valve spool. During neutral, or straight-ahead, operation, the valve spool is centered in the valve assembly by one or more centering springs. In this position, the oil circuits through the valve will impose equal pressure on both sides of the piston in the booster cylinder. As a result of this, there is no tendency for the booster cylinder to exercise any action.

Figure 38-36 illustrates a cutaway view of the valve assembly. In it you can see the centering springs for holding the valve spool in the centered position while you are driving straight-ahead.

When a turn is made, the pitman arm swings in one direction or the other, thus causing the valve action already mentioned. Figure 38-35 shows what happens when a turn is made. Turning the steering wheel to the left, as shown, makes the pitman arm swing to the right. The ball on the end of the pitman arm moves the valve spool to the right. Now oil under pressure from the pump

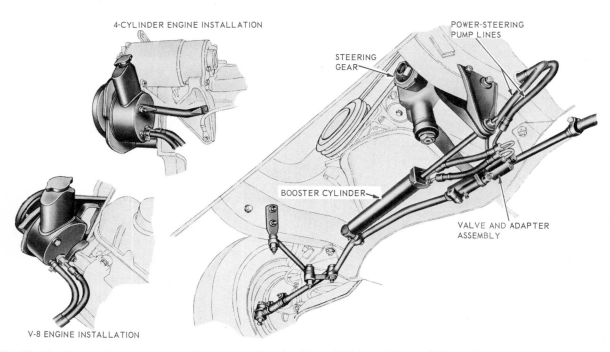

4-CYLINDER ENGINE INSTALLATION

POWER-STEERING PUMP LINES

STEERING GEAR

BOOSTER CYLINDER

VALVE AND ADAPTER ASSEMBLY

V-8 ENGINE INSTALLATION

Fig. 38-34. Linkage-type power-steering system. *(Pontiac Motor Division of General Motors Corporation)*

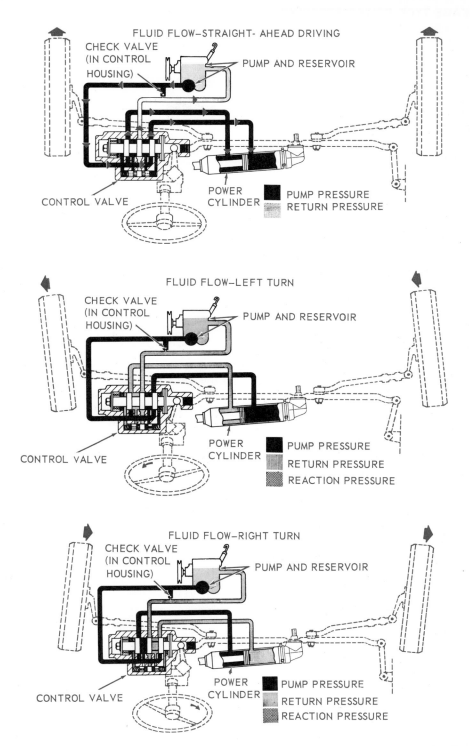

Fig. 38–35. Schematic views of the linkage-type power steering shown in Fig. 38–34. Arrows show direction of oil flow during straight-ahead driving and when turns are being made. Large arrows show the directions in which steering wheel and front wheels turn. *(Lincoln-Mercury Division of Ford Motor Company)*

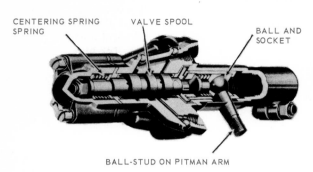

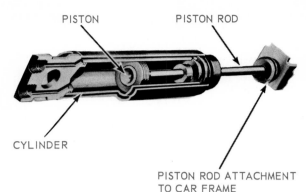

Fig. 38–36. Cutaway view of a valve assembly, showing valve spool, centering springs, and ball-and-socket attachment of the pitman arm to the valve-spool stem. *(Lincoln-Mercury Division of Ford Motor Company)*

Fig. 38–37. Cutaway view of a booster cylinder, showing the relationship of the piston, rod, cylinder, and rod attachment. *(Lincoln-Mercury Division of Ford Motor Company)*

can flow through the valve body to only one side of the piston in the booster cylinder. In the figure, oil flows into the cylinder on the right side of the piston as shown by the arrows. Since the piston is fastened to the car frame by the piston rod, it cannot move. Therefore, the hydraulic pressure in the cylinder causes the cylinder itself to move. The cylinder is fastened to the connecting rod. Thus, the major effort of steering is supplied by the booster cylinder. As the cylinder moves to the right (in the figure), the oil in the left-hand side flows back to the reservoir through the valve body as shown by the arrows. Note that movement

of the valve spool to the right has connected the left-hand side of the cylinder to the reservoir.

2. Booster cylinder. Figure 38–37 is a cutaway view of the booster cylinder. The cylinder is made up of two concentric shells. Oil flows between the two shells to enter the piston-rod end of the cylinder. The end of the piston rod is attached to the car frame by a flexible connection so that some movement of the rod can take place to permit alignment of the rod with the cylinder as the cylinder moves back and forth during steering.

3. Integral valve and power cylinder. Figure 38–38 shows the linkage-type power-steering

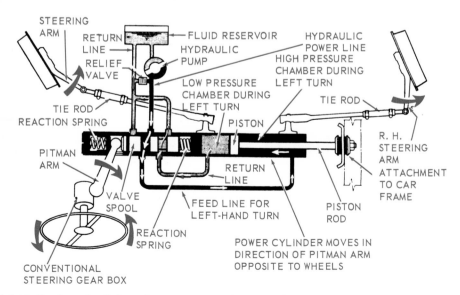

Fig. 38–38. Schematic view of a linkage-type power-steering assembly, showing oil flow and the movement of parts when a left turn is made. *(Monroe Auto Equipment Company)*

496

unit in which the valve assembly and power cylinder are one unit. The piston rod of the power cylinder is attached to the car frame. The cylinder is linked to the steering linkage, forming a part of the linkage. Note that this assembly is called the *power link,* since it is a part of the linkage and, at the same time, supplies steering power.

Figure 38–38 shows the actions during a left turn. When the steering wheel is turned, the ball on the end of the pitman arm shifts the valve spool to the right. This permits oil to flow from the pump under pressure, through the ports in the valve section of the assembly, and into the right-hand side of the power cylinder. The high-pressure oil then forces the cylinder to move to the right. It is this movement of the cylinder which provides the major mechanical steering effort within the car.

Review Questions

1. Define "front-end geometry".
2. What is camber? What is positive camber? Negative camber?
3. What is steering-axis inclination? What is its purpose?
4. What is the included angle?
5. When the point of intersection is below the pavement, will the wheel tend to toe in or toe out?
6. What is caster? What is its purpose? What is negative caster?
7. What is meant by toe-in?
8. What is meant by toe-out on turns? How is it achieved?
9. Describe typical steering linkages.
10. Describe the construction and operation of a tilt steering wheel. Of the movable steering column.
11. Describe the construction and operation of a typical steering gear.
12. Describe the hydraulic system in the in-line power-steering system. Explain how it works when a turn is made.
13. Describe the construction and operation of the in-line power-steering unit. The rotary-valve unit.
14. Describe the construction and operation of a linkage-type power-steering system.
15. Describe two types of collapsible steering columns.

Study Questions

1. Sketch front wheels with positive camber.
2. Make a sketch of front wheels with toe-in.
3. Make a sketch showing the meaning of "included angle."
4. Write an essay explaining the purpose of camber, caster, steering-axis inclination, toe-in, and toe-out on turns.
5. Write an essay explaining the operation of a typical steering gear and linkage.
6. Make a sketch and write an essay explaining the operation of the hydraulic system on one of the power-steering systems.
7. Write an essay explaining the operation of a power-steering system.

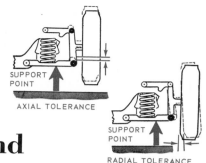

SUPPORT
POINT

AXIAL TOLERANCE

SUPPORT
POINT

RADIAL TOLERANCE

CHAPTER
39

Steering and
Suspension Service

This chapter discusses various steering and suspension troubles and relates them to possible causes. It also outlines the various servicing and overhauling procedures required on steering gears and suspension systems and discusses different front-alignment checks and adjustments.

§ 39-1. NEED FOR LOGICAL PROCEDURE If you are able to relate various steering and suspension complaints to the conditions that cause them, you are much better off than the fellow who seeks blindly to find what is causing the trouble. You will know what to check and correct to eliminate the trouble. You can save a great deal of time and effort when you know where to look.

The following articles tell you where to look when various complaints are made regarding the steering or suspension.

§ 39-2. TROUBLE DIAGNOSIS A variety of steering and suspension troubles will bring the driver to the mechanic, but it is rare that the driver will have a clear idea of what causes his trouble. He can detect an increase in steering difficulty, hard steering, or excessive play in the steering system. But he probably will not have a very good idea of what causes those conditions. The following articles describe various steering and suspension troubles and discuss their causes and corrections.

§ 39-3. EXCESSIVE PLAY IN SYSTEM Excessive play, or looseness, in the steering system means that there is excessive free movement of the steering wheel without corresponding movement of the front wheels. A small amount of steering-wheel play is desirable in order to provide easy steering. But when the play becomes excessive, it is considered objectionable by most drivers. Excessive play can be due to wear or improper adjustments in the steering linkage, to worn steering-knuckle parts, or to loose wheel bearings.

The tie rods and linkage may be checked for looseness by jacking up the front end of the car and then grasping both front wheels, pushing out on both at the same time and then pulling in on both at the same time (Fig. 39-1). Excessive relative movement between the two wheels means that the linkage connections are worn or out of adjustment.

Worn steering-knuckle parts and loose wheel bearings can be detected by jacking up the front end of the car and then grasping the wheel top and bottom and checking it for side play (Fig. 39-2). Try to see how much you can wobble the wheel. Excessive looseness indicates worn or loose parts either in the steering knuckle or in the wheel bearing. The bearing should be readjusted to see whether the looseness is in the bearing or in the knuckle.

A rough check for looseness in the steering gear can be made by watching the pitman arm while an assistant turns the steering wheel one

Fig. 39-1. Checking tie rods and linkage for looseness. *(Bear Manufacturing Company)*

Fig. 39-2. Checking for wear in the steering knuckle and wheel bearing. *(Bear Manufacturing Company)*

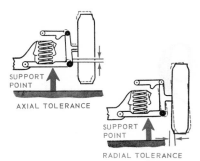

Fig. 39-3. To check ball joints for wear on suspension system with spring on lower arm, support wheel under arm, as shown.

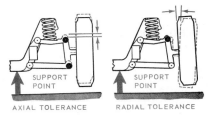

Fig. 39-4. To check ball joints for wear on suspension system with spring on upper arm, support front end on frame, as shown.

way and then the other with the front wheels on the floor. If, after reversal of steering-wheel rotation, considerable initial movement of the steering wheel is required to set the pitman arm in motion, then the steering gear is worn or in need of adjustment.

Ball joints can be checked for wear by supporting the wheel as shown in Figs. 39-3 or 39-4, according to the type. Axial play is checked by moving the wheel up and down. Radial play is measured by rocking the wheel back and forth.

§ 39-4. HARD STEERING If hard steering occurs just after the steering system has been worked on, the chances are that this is due to excessively tight adjustments in the steering gear or linkages. If hard steering develops at other times, it could be due to low or uneven tire pressure, to abnormal friction in the steering gear or linkage or at the ball joints (or kingpin), or to improper wheel or frame alignment.

On a car equipped with power steering, failure of the power-steering mechanism will cause the steering system to revert to straight mechanical operation and to require a considerably greater steering effort. In such a case, the power-steering

unit and the hydraulic pump should be checked.

The steering system can be checked for excessive friction by jacking up the front end of the car and then turning the steering wheel and observing the steering-system components to locate the source of excessive friction. Disconnect the linkage at the pitman arm. If this eliminates the frictional drag that makes it hard to turn the steering wheel, then the friction is either in the linkage itself or at the steering knuckles. If the friction is not eliminated when the linkage is disconnected at the pitman arm, then the steering gear is probably at fault.

If the trouble does not seem to be due to excessive friction in the steering system, the chances are that it is due to incorrect front-wheel alignment or to a misaligned frame or sagging springs. Excessive caster, especially, will cause hard steering.

§ 39-5. CAR WANDER Car wander is experienced as difficulty in keeping the car moving straight ahead; frequent steering-wheel movements are necessary to prevent the car from wandering from one side of the road to the other. An inexperienced driver may sometimes complain of car wander. This is because he tends to over-steer, so he has to keep moving the wheel back and forth unnecessarily to stay on his side of the road.

A considerable variety of conditions can cause car wander. Low or uneven tire pressure, binding or excessive play in the linkage or steering gear, or improper front-wheel alignment will cause car wander. Any condition that causes tightness in the steering system will keep the wheels from automatically seeking the straight-ahead position. The driver therefore has to correct the wheels constantly. This condition would probably also cause hard steering (§ 39–4). Looseness, or excessive play, in the steering system might also cause car wander; this would tend to allow the wheels to waver somewhat and permit the car to wander.

Excessively low caster, uneven caster, or a point of intersection too far above or below the road surface (from wrong camber angle) will tend to cause the wheels to swing away from straight-ahead so that the driver must steer continuously. Excessive toe-in will cause the same condition.

§ 39–6. CAR PULLS TO ONE SIDE (NORMAL DRIVING)

If the car persistently pulls to one side so that pressure must more or less constantly be applied to the steering wheel to maintain forward movement, the trouble could be due to any of the following: uneven tire pressure, uneven caster or camber, a tight wheel bearing, uneven springs, or improper wheel tracking (rear wheels not following in the tracks of the front wheels). Anything that would tend to make one wheel drag or toe in or toe out more than the other will make the car pull to that side.

§ 39–7. CAR PULLS TO ONE SIDE (DURING BRAKING)

The most likely cause of this condition is grabbing brakes. This could be due to the brake linings becoming soaked with oil or brake fluid, to brake shoes unevenly or improperly adjusted, to a brake backing plate loose or out of line, or to other reasons that would cause the brake at one wheel to apply harder than the brake at the corresponding wheel on the other side. The other conditions listed in § 39–6 could also cause pulling to one side during braking, since the condition, from whatever cause, tends to become more noticeable when the car is braked.

§ 39–8. FRONT-WHEEL SHIMMY (LOW SPEED)

Front-wheel shimmy and front-wheel tramp (§ 39–9) are sometimes confused. Low-speed shimmy is the rapid oscillation of the wheel on the ball joints. The wheel tries to turn in and out alternately. The action causes the front end of the car to shake from side to side. On the other hand, front-wheel tramp, or high-speed shimmy, is a tendency for the wheel and tire assembly to move up and down and, when the condition is severe, actually to leave the pavement. Even when the tire does not leave the pavement, tramp can be observed as a rapid flexing-unflexing action of the part of the tire in contact with the pavement. That is, the bottom of the tire first appears deflated (as the wheel moves down) and then inflated (as the wheel moves up).

Low-speed shimmy can result from low or uneven tire pressure, loose linkage, excessively soft springs, incorrect or uneven wheel camber, or irregularities in the tire treads.

§ 39–9. FRONT-WHEEL TRAMP

As explained in the previous article, front-wheel tramp is often called *high-speed shimmy*. This condition causes the front wheels to move up and down alternately. Two of the most common causes of front-wheel tramp are unbalanced wheels and wheels that have too much run-out. An unbalanced wheel is heavy at one part; as it rotates, the heavy part sets up a circulating outward thrust that tends to make the wheel hop up and down. A similar action occurs if the wheel has too much run-out. Run-out is the amount the wheel is out of line with the axle so that one part of the wheel "runs out," or moves to the side, more than other parts of the wheel. Defective shock absorbers, which fail to control natural spring oscillations, will also cause wheel tramp. Any of the causes described in the previous article may also cause wheel tramp. Following articles describe the servicing of the wheel and tire so that they can be restored to proper balance and alignment.

§ 39–10. STEERING KICKBACK

Steering shock, or kickback, becomes evident as sharp and rapid movements of the steering wheel when the front wheels encounter obstructions in the road. Normally, some kickback to the steering wheel will always occur. But when it becomes excessive, an investigation should be made. This condition could result from incorrect or uneven tire inflation, sagging springs, defective shock absorbers, or looseness in the linkage or steering gear. Any of these defects could permit road shock to carry back excessively to the steering wheel.

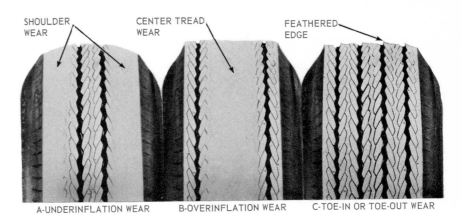

SHOULDER WEAR   CENTER TREAD WEAR   FEATHERED EDGE

A-UNDERINFLATION WEAR   B-OVERINFLATION WEAR   C-TOE-IN OR TOE-OUT WEAR

ONE SIDE OF TREAD WORN EXCESSIVELY   ROUNDED EDGE OF OUTSIDE SHOULDER   CUPPED

ROUGH SURFACE FROM ABRASION

D-SIDE OR CAMBER WEAR   E-CORNERING WEAR   F-MULTI-PROBLEM WEAR

Fig. 39-5. Patterns of abnormal tire tread wear. *(Buick Motor Division of General Motors Corporation)*

§ 39–11. TIRES SQUEAL ON TURNS If the tires skid or squeal on turns, this may be due to excessive speeds on the turns. If this is not the cause, then it is probably due to low or uneven tire pressure or to misalignment of the front wheels (particularly camber and toe-in).

§ 39–12. ABNORMAL TIRE WEAR Various types of abnormal tire wear can be experienced. The type of tire wear found is often a good indication of a definite defect in the suspension or steering system or of improper operation or abuse. For example, if the tire is operated with insufficient air pressure (underinflated), the sides will bulge over and the center of the tread will be lifted clear of the road. The sides of the tread will take all the wear, the center being barely worn (Fig. 39–5). Uneven tread wear shortens tire life. But even more damaging is the excessive flexing of the tire side walls that takes place as the underinflated tire rolls on the pavement. The repeated flexing causes the fabric in the side walls to crack or break and the plies to separate (Fig. 39–6). Naturally, this serious-

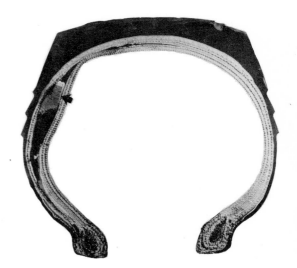

Fig. 39-6. Separation of plies in the side wall of a tire resulting from operation of the tire in an underinflated condition. A piece of wood (arrowed) has been inserted between the plies to show clearly where the separation has occurred.

ly weakens the side walls and may soon lead to complete tire failure. Aside from all this, the tire that is underinflated is unprotected against rim bruises. That is, if the tire should strike a rut or stone on the curb a little too hard, the tire will flex so much under the blow that it will actually be pinched on the rim. This breaks plies and leads to early tire failure.

Overinflation causes the tire to ride on the center of its tread so that only the center of the tread wears (Fig. 39–5). This uneven tread wear shortens tire life. But more damaging than this is the fact that the overinflated tire does not have normal "give" when it meets a rut or bump in the road. Instead of "giving" normally, the tire fabric takes the major shock of the encounter. This may cause the fabric to crack or break and the tire to fail.

Excessive camber of the wheel causes one side of the tire tread to wear more rapidly than the other, as shown in Fig. 39–5.

Excessive toe-in or toe-out on turns causes the tire to be dragged sideways while it is moving forward. The tire on a front wheel that toes in 1 inch from straight ahead will be dragged sideways about 150 feet every mile. This sideward drag scrapes off rubber, as shown in Fig. 39–5. One characteristic of this type of wear is the featheredges of rubber that appear on one side of the tread design. If both front tires show this type of wear, the front system is misaligned. But if only one tire shows this type of wear (and if both front tires have been on the car for some time), then this indicates a bent steering arm. This causes one wheel to toe in more than the other.

Cornering wear (Fig. 39–5), caused by taking curves at excessively high speeds, can be mistaken for camber wear or toe-in or toe-out wear. Cornering wear is due to centrifugal force acting on the car and causing the tires to roll as well as skid on the road. This produces a diagonal type of wear which rounds the outside shoulder. In severe cornering wear, fins or sharp edges will be found along the inner edges of the tire treads. There is no adjustment that can be made to correct the steering system for this type of wear. The only preventive is for drivers to slow down on curves.

Uneven tire wear, such as shown in Fig. 39–5, where the tread is unevenly or spottily worn, can result from a number of mechanical conditions. These include misaligned wheels, unequally or improperly adjusted brakes, unbalanced wheels, and incorrect linkage adjustments.

High-speed operation causes much more rapid tire wear because of the high temperature, greater amount of scuffing, and rapid flexing to which the tires are subjected. The chart (Fig. 39–7) shows how tire wear increases with car speed. According to the chart, tires wear more than three times faster at 70 mph (miles per hour) than they do at 30 mph. More careful, slower driving and correct tire inflation will increase tire life greatly.

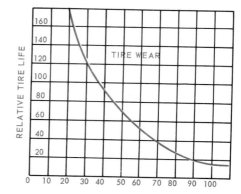

Fig. 39–7. How tire wear increases with speed.

§ **39–13. HARD OR ROUGH RIDE** A hard or rough ride could be due to excessive tire pressure, improperly operating shock absorbers, or excessive friction in the spring suspension. Make correction by lubricating springs, shackles, and bushings (on types where lubrication is specified) and by loosening the shock-absorber arm linkages, shackle bolts, and U bolts. Then retighten the U bolts, shackle bolts, and shock-absorber linkages in that order. This procedure permits realignment of parts that have slipped to cause excessive friction.

Shock-absorber action on cars giving a hard or rough ride may be roughly checked by bouncing each corner of the car in turn. This is done by seizing the bumper, pulling up and pushing down on it several times so that the car bounces, and then releasing the bumper.* If the shock absorber is operating normally, the car will come to rest immediately. If the car continues to bounce after the bumper is released, the shock absorber is probably defective. A more accurate check can

---

* Some direct-acting shock absorbers, as, for instance, those used on Plymouth, cannot be tested in this way, since they are valved to permit slow spring oscillations in the interest of smoother riding.

be made by disconnecting the shock-absorber linkage so that the shock absorber can be operated. Then note the resistance to shock-absorber movement. If the resistance is small or is not uniform through the full stroke or if the movement is very stiff, the shock absorber will require service. As a rule, shock absorbers are serviced by complete replacement. Special tools are required for shock-absorber repair.

§ 39-14. **SWAY ON TURNS** Sway of the car body on turns or on rough roads may be due to a loose stabilizer bar or shaft. The attachments of such bars or shafts to the frame, axle housing, or suspension arms should be checked. Weak or sagging springs could also cause excessive sway. If the shock absorbers are ineffective, they may permit excessive spring movement which could cause strong body pitching and sway, particularly on rough roads. If the caster is excessively positive, it will cause the car to roll out, or lean out, on turns. This requires front-wheel realignment.

§ 39-15. **SPRING BREAKAGE** Breakage of leaf springs can result from excessive overloading; loose U bolts, which cause breakage near the center bolt; loose center bolt, which causes breakage at the center-bolt holes; an improperly operating shock absorber, which causes breakage of the master leaf; or tight spring shackle, which causes breakage of the master leaf near or at the spring eye. Determining the point at which breakage has occurred will indicate the cause.

§ 39-16. **SAGGING SPRINGS** Springs will sag from overloading or if they have become weak (as, for example, from habitual overloading). Loss of the shim from the coil-spring seat on the coil-spring suspension (from failure to return it during overhaul) will cause the spring to seem shorter and to sag. Not all coil springs require or use shims. Defective shock absorbers may tend to restrict spring action and thus make them appear to sag more than normal.

§ 39-17. **NOISES** Noises produced by spring or shock-absorber difficulties will usually be either rattles or squeaks. Rattling noises can be produced by looseness of such parts as spring U bolts, metal spring covers, rebound clips, spring shackles, or shock-absorber linkages or springs. These can generally be located by a careful examination of the various suspension parts. Spring squeaks

can result from lack of lubrication in the spring shackles or at spring bushings (on the type requiring lubrication) or in the spring itself (leaf springs requiring lubrication). Shock-absorber squeak could result from tight or dry bushings. Steering-linkage rattles may develop if linkage components become loose. Under exceptional circumstances, squeaks during turns could develop owing to lack of lubrication in steering-linkage joints or bearings. This would, of course, also produce hard steering.

§ 39-18. **SERVICING STEERING LINKAGES AND SUSPENSIONS** Steering and suspension service includes removal, replacement, and adjustment of tie rods; removal and replacement of other linkage parts, such as the steering idler and the upper and lower control arms; removal and replacement of springs; removal and replacement of wheel hub and drum; and so on. In addition, the steering gear may require adjustment or removal, overhaul, and reinstallation. Also, the front wheels may require alignment (adjustment of caster, camber, toe-in, and so on).

For service on any of these components, refer to the shop manual on the model and make of car being worked on. Discussions of front-end alignment, wheel balance, and steering-gear adjustments and service follow.

§ 39-19. **FRONT-END ALIGNMENT** A variety of alignment equipment is in use. The purpose of this equipment is to measure the caster, camber,

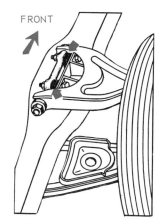

Fig. 39-8. Location of caster and camber adjusting shims (indicated by heavy arrows). Note that the shims and upper control-arm shaft are *inside* the frame bracket. (*Bear Manufacturing Company*)

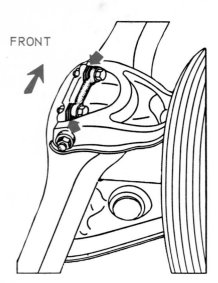

FRONT

Fig. 39-9. Location of caster and camber adjusting shims (indicated by heavy arrows). Note that the shims and upper control-arm shaft are outside the frame bracket. *(Bear Manufacturing Company)*

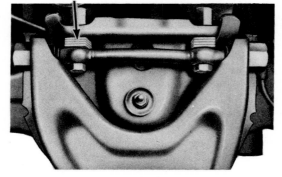

CASTER ADJUSTMENT — REMOVE OR INSTALL SHIMS AT EITHER FRONT OR REAR BOLT

CAMBER ADJUSTMENT — REMOVE OR INSTALL EQUAL SHIM THICKNESS AT BOTH BOLTS

ADJUSTING SHIM STACK

MAXIMUM DIFFERENCE BETWEEN SHIM STACK THICKNESS—1/8 INCH
MAXIMUM THICKNESS AT EACH SHIM STACK—5/8 INCH

Fig. 39-10. Caster and camber shim location. *(Ford Motor Company)*

steering-axis inclination, toe-in, and toe-out on turns. Adjustment procedures to correct these various elements vary with different cars.

Caster and camber are adjusted on many cars by installing or removing shims at the upper control-arm shafts. These shims are located in two places. Figure 39-8 shows their location on many General Motors cars (Buick, Chevrolet, Pontiac, etc.). Figure 39-9 shows their location on many Ford vehicles. When the shims and shafts are inside the frame bracket (Fig. 39-8), adding shims will move the upper control arm inward and thus reduce positive camber. If shims are added at one of the attachment bolts and removed from the other, this will shift the outer end of the upper control arm one way or the other, thus increasing or decreasing caster. Figure 39-10 shows the location of the shims on a car.

Toe-in is changed by turning the adjuster sleeves in the steering linkage (see Fig. 38-14).

§ 39-20. PRELIMINARY CHECKS
Before front alignment is checked, the following items must be checked and corrected if necessary:

1. Tire inflation
2. Wheel bearings
3. Wheel run-out
4. Ball joints
5. Steering linkages
6. Wheel balance
7. Shock absorbers
8. Tracking

If tires are incorrectly inflated, or if wheel bearings, ball joints, or steering linkages are worn or out of adjustment, then alignment of the wheels cannot be accurately checked. Likewise, if the wheel is bent or out of balance, alignment adjustments would mean little; as soon as the car went out on the highway, the bent or out-of-balance conditions would cause steering trouble. If the shock absorbers are faulty, they may cause steering trouble. Also, failure to track (failure of rear wheels to follow in the tracks of the front wheels) because of a bent frame or other parts would cause steering trouble that could not be corrected by alignment adjustments.

§ 39-21. STEERING-GEAR SERVICE
Manual steering gears have two basic adjustments, one for taking up the worm-gear and steering-shaft end play and the other for removing backlash between the worm and sector (or roller or lever studs). In addition, some designs have a means of adjusting the sector-shaft (pitman-arm-shaft) end play. In addition, on power-steering units, various other adjustments may be required. Always follow the instructions in the applicable shop manual to adjust or overhaul a steering gear.

Review Questions

1. What could cause excessive play in the steering system?
2. What could cause hard steering?
3. What could cause car wander?
4. What could cause the car to pull to one side during normal driving?
5. What could cause the car to pull to one side during braking?
6. What could cause front-wheel shimmy at low speeds?
7. What could cause front-wheel tramp (high-speed shimmy)?
8. What could produce steering kickback?
9. What causes tires to squeal on turns?
10. Describe various types of abnormal tire wear, and explain what could cause each.
11. What could cause a hard ride?
12. What could cause the car to sway on turns?
13. What are causes of spring breakage?
14. What causes springs to sag?
15. Explain how to check the steering linkage for looseness.
16. Explain how to check front-wheel bearings for wear or improper adjustment.
17. Explain how to check the steering system for excessive friction.
18. Describe a method of checking shock-absorber action.
19. Describe two methods of making caster adjustments.
20. What are the preliminary checks to be made before front alignment is checked?

Study Questions

1. Make a list of the various steering and suspension troubles and their causes and corrections.
2. Refer to a manufacturer's shop manual, and write a service story on steering-linkage service, including removal, replacement, and adjustment.
3. Refer to a manufacturer's shop manual, and write a service story on aligning a front end, including preliminary checks such as balancing wheels, adjusting front-wheel bearings, and so on.
4. Refer to a manufacturer's shop manual, and write a service story on a manual steering gear, including removal, disassembly, reassembly, replacement, and adjustment.
5. Write a similar service story on a power-steering unit.

40

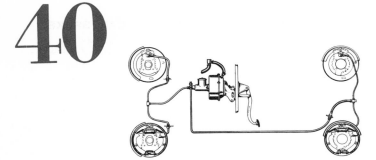

This chapter describes the construction and operation of the various types of brakes used on automobiles. Since most automotive brakes in use today are hydraulically actuated, the chapter contains a review of hydraulic principles and explains their appli- cation to brakes. Also, since brakes operate by friction, some of the principles of friction are reviewed. Brakes have already been discussed briefly (in § 1–13). Note that there are two basic types of brakes, drum and disk. The drum type uses curved shoes that fit the curvature of the drums. The disk type uses flat shoes or pads that fit the flat surfaces of the disks.

Automotive Brakes

§ 40–1. FRICTION As already noted (§ 4–6), friction is the resistance to motion between two objects in contact with each other. Three types of friction were discussed in § 4–6: dry, greasy, and viscous. Generally, we are concerned only with dry friction in connection with brakes (but sometimes we have greasy friction if the brake linings are greasy or oil-soaked). Friction varies according to the pressure applied between the sliding surfaces, the roughness of the surfaces, and the material of which the surfaces are made. Suppose, for example, that a platform and its load weigh 100 pounds and that it takes 50 pounds of

pull to move it along the floor (Fig. 40–1). If you reduced the load so that the platform and load weighed only 10 pounds, you would find that it required only 5 pounds pull to move it along the floor. *Friction varies with the load.*

If you went over the floor and the sliding part of the platform with sandpaper and smoothed them off, you would find that it would require less pull to move the platform on the floor. *Friction varies with the roughness of the surfaces.*

Friction also varies with the type of material. For example, if you dragged a 100-pound bale of rubber across a concrete floor, you might find that

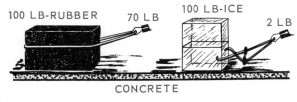

Fig. 40–1. Friction varies with the load applied between the sliding surfaces. *(Pontiac Motor Division of General Motors Corporation)*

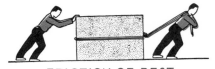

FRICTION OF REST

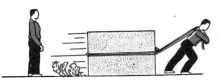

FRICTION OF MOTION

Fig. 40–3. Friction of rest is greater than the friction of motion. In the example shown, it takes two men to over- come the friction of rest, but only one to overcome the friction of motion (after object starts moving). *(Pontiac Motor Division of General Motors Corporation)*

Fig. 40–2. Friction varies with the type of material. *(Pontiac Motor Division of General Motors Corporation)*

it required a pull of 70 pounds (Fig. 40–2). But to drag a 100-pound cake of ice across the same floor might require a pull of only 2 pounds.

§ 40–2. FRICTION OF REST AND MOTION

It requires more force to put an object into motion than it does to keep it in motion (Fig. 40–3). In the example shown, it takes two men to get the object started, but once it is started, only one man can keep it moving. Thus, the friction of an object at rest is greater than the friction of an object in motion.

Engineers do not usually refer to these two kinds of friction as friction of rest and friction of motion. Instead, they call them *static friction* and *kinetic friction*. The word "static" means at rest. The word "kinetic" means in motion, or moving.

Thus, static friction is friction of rest, and kinetic friction is friction of motion.

§ 40–3. FRICTION IN THE CAR BRAKES

We have mentioned that friction is used in the car braking system. The friction between the brake drums or disks and brake shoes slows or stops the car. This friction slows the rotation of the wheels, and then friction between the tires and road slows the motion of the car. Note that it is the friction between the tires and the road that results in the stopping of the car. That being the case, would the car stop more quickly if the wheels were locked (so that the tires skidded on the road)? The answer is that the car would not. If the brakes are applied so hard that the wheels lock, then the friction between the tires and road is kinetic

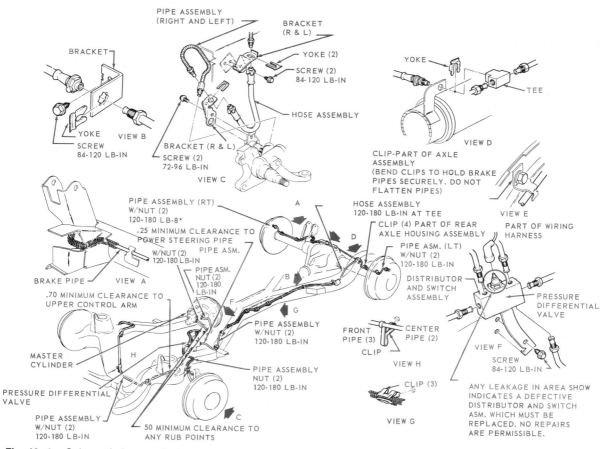

Fig. 40–4. Schematic layout of a hydraulic-brake system. This is one of several layouts shown in a recent shop manual. The illustration supplies details on how all components of the system are arranged. *(Buick Motor Division of General Motors Corporation)*

507

friction (friction of motion as the tires skid on the road). When the brakes are applied a little less hard, so that the wheels are permitted to continue rotating, then it is static friction that works between the tires and road. The tire surface is not skidding on the road but is rolling on it. Since this produces static friction between the road and tires, there is considerably greater braking effect. The car will stop more quickly if the brakes are applied just hard enough to get maximum static friction between the tires and road. If the brakes are applied harder than this, then the wheels will lock, the tires will skid, or slide, and the lesser kinetic friction will result. See § 40–12 on antiskid devices.

§ 40–4. BRAKE ACTION Figure 40–4 shows, schematically, a typical hydraulic braking system. The system includes two essentials, the master cylinder with brake pedal and the wheel brake mechanism, together with the connecting tubing, or brake lines, and the supporting arrangements.

In operation, movement of the brake pedal forces a piston to move in the master cylinder. This applies pressure to liquid ahead of the piston, forcing the liquid, under pressure, through the brake lines to the wheel cylinders (Fig. 40–5). In the drum type of brake, each wheel cylinder has two pistons, as shown. Each piston is linked to one of the brake shoes by an actuating pin (or the end of the shoe rests on the piston). Thus, when the liquid is forced into the wheel cylinders, the two wheel-cylinder pistons are pushed outward. This outward movement forces the brake

shoes outward and into contact with the rotating brake drum.

The brake shoes are lined with a tough asbestos material that can withstand the heat and dragging effect imposed when they are forced against the disk or drum. During hard braking, the shoe may be pressed against the disk or drum with a pressure as great as 1,000 pounds. Since friction increases as the load (pressure) increases, this produces a strong frictional drag on the brake drum or disk and a strong braking effect on the wheel.

A great deal of heat is produced, also, by the frictional effect between the brake shoes and drum. When you rub your hands together vigorously, they become warm. In like manner, when the drum rubs against the shoe, the drum and shoe get warm. In fact, under extreme braking conditions, temperatures may reach 500°F. Some of this heat goes through the brake linings to the shoes and backing plate, where it is radiated to the surrounding air. But most of it is absorbed by the brake disk or drum. Some brake drums have cooling fins to provide additional radiating surface for getting rid of the heat more quickly. Disks have hollow spaces between the two sides. There are fins in these areas to help get rid of the heat. Excessive temperatures are not good for brakes, since they may char the brake linings. Also, with the linings and drums hot, less effective braking action results. This is the reason that brakes "fade" when they are used continuously for relatively long periods, as, for instance, in coming down a mountain or a long hill.

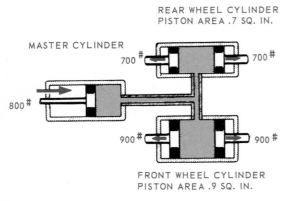

REAR WHEEL CYLINDER
PISTON AREA .7 SQ. IN.

MASTER CYLINDER

700 #   700 #

800 #

900 #   900 #

FRONT WHEEL CYLINDER
PISTON AREA .9 SQ. IN.

Fig. 40–5. As the brake pedal is moved, the piston in the master cylinder applies pressure to the liquid, forcing it, under pressure, into the wheel cylinders. Shown here is the drum type of brake system. *(Pontiac Motor Division of General Motors Corporation)*

METALLIC PADS ON BRAKE SHOES

Fig. 40–6. Details of a brake assembly using metallic pads instead of brake lining. *(Chevrolet Motor Division of General Motors Corporation)*

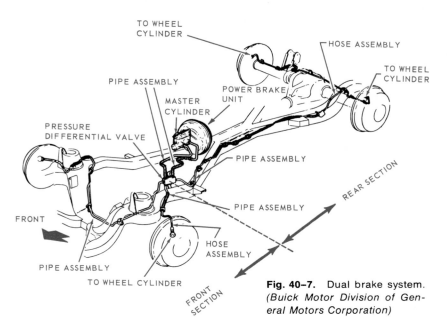

Fig. 40–7. Dual brake system. *(Buick Motor Division of General Motors Corporation)*

Some special-performance vehicles, such as racing cars, are equipped with metallic brakes. Instead of linings of asbestos material, these brakes have a series of metallic pads attached to the brake shoes (Fig. 40–6). These brakes can withstand more severe braking and higher temperatures and have less tendency to fade.

The pistons are usually larger at the front wheels because, when the brakes are applied, the forward momentum of the car throws more of the weight on the front wheels. A stronger braking effort at the front wheels is therefore necessary to achieve balanced braking effort.

§ 40–5. DUAL BRAKE SYSTEM In older-model cars, the master cylinder contained only one piston and its movement forced brake fluid to all four wheel cylinders. In recent years, however, the

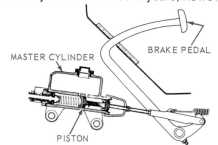

Fig. 40–8. Relationship between the brake pedal and the master cylinder. *(Pontiac Motor Division of General Motors Corporation)*

hydraulic system has been split into two sections, a front section and a rear section (Fig. 40–7). With this arrangement, if one section fails due to damage or leakage, the other section will still provide braking. This system also includes a warning light that comes on when one section has failed.

§ 40–6. MASTER CYLINDER In the older braking system, the master cylinder had but one piston. The dual braking system has a master cylinder with two pistons, set in tandem. Figures 40–8 and 40–9 show the two types. The operation is similar in both systems, except that in the dual system there are two separate sections functioning semi-independently. The master-cylinder pistons are linked to the brake pedal through a lever arrangement that provides a considerable mechanical advantage. For example, in the arrangement shown in Fig. 40–8, a push of 100 pounds on the brake pedal will produce a push of about 750 pounds at the piston (as brakes are first applied).

As the piston moves in the master cylinder, it moves past the compensating port (see Fig. 40–10). This traps the brake fluid in the cylinder that is ahead of the piston. Pressure rises rapidly, and the fluid is forced through the brake lines to the wheel cylinders.

§ 40–7. WHEEL CYLINDERS Figures 40–10 and 40–11 show the construction of a wheel cylinder for the drum-type brake. Hydraulic pressure ap-

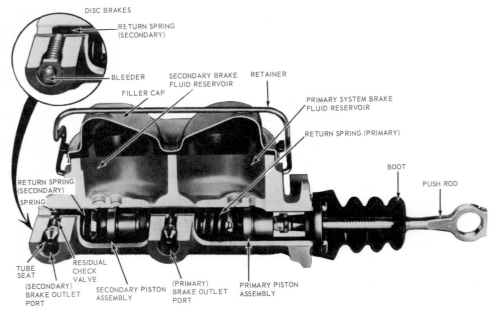

Fig. 40-9. Cutaway view of a dual master cylinder. (Ford Division of Ford Motor Company)

plied between the two piston cups forces the pistons out. Thus, the brake-shoe actuating pins force the brake shoes into contact with the brake drums. The piston cups are so formed that the hydraulic pressure forces them tightly against the cylinder wall of the wheel cylinder. This produces a good sealing action that holds the fluid in the cylinder.

§ 40-8. RETURN STROKE On the return stroke, spring tension on the brake linkage and spring pressure against the master-cylinder piston force

the piston to move back in its cylinder. Fluid now flows from the wheel cylinders to the master cylinder, as shown in Fig. 40-12. The tension of the brake-shoe springs forces the brake shoes away from the brake drums and thus pushes the wheel cylinder pistons inward. Fluid is thus returned from the wheel cylinders to the master cylinder, as shown by the arrows. However, in the system shown, some pressure is trapped in the lines by the check valve at the end of the master cylinder (see Fig. 40-10). As the pressure drops, the check

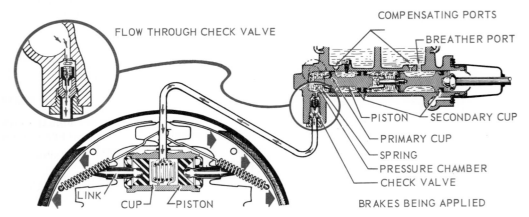

Fig. 40-10. Conditions in drum-type brake system with brakes applied. Brake fluid flows from master cylinder to the wheel cylinder, as shown, causing the wheel-cylinder pistons to move outward and thereby apply the brakes. (Buick Motor Division of General Motors Corporation)

510

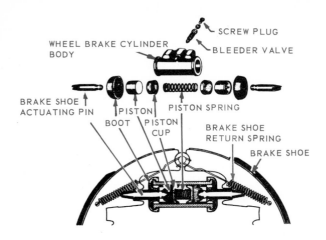

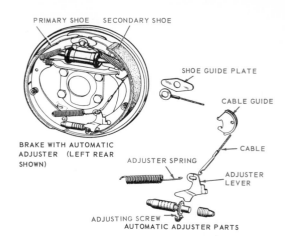

Fig. 40–11. Disassembled and sectional views of a wheel cylinder for a drum-type brake. *(Pontiac Motor Division of General Motors Corporation)*

Fig. 40–13. Brake assembly of drum type with automatic self-adjuster and adjuster parts disassembled. *(Bendix-Westinghouse Automotive Air Brake Company)*

valve closes, trapping a few pounds of pressure in the lines and wheel cylinders. This pressure has the purpose of keeping the wheel cylinders from leaking and also of reducing the chances of air leaking into the system.

§ 40–9. SELF-ADJUSTING BRAKES (DRUM TYPE)
Most modern automotive brakes have a self-adjusting feature that automatically adjusts the brakes when they need it as a result of brake-lining wear. Figures 40–13 and 40–14 illustrate typical arrangements. The adjustment takes place only when the car is moving backward and the brakes are applied. When this happens, an adjustment will be made if the brake linings have worn enough to make adjustment necessary.

As the brakes are applied when the car is moving backward, friction between the primary shoe and brake drum forces the primary shoe against the anchor pin. Then hydraulic pressure from the wheel cylinder forces the upper end of the secondary shoe away from the anchor pin and downward. This causes the adjustment lever to pivot on the secondary shoe so that the lower end of the lever is forced against the sprocket on the adjustment screw. If the brake linings have worn enough, then the adjustment screw will be turned a full tooth. This spreads the lower ends of the brake shoes a few thousandths of an inch, or enough to compensate for the lining wear. On some cars, the adjustment feature will operate with the car moving forward when the brakes are applied.

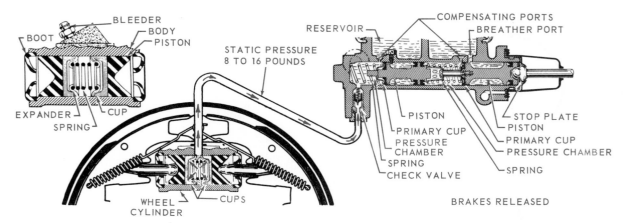

Fig. 40–12. Conditions in drum-type brake system when brakes are released. Brake fluid flows to the master cylinder, as shown. *(Buick Motor Division of General Motors Corporation)*

511

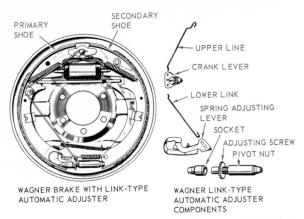

PRIMARY SHOE

SECONDARY SHOE

UPPER LINE

CRANK LEVER

LOWER LINK

SPRING ADJUSTING LEVER

SOCKET

ADJUSTING SCREW

PIVOT NUT

WAGNER BRAKE WITH LINK-TYPE AUTOMATIC ADJUSTER

WAGNER LINK-TYPE AUTOMATIC ADJUSTER COMPONENTS

Fig. 40-14. Wagner drum-type brake assembly (at left rear wheel) with link-type automatic self-adjuster, and adjuster components. *(Bendix-Westinghouse Automotive Air Brake Company)*

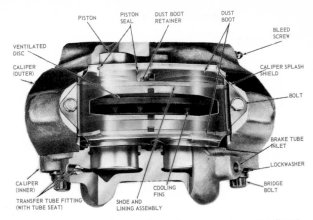

PISTON

PISTON SEAL

DUST BOOT RETAINER

DUST BOOT

BLEED SCREW

VENTILATED DISC

CALIPER (OUTER)

CALIPER SPLASH SHIELD

BOLT

BRAKE TUBE INLET

LOCKWASHER

BRIDGE BOLT

CALIPER (INNER)

TRANSFER TUBE FITTING (WITH TUBE SEAT)

SHOE AND LINING ASSEMBLY

COOLING FINS

Fig. 40-16. Top view partly cut away to show the fixed-caliper assembly of a disk brake on each side of the disk. *(Chrysler-Plymouth Division of Chrysler Motors Corporation)*

§ 40-10. DISK BRAKES The disk, or caliper, brake has a metal disk instead of a drum and a pair of pads, or flat shoes, instead of the curved shoes used with the drum brakes. There are two general types, fixed-caliper and floating-caliper. In the fixed-caliper type (Figs. 40-15 and 40-16), the two flat shoes are located on each side of the disk. In operation (see Fig. 40-17), the shoes are forced against the disk by hydraulic pressure from the master cylinder. The shoes in effect grip the disk, just as you would squeeze a piece of paper between your thumb and first finger as you picked it up. The friction between the shoes and revolving disk then provides the braking action.

In the floating-caliper type of disk brake (Figs. 40-18 and 40-19), the caliper can pivot, or swing in or out. It requires only one piston in contrast to the type previously described, which uses four

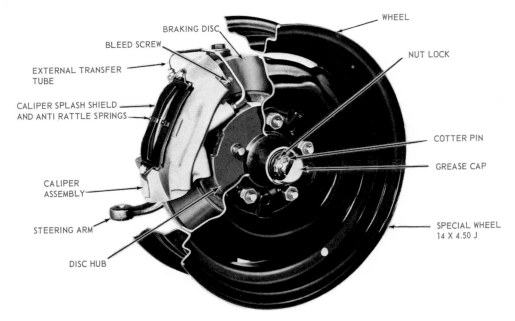

BRAKING DISC

WHEEL

BLEED SCREW

NUT LOCK

EXTERNAL TRANSFER TUBE

CALIPER SPLASH SHIELD AND ANTI RATTLE SPRINGS

COTTER PIN

GREASE CAP

CALIPER ASSEMBLY

SPECIAL WHEEL 14 X 4.50 J

STEERING ARM

DISC HUB

Fig. 40-15. Disk brake assembly (Kelsey-Hayes), partly cut away so that the location of the caliper assembly on the disk can be seen. *(Chrysler-Plymouth Division of Chrysler Motors Corporation)*

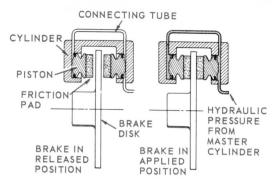

Fig. 40-17. Sectional views showing how hydraulic pressure forces friction pads inward against the brake disk to produce braking action. *(Studebaker Corporation)*

Fig. 40-18. Disk brake assembly of the floating-caliper type. *(Ford Division of Ford Motor Company)*

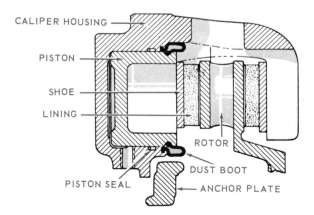

Fig. 40-19. Sectional view of floating-caliper type of disk brake. *(Ford Division of Ford Motor Company)*

pistons. In operation, the floating-caliper disk brake is actuated by hydraulic pressure back of the piston. This forces the shoe against the disk. At the same time, the pressure of the shoe against the disk causes the caliper to pivot inward so that the fixed brake shoe on the opposite side is also brought into contact with the other side of the disk. Now, the braking action is the same as with the other type of disk brake.

Disk-brake systems include a metering, or proportioning, valve. This valve, in some systems, prevents front brake application until pressure of 100 to 135 pounds per square inch has built up in the hydraulic system. This assures that the rear brakes will apply at the same time as the front brakes. The proportioning type of valve, used on some Chrysler-built automobiles, regulates the hydraulic pressure applied at the rear-wheel brakes. This limits rear-brake action when high pressures are required at the front brakes. Premature rear-wheel skid is thus prevented.

§ 40-11. WARNING LIGHT In the dual braking system, a pressure differential valve is used to actuate a switch for the warning light. The valve (Fig. 40-20) has a piston that is centered when both the front and the rear brakes are operating normally. However, if one section fails, then there will be low pressure on one side of the piston. The high pressure, from the normally functioning section, will move the piston and cause it to push the switch plunger upward (Fig. 40-21). This closes contacts which turn on the warning light on the instrument panel. The driver is thus warned that either the rear-wheel or front-wheel brakes are failing.

§ 40-12. ANTISKID DEVICES As mentioned earlier (§ 40-3), the best braking takes place when the wheels are still revolving. If the brakes lock the wheels so that the tires skid, then kinetic friction results and braking is much less effective. To prevent skidding and thus provide maximum effective braking, several devices have been proposed. The most common provide skid control of the rear wheels only. Others provide control at all four wheels. What is meant by "control" is this: As long as the wheels are rotating, the antiskid device permits normal application of the brakes. But if the brakes are applied so hard that the wheels tend to stop turning and thus a skid starts to develop, the device comes into operation and partly releases the brakes so that the wheels continue to rotate.

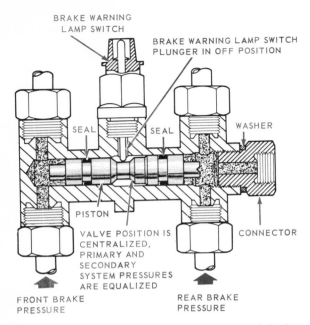

Fig. 40-20. Sectional view of pressure differential valve with both rear and front brake systems operating normally. *(Ford Division of Ford Motor Company)*

BRAKE WARNING LAMP SWITCH

BRAKE WARNING LAMP SWITCH PLUNGER IN OFF POSITION

SEAL

SEAL

WASHER

PISTON

VALVE POSITION IS CENTRALIZED, PRIMARY AND SECONDARY SYSTEM PRESSURES ARE EQUALIZED

CONNECTOR

FRONT BRAKE PRESSURE

REAR BRAKE PRESSURE

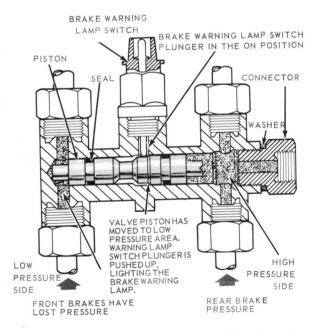

Fig. 40-21. Sectional view of pressure differential valve showing conditions when front brake system has failed. *(Ford Division of Ford Motor Company)*

BRAKE WARNING LAMP SWITCH

BRAKE WARNING LAMP SWITCH PLUNGER IN THE ON POSITION

PISTON

SEAL

CONNECTOR

WASHER

VALVE PISTON HAS MOVED TO LOW PRESSURE AREA. WARNING LAMP SWITCH PLUNGER IS PUSHED UP, LIGHTING THE BRAKE WARNING LAMP.

LOW PRESSURE SIDE

HIGH PRESSURE SIDE

FRONT BRAKES HAVE LOST PRESSURE

REAR BRAKE PRESSURE

However, braking continues. But it is held to just below the point where a skid would start. The result is maximum braking effect.

One antiskid control system, called the Sure-Track (Fig. 40-22) uses mechanically driven electromagnetic sensors at the two rear wheels. It also includes an electronic control module, mounted under the glove compartment, and a vacuum-powered actuator to modulate hydraulic brake pressure to the rear wheels. The wheel sensors consist of steel rings having teeth on their outer diameters. These are pressed onto the axle shafts, just outside the wheel bearings. The teeth rotate past corresponding teeth on the inside diameter of stationary, ring-shaped, permanent magnets, and coils of wire are mounted on the bearing retainers. These coils of wire are connected to the electronic control module.

As the wheels rotate, the rotating teeth on the axle rings produce alternating current in the wire coils. This is because the teeth change the shape of the magnetic fields from the permanent magnets. Thus, magnetic lines of force are cutting through the coils of wire, producing the alternating current. This alternating current is carried to the control module. As long as the wheels are rotating, normal braking can take place. But if the brakes are applied so hard that a skid tends to start, the sudden deceleration of the rear wheels causes a sudden change in the frequency of the alternating current going to the control module. The control module acts on this information and causes the actuator to cut off some hydraulic brake pressure to the rear wheels. This eases up somewhat on the braking so that the wheels do not skid. During hard braking, therefore, just enough hydraulic pressure is released to the rear-wheel braking to permit maximum braking without skidding.

§ 40-13. BRAKE FLUID The liquid used in the hydraulic braking system is called *brake fluid.* Brake fluid must have very definite characteristics. It must be chemically inert. It must be little affected by high or low temperatures. It must provide lubrication for the master-cylinder and wheel-cylinder pistons. And it must not attack the metallic and rubber parts in the braking system. For these reasons, the brake fluid recommended by the car manufacturer must always be used when the addition of brake fluid becomes necessary.

● CAUTION: Mineral oil must never be put into the brake system. Mineral oil will cause the

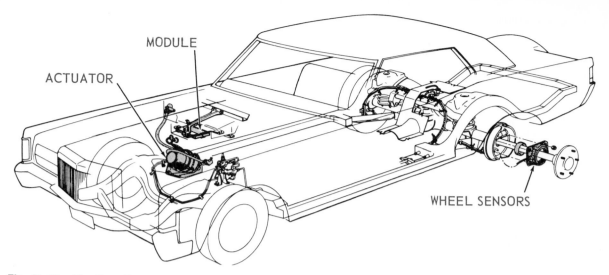

Fig. 40-22. The Sure-Track antiskid components. *(Ford Motor Company)*

rubber parts in the system, including the piston cups, to swell and disintegrate. This will, of course, cause faulty braking action and possibly complete brake failure. Nothing except the fluid recommended by the manufacturer must be put into the hydraulic brake system.

§ **40-14. BRAKE LINES** Steel pipe is used between the master cylinder and the frame connections and between the rear-axle T fitting and the rear-wheel cylinders. Flexible hose connects the brake pipe to the front-wheel cylinders and to the rear-axle fitting. These various hoses and pipes can be seen in Fig. 40-4. If a section of pipe or a hose becomes damaged, be sure to replace it with the proper pipe or hose as specified by the manufacturer. Since these lines are required to withstand considerable pressure, they are special. Ordinary copper tubing, for example, would not be satisfactory.

§ **40-15. HAND BRAKES** Hand, or parking, brakes are operated by a lever, pedal, or pull in the driving compartment. The lever, pedal, or pull is connected by linkage and cables to the rear-wheel brake shoes or to a separate brake on the transmission shaft. Figure 40-23 illustrates a parking brake using the rear-wheel brake shoes. As the hand lever is pulled, the brake shoes are forced into contact with the brake drum.

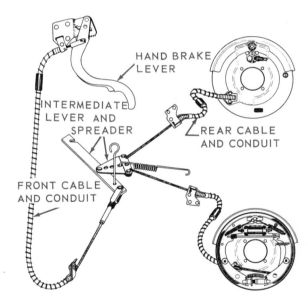

Fig. 40-23. Schematic layout of a parking-brake system. Operation of the hand-brake lever causes the intermediate lever to pivot forward. This pulls on the two rear cables so that the rear brakes are mechanically applied. *(Pontiac Motor Division of General Motors Corporation)*

§ **40-16. POWER BRAKES** For hard braking and fast stops, considerable pressure must be exerted on the brake pedal with the braking system described above. Also, the heavier the vehicle, the greater the braking effort required. For many years,

515

buses and trucks have used special equipment that assists the driver to brake the vehicle. This equipment may use either compressed air or vacuum. When the driver applies the brake, the compressed air or vacuum then supplies most of the effort required for braking. There is another system that uses an electrical means of braking.

In recent years, passenger cars have been supplied with vacuum-assisted braking systems called *power brakes*. Essentially, they all operate in a similar manner. When the brake pedal is moved to apply the brakes, a valving arrangement is actuated. The valves admit atmospheric pressure on one side of a piston or diaphragm and apply vacuum to the other side. The piston or diaphragm then moves toward the vacuum side; this movement supplies most of the hydraulic pressure, through the brake fluid, to the wheel cylinders.

§ 40-17. ATMOSPHERIC PRESSURE AND VACUUM
If we arranged a simple cylinder and piston as shown in Fig. 40-24 and then applied atmospheric pressure to one side and vacuum to the other, the piston would move toward the vacuum side, as shown. It is this movement that is utilized in power brakes. The vacuum is supplied by the automobile engine intake manifold. The vacuum side of the power-brake cylinder is connected to the intake manifold so that it can utilize intake-manifold vacuum.

If we add a hydraulic device to the cylinder and piston of Fig. 40-24 as shown in Fig. 40-25, we can utilize the push on the piston to produce hydraulic pressure. All the pressure on the piston is carried through the piston rod and into the hydraulic cylinder. If the hydraulic cylinder is connected to the wheel cylinders, the hydraulic pressure produced will result in braking action.

§ 40-18. TYPES OF POWER BRAKES
There are several types of vacuum-assisted power brakes, integral, multiplier, and assist.

1. *Integral type.* This type of power brake (Fig. 40-26) has the brake master cylinder as an integral part of the power-brake assembly (see Fig. 40-29). When the brake pedal is operated, it actuates a valve in the power-brake assembly that applies atmospheric pressure to one side of a piston or diaphragm and vacuum to the other side. This causes the piston or diaphragm to move, and the movement forces a piston to move in the master cylinder. This applies the brakes. Most passenger cars and light trucks use this type of system.

2. *Multiplier type.* This type of power-brake system (Fig. 40-27) multiplies the pressure produced by the master cylinder. The pressure from the master cylinder is directed to the multiplier unit through a brake tube. In the multiplier unit, the pressure of the brake fluid actuates a valve. The valve causes atmospheric pressure to be directed to one side of a diaphragm and vacuum to the other side. The diaphragm is thus forced to move, and this moves a piston in a hydraulic cyl-

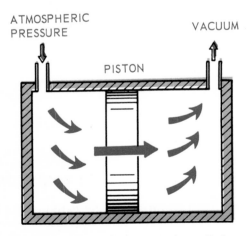

Fig. 40-24. If atmospheric pressure is applied on one side of a piston and vacuum on the other side, the piston will move toward the vacuum side, as shown.

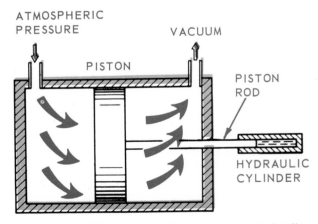

Fig. 40-25. If the piston rod is placed in a hydraulic cylinder, the pressure on the piston in the atmospheric-pressure chamber will be translated into hydraulic pressure.

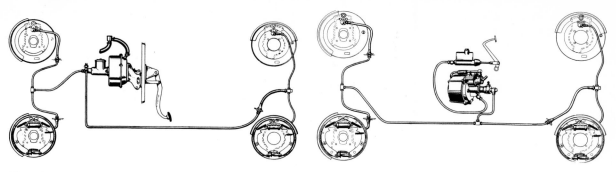

Fig. 40-26. Typical power-brake system of the integral type. *(Bendix-Westinghouse Automotive Air Brake Company)*

Fig. 40-27. Typical power-brake system of the multiplier type. *(Bendix-Westinghouse Automotive Air Brake Company)*

inder that is part of the multiplier unit. This produces a high hydraulic pressure which is carried by brake lines to the wheel cylinders.

3. *Assist type.* This type of power-brake system (Fig. 40-28) has a power-cylinder assembly that assists in applying the brakes through mechanical linkage. When the brake pedal is moved, linkage to the power cylinder is actuated, causing valve action and thus movement of a diaphragm or

bellows in the cylinder. This movement is carried through linkage to the master cylinder, thereby increasing the total force being applied, which in turn increases the braking action.

§ 40-19. POWER-BRAKE OPERATION To describe the operation of a typical power brake, we will use the Bendix unit shown in Fig. 40-29. This

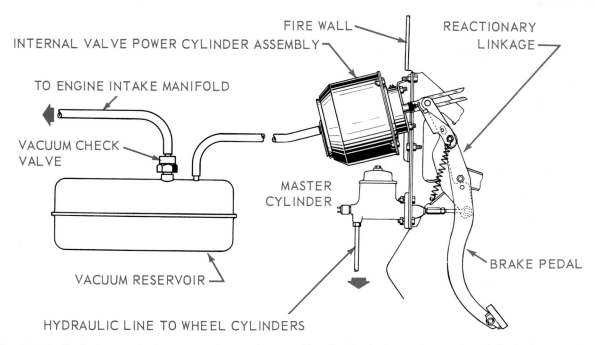

Fig. 40-28. Typical power-brake system of the assist type. *(Bendix-Westinghouse Automotive Air Brake Company)*

517

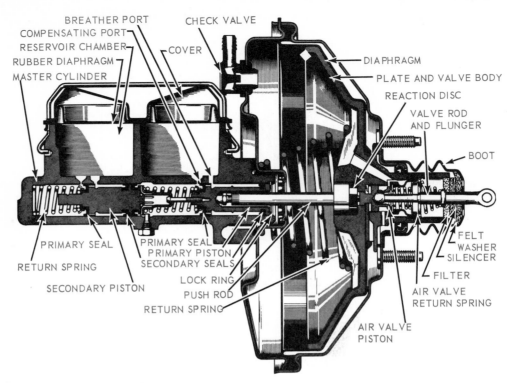

Fig. 40-29. Sectional view of a Bendix dual-master cylinder and power unit. *(Buick Motor Division of General Motors Corporation)*

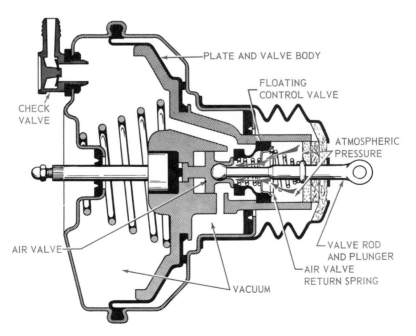

Fig. 40-30. Power-brake unit in the released position, with brakes off. *(Buick Motor Division of General Motors Corporation)*

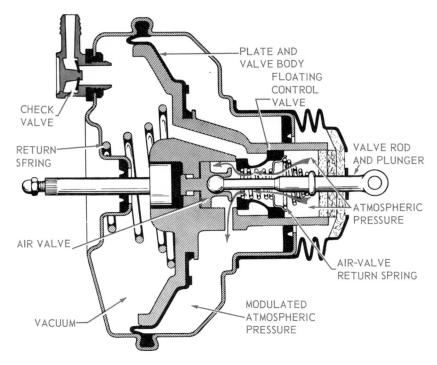

Fig. 40–31. Power-brake unit in the applied position, with brakes on. *(Buick Motor Division of General Motors Corporation)*

has a dual master cylinder (not shown in Figs. 40–30 and 40–31). Figure 40–30 shows the situation in the released position. The floating control valve is seating against the air valve so that no air can pass into the vacuum part of the unit. However, when the brakes are applied, the valve rod and plunger are moved to the left (in Fig. 40–3l). This opens the passage for the air to pass through and into the area to the right of the plate and valve body. At the same time, the floating control valve changes shape, because of the spring pressure released by the air-valve movement. This change of shape permits the left part of the valve to seal off the passage through the plate. Thus, air cannot pass to the vacuum side of the plate. With vacuum on the left side of the plate, and atmospheric pressure to the right, the plate is forced

to the left, as shown in Fig. 40–31. This movement forces the hydraulic piston into the master cylinder, thus applying hydraulic pressure, through the brake lines, to the wheel cylinders. Braking takes place. Only a small amount of foot pressure on the brake pedal is required to produce the actions described. Most of the braking effort is produced by the movement of the plate in the power unit.

When the brake pedal is released, the return springs move the power piston and hydraulic piston to their released positions, as shown in Fig. 40–30. Atmospheric pressure is shut off from the right-hand side of the power piston, and vacuum is applied by the action of the air valve.

In case of vacuum failure, the brakes can still be applied, but since there is no power assist, much heavier brake-pedal pressure is required.

Review Questions

1. What is static friction? Kinetic friction?
2. Name the different conditions that cause friction to change.
3. Generally speaking, will the car stop more quickly if the wheels are locked or if the wheels continue to turn when the brakes are applied?
4. What are the two basic types of car brakes?
5. Define the term "dual brake system".
6. Describe the actions that take place in the master cylinder when the brakes are applied. In the wheel cylinders.
7. How hot may brake shoes and drum get during extreme braking?
8. Explain how self-adjusting brakes work.
9. What are the two types of disk brakes?
10. Explain how a disk brake works.
11. What is brake fade?
12. What are metallic brakes?
13. Why must mineral oil never be used in a brake system?
14. Explain how the pressure-differential valve works.
15. Explain the purpose and operation of an anti-skid device.
16. Describe the construction and operation of a power-brake system.

Study Questions

1. Make a simple sketch of a hydraulic braking system, and describe its operation.
2. Write a short essay explaining why braking action is better when the wheels continue to roll (as opposed to when brakes are applied so hard that the wheels skid).
3. Make a sketch of a power-brake system, and describe its operation.

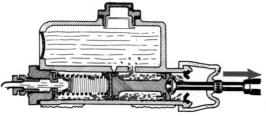

CHAPTER

41

Brake Service

This chapter discusses the trouble diagnosis, adjustment, removal, repair, and reinstallation of the various hydraulic-brake-system components.

§ 41-1. BRAKE TROUBLE DIAGNOSIS The article that follows relates various braking troubles to their possible causes and corrections. This information gives you a means of logically tracing down troubles to their actual causes. This permits quick location of causes and quick correction. If the cause is known, the trouble is usually relatively easy to correct. Following the trouble-diagnosis article are several sections that discuss the adjustment and repair procedures on different types of hydraulic brakes.

§ 41-2. TROUBLE DIAGNOSIS – DRUM TYPE This article gives you a good idea of the types of trouble that may develop in drum-type hydraulic braking systems and their causes and corrections. Let us discuss these troubles in more detail. Following articles will explain how to make corrections.

1. Brake pedal goes to floor board. When this happens, it means that there is no pedal reserve, since full pedal movement does not provide adequate braking. This would be a very unlikely situation with a dual-brake system. One section might fail (front or rear) but it would be rare for both to fail at the same time. If this happens, chances are the driver has been driving for some time with one section out. Causes of failure could be lack of brake fluid, air in the system, pedal or linkage out of adjustment, or worn brake shoes. If both sections have failed, check for a burned-out warning light or a stuck pressure-differential valve.

2. One brake drags. This means that the brake shoes are not moving away from the brake drum when the brakes are released. This could be due to incorrect shoe adjustment, to a clogged brake

line which does not release pressure from the wheel cylinder, to sticking pistons in the wheel cylinder, to weak or broken brake-shoe return springs, or to a loose wheel bearing which permits the wheel to wobble so that the brake drum comes in contact with the brake shoes even though they are retracted.

3. All brakes drag. When all brakes drag, it may be that the brake pedal does not have sufficient play, so that the piston in the master cylinder does not fully retract. This would prevent the lip of the piston cup from clearing the compensating port, so that hydraulic pressure would not be relieved as it should be (see Figs. 40-10 to 40-12). As a result, the wheel cylinders would not release the brake shoes. A similar condition could result if mineral oil had been added to the system, since this would be likely to cause the piston cup to swell. If it swelled enough, it would not clear the compensating port even with the piston in the "fully retracted" position (Fig. 4I-1). A clogged compensating port would have the same result. Do not use a wire or drill to clear the port; this might produce a burr that would cut the piston cup. Instead, clear it with alcohol and compressed air. Clogging of the reservoir vent might cause dragging brakes, since this could trap pressure in the reservoir which would prevent release of pressure. But this would be just as likely to cause leakage of air into the system (see item 9 below).

4. Car pulls to one side. If the car pulls to one side when the brakes are applied, this means that more braking pressure is being applied to one side than to the other. This happens if some of the brake linings have become soaked in oil or brake fluid (so that they lose braking effectiveness),

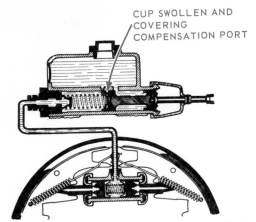

CUP SWOLLEN AND COVERING COMPENSATION PORT

Fig. 41–1. If the primary piston cup swells badly, it can close off the compensating port to the reservoir with the piston fully retracted, as shown. This causes dragging or locked brakes, since the hydraulic pressure will not release. *(Pontiac Motor Division of General Motors Corporation)*

if brake shoes are unevenly or improperly adjusted, if tires are not evenly inflated, or if defective wheel cylinders or clogged brake lines are preventing uniform braking action at all wheels. In addition, a loose brake backing plate or the use of two different types of brake lining will cause the car to pull to one side when the brakes are applied. Also, a misaligned front end or a broken spring could cause this.

Linings will become soaked with oil if the lubricant level in the differential and rear axle is too high, since this usually causes leakage past the oil seal (Fig. 41–2). The oil leaks onto the brake linings and soaks them. At the front wheel, brake linings may become oil soaked if the front-wheel bearings are improperly lubricated or if the oil seal is defective or not properly installed. Wheel cylinders will leak brake fluid onto the brake linings if they are defective or if an actuating pin

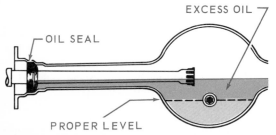

EXCESS OIL

OIL SEAL

PROPER LEVEL

Fig. 41–2. A high lubricant level in the differential and rear-axle housing may cause leakage past the oil seal, resulting in soaked brake linings. *(Pontiac Motor Division of General Motors Corporation)*

has been improperly installed (see item 10 below). If the linings at a left wheel become soaked with brake fluid or oil, for example, the car will tend to pull to the right. This is because the brakes would be more effective on the right side.

5. Soft, or spongy, pedal. If the pedal action is soft, or spongy, the chances are that there is air in the system, although out-of-adjustment brake shoes could cause this. Refer to item 9 below for conditions that could allow air to get into the system.

6. Poor braking action requiring excessive pedal pressure. If the brake linings are soaked with oil or brake fluid, they will not hold well, and excessive pedal pressure is required for braking action. Improper brake-shoe adjustment or the use of the wrong brake lining could cause the same trouble. Sometimes, when brake linings have become wet after a hard rain or after driving through deep water puddles, they will not hold very well. In this case, normal braking action will be restored after the brake linings have dried out. But if the linings are soaked with oil or brake fluid, they must be replaced, since it is not feasible to cleanse the linings of these contaminants. Another possible cause of poor braking action is excessive temperature. After the brakes have been applied for long periods, as in coming down a long hill, they begin to overheat. This overheating reduces braking effectiveness so that the brakes "fade." Often, if brakes are allowed to cool, braking efficiency will be restored. However, excessively long periods of braking at high temperature may char the brake linings so that they must be replaced. Further, this may glaze the brake drum so that it becomes too smooth for effective braking action. In this case, the drum must be ground or turned to remove the glaze. Glazing can also take place even though the brakes are not overheated.

7. Brakes too sensitive or grab. When the brakes are too sensitive and brake hard or grab with slight brake-pedal pressure, it may be that the linings have become greasy (if linings are greasy, the brakes are apt to grab, but if they are soaked with oil, they will not produce much braking effect at all). If the brake shoes are out of adjustment, if the wrong lining is being used, or if drums are scored or rough (Fig. 41–3), grabbing may result as the linings come into contact with the drum. A loose backing plate may cause the same condition; as the linings come into contact with the drum, the backing plate shifts to give hard braking.

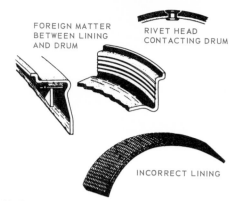

FOREIGN MATTER
BETWEEN LINING
AND DRUM

RIVET HEAD
CONTACTING DRUM

INCORRECT LINING

Fig. 41-3. Brake drums can be scored by foreign matter, such as dirt particles between the lining and drum, by worn linings that permit the rivet head to contact the drum, or by very harsh linings (especially on steel drums). *(Pontiac Motor Division of General Motors Corporation)*

8. Noisy brakes. Brakes will become noisy if the brake linings wear so much that the rivets come into contact with the brake drum (see Fig. 41-3), if the shoes become warped so that pressure on the drum is not uniform, if shoe rivets become loose so that they contact the drum, or if the drum becomes rough or worn. Any of these conditions are likely to cause a squeak or squeal when the brakes are applied. Also, loose parts, such as the brake backing plate, may rattle.

9. Air in system. If air gets into the hydraulic system, poor braking and a spongy pedal will result. Air can get into the system if the filler vent becomes plugged (Fig. 41-4), since this may tend to create a partial vacuum in the system on the return stroke of the piston. Air could then bypass the rear piston cup, as shown by the arrows, and enter the system. It is possible accidentally to plug the vent (by wrench action) when the filler plug

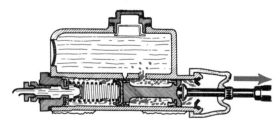

Fig. 41-4. If the filler vent becomes plugged, air may be drawn into the system on the return stroke of the piston, past the rear piston cup, as shown by the small arrows and bubbles. *(Pontiac Motor Division of General Motors Corporation)*

is removed. Always check the vent and clean it when the plug is removed and replaced. Air can also get into the system if the master-cylinder valve is leaky and does not hold pressure in the system. This could allow air to seep in around the wheel-cylinder piston cups, since there would be no pressure holding the cups tight against the cylinder walls. Probably the most common cause of air in the braking system is insufficient brake fluid in the master cylinder. If the brake fluid drops below the compensating port, then the hydraulic system will draw air in as the piston moves forward on the braking stroke. Air in the system must be removed by adding brake fluid and bleeding the system as described in a following article.

10. Loss of brake fluid. Brake fluid can be lost if the master cylinder leaks, if the wheel cylinder leaks, if the line connections are loose, or if the line is damaged. One possible cause of wheel-cylinder leakage is incorrect installation of the actuating pin (Fig. 41-5). If the pin is cocked, as shown, then the side thrust on the piston may permit leakage past the piston. Leakage from other causes at the master cylinder or wheel cylinder requires removal and repair, or replacement, of the defective parts.

Fig. 41-5. Incorrect installation of the actuating pin will cause a side thrust on the piston which will permit leakage of brake fluid from the wheel cylinder. The pin must always align in the notch in the brake shoe. *(Pontiac Motor Division of General Motors Corporation)*

11. Warning light comes on when braking (dual system). This is a signal that one of the two braking systems has failed. Both systems (rear and front) should be checked so that the trouble can be found and eliminated. It is dangerous to drive with this condition, even though braking can be achieved, because only half the wheels are being braked.

§ 41-3. TROUBLE DIAGNOSIS—DISK TYPE Many of the troubles in the disk type of brake system are similar to those that may be found in the drum type.

1. *Excessive pedal travel.* This could be caused by excessive disk wobble or runout, air or leaks in the hydraulic system, warped or tapered shoe, loose wheel bearing, damaged piston seal, or power-brake malfunction.

2. *Brake roughness or chatter* (*pedal pulsation*). This could be due to excessive disk run-out, disk out of parallel, or a loose wheel bearing.

3. *Excessive pedal effort required.* Possible causes of this condition could be malfunctioning power-brake unit, brake linings with grease or brake fluid on them, worn or incorrect linings, or frozen or seized caliper pistons.

4. *Car pulls to one side.* This could result from linings with oil or brake fluid on them, frozen or seized caliper pistons, incorrect tire pressure, distorted brake shoes, front end out of alignment, broken car-suspension spring, restricted or clogged brake line, or unmatched linings.

5. *Noises.* Some brakes have brake shoes with tabs that start to scrape on the brake disk, producing a scraping noise, when the brake linings have worn down to the point where they should be replaced. Another noise is a rattle which could come from excessive clearance between the shoes and caliper. This can be cured by installing new brake shoes and linings. In some installations, there will be a slight groan that is produced when the brakes are just released so that the shoes still contact the brake disk. It can be eliminated by fully releasing or increasing pedal pressure.

6. *Brakes heat up during driving and fail to release.* This could be due to a power-brake malfunction, sticking pedal linkage, driver riding the brake pedal, or frozen or seized caliper pistons.

7. *Leaky wheel cylinder.* This could be due to a damaged or worn piston seal or to scores or corrosion on the surface of the piston.

8. *Grabbing or uneven braking action.* This could be due to a malfunction of the power brake or of the proportioning or metering valve. Also, it could be due to conditions discussed under 4.

9. *Brake pedal can be depressed without braking action.* This is a very unlikely situation with the dual-brake system. One section might fail (either front or rear brakes), but it would be rare indeed for both to fail at the same time. If this happens, chances are the driver has been driving for some time with only half the system working. Causes of failure in one section could be leaks in the hydraulic system, damaged piston seal in a caliper or master cylinder, air in system (probably due to loss of brake fluid). Also, improper

servicing can result in this condition. For example, failure to install the caliper pistons corectly, incorrect bleeding of the system, or incorrect servicing of the master cylinder could cause brake failure.

Consider also the possibility that the pressure-differential valve is stuck or the warning light is burned out if both front and rear sections have gone out. The driver might have been driving for some time with one section defective but the warning system did not work to warn him of the trouble.

§ 41-4. BRAKE SERVICE Whenever you encounter a complaint of faulty braking action, always try to analyze it and determine its cause, as noted in the previous articles. Sometimes, all that is necessary (on earlier drum-type brakes) is a minor brake adjustment to compensate for lining wear. On later brakes with the self-adjuster (Figs. 40-13 and 40-14), the brakes automatically adjust themselves to compensate for lining wear. Other brake services include addition of brake fluid, bleeding the hydraulic system to remove air, repair or replacement of master cylinder and wheel cylinders, replacement of brake linings, and refinishing of brake drums.

§ 41-5. ADJUSTMENT OF BRAKES On earlier drum-type brakes, periodic adjustments were required to compensate for brake-lining wear. On the self-adjusting type, no adjustment is required except perhaps just after new linings are installed. Procedures vary from car to car; so always consult the manufacturer's shop manual before attempting any adjustment of a brake.

§ 41-6. BRAKE LININGS On drum-type brakes, the brake shoes are curved. The brake linings are either riveted or cement-bonded to the shoes. If linings are excessively worn, new linings or shoes should be installed. On the riveted type, new linings can be installed on the shoes by knocking out the old rivets and then riveting the new lining in place. The cement-bonded type of lining requires a special oven, so that the automotive manufacturers using this type of brake lining recommend that the lining and shoe be replaced as a unit.

To establish a good fit, some manufacturers recommend a preliminary grinding of the lining, either before the shoe is installed or afterward.

On disk-type brakes, new brake shoes can be

Fig. 41-6. Installing a new brake shoe in a caliper. *(Chrysler-Plymouth Division of Chrysler Motors Corporation)*

installed after removing the wheel (Fig. 41-6) and, on some designs, the caliper itself (Fig. 41-7). This is a relatively simple operation, but the shop manual should be referred to.

§ 41-7. BRAKE DISKS AND DRUMS

Brake disks will require replacement only if they become deeply scored or are warped out of line. Light scores and grooving are normal and will not affect braking. Some manufacturers say that you must never attempt to grind down or reface a scored brake disk. This will adversely affect performance.

Instead, replace it, they say. Other manufacturers (Ford, for example) supply a special disk-refinishing tool. Check the manufacturer's shop manual for details.

On the drum-type brake, the drums should be inspected for distortion, cracks, scores, roughness, or excessive glaze or smoothness (glaze lowers friction and braking efficiency). Drums that are distorted or cracked should be discarded and new drums installed. Light score marks can be removed with fine emery cloth. All traces of emery must be removed after smoothing the drum. Deeper scores, roughness, and glaze can be removed by turning or grinding the drum.

● **CAUTION:** Removing excessive amounts of material will result in overheating of the drum during braking action, possible warping, and faulty brake action. Not more than about 25 percent of the total thickness of the drum should be removed in any event. If more than this amount must be removed to take out deep scores or roughness, new drums should be installed.

§ 41-8. WHEEL AND MASTER CYLINDERS

Wheel and master cylinders must be disassembled and assembled with extreme care in order to avoid getting the slightest trace of grease or dirt in them. Hands must be clean—washed with soap and water, not gasoline—since any trace of

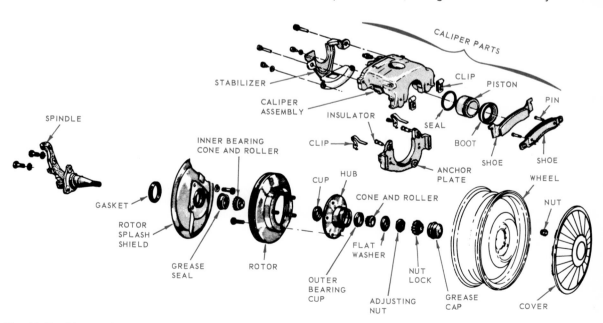

Fig. 41-7. Disassembled view of a floating-caliper type of disk brake. *(Ford Division of Ford Motor Company)*

oil or gasoline on the cylinder parts may ruin them. The bench and the tools must be clean.

To remove a wheel cylinder from the car, the wheel and the drum must be off, and the brake pedal should be blocked up to prevent its operation. Then the tube or hose should be disconnected from the cylinder and the cylinder removed by taking out the attaching bolts. The tube end at the wheel should be taped closed to prevent entrance of dirt. The cylinder can be disassembled by rolling off the rubber boots or taking off the covers. All parts should be washed in brake-system cleaning fluid. Old boots and piston cups should be discarded if they are not in excellent condition. Some manufacturers recommend replacement of these parts every time the cylinder is disassembled. If the cylinder is scored, it should be polished with crocus cloth (not sandpaper or emery cloth). Some manufacturers permit the use of a hone if the diameter of the cylinder is not increased more than a few thousandths of an inch. If scores do not come out, the cylinder should be replaced. Also, cylinder and pistons should be replaced if the clearance between them is excessive. When reassembling the cylinder, lubricate all parts with brake fluid.

● **CAUTION:** Never allow any grease or oil to come in contact with rubber parts of the brake system, since this would cause them to swell so that braking action might be destroyed.

To remove a master cylinder, detach the brake pedal and the brake line, and take out the bolts holding the cylinder to the frame. Then, drain out the brake fluid, and disassemble the cylinder by taking off the boot and removing the push rod, snap ring, or stop plate so that piston, cup, spring, valve, and other parts will come out. Use extreme care to keep all parts clean and free of grease or oil. All old rubber parts that appear at all deteriorated should be discarded. Some manufacturers supply master-cylinder repair kits and recommend that the parts in such a kit be used to replace the old parts whenever a master cylinder is disassembled.

All parts should be washed in brake-system cleaning fluid. If the cylinder is scored, it should be polished with crocus cloth (not sandpaper or emery cloth). Some manufacturers permit the use of a hone provided the diameter of the cylinder is not increased more than a few thousandths of an inch. However, if light polishing or honing does not remove scores, the cylinder should be replaced.

Check the fit of the piston to the cylinder, and if they do not fit within specifications, replace them.

On reassembly, lubricate the parts with brake fluid. Never allow grease or oil to come in contact with any rubber parts of the brake system.

§ 41-9. DISK-BRAKE SERVICE On some applications, the brake shoes can be replaced without removing the caliper assembly (Fig. 41-6). First, the car must be put on a hoist or jackstands and the wheel and tire assembly must be removed. Then, with two pairs of pliers, take hold of the shoe tabs and pull the shoe out. Next, the pistons must be forced down into their bores with a flat metal bar. Exert steady pressure. This will force brake fluid back up into the master-cylinder reservoir. So, before you do this, take some of the brake fluid out of the reservoir. After installation of the new shoes, pump the brake pedal several times until you get a firm pedal.

● **CAUTION:** Do not attempt to move the car before pumping the brake pedal, because you will not have brakes until you do.

Check and refill master-cylinder reservoir as necessary. Drive the car and make several heavy 40-mph stops to seat the brake shoes.

Other disk-brake designs require removal and disassembly of the caliper assembly before the new shoes can be installed (Fig. 41-7). The design shown in Fig. 41-7 is the floating-caliper type, using only one piston.

If pistons or seals require replacement, the caliper assembly must be removed. A special tool should be used to pull the pistons from the caliper, because they must come out straight, without cocking. If they cock, the bore is apt to be damaged. When installing new seals in the piston bores, be sure that they go in straight and are not twisted. Dipping them in clean brake fluid will help.

Slight roughness or corrosion in the piston bores can be cleaned up with a special hone, but if the bore diameter must be increased more than 0.002 inch, discard the old caliper and use a new one. New pistons are required, also, if the old show signs of wear sufficient to remove the chrome plating.

NOTE: Wheel bearings (front wheels) must be adjusted to specifications. Excessive play will have a bad effect on disk-brake action.

§ 41–10. INSTALLING BRAKE TUBING Special steel tubing must be used for hydraulic brakes, since it is best able to withstand the high pressures developed in the system. Tubing must be cut off square with a special tube cutter. Tubing must not be cut with a jaw-type cutter or with a hacksaw. Either of these methods may distort the tube and leave heavy burrs that would prevent normal flaring of the tube. After the tube has been cut off, a special flaring tool must be used to flare it.

§ 41–11. FLUSHING HYDRAULIC SYSTEM If dirt or damaging liquid has been introduced into the hydraulic system, it will be necessary to flush out the system. We should like to repeat here that mineral oil should never be put into the system, since this will cause the rubber parts to swell and deteriorate so that braking action may be completely lost. In flushing the system, only the special flushing compound recommended by the car manufacturer should be used. Anything else is likely to cause damage in the system.

To flush the system, remove the bleeder-valve screws at all wheel cylinders, and attach bleeder drains.

● CAUTION: Clean dirt and grease from around the valves so as to avoid getting any dirt into the cylinders. Any dirt at a valve or in a drain tube may get sucked into the cylinder on the brake-pedal return stroke. This could cause subsequent failure of the wheel cylinder and brakes at the wheel.

Put the lower ends of the drain tubes into clean glass jars (one tube in a jar is shown in Fig. 41–8). Unscrew the bleeder valves about three-quarters of a turn. Then operate the brake pedal full strokes to force all fluid from the system. When all fluid is out, fill the master cylinder with brake-system cleaning fluid (use only recommended brake-system cleaning fluid). Use a master-cylinder filler, such as is shown in place in Fig. 41–8, so that the reservoir will be replenished as the cleaning fluid passes through the system. Operate the brake pedal full strokes until all the cleaning fluid in the reservoir and in the filler has passed through the system. Then use dry, clean air, applied through the master cylinder, to blow out all the liquid from the system. Do not apply too much air pressure. Finally, add new brake fluid, and bleed the system as outlined.

§ 41–12. FILLING AND BLEEDING BRAKE SYSTEM When a hydraulic brake system has been flushed, when the fluid has become low, or when air has leaked into the system, the system must be bled to eliminate the air. Air in the system will cause a soft, or spongy, brake-pedal action; the air will compress when the brakes are applied, and poor braking action will result. Air is eliminated by adding brake fluid and bleeding off a little of the fluid from each wheel cylinder. To add brake fluid, first make sure that the bleeder valves are closed at all cylinders. Then, either a master-cylinder reservoir filler, such as the one shown in Fig. 41–8, or a pressure tank, such as the

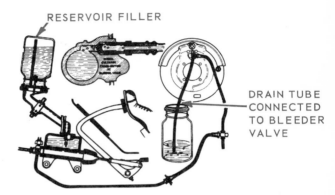

RESERVOIR FILLER

DRAIN TUBE CONNECTED TO BLEEDER VALVE

Fig. 41–8. Bleeding a hydraulic system with a master-cylinder reservoir filler. *(Pontiac Motor Division of General Motors Corporation)*

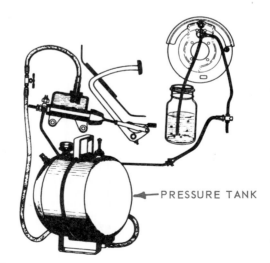

PRESSURE TANK

Fig. 41–9. Bleeding a hydraulic system with a pressure tank. *(Pontiac Motor Division of General Motors Corporation)*

one shown in Fig. 41–9, can be used. In either case, the reservoir filler or pressure tank should contain approved brake fluid.

When the reservoir is filled and the filler is in place (or pressure tank connected), install a bleeder drain and jar at one wheel cylinder (make sure that dirt is cleaned from around the connection so that dirt will not get into wheel cylinder). Open the bleeder drain. When using the reservoir, have someone get into the car and pump the brake pedal full strokes, allowing it to return slowly (Fig. 41–8). Continue until the fluid flows from the drain tube into the glass jar in a solid stream that is free of air bubbles. Make sure the end of the tube is below the liquid level in the jar. This prevents air from being sucked into the system on the brake-pedal return strokes. Tighten the bleeder valve, remove the drain tube, and replace the screw in the valve. Repeat the operation at the other wheel cylinders. Be sure to maintain proper fluid level in the master-cylinder reservoir. When the bleeding operation is complete, remove the master-cylinder filler. Make sure that the fluid level in the reservoir is correct, and then install the filler plug and gasket. Be sure the vent is open.

When the pressure tank is used (Fig. 41–9), no assistant is needed. The pressure tank is partly filled with brake fluid. Then, air is compressed in the tank by use of the tire-inflating equipment. The brake fluid is therefore under pressure in the tank. When the tank is connected to the master cylinder, as shown in Fig. 41–9, and the valve is turned on, brake fluid flows from the tank, under pressure, to the master-cylinder reservoir. Brake fluid is therefore forced through the brake line and wheel cylinder to which the drain tube has been connected, as shown. With the pressure tank, the valve in the line from the tank to the reservoir is turned on. Brake fluid is allowed to flow from the tank into the brake system until the brake fluid runs from the drain tube in a solid stream without air bubbles. Then, the valve is tightened, the drain tube removed, and the screw replaced. The operation is repeated at each wheel cylinder.

Do not attempt to reuse the brake fluid in the glass jar. It is likely to be contaminated or dirty.

Review Questions

1. What conditions could cause the brake pedal to go all the way to the floor board (drum brakes)?
2. What could cause one brake to drag (drum brakes)?
3. What could cause all brakes to drag (drum brakes)?
4. What could cause the car to pull to one side when the brakes are applied (drum brakes)?
5. What causes a soft, or spongy, pedal (drum brakes)?
6. What is the cause when excessive pedal pressure is required to produce braking (drum brakes)?
7. Why do brakes become too sensitive (drum brakes)?
8. What causes noisy brakes (drum brakes)?
9. What could cause excessive pedal travel (disk brakes)?
10. What could cause pedal pulsation (disk brakes)?
11. What could cause excessive pedal pressure (disk brakes)?
12. What could cause the car to pull to one side (disk brakes)?
13. What could cause noises during braking (disk brakes)?
14. Describe the procedure of installing new brake linings in drum brakes.
15. How is the brake drum serviced if it is only slightly scored? If it is deeply scored and rough? How much material can be removed from the brake drum?
16. Explain how to remove and replace a brake shoe on disk brakes.
17. Describe the procedure of flushing the hydraulic system.
18. What would be the effect of introducing mineral oil into the hydraulic braking system?
19. What is the purpose of bleeding the hydraulic system? How is this procedure carried out?

Study Questions

1. Make two lists of various types of braking difficulty (one for drum brakes and one for disk brakes), noting under each the possible causes and corrections.
2. First, select a particular brake adjustment. Then, refer to the shop manual, and write a sequence story in which you list the steps that are required to make these adjustments.
3. Write a sequence story on the procedure for flushing a hydraulic system.
4. Write a sequence story on the procedure of bleeding the hydraulic system.
5. Write a sequence story on replacing brake shoes on a disk brake.

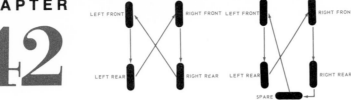

CHAPTER 42

Tires and Tire Service

This chapter describes tires and tire service, including tire removal and replacement and tire and tube repair.

---

§ 42–1. CONSTRUCTION OF TIRES Tires have two functions. First, they interpose a cushion between the road and the car wheels to absorb shocks resulting from irregularities in the road. The tires flex, or give, as bumps are encountered, thus reducing the shock effect to the passengers in the car. Second, the tires provide frictional contact between the wheels and the road so that good traction is secured. This permits the transmitting of power through the tires to the road for rapid accelerating, combats the tendency of the car to skid on turns, and allows quick stops when the brakes are applied.

Tires are of two basic types, solid and pneumatic (air-filled). Solid tires have very limited usage, being confined largely to specialized industrial applications. Only pneumatic tires will be considered here. Pneumatic tires are of two types, those using an inner tube and the tubeless type. On the type with an inner tube, both the tube and the tire casing are mounted on the wheel rim, with the tube inside the casing. The inner tube is inflated with air, and this causes the

tire casing to resist any change of shape. The tubeless tire (Fig. 42–1) does not use an inner tube. This tire is mounted on the rim in such a way that the air is retained between rim and tire casing (Fig. 42–2).

The amount of air pressure used depends on the type of tire and operation. Passenger-car tires are inflated to about 22 to 30 pounds [actually, pounds per square inch (psi)]. Heavy-duty tires on trucks or buses may be inflated up to 100 psi.

Tire casings (and tubeless tires) are made up of layers of cord impregnated with rubber over which the rubber sidewalls and tread are applied (Fig. 42–1). The layers of cord (called the *plies*) are formed over a spacing device and rubberized, and the sidewall and tread material is applied and vulcanized into place. The term "vulcanizing" pertains to a process of heating the rubber under pressure. This process both molds the rubber into the desired form and gives it the characteristics required. The number of layers of cord (plies) varies according to the use to which the tire will be put. Passenger-car tires usually have

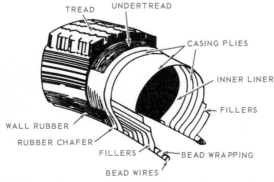

Fig. 42–1. Cutaway view of a tubeless tire, showing its construction.

Fig. 42–2. Sectional view of a tubeless tire, showing how the tire bead rests between the ledge and the flange of the rim to produce a good seal. *(Pontiac Motor Division of General Motors Corporation)*

2 or 4 plies. Heavy-duty truck and bus tires may have up to 14 plies, whereas tires for extremely heavy-duty service, such as earth-moving machinery, have been made with 32 plies.

Various shapes of treads are used. The tread designs provide traction and reduce the possibility of skidding.

Air is introduced into the tire (or inner tube) through a valve that opens when the chuck on the air hose is applied. On the tire with an inner tube, the valve is mounted on the tube. On the tubeless tire, the valve is mounted on the wheel rim (Fig. 42–2).

§ 42–2. TYPES OF TIRES AND TUBES We have already mentioned that the number of plies in tires varies according to the type of service for which the tires are built. Of course, the heavy-duty truck tire is much larger than the passenger-car tire. The typical passenger-car tire today (the low-pressure type) is designed for use on a rim 14 inches in diameter. They are called low-pressure tires (or *extra*-low-pressure tires), because they are normally inflated from 20 to 28 psi.

1. Tire sizes. Tire sizes are marked on the side of the casing. A tire might be marked 8.00 × 15, for example. This means that the tire fits on a 15-inch rim and that it is 8 inches larger in radius than the rim (when properly inflated but without load). Thus, the diameter of the tire, when inflated but unloaded, is 31 inches (8 + 15 + 8).

2. Tubeless tires. Most late-model cars are equipped with tires that do not use tubes. The rim used with this type of tire must be sealed, and it must have a sealed-in tire valve. The tire bead is so constructed that it seals tightly against the rim flange; thus the air pressure will be retained when the tire is inflated.

3. Puncture-sealing tires. Some tubeless tires have a coating of plastic material in the inner surface. When the tire is punctured, this plastic material is forced, by the internal air pressure, into the hole left when the nail or other object is removed. The plastic material then hardens to seal the hole.

4. Tubes. Three types of rubber, one natural and two synthetic, have been used to make tubes. Today, the most common tube material is butyl. You can identify a butyl tube by its blue stripe. The other synthetic rubber tube (GR-S) has a red stripe. Natural rubber is not striped.

5. Puncture-sealing tubes. Some tubes have a coating of plastic material which acts like the plastic material used in the puncture-sealing tire. It flows into and seals any holes left by punctures. In some tubes, the plastic material coats the inside of the tube. In others, the material is retained between an inner rubber diaphragm and the tube in a series of cells. This latter construction prevents the material from flowing as a result of centrifugal force and thereby from building up in certain spots in the tube. If the material were allowed to build up, it would cause an unbalanced condition.

6. Safety tube. The safety tube is really two tubes in one, one smaller than the other and joined at the rim edge. When the tube is filled with air, the air flows first into the inside tube. From there it passes through an equalizing passage into the space between the two tubes. Thus both tubes are filled with air. Now let us see what happens if a puncture or blowout occurs. In this case, the air is lost from between the two tubes. But the inside tube, which has not been damaged, retains its air pressure. It is sufficiently strong to support the weight of the car until the car can be slowed and stopped. Usually, the inside tube is reinforced with nylon fabric so that it can take the suddenly imposed weight of the car when a blowout occurs without giving way.

7. Bias-ply and radial-ply tires. There are two general methods of laying down the tire plies, radially and on the bias. These differences are shown in Fig. 42–3. For many years, the bias-ply tire was standard in the United States. The layers, or plies, are laid down on a bias so that they cross, as shown. These are called the *carcass plies*. In the radial tire, now coming into widespread use, the carcass plies are laid down at right angles to the circumference of the tire. An additional belt of cord (called the *tread ply*) is added directly under

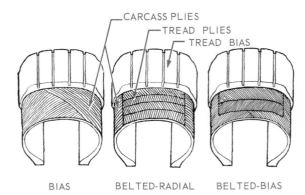

Fig. 42–3. Bias, belted-radial, and belted-bias tire constructions.

the tread. These tires are called *belted-radial tires.* According to a recent publication from one of the automotive manufacturers, the advantages of the radial tire are improved fuel economy, longer tread life, improved traction, increased skid resistance, and more positive braking. Disadvantages, according to this publication, include low-speed harshness, greater difficulty in mounting them, greater steering effort, and an appearance of being underinflated.

A compromise arrangement, said to have many of the advantages of the radial without many of the disadvantages, is shown at the right in Fig. 42–3. Here, the plies are on the bias, but the additional belt of cord under the tread is the same as on the radial. The tire is called a *belted-bias tire.* A modern arrangement is to make the two carcass plies of polyester fiber cord and the two tread plies of fiberglass.

Some radial tires, made in Europe, have a layer or two of fine steel mesh embedded in the tread plies as an added protection against tire damage.

8. The two-ply, four-ply rating tire. This tire has only two plies, but they are twice as strong as the plies used in the four-ply tires, according to tire makers. Advantages claimed for the two-ply, four-ply rating tire is that it improves fuel economy, makes steering easier, and has improved high-speed durability because it runs cooler.

9. Snow tires. Snow tires have special heavy treads which provide a much better grip.

10. Studded tires. These tires have steel studs anchored in the tread. The steel studs provide still better traction in snow and on ice than the standard snow tire. Neither the snow tire nor the studded tire is considered to be good for use at medium or high speed on clean highways. They would be noisy and, because of their extra heavy tread, would make steering more difficult. Further, they would tend to overheat.

11. Wear indicators. Some tires have wear indicators which are filled-in sections of the tread grooves. When the tread has worn down enough to show the indicators (Fig. 42–4), tire replacement is due.

§ 42–3. TIRE SERVICE Tire service includes periodic inflation to make sure that the tire is kept at the proper pressure, periodic tire inspection so that small damages can be detected and repaired before they develop into major defects, and tire removal, repair, and replacement. These services are covered in detail below.

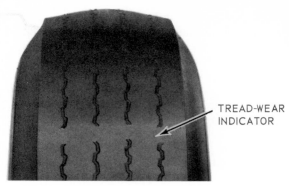

TREAD-WEAR INDICATOR

Fig. 42–4. Tread-wear indicator. The tread has worn down enough to require tire replacement. *(Chrysler-Plymouth Division of Chrysler Motors Corporation)*

§ 42–4. TIRE INFLATION As we have noted in previous chapters, incorrect tire inflation can cause many types of steering and braking difficulty. Low pressure will cause hard steering, front-wheel shimmy, steering kickback, and tire squeal on turns. Uneven tire pressure will tend to make the car pull to one side. Article 39–12 covers, in detail, the effects of improper tire inflation on the tires themselves. Low pressure wears the sides of the treads (Fig. 39–5), causes excessive flexing of the side walls, and results in ply separation. A tire with insufficient pressure is also subject to rim bruises; this could break plies and lead to early tire failure. Excessive pressure likewise causes uneven tread wear; the tread wears in the center. Also, a tire that is excessively inflated will give a hard ride and is subject to fabric rupture, since the pressure may be so high that the tire does not give normally. Thus, when the tire meets a rut or bump, the fabric takes the shock and cannot give, or flex, in a normal manner. Figure 42–5 shows the effect of proper and improper inflation on the tread contact with the road. See also Fig. 42–6.

For these reasons, it is very important to maintain proper pressure in the tires. There are a few points you should remember when inflating tires:

1. Don't inflate a tire when it is hot, as, for instance, after hard driving on the highway. This increase in temperature increases the air pressure in the tire. If you check pressure with the tire hot, you may find it is high, and your first impulse might be to bleed some of the air out to reduce the pressure. But if you did this, you might excessively reduce cold-tire pressure. That is, when the tire cools off, the pressure drops. If you adjust the pressure to the proper value with the tire hot,

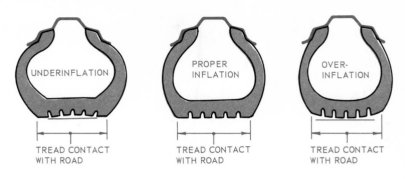

Fig. 42–5. Effects of proper and improper tire inflation on the contact that the tread makes on the road. *(Pontiac Motor Division of General Motors Corporation)*

CONDITION	RAPID WEAR AT SHOULDERS	RAPID WEAR AT CENTER	CRACKED TREADS	WEAR ON ONE SIDE	FEATHERED EDGE	BALD SPOTS
CAUSE	UNDER INFLATION	OVER INFLATION	UNDER-INFLATION OR EXCESSIVE SPEED	EXCESSIVE CAMBER	INCORRECT TOE	WHEEL UNBALANCED
CORRECTION	ADJUST PRESSURE TO SPECIFICATIONS WHEN TIRES ARE COOL			ADJUST CAMBER TO SPECIFICATIONS	ADJUST FOR TOE-IN 1/8 INCH	DYNAMIC OR STATIC BALANCE WHEELS

Fig. 42–6. Tire wear patterns, their causes and corrections. *(Chrysler-Plymouth Division of Chrysler Motors Corporation)*

then when the tire cools, the pressure will be too low. Pressures specified by the manufacturers are for cold tires.

2. Always replace the cap (where used) after checking air pressure or inflating a tire. The cap helps maintain the air pressure in case the tube valve is leaky. Also, it protects the valve from dirt. If dirt gets into the valve, it may cause the valve to leak. If you release air pressure when you take a cap off, it may be that the valve has become dirty. A new valve core should be installed if the old valve leaks. This simply requires screwing out the old core and screwing in a new one.

§ 42–5. TIRE INSPECTION There are certain types of damage and wear you can spot by examining the outside of the tire casing. Thus, abnormal wear, which indicates certain abnormal conditions in the steering, alignment, and brake system (§ 39–12), can be easily seen. This abnormal wear is a tip-off that the steering, suspension, or braking system requires service. The

effects of overinflation or underinflation on tire treads are also obvious. Less obvious are the internal damages from rim bruises or fabric breaks. Sometimes a tire can be bruised badly enough for fabric to break, and yet there will be little indication of the trouble on the outside of the casing. Thus, the only way to give a tire a thorough inspection is to remove it from the wheel rim so that it can be examined inside and out.

Removing the tire from the wheel rim also permits inspection of the tube (where the tire has a tube). Tubes give little trouble if they are installed correctly. However, careless installation of a tube may give trouble. For example, if the tire rim is rusty or if the tire bead (at the rim) is rough, the tube may chafe through. Rust and roughness should be sanded off. Naturally, if the tube is pinched between the tire and rim or at the valve stem, it will probably wear through at the pinch and fail. Dirt in the tire casing will also cause chafing of the tube. Another condition that may cause trouble is the installation of too large a tube

A—DEFLATE TUBE
REMOVE FIRST BEAD
STARTING NEAR VALVE STEM

B—REMOVE TUBE

C—REMOVE WHEEL

Fig. 42-7. Removing a tire from a wheel. After the tube is deflated, the bead on the upper side (at A) should be pushed down off the rim flange. The tire bead can then be worked up over the rim, as shown at A and C. *(Buick Motor Division of General Motors Corporation)*

in a tire casing. This could happen if the wrong tube were selected. It could also happen if an old tube were used in a new tire. Sometimes, an old tube has stretched a little. Here is what may happen when you put a tube that is too large in a tire casing: The tube overlaps at some point, and this overlapped area tends to wear both the tire and the tube.

§ 42-6. TIRE REMOVAL The removal and replacement of tires are not difficult on smaller vehicles, but on large, heavy-duty applications special tools are required to remove and handle them. Air must be released from the tube or tire as a first step in tire removal. The bead on one side of the tire should then be pushed in toward the center of the rim (Fig. 42-7). A tire tool or flat stock can be used to pry one part of the bead up over the rim flange (start near the valve stem).

Fig. 42-8. Commercial tire changer. *(Jack P. Hennessy Company, Incorporated)*

Care must be exercised to avoid damaging the tire bead or inner tube. After the bead is started over the rim flange with the tool, the remainder of the bead can be worked out over the flange with the hands. The other bead of the tire is removed from over the same side of the rim flange in a similar manner.

In tire shops where many tires are being changed daily, special tire-changing machines are used (Fig. 42-8). In these, the wheel is put into place and air pressure is used to force the tire bead away from the rim. This machine will remove a tire from a wheel rim in a few seconds. Further, it can be used to quickly install a tire on the rim.

● **CAUTION:** On tubeless tires, do not use tire irons to force the beads away from the rim flanges; this could damage the rim seals on the beads and cause an air leak. Instead, use a bead-breaker tool.

The tire using a tube requires one mounting procedure, the tubeless tire another, as follows:

1. Tire with tube. Before replacing the tire, inflate the tube until it is barely rounded, and put it into the casing. The inside and outside of the tire bead may be coated with a vegetable-oil soft soap to facilitate installation of the tire. Never use grease or oil, for these will damage the rubber. In replacing the tire on the rim, install one bead first, following with the second. Pressing down on the side wall of the tire will facilitate slipping the second bead over the rim flange. After the tire is in place, make sure that the beads are up on the bead seats in the rim and that they are uniformly seated all around the rim. Inflate the tube, making sure that it is properly centered in the tire and that the valve stem is square in the rim valve-stem hole. Deflate and then reinflate the tube. This last operation assures good alignment of tire, tube, and rim.

● **CAUTION:** If a tire has been deflated, never inflate it while the car weight is on the tire. Always jack up the car before inflating the tire so that the tube can distribute itself around the tire evenly. If this is not done, some parts of the tube will be stretched more than other parts, and this puts a strain on the tube that might cause it to blow out.

2. *Tubeless tire.* Examine the wheel rim carefully for dents and for roughness or rusting of the rim flanges (where tire beads fit). Straighten out any dents with a hammer. Use steel wool to clean off rim flanges. Use a file to remove roughness of the butt weld (where rim flange attaches to rim). All these areas must be smooth so that the tire bead will seal tightly against the rim and not allow air leakage.

Make sure that the valve is sealed tightly in the rim. Most rims have round holes (and require round washers), but some have oval holes (and require oval washers). Rubber valves do not use washers but are snapped into the hole in the rim (vegetable-oil soap makes this job easier).

To replace the tire, install the two beads over the rim, as noted above (for tire with tube). Coating the beads and rim flanges with a vegetable-oil soft soap makes the mounting procedure easier (never use grease or oil, since they will damage

Fig. 42-9. Using a commercial tire-mounting band or a rope tourniquet to spread beads during mounting of a tubeless tire.

the rubber). After the tire is mounted on the rim, apply a blast of air to the valve. The valve core should be removed, since this will permit the air to enter more freely. The blast of air should force the tire beads outward and into contact with the bead seats on the rim. If it does not and air escapes so that the tire will not inflate, then the beads must be spread by constricting the tread center line. This can be done with a commercial tire-mounting band or with a simple rope tourniquet (Fig. 42-9). As soon as the beads seat, the tire will inflate normally. Remove the band or tourniquet, replace the valve core, and inflate to recommended pressure.

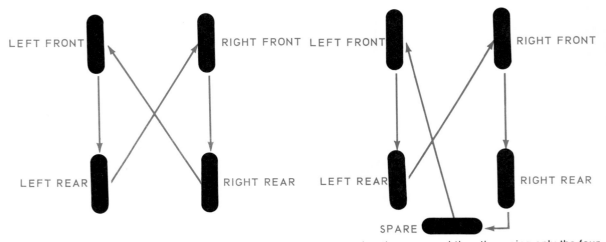

Fig. 42-10. Two procedures of rotating tires to equalize wear, one using the spare and the other using only the four mounted tires. *(Chrysler-Plymouth Division of Chrysler Motors Corporation)*

§ 42-7. ROTATING TIRES The amount of wear that a tire receives varies according to its location on the vehicle. The right rear tire, for example, wears more than twice as fast as the left front tire. Of the four tires, the right rear tire wears most rapidly, the left rear tire is next, the right front tire is third, and the left front tire wears least rapidly of all. To equalize tire wear, it is recommended that tires be rotated every 5,000 miles of operation. The diagrams in Fig. 42-10 illustrate two tire-rotation plans. In the one shown to the left, the right front tire is moved to the right rear, the right rear tire becomes the spare, the spare goes to the left front, the left front goes to the left rear, and the left rear tire goes to the right front. This distributes the wear more evenly and also changes the direction of tire rotation periodically.

§ 42-8. TUBE AND TIRE REPAIR A number of repairs can be made on tires and tubes, ranging from the patching of nail holes, punctures, or cuts to vulcanizing new tread material to the tire casing. This latter operation is known as *recapping*, since a new cap, or tread, is placed on the tire. Repair procedures vary according to whether the tire is or is not of the tubeless type.

With the tube type, puncture repair requires removal of the tire so that the puncture in the tube can be patched. This is done with a special kit. Patches require curing, or vulcanizing, at a temperature of around 300°F.

Tubeless-tire punctures can usually be repaired without taking the tire off the rim. One method uses a rubber plug which is inserted into the puncture hole along with special cement. After the cement dries and the plug is trimmed flush with the tread, the repair is complete.

Larger holes and cuts in tires can be repaired by applying a patch on the inside. In addition, when treads have worn down, new treads can be vulcanized onto the casing provided the casing is in good condition.

Review Questions

1. What two functions do tires perform?
2. How are tire sizes designated? For instance, what does 8.00 × 15 mean?
3. Describe the special features of a tubeless tire. Of a puncture-sealing tire.
4. Explain what a bias-ply tire is. A radial-ply tire. A belted-bias tire.
5. Describe the procedure of properly inflating a tire.
6. Discuss the procedure of inspecting a tire.
7. Explain how to remove and replace a tire which has a tube.
8. Explain how to remove and replace a tubeless tire.
9. Explain "tire rotation". Give an example.
10. How do you repair a punctured tube?
11. Explain how to repair a tubeless tire that has a small puncture.
12. Explain how to repair a tubeless tire that has a fairly large hole in it.

Study Questions

1. Make a sketch of a tire casing, and explain how it is constructed.
2. Write an essay describing various types of tires.
3. Write an essay explaining what could happen to a tire that does not have enough air.
4. Explain how to remove, repair, and replace a tire that uses a tube. A tubeless tire.

CHAPTER

43

Air Conditioning

This chapter discusses the construction and operation of the air-conditioning equipment used in automobiles. For specific servicing instructions on this equipment, refer to the manufacturer's shop manual.

---

§ 43–1. AIR CONDITIONING An air-conditioner does two things when it "conditions," or treats, the air. First, it takes heat from the air (by refrigeration), thus lowering the temperature of the air. Second, it takes moisture from the air, thus drying the air. Thus, the air-conditioner cools and dries the air.

Air-conditioners have been used for many years in public buildings, theaters, restaurants, and homes. A few installations of air-conditioning equipment were made on passenger cars a number of years ago. But it has been only recently that the major car companies have made air conditioning generally available, as accessory equipment, on their cars.

§ 43–2. AUTOMOBILE AIR CONDITIONING Figures 43–1 to 43–5 show various automotive air-conditioning systems. The essential parts include the compressor, condenser, receiver-drier, expan-

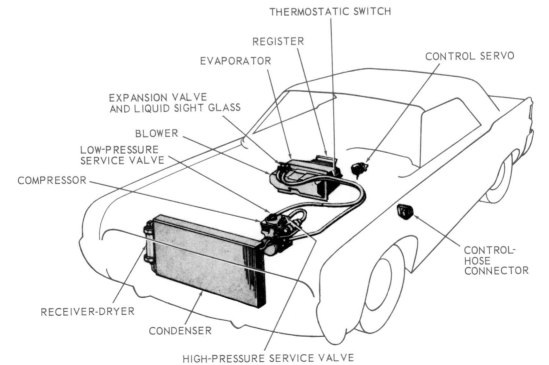

Fig. 43–1. Installation of an air-conditioning system in a passenger car. *(Lincoln-Mercury Division of Ford Motor Company)*

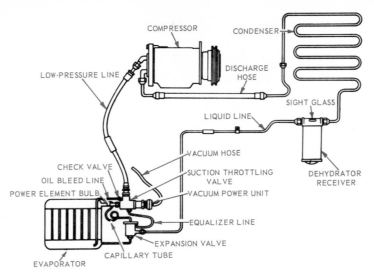

Fig. 43-2. Schematic layout of an automotive air-conditioning system. *(Cadillac Motor Car Division of General Motors Corporation)*

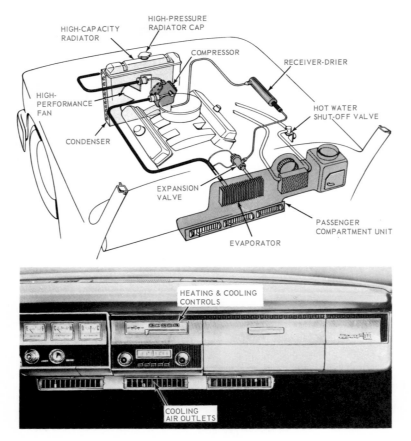

Fig. 43-3. Top, layout of air-conditioning system on a car. Bottom, instrument panel controls of system. *(Dodge Division of Chrysler Motors Corporation)*

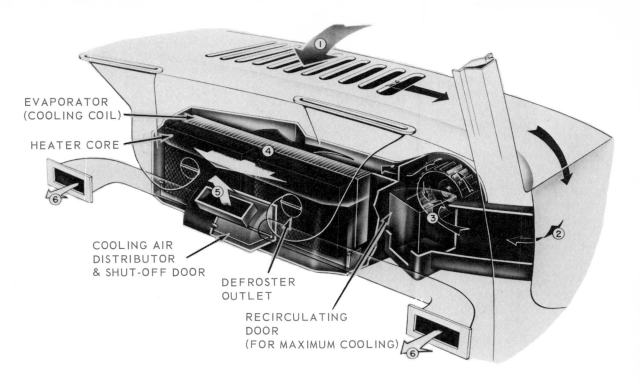

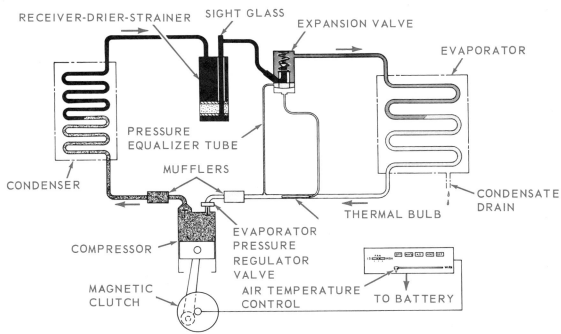

EVAPORATOR (COOLING COIL)

HEATER CORE

COOLING AIR DISTRIBUTOR & SHUT-OFF DOOR

DEFROSTER OUTLET

RECIRCULATING DOOR (FOR MAXIMUM COOLING)

RECEIVER-DRIER-STRAINER

SIGHT GLASS

EXPANSION VALVE

EVAPORATOR

PRESSURE EQUALIZER TUBE

CONDENSER

MUFFLERS

CONDENSATE DRAIN

THERMAL BULB

COMPRESSOR

EVAPORATOR PRESSURE REGULATOR VALVE

AIR TEMPERATURE CONTROL

TO BATTERY

MAGNETIC CLUTCH

Fig. 43-4. Top, air circuit in air-conditioning system. 1. Outside air entering. 2. Air passing through side cowl. 3. Air entering blower. 4. Blower forcing air through cooling coil and heater core. 5. Conditioned air discharging through center outlets. 6. Conditioned air discharging through side outlets. Bottom, schematic layout of system. *(Dodge Division of Chrysler Motors Corporation)*

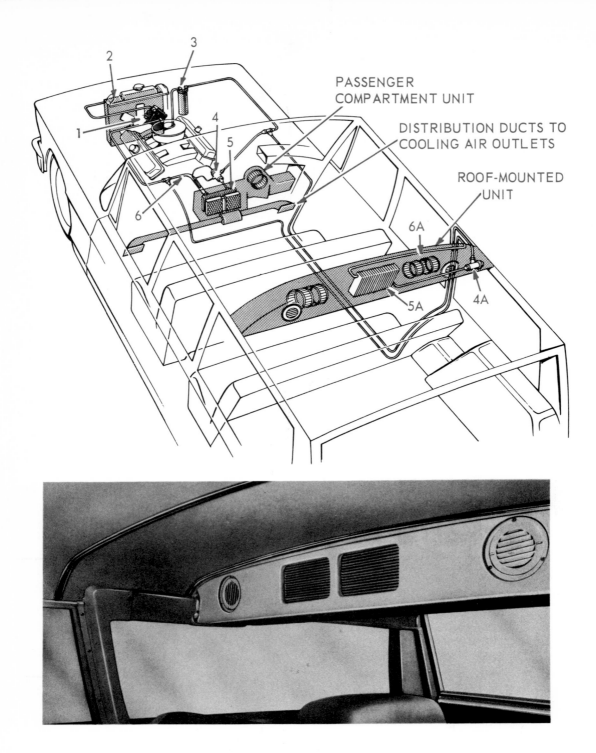

Fig. 43–5. Air-conditioning system for a station wagon. This system has an additional rear unit. Flow of refrigerant is from compressor (1) to condenser (2), receiver-drier (3), expansion valves (4 and 4A), evaporators (5 and 5A), and return lines (6 and 6A), back to compressor. *(Dodge Division of Chrysler Motors Corporation)*

sion valve, evaporator, connecting tubes, and the controls. Let us see how these various components work.

NOTE: The air-conditioning systems shown and discussed in this chapter are only a few of a number being used in automobiles. They are, however, typical and will serve to describe how these systems function.

§ 43–3. COMPRESSOR   The compressor is mounted on the side of the engine and is driven by a V belt from a special pulley on the engine crankshaft. In some systems, the compressor is driven all the time that the engine is operating. In other systems, the compressor drive pulley contains a clutch (electrically operated) which declutches the compressor from the pulley when cooling is not wanted.

The function of the compressor is to compress the vaporized refrigerant after it leaves the evaporator. The compressed vapor is than delivered to the condenser.

§ 43–4. CONDENSER   The condenser and receiver are mounted at the front of the car. The condenser consists essentially of a series of tubes on which fins have been mounted. The compressed vapor passes through the tubes.

Air passes around the fins and between the tubes. In this way, heat is removed from the compressed vapor. As the vapor is cooled, it begins to condense, or return to liquid form. The liquid then runs into the receiver.

§ 43–5. EXPANSION   VALVE   The expansion valve is the controlling valve in the refrigerating system. When the system is in operation, refrigerant passes, under high pressure, to the condenser (where it is cooled and condensed). Then, it moves into the receiver. Refrigerant, in liquid form, passes from the dehydrator-receiver (which removes dirt and moisture) to the expansion valve. The expansion valve holds back the high pressure from the condenser and admits liquid refrigerant to the evaporator in a relatively small stream and at low pressure. As the liquid refrigerant passes into the evaporator, at low pressure, it begins to evaporate. This evaporation "soaks up" heat. The evaporated refrigerant is then pumped back through the compressor and is delivered, at high pressure, to the condenser.

§ 43–6. EVAPORATOR   The evaporator consists of tubing and radiating fins. Air from a blower passes around the tubing and fins and is cooled. This air is then directed into the car as desired by adjustment of louvers or air nozzles.

Review Questions

1. Explain the purpose of the condenser.
2. Explain the purpose of the compressor.

3. Describe expansion-valve operation.
4. Explain the purpose of the evaporator.

Study Questions

1. Write a step-by-step story on the servicing procedures required on the different components of a car air-conditioning system.

2. Explain how the car air-conditioning system functions. Make sketches to illustrate your explanation.

ACKNOWLEDGMENTS

Many individuals and organizations have contributed to the present and previous editions of *Automotive Mechanics.* The author gratefully acknowledges his indebtedness and tenders his sincere thanks to the many, many people in industry and in education who, by their advice and counsel, so ably assisted in the preparation of the present edition of the book. All cooperated with the aim of producing complete and accurate information that would be useful in the training of automotive mechanics. Special thanks are due to the following organizations for information and illustrations that they supplied: AC Spark Plug Division, Buick Motor Division, Cadillac Motor Car Division, Chevrolet Motor Division, Delco Products Division, Delco-Remy Division, Detroit Diesel Engine Division, Frigidaire Division, Oldsmobile Division, Pontiac Motor Division, Saginaw Steering Gear Division, and United Delco Division of General Motors Corporation; Allen Electric and Equipment Company; Akron Equipment Company; American Motors Corporation; American Petroleum Institute; Barrett Equipment Company; Bear Manufacturing Company; Bendix Products Division of Bendix Aviation Corporation; L. O. Beard Tool Company; Black and Decker Manufacturing Company; Carter Carburetor Company; Dodge Division, and Chrysler-Plymouth Division of Chrysler Motors Corporation; Clayton Manufacturing Company; Henry Disston and Sons, Inc.; Eaton Manufacturing Company; E. I. du Pont de Nemours & Company, Inc.; Electric Auto-Lite Company; Federal-Mogul Corporation; E. Edelmann and Company; Federal Motor Truck Company; Ford Motor Company; Gemmer Manufacturing Company; B. F. Goodrich Company; Greenfield Tap and Die Corporation; Hall Manufacturing Company; Hercules Motors Corporation; Hobart Brothers; International Harvester Company; K-D Manufacturing Company; Kelsey-Hayes Wheel Company; Kent-Moore Organization, Inc.; Johnson Bronze Company; King-Seeley Corporation; Lincoln-Mercury Division of Ford Motor Company; Linde Air Products Company; Mack-International Motor Truck Corporation; Metalizing Company of America; Alexander Milburn Company; Monmouth Products Company; Monroe Auto Equipment Company; Muskegon Piston Ring Company; New Britain Machine Company; North American Electric Lamp Company; Perfect Circle Company; The Pure Oil Company; Ramsey Accessories Manufacturing Company; Rottler Boring Bar Company; The Rover Company Ltd.; A Schrader's Son Division of Scovill Manufacturing Company, Inc.; Sealed Power Corporation; Snap-on Tools Corporation; South Bend Lathe Works; Spicer Manufacturing Corporation; Standard Oil Company; Standard-Triumph Motor Company, Inc.; Storm Manufacturing Company, Inc.; Studebaker Corporation; Sun Electric Corporation; Sunnen Products Company; Thompson Products Inc.; United Specialties Company; United States Rubber Company; Van Norman Company; Walker Manufacturing Company; Warner Electric Brake Manufacturing Company; Waukesha Motor Company; Weaver Manufacturing Company; Wilkening Manufacturing Company; and Zenith Carburetor Company.

Special thanks are also due to the hundreds of people in education who helped the publisher and the author plan the revision so that the new edition of *Automotive Mechanics* would be more useful to them than ever before. Scores of automotive-mechanics instructors offered advice, comments, and criticisms with the aim of making the new edition of the book a more useful and more perfect teaching tool. To all these people and the organizations they represent, sincere thanks!

WILLIAM H. CROUSE

INDEX